The Management
of Organizations

Wiley Series in Management

The Management of Organizations

Franklin G. Moore
University of Michigan

JOHN WILEY & SONS
New York   Chichester   Brisbane   Toronto   Singapore

Library of Congress Cataloging in Publication Data:

Moore, Franklin G., 1905-
  Management of organizations.
  (Wiley Series in management)
  Includes index and glossary.
  1. Management. 2. Organization. I. Title. II.
Series: Wiley Series in Management.

HD31. M623   658   81-4665
ISBN 0-471-87691-7   AACR2

Printed in the United States of America

10 9 8 7 6 5 4 3 2 1

Preface

This book addresses itself to the *effective management of organizations.* Organizations are viewed as ongoing entities which have established positions in their environments. They are made up of people who have certain strengths and weaknesses and capabilities in areas related to the work of their organizations. The work of these people has to be directed, managed, and coordinated. These organizations also have physical assets, monetary assets, and consumer acceptance of their products or services and a place in the competitive economy. These assets, too, have to be managed.

Organizations are always in the process of change. Their people grow old and are replaced. So also the nature of the economy as well as market opportunities and technologies change. In the last decade, responsibilities to society became more important. Managers have to be aware of such changes and try to cause their organizations to change and to react in appropriate ways so that they will continue to be effective under the new conditions.

Managing and organizing go on at all levels in all organizations, so the study of this subject deals with what goes on at both higher and lower levels. High level managers are concerned with matters of major policies, strategies, and objectives, while lower level managers are more concerned with getting today's work done.

The subject of management and organization has universal application. All organizations—schools, cities, states, federal governments, armies, hospitals, churches, political parties, as well as business firms—need to be managed. Management and organization fundamentals apply to all of them. Yet there are differences in objectives, constraints, and environments, which determine how managerial and organizational fundamentals are applied. These differences sometimes change the methods and the points of emphasis.

The rationale of this book is that people wanting to learn about organization and management should be introduced to the prevailing ideas of both theory and practice. Consequently, the attempt is made to weave together the findings of social science researchers and the thinking of practicing managers.

In the interest of maintaining a smooth flow of the text, we have used reference notes sparingly. If one were to supply footnote or endnote references to the sources of all of the ideas discussed, they would number in the thousands. Readers who wish to explore further the ideas treated in the text may want to refer to one or more of the sources listed at the close of each chapter under the heading, "Suggested Supplementary Readings."

The objectives of each chapter are set out at the start of each chapter so that readers will know what to look for. Review questions relating to the chapter contents are also provided at the end of each chapter to help readers fix in their minds the salient points brought out in the chapter.

At the close of each chapter, we have also provided several questions for analysis and discussion. These are thought-provoking questions and situational cases dealing with the subjects of the chapters. These questions differ from the review questions in that they go beyond the text presentation and bring out some of the real-life difficulties in applying the ideas discussed in the chapters.

Most of these thought-provoking questions and problems have been brought up by mature students in regular college courses and by managers in executive training courses. They have been selected because they generated stimulating discussions in regular college classes and in training programs. Teachers may find that, when discussing these problems, they will be teaching almost as much from the problems as from the text.

Better understanding is also developed by studying cases which pose difficult problems and which often cut across several subject areas. The text provides two kinds of cases to meet this need. Short cases are provided at the end of most chapters while longer cases are provided at the end of each section of the book.

Since nearly all of the material in this book has been tested in classes with undergraduate students, graduate students, and managers in executive training programs in both the United States and Europe, and since a number of people have reviewed the text material, I have had the benefit of thoughtful suggestions from many people. The suggestions of George Odiorne, William Werther, Robert Swindle and Johannes Pennings were particularly helpful. I want to thank these people and all of the others who have offered suggestions for their helpful ideas.

Contents

Case List

The Management
of Organizations

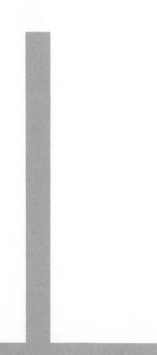

Managers have many different ideas about how best to manage. Some of their ideas have just grown up out of general practice while others of their ideas have come from teachers and other scholars who have developed theories based on their research about how organizations operate. Like the ideas developed from general practice, these theories also differ from each other.

Chapter 1 presents the setting for our subject and provides an overview of managerial work. Chapter 2 gives a brief history of early organizational theory and the thinking of the most important early organizational theorists. Chapter 3 continues this survey of the views of the leading scholars and researchers since the days of the pioneers.

Objectives of Chapter One

1. To acquaint the reader with the nature of the work of managers in organizations.
2. To show how managers can be effective in molding the future of their organizations.
3. To show that, in order to be effective, organizations need to be flexible and designed to suit the current environment.
4. To point out the differences between the operations of business and nonbusiness organizations.

Managers in Organizations

1

*Managers are to an organization
as the mind is to a person.*

Managers are an organization's prime movers, its catalysts. They decide what the organization is to try to do. They decide what work will need to be done and they recruit people and build up an organization to do these things. They decide what equipment and other physical assets will be required and they raise the money to pay for these things by selling stock or by borrowing money.

As managers do these things, they *plan, organize, staff, direct,* and *coordinate* the work of their organizations. They also see that their organizations have *communication systems* and they try to *control* their organizations' work.

Managerial and organizational work goes on in all organizations, nonbusiness as well as business. Nonbusiness organizations, such as the Massachusetts General Hospital, the University of California, and the United States Department of Agriculture, all require managers. Even voluntary organizations, such as the Girl Scouts of America and the American Red Cross, need managers. In the past, many people in nonbusiness organizations did not appreciate the need for their managers to have managerial skills. In recent years, however, such organizations have been paying more attention to how to manage and to the selection and training of their managers.

One Year at Borden

We have just said that managers are "catalysts." It is sometimes said that, "managers set objectives," "managers do things," and "managers make things happen which would not otherwise have happened."

We can illustrate the meaning of these statements by looking at some of the things done in a typical company. We have selected the Borden company. A review of some of its actions in a recent year will give us some appreciation of what managers do.

Most people know the Borden Company as a milk company. It is, in fact, the second largest milk company in the world. In a year, it sells $4.5 billion worth of products (only one quarter of which are milk products). On these sales, Borden earns 3 percent or some $135 million annually. Employment averages nearly 40,000 people.

An overbrief list of things done at Borden (in a recent Annual Report) includes the following:

· Restructured the company's Foods division into twenty profit centers, entered TV advertising on a national scale. Established an Energy Saving Task Force.
· Introduced new non-allergic Marcelle cosmetic products, developed two new inks for lithographing, added Kava, a new acid free coffee, introduced non-fat dry milk and onion flavored potatoes, expanded the sales of Swiss Style Yogurt, introduced X-nog, a drink to help in taking stomach X-ray pictures, expanded Cracker Jack and Elmer's Glue operations, and acquired Calo Pet Food Company.
· Added sixty new field outlets for selling fertilizers, expanded plywood and particleboard production. Added five ships to its shrimp fleet fishing off Costa Rica.
· Added to an ammonia-urea plant in Geismar, Louisiana, started a $50 million program to develop new reserves of phosphate in Florida, opened up a new synthetic resin plant in the Philippines and another in Malaysia, a phenolic plant in Mexico, another in Australia, and a plastic film company in Nicaragua, expanded a methanol plant in Culbato, Brazil, opened a tin can making factory in Chuba, Japan, and built a freezing plant in Dublin, Ireland.
· Not all of Borden's operations were successful, so the company had to close down plants in Lake Wales, Florida; Waukesha, Wisconsin; and Bound Brook, New Jersey,

making candied fruit, malted milk, and disposable diapers, respectively.

· In addition to the activities above, the company suffered a crippling explosion in an acetic acid plant. It also suffered a five-month strike at a coated fabrics plant in Columbus, and it defended itself against several Federal Trade Commission lawsuits. As a result of one such suit, Borden sold certain Midwest milk operations.

Although our list has been condensed to one page, it shows that Borden's executives were *managing* on a broad front. They organized the work of their subordinates, they marshalled resources and took actions. Not only did they manage their milk business successfully during this period, but they extended the company's operations into several new areas. They expanded certain activities and they cut off certain other activities. They *managed* in that they tried to guide their organization and to steer it in the direction they chose.

Borden is the company that it is today because of activities such as those listed above which were undertaken in years past by its managers. But Borden does not make dacron thread nor camera film nor does it refine oil because its managers did not decide to do these things. Nor does Borden operate in certain geographic areas because its managers did not move into them. And, finally, Borden no longer makes candied fruit because its attempts to do this resulted in failure.

Borden's accomplishments were not the direct accomplishments of its top administrators. These accomplishments were made with the support of and as a result of the work of many managers down through the organization. Many middle-level managers managed the sub-parts of the work which lay behind the important accomplishments.

This recounting of accomplishments at Borden is, however, a report of accomplishments rather than an analysis of how the organization achieved them. From our list, we see that Borden's managers must have set goals, conceived strategies, studied problems, considered alternatives, made decisions, reacted to their environments, made and implemented plans, received reports and took corrective actions. These are all essential parts of organizing and managing. Borden's managers did things and caused things to happen which would not otherwise have happened.

Management Concerns

In order to manage well, managers need to have considerable knowledge about management as a process, as well as considerable knowledge about people since they must manage through other people. This section will consider these matters as well as the question of the need for managers having expertise in the work areas over which they have direction.

Management — A Multifaceted Job

Our example of Borden has given us a flavor of what "management" means. But, as yet, we have said little about people. Since *people* have to carry out the work of organizations, managing people is almost always the most important part of managerial work.

Managing people is so important that scholars of organization and management sometimes overlook almost everything else. But, people in organizations are like actors in a play. They *are* very important. But so is the play itself, the theater, its location, the time of year, the weather, and the competition. So are the ticket prices, the stage effects, and the type of audience.

Important though people are, managing people in organizations is not the whole story. Machines, materials, products, services, and money need managing. Managers have to decide whether to spend money for advertising, or for research or for new machines. Airlines have to be concerned with flight routes and air terminals as well as with people.

Furthermore, the work of every organization has to be carried on in a social and economic environment. There are consumer attitudes and there are competitors, laws, ethics, money limitations and other constraints to live with.

Managers need also to be concerned with their internal organization. They have to be concerned with the nature of the organization's main activities and to develop their organization's strengths to suit these needs. Business organizations selling to consumers need to be strong in selling whereas airplane companies need to be strong in engineering.

The Pervasive Nature of Management at All Levels

At Borden, the company president did not himself bring about all of the accomplishments we listed earlier. He did not, himself, decide to add the sixty new outlets for selling fertilizer, nor did he expand the Cracker Jack operations, nor introduce non-fat dry milk. In fact, Borden's top managers probably did very little of the work leading up to most of the accomplishments listed earlier in this chapter. Probably subordinate managers decided that doing these things would benefit the organization. Actually, a great deal of the managerial work done in all organizations is done by middle-level managers and not by top-level managers.

All organizations are made up of people, each of whom does a small part of the total work. In order to carry out his part, each member of the organization needs to know what he is to do and, in order for him to do his part, he also needs to have certain knowledge and skills which he acquires

through training, education, and experience. In order for managers to build organizations made up of such people, they have to select people, give jobs to them, tell them what to do and, in many cases, to coach and train them. Their work has to be directed and coordinated and information has to be communicated back and forth between organizational members at all levels. In a word, their work needs to be *controlled*.

At lower levels, the managerial job content is largely the supervision of the work of other people. It is assigning work, watching over performance, and helping to remove causes of interferences and bad work. It is avoiding doing wasteful work or unnecessary work. It is coaching, motivating, and supervising individuals. It is cooperating with other departments, and it is the receiving of instructions from superiors and advice from staff personnel. It is the making of reports, verbal and written, of work done, reports showing performance compared to plans, and reports showing plans for removing obstacles to effective performance.

At higher levels the nature of the managerial work changes. There is much less direct supervision of the work of others and much more analysis of problems and strategies. There is much more conferring, particularly with staff specialists, over their recommendations concerning major proposals and alternative activities and there is more setting major strategies, objectives and policies.

The Need for Operational Knowledge

Obviously, in order to carry out all of these activities, managers need to know something about how to manage. Yet knowledge of managerial fundamentals is usually not enough by itself to assure that a manager will be able to direct an organization's operations successfully. Besides managerial knowledge, every manager has to direct some kind of activity, some kind of work, so he needs to have a reasonable amount of knowledge and technical expertise relating to the organization's main work.

A banker needs to know something about how to run a bank just as the manager of a steel mill needs to know something about how steel mills operate. People who advance into managerial positions through promotions up the ladder already know a good bit about the technology of the industry they are in and how to manage a company in that business. But, in the few cases where managers transfer to new situations, they may lack the necessary technical expertise. This lack could constitute a serious weakness unless such managers include in their managerial team other people who have the required technical expertise to fill in for their gaps.

The Universality of Managerial Capability

Not all scholars agree with the view just expressed, that managers need to know both about the kind of work the organization is engaged in and about managerial methods as well. Some scholars and many business administrators as well, believe that a capable manager can manage any organization effectively. They believe that he can be an "all-purpose" manager. Some of them believe that, at high levels of abstraction and at high levels in all businesses, managerial work is the same.

This is an appealing idea which no doubt has considerable merit. This is especially true where managers without depth knowledge of the work of the organization, surround themselves with subordinates who *are* knowledgeable in the area of the work of the organization.

Appealing though this idea is, the experiences of companies whose top managers believed it and who have, therefore, moved managers around freely, is mixed. When, some years ago, Ford Motor bought

Philco (maker of television sets, electrical appliances, and electronics), it sent in, one after the other, several of its best managers with automobile production and sales backgrounds, none of whom could turn Philco around. Philco continued to perform poorly. Finally, a good job was done by a manager experienced in appliance manufacture and sales.

General Electric is another company which became disillusioned about the merits of the all-purpose manager idea. For nearly twenty years, GE's successive presidents believed that "a good manager can manage any business." But successive managers of proven capability elsewhere in GE, were, none of them, able to improve GE's computer operations in the 1970s. Ultimately, these computer operations were phased out. Since the mid-1970s, the all-purpose manager idea has been shelved at GE.[1] Managers are now moved around more to broaden them as preparation for higher level jobs.

Admittedly, however, our two examples, from Ford and General Electric, are not really good examples to illustrate our point. In both cases, the competition was so severe that even the best of fully qualified managers would have had trouble. It is nonetheless true that newly appointed managers without expertise relevant to the organization's work do not always surround themselves with subordinates who do have such knowledge. When this happens, it is much more likely that they will be ineffective.

John Nevin, who, in 1980, became president of Firestone Tire & Rubber Company, after having been head of Zenith (television set maker), seems in his early days, to have been successful in turning troubled Firestone around. This, in spite of his having a limited technical knowledge about tires.

Similarly, Michael Blumenthal, once Secretary of the Treasury under President Carter, became president of Burroughs (computer maker) in 1979. He, too, seems to have been successful on his new job in spite of its technology being unfamiliar to him.

Blumenthal had, however, once been president of Bendix (maker of automobile and airplane parts).

The Elusive Question of "What Is Effective Management?"

For many years, K mart has been more successful than Woolworth. Presumably this has been because it was better managed. Yet the discussion here has not said what effective management is. Management is sometimes defined as, "getting work done through people," but this definition does not provide answers to such questions as, "What is *good management*?" "How does a person recognize an effective manager when he sees one?" These are questions which higher-level managers need to try to answer for themselves about their subordinates.

These questions are hard to answer because the differences in the quality of managerial performances are usually in how well better managers do just about the same things that less effective managers do. Players on football teams which lose do most of the same things that players on better teams do but they do them less skillfully.

Judging the quality of managerial accomplishment is also always a matter of judging a totality which is composed of differing degrees of accomplishment of different things. It is hard to speak of effective accomplishment when, in fact, organizations fulfill multiple functions and have multiple goals, some of which are in conflict with others.

Edgar Schein suggests that managerial accomplishments should be judged in terms of the health of the organization. Even this does not, however, simplify the matter of judging effective management very much since, as Schein says, "No one part of managerial performance can provide valid indications of overall organizational health.[2]

Effective management is not only hard to define, it is even hard to detect be-cause effective performance is always related to context. Managerial actions are only some of the factors which cause results. Results are brought about by environmental and other factors as well as by managerial actions.

Lawrence Appley, long-time head of the American Management Associations, listened, over the years, to a great many business managers discuss their successes, their failures, and their problems in AMA seminars. In those seminars, organization theories were also presented and discussed by social scientist researchers. From these experiences, Appley concluded that, in order for managers to get things done through other people they have to answer certain questions:

· Where are we? (take an inventory)
· What do we want people to do? (plan)
· What kinds of men and women will be needed to do it? (organize human resources)
· What will these people need in order to do it? (organize physical resources)
· How well should the work be done? (set standards of performance)
· How well is this work being done? (reviews of performance)
· What help do the people need in order to do it better? (development and controls)
· What is it worth to get the essential work done right? (decide upon rewards and incentives)[3]

Appley's list emphasizes the need to direct and control the organization's *activities* — the things people do — and the need to relate resource use to accomplishment. His list is directed more toward what organizations are trying to do than it is at how people get along with each other. Although Appley's list was formulated a number of years ago, a manager today who follows it will almost surely be managing well.

The Role of Management in Organizations

The job of managers is to plan, organize, staff, and direct and control their organizations. They determine general strategies, identify problems, make decisions, and delegate, direct, guide, and control the work of their people. Doing these things requires the setting of standards of performance goals and the getting back of performance reports.

Managers need also to give middle-level and lower-level managers the authority necessary for the carrying out of their work. Across-channel information links need also to be developed so that departments in different work areas can coordinate and integrate their activities.

Over the years, researchers have sometimes followed managers around and written down what they did. The picture which emerges is, of course, somewhat superficial. Yet one fact invariably emerges. Managers do not lead such orderly lives nor do they go at their jobs in such a logical way as textbooks might imply.

Henry Mintzberg, after such a study, concluded that high-level managers are not reflective systematic planners. On the contrary, they dislike reflective activities and are strongly motivated to action. They do lots of things of short duration, jump from one thing to another, and respond to the pressures of their jobs. They answer mail, see callers, negotiate, handle exceptions, and do things to link the organization to its environment. They also sometimes perform as figureheads and do ritual work such as speaking to customer groups.

Mintzberg reported, too, that high-level managers get most of their information from telephone calls, meetings, observational tours, gossip and conversations. Of these, the telephone calls and meetings are the most important. Noticeably missing from Mintzberg's list are regular written reports.

He suggests that these do not play as important a part as it would seem they should.

In a later study, Neil Snyder and William Glueck reported that managers were more orderly than Mintzberg thought and that they did indeed plan in a somewhat orderly fashion. Snyder and Glueck noted that the many separate kinds of activities observed by Mintzberg were usually associated with information and analysis of matters relating to strategies and plans.[4]

Mintzberg's observations should not, therefore, be taken as indicative of how managers make *important* decisions. When Boeing's managers decide whether to put General Electric or Pratt and Whitney jet engines in the next large airplanes it builds, their decision is based on very careful consideration and study which includes written reports and analyses. Nor do Holiday Inn's managers decide whether or not to put a hotel in Cairo, Egypt, in any casual fashion or on verbal information alone. Even though top managers may not always wade through all of the written reports which come in to them, their subordinates do go over them carefully and report their contents to them.

Managers as Organizational Resources. Since managers exist at all levels in all organizations, some, obviously, must be superior in the hierarchy to others.

Often this has unfortunate consequences because the "superiors" come to regard themselves as superior in knowledge and judgment to their subordinates. Although they may be superior in knowledge and judgment in most cases, this is not so in every individual case. The unfortunate part is that a manager who feels superior often approaches his managerial work with a poor attitude. He wants to "tell" his subordinates how to do their work instead of working with them in a helpful way.

Such managers are unlikely to ask themselves, "How can I help my subordinates to perform better?" Yet their greatest possible contributions to their organizations are to make their units more effective and

Historic Management Philosophy

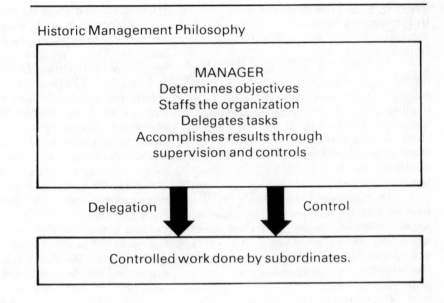

Today's Management Philosophy

Figure 1-1
The philosophy of how managers operated many years ago and today. Today much more attention is given to participation by subordinates.

this is more likely to happen if they regard their major jobs to be helping their subordinates to operate effectively, rather than as being their bosses.

Molding the Future. Since an organization's major decisions are made by its high-level managers, the future well-being of all organizations is largely a high-level responsibility. High-level managers need to think more about tomorrow's operations than about today's operations because it is already too late to do anything about the present.

In order to mold an organization's future, its high-level managers need to try to see where it is headed and where, if the natural course of events is left alone, the future will take it. Then, if these managers do not like what they see, they can lay out other goals and courses of action and try to improve their organizations' prospects.

Defense against Decay and Aggressive Factors. Managers of businesses at all levels are always on a treadmill. This treadmill effect, having to run to stay even, is caused by conditions both inside and outside every business organization. There are always both "decaying factors" and "aggressive factors" which tend to reduce an organization's income and to increase its costs of operation. These factors are always on the move and are always working against effective operations.

Inside all organizations, inefficiencies tend to grow. Taxes and other costs keep edging up year by year. Workers always want more money, often for less work. Department heads grow old and become less efficient and products age and move along their life cycles. Employees quit and have to be replaced by others who are, at the start, less well qualified than their predecessors.

Every business organization's competitors keep eroding away its income by attracting customers away by bringing out new products, by cutting prices and by taking other actions. Consequently, every business organization has to keep developing new products or improving its services or risk falling behind.

Organizational Concerns

We have treated the job of managing from a conceptual viewpoint. Now we turn to matters of organizational concern. Here we will deal with the relationships between people and organizations, differences between accomplishments of different organizations, and differences between business goals and social objectives.

Differences between Accomplishments of Different Organizations

In this text, references will sometimes be made to the operations of specific companies and other organizations such as government agencies. These references will usually be to organizations which have been unusually successful or unusually unsuccessful. The purpose is to try first to identify examples of effective and of less effective management and then to try to look behind end-results into causes and reasons why. This process should help us to discover what it is that effective managers do which differs from what less effective managers do.

The assumption implied in this process is that when two companies face the same opportunities and one company is more successful than the other, effective management is usually responsible for its superior accomplishments. The managers of the more successful companies do better jobs of seeing opportunities offered by the environment and do better jobs of serving society. And they manage their organizations more effectively internally.

Nor are the differences in accomplishment small; in many cases they are large indeed. Sixty years ago, Ford Motor was larger than General Motors. But, today,

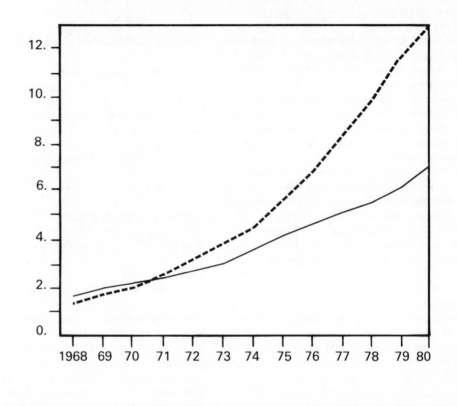

Figure 1-2
Growth of Woolworth and K-mart sales from 1968 to 1979. In this time, K-mart grew at a far more rapid rate than did competitor Woolworth. Yet the advantage in 1968 was with Woolworth.

General Motors is twice as large as Ford. And, as Figure 1-2 shows, K-mart is now ten times as large as it was ten years ago, whereas competitor Woolworth is only three times as large as it was. Such growth under equal competitive conditions could have come only from more effective management.

By way of emphasizing the importance of effective managers, one can point to several cases in business history where a new top manager was brought into a company which was having difficulty and who turned the organization around and made it successful. Ernest Breech did it at Ford Motor after World War II; Harry Cunningham did it at K-mart in the late 1960s; Edward Carlson did it at United Airlines in the 1970s. In all of these cases, the new managers redesigned their companies' organizations and made them more effective.

Business Goals and Social Obligations

Managers of government and of non-profit organizations usually put serving the public well (as they see it) at the top of their lists of objectives. This is what they should be trying to do. Business managers, too, should put serving society high on their lists but, of necessity, they also have to put making at least enough money to survive high on their lists.

One of the fundamental purposes of every *business* organization, therefore, must be to use resources (principally money and the efforts of its people) economically and to distribute goods and services which customers want. Managers should always be trying to increase the quantity and quality of the products and services obtained from the use of resource inputs. Not only does this improve their organizations' well being, but at the same time, it increases the nation's productivity and improves the economy.

Yet, today, this is not enough. Responsibilities to society call for more. Business managers are being asked to use the capabilities of their organizations to help solve social problems. They are being asked to put responsibility to the community high on their lists of objectives.

Environmental Concerns

As they operate, managers have to contend with environmental factors which limit what they can do in certain directions. They also have to deal with economic matters such as the organization's resources and how best to use them. These concerns and the differences between business and nonbusiness operations are considered in this section.

Environmental and Cultural Factors and the Study of Management

Effective management methods are, to some extent, functions of the environment. In high-technology companies where

highly trained scientists make sophisticated new products, a rather informal, loosely structured organization seems to work best. Work assignments are made in general terms rather than being spelled out exactly. Subordinates consult with each other and participate in their superiors' decisions. In contrast, in mature industries, such as textiles or shoes, where the work is more routine, a more structured organization with more exact assignments of duties and with less participation seems to work better.

Similarly, American managers operating overseas have frequently found that their hard driving "do it now" methods, which often work in the United States, are not suitable to the people and the environments of other lands and consequently produce poor results. Responses to work assignments differ in different cultures. Goals, too, differ. Many overseas companies put maintaining sales volume ahead of earning profits. Steady employment is sometimes regarded as so important as to cause companies to lose money rather than to lay off unneeded employees. (This applies, of course, only to the short run.)

Normally, too, both in the United States and in some other social orders, a reasonable amount of participation by subordinates in decision making produces better results than less democratic one-person decision making. But opportunities to participate in decision making are not received in the same way in all cultures. In some countries, subordinates do not want to participate in making decisions lest a decision turn out badly in which case they might lose their jobs. Consequently, they do not want to make decisions nor to participate in the making of decisions.

Differences in Management between Business and Nonbusiness Organizations

Government departments are to carry out service missions. Their purposes are often broad, sweeping, and ill-defined missions. Their delegations do not even say that they are to operate effectively nor economically. Almost never are any control provisions provided for appraising their accomplishments of their goals. Nor is any provision made to apply a test of the quality of service, the cost of service, or the value of the benefits stemming from what they do. It is small wonder that they sometimes operate ineffectively.

Other nonbusiness organizations, such as hospitals, are similar to government departments in that they too have little incentive to operate effectively.

Government departments obviously do not operate in the same way that business organizations operate. Besides their having no incentive to operate economically, there are differences in their goals and objectives. In government units, managers have to translate their broad mission delegations into narrower individual objectives which have to be within the confines of the broad major mission. The United States Federal Trade Commission tries to regulate competition but it stays out of trying to stimulate agriculture. Matters concerning agriculture have been assigned to the Department of Agriculture.

In contrast, business organizations have narrower general objectives. They have to carry on their business in certain selected areas. But they are free to choose these areas. They have more freedom to set objectives than do heads of government departments. RCA's (television and electronics) managers could go into the hotel business or they could (and did) buy a book publishing company (Random House, which they later sold).

The big difference, however, between business and nonbusiness organizations lies in the need for business organizations to operate effectively. If they don't do this, they go bankrupt. They have to take in more money than they pay out. They have to sell products or services to customers in order to get the money to pay the wages and sal-

aries of their employees and to pay for their other expenses such as materials, power, taxes, and buildings and machinery.

Businesses do this in a competitive economy. Other companies are always trying to do the same so all of them have to try to operate economically in order to stay in business. Business managers have to try to control the actions of their organizations and to see that the money spent for activities does indeed produce the desired results. Top business managers appraise the performances of their subordinates and the costs of achieving results and compare them to the worth of the results. Uneconomical activities, and the costs associated with them, are pruned.

In contrast, government agencies do not have to sell services or products to customers in order to generate the money needed to pay wages or salaries or to pay for the buildings they use. Neither the Federal Trade Commission nor the Department of Agriculture can go bankrupt. Their incomes are budgetary allocations and the resources they need in the form of buildings or other assets are supplied to them.

Also in contrast with business organizations, government organizations and nonbusiness organizations such as hospitals, churches, and schools perform services to which cost-value analysis measures can rarely be assigned.

Furthermore, nonbusiness organizations almost always have very weak reward-penalty systems. Poor work does not result in bankruptcy. And down inside most nonbusiness organizations, the rewards for a person who performs well are often nonexistent or are at best of only minor proportions. Similarly, penalties for poor performance are minimal or non-existent. Often poor performers receive the same periodic pay raises that everyone else gets. Federal Civil Service regulations make it almost impossible to dismiss an incompetent employee from a Federal government job.[5] The same is true at high-level jobs. High-level government department heads are paid a salary. If they manage well, they do not get any bonuses. Nor is there any penalty if they do poorly. (Near the end of President Carter's term as President a bonus system was introduced into high-level government managerial jobs. It remains to be seen how effective it will be.)

Decision making, too, as we will see in Chapter 21, is different in government agencies and in other nonbusiness organizations. In government agencies, decision making is a more ponderous procedure and often requires the joint agreement or approval of several agencies. This slows down the whole process and makes everything take longer.

Summary

Management is concerned with directing the efforts of people toward reaching organizational goals. And although managing people is *the* important job, additional factors, such as the work to be done, the environment, and other constraining factors also need to be considered.

Management and organization fundamentals appear to be universal and to apply to all types of organizations. There are, however, differences in the contexts in which fundamentals are applied. This book is oriented largely to considering how business organizations are managed. Most of the discussion in later chapters applies to nonbusiness organizations as well but in some cases this is not wholly so.

Business goals are often said to be to earn profits. But the earning of profits is possible only if these businesses produce goods and services at reasonable costs, and if they maintain reasonable levels of employment, and in general, do things to improve the well-being of the communities in which they operate. Business managers should use the resources entrusted to their care to the best advantage, thus doing their part to improve the nation's well-being.

Business managers should also act and should try to cause their organizations to accomplish results rather than just reacting to conditions and managing by drift. They should look ahead and should do things to prepare their companies to be in positions to do well in the future. Managers also need to be working continually to change and to counteract factors which tend toward decay and which, if not counteracted, will undermine the organization's future.

Review Questions

1. Isn't managing an organization largely a matter of managing people? Discuss.

Managers in Organizations

2. What part do environmental factors play in the way managers should operate? Discuss.

3. At what levels in an organization does management, in the larger sense, go on? At high levels, middle levels, or lower levels? Discuss.

4. Which is more important, knowledge of organization fundamentals or knowledge of the kind of business a company is in? Discuss.

5. Discuss the matter of putting resources to work to best advantage as being the proper purpose of business organizations.

6. Is it true that effective managers do only the same things as ineffective managers but do them better? Discuss.

7. What, according to Lawrence Appley, do managers have to determine in order to "make things happen"?

8. What are some of the factors which make the job of managing business and nonbusiness organizations somewhat different? Discuss the effects of these factors.

Questions for Analysis and Discussion

1. "Good management is more a matter of time, place, and circumstance than it is of fundamental principles." Discuss.

2. In the last decade, several large company presidents were men who had formerly been with Ford Motor. These included the heads of such companies as Bell & Howell, Zenith, Arcata National Corporation, Litton Industries, and several others. None of these firms produce automobiles or auto parts. Yet all of them did well under ex-Ford executives. How could this be explained?

3. One can find quite a few cities in the United States where several family controlled companies have been successful over the years and have, more or less, collectively dominated the economies of these cities. Yet, in several cases, these same companies have not, for the last twenty years or more, kept up with the growth of the national economy. They have grown but their growth has been at a slower rate than the growth of the national economy. Have such companies a right not to try to grow as much as they can in order to serve their communities as well as possible?

4. Should management fight hard against giving pay raises to employees, thus holding down their costs and selling prices? Low selling prices help to generate sales and so help to preserve their employees' jobs and at the same time help to control inflation.

5. A report on business education made a number of years ago by Gordon and Howell[6] concluded that the basic skills and abilities required for business managers are analytical ability and judgment, skill in interpersonal relations, ability to accept responsibility and to make decisions, general administrative skills, breadth and flexibility of mind, imagination, facility

in personal communications, and strong motivation. Is this list still all right or should it be changed? How?

Assuming that this list is reasonably satisfactory, how should a college student go about preparing himself for a managerial career in business? Should he study French, sociology, public speaking, mathematics, accounting, business law, or what subjects?

6. The Exposure Camera Company spends 4 percent of its gross income for engineering. It is possible for it to get a government contract to work on space items unrelated to cameras if it shifts its engineers over and uses them on the proposed contract. The contract will probably keep them busy for nearly two years. What cost, profit, and other implications need to be considered here?

7. Is there any way to get the equivalent of profit motivation into the minds of the heads of government departments? Would this be desirable?

8. Consider these three managerial jobs:

    1. The head of the highway department of the State of California.
    2. The head of the Massachusetts General Hospital.
    3. The head of the federal Department of Health, Education and Welfare.

    · How can one tell if these managers are doing good jobs?
    · Who should make such a judgment?
    · How would one go about making an appraisal?
    · If the incumbent were judged to be doing poorly, who should do what about it?

9. Twenty-five years ago it cost $15 a day to stay in a semi-private room as a patient at a large metropolitan hospital. By 1980, the same room with comparable service cost $150. Yet this particular hospital can hardly pay its bills in spite of being nearly fully occupied and has been pleading for more government support. Under similar circumstances a business corporation would be in bankruptcy. Another hospital in the same city but operated as a private corporation and charging the same rates is making money. If you were sick and had to go into a hospital, which one would you choose? Why?

20

Case 1-1 The Management Training Program

TOP MANAGEMENT
IS NO PLACE FOR AMATEURS

"That's why they rarely make it to the top. And if by some mistake they do
— they're lost when they get there.

"A professional can beat an amateur every time. He's trained to get things done . . .
the right way. . . through other people. He has full command of management skills
and techniques to solve his problems professionally.

"Where did he get that knowledge?"

The above is from an advertisement for management training courses offered by the American Management Associations. Obviously, the AMA's answer to the question, "Where did these professionals get that knowledge?" is, "In AMA training programs."

Passing by the obvious answer and recognizing that the later chapters in this book are still to follow, one might consider at this point, the question of what general areas of subject content need to be dealt with in courses such as AMA's seminars. One could also consider whether the required managerial know-how is something which can be reduced to text form and whether the necessary skills can be learned from a book or in a classroom as compared to being learned on the job.

What are some of the relevant subject areas of knowledge and what is the best way to achieve managerial competence?

Case 1-2 Pacific Southwest Airlines

Pacific Southwest Airlines was started right after World War II by eight former military pilots to provide air service between a number of California cities. Because it did not fly across any state line, it did not fall under the jurisdiction of the Federal aviation laws as do the big trunk airlines (United, American, TWA, etc.).

Pacific Southwest's service was very good and its fares were 20 percent below those of the larger regulated airlines for the same air flights within the state of California. For many years Pacific Southwest was held up by business magazine writers as an example of how successful a privately owned company could be if it was left relatively free from regulation.

Then, in 1970, PSA started to spend some of its retained earnings. It ordered several new extra large "Jumbo Jets." At the same time, in a diversification move, it started buying other kinds of businesses: hotels, car rentals, and radio stations. By the end of 1974, these moves had created serious losses. In mid-1975, there was such a severe financial crunch that the company nearly went bankrupt. The company did survive, however. (It sold off its other businesses and its extra large airplanes, limited its flights to two hours duration with no food service, and continued its frequent flight policy.) By 1980 it was again a very profitable company.

- How could Borden run all those organizations which differed from its basic milk business and succeed, whereas PSA tried just a few and failed?
- What are the similarities and differences between operating an airline and a rental car agency?
- Does this case prove anything for or against government regulation of industry?

Endnotes

1. "GE: Not Recession Proof, But Recession Resistant," *Forbes*, March 15, 1975, pages 26ff.
2. *Organizational Psychology*, 3rd ed., by Edgar H. Schein, Prentice-Hall, 1980, page 117.
3. *Formula for Success*, by Lawrence A. Appley, AMACOM, 1971, page 4.
4. Reported in *Management Review*, August, 1980, page 53. See also "The Manager's Job; Folklore and Fact," by Henry Mintzberg, *Harvard Business Review*, July-August, 1975, pages 49–61. See also, "Managers in Action: A New Look at Their Behavior and Operating Methods," by R.V. Davis and Fred Luthans, *Organizational Dynamics*, Summer, 1980, pages 64–80.
5. As reported by W. Michael Blumenthal when he was Secretary of the Treasury under President Carter. Before becoming Secretary of the Treasury, Blumenthal had been president of Bendix Corporation, maker of automobile and airplane parts. See, "Carter's Harried Businessmen," *Business Week*, May 29, 1978, p. 80. After leaving Carter's cabinet, Blumenthal became president of Burroughs Corporation, makers of computers. See also, "The Nature of Managerial Work: A Comparison of Public and Private Sector Jobs," by Alan W. Lau, Cynthia M. Pavett, and Arthur R. Newman, *Academy of Management Proceedings*, 1980, pp. 9–13.
6. *Higher Education for Business*, by Robert A. Gordon and James E. Howell, Columbia University Press, 1959.

Suggested Supplementary Readings

Blumenthal, W. Michael, "Candid Reflections of a Businessman in Washington." *Fortune*, 29 January 1979, pp. 36ff. (Blumenthal had resigned from the presidency of Bendix Corporation to become Secretary of the Treasury under President Carter. Later he resigned from the Cabinet and became president of Burroughs Corporation.)

Katz, Daniel, Kahn, Robert L. and Adams, J. Stacy, eds. *The Study of Organizations*, Jossey-Bass, 1980.

Newman, William H., and Wallender, Harvey W., III. "Managing Not-For-Profit Enterprises," *Academy of Management Review*, January, 1978, pp. 24–31.

Rumsfeld, Donald. "A Politician-Turned-Executive Surveys Both Worlds." *Fortune*, 1 September, 1979, pp. 88–94. (Rumsfeld resigned from being Secretary of Defense under President Ford and became president of G.D. Searle company.)

Objectives of Chapter Two

1. To explore the beginnings of management and organizational theory.
2. To present, individually, the contributions of the three main proponents of "classical" thinking.
3. To summarize the managerial and organizational thinking at the close of the classical period in the decade after World War I.
4. To consider the main developments in the neo-classical period which ended with World War II.

Early Management Theory

Directing our organization is not difficult.
Our products are so well suited to
our customers' needs that a lad in the office
who is good at bookkeeping could do all
of the necessary work to keep things moving.
A factory owner's view, circa 1850.

Managing 100 Years Ago

Although isolated and fragmentary instances of interest in management and organization fundamentals can be found as far back as the dawn of recorded history, there was no general interest in developing knowledge about management and organization until the late 1800s.

This interest was spurred by the tremendous growth in the size of companies after the Civil War in the United States. Most prominent in this growth were the railroads and the steel producing companies.

After the Civil War, American railroads grew rapidly into large organizations with thousands of employees. (By 1890 the Pennsylvania Railroad had over 100,000 employees.) Thousands of tons of freight from thousands of shippers were picked up by thousands of employees at hundreds of points of origination and shipped to hundreds of destinations. Employees in all of these locations had to do their bits of work to make things go.

Growth was also occurring in other segments of the economy. Besides the steel industry, which was characterized by large scale multi-plant operations, large scale manufacturing was also the rule in the sewing machine, farm equipment, and numerous other industries.

Similar growth was occurring in retailing. Marshall Field in Chicago, Macy's in New York and many other large department stores were well established. Montgomery Ward's mail order catalog had over 500 pages.[1]

The operations of all of these enterprises had to be *managed*. And, as their continued growth attests, they were being managed successfully. But, managed only by yesterday's standards, not today's standards.

Typically these large companies were managed almost as if they were collections of small independent companies. Lower-level managers were given almost complete authority to carry on their operations as they saw fit. Factory foremen did their own hiring, disciplining, and firing of employees. They determined the wages to be paid. Sometimes they even contracted out parts of their inside work to groups of their employees. In retailing, department managers did their own buying and selling as well as hiring their own clerks.

There was no long-range planning, budgets were almost unknown, operations were not planned, costs were often not recorded and, if they were, they were only the direct costs. Overhead costs were not pro-rated to products so no one ever knew what the total costs of products were. There were no production standards, no evaluation of performance, and no control from the top. Central office staff departments were rare.

All of this growth in size was accompanied by an expansion in the number of middle-level managers — salaried employees who were not owners. These employees usually received almost no training in their work and tended to become bureaucratic rather than entrepreneurial in their thinking.

The Quest for Fundamentals

The time was right for someone to appear on the scene who would try to find out how best to *manage*. Frederick Taylor, who appeared in the 1880s, filled this need. He was the first to emphasize that *management* was a very important ingredient in the effective operation of organizations. We will consider his contributions and the contributions of other early scholars of management and organization in the next few pages.

Since Taylor's time, the interest in management and organization has become widespread. Yet, even today, there is disagreement over how best to manage and direct organizations. This occurs in spite of a great deal of time and effort being spent trying to unearth fundamentals which will help managers to direct their organizations more effectively.

College professors of business administration, psychology, sociology, and other subjects have conducted research and have written books and articles in learned journals and magazines devoted to management and organization. Consulting companies, business managers' associations, universities, and teachers' organizations hold meetings devoted to discussing various aspects of how best to manage organizations.

Out of all this welter of scholarly input have come many insights into how people behave, how we are motivated, and how we do or do not respond to stimuli. Not surprisingly, the researchers have found that people are not all alike and that our contacts with each other occur under varying circumstances. So our behavior and our responses are not all alike either.

Perhaps it is because of this that scholars who study the behavior of people in organizations often emphasize different points.

Some people see organizations as social orders. Some emphasize the behavior of groups rather than individuals. Some scholars view organizations largely in terms of decision making. Some see sets of interacting variables and some see systems of communications. Still others see organizations as structures made up of departments doing different things.

An organization *is* a complex entity. It would be surprising if scholars studying organizations did not see different things. This chapter will examine early theories and "classical" concepts.

Classical Theory

The managerial thinking of theorists and practitioners at the close of the last century and the early years of this century has come to be called "classical" theory. The major contributors to classical theory were Frederick Taylor, Henri Fayol, and Max Weber.

Frederick Taylor

The first of the classicists was Frederick Taylor.

In 1880, Taylor was promoted, at age 24, to be a "gang boss" at the Midvale Steel Company in Philadelphia. Being himself a skilled machinist, he knew when his workers were doing well and when they were not doing well. And, being also ambitious, he wanted to do his job well and to have his group perform efficiently.

Almost immediately, he ran into trouble because his men had little interest in working efficiently. All they wanted to do was to work along at a comfortable pace, a pace which Taylor thought was too slow. (He said that they were "soldiering on the job" and that they were not doing a "fair day's work.")

He tried threatening them, which did little good. Then he tried using persuasion, which did little better.[2]

After both threats and persuasion failed, Taylor turned his attention to why he had trouble. Observing his men at their work, he noticed that they did not do things in the same way. Some of their methods took more effort and more time than methods used by other workers. Work methods had always been left up to the workers. Taylor reasoned that there should be one best way to do every job. This led him to the conclusion that work methods should be studied and the best method determined. This method should then be taught to all workers doing

FIGURE 2-1

Workers laboring for $1 a day eyed Fred Taylor with suspicion when he appeared among them with a stop watch and pad and made notes as they worked.

that kind of work. The big change here was a recognition that *management* should undertake the job of developing work methods and also the obligation to teach these methods to workers.

Differing methods were not, however, the whole trouble. Taylor found that, in a great many cases, neither the workers nor the foreman knew just how *much* work men should do. There were no production standards so no one knew what a "fair day's work" was. And so long as the men used different methods, reliable time standards could not be set. So Taylor's first job became to standardize work methods.

Once the proper methods for performing tasks were set up, the next job was to set production standards specifying how many times an hour the worker should perform his work. Taylor developed a new technique, time study, using a stop watch to time the work being done, for setting the production standards. Now he was able to find out how much work to expect and could set work quotas knowing that the expectations were reasonable.

At this point he ran into a new problem. In some cases, the job required physical capabilities that some workers did not have. Men unloading pig iron from railroad cars needed to be big and strong. On other jobs, manual dexterity was more important. This showed that people should be selected for jobs in accord with each job's requirements.

Taylor's predecessors had not been unaware of this fairly obvious need but they had not paid very much attention to it and they had paid very little attention to training new workers in proper work methods.

Taylor also appreciated that, fundamentally, productivity comes about from the joint efforts of all concerned, managers and workers alike, working together cooperatively. He wanted and he tried to develop cooperative attitudes although he was himself not very democratic and often failed to win the cooperation of his workers.

Taylor's main contributions were largely concerned with replacing rules of thumb with organized knowledge based on analytical work done by management. Taylor's work led him to conclude that:

· Jobs should be done in the one best way and it is a management obligation to find out this best way and to teach it to workers.
· Time standards, set by time study methods, should be set for all jobs wherever possible. Taylor was the father of time study.
· Employees should be selected and assigned to jobs in accord with the matchup of their capabilities and the jobs' requirements.
· Close and friendly cooperation between workers and management is the most effective way to become efficient.

"Scientific Management." Taylor's methods were, later on, called "scientific management." They were quite successful so far as improving the efficiency of shop floor work. This was accomplished in spite of more than a little opposition from workers and unions.

Taylor's scientific management differed from the approach of the other well known members of the classical school, such as Henri Fayol and Max Weber. Taylor started at the bottom and analyzed shop floor jobs. Fayol and Weber started at the top and worked downward.

Scientific management, in the Taylor mode, regarded job content as fixed and unchanging. Workers had to mold their movements to the job. One of the negative reactions to scientific management was that it was claimed by detractors that it made automatons out of the workers. Taylor's bid for cooperation between workers and management failed because the power was all in the hands of management. Often the result was resentment and bitterness rather than a helpful joining of hands.

In the conceptual realm, Taylor separated mental from manual work so far as factory jobs were concerned. The mental work, determining how work should be done, was to become part of managerial work. Only the manual work was left for workers. This differed from the practices of Taylor's time which left it up to workers to figure out how to do their jobs.

Henri Fayol

The second of the three most important classicists was Henri Fayol. Fayol was a successful industrialist in coal mining in France. His only book, *General and Industrial Management*, was published in 1916, a year after Taylor's death. Like Taylor, Fayol felt that management was of great importance and was a skill which could be learned.

Curiously, Fayol is recognized today in organizational literature for his early contributions. But, like many pioneers in other subject areas, his recognition came long after his death in 1925. He was virtually unknown in England and the United States until the late 1930s. Today's scholars, however, give him credit for having developed an incisive philosophy of management almost as early as that of Frederick Taylor even though he had little influence on his contemporaries.

Fayol held that the job of managers is to *plan, organize, command, coordinate, and control activities.* He was the first to consider this "functional" approach to management.

He also put more emphasis than others had done on the need for managers to try to *control* the work of their subordinates by exercising surveillance over their work. He thought of management as a closed system rather than an open system and did not emphasize the dynamic relationships between groups.

Fayol considered organizations to be vertical structures with different operating areas being set apart by what they do (by "function"). Power flows down through the hierarchy. He recognized that this made for overly formalized communications and generated bureaucratic rigidities which inhibited lateral communications. This hampered cooperation between different departments. To alleviate this, Fayol proposed to set up "bridges" (coordinative departments) between chains of command so that cooperation could occur.

He formulated what was perhaps the first set of "principles" of management. Managers who used his principles would, according to Fayol, be managing well. The most important of his principles were:

Unity of command. Positions should be so arranged that subordinates have only one superior. Curiously, and in contrast, Taylor never seemed to be concerned with this concept. In fact, Taylor, even tried out eliminating line foremen altogether and substituting a number of functional superiors, each of whom had charge of one phase of a worker's activities. This attempt on Taylor's part was a failure.

Parity of authority and responsibility. The authority of managers should match their responsibilities or come close to matching them.

Span of control. Managers and supervisors should have neither too many nor too few subordinates reporting directly to them. At bottom levels the number should probably be from twenty to thirty people. At top levels it should be five or six.

Max Weber

Max Weber, the third of our three major classicists, also wrote in this early period. Weber, a German, was a sociologist who was interested in capitalism. He saw that numerous large companies developed in capitalistic societies and that such economies were far more productive than any other societies had ever been in history. He tried to figure out why this was so. He concluded that it came from the large companies employing thousands of workers which had grown up in twentieth century capitalistic countries.

This led Weber to giving thought to how these organizations operate. He considered the "Protestant work ethic" to be one of the causes. This concept held, in contrast to the ethic of many societies in the past, that it was not only socially acceptable, but it was, in fact, desirable for people to be motivated by the profit motive to work and produce goods and services. Moreover, people preferred to take the productivity gains in the form of more products and services rather than in more leisure.

Weber's interest in organizations started at the top. He visualized a vertical downward hierarchy of levels of subordinates, each receiving his power from his superior. Like Fayol, he felt that unity of command was important. And, like both Fayol and Taylor, he felt that jobs should be specialized. He also felt, as they did, that the jobs of subordinates should be quite circumscribed. Their job assignments were to be fully defined and formally delegated to them.

Weber felt that the departments which produce the organization's end-product or end-service, the "line" organization, needed advice and help on some matters. This advisory and helping work was to be done by "staff" departments, whose relationships to line departments should be carefully delineated. His view here was quite different from that of Taylor, who also recognized the need for specialized help but wanted to eliminate the line altogether and to have staff-type specialized people supervise low-level operators directly in the area of their expertise.

Bureaucracy. Weber put a great deal of emphasis on the orderly structure of hierarchies in organizations. He wanted administrators to be hired professionals who were completely divorced from ownership. He felt that so long as jobs were filled by promotion from within of the most capable subordinates, the organization would be efficient. He felt that this corrected a weakness that had existed in the past in most societies where people were born into a class or occupation from which they could not break out and where the people who held responsible positions depended on family and birth and not on accomplishments. Because workers could aspire to higher jobs under capitalism, they were strongly motivated to do well so that they might be promoted.

Thus, Weber felt that the *bureaucracy was a favorable aspect of capitalism* because it was impersonal and so unlocked motivation in people by freeing them from fixed class occupations. He did not consider the negative features of rigidities which are today implied by the use of the term "bureaucracy."

In summary, Weber thought that the vertical hierarchy, with unity of command and with staff departments, would be an efficient organization. Because it was impersonal, it offered promotional opportunities to people to lift themselves up and so motivated them to work hard.

Other Contributors

By no means were our three major contributors in the classical area the only people interested in management and organization at that time.

Another contributor, Henry Towne, was a leading businessman-scholar when Taylor came on the scene. Towne, the head of his own company making locks and other hardware items, was trying to develop better management practices in his own company. He wrote several papers on the subject.

Two other early contributors to management thought, Henry Gantt and Carl Barth, came on a little later. Both were collaborators with Taylor in some of his work. Gantt developed a somewhat unusual wage incentive payment plan and also developed "Gantt" charts to help in the planning and control of big projects. Barth developed slide rules which told machine operators how fast to run their metal cutting machines and how much metal to try to take off at each cut.

Another important pioneer was Harrington Emerson who, like Taylor, was a consultant in the first decade of the century. He was an expert in the management of railroads.

Frank Gilbreth and his wife Lillian, of "Cheaper by the Dozen" fame, were well known as job improvement specialists. They were contemporaries of Taylor in his later years and became well known after World War I. After Frank's death in 1924, Lillian went on to fame as an industrial psychologist.

Summary of Classical Theory

Management Principles. The early classical writers felt that there must be a rational underlying set of fundamental truths or "principles" upon which good management was based. These rules were waiting to be formulated. Once formulated, they would constitute a set of laws of management which could be learned and, if followed, would insure good management.

These principles, as developed by the classicists, were pragmatic and were not based on research. Instead, they were their interpretations of what they had observed in their own experiences and the experiences of others.

Taylor, Fayol, and Weber all completed their writing before the end of World War I but their thinking, particularly that of Taylor, influenced the next generation.[3]

Systematic and Orderly Ways for Directing Work. All of these early writers liked systematic and orderly ways of doing things. For the most part, they believed that an organization was a product of rational thought. Top managers were responsible for the organization's work. They knew what work needed doing and accordingly set up jobs and filled them with employees. They planned the work to be done, and set up the organization's structure so that its objectives could be accomplished. People worked at known and fixed jobs whose task content rarely changed. Each subordinate manager was delegated appropriate responsibility and authority. (Two notable exceptions to this kind of thinking were Hugo Munsterberg and Lillian Gilbreth, both of whom were psychologists.)

Specialization of Labor. Most early organizational thinking focused on the specialization of labor (dividing up work so that each individual is assigned only a small collection of duties which he or she performs repetitively, thus acquiring great competence in this limited work assignment). They overlooked the interactions of groups and subparts of the organization.[4]

People as "Instrumental" Employees. Even the attention to individuals was more mechanistic than humanistic. An employee was an "instrumental" person who did work but who was not a personality. Employees were believed to behave logically and rationally in their own self interest and were viewed primarily as means through which the organization's work would get done. According to this view, employees, if they were properly selected, trained, directed, and paid, would respond in a disciplined fashion and would do their work well.

Employee Acceptance of Authority. Classical theory was somewhat legalistic. It seemed to assume that employees, particularly subordinate managers, when they accepted their jobs, had implicitly contracted to do certain work and would, therefore, accept responsibility and strive wholeheartedly to achieve organizational goals. Everything was quite authoritarian.

Early Human Behavior Theory

The rather formalistic classical view of management and organization had widespread acceptance throughout the 1920s and into the 1930s. By then, however, interest in the subject had broadened and there were perhaps two dozen well known writers. Some of these new scholars were beginning to pay more attention to the dynamics of situations and especially were noticing that organizations were made up of people whose reactions by no means always followed the supposed rules. Ordway Tead, Seebohm Rountree, Henry Dennison, and Mary Parker Follett expressed such ideas in the 1920s; Elton Mayo and Chester Barnard carried these ideas further in the 1930s. Although space does not permit us to go into the specific contributions of all these people, we will consider the unusual contributions of Elton Mayo and Chester Barnard separately.

Elton Mayo

The Hawthorne Experiments. Elton Mayo and his group of researchers conducted a series of experiments relating to worker behavior on the job in the late 1920s and early 1930s at Western Electric's Hawthorne factory in Chicago.[5]

The first studies were intended to find out the effects of differing lighting intensities on worker productivity. A group of five workers who were assembling telephone "relays" was selected as an experimental group and set apart in a separate study area.

Lighting intensities were changed up and down. Sometimes the workers were told whether the new intensity was greater or less than before. Sometimes they were intentionally told wrongfully to see what would happen. Surprisingly, in all cases, productivity increased!

Management and the researchers were puzzled. So a new, more extensive study was started. It was proposed that several kinds of changes would be made in order to study their effects. The changes were all to be discussed with the five workers before they were put into effect.

The first change was to put each worker on piece work. Productivity went up. Next, two rest pauses a day were introduced. Productivity went up. Then refreshments were served during the rest pauses. Again, productivity went up. Then the workday was shortened by half an hour. Productivity increased again.

Over a two-year period, a number of combinations of these kinds of change were tried. In all cases, productivity per work hour increased, although productivity per week did not always go up when rest pauses were made more frequently and lasted longer or when the work days or work weeks were shortened considerably.

Puzzled by all of this, the researchers next canceled everything and went back to the initial arrangement. Productivity went up again! And during the whole experiment, absenteeism went down, finally to only 20 percent of what it had been.

Interviews with the workers revealed that they liked all of the attention they were getting and they liked being consulted about prospective changes. They liked the lack of pressure and the almost nonexistent supervision. They liked the greater freedom and to be able to work at their own pace without fear of a reprimand. They liked it when the supervisor took pride in their work and they liked his taking an interest in them as individuals.

This, then, was the secret of why they were so much more productive. Their mental attitude had changed. They were favorable to their work situation. And it all came about because of the changes which had been made in the way they were supervised.

This study was the first of its kind ever made. And since the findings were so different from what practitioners of the day had believed, Mayo's report attracted a great deal of attention. It became a landmark and had a tremendous impact on the thinking of social scientists and, to some extent, on practitioners in the following years.

The "Hawthorne" Effect. Scholars today believe that part of the gain in productivity found by Mayo's group came from what is now called the "Hawthorne" effect. This concept holds that when any research singles out a group of workers for study, one of the immediate effects is to generate unusual interest and enthusiasm among the group members. They know that they are the subjects of special attention and usually they respond by working harder and becoming more productive. Unfortunately, over a period of time this extra motivation diminishes and production levels go back down to the old levels (as it did in the Hawthorne experiments after three years). Researchers need to be careful about how they interpret cause and effect relationships based on the initial effects of changed work conditions. The Hawthorne effect will cause improvement initially and this will suggest relationships which may prove, later on, to be only transitory.[6]

Chester Barnard

In 1938, executive-scholar Chester Barnard put forward his "Acceptance" theory of authority.[7] Briefly, the acceptance theory, which we will discuss more fully in Chapter 19, holds that a superior has only such authority as his subordinates are willing to confer on him. Barnard also believed that people in organizations develop behind-the-scenes "informal organizations" whose operation often interferes with the way the formal organization is supposed to operate. Both of these views ran counter to earlier ideas about the delegation of work.

Barnard emphasized that organizations needed to be cooperative entities and that managers needed to design their organizations so that cooperation would come about as a result of conscious, purposeful actions by managers. He felt that the basic function of managers is to *win* the support of their subordinates and also to provide them with the basis for cooperative effort. Such cooperation would be facilitated by the managers formulating objectives and by their providing their subordinates with the resources needed to meet the objectives. Barnard also emphasized the need for good communications as the means for making cooperation possible.

Other Contributors

During the 1930s, social science scholars with backgrounds in government work and other nonbusiness subjects were also writing on the subject of organization. Two of these, Luther Gulick and Marshall Dimock, had backgrounds in public administration rather than in the administration of businesses. Most of the writers with nonbusiness backgrounds put more emphasis on organizational dynamics than on rules and principles.

We mentioned Ordway Tead, Seebohm Rountree, Henry Dennison, and Mary Parker Follett earlier in this chapter. They were early proponents of the idea that organizations were dynamic and that employees were people with individual personalities. Others like James Mooney, Oliver Sheldon, Lyndall Urwick, and Donaldson Brown were interested in the philosophy of organization. Donaldson Brown was the architect of General Motors' "federalized decentralization" organizational structure which has served General Motors for over fifty years.

Although only a few names have been mentioned here and each name has been associated with certain specific single ideas, this is a tremendous oversimplification. From as early as 1910 and continuing to World War II, the close of the early period, many scholars wrote and a substantial literature developed.

Summary of Early Human Behavior Theory

Of the human behavior writers in the development period of the 1930s, only Elton Mayo did research of any consequence. The others, including Chester Barnard, were like the classicists in that they put forward their conclusions from observations of their own experiences and that of others.

But their conclusions were different from those of the classicists in that they brought the human organization into the picture and considered people and their reactions to be important factors in the total situation. These early behavioral scientists felt that their classicist predecessors had too much confidence in top-down management and in authoritarian methods for getting people to do things.

Much of what is now within the scope of behavioral theory still lay in the future, however. Mayo, Barnard, and others of this period opened the door to further investigations of organizational behavior but they did not themselves go very far in the direction of finding out how managers could manage better.

There was some research done in this period along the lines originally intended by the Hawthorne experiments. These projects were directed at learning the effects of lighting intensities on productivity and how fatigue and monotony on the job affected people. At the same time, industrial engineers such as Ralph Barnes were studying learning to see how and what changes occurred as workers learned their jobs. Industrial engineers and managers on industrial jobs also were trying out various wage incentive plans and studying their effects as motivators. Most of this interest had passed before World War II.

Review Questions

1. In general, what was the thinking of the early (pre-1920) writers on the subject of organization?
2. What is the difference between the general viewpoint of the classical pioneers and the early behavioralists?
3. Explain briefly the following terms: soldiering on the job, scientific management, bureaucracy, and the Hawthorne effect.
4. What were Frederick Taylor's contributions?
5. How did the ideas of Max Weber and Chester Barnard differ?
6. What, in general, were the conclusions of the classicists about how organizations operate?
7. What is the "Hawthorne effect"? Of what importance is it in the study of management and organization?
8. What findings came out of the research of Elton Mayo at Western Electric's Hawthorne plant?

Questions for Analysis and Discussion

1. How does it happen that, after many years of research on how best to manage, we still have no general theory of management?

Early Management Theory

2. Mayo's study was based on only five workers (although because of personnel changes some fourteen different people were in the group at one time or another). Isn't it unrealistic to build an edifice of conclusions on what five people did? (There were probably 50 million other Americans working during the time of Mayo's studies.) Discuss.

Case 2-1   Mary Parker Follett on Managing and Teaching

On page one of the fiftieth anniversary issue of the American Management Associations' *Management News*, Mary Parker Follett, a pioneer in organization theory, is quoted as having said, fifty years earlier:

> We shall all agree that it is one of the leader's chief duties to draw out from each man his fullest possibilities. The foreman should feel responsible for the education and training of those under him, the heads of departments should feel the same, and so on all along up the line to the chief executive. In fact, several men at a meeting of the American Management Associations voiced their conviction that 'leader' and 'teacher' are synonymous terms. If we are coming to think that the leader is not the boss, but the educator, that seems to me an indication that business is taking a long step forward.

If, in a manufacturing company, the purchasing agent works for the works manager, should and could the works manager teach him how to be a good purchasing agent? How about the chief chemist?

The dictionary does not mention "leader" in its definition of "teacher" nor vice versa. What is the merit of Miss Follett's views?

Case 2-2   Frederick Taylor at Bethlehem Steel

In the 1890s, Frederick Taylor worked as a consultant at the Bethlehem Steel Company. While there, he conducted several experiments aimed at improving operations and reducing production costs.

One of these studies had to do with the work of the yard labor gang. Sometimes the yard laborers had to shovel coal, sometimes it was iron ore, sometimes it was ashes, etc. There was a great variation in the weight of a shovelful of material. The men furnished their own shovels which were of various sizes. Taylor's experiments showed that the most work was done when about 21 pounds of material was moved in each shovelful. So he had the company buy several sizes of shovels. Large shovels were for ashes, small shovels were for iron ore, etc. Production costs were reduced considerably.

Taylor's second experiment was with pig iron. He decided, after observing men loading pig iron into freight cars from the storage yard, that they were not doing it right. He thought that they used the wrong motions and that they worked too long at a time, became overfatigued, and then rested too long. He believed that the work would be less tiring if the workers did their work differently and took frequent, short rest periods.

The job paid $1.15 a day and the men loaded 12½ tons of pig iron per man per day. Taylor offered one of the laborers, named Schmidt, $1.85 if he would change his methods and follow Taylor's directions about rest periods. Schmidt accepted and earned the $1.85 while loading 47 tons of pig iron. He continued to do this thereafter.

These accomplishments of Taylor did not meet with universal approbation.

· Who would object and why?

Endnotes

1. A good account of this early period is given in, *The Visible Hand: The Managerial Revolution in American Business,* by Alfred D. Chandler, Jr., Belknap Press, 1977. [The Visible Hand = professional management]
2. *Frederick W. Taylor,* by Frank B. Copley, Harper & Brothers, 1923, vol. 1, p. 161.
3. The ideas of these men and of other early writers on management and organizations are discussed in *The History of Management Thought,* 2d ed., by Claude S. George, Jr. (Prentice-Hall, 1972); *The Evolution of Management Thought,* by Daniel A. Wren (Ronald Press, 1972); and in *Classics of Organization Theory,* by Jay M. Shafritz and Philip H. Whitbeck (eds.) (Moore Publishing Co. 1978).
4. Max Weber did not, however, emphasize individuals. He overlooked individuals in his interest in the hierarchical structure.
5. Reported in, *The Human Problems of an Industrial Civilization,* by Elton Mayo, (Macmillan, 1933).
6. "Participative Management at Work: An Interview with John P. Donnelly," *Harvard Business Review,* January-February, 1977, pp. 117–127.
7. *The Function of the Executive,* by Chester Barnard, Harvard University Press, 1938. Barnard was president of the New Jersey Bell Telephone Company and later was head of the Rockefeller Foundation.

Suggested Supplementary Readings

Copley, Frank P., *Frederick W. Taylor,* Harper & Brothers, 1923.

Shafritz, Jay M., and Philip H. Whitbeck, eds., *Classics of Organization Theory,* (Moore Publishing Co., 1978).

Van Fleet, David D. "Management History." *Academy of Management Proceedings* 1979 Meeting at Atlanta, pp. 1–6.

Weber, Marianna. *Max Weber: A Biography,* trans. and ed. by Henry Zohn, (Wiley, 1975).

Objectives of Chapter Three

1. To present the main contributions of each of the several leading contributors to the development of behavioral science after World War II.
2. To summarize the contributions of these pioneer behavioral scientists.
3. To relate the contributions of these pioneers to present day theory.
4. To consider the use of organizational and behavioral theory in practice.

Behavioral Science Comes of Age

3

*All organizations are made up of people
so the study of how people behave singly
and in groups is fundamental to
understanding how organizations function.*

After its early start, behavioral science continued to develop, slowly in the 1940s and more rapidly in the 1950s and on into more recent years. During the early years of this period, social scientists, who distrusted the conclusions of the classicists because they were not based on research, undertook to investigate how organizations function by using controlled research methods. Their findings did not wholly upset the pragmatic knowledge of the past but they did provide deeper insights into organizational behavior. They showed that, in many cases, the old rules were too simplistic and were inadequate to explain organizational behavior.

The development of behavioral science thinking during this transitional period was influenced strongly by the work of a small number of outstanding scholars, each of whom is best known for his contribution in certain areas. We will consider the contributions of these outstanding scholars in this chapter.

Leaders in the Development of Behavioral Science

The leaders in the development of behavioral science in the years after World War II (mostly in the 1950s and 1960s) and the ideas with which their names are most commonly associated are:

Kurt Lewin	Group Dynamics
Rensis Likert	Participative Management, System 4
Abraham Maslow	Hierarchy of Needs
Douglas McGregor	Theory X and Theory Y
Frederick Herzberg	Dissatisfiers and Satisfiers
Chris Argyris	Stultifying job requirements
Robert Blake and Jane Mouton	Managerial Grid

Kurt Lewin: Group Dynamics

Kurt Lewin, one of the very early social scientists who was interested in organizational behavior, is given credit for developing the idea of "group dynamics."[1]

Group dynamics holds that *groups of people are entities apart from the individuals who make them up.* Groups develop identities and sub-cultures all of their own. People in groups act differently from the way they would act as individuals.

Groups are sometimes employees who work in one department of an organization. When they operate as groups, they often develop departmental objectives compatible with their self-interest. Such group objectives often do not advance the whole organization's objectives very much. They may even run counter to organizational objectives and harm organizational accomplishment.

Group cultures usually require that their members comply with the group's informal objectives (which are often protective over things hurtful to the group). These group objectives may be in conflict with the personal objectives of some of the individuals in the group. Sometimes the peer pressure from other group members is quite strong on reluctant members. So, even unenthusiastic members of the group go along in order to continue their acceptability to the group. The desire to be accepted and to belong to the group is very strong in many people. We all want to be accepted — warts and all.

Group loyalty and cohesiveness and support for goals which the individual would not himself choose (perhaps he or she would rather not restrict output to the group-generated norm) depend a great deal on the attractiveness of the group's goals. In order for group goals and the goals of group leaders to win respect and support, these goals need to be largely congruent with the predominant individual goals.

Not every collection of people is a "group" in the sense that they act in some concerted way to support a goal or action which all members accept. A college class is not a "group," at least not at first. It is merely a collection of individuals. Such collections of people may develop into one or more "groups" and they sometimes do. But at first they are only individuals. As such they do not subordinate personal goals to those of the group. But later, perhaps as group feelings develop and coalesce, their individual goals and those of the group begin to merge and become the same. The summation of the goals of individuals becomes incorporated into the group's goals while group goals at the same time mold individual goals.

Rensis Likert: Participative Management, System 4

Rensis Likert developed Lewin's group dynamics idea further and added such ideas as the superiority of democratic, participative leadership styles over authoritarian methods.[2] (By no means was Likert alone, however, in espousing participative leadership.) Likert is also one of many behavioral scientists who believe that, fundamentally, power is more or less evenly divided between organizational superiors and subordinates and that there ought to be a "power-equalization" mental set in organizational decision making. Subordinates will respond better if they are consulted and allowed to participate in decisions affecting them.

Likert classified leadership styles of managers into four "systems":[3]

System 1: Exploitive Authoritative.

System 1 managers make the decisions, give orders and have little trust in their subordinates. They use penalties and rewards with the emphasis on penalties. The fear motivation is strong.

System 2: Benevolent Authoritative. System 2 managers delegate some decision making, accept suggestions from subordinates, have a condescending confidence and trust in subordinates, and use penalties and rewards with the emphasis on rewards.

System 3: Consultative Management. Managers consult more with their subordinates and let them help make decisions. There is more up and down communication. But superiors do not have complete confidence and trust in subordinates. Penalties are rare and there is less emphasis on rewards.

System 4: Participative Group Management. System 4 managers are participative with individuals and with groups. Such managers have complete trust in their subordinates and allow them to make decisions. Participation and involvement by subordinates in problem solving is encouraged. Upward and downward communications are maximized and cooperation is encouraged. Penalty and reward systems almost disappear.

Of these four systems, Likert feels that system 2 is the most prevalent system in American industry but that system 4 is the most effective.

Likert feels that the use of strong power should be avoided because it tears down what he calls "intervening variables," in the organization. These variables are organizational empathy, loyalty, motivation, morale, and favorable attitudes toward organizational objectives. He believes that managers should be "employee-centered" (as against "production-centered") and supportive of their subordinates. Likert believes that production-centered managers get poorer results in the long run.

Because Likert believes that authoritarian leadership often harms the organization, and that this is not reflected in the usual reports of accomplishments of individual members, he recommends the development of more incisive reports. This idea grew into "human resource accounting" which would include in each manager's report credit for the improvement to, or a charge for the harm done, to the human organization by a manager. This idea got some play in the 1970s but now seems to have been discarded because of the impossibility of measuring such subjective things as changes in the quality of the organization.

Abraham Maslow: Hierarchy of Needs

Credit for being the first to set up a conceptual hierarchy of the needs of people as they relate to motivation is generally given to Abraham Maslow.[4]

According to Maslow, people's needs operate according to a hierarchy. These needs are of five kinds:

1. Physiological
2. Security and safety
3. Belongingness and love
4. Self-esteem and the esteem of others
5. Self-actualization

As Figure 3-1 shows, physiological and security needs are the most fundamental and universal of all motivations. People everywhere will work hard to meet their needs to eat and to stay alive. They are motivated to do whatever is necessary to meet these needs. In our monetary economies in the Western world, this means to earn enough money to be able to get along in a minimum way.

Once these primary needs are met on a continuing basis, offering a person more money for greater contribution to organizational accomplishment has, according to Maslow, only a weak motivational value. Motivation to further effort has, according to him, to be on a higher plane. The appeal

has to be to the desire to belong, to succeed, to be esteemed by others, to accomplish something, and to use one's higher capabilities. These become the important motivators. Managers need to offer subordinates opportunities to fulfill these higher level desires if they are to bring out the best in them.

Although Maslow himself had a considerable influence on other social scientists, his thinking had an even greater impact on the general acquaintance of people with his ideas because both McGregor and Herzberg were influenced by his views.

Many of today's social scientists doubt that there really is a hierarchy of motivations as Maslow thought. Research since Maslow's day indicates that people's biological needs (the need for food, shelter, and security) do indeed come first. But, once a person has a job so that these needs are satisfied, then other motivations come into play, but not as a sequential hierarchy as Maslow visualized. Instead, the higher level motivations differ considerably among people. In some people, esteem is more important than self-actualization, but in others, the reverse is true.[5] Psychologist Ruth Armstrong even says, "I question whether self-actualization is even a viable concept, since individual potential remains always a mystery."[6]

Douglas McGregor: Theory X and Theory Y

Douglas McGregor put forth his "Theory X" and "Theory Y" postulates in 1960.[7]

Theory X said that the average person dislikes work and avoids it when he can. To get people to work, they have to be forced, controlled, directed, and motivated by rewards and the fear of punishment. People have little ambition, prefer to be directed, and seek only security.

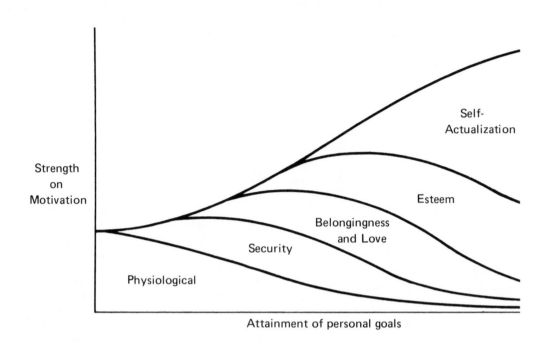

Figure 3-1
Maslow's hierarchy of needs related to motivational strength.

McGregor's Theory Y, on the other hand, held that, for most people, putting effort into work is as natural as play and that external control and threats are not good means for getting people to do work. If people's egos and self-actualization needs are met, and if they are allowed to exercise self-direction and self-control, they will not be resistant to organizational needs. They will seek responsibility and will work with imagination, ingenuity, and creativity toward organizational goals.

According to McGregor, managers with a Theory Y philosophy will manage differently and more effectively than Theory X proponents. And, according to McGregor, too few managers subscribe to Theory Y. (McGregor thought that most workers were Theory Y people.)

McGregor saw Theory X and Theory Y largely as opposites with no intervening positions. Gene Dalton and Paul Lawrence believe that this is too extreme. They say that "McGregor simplifies and polarizes some things which are not discontinuous but all lie on an underlying continuum."[8]

Theory X and Theory Y also do not consider individual differences in employees. Obviously, some people are Theory Y people and are energetic and highly motivated. But others are Theory X people. They are less energetic and less highly motivated. A few are even lazy. So, since not everyone is a Theory Y person, it follows that Theory Y leadership is not the best in every case.

The desire to work may be wholly natural to a great many people, just as

McGregor says. But, such innate desires probably do *not* relate to every specific kind of work, particularly to jobs which are inherently uninteresting. The work of cutting "eyes" out of 1,000 tons of potatoes used to make French fried potatoes for McDonald restaurants is not likely to fulfill very many people's desires to work. Managers can't always provide the kind of work which will satisfy this desire but they should try to make jobs as interesting as they can.

The fact that McGregor overdrew his points to dramatize and strengthen their impact did not keep them from being well received and from influencing the thinking both of other scholars and of practitioners.

Frederick Herzberg: Dissatisfiers and Satisfiers

Herzberg holds that motivations on the job come from two different sets of elements, "dissatisfiers," and "satisfiers," and that they are not the opposites of each other. This theory is sometimes called the "deficiencies or abundance" theory.[9]

One set of elements is associated with what Herzberg calls "hygiene" or "mainte-nance" factors. Hygiene factors include *working conditions; supervision; interpersonal relations; policies and administration; and money, status, and security.*

Herzberg says that these elements contribute mainly to *dissatisfaction.* They create dissatisfaction if they are *not* present, but they do not create satisfaction if they *are* present. So changes in them will *not* increase satisfaction. These job elements are essentially "dissatisfiers."

In contrast, Herzberg feels that satisfaction comes from "motivators," or "job content" factors, which are not the opposites of dissatisfiers. These "satisfier" elements include *challenging work, increasing responsibility, growth and development, achievement, and recognition for accomplishment.*

Changes in these motivators (which do not include pay), and *only* such changes, can motivate people to high satisfaction and high performance. A manager wishing to improve the performance of his organization should, therefore, try to provide the proper environment by reducing the dissatisfiers. Then he can turn to trying to build up the satisfiers. But, reducing the dissatisfiers will not, by itself, cause improved performance.

Herzberg's views on money as being a dissatisfier sound, at first, as if he had in

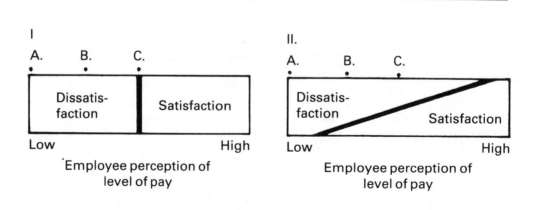

Figure 3-2

mind a situation such as that depicted in section I of Figure 3-2. A person getting a pay raise from A to B would be only less dissatisfied. Even a pay raise to C would not generate any satisfaction.

Section II of Figure 3-2 is a better illustration of how Herzberg believes that pay is related to dissatisfaction and satisfaction. In part II, a pay raise from A to B, for the most part, only reduces dissatisfaction. It does, however, generate a small amount of satisfaction. A pay raise to C, on the other hand, eliminates much more of the dissatisfaction over pay and generates an increasing amount of satisfaction.

Herzberg is also among the leading advocates of job enrichment (making jobs more interesting by adding varied duties). He feels strongly that managers can get extra productivity from workers whose jobs are designed to be interesting jobs.

Chris Argyris: Stultifying Job Requirements

According to Chris Argyris, the demands which most organizational controls put on employees are harmful.

These controls, says Argyris, ignore the social and egoistic needs of employees and work against their natural desires for self-actualization. The way most jobs are structured do not meet the individual's growth needs. Argyris says that most organizations need innovative behavior from the individual but that the controls exercised stifle people causing them to feel submissive and dependent. They are kept in an immature and dependent state and not allowed to develop maturity and independence. As a consequence, the employee develops dissatisfaction and apathy or conflict.[10]

Argyris also puts a great deal of emphasis on the need for job rewards and satisfactions to match up with people's goals. He holds that one person cannot motivate an-

other person but that motivation comes from an individual being able to meet his personal goals. So managers should manage in such a way as to reward people by satisfying their motivational desires.

If accomplishing these two sets of goals (personal and organizational) are not made to match up, then the result will be dissatisfaction, apathy, and sometimes tension, subversion, and conflict. In particular, Argyris feels that superiors should offer job challenge and opportunity to their subordinates.

Argyris is as well known because of his interest in sensitivity training and T-Groups as he is for his other contributions to organizational thinking. (Sensitivity training and T-Groups are discussed in Chapter 16.)

Robert Blake and Jane Mouton: Managerial Grid

Robert Blake and Jane Mouton are known for their "Managerial Grid."[11] The grid is a square diagram (see Figure 3-3) with a vertical scale marked off in degrees from 1 to 9 of concern for people. The horizontal scale represents degrees from 1 to 9 of interest in production. A 1.9 manager would be high on the vertical scale and low on the horizontal scale and would be interested in people but not in production. A 9.1 manager would be high in interest in output but would have little interest in subordinates.

Blake and Mouton emphasize that the manner in which these two concerns (concern for output and concern for people) are linked together is important. The ideal is a 9.9 style of management. Here the manager tries both to get people involved in their work and at the same time to have them strive to contribute to organization purposes. This combination of interests by the supervisor characterizes the best managers.

The process of developing managers into 9.9 people consists of a six-phase pro-

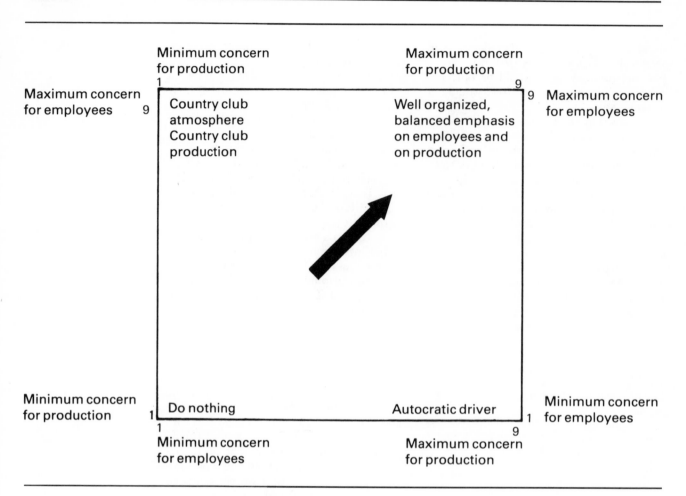

Figure 3-3

gram which may take three years or more. These phases are:

1. Problem solving seminar, concentrating on situations involving interpersonal behavior and emphasizing task performance.
2. Study of managerial styles as revealed in phase 1.
3. Development of group-to-group relationships.
4. Development of new organizational goals.
5. Study of total organization problems.
6. Evaluation of results and continued attention to remaining problems.

Contributions of Behavioral Scientists to Management and Organizational Thought

Theories and Principles

The history of the development of management thought reveals a persistent search for universal truths and generalizations. The classicists searched for "principles," whereas social scientists tried to develop "theories." Both, in fact, searched for generalizations which would have widespread applicability.

Many early social scientists rejected the idea that there could be principles, and certainly some of the "principles" favored by the classicists were too dogmatic. They just did not apply in every case. The principle of "unity of command," for example, held that a subordinate should have only one superior. Yet, in fact, an organization can get along, sometimes quite well, where there are some situations in which people have two superiors.

Because they disliked the principles idea, social science researchers called their conclusions "theories." These theories were intended to describe how most people behaved and why. As time has passed and as more research evidence has piled up, many of the theories of the early behavioralists have been found to have only limited applicability. Today, social scientists believe that although generalizations can have widespread applicability, there are so many different situations that how theories as well as principles will operate is conditional and is dependent on the situation. If a quick decision is needed, for example, then an autocratic decision-making process is probably the best way. But with more time, a consultative process would probably be better.

Differences in people also matter. Some people don't want to be consulted about decisions; others, possibly most others, do want to be consulted. "Contingency theory," which covers such differences, has emerged. Contingency theory (to be discussed in Chapter 14) holds, in effect, that the best way to manage depends upon the interaction of several variables according to the situation.

People as Human Beings

Social scientists showed that human reactions in organizations do not always follow rules. Organizations are made up of people and people are not inanimate and passive machines. They have different capabilities and skills and they have ambitions and hopes and fears. When they are told to do something, they respond like people; that is, they may do what they are told to do or they may not, or they may not do it in the way their superior wants it done. And the reasons why they react as they do are not always very logical, at least not as a rule-bound superior would see it.

Early behavioral scientists generally associated worker satisfaction with productivity and believed that increasing worker satisfaction would lead to increased productivity. Today's scholars regard this conclusion as being too simplistic. It does not consider individual differences in people nor does it reflect a very deep understanding of human motivations. Added research over the years has found that although employee satisfaction and productivity usually go hand in hand, this is not always so. Satisfied workers are by no means always productive and dissatisfied workers are not always unproductive.

Self-Actualization

Social science research indicates that a great many of us, at least in the Western world, seem to have within us a deep-seated urge for "self-actualization" or "self-fulfillment."[12] We have inside us a need to achieve and to accomplish something we can claim as our own. This was Maslow's highest level motivator.

This need for self-actualization poses a serious challenge to managers because a great many jobs have only limited self-actualization potential. There is actually very little that a manager can do to increase the self-actualization possibilities on, say, the job of an employee who nails heels onto shoes in a shoe factory. Yet this is the challenge. Managers need to try to do what they can to make the work of their people more interesting. Just talking to them and telling them what is going on will help make them feel that they are part of the organization.

People's desires for self-actualization may also make problems when their desires outstrip their capabilities. Not every young man can become an All-American football player just because he wants to do so. This situation is similar to the cases where people have capabilities not related to their work. A person whose capability is to play a violin well is unlikely to find self-fulfillment on a job as a bank teller.

Fortunately, the need for self-actualization is often met by off-the-job activities not related to people's regular employment. It will be recalled, from our description of Maslow's ideas, that more than a few social scientists believe that self-actualization is not so serious a matter as Maslow thought. Edgar Schein says that self-actualization needs *are* important to high-level members of organizations such as managers and professionals. But, says Schein, many lower-level employees have only low self-actualization needs.[13] We know, too, that educators tell us that in school some students are "underachievers" who do not seem to want to achieve all that they might. Some adults seem also to be underachievers with low self-actualization needs.

Role Development

Behavioral scientists also showed that delegation of work is a much less precise activity than early scholars had felt it to be. As we will see in Chapter 17, delegations of work are usually only frameworks which subordinates fill in for themselves. The work which they actually end up doing is partly dependent on their own perceptions of what they see as needing to be done. In almost all cases, their perceptions are colored by their views of how their self-interest will be affected. Their views are further modified by their

doing what they like to do and avoiding doing things they don't like to do. Consequently, what they end up doing may not be quite in accord with their original delegation, at least as the superior views their original delegation.

Role Conflict

Another idea brought to light by social scientists concerns "role conflict." Employees sometimes have to try to meet conflicting demands or expectations and thus feel role conflict. Probably all jobs contain certain elements of role conflict.

A factory supervisor is supposed to run his department well. He is expected to get out a given quantity of production at minimal cost. He is part of management and he represents management to his subordinates. At the same time, however, he represents his employees to management. He needs to have good and smooth working relationships with his employees, to understand their problems, and to provide support to protect their interests.

In cases in which the goals and actions of subordinates do not mesh with the goals of management (as when employees do not work hard enough to keep costs down) the supervisor is torn between trying to maintain good relations with his employees and trying to comply with the desires of management and to operate the department effectively. He has to try to meet the expectations of both superiors and subordinates and sometimes these are in conflict with each other.

More complicated is the situation in which an employee has to play two or more roles simultaneously. A social worker in the personnel department might experience a conflict between being an employee of the company (thus required to favor the interests of the company) while on the other hand his professional instincts dictate that he or she violate the company's interests. Perhaps an employee has an alcohol or a drug problem. For the employee's best interest, he should be given help and tolerant supervision. But for the organization's best interest, the employee should be dismissed.

Role conflict in such a situation may cause conflict in the mind of the individual, causing frustration. Role conflict can lead to outward actions of hostility and it can lead to inward difficulties such as nervous breakdowns and ulcers.

A reasonable amount of role conflict seems not to disturb most people. Sometimes it is like the mental conflict which goes on in our minds when we choose not to spend money today for something we would like to have in order to save money for a vacation trip which we also want. The mental conflict is not of serious proportions. In job situations, too, minor role conflict rarely makes much trouble.

Probably it is impossible to eliminate role conflict altogether because goals do sometimes conflict. Yet managers should recognize this as a problem and try to keep it from growing to harmful proportions and causing people to quarrel, argue, and refuse to cooperate with each other.

Groups

Kurt Lewin noted that people in groups behave differently from the way they behave by themselves. Before Lewin, the classical scholars had given very little attention to groups. Informal groups seem to grow up in all organizations and often play a part in how organizations function. They have power to aid or to hamper organizational activities. Since they are usually protective of group interests, they often favor retaining the status quo and make it harder for managers to make changes.

It is hard to put group influence into the proper perspective because it is only sometimes that groups play a very significant part. In one early research project, Robert Dubin found that two-thirds of the workers in his study did *not* possess any group identification with their work colleagues. Dubin found that status and wage differentials led to the continual erosion of the solidarity of the work group, as did specialization of the work, particularly along assembly lines.[14]

Thus, informal groups are not always very important. Against Dubin's findings, however, research and history provide us with considerable evidence that groups often do play a part. Managers need to be aware of them and to manage accordingly. We will consider informal groups more fully in Chapter 16.

Leadership and Motivation

Early organization scholars devoted very little attention to leadership and motivation. They assumed that the heads of organizations had the power to make decisions and to issue directions which organization members would carry out. They seemed not to recognize that leadership styles would themselves have any bearing on the way subordinates carried out their work. Similarly, classical scholars did not concern themselves with motivation. They assumed that when people accepted jobs they would apply themselves diligently to carrying out the organization's objectives.

Behavioral scientists have done a great deal of work in these two areas and have found that a better understanding of leadership and motivation is of the greatest importance in effective operations. Leadership and motivation are discussed in Chapters 14 and 15.

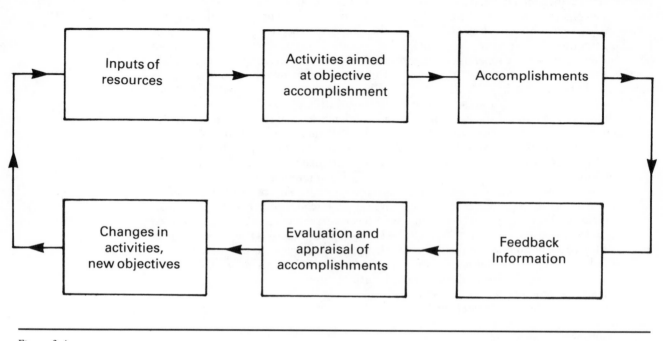

Figure 3-4
A closed loop system.

Recent Organizational Thought

Today there is a very substantial literature of organizational thought. Research into how organizations operate has mushroomed, and scholars now conducting research and presenting their findings number in the hundreds. The areas of their interests and points of emphasis are so varied that it is impossible to cover all of their ideas in any brief summary.

And like so many of the earlier scholars, most recent researchers also have broad interests and their names cannot properly be associated with only one idea. For the most part, their research has been devoted to refining and reinvestigating the subjects investigated by their predecessors. But they have also investigated other areas, too, some

of which were neglected by the earlier researchers. *

Systems

The "systems" concept merits separate attention here because it came to the fore along with behavioral thinking but it is more or less outside the behavioral school of thought.

The systems concept holds that the complete system is more than the sum of its

---

*Rather than attempting a listing of the current leading scholars of organizational thought, we have chosen to give them recognition through text references wherever this is appropriate. As we discuss the subjects covered in this book, we will refer to journal articles and books on these subjects. The reader will thus become acquainted with the names of scholars and their ideas through these references.

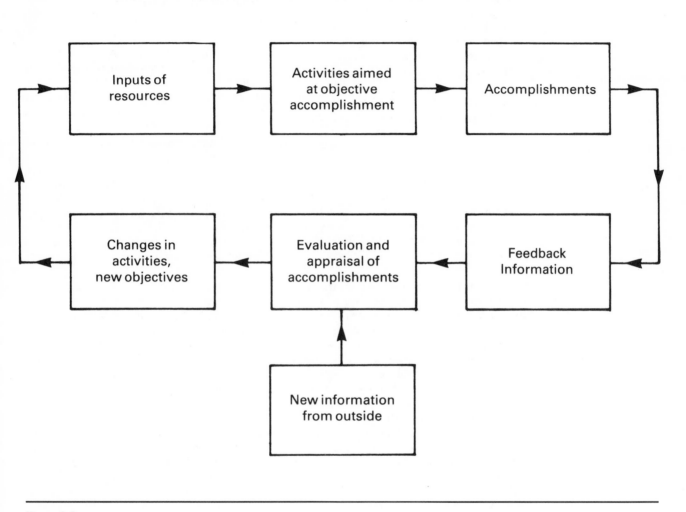

Figure 3-5
An open loop system.

parts. It is itself a totality which is something different from just a collection of parts.

In the study of organizations, the systems concept is usually cast in a communications setting. It has to do with the flow of communications which reveals what is going on and how what is going on affects the different parts of the system and how it affects the whole system.

It emphasizes the "complete circuit" idea. Managers get reports of results of actions, evaluate the results, make new decisions, and carry on new activities designed to reach goals. Then they get reports again and the cycle repeats. Systems proponents emphasize the effects of single actions on the totality.

Systems may be "closed" or "open."

- *Closed systems* (see Figure 3-4) are systems which have internal flows, much as a person's blood flow system is a closed system. It continues on without outside stimulus and is largely non-responsive to outside stimuli.

- *Open systems* (see Figure 3-5) have internal flows but they receive inputs from the outside and react to them.

The value of the systems approach in a study of how organizations operate is in the recognition that organizations tend to become closed systems and not to be responsive enough to outside factors, whereas they *should* be responsive to such factors.

It is probably true that, in the most literal sense, and even in the physical world, there can be no such thing as a *completely* closed system (an automatic washing machine and a spring wound clock are closed systems only for a short while). And certainly no organization could ever be wholly a closed system. On the other hand, most of us have had frustrating experiences with government agencies or with businesses which seem, at times, not to be responsive to our needs. Public school systems, hospitals, governments, and sometimes businesses, too, are often not responsive enough to outside influences. They tend to become closed systems and to lag in their adaptations to environmental needs.

Part of the trouble is often within the system itself. The organization's people, those at its boundaries, where environmental changes can be sensed, do not convey information into the organization's internal information flow system. Hence the organization cannot respond appropriately. Difficulty can arise, too, from failures of internal units receiving input information reacting appropriately to it.

Managers' Use of Organization Theory

Most business managers do not go all the way with organization theorists. Many of them feel that the theorists' ideas are untested, or are too soft and impractical. (Most behavioral scientists would object to this charge and claim that employee-centered management does not have to be, nor should it be, "soft" management.) Many executives also think that theorists concern themselves too much with people-satisfactions and too little with getting work done. They also feel that theorists equate the effective management of people with the totality of effective management, forgetting the other facets of the managerial job, such as making products, selling them, paying debts, obeying laws, operating according to a labor contract, and such things.

Many companies actually make considerable use of the findings of social science researchers; some even employ behavioral scientists full time. Texas Instruments, American Airlines, Armstrong Cork, and TRW are among the many companies which employ full time psychologists and sociologists whose job it is to use behavioral research findings in their organizations whenever they apply. And the names of the companies which have called on the services of the people named in this chapter to serve them as consultants include many of the largest companies in the country.

Some managers who have tried certain specific ideas remain unconvinced of their value. A few would even agree with sociologist Charles Perrow who says:

The attempt to produce change in an organization through management grids, sensitivity training, and even job enrichment and job enlargement is likely to be fairly ineffective for all but a few organizations. Critical review of research in all of these fields show that there is no scientific evidence to support the claims of the proponents of these various methods.[15]

Most social scientists and many managers, too, would probably disagree with Perrow and would say that he is too critical in his statement.

One widespread effect of the work of behavioral scientists has been a growth of more democratic management methods. Perhaps this would have evolved without the behavioral scientists. But whether it would have or not, today's managers, and particularly business managers, use more democratic methods than they used to. Yesterday's dictatorial manager is less common today than in years past.

Summary

Soon after World War I new social scientists began to point out that things were by no means so orderly as their predecessors had thought. Not only were organizations complex entities but they were made up of people who were in many ways alike but were also at the same time individuals and therefore always and forever different. This meant that there could be no true principles about their behavior patterns.

Since World War II, social scientists have done a great deal of research trying to find out more about how organizations operate and how people work when they are members of organizations. Out of this research have come, not principles, but many generalizations and theories which can help managers to manage better.

Researchers have found that, in the American culture, a great many, perhaps most, people seem to want their work to provide an opportunity for self-fulfillment. And most people seem to like to participate in the making of decisions which will significantly affect their work. According to these theories, their desires for more money, once a reasonable income has been achieved, seem to become secondary to factors which make their work more self-fulfilling.

Review Questions

1. In what way did the contributions of social scientists change the direction of thinking about how organizations operate?
2. What is meant by "group dynamics"? What has it to do with organizational behavior?
3. Discuss and compare Likert's four systems. Which is the most common? Which does Likert prefer and why?

4. What difference does it make whether there is a hierarchy of needs, as Maslow held, or not?

5. What are "Theory X" and "Theory Y"? Where did these ideas originate? Of what use are they?

6. Explain Herzberg's "deficiencies or abundance" theory. In what way should a manager who accepts Herzberg's ideas manage?

7. Behavioral scientists avoid using the word "principles." Yet they accept "theories," such as those of Maslow, McGregor, etc. Aren't they being inconsistent? Aren't theories the same as principles?

8. Why should role conflict exist? Discuss.

Questions for Analysis and Discussion

1. "Principles (enduring generalizations) pose a dilemma because on the one hand they must exist, yet on the other hand they cannot exist."

    Discuss this statement from the point of view of (a) social scientists, and (b) traditional theory.

2. If a man or woman drinks a quart of whiskey, he or she will get drunk — whether a research study proves it or not. Of what use is research into human behavior? Don't we know pretty well what people are like?

3. "The hunches, suspicions, and superstitions of yesteryear have been replaced by valid, reliable data leading to the formulation of sound theories that can be used to explain and predict people's behavior." So says the advertisement for a two-day seminar on "What Managers Should Know About Behavioral Science" (fee, $200). This seminar was to be conducted by a discussion leader who had a Ph.D. degree.

    Comment on this advertisement.

4. Some people believe that group reactions and feelings are more important than individual feelings. Is your college class, studying organization and using this book, a group? Or is it a collection of individuals? Is there a cohesive group attitude on problems? Is it the same in business organizations?

5 European managers generally delegate less than do American managers. Is this because European lower-level managers have less desire than Americans for self-actualization?

6. "My idea of self-fulfillment and self-actualization is to become the company president. I am now 40 years old and am the head of a major department next below the vice-president level. But the president is only 45 years old."

    How can this manager be well-adjusted and be an effective member of the organization with probable frustration facing him?

7. What should be done with a middle-level manager who wants to swing his weight around and impinge on other people's work areas because he feels that this is necessary for his self-fulfillment?

8. In 1981, the recession forced numerous employment reductions. Jobs were hard to find. A laid-off space engineer found a job on his state's payroll as a statistician. A laid-off personnel director ended up driving a taxicab. A newly-graduated school teacher went to work in a gasoline filling station.
    Should we forget about self-actualization?

9. A business manager who rejects most organizational theory says that "Professors place too high a value on autonomy, inner direction, and the quest for self-development." Discuss this viewpoint.

10. Are people more alike than they are different? Or are they more different than they are alike? What have the answers to these questions to do with organizational matters?

Case 3-1   The Man in the Grey Flannel Suit

A number of years ago, novelist Sloan Wilson wrote a best selling book called, *The Man in the Grey Flannel Suit* (published by Simon and Schuster). It became a best selling movie as well, featuring Gregory Peck.

The theme was that people who work in large companies must conform to the organization's customs and mores, even to wearing the approved kinds of clothes (hence the title). In the end Peck as the hero finds that the demands of the organization are too much and he opts out. He gives up a lucrative and promising career in a dairy company to do his own thing.

Break the class into discussion groups of six members each. Have each group prepare a brief, as follows:

Odd numbered groups; "Resolved that a person cannot find fulfillment, self-expression, and personal satisfaction working for a large organization, whether it be a corporation, the government, or a large, non-profit organization."

Even numbered groups: "Resolved that a person can, by giving up trivial things (like dress, hours, and petty conveniences and indulgences), make substantial contributions to society, and find personal growth, satisfaction, and self-expression, while working for a large organization, whether it be a corporation, the government, or a large non-profit organization."

Have a spokesman from each group in alternate order present their arguments. After the presentation, have a show of hands reflecting the personal choices of the class members.

Behavioral Science Comes of Age

Case 3-2   Initiative at Lower Supervisory Levels

An official of a large steel-making company says, "Industry has not yet provided opportunity for the first line supervisor of a large corporation to feel the same thrill of individual initiative as does the top-level executive or the man in charge of his own business. This is a problem and possibly something can be done about it. But, we, as managers, have immediate and pressing jobs to reduce costs, improve methods, improve quality, and earn a profit. We just do not have the time during the business day to take on social problems. Perhaps those specializing in sociology can give more attention to this matter and can devise some way for improving this situation. Up to now, we have had almost no success with recruiting college graduates for foremen."

· Is the lack of the thrill from exercising individual initiative a problem?
· If this company put a manager in charge with full power to act on such a situation, what should he do?

Endnotes

1. Lewin's writing, most of which was done in the 1940s, is discussed in *The Practical Theorist: The Life and Work of Kurt Lewin,* by Alfred J. Morrow (Basic Books, 1969).
2. *The Human Organization: Its Management and Value,* by Rensis Likert, (McGraw-Hill, 1967).
3. A good discussion of these leadership styles is given in *Systems of Organization,* by David G. Bowers, (University of Michigan Press, 1976), pp. 100–109.
4. *The Further Reaches of Human Nature,* by Abraham H. Maslow, (Viking Press, 1971). This book brings together the ideas presented in Maslow's earlier publications.
5. "A Causal Correlation of the Need-Hierarchy Concept," by E. Lawler and J. Settle, *Organizational Behavior and Human Performance,* April, 1972, pp. 265–287.
6. "No Future for the Me Generation," by Ruth Armstrong, *Graduate Women* January–February, 1980, p. 43.
7. *The Human Side of Enterprise,* by Douglas McGregor (McGraw-Hill, 1960).
8. *Motivation and Control in Organizations,* by Gene W. Dalton and Paul R. Lawrence (Richard D. Irwin, 1971), p. 19.
9. *Work and the Nature of Man,* by Frederick Herzberg (New American Library, 1973). This book includes the ideas Herzberg introduced in his earlier writings.
10. *The Applicability of Organizational Sociology,* by Chris Argyris, (Cambridge: The University Press), 1972.
11. *The New Managerial Grid,* by Robert R. Blake and Jane S. Mouton (Gulf Publishing, 1978).

12. Warren Bennis gives Maslow credit for originating this idea. See, "Chairman Mac in Perspective," by Warren Bennis, *Harvard Business Review,* September-October, 1972, p. 141.
13. Schein, *op. cit.,* p. 69.
14. "Industrial Workers' Worlds, A Study of the Central Life Interests of Industrial Workers," by Robert Dubin, *Social Problems* 3 (1956); 131–142.
15. "The Short and Glorious History of Organizational Theory," by Charles Perrow, *Organizational Dynamics,* Summer 1973, p. 13.

Suggested Supplementary Readings

Koontz, Harold. "The Management Theory Jungle Revisited." *Academy of Management Review,* April, 1980, pp. 175–187.

Likert, Rensis. "Management Styles and the Human Component," *Management Review,* October 1977, pp. 23ff.

Natemeyer, Walter E., ed. *Classics of Organizational Behavior* (Moore Publishing Co., 1978).

Ryan, William G. "Management Practice and Research — Poles Apart," *Business Horizons,* June 1977, pp. 23–29.

Whettin, D.A. "Coping With Incompatible Expectations: An Integrated View of Role Conflict." *Administrative Science Quarterly* 23 (1978): 254–271.

Case for Section I Welch Chemical Company

The Welch Chemical Company, a maker of a diversified line of chemicals with sales of $150 million a year, is small compared to the giants of the industry.

Heavy emphasis on research in the chemical industry causes rapid change and often product obsolescence. In order to survive in this highly competitive industry, firms find it necessary to allocate a much higher percentage of their gross sales income to research (in the range of 6 to 12 percent) than do most other manufacturing industries.

James Welch, president of Welch Chemical, believes that no expense restrictions should be put on the scientists who are engaged in research. Consequently, the budget for this work is generous. Some of Welch's scientists are engaged in experiments of kinds which may not produce any ultimate financial return to the company. The large sums spent on research have held down the company's earnings but there has been no consequential complaint from stockholders.

Behavioral Science Comes of Age

Among the products which Welch Chemical has been actively developing and making are pesticides and insecticides. Such products account for over one-third of the company's sales. The use of these products has, however, over the years, attracted wide public attention over the harm which they might do to people and to wildlife and fish. Various government agencies have been studying the effects of the use of these chemicals.

Several conclusions have been drawn from these government studies. On the positive side, it is generally agreed that the yield of farm crops is higher, that the quality of harvested products is better, and that insect control, which is necessary also for human health, is improved. On the negative side, it is generally believed that some of these chemicals accumulate in minute quantities on or in the vegetables, fruit, and meat that people eat. And even these small quantities may be harmful to wildlife other than insects. There is, however, no evidence that such minute quantities of these chemicals are harmful to human life and the harm to wildlife other than insects is debatable. Government studies of the possible harm from the use of these chemicals in the quantities normally used have been inconclusive, but, as a safety measure, regulations covering their use have been set up.

Certain ecology groups have been pressing James Welch to have his company stop making these chemicals. Welch feels, however, that the possible harm from using these pesticides and insecticides has been blown up far out of proportion by the activities of ecology groups. He points to the need for the whole world to increase crop production, which the use of pesticides accomplishes. He agrees that restrictions possibly may be appropriate near game preserves.

Welch also has been criticized by some of the company's stockholders for spending so much on research. They suggest that he spend less and pay out the money saved in dividends. Research into the long-range effect of these chemicals upon plant and animal life is an expensive undertaking.

If Welch were to stop producing pesticides and insecticides, it would lose one-third of its sales, which in turn would cause substantial layoffs of employees in addition to the reduction in profits. Furthermore, almost certainly some of the company's competitors would not stop making these products so they would still be available on the market and would be bought by the same people who now buy them. James Welch believes that the Welch Company is filling a need by continuing to produce them.

· What should Welch do? Why?

All organizations have purposes: they exist in order to do something. In businesses, these purposes are spelled out in corporate charters and company boards of directors have the responsibility for hiring officers to carry them out. In governments, purposes are stated in laws and statutory delegations and the responsibility for carrying them out is vested in certain administrative officers.

Original statements of purpose for all kinds of organizations are often not true reflections of their current purposes. Purposes are subject to evolutionary change when laws, economic conditions, and even the organization's personnel change. Purposes are also shaped by the interpretations of their missions by managers as well as by organizational responses to environmental constraints and needs and to the opportunities which present themselves. The administrators of organizations choose strategic goals and define policy guidelines within which lower managers are expected to operate in their pursuit of organizational objectives.

Down within organizations, individuals, departments, and other groups actually develop their own objectives which should always be but in fact are not, always in harmony with overall organizational objectives.

Purposes need to be implemented by plans and actions. If during the making of plans it appears that objectives cannot be achieved, then the objectives themselves may have to be changed to bring them into line with reasonable expectations.

The four chapters in this section deal with management's responsibilities for setting objectives and planning for the organization's future.

Section Two

Organizational Purposes

Objectives of Chapter Four

1. To point out the value of managers setting formal objectives.
2. To consider the kinds and purposes of objectives.
3. To discuss the difficulties encountered in setting objectives and in reaching them.
4. To call attention to the need for organizational objectives to be related to the personal objectives of organizational members.

Objectives and Strategies

4

*If you don't know where you want to go,
any path will take you there.
Alice in Wonderland*

An *objective* is a goal to be reached. It provides a focal point around which to develop plans and to allocate resources. *Strategies* are the means chosen for reaching objectives.

The history of the Textron company in the last thirty years illustrates how objectives can guide the organization. Textron is America's original conglomerate (multi-industry) company. Today, Textron is a far cry from what it was in the early 1950's.

Thirty years ago the Textron company was a relatively small, profitless, textile company making cloth. In 1952 it lost $4 million on sales of just under $100 million. The company had not been able to reach its objective of operating profitably in the textile industry.

Royal Little, Textron's president, decided that the future looked bleak so he decided to adopt a new strategy and to set new and different objectives for Textron. The new strategy was to shift the company out of textiles into industries with greater growth potentials. Since the company's physical assets were themselves not transferrable to other uses, implementing this strategy meant changing the use of Textron's capital and putting it to work in other industries.

In the years since this program was instituted, Textron has sold all of its textile operations and has bought more than fifty non-textile companies.

Among the many products which Textron makes today are Bell Helicopters, Gorham silverware, and Homelite chain saws. Textron also makes outboard motors for boats, work shoes, poultry feed, rocket engines, eyeglasses, and a long list of other products.

Figure 4-1 shows how the make-up of Textron's business has changed over the years. In the years since the decision to change was made, Textron has grown by thirty times. Today it has 75,000 employees. Sales are now close to $3 billion and profits are over $125 million annually. This is a 5 percent return on sales and 8 percent on the stockholders' investment. These returns are not extraordinary but they are much better than most textile companies earn. This has come about because the company changed its objectives.

Every company and every other kind of organization has objectives. They exist in order to do something. Yet some organizations are more successful at reaching their objectives than others. And, as time passes, some organizations are more successful at recasting their objectives so that they are in step with current conditions. Setting such organizational objectives is the subject of this chapter.

Strategic objectives are those organizational purposes and goals which would change the character and direction of the organization (such as Textron adopted). They come out of managers trying to answer such questions as, "Are we doing the right things?" and "Who will tomorrow's customers be and what will they want?" Such questions need to be asked and answered from time to time if the organization's objectives are to stay in tune with the times.

Strategic objectives are established by high level managers with the concurrence of the boards of directors. Such objectives are almost always multi-year in character and reach out from three to five years or more into the future. How to reach them is not very predictable and the degrees of accomplishment are often unmeasurable.

Operational objectives and goals are lower-level subordinate objectives. They have shorter time horizons and reach out no more than a year or two into the future. They are more in the nature of specific goals. Many operational objectives relate only to limited segments of the organization. They are designed to foster effective middle and lower level operations. Since they are usually responsibilities of single department heads and for short periods only, they are fairly predictable and fairly measurable.

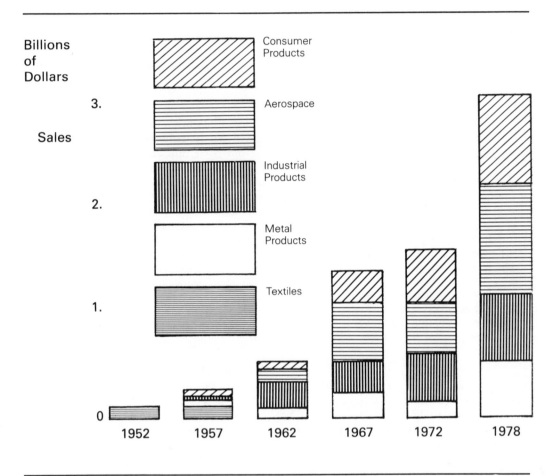

Figure 4-1
Changes in the nature of Textron's business in the years when it was changing its product lines and its place in the economy.

Characteristics of Objectives

In businesses, objectives are related to where the organization is now, to what its present capabilities are, and to what its top managers would like for it to become in order to achieve the things they want it to achieve.

This section will deal with the way objectives are related to each other and to the way they affect organizational performance.

The Need for Overall Objectives

One of every company's objectives has to be to succeed *in certain businesses.* Safeway operates stores and sells groceries and Amoco Oil produces and sells gasoline. These companies are in the businesses they are in because, over the years, success in these businesses was the goal which their managers pursued successfully.

Determining the organization's overall strategy and determining its major objectives are, in business organizations, two of top management's most important jobs.

· If Safeway's managers were to choose a strategy of becoming more vertically integrated, they would themselves make more of the products they sell rather than buying them. Quite possibly they would consider making the soap and detergents which their stores sell.

· If Safeway's managers wanted to diversify and follow a conglomerate strategy, they might buy an amusement park such as Disney World.

Safeway's managers have not made these choices, but if they did, their adoption would lead on to objectives which would change the configuration of their organization and the activities in which they would engage. Organization resources would have to be committed to these new uses in order to develop the necessary new and different capabilities.

Small companies have less possibility than large companies have of setting up and using formally set long-range objectives. Theirs is more an existence in the present, and they get along more by fitting in with current conditions. Their strategy should be more to live on a day-to-day basis and probably they should not spend much time or money developing carefully thought out distant future objectives. It isn't that they do not need to look ahead but that they cannot afford the costs of market surveys, thorough forecasting, and extensive research.

Formally Set and Implicit Objectives

There are many organizations which operate with little overall planning and without carefully thought out objectives. Their managers would say that they "play it by ear." The unpredictable nature of the future is often cited by such people as the reason for their not defining their objectives. Perhaps too, such managers appreciate the fact that setting objectives has its risk-taking aspects. Objectives set, if not reached, represent failures.

Actually, it is not necessary, in all cases, to give much thought to overall objectives because they are obvious. A gasoline filling station's purpose is to sell gasoline and perhaps to do minor repairs on cars, and to do these things economically enough so that the operations will be profitable. The purpose of a shoe store is to sell shoes, again while operating economically enough to show a profit. Carefully spelled out objectives are, in such cases, rarely of critical importance.

It is different, though, in large organizations where so many things can be done that some guidance to activities needs to be given. Consciously set objectives, such as Royal Little set up at Textron, provide guidelines by which to determine priorities and to judge borderline activities. An objective of achieving a 20 percent market share or putting in four new branches in the South this year provides a guide. Effort and money are not frittered away on off-the-main-channel activities which do little to further organizational goals.

Organizational objectives are sometimes difficult to define, particularly in non-business organizations. It is difficult, for example, to say exactly what the objectives of a university should be. Nonetheless, administrators of universities and other non-business organizations have to have some notion of what they are trying to do because they have to hire people and put them to work doing certain things and not put them to work doing other things. They ought to try to set up their objectives in an organized way.

Objectives need to be responsive to technological developments and to the actions of outside factors such as competition and to regulating bodies such as government units. So, formally set objectives need to be reviewed from time to time and changed as conditions change.

When Reynolds Industries, originally a tobacco company (Winston, Salem, and Camel cigarettes and Prince Albert smoking tobacco), was confronted in the early 1970s with the rising legal and social opposition to cigarette smoking because of its harmful effects on health, Reynolds' managers decided to make the company less dependent on tobacco products. They adopted a new strategy of plowing earnings available for reinvestment into non-tobacco activities. Today, Reynolds is largely a non-tobacco company, being in the shipping, foods, oil, and packaging materials industries as well as tobacco.

Changes in the environment caused Reynolds' managers to change its objectives and the company is surely in a better position from their having done that.

Strategic Objectives and Major Units. Giant companies are so large and are made up of such diverse subordinate units that organization-wide objectives are set up only in the most general terms. Each major part of the company sets up its own more specific objectives and its own plans for reaching them. At General Foods, for example, Birds Eye (frozen vegetables), Maxwell House (coffee), and Gaines Dog Food each decides its own objectives.

Establishing Objectives

Managers have to set the objectives of the organization with due respect to quite a number of limiting factors. What they would like to have the organization accomplish is a starting point; then the limitations must be considered. The objectives actually set up should be realistic and appropriate to the limitations. Furthermore, strategy and objective formulation should not be just a one-time affair but should be a dynamic, continuing process.

Among the considerations are the many internal supporting objectives which need to be accomplished in order for major objectives to be reached. This section considers these factors and the part they play in the determination of objectives.

Major Objectives

At any given time, an organization's major objectives are all carryovers from the past. A newly appointed president of the Bank of America or of Goodyear Tire & Rubber would not really have to set up his company's major objectives because they would already be set up, implicitly if not explicitly. This new president would inherit an organization, and products or service lines, and customers — in a word, he would inherit a place in the economic world. The president would not, as part of his job, have to decide these matters.

On the other hand, this is just where managing begins. High-level managers should not feel too much restricted by having to continue with today's organization and with today's activities. If tomorrow's needs will be different, new capabilities may have to be developed while other things may have to be cut out.

It is important, too, to get the right answers to questions about objectives. If the managers of General Foods were to ask themselves what their objectives should be, they might well answer, "to succeed in the packaged food business." But, instead, they might answer that their objective is "to save the time and work of housewives." This answer would probably lead them to consider the development of pre-washed, pre-peeled, pre-cooked, and pre-mixed foods, any of which might be overlooked by a company whose managers think that they are just in the packaged food business.

Several years ago, the managers of Ford Motor wanted to get more into the government defense and electronics businesses, so they bought the Philco company. This gave Ford an immediate entry into these industries.

Determining major strategies and major objectives implies trying to reach them. Having set objectives, managers then commit resources and do things which they would not have done without the objectives. Ford wanted more defense business (the objective); it bought Philco (the resource commitment and the action); it became a bigger defense products supplier, thus achieving its goal (the desired end state of affairs which would not have happened by itself).

The "Reaching" Nature of Major Objectives. Major objectives look into the future but they should be more than mere forecasts. They should be "reaching" objectives which can be achieved only if the organization stretches itself and puts forth a plus effort. In order to achieve them, the organization will have to do things which it would not otherwise do.

"Reaching" objectives should reflect hidden as well as visible potential.

A manager of a company which makes and sells sewing machines whose forecast tells him that the company is likely to sell ten million dollars worth of sewing machines next year might change the forecast and set the figure a little higher. This would make him give thought to doing something more in order to reach the higher figure. To reach it, the company might have to go into other markets. Or perhaps its product designers could develop a new children's model which would sell well. Or maybe the company could sell accessories to do fancy stitches or little cabinets to hold sewing.

Obviously, "reaching" objectives should not reach too far. Lockheed won't displace Boeing, nor will Chrysler displace General Motors in the foreseeable future. There would be no point in either Lockheed or Chrysler spending money investigating the size of plants they would need to reach this "objective," because it is unrealistic. Furthermore, objectives which reach beyond reasonable accomplishments discourage people rather than encourage them.

Limitations to Freedom to Set Major Objectives. Not only do objectives need to be realistic, but, as earlier discussions brought out, the scope of the managerial job varies among organizations. This carries over into setting major objectives. A manufacturing company's managers can choose to become more vertically integrated and to make more of the things it now buys, or they can choose to diversify. But a banker cannot do much in either of these directions. A banker's opportunities to set reaching objectives are more limited by laws and regulations. Nor can United Airlines fly its airplanes to Europe because it has not been given permission.

Often the most serious limiting factor to managers' ability to set realistic objectives is the competition. An objective always anticipates accomplishment in some specific area. But, there are no vacuums. Just as there are competitors in a company's present product line area, so are there competitors in all other alternative areas. One of the most common failures of managers in setting objectives is to underestimate the strength of the established competition in the areas the managers are thinking of entering.

Members of government organizations also are usually limited to their major objectives as set by law. The Federal Trade Commission deals with fair trade and not with labor disputes. Its objectives, set by law, restrict it to a limited area.

Product-Line Objectives

Long Term Growth Potential
   We will try to develop and sell products for which future markets offer long-term prospects of increasing demand. Desirable products from the standpoint of growth include (1) those with an increasing rate of consumption for existing uses; (2) those offering expansion possibilities through new uses; and (3) those for which demand can be expected to increase through natural growth in the size of markets (for example, population growth of the country).

Profitability
   Each of the company's major product lines shall be profitable and shall earn a fair share of total company profits based on its proportionate utilization of total capital and facilities and of executive activities required to manage the line.

Breadth of Lines
   We want our product lines to be broad enough to provide wide diversification of markets and contribute a long-run stability of demand and profits. Each major category of products should offer a wide enough selection to maintain a strong position for that line in a given market.

Market Concentration
   Sales of a given line of products to a single customer shall not exceed 10 percent of the total company sales of that product line.

Product-Line Planning
   The company will conduct an organized, vigorous, and continuing appraisal of its product lines, with the objective of maintaining the strongest possible position in each of its markets.

Figure 4-2
A statement of product line objectives.

The Realm of Alternative Objectives

The full consideration of all possible alternative strategies and objectives is not always carried through, even when managers give conscious attention to them. One reason is that it is manifestly impossible for managers to be aware of every possibility which might arise. Nor could managers, were they aware of every possibility, consider carefully every possible course of action. The job would be too great.

Actually, there is no need for managers to consider every possibility. They don't need to consider actions which are far afield. United States Steel company probably has never "decided" not to make automobiles, nor has Florsheim Shoe "decided" not to make television sets.

It should be different though with related activities.

A few years ago, TWA bought the overseas Hilton Hotels chain. Now TWA not only flies airplanes but it also operates hotels so that it can fly passengers to remote parts of the world and then provide them with hotel rooms after they get there.

It is here, in choosing strategies or ruling out strategies in areas which are closely related to the company's existing operations where choices of objectives should be made consciously and after careful study of the organization's capabilities and of the opportunities and constraints presented by the environment.

Multi-Industry Company Objectives. Managers of many of today's multi-industry companies would object to this "closely related" criteria we have just been talking about because such companies range widely. Rare until the late 1960s, multi-industry companies ("conglomerates"), such as General Tire, Textron, Litton, Gulf and Western, and Avco, are now numerous. Each of these companies operates in many industries. One of them, General Tire, makes automobile tires, iron pipes, motion pictures, space missiles, and also operates television stations. In all, General is in twenty-six industries.

Operating successfully in such different areas are major objectives in their own right. Nonetheless, success in any single area of business should be secondary to the overall objective — using capital to the best advantage.

Achieving versus Becoming Capable

In order to achieve, an organization must be capable of achieving. Managers sometimes run into trouble because they set objectives without paying enough attention to whether or not their organization has the necessary capabilities.

Presumably, when managers choose objectives which require capabilities which their organizations don't now have, they assume that these capabilities can be developed if a reasonable amount of money is spent developing them. Managers *do* have it in their power to channel resources in given directions. In some cases, this power can be considered to be almost the same as developing the needed capabilities. If J.C. Penney spends $5 million to open a new shopping center, the shopping center will almost surely be opened and Penney will become capable of selling in one more area.

But spending money by no means always gets results. It is surely true, for example, that not every new Penney store proves to be as profitable as was hoped. Nor did General Electric's spending $500 million developing computers in the 1960s and 1970s pay off. GE's computers never sold well and its money was lost.

Conflicting Objectives

Managers often have to choose from among conflicting objectives and trade off advantages and disadvantages. It is really not possible, for example, for a company to serve the public, its customers, its suppliers, its employees, and its stockholders, and do its best for each group, all at the same time because the interests of these groups conflict.

High prices are fine for employees and stockholders because they provide the means for the payment of high wages and dividends. But high prices are not part of good customer service. When one group is favored, it is at the expense of others. Choosing objectives is an exercise in trade-offs.

Managers also make choices which are heavily influenced by their personal goals, which are sometimes in conflict with organizational goals. Internal sub-group objectives also sometimes run counter to organizational objectives and so warp or even displace them. The sales manager would like to sell to everybody, cash or credit, but the credit manager does not want sales to be made to poor credit risks because this would increase bad debts.

Obviously, when objectives and goals are in conflict with each other, some kind of priority system will develop. Money and other resources will go for high priority goals, while low priority goals get what's left.

Objectives in Government Agencies

A manager of a government agency would probably object to our discussion of objectives and say that it emphasizes the freedom of managers to choose objectives too much.

We said earlier that the objectives of government agencies and departments are usually set by legislative bodies. These pre-set objectives are, however, stated only in mission terms. The actual objectives are the interpretations that the managers put on them. (We will consider the interpretations of their missions by heads of government departments in Chapter 17.) The heads of major government departments do, in fact, have some freedom to set objectives.

But they are also influenced and hedged about by other outside factors and by public interest groups, pressure groups, and the press. They also have to spread their spending around the nation so that each geographic area and each consequential group of voters will share in the benefits. Even the bureaucracy that a government agency head administers may be intractable. Forces such as these bear upon many government administrators and restrict their freedom to set objectives.

There is one area, however, in which government department heads probably all add one particular undelegated objective to their missions. This is growth. In Chapter 25, we will report that Peter Drucker says that, to a government department administrator, a bigger department is success. To him, this is evidence of the importance of the work of his department as well as of his

success in making it grow and of the department serving the public better. Businessmen, too, like to see their organizations grow, but only if sales and profits grow at the same time.

Value Judgments and Biases in Setting Objectives

Strategies and objectives always incorporate value judgments made by the managers who choose them. A company's managers might decide that their company should be a leader in the industry in research, because they think that carrying on research is very important. Or a hospital director might decide to provide for special care of diabetics but not to provide facilities for kidney transplants. These would be value judgments.

Such value judgments put biases into decisions in the sense that other managers would probably choose other decisions. A scientist would probably choose different strategies and goals from those a banker would choose, and young people would probably choose differently from older people because their value systems are different.

Goals also depend upon the drive and motivation of the organization's top managers. Many top managers aim only for "satisficing" goals (goals which satisfy them but which fall short of what can reasonably be accomplished). Furthermore, managers down within organizations are not all very responsive to organizational goals just because someone higher up has set them.

Goals are heavily influenced by the past. What an organization has been able to accomplish in the past gives its managers a good clue as to what it may be able to accomplish in the future. While this is reasonable, it is unfortunate because an organization's past shortcomings may circumscribe its future more than they should.

The most important objective of almost every organization is to perpetuate itself. And almost always this means that it must make a contribution to society which is commensurate with its cost. In the case of business organizations, the most important operational objective really ought to be to make the most effective use of the organization's resources so that it will stay alive.

Actually, a good many top managers put other objectives and goals at the top of their priority lists. They try to get their organizations to capture a certain share of the market, or to achieve certain market coverage, or to grow rapidly. Or they try to reach a certain degree of integration, or a desired degree of diversification, as Reynolds Industries is now doing. Or they strive for research leadership, as RCA did for many years. Some managers go for sheer size, others for a large cash flow. Some aim for a given capital structure. And there are other goals.

None of these goals is wholly congruent with using resources to the best advantage; nonetheless, these goals are sometimes selected. Managers who choose such goals probably more or less equate, in their minds, reaching them as constituting success in operating their organizations effectively.

Growth as a Goal. One of the most commonplace goals of American businessmen is to have their organizations grow. (In fact, since our economy continually grows, a company which does not grow is actually falling behind relatively.) In the United States, there is an almost religious worship by managers of the desirability of having their organizations grow. And it is generally accepted that growth is evidence of successful management. Even more important, growth supports and makes possible increases in jobs and pay raises for all.

Growth does not occur everywhere. It is largely concentrated in growth industries and in growth geographic areas. In the last decade, in the United States, the electronics, pharmaceuticals, chemicals, and oil industries have been growth industries. The "Sun Belt" areas (the South, Southwest, and West) have been the most rapidly growing geographic areas.

Quite a few companies not originally in these industries or areas have grown anyway by joining the trend. They have moved into growth industries and areas. Usually such moves came after the company's long-range planners had investigated and decided that there were opportunities there.

Low wage levels have, in the past, been an important factor in this movement. But factors behind the scenes also played an important part. These factors included the building of dams along the Colorado River, thus making water available to Southern California and Arizona. Also important were the development of air conditioning and heavy government spending in these geographical areas for aerospace and defense products. These changes in the environment helped the companies located there to grow rapidly.

Outside-the-company factors also sometimes play a big part when companies do poorly. Sometimes whole industries are depressed. The financial difficulties of most of the nation's railroads in the last decade caused them not to order new equipment. This depressed the railroad equipment industry.

Important though the decision making of managers is, factors beyond their control often contribute a great deal to their organizations' successes or failures.

Internal Operational Objectives

Important though major objectives are, smaller internal operating objectives are also important. High-level managers can lay out strategies and formulate major objectives but these cannot be achieved unless secondary objectives which support major objectives are set and reached. Most of these secondary objectives have to be set by middle and lower level managers, keeping in mind both the part they should play in contributing to major goal accomplishment and the resources and capabilities available in lower departments. Normally, such goals are decided by superiors and subordinates sitting down together and jointly agreeing upon them.

Because many internal objectives are short-term and are goals to be reached within weeks or months, managers need to be developing new objectives all the time. These take the form of sales quotas by territories for given periods of time, ratios of selling expense to sales volume, ratios of sales coverage to potential customers, or labor cost per unit, etc. Goal setting of this kind has to be done over and over again.

Objective and Subjective Goals

Psychologists sometimes make a distinction between objective and subjective goals. Sometimes these are called "hard" goals and "soft" goals. In a factory, objective goals ("hard" goals) are productivity against standards, scrap-ratio goals, meeting production schedules, reducing machine downtime, etc. Subjective goals ("soft" goals) are Likert's "intervening variables" (discussed in Chapter 3). Recall that these include employee empathy and morale, communications effectiveness, cooperative attitudes, level of performance, motivation, and group cohesiveness.

Likert feels that there is a danger, in the drive by managers toward objective goals, that subjective goals, which are not usually formalized, will get downgraded. Possibly wrong actions will be undertaken, actions which prevent reaching soft goals, which, in turn, in the long run, prevent reaching hard goals.

There is a danger that managers will feel that objective goals are more valid. In a sense, this is true. They *are* what the organization has to accomplish. But, if soft goals are essential to the reaching of hard goals, then they become just as important and just as relevant.

Personal Objectives

We all have personal objectives. First of all, nearly everyone who is a member of any organization wants to keep his job and to enjoy his work life and to be accepted by his or her fellow workers. Besides this, most people seem to want money, power, prestige, interesting work, and a chance to do something on their own. They want most of the things on Maslow's list given in Chapter 3. On the other hand, organizational objectives can be reached only if the organization's employees work cooperatively toward organizational objectives.

These two kinds of objectives (personal objectives and organizational objectives) do not automatically mesh. Many managers, for example, do not like to take chances because if something goes wrong they might lose their jobs. So, their first objective becomes keeping their jobs and staying on the payroll. Consequently, they sometimes avoid taking actions which would probably benefit the organization if taking these actions involves any risk at all.

A great many people also seem to like to do their work well and sometimes they do their work too thoroughly, thus causing inordinately high costs. Superiors may need to curb the desires of subordinates to do things too well.

Scientists, engineers, and other professionals often have to be willing to subordinate their desire to identify with their subject areas to identifying with the company. Young employees frequently identify more with the kind of work they are trained to do and which they like to do (an accountant may think of himself more as an accountant than he does as a member of the XYZ company team), whereas older employees identify more with the organization. Those who identify with their organizations will more readily accept doing what needs doing for organizational benefit.

High-level managers need always to try to be aware of the personal objectives of their subordinates and to manage so that subordinates who accomplish goals will at the same time be accomplishing their personal goals.

Unfortunately, saying that "high-level managers need to be aware of the personal objectives of their subordinates," seems to say more than it does. Subordinates, like most people, may hardly be conscious of having any personal objectives at all, beyond keeping their jobs and getting a pay raise once in a while.

The personal objectives of middle level managers and of lower-level people as well are mixed bags of varied things about which they may feel strongly or less strongly. A superior with a dozen subordinates also has to deal with a dozen sets of individual differences in personal objectives. About all that he can do is to be aware of general theories of motivation, such as Maslow's, and to try to manage as if his people would all respond to these motivations.

Summary

Managers of organizations should direct their efforts toward having their organizations follow established strategies and achieving consciously-selected objectives. But a good many managers are not well organized and they do not set up objectives in any organized way. Consequently, they are sometimes not quite clear in their own minds about the objectives which they should be trying to have their organizations reach.

This failure usually does not occur, however, wholly because they don't pay attention to objectives. Rather. it happens because most organizations are always working toward several or many objectives, some of which conflict. Managers continually have to compromise and to try to strike a balance between conflicting objectives.

Superiors also have to recognize that their organizational subunits develop their own departmental goals and usually tend to work toward them. When these goals are not congruent with organizational objectives, the result is that they sub-optimize, to the detriment of organizational objectives. Managers need to try to contain this tendency.

The setting of an organization's strategies and major objectives is a job for top managers. But such setting of objectives would have little value if this were not supported by the lesser goals which lower departments need to achieve in order for the big objectives to be reached. In order for these lesser goals to be achieved, the support of middle and lower managers is necessary. And, in order to win this support, it is necessary to consider the personal goals of middle-level managers.

Review Questions

1. What gains might one expect from thinking through carefully the organization's objectives and putting them down in writing?
2. Why is it usually hard to say just what an organization's objectives are?
3. What *should* be the objectives of a business organization?
4. If objectives are flexible, they can be (and often are) changed. But, do you have an objective at all if it is constantly changed? What good are flexible objectives?
5. What are "reaching" objectives? Should they be used? Why?
6. What kinds of clashes between objectives might occur in business organizations? What can a manager do to resolve such clashes?
7. What are the differences between hard and soft goals? Which are better? Why?
8. What part do personal objectives play in accomplishing an organization's objectives?

Questions for Analysis and Discussion

1. John Kenneth Galbraith says that one of business managers' biggest objectives is to eliminate risk. Is this so? Is security essential for efficient operations? Cannot a manager eliminate most risks just by doing nothing new or different?
2. The president of the Allen Food Company asked each of his top managers to jot down what he thought the basic goals of the company were. He found that they all had different ideas. What difference does this make? What should the president do? How can he make something productive out of this?
3. Suppose that the president of Firestone Tire decided to try to become "The biggest name in rubber." (Goodyear is considerably larger than Firestone.) What would such a goal cause him to do which he would not otherwise do? Is this a reasonable objective?
4. Is profit maximization really the goal? It if is, then how can a manager reconcile the following circumstances with the goal? The company gives separation payments to all employees who are laid off or who are discharged. There is also a well kept lawn around the factory. Yet, at the same time, the company sets prices as high as competition will allow.
5. The Aetna Life Insurance Company is a corporation with shares of stock outstanding (it is a profit-making organization). Metropolitan Life, a

mutual company, is not (profits, if any, are refunded to the policy holders). Is it probable that this difference has any important effect on the operations of these companies? Discuss.

6. The controller of a large steel company says, "We're not in business to make steel, build ships, or erect buildings. We're in business to make money."

   Why should any company need, as a company goal or objective, anything more than simply a statement that its managers should try to make as much money as they can provided it is done by means which are both ethical and legal?

7. "My boss tells me to keep the profit impact of my actions in mind when I do things."

   Does this mean that a store manager should pay his clerks as little as possible? Discuss.

8. A reviewer of this text commented, "Most of the time you discuss the goals of organizations as being formulated and implemented by top administrators. The rest of the organization will follow. To me this is unrealistic. I cannot see the top administrator as a person who dictates what the goals are. Complex organizations are too complex for things to work this way." Discuss.

9. Psychologists sometimes express concern over the drive toward "hard" goals (production quantities, meeting schedules, etc.), causing harm to "soft" goals (organizational empathy, mutual cooperativeness, etc.). Will it matter if this occurs? The company president asks his personnel manager how he can measure soft goal accomplishment so that he can judge his subordinates' performances better. What should the personnel director tell him?

10. In a later chapter in this text, it is reported that well managed companies are invariably said to be good at cost control. Texaco, for example, for many years and long after it became a giant company, required its officials to fly economy class when they fly. Why not go first class? Why try so hard?

Case 4-1   Chrysler's Objectives

A 1975 *Fortune* article about the Chrysler company said, "Chrysler is in trouble because its management has never adequately answered the fundamental question: What is our purpose? Whom are we trying to serve? Chrysler's managers have never been able to decide what kinds of cars they want to build or what kinds of customers they want to attract. They have no steady vision of what their company is or should become, and as a result, they have continually shifted gears, thus accentuating its weaknesses and failing to capitalize on its strengths." (*Fortune*, May 1975, p. 176.) In 1980, Chrysler had to have help from the government to avoid bankruptcy.

• What has steadiness of vision to do with Chrysler's problems?

Case 4-2   Unilever's Objectives

The Unilever company, owned half by British and half by Dutch owners, is a multi-national company with $20 billion of sales annually. Its sales come from world-wide operations. Unilever is both the world's largest food company and the largest toiletries company. It is, in fact, a larger soap company, except in the United States, than Procter & Gamble. In a recent 10-year period, its sales went up 75 percent but its profits went up only 1 percent.

Unilever had long pursued a goal of emphasizing sales volume first and profits second. But this period of stagnant profits caused its managers to change their minds. An American consulting company, McKinsey & Company, was called in to study Unilever's problems and to recommend changes. Out of this came a new goal, to emphasize profits more. As a result of the adoption of a program aimed at improving profits, in the next five years, sales went up 10 percent, while profits went up 25 percent.

Later, when discussing this change, Geeret Klijnstra, head of the company, said, "It's a hard job for a large organization like ours to get the message through that the goal isn't just to sell more products in the market, but to improve profitability by cutting down on inventories and improving efficiency in manufacturing." To get the message through, Klijnstra said, "We are now getting more active management from the top. We have gone from a passive direction to an active direction from the top. We have also been changing our product lines and have shifted away from commodities into convenience foods such as frozen foods. We have also been able to revive our big margarine business by bringing out new varieties — health margarine, for example."

Reminiscing about Unilever's poor profits earlier, Klijnstra commented, "I don't want to criticize myself or my predecessors, but life in years past was easier. Although I was not in charge, I was a board member in those days. Given the European mentality toward competition, it was more difficult to get high profit margins than it was in the United States where making a profit was not a crime." Klijnstra reported that the old attitude has changed because, far too often, the pursuit of volume to the neglect of profit margins has, in the past, led only to corporate disaster.

• Are the objectives of worldwide companies different?
• How could it be that an outside consultant, and an American consultant at that, would have anything to offer here?
• What would be the problem of making it known that earning profits should come above sales volume as an objective?

Endnotes

1. Managing by group objectives is discussed in, "MBGO, Putting Some Team Spirit Into MBO," by Rensis Likert and M. Scott Fisher, *Personnel,* January-February 1977, pp. 40–47.
2. "Different Goal Setting Treatments and Their Effects on Performance and Job Satisfaction," by John M. Ivancevitch, *Academy of Management Journal,* 20 (1977); 406–416.

Suggested Supplementary Readings

Glueck, William F. "Strategies Chosen by Large American Corporations, 1930–1974." *Academy of Management Proceedings,* 1977, pp. 113–117.

Quinn, James B. "Strategic Goals: Process and Policies." *Sloan Management Review,* Fall 1977, pp. 21–37.

Thomas, Dan R.E. "Strategy is Different in the Service Industries." *Harvard Business Review,* July–August 1978, pp. 158–165.

Vancil, Richard F. "Strategy Evaluation in Complex Organizations." *Sloan Management Review,* Winter 1976, pp. 1–18.

Objectives of Chapter Five

1. To bring out the relationships between policies and objectives.
2. To consider the problems encountered in the development of beneficial policies.
3. To investigate the effects of policies on organizational behavior and practices.
4. To learn about the advantages and the possible disadvantages of policies.

Policies

5

Question: Why do you do it that way?
Answer: There isn't any reason,
it's company policy.

Nature of Policies

Policies are courses of action which managers follow while trying to reach objectives.

For many years every door to Gimbel's New York department store displayed the sign, "Nobody, But Nobody, Undersells Gimbels." Gimbel's is one of many stores which have adopted the policy of meeting every price of a competitor.

Maytag makes washing machines, dryers, disposers and dishwashers — but only under its own name. It does not make special lower quality and lower cost models and put private brand names on them for Sears, Roebuck or Montgomery Ward.

This is part of Maytag's product line and sales distribution policy. Maytag, as another part of its product line policy, until 1980, concentrated on its four lines of products and did not make stoves or refrigerators. (In 1980, it bought a stove manufacturing company.) And, as still another part of its distribution policy, Maytag distributes products directly to dealers and does not go through wholesalers.

Policies are intended to help the organization reach its objectives in the most economical manner. The statement above that "there isn't any reason" should not be so. Nor should the people who have to carry out the policies think that there are no reasons for them because of their not knowing about the reasons. Subordinates should be told the reasons why.

The post office, the utility company, the bank, or the university registrar's office which persists in enforcing a policy which does not appear to be related to the proper purposes of the organization irritates people. The reasons for the policies may need to be explained to them. When people understand the reasons for policies, they accept them more readily.

Major policies, however, often relate to economic matters and do not need to be explained to either employees or customers. Holiday Inns owns very few motels itself but instead enfranchises other owners to use the Holiday Inns name. Policies such as this do not require explanation.

The importance of an organization's *major policies* can hardly be overemphasized. They concern such matters as, Should K-mart sell its own brands of products or only well known other brands? Should Exxon join in drilling for oil in the North Sea? Should a hospital develop capabilities for heart transplants?

The policies followed by organizations depend on the answers to such questions. They determine their organizations' configurations and, along with objectives, determine their organizations' activities and the directions their organizations will go.

Furthermore, major policy decisions are big-picture matters. Managers making such decisions need to be broad-gauged and not narrow functional specialists. Managers with policy making responsibilities have to rise above the levels of individual subject area expertise.

Relationships Between Policies and Objectives

As Figure 5-1 shows, objectives are at the top of the objective-policy edifice. They are supported by policies, major and minor. Minor policies are often embodied in procedures and, at the lowest levels, become rules, regulations and methods. All, however, are designed to lead toward objective accomplishment.

Conceptually, it would seem that objectives should always come first and then policies, large and small, should be shaped to fit. It seems logical to decide first where you want to go and then decide how to get there.

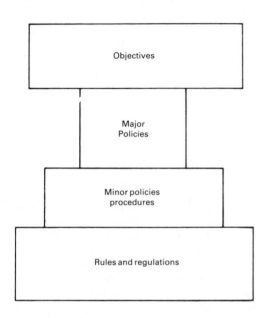

Figure 5-1
Policies in their role of supporting objectives.

But things don't always work out this neatly and it may be that after an organization has investigated how it might go about accomplishing an objective and at what cost, it might reverse the process and mold the objective to suit the means for achieving it. The Eli Lilly company (maker of pharmaceutical products) might, for example, decide that it wants to set an objective of curing cancer.

This is a noble objective which would benefit mankind, and would insure fame and fortune for Lilly. But the cost of the research and the technical state of the art might indicate that the amount of investment required would be so large that before this objective could be achieved, the company would be bankrupt. Lilly might, therefore, decide to settle for lesser worthwhile objectives such as developing a pain killer or a remedy for an allergy. Since man-

agers need to consider how they will reach objectives, it is not a hard and fast rule that objectives come first and policies second.

Indirect Relationships Between Policies and Objectives. The relationships of policies to objectives is not always direct. Some policies aim at achieving objectives indirectly.

Eastman Kodak, for example, has for many years sold cameras at low prices so that consumers would take lots of pictures. Kodak made considerably more money from selling film than on the cameras themselves. The price policy for cameras benefited the organization indirectly by fostering the sale of films.

Similarly, in nearly all organizations, employees must come to work and on time. Too much absenteeism and tardiness hamper effective operations so penalties are provided for excesses. The objective of effective operation is supported by policies covering how to handle absenteeism and tardiness.

Levels of Policies

Policies are needed at all levels in organizations. Major policies need the support of subsidiary policies. We will consider them at three levels of importance; major, intermediate, and minor.

Major Policies. "We are fundamentally a company which designs, builds and sells products based on motors."

This has been General Motors' main overall policy for more than a half century. Following this policy, General Motors has stayed out of vertical integration. GM does not make its own steel, glass, paint, nor automobile tires, and it has also stayed out of owning auto dealerships.

Many electrical appliance makers produce full lines of related products so that their dealers won't have to handle any products of competitors. Yet Maytag has done well with an opposite policy and has concentrated on washers, dryers, disposers and dishwashers. Dealers selling these Maytag products have to carry other appliances made by Maytag's competitors if they are to carry a full line of appliances.

Because the effectiveness of particular policies is so hard to judge ahead of time and because different policies always have different advantages and disadvantages, competing companies rarely pursue exactly the same policies even when they are faced with the same market conditions. Figure 5-2 shows the distribution policies of five leading manufacturers of low cost computers ($5,000 to $25,000) in 1980.[1]

As we move into the 1980s, it is not clear which of these sets of policies will work out the best. So far, all of these companies have been quite successful with the policies they have followed.

Intermediate Policies. Many policies are not quite so vital, yet they are far from minor. The example given at the beginning of this chapter of Gimbel's policy of meeting competitive prices is perhaps not a matter of major policy, yet it is hardly minor either.

Other examples of policies which perhaps should be considered intermediate rather than major are "We will always give office people pay raises to match those given in the factory," "We will do our growing out of retained earnings, and not borrow money," and "We will operate a company-owned cafeteria for our employees."

Minor Policies. Minor policies extend all the way down to such trivia as who gets favored parking lot locations, who may make long-distance telephone calls, and who gets to use a company car. Minor policies are not all so trivial as these, however. A policy not to keep a retail store open on Sundays is minor yet not trivial.

Establishing Policies

The setting of policies is too important to be left to chance nor should policies be allowed to grow up only from repetitive decisions made at low levels lest they be inconsistent or poorly thought through. Policies should not be merely outgrowths of common practice. In this section we will consider the factors which managers need to consider as they set the organization's policies.

Policies and Motivations

Policies ought to be motivators which will cause the organization's members to take actions which will help goal accomplishment. Paying salespeople on a commission basis instead of salaries in order to mo-

Company	Systems houses	Manufacturer's sales force	Manufacturer's retail stores	Authorized wholesalers	Office equipment stores
IBM		*	*		
Xerox		*	*	*	
Tandy	*	*	*	*	*
Hewlett-Packard	*	*		*	*
Apple	*	*		*	*

Figure 5-2
Method of distribution

tivate them to sell more products is such a policy. The common use of commissions for salespeople attests to the effectiveness of this motivation-type policy.

Policies should not, however, motivate the organization's people to do things which harm organizational well-being. Since control policies and control methods do sometimes motivate people to do things which do not help the organization, they need to be designed carefully in order to avoid having this happen.

A case of this sort, in which managerial policies did cause employees to do things harmful to the organization, occurred a number of years ago at Eastern Airlines.

The employees of Eastern who met the public had a widespread reputation for being surly and discourteous. This was a contributing factor to the company running into financial difficulties. As a result, the company got a new president who made the employees take a training course in courtesy. Their attitudes improved immediately and on the surface it seemed that this improvement resulted from the course.

Actually, it was the *policies* in the past which had caused the employees to act the way they did. The root cause for the improvement was really certain changes in company policies and not just from the employees taking a course in courtesy.

Before the new president came on the scene, Eastern had had a monopoly on certain heavily traveled north-south air routes in the eastern United States. In order to operate with full airplanes, only a limited number of flights were scheduled. And in order to be sure that there would be no empty seats because of "no-shows," Eastern overbooked reservations. This, the overbooking, caused the trouble. (Other airlines sometimes did this too but Eastern had the reputation for being the worst.)

Ticket sellers were required to overbook and then when there were only a few no-shows, they were faced with turning away irate customers at the last minute. Naturally, these customers complained bitterly to the lower-level employees with

whom they came into contact, notwithstanding that they were not really to blame and could not remedy the situation. And, naturally, the employees became surly and discourteous.

At this point the government granted other airlines the right to fly these same routes. Eastern's airplanes were suddenly only half full, the company lost money, and the president lost his job. The setting was ripe for the new president's "be courteous" campaign to be effective.

The Selection of Policies

Obviously, managers should try to select policies which will benefit the organization. Policies which will help the organization need to be compatible with the organization's human and other resource capabilities. They also should be compatible with the organization's established position in the economy and with the nature of the competition and should involve only an acceptable degree of risk. Beneficial policies will use the organization's strengths to best advantage and not get the organization into activities where it is weak.

In order to be effective, policies should also be easily understood, capable of ready interpretation, and acceptable to the organization. Only if a policy is acceptable will the organization members support it enthusiastically.

In spite of what we have just said, however, it is often difficult to judge which one of several alternative policies is the best. Every policy has both advantages and disadvantages which need to be weighed against each other. In the Maytag case, its policy of not selling private brands of appliances to Sears and Montgomery Ward helps support its dealers. But, by making this choice, Maytag has cut itself off from Sears' and Wards' and other chain store business. This is a large segment of the market.

The policies of K mart and Sears, Roebuck in the last decade make an interesting study in contrasts.

K mart emphasizes well known brands of products at discount prices. Sears, Roebuck emphasizes its own brands of products at low prices. K mart builds its K marts as free-standing stores which are not integral parts of shopping centers. Sears stores are often integral parts of shopping centers.

In all of these areas, pricing, product lines, and the separation of their stores from other stores, these two companies have followed different policies. And how have they fared? In the 1970s Sears' sales doubled to $18 billion annually. But K mart's sales grew by six times to $13 billion per year. Although many factors played a part in the performance of these two companies, the comparison favors K mart and is presumptive, although not conclusive, evidence that K mart's policies were better suited to the environment.

Effective or ineffective policies are not wholly dependent on an organization's present strengths or weaknesses because, over a period of time, its managers can change these things. In fact, as time goes along, a company's policies may determine its organization as much as the other way around. Today, Sears, Roebuck and J.C. Penney both sell on credit whereas years ago they sold only for cash. In order to make this change, both of these companies had to set up credit departments to evaluate charge account applicants and to handle collections. They developed the capabilities needed in order to carry out the policy.

Compatibility of Policies with Each Other

Most of the time, policies need to be consistent and compatible with each other so that they reinforce instead of work against each other. Maytag's policy of not making private brand appliances reinforces its other policies of using exclusive dealers and trying to build a quality image for Maytag products. These policies are consistent with each other.

Yet, too much consistency of policies is one reason why, years ago, department stores let discount stores, such as K mart, grow up unopposed for a long time. The department stores' policy of wide coverage of product variety (and hence low inventory turnover) with liberal price mark-up margins ran counter to a policy (which the department stores did not adopt), of carrying only the popular sizes at low mark-up prices. In this case, the department stores probably should not have followed the wide-line, ample-mark-up policy for all products.

Ethics

Ethics are codes of behavior. Just as individuals need to have codes of behavior, so also do organizations. Organizations need codes of their own because the codes of individuals vary, whereas, in an organization, all members should follow a common code. Organizations need to have ethical standards which their members are all expected to meet.

In our Western culture, we claim to have high ethical standards. Yet, in the mid 1970s, the business world in the United States was rocked by disclosures of bribery. The first shocks were disclosures by Lockheed Aircraft of bribes paid, usually to government officials in various countries around the world, in exchange for Lockheed receiving contracts for airplanes. In overseas transactions, such payments are not always so crudely put as to be direct bribes. Instead, a third party national, known to have connections, offers himself, in exchange for a substantial payment, to "use his influence" to get a contract for the seller. If he gets the money, the contract comes through.

Once these initial disclosures about Lockheed became known, investigations by government officials both in the United States and in other countries revealed that a great deal of this kind of activity went on.

There are actually many countries in the world where a company can get its taxes cut or receive other privileges if it pays off the right people. National businessmen in such countries sometimes do just that and it is not considered to be a very bad action. It is said that in Rome, some of them slip *bustralla* in little envelopes to favorably placed government employees. In Hong Kong, it is *hai yo* (oil to calm troubled waters). In the Middle East, *baksheesh* greases the wheels of commerce. In Africa, it is *dash,* and in South America, it is *mordita.* Undoubtedly a certain amount of this also goes on in the United States, too, but here it is considered to be unethical.

Perhaps a person should always hold fast to strict ethical standards and say that the examples given above of practices in some other parts of the world are examples of unethical practices. The United States government goes so far as not to allow anyone in a position of placing government orders to accept even a free meal from a company selling anything to the government, lest he be influenced by it. Nor does the United States Internal Revenue Service allow companies to consider payments made to individuals in other organizations for the purpose of influencing them to be considered as costs of operation when they calculate their income taxes.

Ethics, is not, however, always a matter of all good or all bad. There is, in fact, often a real question of whether a payment is a bribe or an extortion payment. By no means does the initiation of the transaction always come from the seller. The customer's purchasing agent or the government official may demand a kick-back or a payoff. How unethical is it to pay extortion? (No

one who pays extortion to a kidnaper is considered to have been unethical.)

In Latin America, it is customary to make small payments to government officials (an American driving his car into Mexico will, at some locations, find it easier at the border if he gives the official there a small amount of money). Such payments are more or less in the nature of tips and are not considered unethical.

Or, on a different plane, is it unethical for a person to contribute money to the campaign funds of candidates for office whose views agree with his? Or, is it unethical to hire an employee who last worked for a competitor company and who might have some helpful ideas?

A good many of us would not feel wholly comfortable labeling every one of these actions as unethical. There are gray areas. In the United States, in business and government, there is a rather widespread acceptance of the idea that the magnitude of the act can serve as a reasonable yardstick for borderline activities. If a salesman gives a customer company's purchasing agent a couple of bottles of liquor at Christmas, no one will think that he has bribed him, but a TV set, no. Here, the size of the gift decides our attitude.

Arjay Miller, one time president of Ford Motor and later dean of the Business school at Stanford University, suggests that the TV rule is a good guide. Don't do anything that you would feel uncomfortable about if you had to explain it on TV.

Conflicts of Interest. Company administrators need to be particularly careful about conflicts of interest. In years past, officials sometimes had their organizations do things which were more for their personal benefit than for the organization's good.

Years ago, the partners of New York financial companies often were also directors on the boards of many large companies. If these companies wanted to sell a bond issue or a new issue of stock, these directors saw to it that their financial companies got the jobs of selling the securities and collecting the usual fees for selling them. Such ties have not disappeared altogether, but today such directors need to be sure that if their financial companies get the business of selling the securities, they get it on their competitive merits and not because of inside pull.

Nor are officers of one company allowed to be directors of either a supplying company or a customer company lest their main company interests cause them not to have the other company's best interests at heart. High officials in most large companies today are very aware of these dangers and they try to avoid conflicts of interest.

The Right to Dissent Versus Organizational Loyalty. A difficult situation sometimes arises when an employee of an organization conscientiously believes that his organization is doing something which he thinks is morally or legally wrong.

Organizational loyalty says that he should accept the organization's objectives, policies and actions. But, has he no right (or moral obligation?) to dissent?

Today, many people would answer, yes, that he has an obligation to himself to dissent and that he should have the right to do so. He does, in fact, have such a right, but when he disagrees with the view of his superiors, they, of course, disagree with *him*. They think that *he* is wrong and that *they* are right. If he persists, they regard him as a trouble maker who does not accept his job as it has been assigned. They are likely to discipline him or even to fire him.

Alan Westin, in a book, *Whistle Blowing*, examined ten cases in which employees persisted in objecting to something the company was doing.[2] Most of these were cases of honest differences of opinion. A Ford Motor engineer thought that the Ford Pinto car was being made too light weight to be fully safe. An Eastern Airlines pilot thought that the automatic pilot was not reliable enough. In neither case did the complainer get a favorable reception and his

progress in the company suffered. Nothing serious happened in either case but, in both cases, improvements were made later on.

In another case, an auditor in a utility company was finally fired for objecting to the company not dunning welfare families which had not paid their bills. The company just marked such past due bills as "uncollectable" and billed the state's relief agency.

None of Westin's cases were as bad, however, as one which is described in Chapter 23. Olin Company's Niagara Falls division falsely and grossly understated the amount of mercury waste it was dumping into the Niagara River. The company was fined $750,000 for this. Down inside the company, there must have been several employees who knew of this falsification but not one of them "blew the whistle." The government had to find this out from its own investigation.

An employee in possession of knowledge of such a violation would be in a difficult position, knowing that it was wrong but knowing also that he might lose his job if he reported it.

"Essential" Policies

Our discussion about policies has been wholly in a framework of managerial decision-making options. We have treated policies as if managers were free to decide what policies they should follow in order to have their organizations benefit the most.

Such an approach overlooks the fact that some policies are mandated by law. These are "essential" policies. The equal employment opportunities law, for example, requires that employers follow policies of nondiscrimination in hiring, in job assignments, and in promotions.

Such essential policies need to be spelled out and disseminated throughout the organization. In order to implement the requirements of the equal employment opportunities law, it is necessary to use job descriptions and to follow a policy of posting notices of job vacancies on bulletin boards before filling them so that eligible employees who would like to have such jobs can "bid" for them.

Similarly, safety laws make it necessary to establish safety policies. (Employees at grinding wheels must wear safety glasses and penalties for noncompliance need to be set up, etc.)

Policies also need to be set up covering practices where ethics might enter in. Policies answer questions such as, can a buyer in the purchasing department accept a free turkey as a Christmas gift from one of the company's suppliers? What gifts or favors can a sales representative offer to a prospective customer?

Ethics were discussed earlier in this chapter but the point here is that policy positions need to be taken and policy statements need to be made in order to be sure that all organizational subunits are complying with the organization's position. In contrast with most policies, these policies are not aimed at fostering more effective operations.

The Policy of "Good Enough"

Whenever a policy is carried out, it is always at a price, which can be too high. Similarly, products and services can be better than they need to be for the purpose and consequently they cost more than they need to cost. Policies should always consider the need to try to reach objectives in the most economical way possible. Products and services should be only "good enough" to fill the need.

Cardboard milk cartons are not as good as glass bottles but they cost much less to make and are good enough for the purpose they serve. A newspaper is made out of poor quality paper, as it should be. The quality of the paper used is good enough for the purpose and any added cost for higher quality paper would be wasteful.

The need to confine quality to the good-enough level is not limited to products; it also relates to how people do their work. People usually take pride in their work and like to do their work well. Unfortunately, they sometimes do it too well and too perfectly and consequently at too high a cost. This danger is particularly great in staff work. In their desire to serve, staff personnel tend to serve beyond real need, forgetting the cost-value of their work. (Curiously, this desire to serve well sometimes seems not to apply to clerks and waiters. Some people serving customers seem not to care very much about the quality of the service they give.)

Policies and the Time Element

Unfortunately, no one can always and forever be following the most appropriate policies because circumstances change, while some policies result in long-term commitments or in positions in the economy which cannot be changed easily.

The Texaco oil company is being hurt today by policies followed by its managers of many years ago. Texaco went heavily into developing oil wells in Arabia, whereas most other major oil companies went much more heavily into Western hemisphere sources. Up until a few years ago, this difference in strategies favored Texaco as against its competitors.

In recent years the situation has become reversed since the Arabs and other oil-producing nations nationalized their oil wells and raised their prices to outside companies producing oil there. Texaco has, accordingly, shifted its emphasis to greater exploration in the United States.

Advantages and Disadvantages of Policies

Advantages of Policies. In their capacity as guidelines, policies can be advantageous in several ways:

· They help produce order, rationality, and predictability in actions and help reduce errors.
· They reduce the waste which would come from the need to restudy and reevaluate every new decision. They help assure equitable and consistent treatment. They allow knowledge gained from past experience to be used.
· They allow managers to think through future decisions and their effects in a non-crisis atmosphere. They let managers consider the long-run well-being of the organization and its people and customers, in ways which might not be thought of if all decisions were made on the spur of the moment.
· They rephrase laws, regulations, and matters of public interest into language which has meaning to organizational members.
· They provide answers to questions, in some cases, even before they are asked. A policy statement such as, "This firm does not compete with its customers," tells a sales representative what he should do when he wonders whether he should accept a certain order. If it is a company policy to distribute its products only through wholesalers, then the sales representative cannot sell directly to retailers because they are customers of wholesalers.

Disadvantages of Policies. Well thought-out policies rarely make problems, but there are several possible disadvantages:

· Policies may become too rigid and inflexible, thus standing in the way of appropriate actions.
· Policies may be inappropriate to new conditions.
· The difficulty of expressing policies in words sometimes makes them ambiguous.
· Sometimes policies need to be unpublicized where public dissemination could be turned against the organization.

Thus if a retail store follows a policy of not prosecuting cases of minor shoplifting, publicizing this policy would probably encourage more minor shoplifting. Furthermore, the firm might be accused of unfairness if, for unusual reasons, it did prosecute in one case when it had not prosecuted in another case.

Similarly, there is danger in publicizing personnel policies. Courts are starting to interpret personnel policies as being contractual relationships. If a company prints up its policies and distributes them to employees, and then fails to follow them *in every case*, and for whatever reason, it stands a better chance of being sued and of losing the suit than if it had never printed anything at all.

Summary

Policies are the general practices or general courses of action which an organization follows as it implements its strategies and works toward its objectives. As in the case of objectives, policies sometimes are not well thought out even though they should be. Major policies ought to be formulated by the organization's top managers. Then lesser policies can be formulated in such a way as to fit in with major policies.

Minor policies, however, sometimes grow up out of repetitive decisions made at bottom levels. Policies developed this way have the merit of being related to the needs of actual circumstances. But they may, at the same time, be unwise policies because they are made by many lower-level people and they may not be consistent. And they might not fit well with major policies because they are being made by people who are not high enough up to see the total picture.

Business managers sometimes have to decide matters of policy which involve ethical standards. Often these are difficult problems because so often they are not all black or white. There are many in-between grays. Furthermore, ethical standards vary somewhat in different social cultures. Business managers probably should always operate well within the ethical standards of the economies in which they operate.

Review Questions:

1. Isn't it really unnecessary to explain policies so that members of the organization will know the reasons why? Discuss.
2. Managers do not formulate policy. It formulates itself as it evolves out of a succession of decisions. Does it? Should it?
3. Is it true that every objective has to have a supporting policy? Which comes first, policies or objectives? Discuss.
4. Can policies be motivators to draw forth extra effort? If not, why not? If yes, how?
5. Surely there must be helpful policies and harmful policies. How can a manager tell before a policy goes into effect whether it will be helpful or harmful? What does a helpful policy have that a harmful policy does not have, and vice versa?
6. To what ethical standards should an organization try to adhere? Why?
7. What practical effect does the attitude of the United States Internal Revenue Service have on the ethical practices of the overseas operations of American companies?
8. What are "essential" policies? Who determines that they are essential and how does this affect an organization's operations?

Questions for Analysis and Discussion

1. Books on policy and books on quality never seem to discuss the policy of "good enough," meaning, don't do things too well. Why not?

2. Some companies set up policy "creeds." The IBM creed includes a statement that the company should be administered "with a sense of competitive urgency." How could this policy be implemented?

3. General Electric makes household appliances, including some for use in the kitchen and utility room. Zenith, however, stays out of the kitchen and utility room. Which is the better policy?

4. Is a policy more acceptable to a group if its members helped decide it? How about its acceptability to members of the group who opposed it? How about policies which a manager's predecessors developed but which he does not like?

5. K mart follows a policy of putting several K marts in a general area to "saturate the market." Sears and Wards do not. Which is the better policy?

6. "We don't do it because it's not our policy." Is this an intelligent statement or an unintelligent statement? Why?

7. The president of Interstate Department Stores says that its policy is "Thick on the best, thin on the rest." Discounters say, "Thick on the best, to hell with the rest." (Macy's department store in New York carries over 100 styles of men's shirts at all price levels. K mart stores carry 35 styles, all priced at from $2.99 to $12.00.) Which policy is the better?

8. In the Jackson Foods Company, the assistant to the president found that its breakfast foods division extended credit on very different terms from the credit terms allowed in the frozen vegetable division. Is this all right, or should the company have one and only one policy for extending credit?

9. "Each company has to find its own threshold of what is comfortable to do from an ethical standpoint." Isn't this too liberal a point of view? Wouldn't a person with a questionable standard of ethics find this a very acceptable statement? Discuss.

10. One of Morton's big customers, the Watson Company, demands a big discount, so big that Morton's managers feel sure that it would violate the law if they gave it. What should Morton's managers do?

11. The Celsius Corporation's sales have been declining and several employees are going to have to be laid off, at least for the present. Should the company follow a policy of laying off those most recently hired? If so, this will reduce the proportion of women and minority groups among the remaining employees since they were largely hired recently. Is there any policy problem here? Discuss.

12. We are bidding on a $10 million contract to sell road-building equipment to the country of Ruratania. There seems to be no way, however, for us to get the contract unless we pay off several government officials. They are not well paid and it might cost as much as $250,000 to pay them off. If we

get the contract it will mean one year's work for 300 of our employees who might otherwise be laid off. Decide on a course of action and defend your position.

Case 5-1   Crown Cork & Seal Company Creed

Some companies put out statements of fundamental policies in written form as their "creeds." Here is the creed of the Crown Cork & Seal Company (which they label as "This we believe"):

That a business enterprise is a living, functioning institution, existing to perform a needed, satisfactory service.

That a business enterprise does not exist solely for the benefit of any one group, neither customers, nor stockholders, nor public, but that the benefits for all groups must be in balance and that the resulting benefits are the products of a well-run business.

That the rights, interests, and obligations of these groups are inseparable.

That our opportunities in the Company carry with them great responsibilities, both economic and social.

That these obligations and responsibilities require from each of us a high degree of competence and performance in our jobs, and a high order of good citizenship.

That our individual and our Company relationships should be governed by the highest standards of conduct and ethics.

That within this Creed, we should devote our efforts toward achieving and maintaining a position of acknowledged leadership in industry.

That to meet our responsibilities and to reach a position of leadership, we must strive constantly to *achieve these objectives.*

• Would any of these statements actually have any effect on an organization's operations? In what way?
• Which of the items are actually restrictions imposed by society and not really determined by the company's managers?

Case 5-2   Asamera Oil Company

"Under-the-table" payments akin to bribery became a cause celebre in the 1970s in the United States after Lockheed Aircraft disclosed that it had made payments to government officials in various countries around the world where it sold airplanes. The United States Congress passed laws forbidding this practice and disallowing such costs from consideration as costs of doing business in corporate income tax calculations.

Both government and industry officials in the United States took outspoken positions against business making under-the-table payments abroad. Such sentiments are, however, far from universal. Under-the-table payments are, in fact, common in many parts of the world. Even Canada has a somewhat different view, which would give Canadians an edge in parts of the world where "consideration" is the norm.

Calgary-based Asamera Oil Corporation, specializing in oil drilling operations outside Canada, in 1977 filed documents with the U.S. Securities and Exchange Commission showing that it had made "expediting and facilitating" payments in the past. (Asamera filed with the SEC because its shares are traded in United States stock exchanges.)

The disclosures caused little comment in Canada. "It's a matter of operating where different moral and ethical standards prevail," says Hans Maciej, technical director of the Canadian Petroleum Association, the industry trade group. "Canada is not trying to be the moralist of the world." Maciej calls the Asamera disclosure "an individual corporate decision based on the facts of life in the parts of the world in which they operate."[3]

• Take a position on this issue and defend it.

Endnotes

1. A more complete comparison of the distribution policies of the companies in this industry is given in, "Tapping the 'mom and pop' market." *Business Week,* 27 October, 1980, pp. 165–169.
2. *Whistle Blowing,* by Alan F. Westin (Mcgraw-Hill, 1980).
3. This occurrence was described in "Canada's Flexible Bribery Standards," *Business Week,* 13 June, 1977, p. 35.

Suggested Supplementary Readings

King, William R. and David I. Clelland. *Strategic Planning and Policy.* Van Nostrand Reinhold, 1978.

Pitts, R.A. "Diversification Strategies and Organizational Policies of Large Diversified Firms." *Journal of Economics and Business,* Spring 1976, pp. 181–188.

Saul, George K. "Business Ethics: Where are We Going?" *Academy of Management Review,* April 1981, pp. 269–276.

Stevens, Edward. *Business Ethics.* Paulist Press, 1979.

Objectives of Chapter Six

1. To become acquainted with what management by objectives is and with its unique features.
2. To learn how management by objectives is set up and how it operates.
3. To summarize the several ways management by objectives can help an organization to function better.
4. To examine the reasons why this useful tool is not universally used and to consider what should be done about the reasons why it sometimes falls short of its promise.

Management by Objectives

It is not enough to be busy . . .
the question is, what are we busy about?
Henry David Thoreau

Management by objectives is a system in which every manager sits down at least once a year with each of his subordinate managers and together they jointly define the responsibilities of the subordinate and agree upon the conditions or accomplishments which will be deemed to comprise success or failure on his part during the year. MBO emphasizes what subordinates are supposed to get done in a period of time.

MBO is concerned with short-term operational objectives, in contrast with long-term overall objectives. They cover one year at the longest. They are line- rather than staff-oriented, and, in a manufacturing company, predominate in production and selling.

The object of MBO is to change the ways subordinates view their work and to put the emphasis on accomplishing desired results rather than on their doing functional work. Most people view their work functionally, as being what they do. People in the purchasing department buy things. They make out purchase orders and send them to vendors. People in the personnel department put advertisements in the newspaper and interview and hire employees.

These are "functional" ways of looking at work. People often come, in their minds, to mis-identify the things they do as being the ends to be achieved. Salespeople might call on numerous prospective customers. Doing this is, as they view it, their jobs. But their jobs are to sell products or services and if they do not sell very much they are not accomplishing their purposes. Or the purchasing staff has not done its job even though they have sent out purchase orders if the material does not arrive on time or is not of the right quality when it arrives. Viewed functionally, there are no failures here because the functional work was done. But, as

MBO would view these cases, they are both failures since the objectives were not achieved.

MBO helps to clarify work assignments by focusing on purposes and accomplishments providing answers to the following questions:

· What are my major responsibilities? What is the order of priority among my responsibilities? Which are the most important?
· What goals am I expected to reach in each accomplishment area?
· What resources will be available and what help will I get from my superior?
· What information will I get as I go along, to tell me how well I am doing?
· How much freedom will I have to do things my own way as I try to reach the agreed upon objectives? (If I have a great deal of freedom, I can be my own self-rewarder, punisher, and behavior change agent, as I try to reach the goals.)
· What rewards can I expect if I reach the goals and what will probably happen if I don't reach them?

Without MBO, subordinates are rarely provided with answers to any of these questions. Their having answers helps them focus on the important things needing to be done and at the same time helps overcome many of the ambiguities and uncertainties which so often cause discontent and mediocre performance.

Setting MBO Goals

In the process of setting MBO goals, it is necessary to consider how to express goals and how to know if they are being achieved. These and other matters relating to MBO goal setting are discussed in this section.

Goal Setting — The Process and the Product

The process of setting MBO goals entails a back and forth dialog, a discussion, and a meeting of the minds of superior and subordinate about the goals. This is confirmed by an end-product, a memorandum of agreement which is put in writing. Each party retains a copy.

As the year goes along, the superior and subordinate get together in periodic review sessions. They go over the results for the year to date and compare them to the agreed upon intermediate targets. If remedial actions are needed to help lagging goal accomplishment, these can be agreed upon. Doing this improves the quality of both the goals established and the quality of the accomplishment.

Some superiors try to run things almost wholly by written memos and downplay or even omit the two-way discussions. Such an omission is usually unfortunate because it prevents bringing about a genuine meeting of the minds between superior and subordinate. Participation by the subordinates is essential since only they know what they might be able to accomplish. Their participation is also essential in the development of attainable goals and in winning their support for such goals.

Group Goal Setting. Some objectives are really group objectives. They fall within the domain of the superior but require the close coordination and cooperative efforts of two or more of his subordinate managers. In such cases, the superior ought to meet with all of those concerned as a group as the goals are determined.

Such joint meetings have several advantages. They bring to light things which might have slipped through the cracks between the several individual responsibility agreements. And they allow everyone to consider matters of joint interest and to develop group goals. Out of this come goals for members to do specific things in order to reach the group's goals. Teamwork is fostered.[1]

Among the values of such meetings are clearer definitions of joint responsibilities. Meetings in which shared goals are considered jointly provide a viable way for deciding who will do what.

It is important, too, when setting joint responsibility objectives, to keep the reward structure in mind. *Each* of the managers jointly concerned should receive individual recognition in the reward system for both the accomplishment of the goals and for his cooperation toward the accomplishment. If two or more people contribute to a result, they should both or all be rewarded. There should be no attempt to find out how much contribution each person makes lest this generate dissatisfaction and bickering.

The Nature of Operating Objectives

Every manager's agreed upon list of objectives will include some which are more important and possibly harder to achieve than others. The real test of a manager's performance is in how well he accomplishes the objectives which are high in importance and which, at the same time, are difficult to reach.

Routine Specific Objectives. Most of the ordinary and routine accomplishments of a great many positions can be expressed in countable and measurable terms. Typical of such kinds of measurable outputs for a general manager's job are the following: dollar volume of sales, return on investment, dollar volume of receivables, inventory investment in dollars, total production in units, and accident frequency. An objective figure could be agreed upon for each one of these

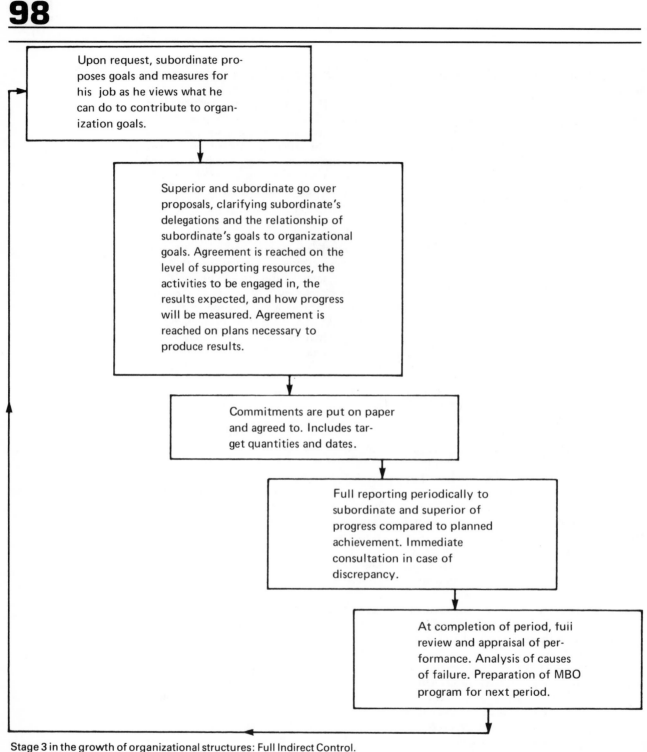

Stage 3 in the growth of organizational structures: Full Indirect Control.

Figure 6-1
Steps in the development and carrying through of an MBO program.

facets of the business which the general manager would try to reach each period.

Problem Solving Objectives. Problem solving objectives are less likely to be measurable; rather they take the form of statements covering the present condition and the desired condition in some area where there is a shortcoming in performance. The means by which the desired condition is to be achieved may be specified or this may be left to be worked out later. Actually, since MBO contributes to reaching problem solving objectives, it is really more helpful here than in areas where tasks are more highly routinized.

Innovative Objectives. People such as engineers, economists, market researchers, personnel development specialists, attorneys, or other such staff workers deal almost wholly with innovative, subjective goals. Few of these goals are measurable although the objectives themselves can often be stated as conditions which will exist if the goal is achieved.

Sometimes, when an innovative goal is a major matter, it is stated in "project" terms. The use of PERT charts, flow charts, or time and money budget statements, often meet the requirements of the innovative goal statement. (Charts and budgets are discussed in Chapters 22 and 25 respectively.)

Defining Goals Numerically

When it is reasonably possible, goals should be put into numbers and have dates attached. To illustrate, a plant superintendent's objectives might include reducing costs by $10,000 by July 1. Or they might include holding the costs of supplies used by the factory to the equivalent of eight cents per worker hour during the month of March. These are statements of achievement stated numerically, not mere descriptions of functional work, and they have dates attached.

In almost all cases of this sort, however, a range of numbers would probably be better than a single number. In the case of costs, a low number could be considered to show desired accomplishment, a higher number would be acceptable, and a still higher number would be disappointing. It might be well to set some "poorest acceptable" number which would mean that something more probably needs to be done.

Verifiable Non-Quantitative Goals

Goals do not have to be numerical to be useful, provided they are verifiable. When numerical measurement of goals is impossible, the goals can be expressed as descriptions of conditions which are to be brought about. An objective of, "Modernize the 1280 and 1850 product lines," is not quantifiable. But it is reasonably verifiable and could be included in an MBO program together with implementation plans and programs showing expected accomplishment dates.

On the other hand, a goal of a college dean, "to establish better student-faculty relationships," is laudable but is neither quantifiable nor verifiable. Sometimes non-verifiable objectives can be restated in verifiable form and so become useful. For example, putting one or more students on faculty committees is verifiable.

When trying to unearth reasonable goals, one may find it helpful to ask questions related to the manager's work. For a foreman's job, one might ask such questions as, Is there much variation between the estimated and the actual costs? Do maintenance costs seem to be too high? Is the reject rate too high? Answers to these and similar questions help in developing objectives in hard to define areas.

Management by Objectives in Staff Departments

Management by objectives can be quite effective in measuring the work of line managers (who supervise and direct the organization's mainstream work) but it is less effective for staff departments because it is almost impossible to express very much of the work of staff departments in terms of quantifiable objectives. Much of what they do can't be counted.

Staff work is often advice, service, new knowledge, or information rather than pounds, tons, dollars, and the like. Much of the work of high-level staff departments is in shaping the final form of strategic objectives. This work is anticipatory in nature and has to be done well in advance of the operating year and so can hardly be related to any end-accomplishment in the current period.

In spite of these weaknesses, MBO is a decided improvement over other methods for administering staff work. Almost always some parts of staff work can be expressed in terms of goals, dates, and costs. In the purchasing department, the number of purchase orders can be expressed numerically. In accounting, "responsibility accounting," described in Chapter 24, ties money spent to the person responsible and so can be used in management by objectives. To the extent that part of the work done by staff departments can be quantified, MBO can be used to improve appraisals of accomplishment.

"Reaching" Goals

We said in Chapter 4, that in order to achieve improved accomplishment, major goals should be "reaching" goals. MBO goals, although they are only short-range goals, should also be "reaching" goals which call for improvement in accomplishment rather than just hold-the-line accomplishment.

Normally, superiors have most to do with adding the reaching element because they know the total organizational goals and they can add to the resource inputs if necessary. On the other hand, thinking of the part

played by superiors first and the part played by subordinates second may not always be the best way to bring reaching goals into the picture. If lower managers are left more wholly on their own, possibly they would set even higher goals for themselves, particularly on matters of operating effectiveness.

Authorities differ on the point of whether people will actually set higher goals for themselves. Psychologist Charles Hughes once said, "When employees have an opportunity to set standards for themselves, they set higher and more difficult achievement goals."

In contrast, John Ivancevitch, in his research on this point, found just the opposite. He found that letting subordinates participate in setting their goals did *not* result in their setting higher and more difficult goals. He said that, in fact, goals set by superiors were better both in producing accomplishment and in generating employee satisfaction than were goals set by participation.[2]

On the whole, organization scholars subscribe to Hughes' position and not to that of Ivancevitch. Quite possibly, however, Hughes and Ivancevitch are not really in disagreement at all. There is little disagreement if Hughes is referring to the goals which subordinates would expect to try hard to accomplish *if they had ample resources,* and if Ivancevitch is talking about goals which they will try hard to reach *if resources are limited.*

Every tax-supported state university always asks the state for more money than it gets. It sets high goals for itself which it really expects to try to reach if it gets the money for which it asks. Later, after a lower appropriation is received (which always happens) the higher goals are scaled down.

Requirements for Making an MBO Program Work

Management by objectives programs sometimes fail from lack of follow-up and continued interest by superiors. A program gets off to a good start with subordinates setting objectives and working toward them, sometimes reaching them. In one company where this sequence of events occurred, only silence from above followed. There was no praise, no reward, nor any review of accomplishment against goals. Not unnaturally, lower-level managers felt let down and lost their enthusiasm for management by objectives. So one requirement to make an MBO program work is top management interest, both at first and on a continuing basis.

The Need for True Participation. We have said that managers should sit down with subordinates and jointly develop objectives. And we also said that it is well to include the subordinate's plans for how he will reach the objectives.

Managers should try to make such objectives be truly jointly determined. They should accept the subordinate's viewpoints if at all possible. Otherwise there is a danger that the resulting objectives and plans will be more superimposed from the top than developed by lower people. If enough pressure is put on a subordinate he will agree to and even make up plans to accomplish whatever the higher manager insists on. But his agreement will be reluctant and he will not feel the commitment to accomplish his boss's goals that he would to accomplish his own goals. If he feels that the goals are really his own, he will have a vested interest in accomplishing them. Almost everyone will work hard to reach *his* goals.

Feedback. Another requirement for a successful MBO program is a good information feedback system. Reports of accomplishment should be made directly to subordinate managers soon after events in a form which allows subordinates to see if accomplishment is proceeding satisfactorily. Then each subordinate can try to solve his own problems.

Appraisals and Incentives. Still another requirement for making MBO plans work comes out of the need for continuing interest and appraisals by superiors. This is the need, on the part of subordinates, for praise and for rewards for accomplishments. High performance should be rewarded. MBO might even become CBO ("compensation-by-objectives").

Unfortunately, appraisals will sometimes be unfavorable. Some kind of notice needs to be taken here too. The notice can be as little as a verbal comment. Or it can be just looking bad before one's peers. Some companies, Procter & Gamble, for one, review the accomplishments of managers in meetings where everyone gets to see everyone else's accomplishments. Wanting to make a favorable showing before their equals provides a strong incentive to accomplishment. The people try to outdo each other. (Perhaps this is what Charles Hughes had in mind when he said that managers will set high goals for themselves.)

In any case, accomplishments, satisfactory or unsatisfactory, should produce appropriate responses. Furthermore, responses should be frequent rather than occasional and should come quickly after events. A manager should know what will probably happen if he meets his goals and what will probably happen if he does not meet them.

Advantages and Disadvantages of MBO

Management by objectives has a number of advantages and produces a number of gains. But MBO is not always successful. As we said, this is sometimes because of neglect or mishandling of its application, but there are also other disadvantages and weaknesses which have, in some situations, contributed to its failing to come up to expectations. We will consider both the advantages and disadvantages in this section.

Gains from Using MBO

Clarification of Assignments. Perhaps the major gain from MBO comes from subordinate' knowing what is wanted and on what they will be judged. It helps if, at the start of the goal setting procedure, the superior writes down, for each key subordinate, what his major areas of responsibility are and how he, the superior, will measure each subordinate's accomplishment at the end of the period. At the same time, the subordinate can be asked to list what he thinks his areas of responsibility are and what he thinks his superior wants done. When such lists are compared, it is sometimes found that the area of overlap between the superior's and the subordinate's list is as little as 25 percent.

Although part of the difference is just that no two people ever describe the same thing the same way, another part of the difference comes from their having different understandings of the same job. Thus, to some extent, the subordinates are marching down different roads from the ones the higher-level managers think they are marching down. Nor do the subordinates know that they are on the wrong road. They don't know that they are not trying to accomplish what their superiors want them to accomplish. Obviously, they can't "succeed" according to the superior's evaluation. With MBO this is different. Subordinates, having before them clearly understood goals, can strike out to accomplish them.

Emphasis on Purposes and Economic Uses of Resources. With MBO, both supervisors and subordinates usually do more purposeful work. Ideally, subordinates should become concerned about doing functional work only when it advances them toward MBO goals. Ideally, too, they would cut out functional work which is not relevant to goal accomplishment. This causes resources to be used more economically.

They also cut down on the time they spend doing the things they like best to do if such work is done at the expense of main mission work. Everyone has his preferences and finds it easy to postpone work he does not like to do. MBO keeps reminding everyone that work directed at main goals needs to come first.

Appreciation of Cost-Value Relationships. Another gain is that managers get to thinking in terms of cost-value relationships. This comes out of accomplishment goals being tied in with cost limitations. Subordinate managers begin to consider whether desirable, but costly, activities will contribute enough to goal accomplishment to justify their being carried forward. MBO tries to get them to think about the financial impacts of their activities, with the hope that activities of small value will be cut out.

Reduction in Role Conflict. Elsewhere we have said that most jobs contain a certain amount of ambiguity and role conflict and that managers often have to try to accomplish conflicting goals. (As, for example, when a sales manager would like to increase sales by selling to more doubtful credit risks than he has in the past, but at the same time, he does not want to increase bad debts.) MBO cannot wholly eliminate such conflicts, but superiors and subordinates can weigh them and jointly agree on a priority scale. When this is done, the role conflict and ambiguity remaining in the subordinate's job is reduced.

Admittedly, however, ideal solutions cannot always be found. A social worker, for example, tries to keep families together but he or she also tries to remove children from bad homes and put them into better environments. Often one goal has to be sacrificed in order to try to reach the other one.

Closer Ties between Departmental and Organizational Goals. Without MBO, middle- and lower-level goals are often only loosely tied to the organization's larger objectives. MBO ties them in more closely. Lower level managers who help set their own goals in conference with their superiors become aware of ways to fit their efforts into accomplishing what needs to be accomplished to further total organizational objectives.

Actually, a great many individual departmental goals do not have to be directly associated with any specific organizational overall goal other than to operate as effectively as possible. The goals may merely be to carry on day-to-day operations more effectively. Subordinates could (and occasionally will) set such goals whether there is an MBO program or not. Yet, with a program, there is more thrust and more concerted effort directed at unearthing opportunities.

Integration of Planning and Control. Another improvement comes out of the integration of planning and control. Managers develop plans for achieving goals at the same time that the goals are set. Subordinates get to ask questions and to ask for more support if they need help in order to do the work. And they can point out possible pitfalls to be considered and possibly how to avoid them. Thus, both plans and goals become more realistic because they are integrated and coordinated.

If plans are left out of MBO, it is more likely that unattainable objectives will be agreed upon but they won't be known to be unattainable until they become after-the-fact failures.

Better Communications. MBO also becomes an early warning system, reporting progress or its lack toward goal accomplishment. MBO envisions frequent back and forth discussions between managers and subordinates about progress toward goals. If progress is too slow, managers find out about it long before the end-accomplishment date. If there is anything that they can do to improve things, they find out about it early in the game.

Improvement of Superiors. With MBO, higher-level managers also probably are improved. Besides becoming more goal oriented themselves, they become more participation-minded. Without an MBO program, many higher managers would rarely consult with their subordinates or talk with them about their jobs. But, with a program, they have to become more open to suggestion and more responsive to the thinking of their subordinates. When management by objectives is used, subordinates will not feel like the lower-level manager who lamented, "Doesn't anyone up there [higher management] know or care about what I am doing?" It is hoped that superiors will see themselves as resources whose principal responsibility is to help their subordinates get the organization's work done.

Personal Interest in Organizational Accomplishment. One hoped for gain from using MBO is that when a subordinate manager fails to reach his goals, he will see it as *his* failure. This differs from the usual situation where a subordinate manager excuses his failure because of lack of tools, money, personnel, or noncooperation or malfeasance by someone else or some other department. Any or all of these factors may have contributed to the failure, but so also may have the lack of diligent application on his part. As long as any part of the cause of nonachievement lies within the subordinate's sphere of responsibility, he should regard the failure as partly *his own*, particularly if he has not performed his work well.

Greater Feeling of Responsibility by Subordinate Managers. MBO tries to get lower managers to feel a share of the responsibility for reaching the organization's overall objectives. It tries to develop in them a feeling that they are part of the big picture. It tries to develop a feeling of accomplishment when overall objectives are reached and to feel disappointment if they are not reached — even when it appears to each subordinate, individually, that he and his group did all that could be expected of it. The hope is that managers will develop the spirit of a basketball team where every team member is happy when a teammate scores and everyone is disappointed when a teammate misses.

The hope is to develop a healthy organizational climate which will contribute toward developing a sense of mission in the minds of these subordinates. Hopefully, subordinates will rise up to their superior's level and mentally step upward and share with their superior managers the full responsibility for accomplishing the organization's total results. Then they will feel a need to accomplish their own objectives in order to help accomplish overall objectives.

More Appreciation of Broader Problems. If the proper organizational climate is developed, then middle level managers will feel concern for overall objectives. They will see more opportunities to achieve and will be more likely to do their share in reaching joint interface goals which require the collective efforts of several department heads. They will not be afraid to step beyond their normal domains and into another peer manager's area if doing so will help. They will not feel that their job descriptions put them into fenced in compartments.

Support for Superiors. MBO may also generate a greater feeling by the organization of support for superiors. The head of every organization actually has a lonesome job. There are no doubt quite a few times when he feels that he is carrying the whole load and that no one else cares. He feels that he is alone in trying to stimulate organizational accomplishment. It may seem to him that most of the members of the organization are not really helping him very much and they may even be opposing his attempts to get the organization to operate effectively.

The gain here is that organizational heads may themselves try harder to be more effective if they feel that the organization is with them instead of against them. It helps *their* morale to know that someone else is interested too.

Dangers and Weaknesses of MBO Programs

MBO programs sometimes fall short of their greatest possible success. Ordinarily, these difficulties can be overcome, but managers need to recognize the pitfalls and take steps to avoid them.

Costs in Time and Money. An MBO program costs a certain amount of money, largely in the form of time, effort, and paperwork, to administer. This is not a high cost since probably no extra employees are added to the payroll, yet the time costs involved in deciding objectives and how to implement them as well as the costs of the few extra reports should not be overlooked when judging the overall worth of an MBO program.

Downgrading of Unlisted Objectives. Since probably no one extra is added to the payroll, the true costs of MBO programs are in the nature of opportunity costs represented by the worth of the work which subordinates don't get done because of the extra time demands of the MBO program. Perhaps the greatest danger in using MBO programs lies in this area, in the hurt which might occur to any activity not directly covered by MBO objectives. This could include soft goals (morale, empathy, etc.) and could well include most innovative activities and work with only long-range payoff prospects.

MBO programs also may keep people from trying to accomplish hard to define partially controllable goals. Usually there are certain things which would be helpful to the organization which a person wants to get done but which he knows he might not be able to accomplish because of factors beyond his control. If he puts reaching any of these goals forward as an MBO goal and then is prevented from reaching it, for whatever reasons, he is looking at a goal failure. This he does not want to happen (he did agree to putting them on the list), so he avoids getting such goals into the record by not, at the start, calling attention to them. A college professor might not want to list publishing a prospective article in a learned society journal as one of his objectives for the year lest he not get it written or lest the editors turn it down.

The loss here is that without MBO the employee would try and would succeed in accomplishing some of these hard to define and only partially controllable goals. But with MBO he won't put them down and not having put them down, he doesn't try very hard to accomplish them. The goals listed take on a higher degree of essentiality and trying to reach them takes all of the person's time.

Over-Emphasis on Goal Achievement. The dangers from using MBO also include the possibility that it may actually discourage joint area problem solving rather than encourage it. MBO goals are "hard goals." In pushing toward their own MBO goals, managers may develop elbows-out intra-organization competition and suboptimize. Managers may feel that they are being driven instead of being helped along.

These dangers ought not normally be serious because MBO programs try to create a healthy organizational climate as well as to tie departmental objectives in with larger organizational objectives. Superiors know about the organization's long-range goals and certainly should not want to make minor short-range gains at serious impairment of important long-range considerations. Also, higher managers ought to recognize the need for subordinates to see themselves as partners in joint problems (because they really are partners) and set up the appraisal system in such a way that it encourages this kind of feeling. The goals set should not overlook the interdependency of jobs.

Need for Reports to Truly Reveal Total Performance. Another weakness of MBO is the possibility that control reports may not truly reflect total accomplishment. Control reports should be designed to show each manager his progress toward each of his goals and they should only incidentally be reports of functional activities accomplished. MBO may, therefore, require that new reports be designed.

A further problem is that MBO reports give credit only for results accomplished whereas often unanticipated but very real difficulties crop up which stand in the way of accomplishment. The production goal is missed because a supplier of raw material has a strike and doesn't deliver materials on time, or a flu epidemic causes more absenteeism than usual.

A subordinate manager may actually do very well in such circumstances and yet not reach his goals. Reports usually do not show interfering circumstances nor do they give the subordinate credit for doing well in spite of adversity. The superior needs to make allowances for these matters which do not show in the reports.

Evaluating the Totality of a Mixed Performance. It is highly likely that a subordinate manager's report will show mixed achievement. Figure 6-2 shows how one personnel director's accomplishments related to his MBO goals. He did well on some items and less well on others.

For MBO purposes, it is not necessary to combine these into one single evaluation. They can be left standing as individual facets of his job and remedial and extra effort can be devoted, in the future, to remedying the failures to meet goals in the past period.

But, for reward purposes, pay raises and bonuses, there needs to be one single evaluation which gives due weight to the various accomplishments and to the importance of the areas of high accomplishment and of low accomplishment. It is difficult to arrive at one single appraisal valuation which will be regarded as fair by all subordinates.

Lack of Empathy on the Part of Subordinates. Nor is the hoped for greater feeling of empathy going to develop in all cases. MBO can easily be thought of as being superior-oriented. Subordinates do not come into the offices of higher managers and suggest that MBO be instituted. Rather, superiors sit down with subordinates and ask them how they can help them to operate more effectively and what goals might be reached.

As an end-effect, MBO programs try to direct and to channel the work of subordinates in certain directions and to get them to

1. Complete clerical selection test validation study by February 11.

2. Hire three black professional-level (exempt) employees by June 30.

3. Ensure the promotion of two women into first-line supervisory jobs in the personnel department by June 30.

4. Rewrite and up-date the job descriptions for the six classifications in the programmer/systems analyst job family by March 6.

5. Complete local survey of rates of pay for twelve, non-exempt benchmark production and maintenance jobs. Report due on September 30.

6. Personally present a written report of the attitude survey findings to each of the nine department managers by April 21.

7. Revise non-management employee grievance procedure and secure approval of executive personnel committee by November 10.

1. Study completed satisfactorily and on time.

2. One black professional hired.

3. One additional female employee promoted into a first-line supervisory job.

4. Job descriptions revised and approved on time.

5. Survey well done but not completed until December 18.

6. Attitude survey feedback handled well and on time.

7. Revised grievance procedure approved by the executive personnel committee on June 15.

Figure 6-2
MBO Performance report for a personnel director. Source: Linking Financial Rewards to Employee Performance: The Roles of OD and MBO, by Thomas H. Patten, Jr., *Human Resource Management*, Winter 1976, p. 13.

do things which they might not otherwise do. So, although the participation may help develop empathy, the constraining effects of spelled out goals and the reaching nature of such goals have a good chance of working against greater empathy.

Furthermore, since the heads of different departments are always being compared to each other, supervisors who hope for advancement often do not want to help anyone else make a good showing. Were this to happen, they would suffer by comparison. A professional basketball player who is sitting on the bench is not always happy when his teammate who is playing scores a basket. The greater the success of his teammate, the more surely the substitute is going to remain a lower paid substitute who rarely plays. He might prefer that his teammate break a leg

Another hoped for gain from using MBO, which we mentioned earlier, is that it might help develop in subordinates a feeling of joint responsibility with their superior and that they might mentally step upward and share his responsibility. Some subordinates might well develop such a feeling but more than a few would not.

Some subordinates just do not want to take on any more responsibility. They would say that these things are the boss's problems and they are glad that they are not their problems to achieve. Still others would say, "The boss is paid to handle such problems, so let him do it." Or they might say, "They don't pay me for doing that; it isn't my job. If they want me to do part of the boss's work and will pay me for it, I'll do what I can."

Lack of Enduring Motivation. And, finally, there is some tendency for management by objectives to become old hat and to wear thin. There is the question of, "What do we do for an encore?" MBO programs always ask for more, and then again for still more. It is not surprising that they lose some of their motivating power as time goes along and degenerate into lifeless slogans or rituals of mechanical nature.

There also does not seem to be enough reward for accomplishment. Superiors should remember that subordinates often ask themselves, "What's in it for me?" The probability of tangible positive rewards helps win the support of subordinates. Often, however, MBO programs seem not to provide for much reward for accomplishment.

Failure to Measure Up to Promise. In our discussion of the strengths and weaknesses of MBO, the balance appears to be substantially in favor of MBO. Yet MBO is by no means universally used. There have been many cases where it was tried and then discarded. Part of the reason for the lack of MBO's greater success is that it is as much a philosophy as it is a methodology. It tries to bring out the entrepreneurship in managers — it tries to get them to manage with "the eye of the owner." But a good many subordinate managers are more bureaucrats than they are entrepreneurs. They still emphasize the activities of their departments instead of overall organizational purposes. They don't want to broaden their jobs.

Summary

The use of management by objectives has become widespread. This appears to be a logical development since MBO tries to get managers to view their work as being for the purpose of accomplishing certain results. It tries to get people not to think of their work functionally lest the reason why work is done be lost. The gains from MBO should be from the greater concentration by everybody on doing work which will further the organization's objectives and cutting out work which does not contribute to goal accomplishment. The greatest value from using MBO probably comes, however, from its being thought of as a continuing process and not as being a "program."

MBO is often closely associated with organizational development activities which aim to promote a healthy open give-and-take atmosphere. In such an atmosphere it is reasonable to hope that middle-level managers will discriminate among the activities they might engage in, and perform only work which helps the whole organization the most.

MBO is not without its disadvantages, however. Perhaps most serious are, first, the tendency to put both short-range goals and hard goals into too commanding a position, vis-a-vis long-range goals and soft goals. And, second, there is the danger that MBO goals, since they can't cover a manager's whole job, might omit important things which will, as a consequence, get little of his attention.

Review Questions

1. In what way is "management by objectives" different from management in a company where this term is not used?
2. It would seem that the objectives set in an MBO program should be set up by superiors since superiors are responsible for reaching the organization's goals. Is this the way MBO objectives should be set, according to the text? How should they be set? If subordinates are allowed to participate in setting their own objectives, won't they set easy-to-reach goals?
3. Groups rather than single individuals are often involved in accomplishing work. Can MBO be used with groups? Explain.
4. Can MBO be used when goals are not quantifiable? When they are not verifiable? When they are neither quantifiable nor verifiable? Explain.
5. Can MBO be helpful in controlling the work of staffs? So much of the work that staffs do is not measurable that it would seem to preclude any use of MBO. Discuss.
6. What gains do people who favor MBO claim ought to result from its use? How valid are these claims?
7. Some people worry over certain possible weaknesses of MBO. What are these weaknesses and how important are they likely to be?
8. How can management by objectives ever be anything but imposed from above? And, if it can only be imposed from above, how can it ever be participative? Discuss.

Questions for Analysis and Discussion

1. Foreman Tom Walker, in answer to the superintendent's request, brought in a list of his objectives. They included:

   • "To perform all of my duties in a superior manner."
   • "I will show more diligence in executing the duties assigned to me."
   • "I will channel my energies more effectively toward company prosperity."
   Discuss these statements as objectives.
2. Complete the following statement as applicable to the setting up of standards for appraisal of a hard-to-appraise job: "A plant manager's performance in selecting supervisors is satisfactory when. . . ."
3. Isn't it just double talk to say that goals are the subordinate's goals when they are set by him and his superior sitting down together and "jointly determining them"?

4. Although MBO is common, probably most companies still do not use it. How do other companies probably set departmental objectives? How do they go about trying to tie departmental objectives in with overall organization objectives?

5. "I still don't like MBO. It is just another method to get me to work harder." Discuss.

6. Discuss, in the light of MBO, subordinates lifting themselves up and trying to solve interface problems with other departments and also to share in their boss's other problems.

7. Isn't conflict more likely to occur than cooperation at interface meeting places between two departments? Isn't it too much to expect that MBO will change these relationships into points of cooperation? Discuss.

8. An Army officer says that with an MBO program, lower managers should see joint problems and that their solving them together ought to be expected. Lower managers should do this automatically and not push problems upstairs to the boss unless they have problems which they can't solve. Will an MBO program foster or will it hamper this kind of cooperation?

9. "The trouble with MBO is that it does not allow for individual differences. Some people work well when they have established goals to work toward but others do not." Wouldn't the joint discussions and the joint agreement on goals take care of individual differences? Discuss.

Case 6-1   The Quick-Grow Company

At the Quick-Grow Company, a producer of animal feeds, sales had been running at a level which kept the company's factory operating at nearly 70 percent of capacity. At this level, the company earned no profit but suffered no loss.

Obviously, a higher operating rate would reduce the cost per ton of feed. Accordingly, Quick-Grow's managers decided to try for more volume, enough to keep the plant operating at 80 percent of capacity. At this level and at current prices, the company would earn a comfortable profit.

The managers exerted pressure on the sales department to bring in enough additional orders so that the plant would be operating at 80 percent of capacity. In order to do this, the sales department eased its credit requirements and increased its sales to somewhat dubious credit risk customers. This resulted in enough more business to bring the plant up to 80 percent of capacity.

Unfortunately, the following winter, when the bills came due, collections fell off. The losses from bad debts increased so much that they wiped out the prospective profits which the added sales had produced.

Management by Objectives

At this point, it happened that a consultant specializing in management by objectives, was just starting an assignment at Quick-Grow to install MBO. He was asked how MBO might help.

• How might MBO help here?

Endnotes

1. Managing by group objectives is discussed in, "MBGO, Putting Some Team Spirit Into MBO," by Rensis Likert and M. Scott Fisher, *Personnel*, January-February 1977, pp. 40–47.
2. "Different Goal Setting Treatments and Their Effects on Performance and Job Satisfaction," by John M. Ivancevitch, *Academy of Management Journal*, 20 (1977): 406–416.

Suggested Supplementary Readings

Greenwood, Ronald G. "Management by Objectives: As Developed by Peter Drucker, Assisted by Harold Smiddy," *Academy of Management Review*, April 1981, pp. 225–230.

Latham, Gary P., and Edwin A. Locke. "Goal Setting — A Motivational Technique That Works," *Organizational Dynamics*, Autumn 1979, pp. 69–80.

Schnake, Melvin E. "Management by Objectives — Review and Evaluation," *Management Planning*, March/April 1979, pp. 19ff.

Snyder, Charles A., and Kevin W. Mossholder. "Application of MBO in Service Organizations." *Proceedings of the Midwest Academy of Management Division*, 1980, pp. 313–321.

Objectives of Chapter Seven

1. To bring the importance of long-range planning to the reader's attention.
2. To relate long-range plans to other kinds of plans and to bring out the proper function of each kind of plan.
3. To discuss the planning process and the problems involved in developing realistic, workable plans.
4. To investigate the reasons why plans sometimes fail and to consider what can be done to improve their success rate.

Planning

7

Today is the tomorrow you have to live with if you planned, or didn't plan, *yesterday.*

Planning is the conscious determination of actions designed to reach specific goals. A plan is a statement which lists things to be done. It shows what, when, by whom, by what means, and at what cost, certain actions will be taken. Plans are action programs and are not mere forecasts of results.

In part, an organization's future can be of its own making. If managers plan their work and then try to work their plan, the future, as it becomes the present, will be more nearly the future which they want instead of the future which would come of its own accord.

Plans may be long-range and look ahead for five or more years. Or they may be for shorter periods of time and deal with only near future accomplishments. These are "operational" plans.

Long-Range Plans

Today, nearly all large companies do formal long-range planning and develop strategies for the future. They try to look ahead for five years or more to see what kind of an economy they will be living in and how they will fare in that economy. They try to figure out what things the organization should be doing today so that they will be ready for the future. Thus, long-range plans do not deal so much with future decisions and future activities as they do with the futurity of present and near-future decisions and activities.

In long-range planning, the important thing is what people will buy. If we do not now have the production capability to make what people will buy, we can probably develop the production capability.

Long-range plans, therefore, nearly always start on the selling end with the planners trying to figure out what products and

services tomorrow's customers will want to buy. Managers then prepare to make the products and to provide the services which will be needed, regardless of the organization's present capabilities.

Sometimes an improved insight into the future comes out of also asking the question, "If we were not in this area already, where would we want to be?" The answer to this question might well indicate that the organization should discontinue certain of today's activities. Long-range planning thus becomes both a pattern for what to do and what not to do in the future.[1]

Long-Range Planning Practices

Some business managers, even in large companies, do not have much faith in long-range strategic planning because it does not always get results. Sometimes, too, managers don't plan much because they are in mature industries where changes are few. Companies making bread or shoes don't need to do much long-range planning. And some managers don't plan much because they prefer just to "muddle through" and to manage by drift.

George Steiner found, in his research on long-range planning, that some managers claim that they do long-range planning when all they do is a little "intuitive-anticipatory" planning based on reflective thinking rather than on any kind of analysis. Although this kind of planning is rough and not very elegant, Steiner reported that sometimes it works reasonably well.[2]

Henry Mintzberg goes farther than Steiner. Mintzberg says that managers dislike reflective activities and that most of their plans are more apparent than real and exist only in their heads.[3]

Formal Plans. It is true that an idea in a manager's mind can be a plan, yet so long as a plan remains only an idea in a manager's mind, it isn't much of a plan. But, if he formalizes it and puts it down in writing, he is more likely to carry it out.

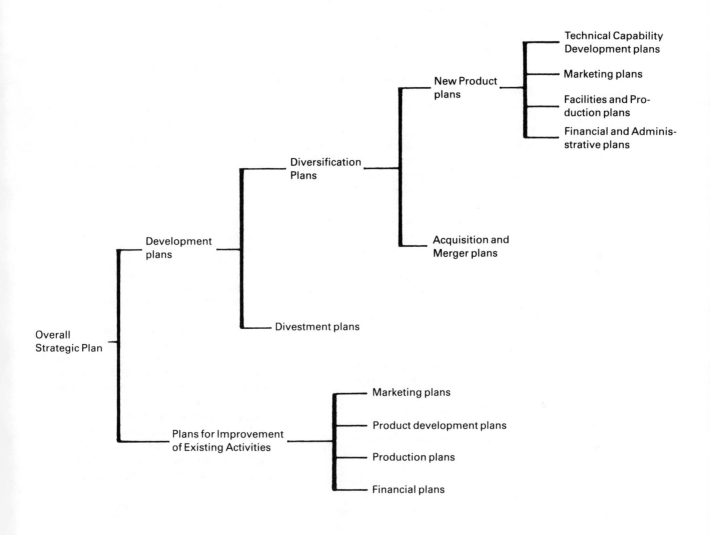

Figure 7-1
Long-range plans need to be made up as a collection of integrated plans covering the major interrelated activities required.

Planning

116

A statement such as, "We plan to increase our business" is an inadequate statement because it doesn't go far enough to be helpful. The manager needs to go on and say, "We plan to increase our business in eleven Western states by seventeen per cent in the next two years." And then he should go on farther: "In order to do this, we will put four more salesmen into this territory, and enfranchise fifteen new dealers. We will bring these dealers into the home office for a one week's training program to acquaint them with our products, etc."

Plans should show numbers, goals and dates. They should include listings of planned sales by product, by area, and by period of time. They should include the necessary money plans (budgets) and the allocations of specific work to specific people. Only when managers do all of these things will they know whether their plans are feasible, and only if they do these things are the plans likely to be carried into effect.

Formalizing a plan makes a manager think about how to carry it out. Plans are sterile until someone puts them into action. They have to degenerate into work. A written plan becomes a kind of commitment which tells everyone that the organization is going ahead with an approved, prescribed, and organized effort, thus making it more effective than just talk about hopes.

Planning Payoffs. Although planning does not always pay off, it does most of the time. Several research studies on this point have found that companies which do long-range planning outstrip non-planning companies in sales and profits by double or more.[4]

Long-range planning is of even greater importance in nonprofit organizations which depend on money from the government or on grants of money from foundations. This is not at all because they are innately long-range oriented. Rather, the managers of these organizations do long-range planning because grants of money from government agencies and from foundations

are made *only after the appropriate agency has approved the organizations' long-range plans.* Without a plan, an organization receives no grant. So, managers of such organizations have to do long-range planning.

The "Total Opportunity" Approach to Long-Range Planning

Long-range planning is as much searching for opportunities as it is planning to take advantage of future conditions. As Figure 7-2 shows, long-range planning is not confined to studies of the future of markets as they exist today.

At General Electric, the corporate planning staff is a "think tank" of forty professionals who study the expected future environment. They search out what they believe to be opportunities in the future. Then they set corporate goals to take advantage of the opportunities they see, no matter in what direction these opportunities lie.

If a company needs to change its nature in order to become an organization which can succeed in this future, such a planning department as GE has develops the plans for making the changes. With this kind of thinking, the organization's present resources and capabilities are regarded as only starting points. It is expected that these capabilities can be reshaped into resources which will take best advantage of the total opportunities which the future will offer.

Long-Range Plans in Operation

A long-range plan is a projection of the company's desired future business. It should incorporate strategies and should provide for implementing actions directed toward accomplishing goals appropriate to the expected future. It should include the following:

Organizational Purposes

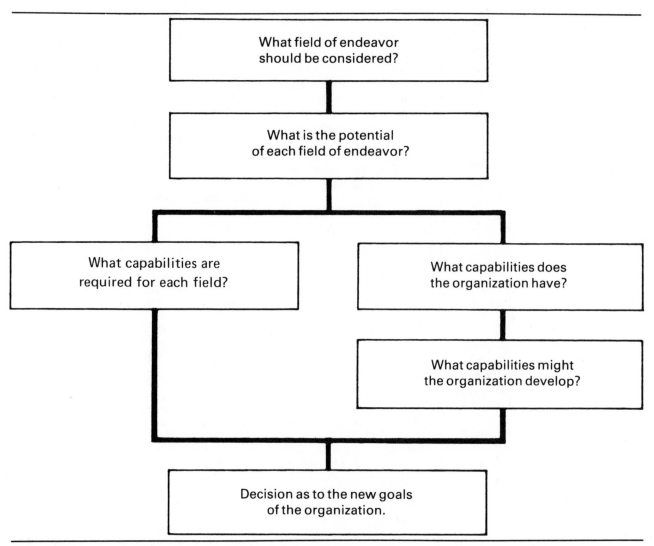

Figure 7-2
Process of arriving at organizational goals while giving consideration to organizational capabilities.

1. The long-range plan should include a statement of five-year (or more) objectives and statements outlining what will have to be done in order to meet these objectives.
2. The plan should consist of separate single-year plans, with plans for the next two years being in considerable detail.
3. The plan should be subject to frequent periodic review. First year objectives and accomplishments should be reviewed quarterly and adjusted when necessary. Plans for the farther ahead years should be reviewed annually.

Planning

118

4. The plan should specify the criteria by which the organization's accomplishments are to be judged. Such criteria may be profit margins, growth in sales or profits, return on investment, or others.

5. Long-range plans should include expected (or "pro forma") profit and loss statements and balance sheets for each of the years covered by the plan.

The overall plans for future years should also be supported by subsidiary plans, although these need to be only in general terms for more distant years. Expected sales would probably be shown in both dollars and in units for the near future years, but only for classes of products and not for each product individually. (A shoe manufacturer would probably list the expected sales of tennis shoes and ski boots apart from each other and from other shoes but would not show figures for the expected sales of size nine tennis shoes or ski boots.)

The plan should also show the facilities required and the expected additions to or subtractions from plants, equipment, and the work force, including managers. If more money will be needed, the plan should show how much, and when, and where it is expected to come from. If a restaurant chain, such as McDonald's, is planning to open up more restaurants, their number and desired locations should be indicated, as should the number and locations of supporting facilities such as warehouses, etc.

Advantages of Long-Range Plans

A long-range plan gives top managers an opportunity to stand back and take a look. It helps a company to avoid staying in stagnant, low-return industries and it helps it to get into growth industries. This was illustrated in the case of the Textron company, discussed in Chapter 4.

Long-range plans also help managers make the most use of their organizations' strengths and they help managers to correct their weaknesses because they force them to take stock of their organizations. They have to make audits of their capabilities. A manager might, for example, ask himself, "What threats, risks, and opportunities are there? Why did we get a certain order? Why did we lose a certain order? What are our strong points? Our weak points? Are we making the best use of our strong points? (If we are not, then the organization's capabilities are only potential or latent energy which long-range plans might release.)"

It was just this kind of thinking in the late 1950s which led what was then the Kresge Company into its very successful K mart activities. At that time a committee was appointed to analyze the company's strengths and weaknesses. This committee decided that the company's greatest strength was in being able to buy advantageously (this was an advantage only because Kresge's buyers did their buying well and not because of any fortuitous set of circumstances).[5]

This led to the conclusion that the company's future success lay in becoming a leading discounter type chain of stores of the K mart type. The years since have proved the wisdom of this choice since K mart has more than quintupled in size and profitability.

Long-range plans also provide a *plane of reference* if things go wrong. When unforeseen stormy weather comes, managers need to do some critical rethinking. Their plans might, for example, call for sales going up when they are actually going down. Their forecast of the future did not anticipate declining sales so their plan needs to be adjusted to give consideration to the conditions they now find.

Long-range plans also *make changes more acceptable to the organization's people.* They know about coming changes and the reasons for them. When the changes come they are better received because they are not surprises.

Impact on Present Work

When a company recruits college graduates in the spring of the year, this is not because it needs them right away. Rather, it is a present action caused by a plan for the future. The company's plan to hire and develop future managers causes recruiting to be done today.

Plans push in on the choices made about what to do today and the resource commitments made today as well as on the priorities assigned to today's activities. Plans tell managers that they have to do certain things today and certain things tomorrow. They focus resource inputs on activities which will lead toward plan accomplishment and they screen out certain other activities and other resource commitments. Thus plans result in the economical use of organizational resources.

The time schedules embodied in planning also require people to set priorities to current activities. A textbook author agrees to send a manuscript to a publisher by a certain date. Often, in order to meet the date, he finds that he must work week-ends and evenings, giving up other activities for the moment. The schedule establishes a priority guide for the things he does.

The time schedule attached to plans also imposes quality restrictions. There is no end to the possible further improvements which continued rewriting can add to a manuscript. But there must finally come a time to stop such improvements and move on to publication. In effect, plans set quality cut-off limits.

Manufacturing companies face similar problems with product design. Improvements can be made forever. But, again, there has to be a cut-off point where design improvements have to be stopped and frozen for the time being so that products can be made and sold.

Plans impose similar restrictions on costs. The contemplated work is supposed to get done within the cost limits allowed. Such cost limitations often determine how thoroughly work can be done.

Other Kinds of Plans

Long-range plans can have so much to do with a company's long-run success that it is easy to overlook the more prosaic multitude of short-range plans. These plans are of even greater importance to successful current operations than are long-range plans. This section deals with the several kinds of short-range plans.

"Standing" Plans

Enduring plans are sometimes called "standing" plans. A great deal of day-to-day planning is routine and is hardly planning at all. A daily newspaper's staff does a great deal of planning for every issue of the paper (one page for television programs and comics, three for classified advertisements, etc.). But the importance of new creative planning in these activities is minor. This kind of routine planning is largely a matter of reusing old plans. The plans become as much established procedures as they are plans.

Single-Use Plans

In contrast to standing plans are single-use plans. These plans are for things which differ and require new and original planning which has to be unique to the situation at hand. The interest in almost all of the discussion in this chapter is in single-use plans and not in the operation of standing plans. Most plans used in management by objectives are single-use plans. So are most proposals for buying new equipment, or for introducing new products, or for increasing the size of the organization.

Profit Plans

"Profit Plans" try to produce a "forced future." Profit planning is almost another name for setting "reaching" objectives but it differs in the strong emphasis it places on *profits*.

In profit planning, a manager starts with a forecast of the company's future business volumes and of its expected profits, year by year, for several years into the future. This is a forecast, a look ahead, and at first it is only a look ahead. Next, the manager decides that he would like for his organization's future to be better. So he changes the forecast and puts in larger numbers for sales and profits which he thinks could be achieved.

Then he uses the new numbers as goals. Next, working backwards from the new goals, he figures out what activities the organization will need to engage in, in order to reach the newly set goals (see Figure 7-3). He considers what products or what services will be needed to produce the desired income. This leads on to a consideration of what new capabilities the organization may need to develop.

Profit planning is not so much a matter of recognizing opportunities as it is a search for opportunities. It is a setting of objectives which will "stretch" the organization's efforts. And it is a matter of planning to do things which allow the organization to take advantage of the opportunities which are believed to exist.

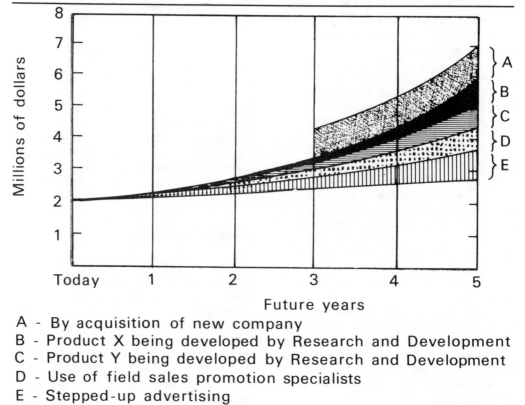

A - By acquisition of new company
B - Product X being developed by Research and Development
C - Product Y being developed by Research and Development
D - Use of field sales promotion specialists
E - Stepped-up advertising

Figure 7-3
Long-range sales projections showing the sources of the expected added sales.

International Minerals & Chemicals Profit Plan. The managers of International Minerals & Chemicals could not seem to increase the sales of their chemicals to fertilizer-making companies so they turned to profit planning. International Minerals' chemicals were good and equal in quality to the chemicals of its competitors' products, and its prices were in line. But IMC had no advantage over its competitors. The problem was how to create a reason for customers to buy *its* chemicals rather than someone else's.

IMC's managers decided to try to develop a "user strategy" plan and to "think customer." It turned out that their customers had a great many problems, including:

· figuring out sales potentials for their territories.
· credits and collections.
· hiring, training, motivating and paying salespeople.
· training and motivating dealers.
· figuring efficient shipping routes and saving freight costs.
· breakage in transit and insurance.
· advertising and sales promotion.

Next, IMC's managers drew up a plan for helping their customers. They established a new management consulting service and an easy-to-use self-help manual to help fertilizer makers solve their problems. The service and the manual were free to customers.

Fertilizer companies now had a good reason to buy from International Minerals instead of its competitors. As a consequence, sales soared. Profit planning produced results which would not otherwise have occurred.

Budgets as Plans

Nearly all plans have a money side to them. Budgets (discussed in Chapter 25) are the financial shadows of plans for activities.

They show the expected costs of reaching goals in money terms. They help managers to be sure that they have provided enough money so that plans appear to be feasible so far as money is concerned.

The Planning Process

Foreseeing the future and making plans to have the organization fit into it is specialized work which is usually assigned to specialists. These people need to work closely with the organization's members who do its main line work so that the plans will be realistic and will be related to the organization's capabilities. This section considers how forecasting is done and how plans are developed.

The Development of Plans

Overall plans to achieve major goals end up being summations of many subordinate plans, each of which is designed to accomplish a part of the total needed in order for the major plan to be achieved. Overall plans usually do not, however, start out as separate subordinate plans which are summed up. Rather they start from the top and come down. Overall plans are at first only frameworks of plans which are to be aimed at implementing important strategies.

So, although planning starts with overall framework plans, final overall plans cannot be determined until the many smaller supporting plans are developed and thus known to be feasible. The process of developing large plans is, therefore, partly one of dividing up the major objective or desired end-accomplishment into smaller segments. After it is known that the smaller segments can probably be accomplished and who is to do what work and when, then the sub-plans can be brought together as supporting parts of the total plan. The total plan is thus known to be feasible.

Planning Premises

"Premises" are the planner's assumptions about the conditions he thinks will exist in the future which will be important to the organization (see Figure 7-4).

The Metropolitan Life Insurance Company has, for many years, been investing hundreds of millions of dollars in apartment buildings and condominiums around the country. It takes twenty-five years or more for these investments to pay off. Obviously, Metropolitan expects that people will keep on wanting to live in apartments and condominiums. These are premises or assumptions that Metropolitan has made about the future.

In many cases, planners need to include, among their premises, their forecasts of such matters as the atmosphere in Washington (financial stringencies, foreign trade matters, tax policies, etc.), and the whole world. National and global matters are becoming more important in long-range planning. Countries all over the world are requiring foreign companies doing business

in their country to conduct their operations more and more for the benefit of the host country's well-being. Realistic plans must allow for growing nationalism.

Even though "the future's not ours to see," some premises are near certainties. In the United States, the nation's growing population is readily apparent to everyone but some matters are more open questions.

People in the United States are already affluent enough to spend a good bit of money for vacations. It seems to be a reasonable premise to assume that vacation expenditures will grow in the future. Managers in vacation and recreational organizations have, however, to decide how they think the money will be spent in the future — whether it will go for domestic or overseas travel or for recreation such as water sports, tennis, golf, skiing, or for visits to Disneylands. Their assumptions in these matters become their premises in their planning.

Cause and Effect Premises. The discussion so far has been about "fact premises," assumptions that certain *situations* will exist in the future. But when a manager

Technological	Economic	Political
· Two-way communication systems for turnpikes	· Inflation will continue at 12 per cent per year	· No shooting war
· Electronically controlled cross-country superhighways by 1990	· Defense spending will come down to 10% below 1980 levels	· No substantial disarmament
· 3-D movies and television by 1990	· Women will become 50% of the employed labor force	· Continued government attempts to control inflation
· Vertical take-off airplanes by 1985	· 20% greater leisure time for work force because of greater worker productivity	· More public welfare programs, and guaranteed annual wages
· Non-narcotic personality changing drugs by 1990	· Continued shift from blue- to white-collar jobs	
· Successful organ transplants for aged people by 1985	· Lower birth rate	

Figure 7-4
Possible premises on which to base forecasts and long-range plans.

plans to bring about a future result, he gets into *cause and effect* premises. He assumes that if he does certain things, certain results will come about. Normally, for example, he assumes that if he hires more salespeople, his sales will go up.

This is a cause and effect premise. But plans based on cause and effect premises sometimes fail because the causes (the input of resources) do not produce the expected results. Results often cost more money to accomplish than they were expected to cost. We come back to cause and effect premises when we discuss their effects on decision making in Chapter 21.

Flexibility of Plans

Several years ago, on a Friday afternoon, the United States Food and Drug Administration announced a ban on the use of cyclamates (a substitute sweetener for sugar) in foods, beverages, and medicines as a result of research which showed that cyclamates might be injurious to health. On the following Monday, the companies making such products had to start massive recalls of their products from the shelves of retailers and to destroy the recalled products. And they had to change all of their formulas and manufacturing processes. Pepsi Cola lost $20 million. Mead Johnson lost $5 million on its weight reducing Metracal. In total, this ruling probably cost the companies affected over $1 billion. They had to change all of their plans for the future.

Plans are frequently upset by unexpected changes in the environment or by the organization's lack of success in the marketplace so they have to be changed. Short-range plans often have to be more in the nature of *reactions* to current conditions than they are parts of long-range plans. Where possible, therefore, plans should be flexible and susceptible to change at reasonable cost.

It is unfortunate that when managers plan, of necessity they must choose certain courses of action and rule out others. They commit resources to one course of action. Ruling out other courses of action and committing resources ties the organization down and takes away flexibility. If the future turns out to be different from what was expected then plans may no longer be suitable and the resources already committed may be lost. So, where possible, large commitments should be made only when drastic changes in the environment are judged to be highly improbable.

Coordination

Work which has to tie together cannot be coordinated without plans.

Before a new model automobile comes out, some employees are working on its design, some are making new dies, and some are arranging to buy materials and components, while still others are working on advertising campaigns. By the time the design of the car is finished, the machines needed to make the new model will have been ordered and when they come in, space in the plant will have been provided so that they can be installed. Raw materials and component parts begin to arrive.

When the first cars roll off the assembly line, *Fortune* and other magazines are carrying double-page advertisements and TV spot commercials are appearing extolling the virtues of the new cars.

Coordination is not, however, all timing and nothing else. Part of the job is to do all of the necessary checking up to be sure that overall plans can be carried out. If, for example, a manager wants to increase his company's sales, he probably will draw up plans to hire more salespeople and advertise more.

But, at this point, he needs to consider what will happen if he gets more business. Can the factory handle it? Douglas Aircraft (now part of McDonnell Douglas) had trouble on this point several years ago.

Douglas' sales department accepted orders for more of its new large airplanes than the factory could deliver by the promised delivery dates. This got the company into serious financial difficulties because of hurry-up costs and penalty charges from late deliveries. Planners need to look at the possible effects, if plans are successful, in all parts of the organization.

Similar troubles occurred in the late 1970s at Wang Laboratories and at Burroughs. Both saw their sales of computers go up so fast that they could not develop adequate well qualified service organizations fast enough. The result was poor service to users and the loss of considerable customer goodwill.[6]

Forecasting

All long- and short-range plans start with forecasts. They start with a look ahead to see, as best one can, what the future will look like. This is essential even though forecasts can never be wholly accurate.

There are many variations in forecasting methods (see Figure 7-5). In general, they can be grouped into four groups:[7]

1. *Jury of Executive Opinion.* Perhaps the most common method used in forecasting is the "Jury of executive opinion." Several high-level managers weigh, in their minds, all of the information they have about conditions (such as what they get from business journals, newspapers, and government statistics), and decide what they think the future will produce.

2. *Grass Roots Information.* This method relies on information from salesmen, dealers, and customers. They are asked about what they foresee in their future sales and buying expectations.

3. *Causal Methods.* This method tries to unearth causal relationships. The fore-caster tries to determine the reasons for changes in the past, to study the causes which are operating today, and to estimate what causes will be operating in the future, and tries to judge what the resulting effects will be.

4. *Statistical Analyses.* Present trends are projected into the future and are used as forecasts of future business expectations. Both underlying trends and seasonal variations are analyzed and combined to give expected figures for future periods.

Probably most large companies use all of these methods combined and add on an element of judgment in their decisions of what forecast to use as the basis for their plans for the future.

Predictability of Factors. Actually, it is possible to predict a good many things with reasonable certainty. At the start of the 1980s, most people in the United States expected that most large metropolitan areas will get larger and that the mass transportation of people within and between cities will become more of a problem. In spite of attempts to control it, there will be continuing inflation. And, in spite of inflation, the spending power of the nation will go up most years because the productivity of the nation will also go up.

There are also occasional surprises which change the course of events. We mentioned the government's ban on the use of cyclamates and its effects on companies. Another event which had a far greater impact was the tripling of oil prices by the Arab countries in the mid-1970s. This caused a serious decline in the sales of automobiles in the United States and caused the public to turn to small cars.

(We will return to the subject of forecasting in Chapter 22 where quantitative methods to aid managerial decision making are discussed. There we will consider the complex economic forecasting models now in use to forecast the future levels of the whole economy.)

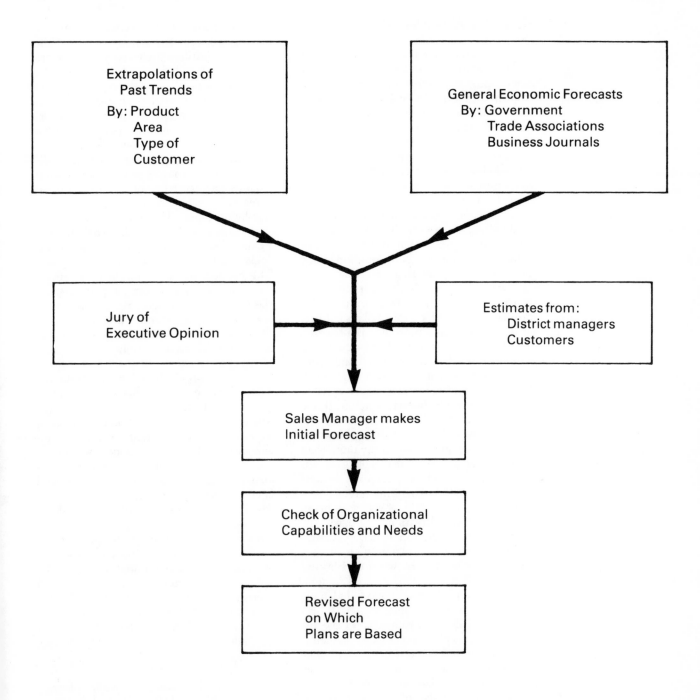

Figure 7-5
Stages in the development of forecasts for use in long-range planning.

Planning

Reasons Why Plans Fail

When President Jimmy Carter was in his last year in office in 1980, he announced that the projected deficit for the Federal government for the fiscal year ending October 1, 1981, would be $15 billion. It turned out to be $60 billion.

How can a forecast be so far off? In the case of governments, political rose-colored glasses cause most of it. But part of such errors comes from just being mistaken about the future.

Governments are not alone in their need to forecast, nor are they alone in often being quite wrong about the future. Unfortunately, planning, both long-range and short-range, does not guarantee that objectives will be reached. This is particularly so in the case of long-range plans. Unfortunately, too, if long-range plans fall very far short, the organization, if it is a business organization, will probably be worse off than if its managers had not planned and spent money for work that has a long-time payoff dimension.

Overly Optimistic Expectations. As was true of Carter's forecast of the government's 1981 deficit, plans are often overly optimistic — hardly more than dreams — and are not really plans at all. How often we read of great expectations from governmental plans in different countries around the world ("We will bring new land under cultivation," "We will increase wheat production by 20 percent," etc.). So often, such "planning" is more a misguided statement of wishful thinking than it is a plan.

Not surprisingly, this kind of plan often fails. This kind of planning is by no means confined to governments, but is common in business planning as well. Benjamin Tregoe and John Zimmerman say that long-range plans of businesses are not much better than government plans and that they, too, are invariably overly-optimistic. They say

that this comes from lower-level managers making projections of improvement. (This, of course, justifies their requests for more money which will be needed to reach the higher goals.)

When all of these lower-level optimistic projections are summed up, the organization's total is really 15 per cent or more too high. But the top managers don't want to have the lower managers lower their goals nor do lower managers want to lower their requests for bigger appropriations, so these unrealistic totals become the organization's equally unrealistic long-range plans.[8]

Lack of Realistic Internal Support Plans. Plans can also fail from not being backed up by the necessary supporting plans. This happens in many cases in which subordinate managers do not get to participate in the making of such supporting plans so the overall plans are sometimes unrealistic. Plans can also fail from the lack of higher level surveillance and attention to support plans.

Too Much Interference from the Top. Having just said that successful plans depend upon top level support, particularly where plans require the spending of money, we now need to note that too much interference from the top often undermines plans.

In his book on his experiences as a General Motors middle-level manager and later as a vice president, John De Lorean describes numerous cases where lower-level plans were emasculated by too much top-level interference. Almost always the harm came from decisions being made at the top, overruling plans of subordinates. Usually the cause of the harm lay in the lack of full appreciation at the top of lower-level problems or of the full impact of the decision in all of the lower-level departments which were affected.[9]

Unforeseen Events.

The Toro Company, maker of lawn mowers and snow blowers, suffered through a dry summer in 1980 and then very little snow in the winter of 1981. Sales of these items declined by more than half (they were down more than $100 million).

Unforeseen events can play havoc with plans. There seems to be no good way to protect against such events. Sometimes their effects are so severe that considerable belt tightening has to be done quickly in order to survive.

Wrong Forecasts of Industry Sales. Sometimes a company is very wrong about its forecast of the whole industry's sales. sales. When this is so its own forecast will also almost surely be wrong. In the early 1970s, twice as many condominiums were built in Florida as proved to be needed. The builders thought that there was a large unfilled demand for condominiums. But they overshot the market and built too many condominiums. Many of the builders went bankrupt and it took several years for the condominiums already built to be sold.

Underestimating the Strength of the Competition. We noted in Chapter 4 that, when setting objectives, managers frequently underestimate the competition. If they make this mistake, it carries over into plans which then become overly optimistic and often fail.

Misguessing Cause-and-Effect Relationships. One reason why companies underestimate the competition is that they overestimate cause-and-effect relationships. They have too much confidence in the expectation that the input of resources will produce results. In the late 1960s and early 1970s, General Electric lost half a billion dollars trying to compete with IBM in computers. GE put large sums of money into its computer efforts but its computers were not well received in the marketplace so GE lost heavily. The resource input did not produce marketplace acceptance.

Misplaced Confidence in the Worth of Technical Excellence. One common kind of wrong estimate of cause and effect relationships occurs frequently in technical areas. Many engineers and scientists have great confidence that technical excellence by itself will produce sales and growth. But sales growth does not come about very often solely because of a product's technical superiority. Unfortunately, too, competing products are often of almost equally high quality, or else they have different advantages and disadvantages, making them hard to compare. In many cases, customers cannot tell which is the better product, as for example, between a Zenith and an RCA television set.

The problem is worse, however. Customers may recognize quality differences but still not buy the best products because they cost too much. They prefer lower priced products even if they are of lower quality. Some people buy a Toyota even though they can afford a Cadillac.

Misjudging the Costs of Activities and Products. Unrealistic cost projections are also frequent reasons for plans failing. Plans anticipate certain cost levels if certain sales volumes are achieved. Such cost projections are forecasts and like all forecasts, they are sometimes wrong, even if the hoped for sales volume materializes. When cost estimates are wrong, almost always they are too low and actual costs exceed the forecasted amounts.

Companies making defense products for the government frequently have had this problem of misguessing the prospective costs of new products. By the time the products are finished, they have cost far more than was planned (part of the increase invariably comes from the government changing designs while production is in progress). It used to be that the government would always make up the difference but this practice has now been stopped.

Summary

Today the managers of most large companies try to foresee the future and then to bend and shape their organizations in directions so that they can thrive as conditions change over the years. Planning allows an organization to operate more purposefully and to make better uses of its resources.

Planning is not, however, without its hazards since, because of it, managers engage in forward looking activities and use current resources for them. Then whenever the future proves to be different from forecasts, both the work and the resources committed may be largely wasted. Yet, in the more probable situation, when forecasts are reasonably accurate, companies which engage in long-range planning are usually better off. As between probable gains and possible harm, the balance seems to favor companies doing long-range planning.

Planning is heavily dependent on the premises which managers make about the nature of the future. Some of these premises relate to matters over which managers have no control but other premises are more controllable in that managers can do something about them. Some plans, called "profit plans," stimulate the search for more productive activities and often result in greater output.

Review Questions

1. Are long-range plans more restricted in their scope than short-range plans? Why or why not?
2. What is meant by the "total opportunity" approach to long-range planning? How is this different from other approaches?
3. What is meant by saying that planning should be "economic?" Discuss.
4. What are "standing" plans? When and where should they be used? What are their advantages and disadvantages?
5. How should a company go about "profit planning?" How effective can profit planning really be when essentially all it does is to plan for doing better the things already being done? Discuss.
6. What are "planning premises?" What effect do they have on long-range plans?
7. What are the most usual methods of forecasting? How is each one carried out?
8. Why do long-range plans sometimes fail? What can managers do to increase the probability of their succeeding?

Questions for Analysis and Discussion

1. As a college student, do you have a long-range plan? How formally should a person of college age try to develop his or her long-range plan? If he has such a plan, how likely is it to do him any good?

2. The Stanford Research Institute did a study for the Weyerhauser Company (lumber and wood products) which projected wood use and tree planting ahead for more than seventy-five years.
   Think back for seventy-five years (few automobiles, few airplanes, no radios, no television, not even moving pictures). Now look ahead seventy-five years. How worthwhile are distant future forecasts? Would the answer be different for a person who works for the telephone company? Or the Union Pacific Railroad? Or the Cincinnati Gas & Electric Company?

3. Bell & Howell uses a continual sixty-month program as its forecast. After each month goes by, another month is added at the far end so that the forecast stays sixty months ahead. B & H reports that keeping the forecast five years ahead (this is a "rolling" five year forecast) helps flexibility rather than hinders it. Would this usually be so?

4. A number of years ago, Monsanto, a chemical company, developed a superior detergent. The established soap and detergent companies did not offer very much money for it. What should Monsanto have done? Should it have gone into the business of selling the detergent at retail? What plans for capitalizing on this development should the company have pursued?

5. The home office staff specialist gave the line manager a copy of his forecast of the company's sales so that the line manager could make up plans for his department's operation. He looked at it and said, "To hell with your forecast. I've got my own forecast and that's the one I'm going to use." The company president hears about this. What should he do and why?

6. The corporate staff has made an optimistic forecast of the economy for the next several years ahead. Each division is required to develop its own plans based on this forecast. Yet, the head of Division A, with one-fourth of the company's business, feels that the future of the company looks bleak. Should he be allowed to plan for poor times when the corporate forecasters see prosperity? Discuss.

7. Large companies often find that there is a "planning gap." Corporate goals are usually more ambitious than divisional goals. So the sum of the divisional expectations comes to less than the corporate goals. What should be done?

8. "All that planning does is to divert the attention of operating managers from sales and production." Discuss.

9. "Planning causes a lot of hard feeling in our organization. Everyone tries to outmaneuver the controller, who keeps a tight fist on the purse strings." Discuss.

10. The text suggests that profit plans let managers pull themselves up by their

Planning

own bootstraps to higher accomplishment. But can a person really get 110 percent accomplishment out of himself or his organization?

11. Among other products, the Northern Company makes powered tailgates for trucks. These tailgates open out and then go down to ground level. A man and his load step on, are hoisted up to truck level and the load is pushed into the truck. When not in use for loading or unloading, the tailgate closes up just as do regular tailgates. Such powered lift tailgates are an accessory installed by dealers after trucks are bought.

• How should a manager go about developing a plan to increase the sales of these tailgates in the central New Jersey area by 15 percent?

Case 7-1   Burroughs Corporation

Several years ago the Burroughs Corporation's top managers decided that the company's sales and profits performances were unsatisfactory. Although sales had grown a little every year, profits had leveled out because costs had been going up steadily.

Some years earlier, in an attempt to deploy their resources to best advantage, and as part of the company's long-range plan, Burroughs had started on a program of heavy investment in computer-related research. Up to this point, results had been disappointing, yet at long last, it appeared that they had developed a superior computer-type bookkeeping machine for use in banks.

Burrough's managers feared that the lackluster performance of their sales department might continue and, if so, that the sales of the new product might not measure up to its potential.

So they decided to try to develop a sense of crisis. They instituted a cost-cutting program which included wage reductions for all salaried personnel, including themselves. They also cut the commissions of the salespeople. Their hope was to eliminate the atmosphere of lethargy.

• Would this probably be a wise course of action or not? Why?

Endnotes

1. A good discussion of this approach is presented in "Peter Drucker on Management," by Peter Drucker, *Management Review*, December 1979, p. 41.
2. *Strategic Planning*, by George A. Steiner, (The Free Press, 1979), p. 8.
3. "The Manager's Job: Folklore and Fact," by Henry Mintzberg, *Harvard Business Review*, July-August, 1975, pp. 49-61.

4. "Does Long-Range Planning Improve Company Performance?" by Zafar A. Malik and Delmar W. Karger, *Management Review,* September 1975, pp. 27–31. See also, "Long-Range Planning and Organizational Performance," by David M. Herold, Robert J. House, and Stanley S. Thune, *Academy of Management Journal,* March 1972, pp. 91–102.
5. These changes at Kresge were reported in, "A Doctrine of Business Management," by Harry B. Cunningham (the head of Kresge's committee and the head of the company during the first decade of the growth of K marts). See *Michigan Business Review,* May 1974, pp. 1–4.
6. As reported in *Business Week,* 24 November 1980, p. 104.
7. *Forecasting Methods for Management,* 3d ed., by Steven C. Wheelwright and Spyros Makridakis (Wiley, 1980).
8. "Strategic Thinking: Key to Corporate Survival," by Benjamin B. Tregoe and John W. Zimmerman, *Management Review,* February 1979, pp. 8–14.
9. *On a Clear Day You Can See General Motors, John Z. De Lorean's Look Inside the Automotive Giant,* by J. Patrick Wright (Wright Enterprises, 1979).

Suggested Supplementary Readings

Larange, Peter. *Corporate Planning: An Executive Viewpoint.* Prentice-Hall, 1980.

Shanklin, William L. Strategic Business Planning: Yesterday, Today, and Tomorrow." *Business Horizons,* October 1979, pp. 7–14.

Uttal, Bro. "How Ray McDonald's Growth Theory Created IBM's Toughest Competitor," *Fortune,* January 1977, pp. 95ff.

Wood, D. Robley, Jr., and R. Lawrence LaForge. "The Impact of Comprehensive Planning on Financial Performance." *Academy of Management Journal,* September 1979, pp. 516–526.

Case for Section II   Boise Cascade Company[1]

"An environment relatively free from job descriptions, organization charts, and other inhibiting restrictions" — such was corporate life at Boise Cascade, according to the company's 1968 annual report. In business schools, the Idaho giant of wood products and real estate development was cited as a spectacular example of "free form" management.

From a small lumber company, Boise Cascade had grown, by means of more than three dozen mergers and acquisitions, into an empire of building materials, paper and packaging, recreational vehicles, land development, and many other interests. In 14 years, its revenues shot up from $35 million a year to more than $1.7 billion. As it expanded, it became known as an exciting, unconventional place for bright young executives to work because it gave them extraordinary opportunities to develop in dozens of near-autonomous groups.

Then came 1970. After nearly a decade and a half of growing, sales in 1970 declined 1 percent below the 1969 level, but profits plummeted 55 percent. Most of the shortfall centered in Boise's real estate operations (the development of recreational areas in California) and construction-related activities (including the construction of low-cost housing in New York City's ghettos), areas which had accounted for two-thirds of the sales and more than half of the profits in 1969.

In trying to solve its problems, Boise scrapped some of the free-form approach. The company's top administrators said, however, that they were not abandoning the methods which, for years, had made Boise so attractive to young MBA's. Robert Hansberger, president, said, "We still believe in decentralizing a high degree of authority and responsibility. But the Boise Cascade Company of the 1970s will be a far more conventionally managed company than it was in the 1960s." (And so it proved to be.)

The trouble in the late 1960s and early 1970s was in Boise's real estate development and in its sales of recreational land. In this sector, expansion came too fast and the operations were too loosely controlled. "The speed with which we grew and the geographical dispersion put strains on the management we had," said William Agee, 33, senior vice president at the time. "We were a little timid about reaching in and seizing control from the former owner-managers of the companies we acquired."

When Boise's land operations ran head-on into the new vigorous movement for a better ecology, the company's managers started rethinking its whole concept of land development. They decided that they were not in the business of speculation. As a result of this rethinking, Boise shelved most of its real estate development plans and has since sold off large parts of its real estate. In the decade since all of this, Boise has gone back to being largely a lumber and related wood products company.

- Discuss this case from the point of view of the setting of objectives.
- Under what conditions is extreme decentralization most likely to work well?
- Why might the extreme loose control not have worked well for Boise Cascade?

Endnotes

The Boise Cascade experience in the 1960s with free form management was written up in a number of magazine articles. One of the most complete of these was "Boise Cascade Shifts Toward Tighter Control," *Business Week,* May 15, 1971. Other magazine articles have also appeared in more recent years.

We usually compliment managers when we describe them as "good organizers." This is a more incisive compliment than might be realized because organizations are complex entities.

In this section we look at the design of organization structures. All modern organizations are set up with departments which specialize in one way or another because specialization increases productivity.

Work can be subdivided into departments and into working modules in several ways each of which will be assigned part of the total work which needs doing. Managers get to choose which of these arrangements to use and to shape their organizations' structures into tall or flat organizations or to use organic, matrix-type organizations or to use other configurations. Most of the alternative structural arrangements have specific effects upon the effectiveness of operations — they can help or they can hinder. Chapters 8 and 9 consider and weigh the merits of the alternative structural arrangements which are available.

Every large organization needs to put certain work into the hands of supportive staff departments. This lets the main-purpose departments concentrate on their essential mission. In large companies there is so much supportive work that staff departments and general office employees sometimes number close to half of all employees. The work of these departments and their interrelationships with other departments are considered in Chapter 10.

Large companies are usually organized on a divisional basis and use profit centers. The merits of this form of structure are discussed in Chapter 11. The last of the five chapters on organization design is Chapter 12 which describes the role that committees play.

Section Three

Organizational Design

Objectives of Chapter Eight

1. To become acquainted with the alternative basic forms of organization structures.
2. To consider the effects of growth in size on organization structure and on managerial methods.
3. To understand "matrix management" and how it differs in its structural relationships from the usual pyramidal structural form.
4. To consider the matter of supervisory spans: the factors which operate to make narrow or wide spans the more advantageous and their relationships to tall and flat structures.

Structural Design

8

"Structures come from and must be suitable to the environment" — but only if managers make them so.

An organization's structure is its arrangement of departments. It is the way in which work assignments are divided up and the way small departments are grouped together into larger departments.

The structure of every organization ought to reflect its needs. J.C. Penney, with its stores in many locations, decentralizes its sales efforts but not its purchasing because purchasing can be done more effectively when done centrally.

Departmental arrangements facilitate the operations of the organization by allocating formal responsibility and authority and determining the location of decision making. Structure also provides balance to the emphasis on activities. It also motivates people to behave in certain ways and to cause certain actions to be taken.

At Oscar Mayer, a meat packing firm, the training of salespeople was assigned to the sales manager. But this did not work out very well. The sales manager wanted to sell products and was not interested in training. After transferring the training work to the personnel department, the training was better done because the personnel manager was interested in training.

One arrangement will result in certain things being done whereas another arrangement will result in other things being done.

Paul Lawrence and Jay Lorsch say that "structure comes from environment," meaning that there is need for the organizational structure to be appropriate to the situation.[1] An airline, for example, operates over widespread geographical areas and so needs to have a structure in which operations are divided up geographically.

Every organization's structure *should* be appropriate to its needs but this does not come about automatically. Managers have to interpret the needs of the situation in which they operate into appropriate organizational structure arrangements. Then they have to try to design their structures to fit their interpretations of the needs. Whether or not an organization's design will be appropriate to the environment will depend on the quality of the managers' interpretations and their success in molding the organization's design to suit their interpretations.

Another complication which we will develop further in later chapters and which bears on an organization's structure is the interplay of the organization's higher level managers and their power positions. High-level managers of major sections of large organizations often have vested interests in resisting changes or sometimes in fostering certain changes. They are often successful in swaying structural decisions in directions which they favor.

Because of such conflicting interest groups, the organization's structure may actually be the result of a sort of bargaining and reconciliation process developed by organizational coalition groups. Environmental needs may be downgraded and not play the part in forming structures which they probably should play.

At the same time, in the long run, neither managers nor dominant power groups are wholly free to set up the organization's design as they prefer it. If they choose a structural form which is not suited to the environment (as, for example, if a large city downtown department store does not open up suburban satellite stores in outlying shopping centers), their organizations will not be as effective as are competing organizations which are structured more appropriately to the environment. Companies whose structures are not well suited to the environment will lose out in competition with the others. Thus, in the long run, the environment will end up playing an important part in determining which organizations survive.

Organizational Design

Basic Structural Patterns

Almost all organizational structures are variations of one basic type. They start at the top with a single head in charge of everything. Below this head are several major departments, each one headed up by a department head. Beneath each of these major department heads, there are lesser department heads, and so on clear down to bottom level operatives. When a chart is made depicting the organization's structure, it is a triangle with the head of the whole organization at the apex.

All structures are not alike, however, in that there are several variants in the way the whole organization's work is divided up into departments and layers of departments. There are three main patterns among the many possible variations:

1. The *pyramidal* structure. This term refers essentially to the triangular appearance of the organization's chart. In a pyramidal structure, the work at the first level down from the top is subdivided "functionally" or on the basis of the *kind of work.*
2. The *organic* structure. Organic structures are really pyramidal structures but with much less formally structured and compartmentalized work assignments. There is more give and take across departmental lines. Organic type structures are also sometimes called "matrix" organizations.
3. The *divisional* structure. Divisional structures differ from pyramidal structures in that the major subdivisions at the top are according to *product line,* or possibly *geography,* or *customer group* and not by the kind of work done.

Both pyramidal and organic structures are discussed in this chapter. Divisional structures are the subject of Chapter 11.

Formal Pyramidal Structures

Our discussion in this chapter deals largely with pyramidal structures. For the most part, it assumes that the work of departments and the jobs of people are defined, set apart, and delineated in a reasonably clear fashion. Most of the attention is devoted to vertical authority relationships.

We recognize that nearly all organizations also develop an informal internal organization and that informal communications systems grow up. They are considered in later chapters.

Organization Charts

An organization's chart is a diagram of responsibility, authority, and communication relationships. It purports to show the general pattern of roles and role relationships between superiors and subordinates.

It is unfortunate that charts cannot be in three dimensions so that they could also show the back and forth exchanges of information, advice, help, and cooperation that go on between departments. Nor do they show the operation of the informal organization. Charts are also static and do not generate action; rather they are more in the nature of information reports.

Charts help show members of the organization how they and their work contribute to the whole and they help everyone keep up with organizational changes. They also show the normal lines of promotion. In some cases, too, they help to clarify the assignments of duties and the lines of authority. Charts also help in organization planning. When changes are to be made, managers can draw up charts showing the different arrangements and study them before settling upon one arrangement.

In spite of the advantages of charts, some people think that they are not very helpful and may even be harmful. In the first place, many people would say that charts don't even approximate what actually goes on. They also complain that, "With charts, people go by the chart when there would be better teamwork if they went across channels more", and "Charts make it harder to change things because they tend to freeze relationships." People may feel blocked into a box. Some people fear that charts will make organizational members become overly conscious of being superiors or inferiors. Each of these objections has some merit; yet, on the whole, they denigrate too much a managerial tool which, when properly used, has proven to be helpful.

The Effects of Growth on Organizational Structures

The structure which suits a company best depends partly upon its size and partly upon its product-line diversification. But even single product-line companies, as they grow from small to large, pass through several stages, each of which is critical in the sense that the owner-manager has to learn to manage differently and also has to make changes in the organization's structure. If these changes in methods and structure are not made, then the organization will outgrow its old arrangements and its operations will suffer.

Growing companies usually pass through five stages, each posing different managerial problems.

Stage 1. Direct Control

A manufacturing company is in the "one manager" control stage — stage 1 — up to about twenty-five employees (see Figure 8-1). The owner-manager can oversee all the work himself with no in-between supervisors. He can delegate work to people who will do the work and not to intermediaries who will tell their subordinates to do it.

At the twenty-five employee mark he would have two or three employees in the office. If the company were a manufacturing company, there would be two or three salesmen, a product designer or two, and maybe fifteen employees making the product. Probably one of these would be a sort of "lead man." He and his better employees would figure out how to make the products that the draftsman designs. They would decide what machines they need and where to put them, and they would keep them in running order. Someone else would keep track of the storeroom and buy materials.

Larry Greiner says that many small companies grow, at first, from the creativity of the owner-manager.[2] Soon, however, this owner-manager has to devote more time to directing the work of others. This would oc-

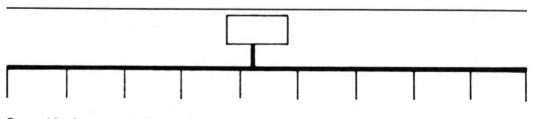

Stage 1 in the growth of organizational structures: Direct Control.

Figure 8-1
Stage 1 in the growth of organizational structures: Direct Control.

cur in most companies as they grow through stage 1.

Stage 2.
Partial Indirect Control

As a company grows beyond the twenty to twenty-five employee mark, and surely before it reaches the forty employee mark, the owner-manager has to introduce one or more intermediate supervisors, as Figure 8-2 shows. When he does this, he moves into the partial indirect control stage, stage 2. In stage 2 he begins to delegate responsibility to subordinates who redelegate the work itself to *their* subordinates. Besides this, it becomes necessary to set up an occasional one- or two-person staff department.

In stage 2, the superior has to work through other people more than in stage 1. He can no longer supervise all of the bottom level operations and he can no longer have as close personal contact with the work itself as he had before. And when things do not go well, he does not always straighten them out himself.

Greiner calls this the "crisis of autonomy" which, as companies grow, necessitates the owner-manager changing from directing to delegating. He has to change his managerial methods and to begin to rely on his subordinates and even on written reports to tell him what is going on. The owner-manager needs also to learn that he has to *train* his subordinates to supervise the work of *their* subordinates and to stop doing bottom level work themselves.

Stage 3.   Full Indirect Control

Stage 2 lasts for a long time, until the company, if it is a manufacturing company, grows into the two- to three-hundred employee range. During this growth period, the top manager has to add more intermediate level supervisors until there are, say, fifteen of them. He will then have introduced supervisors between himself and all bottom level operatives.

Stage 3, full indirect control, begins when the owner-manager finds that there are too many supervisors and staff specialists reporting to him directly. So, he appoints one

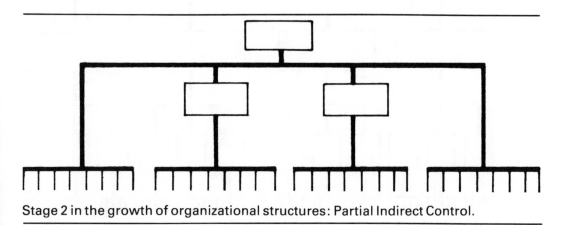

Stage 2 in the growth of organizational structures: Partial Indirect Control.

Figure 8-2
Stage 2 in the growth of organizational structures: Partial Indirect
Control.

Structural Design

of them to be plant superintendent, another sales manager, another chief engineer, and another office manager, etc. When this has been done, there will be a second layer of middle level supervisors throughout the organization, as Figure 8-3 shows.

The managerial job changes considerably as a company moves into stage 3. No longer is the owner-manager's job confined to showing his subordinates how to plan, delegate, and control operative work, but his job is more one of showing *them* how to show *their* subordinates how to do these things.

As a company moves through stage 3, the owner-manager gets even farther removed from lower levels and loses almost all direct touch. This period might be called the "crisis of control" period. It has to be followed by growth through coordination. High-level managers have to depend more and more upon what they learn from others. Reports become substitutes for control by direct supervision. This means setting up a system of written reports and learning how to use them. Managers have their subordinates set up their own goals, budgets, and objec-

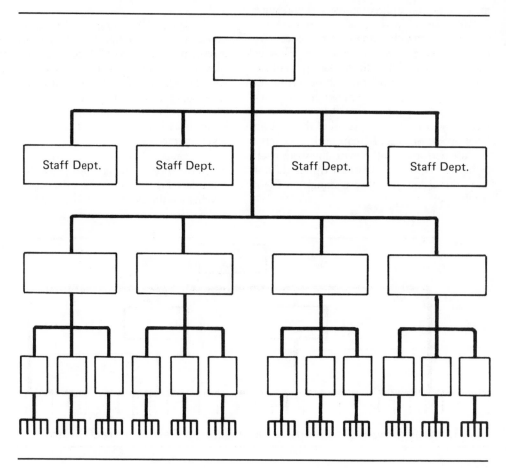

Figure 8-3
Stage 3 in the growth of organizational structures: Full Indirect Control.

tives. All of this indirect control is new. In particular, the paper work part is different and more costly and often less satisfactory than the superior's old control-by-personal-contact method.

Stage 4. Physical Decentralization

As a company grows still larger, it decentralizes both sales and manufacturing and arrives at stage 4. Figure 8-4 shows the organization chart of a stage 4 company with five thousand employees. Besides the vice presidents of sales and production, there are also, in the home office, several sales managers, each in charge of selling one product line. Manufacturing is divided up among six plants in different locations.

This company's arrangement points up a new set of problems which stage 4 companies face. These problems concern what to do centrally and what to delegate to each decentralized unit to do for itself. These problems sometimes make line and staff relationships more difficult and sometimes problems arise concerning the relationships between home office staffs and the staffs in lower units.

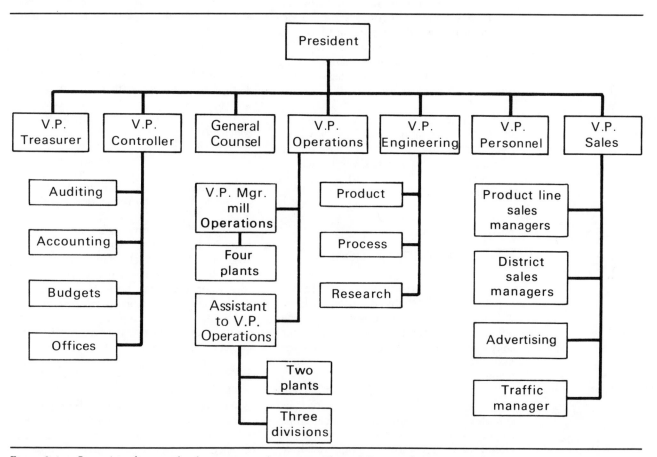

Figure 8-4   Stage 4 in the growth of organizational structure: Physical Decentralization.

Structural Design

Stage 5.
Divisionalized Structures

Ultimately, as a company continues to grow, it probably should change to stage 5, divisionalization, which is discussed in Chapter 11. Alfred Sloan, who pioneered in developing this form of structure at General Motors many years ago, characterized this as "federal decentralization."

The principal difference between stage 4 structures and stage 5 divisionalized structures is that, in stage 5, the top *line departments* are set apart by *product lines* (or possibly by *geographic areas*), and *not by kinds of work*. Manufacturing and sales departments do not become separate departments in stage 5 companies until the second and third level down from the top. The company will have several manufacturing departments and several sales departments, one for each product line.

Almost all of *Fortune's* 500 largest industrial companies are organized divisionally. Size alone does not, however, force a company to adopt a divisional arrangement until it reaches giant size. Diversity of products coupled with size calls for divisional operations.

Organic Structures ("Matrix Management")

Organic structures, depicted in Figure 8-5, are usually regarded as being different organizational arrangements from pyramidal structures. Actually, however, they are only one special kind of pyramidal structure. They are used in "matrix management."

The usual pyramidal structure does not work very well in the making of giant complex products such as space flight ships, advanced types of airplanes, and nuclear electric power generating equipment. This is because these products are at the frontier of technical knowledge so that both their design and manufacture means working in new areas and breaking new ground. It is almost impossible to break up the totality of the work to be done into neat compartmentalized work assignments for departments and for individuals in the concise and circumscribed way that is done in typical pyramidal structures.

In organic structures, which are usually used in these high-science and high-technology organizations, delegations of responsibilities are quite loose and open. There is a great deal of lateral conferring across departmental lines and cooperation as organization members try to get the work done. A person's responsibilities, in organic structure, are more related to his contributing his competence to the organization's tasks, no matter what department he is formally attached to and no matter in what department he makes his contribution. People interact and cooperate with their co-equals laterally as well as vertically.

The difference between organic structures and ordinary pyramidal structures is not in the *form* of the structures but in the *relationships*, the way people work together.

In Matrix management, a *project manager* (or a *program manager*) is appointed to oversee the production of a *project*. He is not a line manager and is not in charge of any department. But he is in charge of the *work* of all employees in all departments who are working on his project. He can give directions to such workers so far as work on his project is concerned.

In any production department, there may be several different projects being worked on at the same time. Several workers will probably be assigned to each project. At the same time, similar assignments of workers are being made to the same or different projects in other departments. Almost always, the individual projects are having

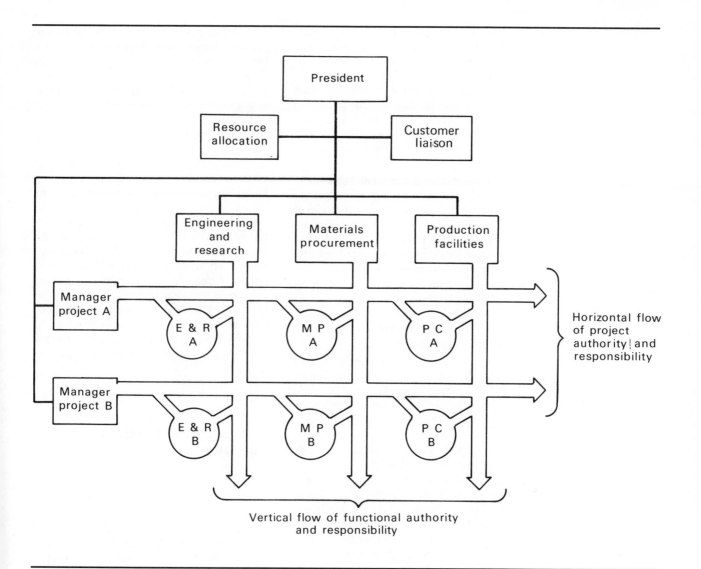

Figure 8-5
The "matrix" form of organization structure.

work done on them in several departments at the same time.

These groups are accountable for their *work* to their project managers rather than to their regular functional department heads. Project managers are usually well qualified technically and they operate as the *technical supervisors* over the employees working on their projects. Regular functional department heads become more *administrative heads* who handle reports and paper work.

Matrix management introduces several problems:

Structural Design

1. Nearly everyone has two or more superiors. The employees who carry out the work are responsible to a functional department head but they are also responsible to the project manager. This violates one of the classical principles of management which holds that people should not have two bosses lest it make trouble (as it often does in matrix management).

2. The functional department head is expected to operate his department effectively yet he does not have full charge of what his people do. He has budgetary responsibility but he can't exercise good control since he does not direct the work that his employees do.

3. Problems stem from the make-up of the group itself. Project managers do not have unlimited power to draft production department employees and to assign them to work on their projects.

4. There is no built-in procedure which assures that the total work load called for by the various projects in individual work areas will stay within bounds. A department's capacity may be underused or there may be more demands than it can handle. Trouble ensues when any department is overloaded.

5. Managers jockey for position in many organizations but a matrix design almost encourages them to do so. Conflicts arise over schedules, priorities, employee work assignments, costs, technical matters, administration, and personalities. It is easy for power struggles to develop.

At one large company which uses matrix management, when a department is overloaded, each project manager has to compete against other project managers for the use of the limited resources and manpower of the department. Project managers sometimes develop a "to-hell-with-everyone-else" attitude.[3]

The possibility of there being greater demands for a department's resources than it has available can occur in any department. To keep such difficulties within reason, some companies make one specific high level manager responsible for watching over the work loads of all departments. When there are overloads, he determines priorities.[4]

By no means is such an assignment (to keep workloads of different departments in line with their capacities) an easy one. Often there is no good measure ahead of time of the amount of work that a project will impose on a department. The work is so often new and at the technical frontier of both engineering and production knowledge that no one knows how long it will take to do certain things. As a consequence, a project often ends up requiring two or three times as much work as was contemplated and uses more of the department's productive capacity. The result is an overloaded department which can't meet its other production schedules.

Tall and Flat Structural Designs

The terms "tall" (or "vertical") and "flat" (or "horizontal") organization structures come from the way their organization charts look when they are drawn up. A tall organization is one with several layers in the vertical hierarchy. Its organization chart is tall and narrow. In contrast, a flat structure has fewer layers between top and bottom. Its organization chart is flat and wide.

In tall organizations, managers supervise directly only a very few, perhaps five to ten, subordinate managers. In a flat organization, each manager supervises directly more subordinate managers, perhaps up to twenty. In general, manufacturing companies use tall structures whereas sales and service organizations use flat structures.

Interest in tall and flat organizational structure in organizational literature was high in the 1950s after which it was dormant in the 1960s and 1970s. But it revived in the 1980s after it was found that the Japanese were having notable success with flat organizations. The typical tall American structure became suspect as being inefficient. We will consider the merits of tall and flat organizations in this section.

Supervisory Spans

The number of subordinates which a manager has reporting directly to him is called his "supervisory span" or his "span of control." There must be some limit to the number of subordinates which a manager can supervise directly. If a manager tries to supervise too many, the result will be less effective operations from the lack of direction and coordination. But if a manager supervises too few, this may also prove to be wasteful because he will not, himself, be very busy or else he will oversupervise his subordinates and not let them do enough on their own.

Studies made of spans actually used in the past years have shown that top executives in large companies usually have from seven to twelve direct subordinates (not counting personal assistants). Extremes run from one to twenty-five. Smaller company managers have fewer subordinates. At bottom levels in all companies, the ratios are usually in the fifteen to twenty-five range with extremes reaching from five to sixty. Actually, these studies of common practice show more dispersion than agreement and provide a wide range to look at rather than a concentration close to any one number.[5]

Factors Which Affect the Ideal Number to be Supervised

Four main factors play a part in determining the ideal number of direct subordi-

nates a superior should have: the superior, the subordinates, the work to be supervised, and the control methods used.

The Superior. Managers differ in their abilities to supervise others. The proper span for one manager is different from that of another. Some managers tell subordinates clearly what they want them to do, thus reducing later supervision time and extending their reasonable spans. Other managers delegate less clearly and so need to supervise more closely, thus reducing their optimum spans.

Nor do managers ever get to spend all of their time supervising. Part of every manager's time is taken up going over things with *his* superior. Besides this, he has certain work of his own to do, work which is different from the work he supervises. So, every department head is, of necessity, not quite a full-time supervisor of the work of others. The smaller the fraction of his time he spends supervising, the fewer subordinates he can supervise.

At the same time, all managers get at least some help in their supervisory work from other people who are not normally thought of as supervisors. Such help allows them to expand their supervisory spans. In a factory, foremen do not do all of the supervising that goes on in their departments. Nearly all of them get supervisory help, usually not recognized as such, from group lead people, inspectors, machine setup mechanics, department clerks and others.

Staff department help also reduces the scope of lower managers' jobs and extends their supervisory spans. In a factory, time-study engineers from the industrial engineering department set job standards. Inspectors (who work for a central quality control department, not the foreman) pass final judgment on the quality of the work done and see that it meets the standards set by the engineering and the quality control departments.

Subordinates. The second important factor in the span of supervision is the capa-

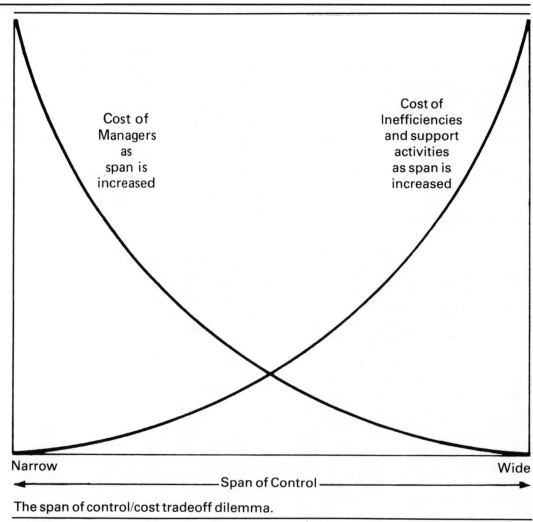

Cost of
Managers
as
span is
increased

Cost of
Inefficiencies
and support
activities
as span is
increased

Narrow

Wide

◄———————— Span of Control ————————►

The span of control/cost tradeoff dilemma.

Figure 8-6

bility and attitude of the subordinates. The more capable and willing they are, the more subordinates a manager can supervise.

The number of workers supervised indirectly also affects supervisory spans. A foreman supervises employees who are not supervisors of anyone else. In contrast, a factory superintendent supervises major department heads who, in turn, supervise other lower-level managers whose main job is also supervision.

The fact that a manager's subordinates have their own next-level-down subor-

dinates cuts down his span a little because there will be times when he (the higher level manager) will have direct contacts with members of the organization in the second level below him or even farther down. He does not exactly supervise them, but he talks to them sometimes and they have occasional access to him and sometimes they come in and talk to him.

Naturally, too, a supervisor can supervise fewer subordinates if they are widely scattered geographically. A manager does not need to be president of a fifty-plant company to run into time-consuming activities which hold down his span. It happens even to department heads whose employees work in two or three separated areas in a plant.

The Work to be Supervised. A third factor which bears upon the proper span of supervision is the nature of the work to be supervised. In mature industries, where products and procedures are fairly stable, managers can have large spans, but where changes are frequent, the spans need to be smaller. Repetitive work allows wide spans; varied work requires narrow spans. Similarly, smaller spans are better where the work of subordinates needs to be closely coordinated.

Physical items also play a part in determining optimum spans. Managers at all levels often have to oversee a number of physical items. They have to oversee machine operations and the handling of materials and other kinds of property. In a retail store, a manager has to deal with merchandise and with moving it around and getting it onto and off shelves and into and out of storage drawers and with marking prices on goods. The more physical items that a supervisor has charge of, the fewer employees he can supervise.

Control Methods. The fourth factor bearing on ideal spans is control methods. When a manager controls his subordinates' work by direct supervision alone, he has to spend considerable time with each subordinate. But a manager can supervise by using fewer direct contacts, using instead more written directions and reports. Good communications systems let him expand his supervisory span.

Advantages of Tall Structures

Both tall and flat structures have their unique advantages so it is often not altogether clear which arrangement will be the more advantageous. The advantages of either form become the disadvantages of the other. In practice, the advantages of tall structures usually cause manufacturing organizations at least in the United States to choose the tall structural form.

Tall structures are generally regarded as being better where work is varied, complicated, and non-routine, where work needs to be coordinated between departments, where jobs are wide scope, and where subordinates are not trained well ahead of time.

Better Supervision

Employees in tall organizations get better supervision than do employees in flat organizations. This probably improves both their performance and their morale since they know that their superiors are interested in what they are doing.

Better Communications

The closer supervision in tall organizations results in more face-to-face contacts between superiors and subordinates which results in better up and down communications. The better communications extend also to relationships between departments. Since managers have fewer subordinates, they have more time to develop better communications with other departments and this helps in the coordination of the work of different departments.

What we have said about better communications needs to be qualified, however, in the case of very large organizations. Even though the closer supervision helps communications, large companies with tall structures have several hierarchical levels. Each layer or level tends to impede communications.

When John De Lorean became the head of General Motors' Chevrolet division a number of years ago, Chevrolet had

140,000 employees (nearly all in manu-facturing activities). De Lorean found *five* hierarchical levels *between* himself and the managers of Chevrolet's factories.

Far from improving communications, the tall arrangement, with its many levels, slowed down communications. It sometimes took months for a proposal coming up to go through all of those levels and just as many more months for an answer to go back down. Worse yet, the information which reached De Lorean had been filtered at each of the five levels before it got to him. He was screened off from almost everything negative.

De Lorean tried to improve the com-munications by eliminating some of these levels and shortening the communications chain. It took him two years to do it, but he eliminated three of the five intervening lev-els. With these reductions, he reported that communications improved a great deal.[6]

More Attention to Non-People Matters

Managers always have to supervise a number of "non-people" matters. They have to be concerned with materials, products, machines, expenses, records, and so on. The jobs in tall structures have a greater fraction of non-people elements than do jobs in flat-span companies. The small spans in vertical companies allow managers to have the time to devote to these non-people aspects of their jobs.

A few years ago, Abbott Laboratories got a new president who found fourteen high level managers reporting to him. This, he thought, was too many so he reorganized and combined work so that only six subordinates reported directly to him.

One of the new lesser heads almost immediately "discovered" the possibilities of an antibiotic drug *Erythrocin* and launched an all-out sales push. Sales and profits soared. Erythrocin had been around for several

years, but under the old wide personnel spans, product emphasis was neglected.

With narrow spans, there is likely to be more time for middle-level managers to pay attention to product possibilities. There are probably many companies which have Abbott Laboratories' Erythrocin problems but don't know about them. Tall structures reduce such problems.

More Opportunities for Promotion

Since there are more managerial jobs in tall structures, there are obviously more opportunities for people to be promoted up the managerial ladder. The odds are perhaps ten to one against a person moving up one level whereas in flat organizations the odds are more nearly twenty to one against one's being promoted.

Advantages of Flat Structures

Flat structures are more suitable than are tall structures in situations where there are widespread activities of a similar kind and where there are few horizontal inter-relationships. They are commonly used by chain store companies in retail selling.

Flat structures are generally believed to be better where the work is repetitive, routine, or highly structured, where little vertical or horizontal communication is needed, where there is little need for coordi-nation between departments, and where non-people matters are minimal.

More Extensive Delegations in Limited Areas

One can wonder where, in flat or-ganizations, managers find all the time it takes to supervise so many subordinates. This brings up one expected advantage of flat structures. Managers do *not* supervise very closely. They delegate more, thus cutting down on the supervision time spent with each subordinate. With wide spans, managers simply don't have the time to oversupervise their subordinates.

The more complete delegation to lower managerial levels is not, however, so broad as it at first seems because lower-level managers have quite limited scope jobs. Flat-structured companies usually rely heavily on standardized instructions. A Safeway store manager does not buy the merchandise he sells, nor does he decide what items he will sell, nor does he do any number of other things that a manager of an independent store would have to do.

More Self-Development of Subordinates

The more complete delegation in flat structures helps to develop good managers. Subordinate managers are more on their own and have to take on more responsibility, which helps them to develop their managerial skills.

Shortened Chains of Communications

Cutting down on the number of

levels shortens the chains of communications. This should improve communications. Ralph Stogdill reported that research on this point found that flat structures did indeed improve communications and led to less time being needed to process decisions.[7]

Need for Fewer Managers

Flat organizations save on the number of managers and, therefore, probably save on managerial salaries. The salary savings may not be quite so large as the reduction in numbers of managers because flat span managers have somewhat more responsible jobs and their pay will probably reflect this.

This advantage of flat structures, the economy of managerial numbers, has interesting productivity implications. Jewell Westerman, management consultant, reports that Ford Motor has 12 levels of managers and that large American companies sometimes have as many as 15 levels of managers. But Japanese automobile companies have only 5 or 6 levels. They get along, and get along very well, with fewer than half as many managers as do American companies. Westerman concludes that flat spans increase managerial productivity.[8]

Summary

An organization's structure is its design or its arrangements of departments. It is the organization's skeletal framework.

Company growth, in the early period of a company's life, should be reflected in changes in the organization's structure. Structures suitable for very small companies need to be changed as the company grows or else the structural arrangement itself will hamper operations. Thus, at any given time, an organization's structure should be related to its size.

Small companies are almost always organized as functional structures with most of their departments being set apart by kind of work. This allows for specialization and is usually the most economical way to set up departments.

Companies which finally grow to very large size often find that they need to "go divisional" and set up their major departments as fairly autonomous units, each responsible for operating a homogeneous segment of the company more or less as if it were an independent company. The change from the usual functional structural form used by most smaller companies is a major change and is sometimes disruptive for a time.

The number of hierarchical levels in organizations has a consequential impact on how the organizations operate. Tall structures with several levels between top and bottom allow middle-level managers to do a better job of supervising because they have a limited number of direct subordinates and can spend more time with each of them. In contrast, flat organizations have fewer levels and managers supervise more direct subordinates. Each arrangement has its own advantages and disadvantages. In general, sales and service companies use flat structures and manufacturing companies use vertical structures.

Review Questions

1. Are organization charts of any value? Discuss their pros and cons.
2. What changes in organization structures occur as companies grow from stage 1 size to stage 2 size? What parallel changes in managerial thinking and managerial practices need to occur?
3. What changes in organization structures occur as a company grows from stage 2 size to stage 3 size? What parallel changes in managerial thinking and managerial practices need to occur?
4. What is matrix management? What are its major strengths and weaknesses?
5. What factors or conditions reduce the proper number of subordinates for a superior to supervise?
6. Contrast tall and flat organization structures. When should each one be used?
7. What disadvantages might one expect to find when wide spans are used?
8. Is it true that managers in wide-span companies really do receive wider delegations? Are they truly larger delegations or are they only wider but less deep? Discuss.

Questions for Analysis and Discussion

1. If a researcher goes into a company which does not use organization charts and asks who reports to whom, he gets answers which are not wholly

consistent. And, if he reverses his procedure and asks people to whom they report, again he gets some inconsistencies. A superior thinks that a person reports to him, but the individual thinks that he reports to someone else, and so on. Is there much of this in most organizations? How bad is this? What harm does it do?

2. One objection made by some people to charts is that they make some employees feel like superiors and some like inferiors. Is this bad? Are not employees necessarily one or the other? Is not a general superior to a private?

3. How can a manager recognize a good organization structural pattern when he sees it? How can he tell when he needs to change his organization's structure?

4. The president of a diversified company says that in his company, "Each group has developed the kind of organization that its operations require." What kind of an organization does the household appliance business require? What does a railroad require?

5. How should the head of an organization decide how many subordinates to have reporting directly to him? If he decides to reduce the number, what would probably be his reasons?

6. How can there be reasonable spans of control when job evaluation plans pay more money for jobs with many direct subordinates?

7. Suppose that a manager has eight direct subordinates and that two quit and two others are promoted to jobs outside the department. How will this manager get his work done? What will happen to his span of supervision? What about delegation?

8. Although the pattern of customer buying in supermarkets varies in different areas, here are the overall figures for the United States. Monday, 8 percent, Tuesday, 8 percent, Wednesday, 11 percent, Thursday, 16 percent, Friday, 29 percent, Saturday, 28 percent (Sundays not counted). Friday and Saturday business is over three times the Monday and Tuesday volume. What does this do to the span of supervision?

Case 8-1   3M's Reorganization Proposal

In the Minnesota Mining and Manufacturing Company (3M), sales had grown rapidly for over thirty years but, in 1980, the increase slowed down considerably (its sales were, nonetheless, nearly $6 billion).

The company managers' analysis of the causes of this slowdown appeared to show that its product lines (including Scotch Tape) had reached maturity and had little potential for further growth. Even more important was the company's failure to penetrate the fast growing office automation market. It had missed out on office paper copying and its word processing efforts had been unsuccessful.

Structural Design

It was felt that the organization's structure was partly at fault. 3M was organized "vertically." Each division and many of 3M's individual product lines were complete entities. They did their own research and their own manufacturing and selling. This, it had been felt, preserved strong entrepreneurial thinking on the part of managers. This had helped 3M to turn home grown innovations into profit makers.

At the same time, however, this arrangement hindered the development of integrated office systems. The individual office machines covered most of the office machine panorama but only as individual products and not as parts of an integrated system.[9]

• What should 3M do?

Endnotes

1. Lawrence and Lorsch came to this conclusion after making their classic study of organization structures. See, *Developing Organizations: Diagnosis and Action,* by Paul L. Lawrence and Jay W. Lorsch (Addison-Wesley, 1969). See also, "Size, Technology, Environment and the Structure of Organizations," by Jeffrey D. Ford and John W. Slocum, *Academy of Management Review,* October 1977, pp. 561–575.
2. "Evolution and Revolution as Organizations Grow," by Larry E. Greiner, *Harvard Business Review,* July-August 1972, pp. 37–46. See also, "Company Growth: Transferring Power in Family Companies," by Louis B. Barnes and Simon A. Hershon, *Harvard Business Review,* July-August 1976, pp. 105–114.
3. This was reported to the author by one of the project managers at that company.
4. "Problems of Matrix Organizations," by Stanley M. Davis and Paul R. Lawrence, *Harvard Business Review,* May-June 1978, pp. 131–142.
5. A good summary of the various research findings on the merits of wide versus narrow spans is given in *Handbook of Leadership,* by Ralph M. Stogdill (The Free Press, 1971), Chapter 26. A more recent investigation of spans of control is reported in, "A Level Specific Prediction of Spans of Control Examining the Effects of Size, Technology, and Specialization," by Robert D. Dewar and Donald P. Simet, *Academy of Management Journal,* March 1981, pp. 5–24.
6. *On a Clear Day You Can See General Motors,* John Z. De Lorean's Look Inside the Automotive Giant, by J. Patrick Wright, Wright Enterprises, Grosse Point, Mich. 1979, p. 114.
7. Stogdill, *op. cit.,* p. 309.
8. "Look Who's Covered in Red Tape," an interview with Jewell G. Westerman, vice president of Hendrick & Company, management consultants, *Fortune,* May 4, 1981, pages 357 ff. See also, "Trust: The New Ingredient in Management," *Business Week,* July 6, 1981.
9. 3M's difficulties are described in *Business Week,* 23 February 1981, p. 84.

Suggested Supplementary Readings

Beyer, Janice M., and Harrison M. Trice. "A Reexamination of the Relations Between Size and Various Components of Organizational Complexity." *Administrative Science Quarterly*, March 1979, pp. 48–64.

Dalton, Dan R., William D. Todor, Michael J. Spendolini, Gordon J. Fielding, and Lyman W. Porter. "Organization Structure and Performance: A Critical Review." *Academy of Management Review*, January 1980, pp. 49–64.

Hill, Raymond E., and Bernard J. White, eds. *Matrix Organizations and Project Management*, Graduate School of Business, University of Michigan, 1979.

Van Fleet, David B., and Arthur G. Bedian, "A History of the Span of Management." *Academy of Management Review*, July 1977, pp. 356–372.

Objectives of Chapter Nine

1. To understand the nature of departments, how they divide up work, and how they combine work.
2. To understand how relationships in the nature of the work play parts in the setting up of departments.
3. To consider the part that chains of authority play in the proper placement of departments in the total structure.
4. To consider the several bases for setting departments apart from each other and the merits of each of the several bases.

Organizational Subdivisions

9

Just as the human body is made up of many sub-parts, each with its specialized task to carry on, so organizations are made up of many sub-departments, each with its specialized tasks to carry on.

The newly appointed president, just promoted from having been the vice president in charge of marketing, asked a leading consulting organization to send in a representative to consult with him about organizational matters. He described for the consultant the company's main structural pattern and then said, "What I really want to know is whether we have the right departments and the best structural arrangements. Does our arrangement hamper or does it facilitate effective operations?"

By no means is such a question an easy one to answer, even for a consultant specializing in organizational matters. Yet it is the kind of question that is sometimes put to consultants and it is the kind of question that the head of every organization might well ask himself from time to time.

In order to arrive at a reasonable answer to such a question, the consultant would need to have, in his repertoire, some knowledge of how departments should be set up. He should know what alternative possibilities there are and he should know the advantages and disadvantages of each arrangement. Then he could move on to trying to develop departmental arrangements which fit the organization's needs the best.

There are two different problems here. One concerns the separation of work into assignments for departments. The other concerns the structural pattern itself, the way that departments are related to each other and the way they are tied into the organizational structure.

The Nature of Departments

Departments are the organization's separate work units. Obviously, it is necessary for organizations to be made up of many subdivisions, each of which does a part of the total work. Just below the top, the organization is divided into a few major departments. These major departments, in turn, are made up of several next-layer-down lesser departments. This subdividing goes on in successive layers down to the lowest level where the final operative work is done.

Departments, Delegation, and Decentralization

The need of organizations to have departments implies the dividing up of work among departments. The process is one of dividing the work up both *horizontally* and *vertically*. An example from Marshall Field, the large Chicago department store, will illustrate these two facets of setting up departments.

1. We will look at dividing up work *horizontally*. Field's could have one single purchasing department buy all of the merchandise it sells. Or it could (and does) let each department (furniture, clothing, etc.) buy its own merchandise. Field's divides up purchasing horizontally and assigns it to its various product line departments.

2. We can view dividing up the work *vertically*. When Field's assigns this work to the product-line departments, it is at the same time, decentralizing this work. It is being transferred down to a lower level in the organization.

    The matter of vertical division of work and decentralization comes up again in the case of satellite stores. How, for example, should Field's handle the buying of shoes for its Old Orchard suburban shopping center? Should the men's shoe buyer in the company's main downtown store buy for it alone, or should be buy for all of the satellite stores as well? (Most department stores would have the main store buyer of shoes buy for the satellite stores.)

In contrast to Marshall Field's decentralization policy, K mart and Sears, Roebuck each have one large centralized purchasing department do all of their buying. Neither the managers of individual stores nor their subordinate department heads do any buying. (The reason for the difference is largely in the importance of styling at Field's. Buyers must buy what the current fashion dictates. This is less important at K mart and Sears.)

Historical Roots of Departments

Every organization's assignments of work to departments are always largely carry-overs from the past. They are probably not wholly the results of yesterday's managers having built an altogether logically arranged structure because, just as today's managers inherited existing structures, so did yesterday's managers. They probably changed departmental assignments whenever they thought that a change would help, just as would the managers of the Safeway grocery company today if they thought that it would help to put in charge accounts. Safeway's managers would have to set up credit departments and accounts receivable departments.

As major departments' duties evolve, they are subject to constraints which keep managers from getting to do what they think should be done. Perceiving that certain work is needed is mental but carrying it out requires resources, capability, initiative, and action. Desirable work may, therefore, not be part of a department's work assignment, because the department lacks the capability necessary to do the work, or its head lacks the motivation to go ahead with it.

The work done by a department is also limited to its degree of success in reach-

ing goals. When a company's personnel department operates the cafeteria, its duties include overseeing a subordinate cafeteria department. But, if the food is not very good, or if the service is poor, or if the prices are too high, the cafeteria's operation may be turned over to an outside caterer. Then there would be no subsidiary cafeteria operating department.

Divisiveness

A department's work differs in some way from the work of other departments. A purchasing department does the organization's buying, but it does not make or sell products because other departments do these things. At the same time, other departments do not buy things.

A disadvantage, *divisiveness*, often arises from the need to have each department working at its specialty. Although the members of each department should think of their work as being part of the total work of the organization, the emphasis tends to get put on the word "their" and not on the word "total."

The feeling of possessiveness over functions, territories, products, customers or whatever, that departments develop can be quite hurtful to effective operations. Such feelings seem to come from something deep within human beings. Sociologists report that primitive societies (and even members of the animal world), develop a "sense of territory" which has to be protected from outsiders.[1] In the animal world the group leader will fight other groups which encroach on what the group considers its domain.

Organizational squabbles and interpersonal conflicts seem often to be similar manifestations of territorial protectionism. Even though all departments are parts of the organization, the pull of the group protectionism is sometimes stronger than the pull of organizational cooperation.

The "Wall Between"

Dividing up work among departments introduces certain difficulties. When one department makes products and another department sells them, their only common superior is the president. No one in the sales organization can actually *tell* (order) anyone in manufacturing to do anything. Nor can anyone in manufacturing *tell* anyone in sales to do anything. No one in either department has strong directive authority over anyone in the other responsibility area.

This is not to say that they cannot talk to each other (although the offices of the heads of these departments are rarely close to each other), but that neither one has strong command authority over the other. There is a "wall between" them (see Figure 9-1). Such authority as either one has over the other is limited to persuasive authority, because every middle-level manager owes his responsibility and his accountability vertically upward to his superior.

The discussion here of the "wall between" uses a manufacturing company's manufacturing and sales departments as examples. The problem exists in all organizations, however, even in governmental units. There are few cross contacts, for example, between a city's police department and its street paving department. Such walls exist at all levels below the common head.

This almost has to be so. Strong authority has to be confined to vertical chains of authority because departments have their own organizations with their own work assignments to carry out. If they let other departments tell them what to do and use up their budgets doing what the others want them to do, they might not get their own

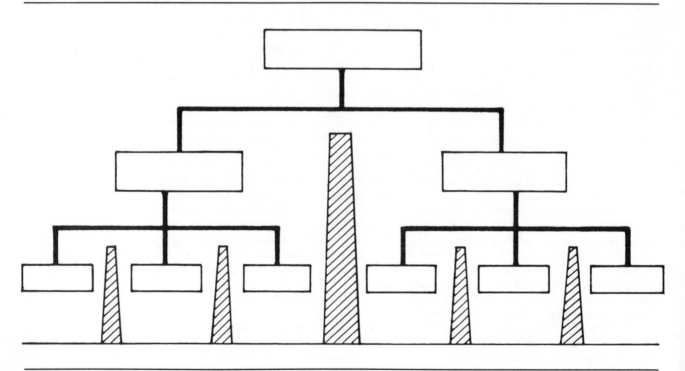

Figure 9-1
"Walls between" different vertical authority chains make horizontal communication and cooperation difficult.

work done. There would surely be a good bit of confusion and duplication of work.

Walls between departments make it difficult for two or more departments to work together on anything. Vertical hierarchical authority chains provide no mechanism for breaking down these conceptual barriers to horizontal communication between departments. It leaves unanswered such questions as, how does the factory find out what products to make? How does the engineering department know what products to design?

Some provision must be made for a horizontal cross flow of information at lower levels. It is not feasible to have every question go up one chain of authority until it reaches the head of the organization, who decides and then sends the word down the other chain to the point where it is put into effect. Lateral information flow systems, including the use of coordinative departments are often used to help alleviate this difficulty. Yet, horizontal information flow systems, if they are confined merely to passing information, cannot become a full solution to the problem of coordinating and integrating the work of different departments because the cross flow of information often needs, in fact, to be essentially a cross flow of *orders*.

When the sales department asks the engineering department to design a product especially to one customer's order, the engineering department is receiving a request for it to do work which will necessitate its spending money and the time of its employees on the requested activity. The request needs almost to carry the weight of an order, yet the sales department cannot exactly tell the engineering department how it must use its budget. The engineering department has other work assignments which also call for the use of its limited resources.

Nonetheless, it is still almost necessary at times for someone in one responsibility area to *tell* someone in another area to do something. And this occurs even though the manager receiving such an order

will then have, essentially, two superiors, his regular superior and the person in the other responsibility area who is telling him what to do and what to spend his department's money for. Such use of the department's resources really should be carried forward only on the authorization of the department's head.

This problem of using departmental resources to fulfill requests for work to be done for other departments, although it is real, has however, been exaggerated in our discussion so far. Sometimes there is no serious problem here.

Departments which serve other departments are expected to get requests from other departments and they are expected to take care of as many of these requests as they can. This is why they exist and why they have budgets. Nonetheless, the "wall between" difficulty often interferes with cooperation between departments. It is an unfortunate by-product of the need to have departments.

Departmental Fundamentals and Situational Expertise

Anyone trying to answer such questions as those at the start of this chapter, "Is our organization set up right?" "Do we have the right departments?" needs to have, in his own mind, some kind of guidelines against which to test what he finds.

To answer these questions, a manager needs to have knowledge in two areas. First, he needs to know what work has to be done. A retail store buys and sells merchandise and an oil company refines and sells gasoline. In each of these cases the organization's departments need to reflect the work to be done.

And, second, the manager needs also to know about organizational fundamentals relating to setting up departments. These include guides for dividing up work and setting up departments in such a way that they will operate together in a smoothly functioning manner. These fundamentals are the subject of the rest of this chapter.

Considerations in Setting Up Departments

Top-level departments are few in number and cover widespread activities. They are collections of two or more successive lower levels of lesser departments. Lower level departments sometimes have close relationships with two or more major departments. When this is the case, thought must be given to their proper placement in the organization's structure. They need to be placed where the whole organization will benefit the most.

Major and Minor Departments

Major departments are composed of successive layers or tiers of progressively smaller subsidiary departments which, taken together, do the major department's work. Every next-layer-down is made up of a half dozen or so subsidiary departments which collectively make up the parent department.

Subsidiary Departments. Most subsidiary departments do part of the parent department's main work assignment. In a retail store, most subsidiary departments sell merchandise; in a factory they make products.

Some subsidiary departments are different, however, in that they assist the departments which do the main stream work. The work that the supporting departments do is almost always quite different in nature from the parent's main work. A department store has a subsidiary department which delivers merchandise to customers. (This department reports to a vice president who has charge of various physical activities of the organization.) An airline has departments which sell tickets. (They report to the vice president in charge of marketing.) Delivering merchandise and selling tickets are supportive kinds of work different from these companies' main work.

An interesting administrative problem is created by lesser departments doing different kinds of work. Major department heads have to administer auxiliary work which is quite unlike their departments' mainstream work. A marketing manager sometimes has to administer the operation of a number of non-selling activities. In our example, in Figure 9-2, one of the subsidiary departments handles real estate matters. The marketing manager may know very little about the work his subordinate real estate department should be doing.

The Proper Location of Minor Departments in the Organization Structure

Usually there is no problem about where minor departments belong in an organization because they have strong ties with one and only one major department. Sometimes, however, the proper home of a subsidiary department is not clear because it has ties with two or more possible parent departments. Credits and collections could be a subsidiary department of the sales, the accounting, or the finance department. And the administration of pensions could be under the direction of the industrial relations or the finance department. In both of these cases, it would be necessary to choose from two or more possible parent departments with which the subsidiary departments have close ties.

Sometimes when minor departments have close ties with two or more major departments, the head of each of the major departments feels quite strongly that the smaller department ought to belong to him rather than to anyone else. Superiors may need to resolve such differences. Sometimes a conflict is not over where a subsidiary *department* should attach but is over which department should do *certain work*. The chief

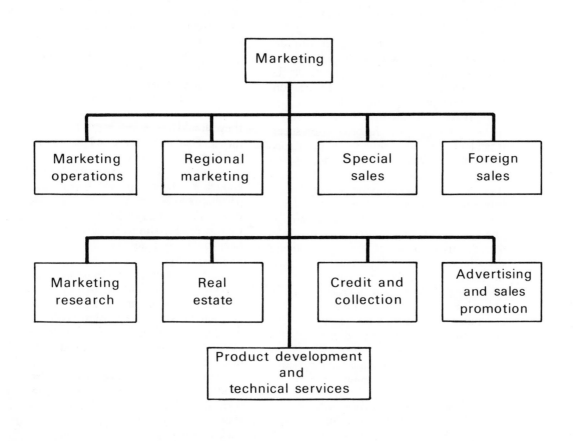

Figure 9-2
Typical marketing department with regional sales departments but also with a department for sales to special customers. Shown also are subsidiary supporting departments which aid in selling but whose work is quite dissimilar to selling.

accountant, for example, usually wants to hire his own accountants, but some personnel directors think that they should have charge of all hiring.

The Need for Major Department Interest in Minor Department Work

The proper placement of minor de-

partments also depends on the interests of major department heads. This was illustrated by the example given in Chapter 8 of the Oscar Mayer company's problem with training its salespeople. This training languished when it was assigned to the sales manager because he was interested only in selling. Reassigning the responsibility for training to the personnel department took care of the problem. The personnel department was interested in training.

Organizational Subdivisions

The Placement of Minor Departments and Motivations

The matter of where minor departments are appended to the organization is often important in the case of staff departments. In a manufacturing organization, the chief engineer might work for the production superintendent or he might report higher. If he works for the production superintendent, he will almost surely do a good job of process engineering and work hard on cost control activities because his direct superior, the production superintendent, is interested in these activities. But, almost surely, he will be less responsive to the product design change needs of the sales department because he does not work for the sales department. If he reported higher, his interests might be reversed.

Joy Manufacturing Company (maker of coal mining and other kinds of mining equipment) recently had to change the alignment of its engineering department because it was not responsive enough to customers' desires. In this case, the difficulty stemmed from faulty communications.

Joy eliminated its central engineering department and transferred engineering work to the company's product-line divisions. Under the former arrangement, the product design engineers were not close enough to customer needs to know what customers wanted. The work was being done at the wrong place in the organization to allow for it to be done well.

Chains of Authority and the Placement of Minor Departments

There are two additional problems concerning where to place subsidiary departments which have not yet been discussed.

First, staff people, those who do helping kinds of work, can serve well only in the several chains of authority under the direction of *their* immediate superior. If they try to serve departments not belonging to their superior there is likely to be trouble since the other departments belong to some other superior.

A second problem deals with communication channels. To operate effectively, departments whose work needs to be closely coordinated need to be able to communicate conveniently. Preferably they should be in the same larger department. This was Joy's problem. When the product design work was centralized, the engineering department was not close enough to the company's several sales departments to be very responsive to customer needs. After engineering was decentralized to the product-line divisions, the several new smaller engineering departments were more receptive.

The matter of communication is especially important in a multinational manufacturing company in its choice of where to assign the responsibility for product development. If, in the case of an American company, product design is attached to the main American company, there may not be enough attention paid to the differences needed for local market areas in different countries around the world. Information about what they need may not filter clearly back to the engineering department in the United States.

Yet, if product development for American products is assigned to the main American company and overseas product development is assigned to the overseas subsidiary, the overseas product development department might well be too small to be economic. Usually, in this situation, it is better to do the product designing in the United States.

Internally Oriented Criteria For Setting Up Departments

Departments are set up on some basis of commonality of their work assignments.

Most departments are wholly internal in that they are designed to meet the organization's internal needs and have little contact with the outside environment. There are several bases of work commonality available for setting up such departments.

Functional Departments

The most common internally oriented way to set departments apart is by *what they do.* In offices, this would be by *function.* In factories this would be by *process.* The word *function* is, however, usually used to refer to setting departments apart by what they do, whether it refers to office work or to factory process departments.

A functional department specializes in one kind of work. A manufacturing de-

partment is a major functional department. The drill press department, the grinding department, and similar departments are subsidiary functional departments of the process type within the manufacturing area. So also, the accounting, industrial relations, and similar departments are functional staff departments.

Functional departments (see Figure 9-3) are the only kind at top levels in almost all companies except divisional (stage 5) companies. And even in divisional companies, the home office staff departments are set apart functionally. And down through most organizations, there are always at least some functional departments at every level all the way down to the bottom.

Advantages of Functional Departments. Functional departments group

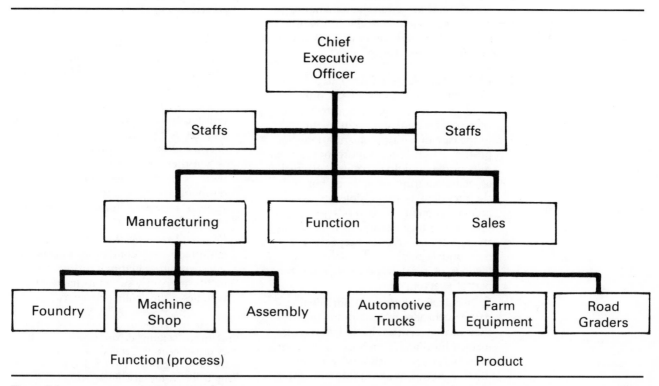

Figure 9-3
Organization structure with primary departmentation on a functional basis. Manufacturing is further subdivided on a functional or process basis but sales is subdivided on a product basis.

Organizational Subdivisions

like work and so benefit from specialization. The advantages include:

1. *Making the best use of skilled workers* because they can be kept busy working all the time at their highest skill.
2. *Work is done under the supervision of specialized supervisors.*
3. *Such departments can make the best use of specialized equipment.* Because the work is concentrated in their area, they can keep expensive specialized equipment busy, thus keeping unit costs down. This is very important where equipment costs are high as, for example, in a steel strip rolling mill where the equipment costs many millions of dollars.

Disadvantages of Functional Departments. It is so economical to combine work of the same kind that the weaknesses of functional departments are, by comparison, small. Yet there are several weaknesses which can, at times, be serious:

1. *Limited Total Responsibility Except at the Top.* Functionalization makes only the head of the organization directly responsible for total accomplishment and, in the case of business organizations, for profits. High-level subordinates are responsible for doing certain work, such as manufacturing or selling, but only the president is responsible for overall accomplishment. This tends to deemphasize the organization as a whole in the minds of everyone except the president and it tends to deemphasize any feelings of total responsibility on the part of everyone else.
2. *Coordination Difficulties.* Individual department heads are responsible only for their own specialties. Each area is under its own head and each area has its own internal "chain of authority" with subordinates being accountable for their work to their superiors who are, in turn, accountable to *their* superiors until all

comes together at the top. This makes it difficult to coordinate the work of different areas of responsibilities.

3. *Lack of Internal Cooperation.* Because functionalization isolates specialists and compartmentalizes knowledge and work areas, it caters to people's natural desires for responsibility possessiveness. Sometimes they become insular, jealous of their prerogatives and resistant to change. The typical functional department head sees things from and only from, his own department's point of view.

For example, sales departments often accept orders and promise quick delivery to customers even though quick delivery often disrupts the factory's production schedules and increases production costs. Or, engineering may ask for near perfection in the making of products which causes extra production costs when less perfection would do.

Such single-mindedness of individual departments often interferes with effective operations in other departments of the organization.

4. *Pushes Decisions Upward.* Functionalization emphasizes the vertical hierarchy and tends to force coordinative type decisions to the top of the organization. When there are differences of opinion, there is no really good mechanism for resolving them. There is no court of appeals between chains of authority except the president.
5. *Product Diversification Difficulties.* In manufacturing companies, both the sales and the manufacturing departments are poorly suited to handle large volumes of diversified products.

It would be hard to conceive of a single manufacturing department or a single sales department in General Electric which made or sold toasters, electric locomotives, light bulbs, X-ray machines, artificial diamonds, jet airplane engines, and electric power generators for nuclear power plants.

6. *Loss of Emphasis on Products.* Functional departments tend to lose emphasis on individual products because no one has the job of doing "total thinking" about them. No one person has the job of figuring out just what the customer wants and designing the product to suit him and getting it manufactured at a cost which will be below the selling price. The product thinking which is done is likely to be disjointed and uncoordinated.

It is also difficult to bring technological advances to bear and to incorporate them into product improvements. Sales departments sell products which are made in completely different lines of jurisdiction. Sales departments have no formal authority over engineering, production, or over the cost of the product.

7. *Difficulty of Judging the Value of Functional Work.* It is difficult, with functional departments, to judge whether activities are worth their cost. Functionalization tends to result in no one looking critically at the *value* or *worth* of any kind of work compared to its *cost*. Functional departments emphasize the kind of work, and not how to do it well or better, and they are not likely to emphasize economical operations.

Functional line departments are said to be responsible for "end results." When there is one big manufacturing department which makes all the products which the company sells, the "end result" for which the manufacturing department is responsible is the *making of products.* And the sales department's desired "end result" is *selling products.* But neither department is inherently very cost- or profit-conscious.

Even if managers want to be cost conscious, it is hard for them to be so because there is a good bit of "common-pot" accounting. The cost of industrial engineering in a factory, for example, is charged into an overhead account which is later assessed against all departments and products on a pro-rata basis. Sometimes this is reasonable, but not if some departments or some products take most of the industrial engineering time. Because of so much "common-pot" accounting it is impossible to get good cost figures for individual products and this makes it very hard to tell if a product is costing too much to make.

Product-Line Departments

In manufacturing, when the sales of any product grows to a large volume, it is often economical to use product-line departments. If a company made sewing machines, typewriters, and lawn mowers, and made each one in considerable volume, it would probably pay to make each one in its own department or even in its own factory.

This would probably be true even though certain of the processes used in making the parts would be similar. The parts could actually all be made in one large parts-making department. But, because of the volume, each product line could also support its own parts-making department and keep it operating at an economical level. This being so, the gains from having each product line under one head and making his own parts would justify using product line departments.

Product-line departments are also commonly used where the nature of the market dictates its use. Sewing machines, typewriters, and lawn mowers are sold through different distribution chains and each one needs market oriented attention. (Product-line departments will be discussed again later in this chapter as examples of externally oriented departments.)

Coordinative Needs of the Work

Sometimes a whole sequence of activities has to be done, one activity after another, in close coordination. These activities may be quite dissimilar yet they follow each other closely. Factory assembly lines, such as are used in the manufacture of television sets and of washing machines, illustrate this. Some workers put pieces in place, some workers solder electrical connections, some weld parts together, while others paint certain parts. Tightening bolts, soldering wires and painting are different kinds of work but because they come in sequence and need to be closely coordinated, these activities should be grouped into one department.

The same thing happens in office work. The factory's production control department, an office department, figures out what materials the factory will need and has the purchasing department buy them. When the materials are received, they go into a raw materials stockroom and are issued to the factory as it needs them to make the products ordered by production control. Meanwhile the accounting department pays the bills.

This whole sequence of activities, mostly office activities, is associated with providing the factory with the materials it needs. The activities need to be closely tied together. For the sake of coordination, the receiving department and the raw materials stockroom are often put under the direction of the production control department.

"Clean-Break"

Somehow the literature has adopted the term "clean-break" to mean: don't break apart work which needs to be closely coordinated and which cannot be separated cleanly and clearly at specific points.

Department stores, for example, make their buyers responsible for both buying and selling merchandise in style goods departments even though buying and selling are quite unlike activities. They do this because they want the buyers to buy what will sell and not to buy what will not sell. With style goods this is very important. Making one person responsible for both buying and selling fixes the responsibility and insures that buying and selling will be coordinated. If one person were not held responsible for both, then superiors could not tell who did a poor job when certain goods did not sell well. It might be from poor selling or it might be that the item should never have been bought. The responsibility for results will not break cleanly so department stores do not separate them.

Competition

All managers in every company are always competing with each other to make the best showing. Some of them may hardly be aware of this and don't respond to the competitive urge very strongly. Managers of government departments and departments in nonprofit organizations are not usually thought of as being in competition with each other. But in most business organizations, most managers try to make good showings vis-a-vis their peers.

In order to highlight the competitive angle, higher-level managers often set up the work of different departments in a parallel fashion. If they can use similar accounting records and reports, then they can compare the performance of various managers. They can compare one store's performance against that of others, and they can compare the performance of departments and even of factories.

Sales campaigns and, in factories, quality improvement campaigns, safety drives, and cost reduction programs pit people and departments against each other. Most people respond to the competitive needle, particularly when it is known that the rewards for accomplishment are pay raises and promotions to higher jobs. Competition keeps people from resting on their oars and failing to push activities they do not care about or oppose.

Fostering competition has its dangers, however. It can get out of hand and hurt cooperation or cause people to try to win at the expense of organization good. To get the most out of competition, there needs to be some control from higher managers to see that it stays within bounds. Poor quality products should not be passed as acceptable by inspectors just to make the product-quality record look good. Nor should the safety record be made to look good by not reporting minor accidents.

Need for Auditing and Inspection to be Set Apart

Auditing and inspecting should *not* be under the direction of the manager whose department is being audited or inspected. No one should be the *final* inspector of his or her own work lest he judge his work to be good when it isn't. Everyone should, of course, check his own work, but it is dangerous for higher managers to accept, at face value, their subordinate managers' evaluations of their own work and to know only what the subordinates choose to tell them.

Large companies sometimes go so far as to have the company treasurer report directly to the board of directors rather than to the president. This gives the board a chance to get whatever information it wants without the information going through the president's hands. And, all the way down through the organization, it is a good idea to set up some kind of a checking arrangement which keeps auditors and final inspectors in chains of authority apart from the chain whose work they inspect.

Externally-Oriented Criteria For Setting Up Departments

Nearly all organizations have re-

lations with the public. Businesses have customers, hospitals have patients, and governments have members of society. Nearly all organizations, therefore, need to set up their departments which meet the public with the needs of their clientele in mind.

Business organizations usually find that one of three departmental arrangements, departments set up by product line, or by geographical areas, or by type of customer, fill this need. Nonbusiness organizations use similar types of departments to interface with their publics.

Product Line Departments

Earlier in this chapter we considered product-line departments from the point of view of internal orientation. But product line departments do not always originate from internal orientation influences (see Figure 9-4). Many times they come from external orientation managerial thinking. They are responses to the needs of customers and other outside influences.

Stage 5 manufacturing companies (divisional companies) are usually set up on a product-line basis. Reynolds Industries, for example, has a tobacco division (Winston, Doral, and other cigarette brands) and a Del Monte division (canned fruits and vegetables). These Reynolds product-line divisions are primarily related to the external environment although, in this instance, they serve internal production-economy purposes at the same time.

Product-line departments are also used in lower organizational levels in retailing. Everyone is familiar with the separate departments which sell furniture, cosmetics, and any number of other products in large stores and with the meat, canned goods, fresh fruits, and other departments in grocery supermarkets.

In selling, product-line arrangements are particularly helpful because the salespeople know their product lines and can help

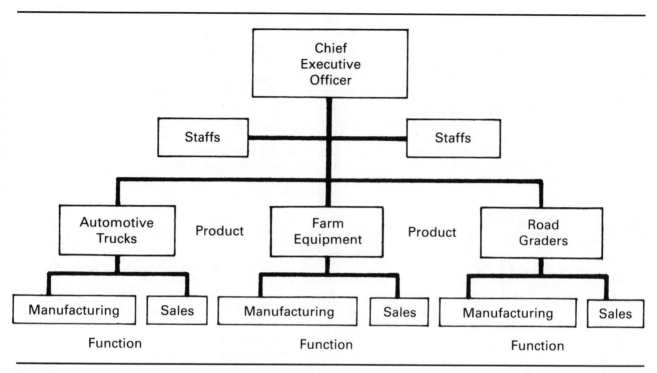

Figure 9-4
Organization structure with primary departments on a product-line basis. Subsidiary departments are on a functional basis.

customers make the choices which will be the best for their needs.

Product-line departments have weaknesses, some of which apply only to giant divisionalized companies so they will be taken up in Chapter 11. But there is one disadvantage which applies especially to lower departments which specialize by product and which needs mentioning here. This is the frequent wasteful use of people and equipment. This can often be seen in a retail store where the clerks are assigned to product areas. The sales clerks in one department may be very busy while clerks in other departments are standing around idle.

Geographical Departments

Geographical departments (see Figure 9-5) are common at top levels in companies whose work is largely concentrated in selling products or services to the consuming public. Such companies need to have outlets in many places. Every grocery supermarket and every gasoline filling station is a geographically decentralized unit.

In a sense, every company has geographical or territorial departments whenever it is spread out — even in one store or factory. Janitors, window washers, and other service people in all kinds of companies serve only certain areas.

The most important advantage of geographical departments is that they allow for good customer service. The employees in the local departments are familiar with local needs and can be responsive to local requirements when these differ from those of other areas.

It is probable, too, that geographical decentralization helps develop managers

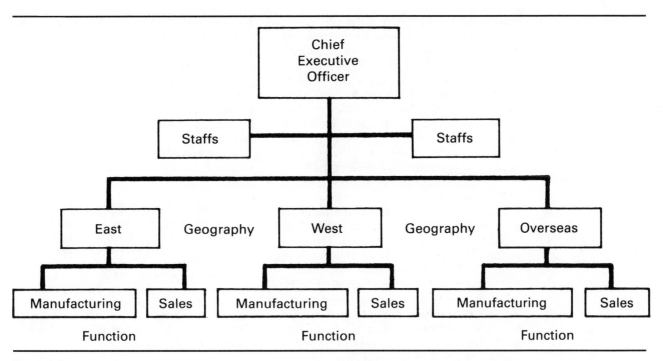

Figure 9-5
Organizational structure with primary departmentalization on a geographic basis with secondary departments on a functional basis.

since the managers of decentralized operations are a little more on their own than are people in functional or product-line departments. They get to see most of the company's problems in miniature. This applies particularly to geographical sales managers, who get very good training for becoming general sales managers.

Geographic departments are uncommon in manufacturing. In manufacturing, geographic departments would often fragmentize production operations too much and so would lose the advantages that large-scale operations can bring in the production area. The possible extra costs (which could be several times higher) from too small-scale operations could be far too much to bear, so manufacturing should not be divided up into many small plant operations.

New product development might also suffer. If the individual geographical units each did development work, they would fre-

quently be making fragmented attacks on problems which could be carried on better all in one place. The separate geographical units might also, unknowingly, be duplicating each other's efforts wastefully.

There is a tendency, however, for neither of these things to happen when manufacturing is divided up geographically. Rather, something quite different happens. There is a tendency for *none* of the managers to do either product or process development work, while hoping that someone else will do it and so relieve them of having to stand the costs of doing it themselves.

Departments by Type of Customer

Individual customers buy automobile tires but so do General Motors and other car makers. So also Greyhound Bus and Yellow Cab, and cities, states, and the Federal government buy tires. Airplane tires constitute another large tire market. There are also large regular tire customers which are only middlemen. Sears, Roebuck; K mart; Standard Oil of California, and other gasoline filling station chains sell tires to individual customers, but tire manufacturers get the contracts to make these tires, perhaps millions of tires, on an all-or-nothing basis.

No local tire dealer in any one city is likely to get any of these large contracts. So much money is involved that the purchase contracts are negotiated by major officials in each of the companies concerned. Tire companies all have special high-level sales groups to sell to their very important customers.

Sales departments often need to be set up by type of customer or market group. A furniture company which makes furniture for schools and restaurants might set up separate sales departments for each of these two market groups. Trying to sell large orders to school board purchasing agents would require a quite different kind of selling effort from selling chairs and tables to restaurant owners. When market groups are as different as this, separate sales departments for each one are more effective than one single sales department.

Similarly, large companies selling to government departments need to have their own inside specialized departments for bidding on such contracts. They need specialized knowledge about the required contract provisions having to do with financing, subcontracting, employment, the inspection of products, and so on.

Combinations of Criteria

Normally, only one criterion of separation and grouping should be used at any one level in an organization. Then the various sub-departments' work assignments, taken together, will be all inclusive, but at the same time they will, individually, be mutually exclusive and will not overlap. If a geographic base is used, there might be an Eastern, Southern, Midwestern, and Western department. The whole country would be covered with mutually exclusive area assignments.

Sometimes, however, there are good reasons for using two or more bases at one level.

Before General Motors sold its Frigidaire operations to White Consolidated in 1979, it had such a problem in selling refrigerators in Canada. GM owned Frigidaire and operated it in the United States as a largely autonomous division. GM also had a Canadian automotive division. These arrangements were not mutually exclusive and left open the question of which division, Frigidaire, or GM of Canada, should sell refrigerators in Canada.

Questions of this sort always arise when two different criteria, in this case, product line and geography, are used at the same level in the organization. Actually, in this case, GM let the product line base override the geographic base. Frigidaire operated its own Canadian subsidiary. Refrigerators are more different from automobiles than Canada is different from the United States. The GM of Canada division handles only automobiles.

Many large companies have similar problems in marketing even in the United States. They have regional sales departments serving every part of the country. But they also have a special sales department to sell to very large customers, such as the United States government, which operate in several regions. Except for the government, such an arrangement is often ambiguous since it is difficult to say where to draw the line and say which large customers belong to a region and which belong to special sales.

Summary

By far the most common basis for setting up departments is by kind of work. A department is a place where one kind of work is done. Such departments are called functional departments.

The mere existence of departments, each specializing in some way, creates problems of divisiveness. Departments tend to become insular and not to cooperate with each other. Problems of common interest to two or more chains of authority tend to be neglected or else forced to the top for decision. Cross-channel communication is often scant and when it occurs, talk alone, although it helps, falls short of getting full cooperation from departments in different chains of authority.

Although functional departments are the most common, there are other bases for setting the work of departments apart from each other. One, the product-line basis, is commonly the main organizational pattern at the top level in giant manufacturing companies. Product-line departments are also used at low levels in both manufacturing and retailing.

Other bases sometimes used include geographical departments and departments by type of customer. Both are more common in selling and distribution than in manufacturing. Down within organizations, and particularly within production organizations, several other bases are sometimes used.

Ordinarily, at any one level in an organization, the subdepartments should be set apart on the basis of only one base. Doing this avoids the ambiguity which comes from mixing bases.

Review Questions

1. What kinds of knowledge are needed in order to set up departments to best advantage? How much should interpersonal relationships play in such decisions?
2. How is it that departmentalization tends to create divisiveness? What can be done about this?
3. What is the "wall between" idea? Is there any way that its pernicious effects can be reduced?
4. How do top managers know which major departments should have the direction over specific lower level departments? Discuss.
5. What factors should an organizational analyst consider when he studies where minor departments should be tied into the organization?

6. What are the advantages and disadvantages of setting up departments on a functional basis?

7. Does using a product criteria for departmentalization (as contrasted with a functional base) make coordination and control more simple or less simple? Discuss.

8. Would you expect to find geographical departments more in sales organizations than in manufacturing organizations? Why?

Questions for Analysis and Discussion

1. The Reed meat packing company has put advertising, sales promotion, and public relations under one vice president. The new president thinks that public relations does not belong there. But he is planning no change for the present because the man in charge will retire in three years. Discuss.

2. A mining company put market research in the finance department because it seemed to be mostly concerned with figures, predictions, and statistics. Soon thereafter the company lost ground to plastics, glass, and compressed wood particle board. Then the president took market research out of the finance department and put it in the marketing department so that it would be more customer oriented. Would things probably improve or get worse? Why?

3. Question two above dealt with a company which put marketing research in the finance department. Would this usually be the right place for marketing research? Why? How can a manager tell if something has been put in the "wrong place"?

4. The board of directors of a growing credit union at a large university asks the university's professor of organization how the credit union should be set up. The board wants to know what departments or officers the credit union needs and what they should do. On what information or knowledge should the professor base his recommendations?

5. Should a college textbook publisher have each of its sales representatives call on only a few schools and call on all departments in these schools? Or should it have a specialist in business administration, another in mathematics, one in economics, etc., each call on many schools but confine himself to his specialty?

6. The White's Clothing store has been growing so there is need to subdivide the work. Should one of the partners say, "Joe, you take the ladies' wear and I'll take the men's wear." Or should he say, "You take the selling and I'll take the buying?" Discuss.

7. Suppose that the president tells his people to break down the "wall between" by establishing informal cross-channel communications.

Are there any bad features in this delegation? What risks does the president run?

8. Is there really a "wall between"? What does the Chief Engineer think he has a budget for if it is not to design products for the sales department?

9. Assume that the head of Department A (there being three departments, A, B, and C) leaves and the question arises as to whether to replace him (thus continuing the same organization structure), or to abolish the position and divide old department A into two new departments, D, and E, or to reassign A's work to B and C. What are the important considerations here?

10. Company A had an outstanding reputation for important production innovations and rapid development of ideas into mass-production items. Nevertheless, there were frequent arguments among research, engineering, and production, as to which department should take the responsibility for the product at what stage in the development sequence. Engineering wanted control of the pilot plant stage. Production wanted control from the time the product entered its physical domain. Research wanted control, as one of its members put it, "until the actual factory yield reaches the theoretical yield." Discuss.

11. Should a hospital have one kitchen which cooks all meals for the whole hospital? Or should it have several kitchens, each specializing in one way or another? And, if they specialize, on what basis should it be done?

12. People who favor using organization charts say that when a company makes up a chart, it will reveal structural faults if there are any. Will it? What is a structural fault? How will a manager know one when he sees it?

Case 9-1   Gulf Oil's Structural Reorganization

In 1975, Gulf Oil departed from typical large oil company practice by changing its organization structure from a geographical pattern to a functional pattern. Formerly, Gulf had had a United States, an Eastern Hemisphere, a Latin American, and, in all, 16 such geographical divisions.

They were replaced by the following newly set up "strategy" divisions based on product lines: (1) Extractive Industries (to explore for and to produce oil, coal, uranium, and other minerals), (2) Refining and Marketing (to process and refine oil), (3) Transportation (to operate Gulf's fleet of oil tankers), (4) Science and Technology, (5) Chemicals, (6) Real Estate, and (7) a 68 percent owned Canadian subsidiary.[2]

• What reasons might be behind this move by Gulf? (Gulf was among the several large oil companies which saw their Arabian oil wells expropriated in the 1970s.)

Case 9-2   IBM's Worldwide Operations

IBM operates worldwide both in manufacturing and selling or leasing its equipment. It also has thirty-two research and development laboratories, of which several are located in Europe. Four thousand of IBM's twenty thousand R&D people work in European laboratories. Each laboratory is assigned certain "missions" to control all technical activities for a product or group of products or service area (such as the use of computers in medical research and health services), which it oversees on a worldwide basis.

There is considerable prestige to the host countries from having advanced technical work done in their country and largely by their own nationals. It has been reported, however, that the physicists, chemists, electrical engineers, and mathematicians working on IBM's overseas research and development work are not wholly happy. The feeling of prestige is partly offset by a feeling of impotence on the part of these people since they have almost no voice in the choice of the missions they are assigned to carry out. Yet if they were given more freedom, there is a possibility that they would be duplicating their efforts or else unintentionally omitting certain needed work. They might even depart from IBM's well-organized one-world product line and develop single country product lines.[3]

- What policy should IBM follow? Why?

Endnotes

1. Lee Grossman has an interesting discussion of how this kind of mental attitude applies in organizations. See, *The Change Agent,* by Lee Grossman (Amacom, 1975), p. 72.
2. This restructuring of Gulf is described at length in *Business Week,* 30 June 1975, pp. 29ff.
3. This difficulty is described in, "R & D on a Global Scale . . . The IBM Approach," by Nancy Foy, *Management Review,* February 1975, pp. 4–10.

Suggested Supplementary Readings

Comstock, D., and W. Scott. "Technology and the Structure of Subunits." *Administrative Science Quarterly* 22 (1977): 177–202.

Duncan, Robert. "What is the Right Organization Structure?" *Organizational Dynamics,* Winter 1979, pp. 59–80.

Ouchi, W. "The Relationship Between Organizational Structure and Organization Control." *Administrative Science Quarterly* 22 (1977): 95–113.

Zeira, Yoran, and Ehud Harari. "Structural Sources of Personnel Problems in Multinational Firms." *Academy of Management Proceedings,* 1977, pp. 332–336.

Objectives of Chapter Ten

1. To set up classes or groups of staff departments according to the nature of their work for other departments.
2. To consider the assignments of staffs and their authority as it relates to the departments they serve.
3. To discuss authority difficulties between lines and staffs at interface points between such departments.
4. To consider how to smooth over possible difficulties and to make staff work more helpful.

Staff Departments

10

An Army marches on its stomach; without its
supportive departments, it is lost.

Staff Functions

Staff work is helping work. Staff departments help the organization to operate effectively. They do not do the organization's main purpose work but instead serve the organization by doing ancillary, supportive work.

The output of staff departments is often intangible and is in the form of proposals, recommendations, information and knowledge. Staff workers are often knowledge workers and their end-products are results of thought processes. Often their recommendations concern the future character and direction of the organization and the main users of their help are high-level managers.

Service work as done by staff departments requires a different kind of managing from that for making and selling products. Staff objectives are less clear, there is more shared responsibility, and staffs work in a longer time frame.

Orientation to Manufacturing Organizations. In this chapter we will consider the work of staff departments largely as they operate in business organizations. More specifically, the discussion in this chapter will be oriented toward manufacturing companies rather than to service organizations. We have chosen this route because there are so many diverse activities which need coordinated direction that staffs in manufacturing organizations play a much greater part than they play in other kinds of organizations. Their work and that of the manufacturing departments is interrelated at almost every step in the manufacturing process.

Service organizations, such as government departments and educational organizations, in contrast, are more independent. Each such organization serves the public in its domain and there are fewer interactions with other departments, whether they be staff or line.

Kinds of Staff Work

Staff work varies all the way from advisory, to actually doing certain kinds of work for other departments. In this section, we will consider these several kinds of staff services.

Advisory Staff Departments. The principal work of some staff departments is to give advice and counsel. (The word "advice" is used narrowly here to mean that their essential work is to give advice and counsel.) In a general way, all staff departments sometimes give advice and counsel. Advisory departments include the legal, economic analysis, market research, parts of the industrial engineering and personnel departments and others. The personnel department would be acting in an advisory way when it advises supervisors on how best to handle grievances.

Functional Control Departments. Functional control departments have "functional authority," meaning that they are supposed to see that their functions are properly carried out everywhere in the organization. These departments include, among others, costs and budgets, accounting, industrial engineering, quality control, and part of the work done by the personnel department.

An inspector, an employee of the quality control department, exercises functional authority when, in a factory department, he says, "This machine is producing too many products which do not meet quality standards. Close it down." A personnel department employee is exercising functional authority when he says, "You cannot promote Smith instead of Jones because Jones, who also wants the promotion, has been with us longer. Promoting Smith would violate our labor contract with the union."

Coordinating Departments. In cases in which the work of several departments needs to be closely coordinated, it may be necessary to have separate coordinating departments since the need for specialization and specialized departments runs counter to the need for coordination.

In manufacturing, the production-control department, a coordinating-type staff department, issues schedules and work orders to the factory's several different producing departments.

Coordinating staff departments issue orders which carry the authority of the high-level official to whom both the staff and the line report. These orders *tell* lower departments and employees to do certain things and when and, to some extent, how. Such staff department orders are binding because the higher line official has approved the overall production program. The production-control department receives deputized authority to develop the individual orders covering the specific things which will need to be done.

Inventory control and finished products distribution are other areas where coordinating departments exercise strong control more or less in the name of the superior.

Coordinating Managers for Products and Projects. Individual products, projects, and programs are sometimes very important. At Procter & Gamble, Crest Toothpaste is such a product. At Westinghouse, the work of designing nuclear powered electricity generating plants is such a program. In most large companies there are several such products, projects, or programs in production at any given time.

If these products are left without special attention they will probably get a proportionate share of attention in all of the departments which perform work on them. Yet when they get only shared attention in every department, there is a missing element. There is no emphasis on the overall product or project and on the balanced coordination of the many sub-bits of work which these products and projects require.

To take care of this lack, many companies set up managers of individual products or of product lines or of large individual projects. These people are coordinators. They are managers but they do not have departments. In most cases where the products are consumer products, this kind of a manager is called a "product manager." In the case of products for industrial customers or for the government, he is called a "project manager," or a "program manager."

Product Managers. Product managers are delegated the responsibility for looking after the best interests of a product or product line in all areas — manufacturing, pricing, advertising, distribution methods, everything.

Kimberly-Clark uses product managers in selling. The Kleenex product manager plans advertising and sales campaigns, makes up plans, sets sales goals, and establishes budgets for selling Kleenex. Kimberly-Clark's product managers also have to determine market strategy, recommend new products and programs, and coordinate the making, financing, and selling of their products.

At Kimberly-Clark a product manager has no staff of his own, but he can draw on the resources of any departments he needs to. He tries to see that his product line earns profits, but he can't set prices and so has no genuine profit responsibility. He has a strong voice, but not the final say, in pricing.

The product manager's job is an ambiguous one. Seldom if ever does his delegated authority come even close to equaling his responsibilities. Often, as at Kimberly-Clark, he has responsibility for his product making a profit yet he has no control over production or marketing costs. But he is mobile and can range persuasively even though not authoritatively up and down and across regular chains of authority. He is expected to be effective yet he operates largely with only persuasive power.

Project and Program Managers. "Project" managers or "program" managers are the counterparts of product managers who operate in heavy industry or in high-science and high-technology organizations. Project managers are almost always used in matrix management.

The work of project and program managers differs from that of product managers (whose products are usually "shelf items" made in large volumes which are sold to the consuming public and customers everywhere) in that projects often are single projects or single contracts for many millions of dollars which take months or years to complete.

Performance Service Departments. Performance service departments *do* things for other departments rather than just advise them. Maintenance departments fix roofs, floors, lights, and so on. Engineering departments design products and purchasing departments buy things. Performance service departments also include research and development, quality control, advertising, and several others. In an army, performance staff departments provide supplies, transportation, and such auxiliary services.

Consultants. High-level managers sometimes need temporary assistance on important matters and call in outside consultants to help. Consultant help is available for any phase of a business, be it finance, building construction, product design, or what not. Consultants can offer a fresh viewpoint from a competent outsider who is not himself a part of either a problem or its solution. These people are usually good at seeing the core problem, which is the first step in the progress toward its solution.

Consultants are agents of change. They will investigate problems and advise or will recommend actions, or they will help the organization's own staff install programs and supervise and train the company's inside staff as a program moves along. Then when the inside group is ready they can take over.

Personal Staffs. Army generals usually have several personal staff assistants who handle details and ease the burden of their superiors. High-level business managers sometimes also have personal assistants. They go by various names, such as, "assistants to," "executive assistants," and other names. Their status in the hierarchy is below that of the manager's subordinates who have charge of departments.

Assistants of this sort have no executive duties and do not make decisions nor do they act in the name of their superiors. They are not seconds-in-command; nor can they delegate; and no one owes them any accountability. They have no authority over anyone. They themselves report directly and only to their superior.

"Assistants to" do many little things, almost all of which are intended to lighten their superior's load. An assistant to might screen visitors and requests for his superior's time. He might help coordinate work by bringing together the parties concerned and he might arrange committee meetings and even act as a committee secretary.

An assistant might design reports, help develop interdepartmental procedures, or prepare organization manuals and keep them up to date. He might relay his chief's messages or look into situations for him and he might even "ghost" his superior's speeches.

In manufacturing companies, assistants to managers sometimes are investigators and "trouble shooters," or "expediters." When something goes wrong, they investigate and try to get things moving again. Or they watch over the production of especially important orders and try to make sure that they stay on schedule.

Corporate Staffs

Staffs exist at high levels and at middle levels of organizations. Most of the employees in the central offices of large companies are staff workers. They help the organization's high level executives and oversee staff work done by the staff people in lower echelons. The work done by central staffs is usually of three kinds:

1. Some central staff work is *upward-oriented work,* as when staffs serve executive officers. Staffs study future opportunities, plan the company's future, make economic forecasts, analyze laws, regulations, and tax and profit implications of decisions. They suggest policies, develop long-range plans, study merger possibilities, and so on. They review and approve or disapprove proposals from lower levels for action programs or capital expenditures.

2. Some central work is *service work for the whole company.* Collective bargaining, when it is done for the whole company, is service work of this sort. Most important real estate matters, too, would be handled by a central staff real estate department. Central staffs also serve the whole company when they keep up with developments in their functional areas.

3. Most central staffs have a number of *downward-looking* responsibilities (see Figure 10-2). Central staffs are usually responsible for seeing that their functions are carried out properly throughout the whole organization.

Corporate Staffs in Divisional Companies. In divisional companies (the subject of Chapter 11), the upward-looking staff duties, the advice and service to the company's executives, are almost wholly in the province of central staffs. So are the company-wide services mentioned above.

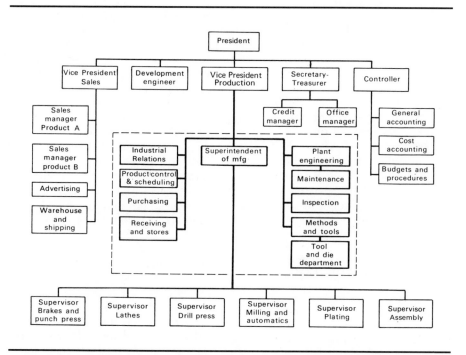

Figure 10-1
Staff departments in the production area of a typical manufacturing company.

Staff Departments

There is a difference, however, in the way downward-oriented staff work operates between functional and divisional companies. In divisional companies the managers of individual *divisions* are largely on their own. They can develop staffs of their own in whatever areas they choose. They can make considerable use of central staffs or not.

Central staffs may, therefore, be quite small in divisional companies (perhaps as few as 50 people in a company with 50,000 employees) since the semi-autonomous divisions might do nearly everything for themselves. Most divisionalized companies, however, have large enough central staffs (perhaps 500 and up in a company with 50,000 employees) so that they can do all three of the kinds of things listed above. Thus, they are large enough to do the necessary high-level advising and also to exercise the needed surveillance over lower-level work. Central staffs should also be able to help out if lower levels need help in their areas of expertise.

In large companies with small staffs, there is neither the surveillance nor available help. The home office more or less abdicates and watches what goes on as a spectator. Such watching as it does is after the fact review of total performance which does not aid the company's administrators in detecting weaknesses ahead of time.

Ambiguous Superior-Subordinate Relationships. Staff specialists at lower levels in almost all large companies are usually in an ambiguous position in that they have line superiors where they work and they also have staff functional superiors at the central office.

A General Motors engineer working for Oldsmobile might, for example, be designing an exhaust system, on which there is a cost ceiling, for next year's Cutlass car. But, while he is doing this for his Oldsmobile superior, he gets help and overseeing from the home office specialists in anti-pollution, who may want him to use a costly kind of catalytic converter.

There is almost always some role conflict in lower staff jobs. It is absent only where there is no superior home office staff group in a specialty area. In divisional companies a lower level staff specialist owes his primary obligation to his divisional line superior since it is highly probable that he will spend his whole working career in this division. His strongest obligation is to serve his division.

On the other hand, the upward promotional path for a staff specialist who does get promoted almost always follows professional lines and leads to a central office staff job in his functional specialty. As a consequence, lower staff personnel need to try to do well for their line superiors but at the same time to try to impress the central staff people with their capability. Figure 10-1 shows how these relationships operate.

The Pernicious Effects of Review Power. The fine line between helpful surveillance which is enough but not too much from central staffs is very important in divisional organizations. Central staff groups, particularly financial staff groups, have, through their authority to review proposals from lower levels from a financial viewpoint, a great deal of power.

The right to review carries with it the implicit power to disapprove. Thus, central financial staffs have near veto power over proposed programs of lower echelons. (If the staff disapproves a proposal, it is unlikely that the company's top executives will override them and approve it.) It is very easy for central review groups to overstep and, from lack of full appreciation of the cost-benefit merits of proposals, to do considerable harm to the operations of divisions.

Functional Overseeing. In order to have consistent policies and practices in labor relations, purchasing, and other staff activities, home office specialists usually have several downward-looking responsibilities. One of these is to tell (or at least to make suggestions which are usually heeded) lower staff personnel how they should do their

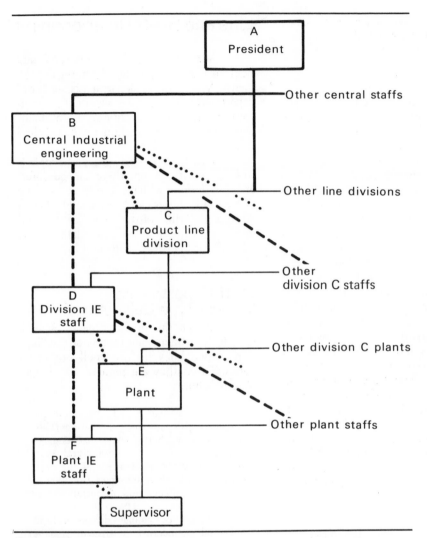

Figure 10-2

The relationship of the central office staff to lower level staffs in Proctor & Gamble's industrial engineering department. The double dashed lines going from B to D and from D to F indicate downward functional overseeing. The single dashed lines going from B to C and from D to E indicate advisory responsibility.

work. They try to insure that the work done in their functional areas in lower level operating units will be well done.

Staffing. Central staffs are usually responsible for recruiting and furnishing trained staff people to all company units.

At Procter & Gamble, the central staffs watch over the staffs all around the country and try to find out who the good juniors coming up are. Then when a more responsible job opens up, they look over the whole crop, not just the local people, and

Staff Departments

suggest who should get the job. In this way P & G is assured that staff work will be well done throughout the organization by the best people available.

Training. Central staffs often have a training responsibility as part of their job of seeing that their function is well performed throughout the organization.

Unfortunately, central staffs usually cannot carry out their general mandate to train functional people in lower echelons very effectively. They can't require lower people to leave their jobs for two weeks, travel 500 miles, and live in a hotel in a central location in order to take a training program. Consequently, they don't reach a good many lower level staff people who ought to get such training. And unfortunately, too, functional specialists in central offices have little opportunity to sit down with their counterpart functional specialists in lower echelons and to coach them and show them how to do their work better.

Advising, Assisting, and Serving Functionally. Central staffs usually stand ready to help out whenever a lower staff needs advice or assistance. If a lower group gets overloaded, one or two central staff people may be sent in to help out for a while. In a similar way, central staffs do things for lower units when they are not prepared to do the work themselves.

At Merck Company (pharmaceuticals), the central engineering department directs the designing and installation of all large construction projects. At Merck, also, if a lower units wants, say, some studies made of the process of fermentation in order to help it develop certain medicinal chemicals, it calls on the central staff for help.

At General Foods, the Birds Eye (frozen foods) unit does not have its own market research staff. So, when it wanted a study made of the market for frozen asparagus, it turned to the central market research staff for help.

Line and Staff Relationships

We have said that staffs serve and help the organization's main purpose departments. Main purpose departments are "line" departments. In a grocery supermarket company, selling groceries is line work. In a manufacturing company, making products is line work, as also is selling.

Any time that one group of people is to help another group, there can be differences of opinion which cause trouble. Some of these difficulties can be avoided by laying down a few "rules-of-the-game" of the kind discussed in the next few pages defining the relationships between staffs and lines.

Staff Departments; Mission-Type Delegations

Delegations or assignments of work to staff departments are usually of the "mission" type. They do not spell out exact duties. Often they are phrased as "charges of responsibility."

At Eastman Kodak, the industrial engineering department's delegation (Eastman calls it a "charter") says that its major responsibilities are "to advise and assist any of the other departments of the company in using their resources (manpower, equipment, space, and materials) more effectively."

Procter & Gamble's delegation to its industrial engineering department is more specific. This department is (1) to aid management in the cooperative search for profit opportunities, (2) to provide consulting services to management in defining solutions for specific problems, (3) to provide design services for management control systems and to audit existing systems for policy and current requirements, and (4) to aid in the design of man-machine systems and to insure a low total cost of operations.

Mission Development. Both the Eastman Kodak and the Procter & Gamble statements delegate missions and do not go very far toward spelling out specific duties. Delegations of missions leave it up to the department heads to decide the specific things their departments will do.

In most cases, the main obvious mission and the responding to calls for service cause most of the workload of staff departments. But there should also be a fraction of each staff department's resources which is devoted to carrying out other work which the staff managers themselves see as needing doing as part of their mission. An example would be the personnel department studying safety laws and trying to see that the company fully complies with these laws. This self-generated obligation coming out of the staff's own interpretation of its mission should not be pushed aside by either the essentiality of hiring new employees or responding to calls from other departments for service.

Work Priorities. When staff departments have more calls for their services than their resources will support (often the case), they have to decide which work to do and which work to let wait. Normally, staff departments themselves decide which work to do first and which to let wait. This practice has far reaching implications because when staff departments decide priorities, they are making judgments about the importance of other people's work. They decide whose work gets done and whose work has to wait.

Often they do not have enough knowledge on which to base an intelligent decision.

This was true in a company where the sales department had been distributing lubricants to small customers by direct shipment from the refinery. The sales manager thought that another method might be less costly so he asked the accounting department to calculate distribution cost comparisons for the proposed and the existing method. Accounting turned him down, saying, "We just don't have the manpower and can't get it done."

There was also the company making golf bag carts which had no seat so that a player waiting could sit down. The sales department asked the engineering department to design a lightweight open-down seat to be attached to the cart. The engineering department, busy with other work, decided that this project would have to wait.

In both of these cases, the staff department decided its own priority list and applied its own value judgment without knowing much about the merits of the rejected projects.

When staffs cannot do all of the work they ought to do, then priorities among important activities should probably be decided higher up at levels where the full import of such decisions can be appreciated.

Activity Cut-Off Points and Quality Cut-Off Points. Higher-level review of priorities is not, however, a complete solution to the priority problem since it only says which work shall wait. But if a tight situation continues, low-priority work never gets done at all because new high-priority work keeps moving in ahead of it. Probably some low-priority work can be dispensed with with little harm being done just as an automobile does not *have* to be washed. But some other low-priority work can be postponed only for so long before it becomes urgent, just as an automobile needs a new tire every now and then. The longer its replacement is postponed, the more urgent its replacement becomes.

The problem then turns into one of cutting off certain low-priority work altogether, or of expanding the staff's capabilities, or of sub-contracting out more work. Here is where high-level review can be important. Higher-level managers can decide the cut-off point which determines which work will be done. This is usually done through budgets. Top executives approve enough money to support work above the cut-off point and not enough to support work below that point.

Another dimension to the matter of cutting off low priority work is the matter of quality limits. It is the "good enough" idea. It is like a barber and his hair cutting (a hair cut takes 15 minutes when other people are waiting, 25 minutes when no one is waiting).

Thus, the work done by staffs, when it is done under budgetary constraints, tends to result in needed work being done yet not being done too thoroughly and low priority work not being done at all.

"Completed Staff Work." "Completed staff work" is a term often used in the military but less often in business organizations. An army general may say to his staff, "Bring me answers, not problems." He wants his staff people to study problems, consider alternatives, make a choice, and hand him a program for him to approve or disapprove. Only then does he think that the staff has done its work. ("Completed staff work," does not mean merely well and capably done staff work. It means more than that and includes the staff deciding on a recommended course of action.)

Many managers in nonmilitary organizations do not rely this much on staffs, nor, in fact, do all generals. In most organizations, staffs are not really supposed to decide. Instead, they study problems, consider alternatives, and lay them, together with the pros and cons of each alternative, before the manager. With all of this to look at, the manager then consults with the staff head who has supervised all of the analytical work, after which he decides.

William Sharwell, of American Telephone & Telegraph Company, however, favors using the completed staff idea in business as well as in the military. He offers the following guidelines for staffs to refer to as they develop their missions:[1]

· Staff assignments should include an initiating responsibility which goes beyond merely processing information.

· Staff work should include interpreting as well as reporting data. Scorekeeping is not enough. Interpretation should accompany data dissemination.
· Staff reports should answer questions, not just raise them.
· On policy issues, staffs should not simply collect relevant data but should analyze and evaluate them, pose alternatives, and recommend a choice.
· Good staff work describes a situation, statistically or verbally, but also explains causes and consequences of situations.
· Staffs should do more than just answer the question asked. They should also raise related relevant questions.
· Staffs need to report results objectively, since their earlier recommendations put them in a position of sharing responsibility for results.

Staff Weaknesses

Valuable though staff work is in adding to the effectiveness of organizational accomplishments, staffs have a number of weaknesses. Among them are that they tend to grow too big and to become inefficient and to become obsessed with doing functional work. Usually, too, there are authority complications where staffs interface with lines.

Growth Tendencies. Because of their desire to serve well, staff departments (as well as service-type organizations) tend to grow in size. At first, the staff provides limited services at low cost. Then the service is improved ("If we see a need we try to take care of it.") and the cost goes up. Then the same thing happens again and still again. It is like Blue Cross insurance. One benefit after another is added until nearly everything is covered and the costs are sky-high, partly because of some benefits which are hardly needed.

In fairness, staffs and service organizations should not always be blamed for growing. In business, staffs are often asked to do one more thing, then another, and still another. And, in cities, people keep asking the government to do more and more things. Schools are asked to provide special teachers for the slow to learn, etc. So, in response to these requests, the services are provided. Then people complain when taxes go up.

This tendency of staffs to grow is, however, abetted from the operation of a quite different factor. The *size* of a staff department might compensate, in the mind of its head, for a lack of authority and prestige that would go with being a line department head; hence the desire for a large department. This is especially true in government organizations. A large department is, per se, an important department and its head has an important job.

The Inefficiency Dilemma. Service departments are all subject to what might be called the *"law of inefficient service departments."* The whole organization operates most effectively only when the service departments, individually, work below their peak efficiency. Maintenance employees in all organizations probably work most effectively when they always have jobs waiting for them to do. Then they never run out of work and are never idle. But, if there are always jobs waiting for them, other departments are sometimes being held up until the maintenance people can get their needed repair work done.

In contrast, maintenance employees can give other departments excellent service only when they themselves have hardly enough to do and are practically standing around waiting for service calls (as fire departments and hospital emergency departments do) which would mean that the service department is itself inefficient. Normally, the most economical arrangement, from the whole organization's point of view, is to organize so that the main activities

operate at their highest effectiveness even though this is at the expense of some loss in the service departments' efficiency.

Dedication to Staff Specialties. Staff people are specialists who usually want to give and are almost dedicated to giving good service in their areas of expertise. Almost always they know more about their specialties than do the people they serve. This gives them a feeling of superiority not only about their specialty but also about the need of line managers for their help. They feel strongly that their service is needed and should be used by lines.

Staffs are often accused of having little feeling of responsibility for anything but performing their specialty. Usually they are not well acquainted with the other activities of the organization and so do not have a full appreciation of the total effects of their activities and recommendations. They do not appreciate either the costs or the consequences within the organization of the changes they recommend.

Judging the Economic Worth of Staff Work. We have said that the end-product of most staff work is advice, reports, and recommendations. These things are intangible and unmeasurable and cannot be separated into countable units. Goals for staffs are therefore hard to define and it is usually not possible to measure progress toward goals in any effective way.

All of this means that it is virtually impossible to judge the economic worth of staff work. It is not possible to say how much it is worth to the organization to have the legal department draw up a sales contract with a customer. Nor is it possible to say how much it is worth to have the production-control department issue directions to factory departments telling them what and how many products to make.

Unfortunately, all of these difficulties facing a high-level manager who is trying to judge the effectiveness of his organization's operations do not let him avoid the problem. He still has to try to see that staff work, as well as production work, is effectively done and that it contributes value in reasonable accord with its cost. About the best the manager can do is to try to get staff department heads to picture themselves as being responsible members of the whole organization and to get them to try to serve well yet economically.

Authority Complications at Line/Staff Interface Points. As we noted earlier, whenever two or more departments join hands to accomplish something, there is a probability that differences of opinion will develop. This sometimes happens in line and staff relationships and conflict may ensue.

Differences of opinion, of course, are not all bad. It is usually good to have different viewpoints brought to bear on problems. Conscientious members of organizations, both line and staff, who are trying to do good jobs *should* sometimes see things differently. If the people involved are cooperative, then line and staff interface points need not result in conflict nor in ineffective operations.

Staffs are, however, in a logical animosity position with lines. Staff people are superior in knowledge in their subject areas to line managers and it is their job to scrutinize, evaluate, judge, and recommend courses of action and sometimes changes. Staff departments are expected to impose their "expertness" on the line. All of this is inherently offensive to line managers who like to think that they are capable of running their departments without so much help.

Although the possible problems are usually matters of lines not wanting to follow staff suggestions, sometimes it is the other way around. There are times when a staff is weighed down with work and so cannot take on any more. The sales department may want the engineering department to carry through extensive product redesigns quickly and at no cost to a customer, but there would be times when the engineering department's work load would be too heavy for it to do this. Problems sometimes arise.

Authority complications often arise as the result of several other factors in operation. These include problems in several areas.

- *Staff Monopolies.* Staff departments are not only available to advise and serve, they have the *exclusive right* to do it. Costly specialists are being supported on the payroll and line managers are not expected to ignore their help and advice, nor to duplicate the staff's work themselves. There are times, however, when lower-level line managers feel that they would be better served if they could take care of their own needs. When staffs have too much to do or when they serve poorly, line managers regard their monopoly as a problem.

- *The Obligation to Serve.* The staff's obligation to serve sometimes makes problems when staff members see a place where they think that their assistance appears to be needed but the line supervisor does not ask for help. If the staff tries to be helpful when no request has been made, the offer is not always well received. This may become a source of friction if both parties do not see the need to cooperate.

- *Lack of Line Options Not to Use Staffs.* Problems sometimes arise because line managers believe that their responsibility for operating their departments is full authority and is a mandate to do what they think is best. Perhaps the subordinate manager thinks that his delegation to run his department effectively means for him to ask for help when he thinks he needs it and not to ask for it when he does not think he needs it.

This is probably not quite what his superior had in mind when he made him a department head. The superior thinks of his subordinates as his agents. He thinks that they need the help of the knowledge workers and he expects them to ask for assistance from time to time and to use the help available. Line managers do not have to ask for help but if they don't, when help is there for the asking, poor performance on their part will be judged more harshly than if they had asked for help.

· *Line and Staff Interface Problems in Organic Structures.* We noted in Chapter 8 that matrix-type organic structures put project managers in an ambiguous position with respect to line managers. Project managers serve in a staff-like way but with considerable, nearly command, authority over lower line managers and operatives. Their authority, which is almost always poorly defined, is close to being in conflict with the formally granted delegation of line managers.

· *Informal Coordinative Communications.* Earlier in this chapter, we discussed coordinative staff departments. Often these formally set up departments are inadequate to produce fully effective coordination. This is especially true in high technology companies. Problems can arise at interface points between departments although they do not have to be serious problems if the organizational atmosphere is one of open, free, across-channel communications.

Integrating the work of different departments is a difficult job in all organizations and is especially difficult in high technology companies. Yet, Paul Lawrence and Jay Lorsch found, in the several high technology companies which they researched a number of years ago, that the lack of coordinative departments did not cause much trouble.[2] In the companies they studied, Lawrence and Lorsch found that where there was no formally set up coordinative department, members of the several chains of authority concerned got together informally and voluntarily, on a face-to-face basis, and tried to coordinate their activities. Coordinated work can and sometimes does get done without the help of formal coordinative departments.

In most pyramidally structured companies it would be difficult for informal cross-

channel communication links of this sort to develop. For one thing, lower-level employees rarely feel much concern about solving organizational problems. And, second, many of the heads of low-level departments do not want their subordinates leaving their jobs and going into other departments, meeting informally with lower level employees there and making commitments about resource uses just to help someone else in another department to solve his problem. A good many such department heads would want to know what is being agreed upon and that it meets with their approval.

Lines and Staffs: The Human Equation

Since line and staff work is performed by people, there are potential problems in their relationships which are more human than they are inherent in the job relationships as such. Sometimes these potential problems flare up and cause trouble. We should emphasize here, however, that although we have been and will be discussing problems and differences of opinions which sometimes come up, the usual situation is mutual respect and cooperation between line and staff groups. Each recognizes that the other is trying to help the organization to perform well.

Both the servers, the staffs, and those served, the lines, usually appreciate the need for such assistance. Normally, too, each group has earned the respect and confidence of the other through proven satisfactory work in the past. Consequently, the two groups work well together in spite of occasional differences of opinion.

Views of Line Managers Which Sometimes Cause Trouble

Whenever there is a lack of cooperation between lines and staffs, it usually comes from one group not fully appreciating the other's contribution. Staff people are said not to recognize that line managers are also specialists and experts who have actual experience with production problems. They have a practical understanding of how to get production out of employees and machines.

Line managers often consider staff work to be less essential than line work. And they can point to examples where this is so. A company can, for example, get along without a company newspaper or magazine. On the other hand, most staff work is just about as fundamental and important as line work. Advertising, personnel, and accounting are staff departments and they are all essential to successful operations in most business organizations. Nonetheless, the fact that some things which staffs do are not highly important is obvious to everyone.

Furthermore, the results of some staff work are neither imminent nor highly visible. The hoped for benefits from a management training program for example, are expected to materialize in the future but not right away. Even if the program is very successful in the long run, not much accomplishment shows in the short run. Nor is the work of the staff very visible when the personnel department analyzes the Fair Employment Practices Act to see what the company has to do in order to be in compliance.

It is also true, as in the case of the management training program, the hoped for result (improved managerial practices) might not materialize at all. And, if it does, people might not notice it. It is very easy for line people to conclude that many staff activities are of little value.

Line managers sometimes say that staff personnel think that they are the smart ones and that they know all the answers. And they say that staff people often do not see the practical problems and don't really want to see them. They sometimes say that staff specialists think in a vacuum and are academic, theoretical, bookish, and ivory tower in their thinking. And they say that

staffs don't give them the help that they need and instead try to push off on them unasked and unwanted help of kinds that they don't need.

Line managers also claim that staff personnel are not "responsible." If staffs give poor advice or make mistakes, they have no accounts to which to charge the cost of their poor work. Line people often say that staffs are not cost-conscious and do too many things which are not worth their cost. But, say line managers, "We have to produce results. We carry those guys. All they do is cost money. We'd like to see the income they produce."

And, they say, staffs are "pushy" and aggressive. Staff people try to take over responsibility. So far as the line is concerned, nearly everything is one-sided; it is all give and no take. Line people do not like being pushed, manipulated, and always expected to "cooperate." They want to make their own decisions.

Staffs are said to be "credit grabbers." They propose plans but other people have to put them into effect. When things go well, the staff may even try to claim the credit. But when things go wrong, it's the line's fault. Not being in entrenched departments, staff personnel are said to be oversensitive to criticism and overeager to prove their worth.

Views of Staff Personnel Which Sometimes Cause Trouble

Turning the coin over, staff people sometimes think that they are the experts and that line managers do not know much. Staff specialists sometimes say that too many line managers decide from narrow viewpoints, and that their work needs the review of staff people who can see the broader implications. Staff people also sometimes say that line supervisors do not use their help when they ought to. And they say that such managers sometimes refuse help when it is proferred. And when they do ask for help, they won't or can't define what they want.

A good many line managers, perhaps most of them, prefer to work their own ways out of their problems rather than call for help. If they do call for help it is only after things have deteriorated seriously. Consequently, even the specialized staff has difficulty straightening things out. This may, however, only convince the line manager of his view that the staff is not of much help. He may say, for example, "I couldn't straighten things out, but neither could they."

Staffs often think that theirs is a life of frustration. The director of the industrial relations department may have been told to help line managers with handling grievances, yet the supervisors don't ask for help and continue to have too many grievances. When things work out like this, it is only natural for staffs to think that a great many line managers are stodgy stand-patters.

Staff people may also feel frustrated because of low promotional ceilings. The way to the top of the organization is more often through the line than through staff departments. The head of a staff department is usually as far as he will get. If he gets that far early in his career, he may, after a few more years, come to regard the work as dull and become frustrated.

Merits of the Views of Lines and Staffs

All of these views of each other by line and staff people are sometimes true. There are times when line managers ought to object to staff advice because the staff is asking for too much. If budgets are regarded as too low or if production or quality standards are regarded as too tight, the line manager should object.

The line's complaint that staffs are aggressive is also sometimes true. Staff people may sometimes feel insecure in their positions since they are not engaged in doing the organization's obvious main work. They may also feel insecure from not having an end-product of their own. Possibly, too, they might feel insecure because some staff activities can be and are reduced in hard times. And if, for whatever reason, they feel insecure, they may try to take on line functions, assume line authority, and try to run the show. They may try to undermine the line.

At the same time, line managers are sometimes too possessive about their rights to operate their departments the way *they* want to. Sometimes they forget that their departments are not theirs to operate as they see fit, but are parts of the organization whose operations have been temporarily entrusted to their direction. They are really agents for their superiors. And they sometimes forget that their delegations do not assume that they have superior knowledge and can make better judgments on every subject. Their delegations assume that they will seek and accept whatever assistance they need.

Actually, line supervisors who say that staffs often offer unasked for and unwanted help are frequently doing staffs a disservice. Most of the time staffs have too small a budget to do all that there is to do so they don't get to push their help on anyone. Instead, theirs becomes a position of deciding whose request they will try to take care of. They will probably help the departments where they are appreciated the most.

The Need for Staffs to "Sell" and Not to "Tell"

Staffs are not, however, always so busy that there are never times when they have to try to get lines to follow their recommendations. Sometimes they have to *win acceptance* for their ideas. When this is so they have to "sell" their ideas to the line. Having to do this keeps them in a healthy frame of mind. It helps to have them thinking, "Who has to use our output?" "How can we help make this person become more effective?" "How can we get this idea across to him?"

Sometimes the selling job amounts to nothing more than explaining a situation which is not clear.

In one company the sales department gave "full case" discount prices to wholesalers who ordered part cases and who wanted small quantities shipped directly to retailers everywhere. This practice had developed slowly over several years. Wholesalers were really entitled to the discount only on full cases delivered to themselves. The sales department employees did not appreciate that they were giving away a good bit of money when they gave low bulk prices on small shipments. When they were shown by the company's controller how much this was costing, they went back to proper pricing. There was no real problem of "selling" them.

The Reality of Staff Authority

"Am I running this plant or is the personnel director running it?" asked the plant manager. "You are," answered the president. "It doesn't seem that way to me," said the plant manager. "I'm glad you feel that way, " the president commented, "because I want the personnel director to be so persuasive that it will bother you when you ignore his advice."

After such an interchange, a plant manager would surely get the idea that he had better take the personnel director's advice in the future unless he had a *very* good reason not to take it. On the other hand, what the president did not say is important. He did not say, "Take the personnel director's advice," which suggests that he thinks that he has left the plant manager with the right to refuse.

Superiors do not like to make positive grants of command authority to staff departments because they want line managers to object in case they feel that the advice or help they get is poor. But the line of demarcation between receiving advice and help and receiving orders is indeed fine. Another plant manager who said, "*The industrial relations department in our company has no 'authority' but lots of influence,*" was describing the ideal relationship.

A great deal has been written about staffs having no real authority. Here are two typical statements: "A line manager cannot delegate his own responsibility to a staff unit." "Staffs never exercise line (strong) authority in the line organization."

Neither of these statements is wholly true, however. A high-level superior *can* delegate whatever he delegates. Probably he *should not* delegate line responsibility to a staff department, but he certainly *can* and some superiors do this. They give staffs strong authority in their areas of expertise.

Strength of Authority of Advisory Staff Departments. Advisory staff departments probably should not have strong functional authority (see Figure 10-3). Line managers should always have the right to appeal. Or, perhaps it should be said that they have an *obligation* to object if they disagree and they should have the right not to follow staff advice if they think that this is best.

Strength of Authority of Nonadvisory Staff Departments. *Service, functional control,* and *coordinative* staff departments need to have stronger authority than advisory departments need. This is especially true of performance-type service staff departments who have both the exclusive right to perform their services and a concomitant obligation to do so. Lower line managers are not allowed to hire their own specialists and do performance-type service work for themselves. Nor should line departments be allowed to ignore the directions of coordinative departments nor the recommendations of functional control de-

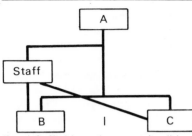

Type I. Staff advises and recommends policies and action to Superior A. who approves them and makes them his orders, which are binding on B and C. Staff neither advises nor gives orders to B and C. This situation is uncommon.

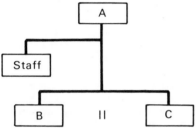

Type II. Staff advises and recommends policies and action to Superior A, who approves staff offering advise and help to B and C. This is the ideal arrangement.

Type III. Staff advises and recommends policies and action (in its functional area) to Superior A, who approves staff putting them into effect as his deputy. Staff gives orders direct to B and C. Type III is typical for coordinating staff work.

Type IV. Acting under general functional control directives from superior A, staff advises and gives orders to B and C or serves them directly. Type IV is the usual arrangement for service staff work.

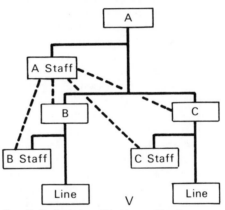

Type V. Similar to type II but in a multi-unit organization. Home office staff advises B and C, lower line officials, and also deals directly with the counterpart staffs in the B and C organizations. Functional control often operates in this direct way.

Figure 10-3

Five types of authority flow between staff and line departments. Solid lines indicate the flow of staff authority. Dotted lines show the downward flow of advice. Any of these five arrangements might be found with *advisory* departments. It is different, however, with *functional control, service* and *coordinating* staff departments. They have solid line relationships with lower line departments, as is shown in Types III and IV. Type V is to be found in multi-unit organizations. The strength of the home office staff authority over lower staffs in Type V situations varies a good bit from company to company. Figure 10-3II shows only dotted downward lines from the central staff, but sometimes they would be solid lines.

Staff Departments

partments. A line supervisor who handles grievances the way he wants to instead of the way the personnel department tells him to may be violating the labor contract or violating the law. He cannot be allowed to do that.

Staff Dominance Over the Line

There is some tendency for staff people to dominate the line, but this should not go so far as for them to usurp the line's authority. Several factors tend to add to the staff's power position, particularly when formal authority is poorly defined (as it is in so many line-staff situations). These factors which add to the staffs' power position include the informal power which automatically accrues to people who are in an advisory position and to staffs being in a good position to influence top managers.

The Advisory Position. A superior-inferior relationship is automatically set up in nearly all staff-line relationships. The technical know-how and expertise of staff members casts them in leadership roles which in turn gives them authority beyond advice giving. Non-staff people look up to them. A specialist who has earned respect by having given good service in the past has an extra degree of authority because his competence has been established.

Status. Staffs get to work on major problems and to do long-range planning and research and are not wholly concerned with day-to-day routines. This gives them a status above line supervisors who have to live more in the present. Staff members report high up in the organization and know the high level managers. This gives weight to their recommendations to lower line people.

Staff members dress well and do not have to meet schedules nor to run their departments to suit other departments. They even get to go to outside meetings at company expense. All of these visible evidences of status contribute to a staff member's power position.

Appeal. Staffs have behind them the shadowy authority of high-level managers. If a lower line manager wants not to follow a staff's advice, the staff member might take the matter up with his superior who takes it up with the high-level line executive to whom the staff reports. This line executive might back up the staff and require the lower line manager to follow the staff's recommendation.

To illustrate, in a factory, the time-study department sets time standards for production jobs. If a supervisor thinks that a particular standard calls for too much production, he can object. Yet, when he appeals to his line superior, the plant superintendent, he is usually overruled because the superintendent regards the time-study engineers as the company's experts in setting standards. Furthermore, he suspects that all his supervisors really want only easy-to-meet standards.

Line Dominance Over Staffs

The factors just discussed probably do strengthen the status position of staffs. But, in spite of this, staffs rarely have enough power actually to dominate lines. Melville Dalton once said, "Staff people don't have the 'roots' that line people have." In fact, *lines sometimes dominate staffs* because their power position is so strong.

Staff personnel have authority because of their *expertise* but line people have authority because of their *positions*. University trained staff members, perhaps even with Ph. D. degrees, are cast in the role of helping less well educated people who have responsible line jobs. A helping role is automatically a secondary role. These line managers are older, have many more subordinates, earn more money, and have higher ultimate promotional ceilings. They are in a strong power position in the organization and have no need to justify their existence.

The discussion up to here about staff dominance over the line seems to go in opposite directions. First, staffs may very well dominate lines and, second, they do not get to dominate lines.

Probably each result occurs at times, yet the apparent discrepancy in the discussion is not so real as it appears. The discussion of staffs dominating lines is low-level oriented whereas the comments about staffs not dominating lines is high-level oriented. Both conclusions could well be true. There is some likelihood that, at lower levels, staffs will dominate lines but there is much less likelihood of this occurring at higher levels. High-level line managers are usually more powerful forces in the organization than are upper-level staff specialists.

Summary

Every organization needs to have certain staff departments which do helping work. Essentially these departments think, advise, and help but do not themselves do the organization's mainstream work. This means that their missions are somewhat ambiguous so far as their relations to mainstream-work departments are concerned.

Large companies often find that their principal products and important projects need to have product or project managers. Without them, various activities needing doing for the good of the product or project often suffer from the lack of coordination and lack of interest in some departments.

Staffs usually receive mission-type delegations and consequently have to develop their own lists of things to do, their roles. Yet they do not have a wholly free hand to do this because of limitations. They must perform their main mission work and they must take care of most calls for service by other departments. All of this is in addition to the work which they themselves decide is needed.

There still remains, however, a considerable area where staff departments set their own priorities and choose which work to do first and which work waits. Budgetary constraints enter here. Rarely do staff departments get enough money to do everything which they might do. So budget limits compel staffs to cut off some work, usually the least necessary. These limits also keep pressure on staffs not to do necessary work too well. Top managers therefore set quantitative and qualitative limits to staff work when they set budgets.

Staff authority is often said not to be strong authority and it should not be really strong in advisory areas. But in service and coordinative staff work, staff directions should probably be stronger. In several of these areas, staffs are acting as deputies for top level managers and their directions should be heeded.

Review Questions

1. What does a staff department having "functional authority" mean? Authority over whom? Over what? Explain.
2. How can a manager be a manager without a department? Does he still have control over anybody? Discuss.
3. What is the "inefficiency dilemma" of service departments? Discuss this concept.
4. Discuss the matter of the strength of the authority of staff departments doing functional control type work.
5. In a divisional organization with home office staff departments, how much functional control should they have over lower level counterpart staff departments? If the central staff is supposed to have functional control over the lower level staff departments, how can this control be exercised? Discuss also the position of the lower-level staff employee and how he relates, on the one hand, to his immediate line supervisor and, on the other hand, to the home office staff department.
6. Since staffs do not work on end-products or produce end-services for sale to customers, is it not proper to consider them to be less essential than line departments which do the organization's mainstream work? Discuss. What difference does it make whether they are considered to be of less, equal, or more importance than line departments?
7. In the text it says that line and staff people do not, in all cases, mutually respect each other. What causes this? Discuss.
8. Staffs receive delegations to carry out their missions so why should they have to "sell" themselves and their services to other departments? Discuss.

Questions for Analysis and Discussion

1. After a visit to Europe, the president said, "The Europeans are going to beat us out. In the plant it's about a standoff, but in the office they make us look like fools. In our plant we have 1,200 hourly paid workers. Its European equivalent has almost 1,300 men. But we have 910 in the office where they have only 220." Why the difference? Presumably, in both cases, most of the office workers work in staff departments. Who is right here?
2. In a West Coast airplane company a newly hired assistant to the president uncovered some irregularities in purchasing. He notified all the vice presidents. This upset the purchasing agent and he told his superior, a vice

president, that he would resign if the assistant were not fired. So, according to the textbook recounting this incident, the president, "had no alternative but to fire the assistant." What should have been done?

3. A *Fortune* article on the Jim Walter construction company describes its central staff's obligation as follows: All of Jim Walter's managers, down to the level of plant and sales office managers set their own goals which are coordinated into company-wide plans. Once this is done, the corporate staff does not second-guess the operating men or tell them how to do their jobs.

    A divisional head said, "They don't issue instructions to my people and if they did, I'd blow up. If you look to a man for profits, you look to him to solve the problems."

    Is this the way it ought to work? Why should the divisional manager feel that it is his right not to use the best capabilities the company has (the advice of the home office staff people)? What if, in the planning stage, the divisional managers set only easy-to-reach goals? What if they plan to spend more money than the company has? What if the company looks to a man for profits but all he produces are losses?

4. How can a central staff exercise functional control over lower-level counterpart staff departments? Must central staff people go around and visit? And when they do, what do they do? Sit at a man's elbow for two days? How can functional control be made to work if there are subsidiary units all over the country?

5. It is indeed unfortunate when lower people regard staffs as being spies for higher ups. Yet sometimes a staff employee finds a local situation which badly needs improving but his recommendations are ignored. He can hardly ignore the situation, yet he does not like to run to headquarters. What should he do?

6. A company manager complained about the consulting help he got. He said, "All that guy did was to invite my men out for cocktails, pick their brains and recommend what they thought should be done." Is this poor consulting? Was the company cheated?

7 A researcher asks a line manager, "What do you do if you disagree with a request by a staff department to do (or not to do) something?" He answers, "I appeal to my boss." Next, the researcher asks a second manager and he answers, "I reject the request and let them take it up through channels." The third manager said, "I say no and tell them why." The fourth said, "I do what they want because I'll probably have to do it anyway." Which is the best answer from the organizational point of view? Why?

8. One foreman said, "If you can't lick 'em, join 'em. I haven't argued a point with a staff man in the last five years." Discuss.

9. In the text, it was said that normally, staff people do not order line personnel around. Can line people issue orders to staff personnel? (Such as, "Stay out of my department; if I need you I'll call you." Or "I don't have the time to get all that information for you.")

10. Foreman: "Mr. Superintendent, who's my boss? That's all I want to know. I thought that you were, but the quality control engineer has been running my department. And now he's trying to run me. How do you think it looks to my men — a twenty-five-year-old kid giving me orders?" "Come back later today, Tom; we'll discuss it when you've cooled off." "I'll be back but I won't be cooled off." Superintendent to himself, "Who *is* his boss; I wish I knew." Discuss.

11. The Wing Company sales department wanted a special attachment to be designed for its recently introduced new model machines. The engineering vice president did not think much of the idea and did not get it done. A few months later, the company's principal competitor introduced such an attachment. Wing's sales dropped from 37 to 32 percent of the market and profits fell one hundred thousand dollars. Because of the smaller volume, eighty factory workers were laid off. The president took no disciplinary action against the engineering vice president. Should he have done anything?

12. A book on organization quotes a staff employee as saying, "We are staff men, but I like to feel that we are line men. I take authority and initiative. If a salesman has a problem, I go directly to him, then I tell his boss. When I talk to the laboratory director, I feel that I am his boss, even though the organization chart doesn't say so. Comment.

Case 10-1   Working in the Home Office

A textbook describes a situation where a man transferred from a line job in a division to a home office said, "At the plant, there's constant pressure. Something's always happening. Somebody's ready to walk out, somebody's complaining about a new conveyor that we put in that doesn't work right. There are a million things going on. Here in the general office, things are quiet and the pace is slow.

"You know, in the plant, you get an idea and you call up a couple of guys to say, 'Come on, let's sit down and talk about it.' Well, in three minutes, you're in action. Here you call up to get three guys together. Well, one guy's out of town for a week. Another fellow is all booked up. You can't get the conference room. (You have to have the conference room, you know, to have a conference.) So it's two weeks before you ever have the first meeting on the damn thing."

"An older fellow who came in here recently to be manager of manufacturing for one of the divisions has nearly gone crazy. He came down to me and said, 'Holy cow, what's going on? I've looked out the window so many times a day, I'm about to go nuts. I gotta do something. What can I do?'"

- What's the problem here? Is the nature of home office work different somehow from line work?
- Are there "staff type" people? Are there "line type" people?
  What can one say about the transferred man in this case and the idea of people developing their own jobs?
- Who should do what in order to have the organization benefit more from this man having been transferred to the central office?

Case 10-2   Home Office Surveillance in Operation

At company A, as the staff representative from the home office prepared to leave after two days of visiting the divisional operations, he asked the local manager, "Is there anything else we can do at the home office to help you?" "Well, yes, there is, you can damn well get on an airplane and go back to New York and stay there and quit bothering me. I've got work to do."

At company B, "Oh yes, we ask the home office for help once or twice a year just to go through the motions. We don't pay any attention to them but the home office knows that we asked them for help and so are trying to manage well. After they leave we go on doing things our way."

- How can home offices overcome such attitudes and become more helpful to operations in the field?
- Suppose the president hears of these two statements; what should he do?

Case 10-3   Administrative and Operational Expertise

An Englishman turned down a high-paying job with an American company. "But why won't you come with us?" asked the astonished president. "You see, sir," the Englishman replied, "I am trained to be an aircraft designer, not an office boy. Here in America I am shocked to learn that your chief designer is what you call an executive: he shuffles papers, has meetings, approves budgets, interviews senior draftsmen. I wouldn't enjoy that at all."

"But," sputtered the president, "I thought you were the chief designer of your company in England." "Oh yes," answered the designer, "but in England the chief designer and his three or four top assistants spend all their time designing aircraft. What you would have me do here in America would be delegated in England to a chief draftsman — to a *clerk!* I am not a clerk — never have been. I am an aircraft designer, the best in the business, so they say. You couldn't get me to be an office boy in America for all the dollars you can mention or all the tea in China."

- Are staff specialist jobs truly superior to administrative jobs?
- Is it necessary for a superior in the hierarchy to be the superior in technical know-how to his subordinates?
- Does it matter if subordinates do not respect their hierarchical superiors? If it does, how can such respect be induced in a case such as that posed here?

Endnotes

1. These are presented and discussed in, "Idea Managers, A New Look at Staff and Line Jobs," by William G. Sharwell, *Management Review*, August 1978, pp. 24ff.
2. This research was reported in *Developing Organizations: Diagnosis and Action*, by Paul L. Lawrence and Jay W. Lorsch, (Addison-Wesley, 1969.)

Suggested Supplementary Readings

"Product Management: Today's Most Demanding Business Job." MBA *Executive*, September 1978, pp. 3ff.

Reimann, B.C. "Parkinson Revisited: A Component Analysis of the Use of Staff Specialists in Manufacturing Organizations." *Human Relations* 32 (1979): 625–641.

Sharwell, William G. "Idea Managers, A New Look at Staff and Line Jobs," *Management Review*, August 1979, pp. 24ff.

William, William W. "Organizational Size, Technology, and Employment Investments in Ancillary Specialists," *Academy of Management Procedings*, 1977, pp. 224–228.

Objectives of Chapter Eleven

1. To bring out the differences between divisional organizations and other types of organizations.
2. To consider the entrepreneurial motivations intended to be developed in the managerial echelons of divisions.
3. To bring out and to compare the advantages and disadvantages of using the divisional form.
4. To investigate the operation of profit centers and to investigate the motivations to managers which come from using profit centers.

Divisional Structures and Profit Centers

*Our organizational concept
is to have centralized policy making
and control
and decentralized operations.*
General Motors

At Greyhound Corporation, primarily an operator of intercity bus transportation, Armour is a separate *division* concentrating on meat packing. Science Research Associates, a book publisher, is a *division* of International Business Machines.

In both of these cases, the *division* is responsible for developing its own products and making and selling them. Neither General Motors nor IBM has a company-wide manufacturing or sales department.

Large companies often are really multi-company companies, as is illustrated in Figures 11-1 and 11-2, which depict the organization structures of Du Pont (chemicals) and Macy (department stores). Both of these companies are really multi-company companies.

We noted in Chapter 8 that companies with a great deal of diversity such as Procter & Gamble (P & G makes soap, detergents, toothpaste, Crisco, Puff paper tissues, Pampers disposable diapers, Folger's coffee, and Duncan Hines cake mixes), usually choose the divisional form of organizational structure. The major segments of divisional companies are allowed to operate much as if they were independent companies. Divisional managers do, however, have available to them the "know-how" and back-up facilities of a central organization at the home office. And they have to operate within the confines of their companies' major policies.

Usually, divisions do not overlap or compete directly against each other for the same business (although General Motors is a notable exception). General Foods' Maxwell House (coffee), Birds Eye (frozen foods), and Post (breakfast foods) divisions each has its own products and does not compete against its sister divisions for business.

Nonmanufacturing organizations also sometimes set up their major departments in a way similar to divisions, although their "products" may be services. The Cincinnati Gas and Electric Company has a gas division and an electric division. The Port of New York Authority has an Aviation department concerned with airports, a Marine Terminals department, a Truck and Bus Terminal department and a Tunnels and Bridges department. Hospitals are set up by type of sickness while universities are set up by subject areas.

This chapter will deal with the way divisional structures operate and their advantages and disadvantages.

The Role of Divisional Managers

The object of divisionalization is to try to develop entrepreneurial motivation on the part of managers below the very top level of the organization. The hope is that this kind of motivation will be developed as a result of pushing wide-scope decision making down one or two levels from the top. The head of each division can then make most of the decisions necessary for the effective operation of his division.

"Entrepreneurial motivation" means "bottom line" (profit) motivation. This is in contrast to "bureaucratic motivation." Bureaucratic motivation means that the manager is largely concerned with doing work. The difference is in the emphasis on having managers keep in mind the impact of what their organizations do on the effectiveness of operations and on end-results such as sales, costs, and profits.

The heads of divisionalized companies are sometimes quoted as saying:

"We want each division head to run his division just as he would if the division were his own company."

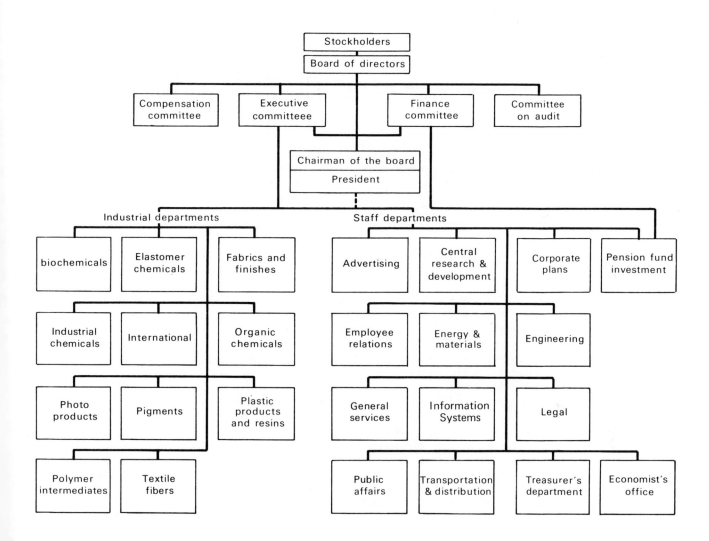

Figure 11-1 Simplified organization chart of E. I. Du Pont de Nemours & Company showing its divisionalization along product lines.

Divisional Structures and Profit Centers

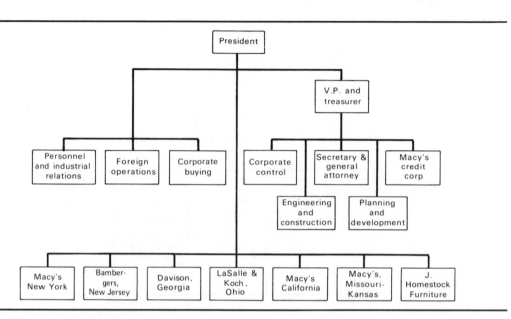

Figure 11-2
Organization chart of R. H. Macy & Company, showing its geographical divisionalization. Each geographical division operates a half dozen or more stores in its area.

This statement, however, goes too far. Owners who run their own companies sometimes do it ineptly and some even go bankrupt. There is no intent, in divisional companies, to allow divisional heads this much autonomy. Furthermore, a company's top administrators want their divisional managers to do things which are helpful both to their divisions and to the company as a whole. The superiors would not want divisional heads to do things which help their divisions but which are hurtful to the whole organization.

Even though wide powers are granted to individual managers, they are at the same time required to do certain things which are regarded as essential by the higher level managers. Divisional heads are, for example, *required* to draw up plans for the future and to make market studies, financial plans, etc. Most divisional companies also *require* each division head to submit detailed monthly reports of accomplishments showing comparisons to plans.

Divisional managers are also expected to operate their divisions well but, in most divisional companies, this means *with the help* of the home office staff specialists. Each division's managers arrive at policies and develop procedures and carry on activities but *with the advice, guidance and, most important, with the approval* of home office specialists.

There are some interesting practical questions as to just what specific things a divisional head is allowed to decide on his own. In most divisional companies, the delegations to divisional managers are not so broad as they appear.

Two examples from General Motors illustrate the limitations typically put on divisional managers:

One had to do with the Cadillac division modernizing its main plant. The other dealt with modernizing an Assembly division car body plant in Detroit.

Both of these proposed actions first went through months of discussion. Then

Organizational Design

each division had to get the approval of the executive committee of the board of directors before it got the go-ahead signal. Both projects started out as informal discussions between divisional heads and the company president and also the board chairman. Given approval to go ahead with their investigations, the Cadillac and the Assembly divisions then "decided" to modernize their plants. The heads of these two divisions decided but "with consultation and approval."

Capital Investment. Usually, divisional managers must get home office approval for all capital expenditure programs of consequence (perhaps expenditures of over $50,000). Such central office review helps the company to channel its resources into their most productive uses. The profits of individual divisions are not theirs to reinvest as they choose. This applies even to highly profitable as well as to less profitable divisions.

Product Lines. Divisional heads usually have almost full authority over their product lines except that they have to stay within their mission confines. In the Singer Company, the divisional manager in charge of making and selling sewing machines cannot start to make television sets without getting approval. But within the limits of their missions, divisional managers themselves decide what products they will make. The sewing machine manager can decide whether to make small portable electric sewing machines or not. Divisional managers also are usually allowed and expected to do whatever research is needed to develop new products in their product lines and to design and make them.

Buying Outside. In large companies, the finished products of one division are often parts or components which are bought by a sister division to put into its end-products. This can make problems because each division's managers are trying to make money for their own division. A-C Sparkplug and New Departure (roller and ball bearings), and all other General Motors

parts supplying divisions can make money if they can charge GM's Assembly division prices high enough to allow for ample profits. But the Assembly division can make money only if it does *not* pay high prices for the things it buys.

Obviously, problems can arise here. It might be, for example, that the Assembly division can buy sparkplugs at a lower price from Champion (an outside company) than from sister A-C Sparkplug division. Should the Assembly division manager be allowed to take advantage of this opportunity and to buy outside? For the good of the assembly division, yes. But, for the good of General Motors, perhaps, no, because of the harm this would do to the A-C Sparkplug division. In such cases, someone high in the GM organization should decide.

Pricing. Divisional managers are usually allowed to set the prices of the products in their product line. This is particularly true where there are hundreds or thousands of products. The 3M company makes 50,000 kinds of products, ranging from sand paper to photocopiers, Scotch tape to traffic lights, skin lotion to electrical connectors, and X-ray kits to artificial hips. Obviously, no one in 3M's central office would be in a position to set these 50,000 prices. Westinghouse makes 8,000 products in 300,000 variations and has over a thousand employees who have price-setting authority.

But it is different if a division has a limited product line and if its products cost a good bit of money. Then a division might be required to get home office approval of its prices. In General Electric, the board of directors would surely want to pass judgment on the prices of the jet airplane engines which GE makes for airplane companies (such engines may cost over one million dollars each), but the board would not want to pass judgment on the prices of stoves or electric irons.

Transfer Prices. Another aspect of the operation of divisions concerns "transfer prices," the prices at which parts and components making divisions sell their products to end-product assembling divisions.[1] (Although this is a very important matter in divisional operations, our interest here is only in the way it affects the behavior of managers.)

Normally, the transfer price is set at a point so that it is a bargain for the buying division. This strengthens the motivation of buying divisions to buy from sister divisions rather than buying from the outside. The lower transfer prices have the effect of the two divisions sharing in the saving from there being no selling expenses.

Personnel. Divisions handle all of their own personnel matters, although they are subject to organization-wide policies. Divisions hire their own personnel and handle all matters of paying and promoting people, so long as they stay within the bounds of company policies. In many large companies, however, divisional managers cannot do their own bargaining with labor unions because the same union represents the employees of several divisions of the company so the bargaining has to be done on a company-wide basis.

Divisional managers, too, usually may not appoint new managers to key jobs in their divisions without home office approval. The central office administrators may want to put certain subordinate managers who come from other divisions into key spots in certain divisions either because they are better managers or because these junior managers need the experience to round them out and to prepare them for still higher jobs.

Essential Policies. Essential policies, which were discussed in Chapter 5, are those required by laws or union contracts. Included, among others, are policies of non-discrimination in employment, affirmative action in employment, and meeting safety and environmental regulations.

In a divisional company, *all* divisional managers are expected to know about such laws and labor contract provisions and to obey them. But, their doing so

is not, in divisional companies, left wholly up to them. Central staffs usually disseminate knowledge of these numerous laws and home office staffs try to see that lower level staffs are informed on these matters. For the protection of the company, the divisional heads are usually not left to do this without home office surveillance.

Merits of Divisions

Today, divisionalization is the accepted way to organize large diversified companies. Nearly all of *Fortune's* 500 largest manufacturing companies are organized divisionally. So are most of the largest non-manufacturing companies.

The advantages, therefore, obviously outweigh the disadvantages by a wide margin. At the same time, however, there are certain disadvantages to divisionalization. To keep these disadvantages from becoming overly harmful, a certain amount of central office surveillance is necessary.

Advantages of Divisions

The principal advantages stemming from divisionalization are that it divides the whole large enterprise into more manageable smaller units while at the same time retaining the advantage of strong motivation of subordinates to manage effectively. These and other advantages are discussed below.

Manageable Units. Divisions split up giantism and reduce the managerial job to managing smaller, more compact units. These smaller units, being more manageable, are usually more efficient and they can respond more quickly to changes in economic conditions and to competition than can large monolithic organizations.

Strong Motivation. Along with the breaking up of giantism is another advantage, strong motivation. Divisional managers, being largely on their own and with whole jobs to do (to produce results and not just to do functional work) generate a more intense identification with their own accomplishments and become greatly interested in performing well. Divisionalization usually develops an entrepreneurial feeling in divisional managers.

Managers are like most other people in having an "effort reserve" or a latent "interest reserve" which is not always tapped. Most people probably try to do their jobs well, yet if the motivation is strong enough they will do still better. Each division's having its own profit responsibility and its own rewards for accomplishment seems to tap its managers' reserves of concern, interest, and effort, and brings greater commitment and better results. Consequently, divisional managers develop organizations which have more life to them and which accomplish more than do major department heads in large functional companies.

American companies try to heighten this motivation by giving extra pay in the form of bonuses to divisional managers and their high-level subordinate managers according to the results achieved *in their respective divisions*. Such bonuses are very effective motivators because they are based largely on the *division's* own performance rather than on the total enterprise's performance.

Development of Managers. The "wholeness" of the work of divisional managers helps develop them. Divisional managers are forced to do "total thinking." They learn to think about the effects of their decisions on all areas under their direction and not just in individual narrow functional areas. And they don't let subordinate department heads quarrel and lose sight of effective operations.

Better Control from Better Appraisals. Divisions help in the appraisal of the performance of managers. Top managers can compare the performance of different divisions according to their profits, rates of return on investments, market penetration, budget variances, and other bases. When high-level managers make such comparisons, their most effective subordinate managers usually stand out.

Reducing Parochial Functional Thinking. Divisional structures reduce the harmful effects of the parochial thinking of functional specialists because division heads must do total thinking. Yet down within each division there is just as much tendency to be parochial by functions as in functional companies. The gain here comes from pushing total thinking down one or two levels in the company, which automatically limits functional parochialism to the still-lower levels.

After one company had changed to a divisional structure, one of the divisional managers said:

When we operated under the old functional basis, the only way we could get people in other functions together to find out what they were doing or to coordinate our work with theirs was to call a committee meeting or to have a conference of some sort. Now we all work right down the hall from one another at division headquarters, so all we have to do is to drop in and clear the matter up in person.

Since we are all being measured and rewarded by the results we achieve from the business we manage and judged in terms of the same yardstick, we find it a lot easier to keep the other fellow informed. I notice now, too, that people are more willing to go out of their way to help the other fellow with his problems.

Disadvantages of Divisions

Divisionalization is not without its weaknesses. But, before we discuss those weaknesses, we should repeat that nearly all large companies all over the world are organized divisionally because no other form of organization has proven to be so effective for large-scale operations. The advantages far outweigh the disadvantages.

Inadequate Surveillance From the Top. Giant diversified companies sometimes have twenty-five or more divisions (General

Electric has more than 100). Many of these divisions are in quite diverse industries. The normal central office light handed surveillance over divisional activities is inadequate to give early warning of trouble spots. Nor are home office staff specialists so expert as to be able to help out in every activity should trouble arise.

Giant companies therefore usually group several divisions for administrative purposes and put a "group executive" in charge of several divisions whose product lines are related to each other. General Electric has, for example, a household appliance group head. His divisions include, among others, the company's electric light bulb division and its washing machine division.

Group executives help solve the problem of inadequate surveillance but not the problem of inadequate home office back-up expertise since the group executive does not have a set of staffs of his own.

Too Much Surveillance and Control From the Top. Just as it is possible to have too little surveillance, it is also possible to have too much. In Chapter 20, on decentralization, we will note that with the passage of time, decision making tends *not* to remain decentralized. Instead, it tends to gravitate upward and to centralize at the top. The two examples from General Motors described earlier in this chapter are illustrations. Both are examples that show the central office people having more to say about a division's operations than they should have if they followed the General Motors organizational concept quoted at the start of this chapter.

In particular, the financial controls exercised by the home office financial unit are often used unwisely. John De Lorean, a one-time GM vice president, cited numerous examples in his book where the home office control over the expenditures of a division were used unwisely. Often the fault came from their not allowing the money required for activities with very good payoff prospects. The central financial staff was

conscious of controlling spending but was not very cost/benefit conscious. De Lorean cited several instances in which programs proposed by lower echelons which would improve operations or products were turned down because of their initial costs.[1]

Failure to Develop Good Top-Level Executives. Although divisions help develop well rounded managers, they do not wholly solve the problem of how to develop good all-around top-level managers. This is because, unless managers on the way up have been consciously moved about as part of executive development training programs, each division's managers know only their own division's work. The head of General Dynamics' Electric Boat division (which makes submarines) would have much to learn if he became head of General Dynamics and had to direct the making and selling of airplanes, chemicals, and the other General Dynamics products.

Excessive Numbers of Staff Personnel. Divisional companies almost always have more staff people, in total, than do functional companies of equal size because each division tends to have a full set of staffs in addition to the home office staffs. Some of these divisional staff units are likely to be too small to be economical.

Large staffs are listed here as a disadvantage, but this is not always clearly so. Presumably, profit-oriented divisional managers will not maintain large staffs unless they believe that they pay for themselves in the value of the assistance that they give. So, surely, most of the time they are worth their cost and their existence is not a disadvantage.

Induction of Parochial Divisional Thinking. The reduction of parochial functional thinking was listed as an advantage of divisions. Unfortunately, this is not all clear gain because divisionalization induces parochial thinking of another kind. Managers are likely to see things only from the point of view of what is good for *their division*. Parochial *divisional* thinking seems to be not quite so bad, however, as parochial *functional* thinking. Divisional thinking retains the profit emphasis, which parochial functional emphasis loses. And it retains a strong product emphasis, which is also beneficial.

Nonetheless, parochial divisional thinking hurts cooperation between divisions. Sometimes a division manager does not even know what is good for other divisions. And even if he does, he may be motivated to put his division's good above the whole company's good.

In one electronics company the manager of a large division will not show his latest production improvements to visiting managers from sister divisions. "Why should I help those guys to look good?" he asks. In another large divisional company, it is easier for an engineer from a competing company to get in and look around than it is for an engineer from a sister division.

Coordination Difficulties. When divisions have to coordinate their work, difficulties may arise from each division being too self-centered. Yet, since each such division is dependent on the other, this may not prove to be a serious problem because, when it is necessary to coordinate the work of different divisions, central office coordinating staffs are usually brought into play.

Coordination is even less of a problem in a good many divisional companies because the work of different divisions is not related, so no cooperation is needed. Borg-Warner has twenty-eight separate divisions. Between many of these divisions there are no relationships at all which would require coordination. The Ingersoll Steel division makes fabricated pieces of steel and the Marbon Chemical division makes adhesives. So, while divisional parochialism is a danger in that it may hurt cooperation, this is, in some cases, a relatively unimportant danger.

Proliferation of Sales Departments. When each division sells its own products, the company has as many sales departments as it has divisions. There are forty-eight different General Electric sales organizations listed at thirty-six different street addresses in the Chicago telephone book! If GE combined them all, it could probably save on both salaries and office rent.

On the other hand, in Chicago, each of GE's sales offices may do enough business to support it, but in, say, Bismarck, North Dakota, it would surely be better for several of GE's divisions to join hands and support a single sales office.

Proliferation of Manufacturing Departments. Manufacturing departments, too, can be too fragmented to be large enough to be economical. Probably for small divisions, such facilities should be combined for two or more divisions in order to have departments large enough to be able to operate economically.

Uncoordinated Customer Relationships.

"Is or is not gas the best for heating?" the architect on the telephone demanded. "Your people can't seem to agree."
The architect was designing a new factory building in Cincinnati. First, a salesman from Cincinnati Gas & Electric Company's gas division called on him. Gas was best and had it all over electricity. Then a salesman from CG & E's electricity division came around and said that gas was all wrong and that electricity was better.

This story is not so bad, however, as some stories one hears about uncoordinated customer relationships in divisional companies. At least CG & E was not likely to lose the customer to any other gas or electric company. But customers form a poor impression of companies when they have such experiences with separate divisions not coordinating their work.

The AMF Company almost got into a much worse spot through one of its divisions' independence. A division on the West Coast was so unhappy with some steel it had bought that it was going to sue the steel company. The home office heard about it just in time to stop it. The steel company was a large customer of two other AMF divisions.

Short-Range Thinking. Divisional managers, motivated to make good showings in the short run, are likely to decide matters on a short-range profit basis. They are not likely to spend money for research with distant pay-out prospects because this hurts short-run profits. General Electric (whose slogan for many years was, "progress is our most important product") reported that the central office had continually to prod the divisions into doing more long-range research.

Making the Division's Record Look Good. Divisional managers sometimes pay more attention to making their record look good than they do to doing a good job. They develop an overriding concern for the appearance of their division's record. Short-range thinking (not doing research or postponing doing needed maintenance work, for example), makes today's record look good.

Divisional managers are also motivated to *do* something if the record shows that things are going badly. Maybe they don't know just what to do so they do something anyway just to show top officials that they are doing something about an unsatisfactory situation. Maybe they fire someone. Desperation firing of employees could well be indiscriminate firing and so be unwise. Recently, in one large electric appliance manufacturing company, one division had three marketing managers in one year. This may well have been justified, but surely when such things happen, it is hard to keep everyone from developing an anxiety neurosis.

Profit Centers and Cost and Service Centers

A profit center is a section of a company whose head is responsible for earning a profit from its operation. It is a unit whose income, outgo, and assets can easily be set apart from the rest of the company.

In contrast, a cost center or a service center is a section of a company whose costs can be isolated but for which it is not possible to calculate an income or a profit figure. A stockroom or an engineering department is a cost center or a service center but not a profit center.

Sometimes the use of profit centers has been called, "unit departmentation." Since the unit can stand alone so far as the records are concerned, its results and its rate of return on its investment can be calculated separately.

Although "divisions" are always profit centers, the reverse is not always true. Profit centers are not always divisions, particularly in selling. Every Safeway grocery store and every Exxon gasoline filling station is a profit center. Each one makes money or it does not, and it is easy to calculate how much. Yet an individual store or filling station is not a division because it is too small and its manager has limited decision making power.

Profit center managers have "profit making responsibility" and are judged on the profits (as expressed by the rate of return on investment) that their parts of the company earn more than on anything else.

Although profit center managers are supposed to earn a return on the company's investment in their division, they are not supposed to put earning a profit above all else. Rather they are supposed to operate their responsibility areas while recognizing the good of the whole company on a long-range basis, and the social obligations which society imposes on business organization managers.

Cost Centers, Service Centers, and Responsibility Centers

Profit centers do not work very well for sections of companies which do not have identifiable sales incomes and costs of their own. So, functional departments and process departments are rarely profit centers. A company's foundry which makes castings for a sister department, the machine shop, is usually only a cost center and not a profit center. (But it could be a profit center if it also sold castings to outside customers.) Similarly, the engineering department is a service center or a responsibility center but is not a profit center. It is not possible in either case to find out the profit they earn.

Heads of these departments are judged on their performance against budgets and on more subjective things, such as the quality of the service they render. In practice, the motivation growing out of such controls seems not to be as strong as that found in profit centers.

Appraisal of Divisional Performance

The main measure of divisional performance is profits as shown by the rate of return on investment (ROI) although admittedly, ROI has weaknesses which keep it from being an altogether excellent measure. Because ROI is not wholly satisfactory, many divisional companies try to develop other procedures to use along with it which make up for ROI's deficiencies.

Such companies try to evaluate each division's market position in its industry, how forward looking its policies are, how well it is developing young managers for the future, its balance between short- and long-range goals, and such things. Obviously, all of these things are important but they are hard to evaluate quantitatively and so require subjective judgments.

Many companies rely a great deal on an annual review by the company's top managers. In these companies, one or two top line executives, plus some staff personnel from the home office visit every profit center at least once a year, sit down with the man-

ager and go over his performance with him. Superiors try to appraise their subordinates on their *total* performance. Rate of return is important, even very important, but it is not the only thing.

Rate of Return

A division's rate of return is calculated by dividing its profits by the value of its assets. Rate of return on investment is the main measure of divisional managers' success at Du Pont, at Armstrong Cork and in a great many other companies. Managers who produce high rates of return in their divisions get bonuses and promotions.

Strengths of Rate of Return. Rate of return as the basis for appraisal makes managers think about everything that influences the rate in any way. Profit center managers think about how to motivate their people and how to win their support. They think about product lines and pricing and which items are the most profitable and how profitable. They think about ways to cut costs, both in production and selling. And they think about the value of things they spend money for, including staff costs and the cost-value worth of more sales.

Profit center managers also think about accounting procedures. They become quite concerned with how home office costs are allocated to them. They also become quite concerned about transfer prices. They delve into the economics of depreciation schedules and whether to capitalize or to expense certain items.

This list of advantages of rate of return is an impressive one. What it amounts to is a claim that rate of return judging makes managers try to manage well.

Weaknesses of Rate of Return. The strengths of ROI usually far outweigh its weaknesses. ROI has, however, quite a few weaknesses which keep it from being a perfect measure of performance and from being the ideal motivator of the behavior of managers.

- ROI ascribes all of the profits to the use of assets used and not to managing the human organization. It gives no consideration to the management of the people who used the assets and produced the profits.
- ROI considers results only. It pays no attention to reasons why. Nor does it pay any attention to any limitations on the freedom of managers to produce results. The Interco Company, for example, would not allow its Florsheim division, maker of high quality shoes, to make cheap work shoes. Divisional managers must also usually buy from sister divisions whether they want to or not.
- ROI also is based on the past and gives no credit for what managers do today for tomorrow's benefit. Nor does ROI give any credit for doing desirable non-profit work such as installing a new cafeteria for workers, reducing air pollution, or reducing noise levels on the job. None of these activities produce a profit and so do not improve a manager's ROI. On the contrary, all of these things reduce profits since they cost money. ROI may make managers too Spartan minded.
- ROI is in part dependent on the way the company's accounts are handled. All central office costs are, at the end of the year, assessed to the divisions. Assessments of shares of the costs of such items as centrally done research, or legal services, are supposed to reflect divisional benefit or use of the service but these assessments can be quite arbitrary and they affect the calculation of divisional profits.
- ROI is high where the assets used are few so it is high where there is much hand work and in service-type work. Accounting firms and consulting firms have high ROIs. In a factory more use of machines and less use of human effort usually increases profits even though the higher investment might reduce the ROI.
- ROI pays no attention to growth. A man-

ager who doubles the size of his operations and earns twice as much money may see his ROI stand still. He has accomplished a great deal but his ROI doesn't show it.
- ROI does not affect very many people directly. Its direct effects are largely felt only by the higher-level managers of profit centers.

These rate of return weaknesses appear to be formidable, yet, in spite of them all, ROI, on balance, has proven to be a very worthwhile managerial working tool. All of these weaknesses are weaknesses only if they cause superiors to make wrong appraisals.

Rate of Return Objectives

The profit making opportunities of the different divisions of a company always differ so it is only reasonable for top administrators to set separate rate of return objectives for each division. DuPont, for example, does not expect the same rate of return from its textile fibers division (nylon, dacron, etc.) that it expects from its organic chemicals division. It would be pure happenstance if the profit-making opportunities were the same in such unlike industries.

It is desirable, therefore, to set for each division a rate of return goal or objective which is reasonable for it. Yet what is reasonable for each division has to be a subjective judgment. DuPont's high-level administrators might decide that its textile fibers division's objective should be 12 percent return on capital and that its organic chemicals division's objective should be 20 percent. This would pose an interesting problem if, in a given year, each one earned 16 percent. Presumably, the textile fibers division's managers, who surpassed their objective, should be congratulated on their excellent performance and should be given substantial bonuses. But the managers of the organic chemicals division, which fell below its objective, should get only moderate praise and smaller bonuses. Yet, in such a case, surely the organic chemicals managers would feel that their goal was arbitrarily set too high.

Superiors cannot escape making such subjective judgments. They have to judge how high a rate a profit center ought to earn before they can judge whether its managers have performed well.

Different rate objectives produce some curious response actions on the part of managers at times. The manager of a 10-percent-objective division will go ahead and propose an improvement program which promises to return 12 percent on its investment because this will raise his overall rate of return. But the manager of a 20-percent-objective division will not even consider an 18 percent project because it would reduce his overall rate.

Summary

Large companies almost always find the divisional form of organizational structure better suited to their operations than the functional form. Whole segments of the company are set apart, more or less, as if they were small independent companies. The basis for such divisionalization is most often product lines although there are other bases.

The principal strength of divisional structures is that they generate "total performance" thinking on the part of divisional managers. They have responsibility over a total enterprise and so manage better than if they were functional heads over one function only.

Divisions are not without their problems, however. One very important matter is the need for well-rounded managers as divisional managers. Divisions also make for divisiveness and lack of inter-divisional cooperation. This comes from the divisional managers, who are judged on their own division's rates of return, putting this above all else. This strong drive for rate of return performance may also induce undesirable short-range decision-making.

When certain segments of a company can be set apart and managed more or less as complete entities (as always occurs in divisionalized companies) with their own money income and outgo, it is possible to use profit centers. Each group of profit center managers are then made responsible for earning profits from the operation of their profit center. The use of profit centers with emphasis on the return on investment (ROI) seems to be very effective in motivating managers to work toward organizational goals.

Review Questions

1. What is the basic philosophy of the divisional form of organization? What is expected to be gained? What are the disadvantages?

Divisional Structures and Profit Centers

2. In divisional organizations, how are prices determined for items made by one division which are bought and used by another division?

3. Discuss the matter of the freedom of divisional managers to make their own decisions.

4. How does surveillance by home office staff departments work in divisional companies? Is this good or bad? Discuss.

5. In the text, it says that divisions reduce parochial thinking. It also says that divisionalization induces parochial thinking. Which does it do? Discuss.

6. Should a company use rate of return (ROI) as the main basis for appraising the performances of divisional managers? Why or why not?

7. What are the requirements for the successful setting up of profit centers? What are they supposed to accomplish? In what way is a profit center different from a cost center or a service center?

8. Is there no way at all to escape from the dilemma of having either the same profit rate objective for all profit centers (which is probably unfair to some profit center managers) or having different rates for each profit center (which requires superiors judging what a reasonable rate is for each center)?

Questions for Analysis and Discussion

1. How can superiors motivate divisional managers to do their best for the company? In fact, how can a divisional manager know what is best for the company?

2. Where, in a divisional company, should the decision be made as to the quality of products to be made and the segment of the market to aim for?

3. In the Dell Company, none of the divisions wants to take on the company's new product X. Product X has a great future potential but only losses and headaches today. What should the president do?

4. An executive of a widely diversified company (which was organized divisionally) said, "The only required interactions in the organization are the vertical ones, the lateral interactions will develop as a result of the self-interest of the parties involved." Is this the way it *ought* to work? Is this the way it *will* work?

5. In one large company, its moving picture camera and projector division could not get its sister lamp making division to develop an improved lamp for its projectors because the lamp division wanted to do its best only for its large outside customers, Kodak and Bell & Howell. Suppose that the president of the company heard about this. What should he do?

6. Divisional head to president: "So if you want a high rate of return in my division, I can produce it for you. All I have to do is to fire fifty engineers.

You'd never see it. If this is the way you want me to run my division, I can do it, but it isn't very smart." Is it possible that such arbitrary and probably unwise actions would not be revealed in the reports received by top management? What should the president do in this situation?

7. At Litton Industries, in a recent year, one of its divisions had such severe losses that they caused the corporate profits to drop substantially. Yet the president said that these losses had been hidden from him. How can a division manager hide his losses and for how long?

8. How can superiors get rate-of-return motivated managers to go ahead with improvements which produce only costs (such as putting in a new employee washroom)? Would it be proper to impute rates of return to such projects?

9. If one division in a company has a 15 percent rate of return goal and another division has a 25 percent goal, should the chief financial officer approve a request for a 20 percent project for the first division if there are any 25 percent or over requests from the 25 percent division? How will the lower profit objective divisions ever get any money for capital projects?

10. The All-Metal Can Company is set up with geographical divisions. How would an area divisional manager probably react to the home office handling the contracts for cans for Del Monte and for Campbell Soup for their canning factories in his territory? He makes the cans and delivers them but he does not get to talk contract prices or other provisions with these customers. How does this affect his profits? Who stands engineering and tool design costs?

11. When setting transfer prices, the selling division's overhead per unit depends upon its volume. Should the transfer price be set based on the cost at the expected volume? What should be done if the volume changes? What if the supplying division's outside business volume changes?

12. The automatic transmission division of the Standard Motor Car Company has developed an automated assembly line at considerable cost. It will reduce costs a great deal in the future. This will result in the division's making a high rate of return. One of the sister buying divisions wants the transfer price adjusted. What should be done?

Case 11-1   Miller Company's Structure

The Miller Company's top management decided to change the company from a functional structure to a divisional structure. To the disappointment of the president, it took nearly seven years for the new structural form to become really effective.

Regarding the experience, the president said, "We had a functional operation in those days — engineering, manufacturing, sales, and finance. The

Divisional Structures and Profit Centers

functional people had tremendous power. They weren't about to let go of it. We had to crack down. Furthermore, I thought that a lot of fellows we took from functional jobs and made general managers would respond to the challenge of being measured. I was wrong. I should have realized that you can't expect a fellow who has been running just a part of it to, all of a sudden, be accountable for the whole thing."

· Had the president known that it would take seven years to make the change effective should he have embarked on the change?

· What decision-making power would the functional people not want to let go? What role would the former functional heads play in the new organization?

· The case mentions the matter of being "measured." What has this to do with the way the change would work out? Should not the managers have been measured before?

· What new competences would the new divisional managers have to acquire?

Case 11-2   Multiplex Company's Disputing Divisions

The Multiplex Company's Chrome Products division head and the head of its Electric Stove division were having a dispute concerning transfer prices. Among its products, the Chrome Products group produces chrome-plated stove tops for the Stove division. Customer complaints about quality in general caused the president of the company to tell the manufacturing staff vice president in charge of quality to improve the quality of the stove tops.

He did get their quality improved but by using a more expensive process which added 45¢ a unit to the stove tops' costs. Consequently, the Chrome Products division wanted to pass on this cost increase to the Stove division, thus increasing the transfer price of the stove tops to $5.00 (outside prices were still higher).

The Stove Division manager said no, he had not authorized the extra costs and could not sell the stoves for any more money so he would not pay $5.00.

• Should the company controller be asked to arbitrate this dispute? If not, how should this matter be handled?

• What should be the authority sphere of a home office staff vice president of quality?

• Where should a product's cost/quality decisions be made in a divisional company?

• How can Multiplex avoid problems similar to this one in the future?

Case 11-3 Washington, D.C.'s Public Transportation System

A number of years ago, the city of Washington, D.C., was thinking about how to improve its public transportation system. The two main proposals were to put in a network of superhighways or to put in a subway system. Either system would cost hundreds of millions of dollars.

General Electric's Transportation Division (makers of electric locomotives and similar equipment) lobbied strongly for the subways. This brought loud complaints from roadway builders to GE's division which made street lighting equipment.

- Should the head of GE try to prevent divisions from working at cross purposes to each other? How could he do it?

- How much sacrifice should a divisional manager who is being judged on his division's rate of return be asked to make to help a sister division make a better showing? (In this case, if either division bowed to the other, it was by no means certain that the sister division would get the contracts.)

Endnotes

1. There are several ways to set transfer prices. These include, cost of production with nominal mark-ups, market prices, market prices less a special discount, negotiated prices, and marginal costs. All of these methods, except for marginal costs, are commonly used.

2. *On a Clear Day You Can See General Motors, John Z. De Lorean's Look Inside the Automotive Giant* by J. Patrick Wright, (Wright Enterprises, 1979), Chapters 2, 7, and 8.

Suggested Supplementary Readings

Allen, Stephen A. "Understanding Reorganizations of Divisionalized Companies." *Academy of Management Journal,* December 1979, pp. 641–671.

Lambert, David R. "Transfer Pricing and Interdivisional Conflict." *California Management Review,* Summer 1979, pp. 70–75.

Lambrix, Robert J., and Surrenda S. Singhui. "How to Set Volume Sensitive ROI Targets," *Harvard Business Review,* March-April 1981, pp. 174–179.

Pitts, Robert A. "Toward a Contingency Theory of Multibusiness Organization Design." *Academy of Management Review,* April 1980, pp. 203–217.

Objectives of Chapter Twelve

1. To consider the nature of committees and how they relate to other organizational units.
2. To see how and where committees can serve most usefully in ways that cannot normally be well handled without committees.
3. To investigate the attitudes and motivations of committee members.
4. To look at the weaknesses of committees and to consider how these weaknesses can be avoided or minimized.

Committees

12

We Athenians, instead of looking on discussion as a stumbling block in the way of action, think of it as an indispensable preliminary to any wise action at all.
Pericles

At Du Pont, the nation's largest chemical company, members of its executive committee meet every Wednesday morning to consider matters of major importance to the company.

Du Pont's executive committee, which is made up of nine of its top administrators, considers such questions as the location of plants, continuance of old products, development of new products, and appropriation requests. It reviews departmental projects and considers what Du Pont calls "Whither" reports, such as "Whither (what is the future of) nylon?" or "Whither titanium?"

The committee also reviews the sales and earnings of every subordinate unit. Managers of departments with slumps or low profits are invited to come in and discuss their problems. The committee gives no orders and department heads can reject its suggestions.

Committees are useful staff-type adjuncts to all organizations of any size. They may be found at any level and usually serve in an advisory capacity to managers, or as aids in coordinating the work of different departments, or as temporary task force groups to give special attention to some unusual problem. Committees can also decide matters which affect several departments. The most important decisions made by managers in most organizations are made only after the careful consideration of the problem by one or more committees.

The Nature of Committees

A committee is a group of employees called together to consider certain specific matters. The group has a responsibility, as a group, to consider these matters and to arrive at a consensus viewpoint.

Except for boards of directors, which are committees elected by the stockholders, committees are always appointed by a high-level manager who asks certain of his subordinates from different departments to meet together to consider some matter of concern to him or to all of them. Normally, he appoints one of them to be the chairperson and does not himself meet with the committee. Normally, too, he follows the committee's recommendations although he is not bound to do so.

Committees are made up of the same people who make up the regular organization, yet they are different.

1. They are only some of the organization's managers, not all of them.
2. Committee members include only those specifically concerned in some way with the matter at hand and whose collective consideration is needed.
3. As committee members, these people are expected, for the moment, to cast aside their usual roles as managers or members of individual departments, and to assume new roles. In their new roles, they are more directly members of the *entire* organization with obligations to consider matters brought before the committee from the viewpoint of the good of the whole organization. (Actually and unfortunately, committee members probably do not act in this detached fashion very often. Instead, they usually act as partison advocates for their subject areas.)
4. The committee acts as a whole, not as individuals. It is to advise, to decide, or recommend, but as a committee, not as separate individuals.

"Ad Hoc" Versus Standing Committees

"Ad hoc" committees are those appointed, usually on short notice, to consider some pressing problem. Their make-up is determined by the need of the situation for certain expertise. When the problem to which the committee addresses itself is taken care of, it is disbanded.

In contrast, certain committees are permanent and have enduring assignments. The Finance committee of the board of directors or the Loan committee of a bank are examples. Such committees, too, are made up of individuals whose expertise is relevant to the committee's mission. They meet periodically on a scheduled basis and consider matters within the scope of their mission. These committees are more numerous than ad hoc committees and since they go on and on, they are, in the long run, almost always far more important than ad hoc committees.

Most of the strengths and weaknesses of committees which we will be discussing apply to standing committees more than to ad hoc committees.

Principal Uses of Committees

For the most part, committees serve in staff capacities in that they help the organization to function better by helping managers to make better decisions. In general, they consider matters of joint concern to several parts of or to the entire organization. They review proposals from lower echelons, decide matters of joint responsibility of several departments, and consider such other matters as they may be assigned.

Advice to Superiors

Managers frequently need the advice and counsel of their specialist subordinates. They need the considered and jointly thought out recommendations made by specialists who have met together and consid-

ered the matter at hand from the angles of their several specialties. Committee recommendations help managers make better decisions and to avoid making mistakes, which they might otherwise make because they are not familiar with all of the relevant details.

Much of the advisory function of committees concerns reviewing proposals from subordinate departments belonging to the manager to whom the committee reports. Someone farther down submits a proposal to the committee for its review. A proponent for the proposal, who may not be a member of the committee, makes a presentation, often complete with charts, slides or moving pictures, to the committee. Agendas are circulated to committee members ahead of time. These agendas contain the essence of the proposal so the committee members come to the meeting with some understanding of the merits of the proposal.

It is unfortunate that proposals are sometimes so important that their approval or disapproval will affect large segments of the organization. Millions or even hundreds of millions of dollars may be spent developing certain products, or going into new markets, or doing other things of equal magnitude. Not unnaturally, there may be conflicts among the organization's major groups as they try to swing the proposed actions in directions which will benefit their departments. This is particularly true when there are two or more alternative choices among proposals, only one of which will be chosen.

Total organizational benefit may be forgotten and eclipsed by the political tugs and pulls of competing groups. The views of the people near the top of the organization who wield the most power in the organization may rule even if they, themselves, are not on the committee.

In spite of such weaknesses of committees, which fortunately do not occur all of the time, using committees is still probably the best way available for resolving such problems.

Deciding Matters of Joint Responsibility

Committees sometimes decide certain matters, especially where two or more departments meet and have a joint interest in the matter (see Figure 12-1). This is frequently the situation in manufacturing companies in matters of product lines and product design. A committee made up of representatives of the departments principally concerned meets periodically to consider the company's product lines, and what changes to make in them and in the designs of individual products.

It could be said, in such cases, that each department concerned has a splinter of the authority needed to decide. Yet, in order for a decision to be made, these splinters need to be joined together. This, essentially, is what the committee does. Otherwise, lower departments would not be able to decide because the decision would affect other departments.

Committees as Coordinators

Committees also are used frequently in a coordinative capacity, particularly in the production of large complex products or the carrying forward of complex projects. Again, a committee of representatives of the various departments concerned gets together and arrives at coordinated schedules which are compatible to all departments. Part of the improved coordination comes from members on committees hearing the views of their colleagues from other authority areas. This gives them a better understanding of their problems and fosters cooperation.

Task Force Groups

Organizations sometimes have unusual situations such as when a downtown department store opens up a new satellite Northland, Southland, or other suburban store. Or, a similar situation occurs when a factory moves to a new location.

In such cases, a temporary committee-like task force may be set up to handle the problem. If the problem is important enough, the task force members may be assigned full time to it for its duration.

Task force groups are also important when they serve as project management teams associated with matrix management, as was discussed in Chapter 10. These groups see the specific project through to completion, even though it may take a year or more.

Companies sometimes use task force teams for such purposes as cost cutting drives. Such programs start with committees at high levels made up of near high-level managers. The goal is put before them and each member is designated to head up a next-level down committee which is responsible for implementing the program in a certain area. As Figure 12-2 shows, this committee, in turn, oversees several still lower-level committees which receive specific assignments to search out cost cutting opportunities and implement programs to reduce costs in their restricted areas.

There is a danger, however, in relying on task forces to handle every problem which concerns two or more departments. There is a tendency in some companies to use task forces for almost everything whereas most problems do not need to involve so many people.

Organization Development Intervention Groups

Organization development intervention groups are somewhat like committees in their operation. Such groups, which are discussed in Chapter 16, do not have formally appointed leaders, nor do they have formally delegated assignments in the same sense that usual committees have.

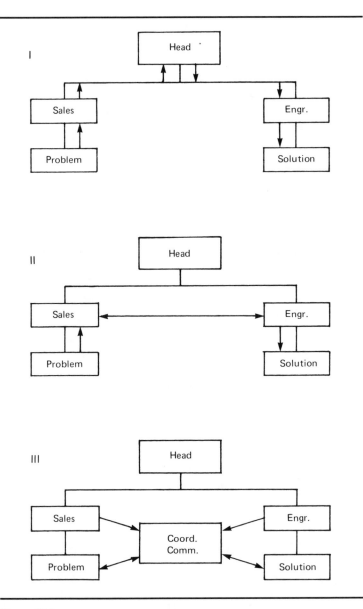

Figure 12-1
Section I depicts how a problem of joint concern to the sales and the engineering departments is sometimes solved. It goes to the top, a decision is made, and a decision comes down. Section II depicts how such a problem might be resolved if the two different chains of command get together on a voluntary basis and settled the problem. This sometimes occurs. Section III shows a coordinating committee in a position of resolving problems of joint concern to the sales and the engineering departments.

Committees

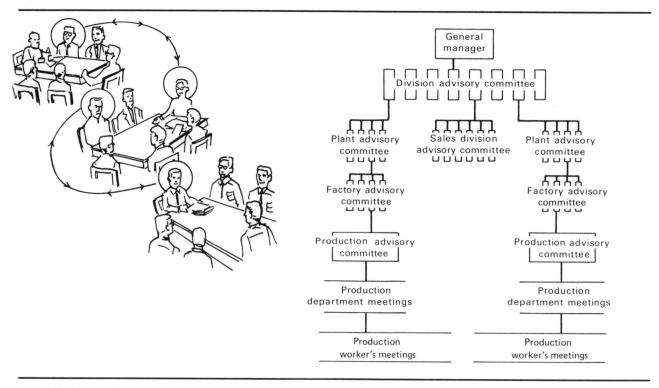

Figure 12-2
How information and task assignments can flow through the organization.

But, organization development intervention groups do meet, often on a regular basis, and they do have objectives. These groups consider any matter which is causing trouble or keeping organizational managers from being as effective as they could be. They try to unearth problems and then solve them. Their thrust is, however, on improving interpersonal relationships between organizational members and not on their functioning as a group.

Committee Strengths

Committees add to the quality of managerial decision making through their contributions in several ways. They bring together the viewpoints of people with different backgrounds on important matters and so help managers to make better decisions. They also let more people in on things and result in more participation.

Clarification of Thinking

In committee meetings, members, in trying to win other members to their viewpoints, often have to justify their positions to the others. This forces them to investigate evidence and to organize their thinking to back up their positions. The challenge to a member's ideas encourages good, hard thinking on his part.

A committee also helps clarify the thinking of the manager who appointed it in that it considers alternatives, divergent views, and possible drawbacks. Only in a committee meeting is there the back-and-forth interchange of ideas and incisive discussion which helps refine and improve the understanding of matters which affect several areas of the organization. Committee discussions are likely to bring out ideas which would not otherwise be brought out. The careful consideration which committees give to problems also prevents hasty decisions.

Exchange of Information and Ideas

Committees afford opportunities for the exchange of information and the cross-fertilization of ideas. Committees let people in on things. Everyone learns about problems or plans at the same time and hears the same statements about them. This lessens the likelihood of anyone hearing conflicting information.

Educational Value

When people serve on committees, they hear other viewpoints on problems, viewpoints different from their own. This broadens each member's knowledge base and sharpens his feel for the organization as a whole. This is especially helpful to young managers as they move up the managerial ladder.

Stimulation of Interest of Subordinates

Committee service is stimulating to many people. Being on a committee is evidence of status. In addition, it offers members opportunities to get away from their regular jobs and to take part in discussions about problems which are different from the problems they encounter on their regular jobs.

Many people have been on their regular jobs long enough that they no longer offer much challenge, so they welcome opportunities to serve on committees.

Some individuals are even more highly motivated. They like to be consulted and to take part in committee discussions which are often about important problems. They like to be in on a "piece of the action" on larger matters. The intellectual exercise is exhilarating to them.

Increase in the Visibility of Members

Since committee service takes each member away from his desk and out of his department, it gives him a chance to meet his peers from other departments. Members become more visible to people in other parts of the organization through the incisiveness of their contributions to the discussions. Their "arena behavior" can impress people. A meeting is a peer-level review.

Proposals are often made to committees for their review and recommendations. These proposals are made by a representative of the department which wants it approved. The person who presents the proposal is, in the meeting, its advocate, its sponsor. He may or may not be a member of the committee. He has to try to sell the idea to the committee members, some of whom are probably not really in favor of it. Aside from wanting the committee to act favorably on the proposal, he wants to impress the committee members with his own capability. His presentation is an opportunity to make a good showing for himself.

Committee members who want to become more visible can also do so even if they don't have opportunities to present proposals. They can volunteer for subcommittee work or to prepare reports for the committee. Greater visibility enhances promotional opportunities. Good presenters are more likely to move up in the organizational hierarchy.

Support for Managers

Group decisions and committee recommendations help win the acceptance of subordinates. They are evidence of participation by the organization. Even members who disagree with a committee's recommendation feel at least some obligation and degree of commitment to support it. They know the reasons for the decision and know that most of their colleagues favored it so they are more sympathetic toward it.

Committee recommendations carry weight with higher-level managers. If a manager takes an action in accordance with a committee's recommendation, and if the action turns out badly, his own superior is likely to judge him less harshly than if he had acted without committee support.

Committees also protect higher-level managers from criticism. If there is an "anti-discrimination in employment" committee or a safety committee, their recommendations, if the manager follows them, serve to protect him from severe personal criticism if something goes wrong.

Check Rein on Authority of One Individual

In government, religious, and educational organizations, committees have the effect of restraining single individuals, even superiors, from having all the power. In universities, various committees, more than administrators, determine policies, curricula, and tenure matters.

Committee Weaknesses

Our discussion so far has been favorable to committees, which is as it should be. Committees are a valuable part of effective managerial practice, a vital managerial tool. Yet, committees almost always get a bad press. A great many people do not like to serve on committees. (see Case 12-2 at the end of this chapter).

Committees get this bad press because of several weaknesses. Not all of these weaknesses are serious even though, taken together, they comprise a formidable list. Probably they should be regarded as things which might happen and which, if they happened, would be harmful, yet they do not have to happen. If the committee chairperson is skillful and if the committee members try to make their committee service into a productive activity, most of these weaknesses will not crop up.

Too Much Discussion and Slow Action

Committee members are just like people in general in that some of them are garrulous and talk more than is necessary. Members who want to impress their colleagues express themselves on every issue and talk too much. So committee meetings tend to stretch out until they use up all of the time available. There is a tendency for minor points, off-the-main-point discussions, and "maybe's" to take up too much time in committees. Furthermore, even if a member would rather keep quiet, he may feel that he has to speak up for defensive reasons, lest the others say, "He never contributes anything."

Sometimes when a committee is supposed to develop a recommendation, no action is taken at first because no one wants to take a position for fear of being in the minority. Everyone waits to see who is for and who is against. And, if strong differences of opinion develop, a committee often recommends further study and the whole thing is delayed further. Some people would say that committees legitimize procrastination and indecisiveness.

Devious managers do not always count slow action as a disadvantage. One university president said,

"I set up committees to keep obstreperous professors busy. They will spend so much time investigating and discussing problems that they wear themselves out and they don't have enough time left over to get in my hair about other troublesome situations."

A good way, as a devious manager would see it, to kill an unwanted suggestion would be to appoint a committee to study it. If this committee doesn't come up with the recommendation he wants, he appoints a new committee to restudy the matter.

Lack of Balanced Discussions

One of the main purposes of using a committee is to see that different viewpoints are put before the group so that the pros and cons of the issue at hand can be explored. But there is no way to judge the importance of the points raised for and against a proposal nor to judge the relative strengths and weaknesses of different positions. Some points raised are both important and are likely to occur. In contrast, other points are both unlikely and trivial. It is difficult, in committees, to weigh and balance properly the viewpoints presented.

There is a tendency for committee discussions to impute equal weight to every viewpoint brought up. Little things become apparent big things, or at least big enough to equal other things. Improbable things receive the same attention that probable things get. Major points tend to be downgraded. Minor points may end up playing a disproportionate part in determining the recommendation.

Low-Grade Recommendations

Discussions in committees often do not settle differences of opinion but just submerge them in compromise. A "yes" by some committee members and a "no" by others usually emerges as a mild recommendation one way or the other. Often there is no decisive recommendation.

Committee recommendations seem also to lean toward the familiar and to exert pressure to preserve the status quo. Occasionally, too, ideas are accepted because no one can think of an objection at the moment. Committees are also geared to the pace of conversation and this makes quickness of comprehension more important than reflectiveness, and fluency more important than creativity. Committees put a premium on the wrong qualities in people, so far as appraisal of ideas is concerned.

Committees seem also to be overly impressed by the elaborateness of a report or presentation and so get a distorted view of the merits of proposals. If a person wants to get his proposal approved, he really ought to over-prepare. Consequently, people either waste time by over-preparing or else run a greater risk of being turned down.

Curiously, committee decisions are sometimes hasty decisions. Some committees don't meet very often and have crowded agendas so, if they dawdle on the matters brought up early in the meeting, they don't have enough time to carry on a thoughtful and incisive consideration of matters farther down on the agenda. Committee members all have their regular jobs to do and these demand most of their time. In the meeting, after a while, someone is likely to say, "Let's agree on something, I've got to get back to work." Matters of considerable importance may therefore end up being considered only superficially.

The discussion here probably overemphasizes low-grade committee recommendations because committee recommendations are by no means always low grade. They are usually what the majority thinks and, since the committee members are presumed to be well qualified, the majority reasoning is probably sound reasoning most, even if not all, of the time.

Recommendations by Unresponsible People

Normally managers put people with various backgrounds on committees in order to get the benefit of their thinking on the matter at hand. Yet, in the case of standing committees, which are more or less permanent and whose membership does not change very often, the expertise of each member is not relevant to every matter considered by the committee. Nonetheless, most members take their committee service seriously and voice their uninformed opinions on every matter brought up and believe that it is their duty to have a voice in every committee recommendation. This is unfortunate because the committee consensus reflects the views of its members, some of whom are uninformed on almost every matter considered by the committee.

Perhaps this does not get to be so bad in business organizations as it sometimes does in universities. There, an accounting professor and a production professor serving on a committee sometimes vote to turn down a request by the marketing staff for a new course in the marketing area. It is unfortunate that the assignment to serve on a committee causes people, feeling their sense of duty, to assume judgment capabilities which they do not have.

Committees tend also to violate the unity of command principle. There is no joint responsibility nor are individual members personally accountable for the recommendations of the committee. Consequently, when a committee is responsible, it is likely that, in fact, no one is responsible. And often when no one is responsible, not much happens. There is, in a sense, a sharing of a lack of responsibility.

In almost all committees there are some members who don't really care what the committee recommends. If they could be made to feel more responsible, they would probably take a greater interest in the recommendation. But committees don't seem to generate strong feelings of responsibility on the part of committee members. There is a lack of emphasis on commitment.

Political Recommendations

Committees are often political even though this is rarely intended. Members are usually chosen either because they know a great deal about a problem or to represent their subject area expertise. They are on the committee so that they can tell the other committee members how the problem looks from the viewpoint of their subject area.

In the case of most committees, the members are not appointed to act as emissaries, deputies, or advocates for departmental interests. Yet, as they serve on committees, members usually feel that they have to protect their department's interests. "What's good for my department" is often their main concern. Committee meetings may almost become battlefields. It is not surprising that, in such cases, committee recommendations on important issues are often expressions of politics more than they are recommendations based on the fundamental merits of problems or on total organizational benefit.

Dominance of a Few

In any group, and committees are no exception, a few individuals will dominate. Some of these people are strong personalities who are trying to make a showing. Some people talk better than others and thus have more influence. A few will almost always do most of the talking in any committee and a few will be the most powerful, although the facile talkers and the powers may not be the same people.

This is a weakness because, if a few individuals dominate, the whole group's opinion is not being brought out and those who give in are actually wasting their time coming to the meetings. It would be a good idea to dismiss them from the committee.

Stifling of Ideas

Committee members sometimes do not speak up in meetings because those who make suggestions often find that other committee members are likely to oppose their ideas. And, if they don't oppose, then the proponent of the suggestion is likely to become a subcommittee of one to look further into the idea or to carry out his own suggestion. If he wants more work or if he wants to become more visible in the organization, this works out well. But, if he already has all of the work he can handle, he will probably keep quiet lest he be assigned more work.

Committees may breed conformity and stifle ideas more directly, however. The members who disagree are sometimes the real innovators, yet after getting squelched a few times, they stop making suggestions. On the other hand, admittedly, everyone finally does have to go the same way. There must finally be conformity in order to move on to consensus recommendations.

Growth Tendencies

In his classic comments about committees, Northcote Parkinson reported that committees tend to grow in size, particularly in governmental organizations.[1] This tendency to grow comes from everyone wanting to be in on the consideration of important matters. There is prestige attached to being on important committees and people on such committees are on the inside. Parkinson also thought that if a committee dies, somehow it generates a new committee which rises up to carry on in its place.

Parkinson also noted that, as committees grow in size, they become unwieldy. After they reach twenty-one members, Parkinson says, a smaller power group develops inside the committee, which meets ahead of regular meetings and decides everything.

Development of Weak Managers

Committees may weaken future managers. Managers raised in an atmosphere of committees are sometimes indecisive, rely on committees too much, and are reluctant to assume responsibility on their own. They use committees as an escape from responsibility.

When and How To Use Committees

Committees should be used only where they work best. Studies of the operation of committees suggest that they are most effective when there are five, six, or seven members. Larger committees tend to become unwieldy and smaller committees don't get the benefit of enough viewpoints.

Normally, too, superiors and their own subordinates should not be put on the same committee because subordinates tend to defer to their superiors. In fact, even when committee members come from different departments, they should be more or less peer equals, for the same reason. Lower-status members are likely to defer to those with higher status.

Committees are thought to be most useful in the following areas:[2]

· Expert advising on problems, objectives, and problem solutions.
· Choosing alternatives.
· Coordinating the work of different departments.
· Judging accomplishment.
· Task force situations.

Committees are thought to be less useful:

· Where one person has the power and the information allowing him to decide without a committee.

- Where sharp, clear responsibility is needed.
- Where subordinates want a leader to look up to.
- Where quick action is needed.
- For making plans, gathering data, and doing research.

Committee Chairpeople

The committee chairperson can help make meetings into productive exercises by drawing up agendas which tell members what subjects will be considered at the meetings. Background or proposal papers can also be circulated ahead to committee members along with the agenda. Members can then think over the matters to be considered ahead of time and they can be prepared by bringing with them any materials essential to the consideration of the subjects on the agenda.

In the meetings themselves, agendas help keep the discussion from wandering too far afield and they help limit the time spent on each subject by reminding everyone of the remaining items to be considered. During discussions, normally the chairperson should remain largely as a background figure who rarely intervenes to express a viewpoint yet who keeps the discussion on the track. He might also improve the exchange of ideas by asking certain people, if they have not expressed themselves, what their views are. He also aids in summing up the "sense of the committee" about the subject being discussed and in bringing the discussion to a conclusion so that the group can move on to the next subject.

During the consideration of a matter before a committee, its members discuss it from their several viewpoints. Often committee members differ in their views. Usually, the discussion leads toward a developing consensus viewpoint which is acceptable to most of the committee members. The committee chairperson then writes up a report which presents the committee's recommendations.

Summary

Committees are necessary and useful adjuncts to every sizable organization. They are particularly helpful when it is desirable to have several viewpoints on problems and where recommendations are needed covering problems which affect several chains of authority. Often, the face-to-face discussion of matters of common interest by representatives from different departments helps everyone to understand better the problems of the departments and promotes cooperation.

At the same time, committees have weaknesses which can cause them to be wasteful. They take up the time of high-salaried people and so are costly. They tend to vacillate and, if there is not a fully agreed upon consensus, to produce watered down compromise-type recommendations.

Nonetheless, their value almost always exceeds their negative features, so they have a place in most organizations.

Review Questions

1. How are committees usually made up? What kind of people are appointed to serve? What are their relationships to each other? What factors should the person appointing a committee consider as he decides who should serve?
2. What kinds of things do committees do best? What kinds of things do they usually do poorly? Discuss.
3. What can a manager do to try to realize the advantages from using committees while at the same time minimizing the disadvantages?
4. Committees are largely advisory. Yet why should committees spend hours considering something which must then go to a higher manager for his decision? The higher manager will finally decide and he is not bound to follow the committee's recommendation. Discuss.
5. What are task force groups? How are they similar to committees and how are they dissimilar? Discuss.
6. Discuss the problem, when committees are used, caused by not everyone on the committee being well-informed or even interested.
7. Discuss the problem, when committees are used, caused by the tendency for committee recommendations to be political recommendations.
8. When should committees be used and what gains should be expected? When should committees not be used?

Questions for Analysis and Discussion

1. In this chapter, it was said that committees help to develop managers because when a manager's ideas are constantly challenged by other committee members, it makes him think. Does it? Or does it just make him keep quiet?
2. In a manufacturing company, how can a product design committee really have the power to decide designs when it does not decide the budgets of the departments which will have to work on the product? Without money-allocating authority, the committee should really not be making decisions which have money consequences in several different departments. Is this logical?
3. In Chapter 17 we will say that an executive does not get rid of his own responsibility when he delegates. But here in Chapter 12, we have said that a top manager does seem to get rid of some responsibility when he submits problems to committees and asks for their recommendations. Can these two diverse positions be reconciled?

4. The pros and cons of problems as brought out in committee discussions sometimes are so far from the true merits as to present a misleading picture. Yet the actual merits are the important things and they will continue to be so in spite of possible warped discussions in committees.

    More than three hundred years ago, Galileo's contemporaries made him recant that the sun was the center of the solar system. But his contemporaries were wrong. Fifty years ago, General "Billy" Mitchell was courtmartialed and demoted in rank by the United States armed forces because he said that an airplane could sink a battleship. But Mitchell was right. How does a person get a fair hearing for his ideas which another committee member labels "unproven theories" or even "superficial mish-mash"?

5. The claim that committees waste a great deal of time is less true than it seems because without committees, committee members might easily waste just as much time at their desks. Is this really so? Discuss.

6. "We meet once a week to iron out really pressing problems, but the discussion invariably runs in circles. The trouble with these people is that they all have their own specialized interests and won't listen to one another. We're wasting valuable time this way, and a lot of friction is developing too." What should a newly appointed chairman of this committee do to improve things?

7. So many committee members vote with the head of the table, that majority rule prevails more in theory than in practice. To get committee approval, a manager must get to the head of the table. Is this so? What can be done about it?

8. A textbook on organization says that the tendency of a few members on a committee to dominate it is common and is "self-destructive." How does this tendency become self-destructive? What might the manager who appoints a committee do to keep this from happening?

9. One executive said, "We need more, not fewer committees in order to insure that important decisions will be based on facts, and not on the opinion of one or two individuals." Is his point a valid one?

10. Joe Williams does not like committees. But, as of today, he is newly promoted and is now a manager. In this capacity he will have to try to weigh the merits of various matters and to solve difficult problems. How might he do it?

11. If the committee chairperson feels that the discussion is not bringing out what he thinks are the important points and if the evolving consensus is different from his view, what should he do? Should he still try to stay in the background? If so, isn't he depriving himself of *his* obligation to serve as a full committee member? Discuss.

Case 12-1   Wolfe Company Reorganization Study

The new president of the Wolfe Company, by the end of his first year, has come to realize that his organization is inefficient and confused, and that the controls are chaotic and inadequate. He sees four alternative approaches to his problem, as follows: (1) Set up a committee to study and recommend changes in the company's organization structure or control procedures; (2) turn the whole problem over to a consultant; (3) give the job to the treasurer (the treasurer has been wanting to set up an organization and control department); (4) hire a good staff assistant and let him work on the problem (possibly later he could head up an organization department, under either the controller or treasurer.)

· Wouldn't this be a good place to use a committee? Who should be on a committee for this purpose?

Case 12-2   The Unwilling Committee Member[3]

Once upon a prodigal time there was a manager who found himself spending four hours a week in a committee meeting where there was much sound and fury, and billows of blowing smoke, but no progress toward solving the problem that they met to consider. And after much frustration he began a thoughtful campaign to rid himself of what he considered to be an odious assignment.

1. He argued mightily and with masterfulness for a compromise solution that would give each committee member some of what he wanted, but there were too many who wanted more, and he was voted down.

2. He argued pleadingly and with passion that the problem should be referred up to a committee of executives who could approach it with a loftier view, but the executives, not having been born recently, would have none of this, and he was voted down.

3. He argued fiercely and with fanaticism for the committee to disband on the basis that the problem was insoluble, but the other members thought this would look bad to the executives, and anyway it was helpful for them to meet and keep each other up to date on items of fateful interest, besides which it used up half a day, and he was voted down.

4. He had his secretary start calling him out of the committee meetings after the first half-hour with fictitious problems, but his superior said it was

important for the department to be represented, and he should be there.

5. He established a regular short conference within his own group and timed it to start at the same time as the committee meeting, so he could at least be late, but his superior said the committee meeting was more important and had him change the time of his conference.

6. Finally he convinced his superior that the distractions of his job kept him from adequately representing the department on the committee and that a better committee job could be done by his ablest subordinate, who was thereupon appointed, with great fanfare but considerable resistance, to take the manager's place on the committee.

Moral: There is nothing like service on a committee to develop a man's initiative.

Or: If at first you don't succeed, delegate.

Endnotes

1. *Parkinson's Law,* by Northcote Parkinson (Houghton-Mifflin, 1957).
2. A good summary of committee strengths and weaknesses appears in, "How to Run a Meeting," by Antony Jay, *Harvard Business Review,* March-April 1976, pp. 43–57.
3. Copyrighted by Jonathan Morley, 1975. All rights reserved.

Suggested Supplementary Readings

Decker, Richard, and Ross H. Johnson. "How to Make Committees More Effective." *Management Review,* February 1976, pp. 34–40.

Meyer, Herbert E. "The Meeting Goers Lament," *Fortune,* 22 October 1979, pp. 94–102.

Murray, John V., Thomas J. Von der Embse, and H.A. Waggener. "Evaluating Disagreement in Committee Action." *Harvard Business Review,* May 1976, pp. 11–17.

Youngblood, Ed. "Use Staff Teams to Solve Management Problems." *Association Management* 29, No. 5 (1977) pp. 61–65.

Case for Section III   World-Wide Company

The World-Wide Company makes agricultural equipment and road grading equipment. Its $1.0 billion annual sales are derived four-fifths in the United States and one-fifth overseas, almost wholly in Europe. Both areas are growing but the European business is growing faster (20 percent a year) than that of the United States.

World-Wide-Europe makes a wide variety of equipment and is organized almost wholly on a geographic basis, with separate English, French and German divisions. Germany also serves Scandinavia and the Netherlands. France serves Italy and southern Europe. England serves all other overseas operations all over the world.

Each of these three divisions makes almost the whole of the World-Wide Company products including making or buying its own parts and sub-assemblies. In total, some 30,000 kinds of parts are used. Of these, each plant makes some 10,000, including most of the items used in volume. Some of the individual machines contain up to 10,000 parts and are sold for more than $100,000.

Although this geographic arrangement has seemed to work well on the surface, it has been uneconomical. Both parts and whole products cost 25 percent more to make in Europe than in the United States, largely because the volume of products made in each country is relatively small.

Because of this, the World-Wide Company sent Wallace Gore, a vice president, to Europe to look into improving the European situation. He called a meeting of the top men in World-Wide's overseas operations. In attendance were Wolfgang Friedricks, vice president of all overseas divisions, Pierre Voiriot, overseas vice president of marketing, Allen Summer, vice president of production, Hans Dierdorf, general manager of German operations, Guy Savoie, general manager in France, and Ian Whitehall, general manager of English operations.

Gore chaired the meeting and asked the group for its recommendations about what to do. He asked the others to consider, among the choices, the closing down of some or all of the making of parts in Europe and having them supplied from the United States, with complete products still to be assembled in Europe. He also suggested that this transfer of work could be carried farther and might include assembly being done in the United States. Other alternatives which might be considered were to "rationalize" production in Europe and to change over to a product-type operation where each product would be produced at one location only. Certain products would be made completely in Germany, others in France, etc.

Committees

There appeared to be several possibilities for carrying out rationalization if this were the course chosen. It could be done for parts only, or for parts and sub-assembly components, or it could be for complete products. Or it could be for new products as they phased in, allowing old products to continue to be made in several places until they phased out. Time, however, was very important since European operations were growing at a 20 percent a year rate. Costs were also important since the inefficient operations were surely costing several million dollars a year.

Voiriot spoke first. He pointed out several difficulties, the need to retool the several factories, the need to move machines between factories, and the difficulty in providing repair service parts which would need to be made on old tooling which would not be available in the new centralized factories. He also called attention to the probable need to move workers from one country to another, to train new workers, and the possibility that some locations might not have enough workers. He was also concerned about the lost production during the change-over period.

Whitehall agreed that there would be problems and called attention also to the greater costs of freight caused by long distance shipping and to the greater import duty costs.

Summer saw things differently. He came back to the high costs and inefficiencies which could not be improved much, if any, unless the operations were rationalized in some way. He pointed out the high cost of short production runs in the factories and to the fact that parts made in different locations didn't always fit perfectly, thus causing still more costs for their reworking. He also called attention to the scheduling problems for shipping back and forth and the high overheads from having all of the plants doing small volumes of the same business.

Dierdorf raised another objection. He pointed out that it helped sales if customers could be told that products were "Made in Germany by German workers." This also helped with government relations. Friedricks wondered if lower prices wouldn't compensate for this difficulty. Both men agreed, however, that rationalizing would make it harder to incorporate minor product design differences which would be needed in different countries. Dierdorf was also concerned about the possible layoffs which would result if an old product phased out and a new one were not assigned to his division to replace it. He was also concerned over the new skills their men might have to learn.

Savoie didn't like the possibility of his plant being locked into certain products and maybe seeing another division get some fine new product with a big future.

- Evaluate the various viewpoints expressed.
- What should World-Wide do?
- If you recommend a change, what would happen to the positions held by the men at this meeting? Would any of them have to make substantial changes in the work they would be called upon to do or to direct? How could such changes be made more acceptable to them?

Much of the study of organizations concerns people and how they work together. People, men and women, are the important factors in almost all organizations. Nonetheless, organizations differ greatly in their accomplishments even when they start with the same capabilities and the same resources and when they face the same opportunities. Some managers are better than others and consequently their organizations accomplish more.

Of the four chapters devoted to the organization's people, the first, Chapter 13, concerns the individuals who fill the organization's jobs. It considers how the organization's staffing needs are determined and how the positions are filled. The next two chapters, Chapters 14 and 15, consider the elusive factors of leadership and motivation and how effective leaders operate. Social scientists' findings on these subjects are reviewed.

The last chapter, Chapter 16, is devoted to organizational development. This term refers to present day attempts to improve organizations through the application of behavioral science theories as they apply to interpersonal and intergroup relationships.

Section Four

The Organization's People

Chapter 13:
Maintaining
the Human
Organization

Chapter 14:
Leadership

Chapter 15:
Motivation

Chapter 16:
Organization
Development

Objectives of Chapter Thirteen

1. To gain an appreciation of the importance of the need to plan for providing for the future managerial needs of organizations.

2. To look at the matter of how to recruit and develop people to fill the organization's managerial needs.

3. To study the methods available for developing managerial capability in managers on the way up.

4. To consider appraisal and the need to judge the performance of subordinates and the problems involved in the appraisal process.

Staffing: Maintaining the Human Organization

*Every French soldier
carries a marshall's baton
in his knapsack.*
Napoleon

Sixty years ago, General Motors was only a small factor in the American automobile market. Soon thereafter, under the direction of Alfred Sloan, General Motors outstripped Ford and became number one in the industry in the United States and in the world, a position it has held ever since. General Motors has, in fact, continually enlarged its share of the market until, for many years now, it has sold over half of all of the automobiles made in the United States.

During the nearly fifty years since Sloan's retirement and under Sloan's successors, thousands of lesser managers have come and gone. And through it all the company has prospered and grown almost without interruption. The changes in General Motors' managers, both at the top and in the middle, did not hurt nor slow down the company *because the company trained and brought on new managers all the time to replace the older managers who moved on.*

One of management's biggest jobs in every organization is the choosing and preparation of tomorrow's managers so that the organization will, in the future, be staffed by well-qualified managers. This chapter will deal with how to build and maintain the human organization.

The discussion in this chapter will be largely concerned with how large organizations maintain their staffs since most employees work for relatively large organizations. Organizations as small as one hundred employees may have to hire no more than twenty new employees a year and only one or two employees at most will be promoted to higher jobs in a year. This volume of hiring and promotion does not permit them to use very formal or sophisticated procedures even though they, as well as large organizations, need to carry on good human relations practices and to know about and obey all laws relating to employment.

The job of providing for tomorrow's managers, in organizations of all sizes, includes selecting, placing, training, motivating, and keeping good talent. And, although developing tomorrow's managers will be discussed in this chapter as if it were a separate subject, managers are actually developed as they learn to do all of the things discussed in this book. When a manager plans, he ought also to be showing his subordinates how to plan. When he makes decisions and delegates work, he ought also to be showing his subordinates how to do these things. And, when he appraises the work of his subordinates, he should also be showing *them* how to appraise *their* subordinates, too.

Not surprisingly, many, perhaps most, middle-level managers are not much interested in training their subordinates to become managers. Probably most middle-level managers are busy doing their day-to-day work; they are comfortable on their jobs and are getting along well. They train their subordinates well enough for them to do a reasonable subordinate job, and there they stop. Their subordinates don't need any more training in order to do their present jobs well and some managers don't want to develop their subordinates into rivals for their jobs.

Consequently, very little conscious training of subordinates to become better managers will occur unless top managers insist that it be done. In order to motivate middle- and lower-level managers to develop their subordinates and to get them ready for promotion, Sylvania Electronics and Otis Elevator are two companies among many which rate managers who do this higher than managers who do not try to develop subordinates. A top Otis official says, "We don't look too kindly on a department head who never has anyone ready for promotion when there is an opening." Such a policy would surely motivate ambitious middle level managers to try to train one or two of their subordinates and get them ready for promotion.

Planning the Future Managerial Organization

Determining Future Managerial Needs. The first step in planning for the organization's future management needs is to find out how many and what kinds of managerial jobs will exist in the years ahead and when they will need to be filled (see Figure 13-1). In most organizations, a projection of managerial job openings in the next five or ten years will show that a surprising number of managers will be needed. In ten years, almost all of the managers who are now over fifty-five years of age and all of those now over sixty will be gone because of deaths, resignations, retirements, and possibly an occasional dismissal. Not only that, but attrition will also remove a few of today's still younger managers.

In addition, the organization's planners need to consider the company's probable growth. Ten years from now, most of today's business organizations will be larger than they are now and will need more managers than they have today. Allowing for growth, the total number of new managers, in many companies will, in the next ten years, be more than one-third as many as there are now. Admittedly, staffing planners cannot foresee very accurately the directions of future growth but they can get some idea of how many and what kinds of managers will be needed.

Interests and Capabilities of the Personnel Available. The second step in the planning of future managerial requirements is to make an audit of the capabilities and the interests of today's managers in middle and lower levels. Curiously, most organizations do keep a record of the experience and training of their present managers but they do not investigate nor keep any record of the interests of today's managers. They don't know their ambitions.

Implementing Planning for Tomorrow's Managers. The third step in planning

for the organization's future managerial needs is to match up (in the plan) today's younger managers with future higher level jobs. The planners can then see what capabilities these younger managers now have and what they will still need to develop in order to be ready for promotion when the time comes. The planners can then lay out programs for these people which will include transfers and promotions to certain jobs so that, as the years go by, these people will develop the added capabilities which will be needed when they move up.

Such a survey will also reveal places where there are no likely prospects now in the organization and where it will become necessary to recruit candidates from the outside.

All of this planning can be laid out neatly on paper but in practice the process is much less precise. People develop differently from the planners' expectations. Openings do not develop on any set schedule; the requirements of jobs to be filled change. And the number of jobs to be filled changes with the company's growth or lack of growth. Sometimes one or more of the promising young prospects resigns. The whole process of planning for staffing an organization's future needs is quite unstructured.

Position Descriptions and Job Classifications

All organizations of any size have several levels of departments and hierarchies of managers in charge of these departments. Nearly all such organizations also keep a file of written position descriptions covering the job content of every job in their organizations, from the bottom up, including all managerial jobs.

For higher-level jobs, these are statements of missions or descriptions of the desired conditions to be brought about. As one goes down through the organization, posi-

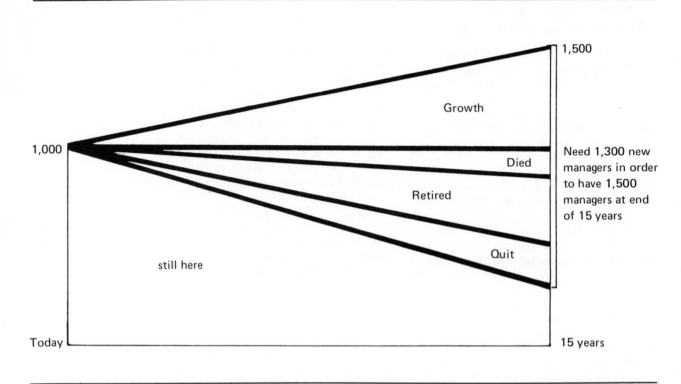

Figure 13-1
One large company's forecast of its managerial manpower needs for the next fifteen years, during which the company is expected to grow by 50 per cent. It would seem, at first glance, that 500 more managers would be needed to expand its present managerial workforce from 1,000 to 1,500. But, instead, because of attrition, the company will have to provide for 1,300 more managers.

tion descriptions change more into lists of duties. In general, position descriptions contain statements of purpose, responsibility, and authority of each position and its relationships to other jobs. Job descriptions also list the educational and experience requirements needed by the person filling the job.

Position and job descriptions serve several purposes:

· They provide a basis for planning organizational staffing needs. We have seen that personnel planners need to develop a

list of expected future job openings which will need filling. But a list of job titles is not very helpful to them. They need to know what *work* needs to be done on each job and what educational and experience qualifications future incumbents will need to have. Position descriptions help fill this need. Usually this is done by having a "job specification" (described below) made out after the job description has been made up.

· Position descriptions help new employees on jobs because they tell them what they are supposed to do. Written position descriptions also help clarify organizational relationships so people know who reports to whom. At the managerial level, position descriptions also help the manager when he is in doubt about the limits of his authority. He can consult his position description and find out what he is authorized to do.

· Position descriptions are used in job evaluation, which in turn, determines the organization's pay structure.

Job evaluation, in government work, uses a graded set of generalized job descriptions. Some ten different grades are set apart by differing definitions of job responsibility and complexity. Low grades are simple jobs and high grades are more difficult and more responsible jobs. Each grade has a specified pay rate.

Then, one by one, individual jobs are compared to these grade definitions to see which one the job fits into. In this process, the job description *is essentially the job* while the comparisons are being made. When a job has been slotted into a grade, its pay rate is the rate for that grade. Often each grade has a specified pay range instead of an individual pay rate. Within the range, each person is paid according to his performance or in accord with his time on his present job.

The job evaluation process is usually different in businesses. Again the description is basic. It is compared to several factors. Each factor is subdivided into, perhaps, five degrees and points are awarded to the job according to the degree which fits the job. A job might, for example, receive ten points for its skill requirements and three points for its physical effort requirements. Usually there are ten or so factors, each of which can earn credit for the job in the form of points. The sum of a job's points from all of the factors produces a total which puts the job into a wage class for all jobs with similar point totals.

Weaknesses of Position Descriptions. Written position descriptions are not wholly adequate for the uses to which they are put. Among their weaknesses are the following:

· It is not possible to capture the full essence of higher-level jobs in words. The position description cannot fully describe such jobs.

· Descriptions tend to stay frozen whereas job content is often dynamic. Thus, descriptions tend to become out-of-phase with actual jobs.

· People may feel restricted by job descriptions. ("That's not my responsibility, it is not in my job description.") They feel that they ought not to do work not specifically listed because the list covers their responsibilities and authority.

This difficulty is often a real stumbling block to flexible action at bottom levels. Factory hourly paid workers, railroad workers, carpenters, and others in many bottom level groups won't do any work beyond their written list of duties. Or, if they do, they want extra pay (at excessive rates). Nor will they allow anyone else to perform any of "their" duties.

· Written position descriptions are not very helpful as job instructions. People soon learn their jobs.

· People who write position descriptions often work for the departments where such descriptions are to be used. Often this results in jobs (as written) being "upgraded by description" (magnified so that they will qualify for higher pay). A typist becomes a "word processor," and a garbage collector becomes a "sanitary engineer." This practice is said to be common in the Federal Civil Service.

Job Specifications. To be of most use in personnel work, a job description needs to be translated into a "job specification." A description tells what the job is. A specification tells what kind of a person is needed on the job.

If a job candidate is to receive his or her complete training on the job, the specification tells what underlying capabilities are needed. A laborer needs to be strong. A prospective assembler of television sets needs to have manual dexterity, and an inspector needs to have good eyes.

If a job candidate is to come to the job already trained, the specification tells what the job's training and experience requirements are. An accountant needs to know accounting and perhaps to hold a college degree in accounting. An electrician needs to know about electricity and perhaps to be licensed. A typist needs to be able to type.

With both job descriptions and job specifications as tools, the people in the personnel department can do a better job of recruiting and placing new people on jobs than if they did not have this information.

Selecting Managerial Prospects

Today's managers should want to select promising candidates for tomorrow's managerial jobs. This raises a question of how today's managers can go about picking good future managers when they hire twenty or twenty-five year old men and women at the start of their careers. It is not easy to look at a young person today and see in him a middle or higher-level manager thirty years later.

Perhaps Napoleon was not quite right when he said, "Every French soldier carries a marshall's baton in his knapsack." Perhaps not everyone has it in him to go clear to the top. But it is probably true that quite a few people have in them, if given the opportunity, the ability to advance up the

managerial ladder. So the attempt should be made to select people with potential.

What should today's manager be looking for when he hires a new employee who he hopes has managerial potential? He should look for people with characteristics generally thought to be common in leaders and less common in followers. These characteristics are considered in Chapter 14 on Leadership. Briefly, they are:

- Ambition: strong task orientation.
- Desire to manage: willingness to assume responsibility.
- Ability to communicate: expresses himself well.
- Analytical ability: intelligent, sees essentials.
- Emotional stability: dependable, does not get overwhelmed.
- Integrity: honesty and loyalty.

It would help, too, for applicants to have training and experience in the work areas where they will be assigned initially to work since promotions usually go to people who succeed in the areas where they work.

Unfortunately, candidates having these characteristics or traits are not thereby guaranteed to become better leaders. As we will see in Chapter 14, leaders do have these characteristics a little more often than do other people but these traits are also often found in non-leaders as well. Unfortunately, too, there is no good way of finding out if job applicants have these characteristics. Interviews and psychological tests help some in the selection process, but neither alone nor together are they really good predictors of an applicant's future success on the job.

Today's anti-invasion-of-privacy regulations prevent prospective employers from asking many of the questions they would like to ask by way of getting an insight into the applicant's character. An interviewer cannot ask, for example, if a person owns his own house, if he pays his bills, or if he has ever served a jail sentence. An interviewer can ask, however, where the applicant has worked and what kind of work he did and he can write to the applicant's former employers to verify these statements.

Psychological Tests. Personnel departments have used psychological tests for many years to help in selection and promotion. (See Figure 13-2) In the case of applicants for employment, practically nothing is known about an applicant's qualifications other than what he tells about himself and that is not very reliable evidence. Since interviewers are not allowed to ask very many questions of a job applicant, psychological tests, which reveal a little more about the applicant, have considerable appeal.

There are limitations, however, to the help that tests can give. In order to be useful as aids in predicting a person's probable success on a job, tests need to be tailored to the job and their reliability as predictors of success validated. Since there are so many kinds of jobs, such special tailoring and validation are not wholly possible.

In the early 1970s, tests came under fire from Federal courts. People denied job opportunities because of low test scores sued in courts claiming illegal discrimination on the basis that the tests did not measure anything relevant to probable job success. In general, the courts have agreed. Now, general intelligence tests may *not* be used as part of either the employment process or the promotion process. Consequently, such tests are used less often.

Filling Government Positions. The heads of government departments are often political appointees whose chief qualification is that they supported the successful candidate for elective office. What we say here about the need to try to pick people who will make good administrators just does not apply.

Furthermore, politically appointed heads have to fill at least a certain number of the jobs in their departments with other loyal followers of the elected candidate. Patronage dictates the choice in many instances. Most state highway departments all over the

	YES	NO	ALMOST ALWAYS	ALMOST ALWAYS
1. Do ideas run through your head that keep you awake?	☐	☐	☐	☐
2. Does it bother you to have people watch you while you work?	☐	☐	☐	☐
3. Can you express yourself better in writing than in talking?	☐	☐	☐	☐
4. Do you believe in God but believe that some people make much fuss over religion?	☐	☐	☐	☐

	ALMOST ALWAYS	FRE-QUENTLY	RARELY	ALMOST NEVER
5. Are you tired when you wake up in the morning? Check: almost always, frequently, rarely, almost never.	☐	☐	☐	☐
6. Do you try to persuade people to do things? Check: almost always, frequently, rarely, almost never.	☐	☐	☐	☐

Figure 13-2
Part of a psychological test. For these particular questions, the answers "no," "no," "no," "yes," "almost never," and "almost always," get high scores. Questions 1, 2, and 5, are part of a set of several questions interspersed in other places in the examination which are intended to reveal a person's emotional stability. Question 3 is one of several designed to reveal a person's stability. Question 4 is a "business values" question and number 6 has to do with self-confidence.

Maintaining the Human Organization

United States, are filled with workers whose work for the winning party is rewarded by giving them jobs in the highway department.[1]

Recruiting Future Managerial Prospects. We return now to business organizations. Since the abilities of every organization's personnel are limited to the innate capabilities of the people it recruits plus the improvement which comes from their training, experience, and maturity, recruitment is fundamental.

Small companies usually cannot pay much attention to a twenty year old applicant's future managerial capabilities when they hire someone to fill a low-level job. Almost everyone they hire is for a low-level entry job and doing low-level work is all that will be required of such recruits for many years to come. Promotions are infrequent.

Large organizations can be more forward-looking in their recruitment. Most low-level jobs are filled by hiring people with only the requirements of these jobs in mind. Ultimately, a few of these people advance into upper levels through promotion. But the normal on-the-job type of experience and growth does not equip such people for high level managerial jobs.

It is here that large companies can be more forward-looking. Specialized college training helps improve the managerial capabilities of those fortunate enough to get such training. Consequently, most large companies try to recruit enough young people right out of college to fill all of the expected future managerial needs plus a few extras to cover losses from turnover. Sometimes these trainees are given brief experience on bottom-level jobs but they are soon given more responsible assignments.

Recruiting Middle- and Top-Level Personnel. Sometimes, although only infrequently, people are hired for middle-level jobs. And, once in a while, an executive is recruited from the outside for a top job.

It might seem that established managers willing to move would be the less capable ones who can't get along where they are. Managers who are willing to move are, however, often quite capable people who would like to move up faster than they can where they are. Sometimes personality clashes cause a capable manager to be willing to move and sometimes capable young managers bump their heads on a ceiling. Their own bosses are not much older than they are so their promotional prospects are dim.

It is often possible to take good prospects away from even the best companies because they often develop more capable managers than they have openings for. Such companies as IBM (more than 100 companies are said to have presidents who are IBM "alumni") and General Electric actually train a good many managers for other companies.

Marketplace Limitations to Staffing. The discussion so far has more or less assumed that an organization's high-level managers have it in their power to decide how they want to be staffed, and that they can then staff the organization with the number and kind of subordinates they want.

Although this is true, it is at the same time too mechanistic a view. Newspapers are usually full of help wanted advertisements, particularly for employees, including managers, with specific skills. (See Figure 13-3) No end of organizations of all kinds are continually trying to hire more people for work of various kinds. This means that most of the time they are operating without the number and kind of employees that their managers think they need.

It is never altogether clear in any organization exactly how many people are actually needed because usually the work is being done today in some fashion without the people who are being sought. One or more additional employees are felt to be needed either because it is believed that without them the work is being inadequately done or that certain desirable work is not being done at all from the lack of someone to do it. Nevertheless, the organization is func-

The Organization's People

Figure 13-3

tioning, so the need for more employees is a "decided" need. Certain managers have decided that more personnel are needed.

On the supply side, it may well prove that the recruitment efforts fail and that not enough new employees of the kind wanted can be hired. In such cases, either the organization continues to get along shorthanded, as its managers see it, or they hire less well qualified people. In either case, the work is not done as well as the managers would like.

Rarely do candidates, even those carefully selected and trained, fit jobs perfectly. Just as a person has to build his house out of the bricks he has or can get, so does a manager have to build his organization out of the people he has or can get and hold. He

may have to put a square peg in a round hole or vice versa. And if he has to put a square peg in a round hole, he makes the peg a little rounder and the hole a little squarer. No organization can escape having to live with some imperfect matching of employees and jobs. Perhaps it would be well for the superior to be an optimistic type; if he is he may give people with known limitations opportunities to show what they can do. Usually some of them develop better than expected.

The "Peter Principle." Laurence Peter says that, because people succeed on lower jobs, they get promoted to higher jobs from where, if they again perform well, they are again promoted up another step. This goes on until they are promoted to jobs beyond their ability to perform. Peter's point is

Maintaining the Human Organization

true sometimes. People with proven competence in one limited area are promoted into jobs requiring broad general capabilities which they don't have.[2]

Peter's idea rests on the assumption that capable people are scarce and that they do not grow and develop. But there is enough truth in his idea that high-level managers need to try to avoid promoting people beyond their depth. They need to appraise a managerial job candidate's prospective capabilities on the new job as well as they can and not rely wholly on how well he performed on his past lower-level jobs.

Selecting Employees to Promote. When a vacancy occurs in a managerial position, the superior should want, of course, to promote the man or woman who will do the best on the job to be filled. This is, however, a deceptively simple statement. It overlooks rewarding employees for what they have done. If a choice has to be made between two people, one of whom is likely to do the job a little better but the other is a longer-service employee who has done a good job where he is now, it may be better to promote the longer-service employee as a reward, lest people conclude that doing a good job over a period of time doesn't count.

But, for highly important jobs, expected superior performance should be put ahead of long service. Sometimes expected superior performance is the ability to get along with people and to get them to cooperate with each other.

When General Eisenhower was made head of all European forces of the Allies in World War II, he was, partly because of his ability to get along with people and to get them to work together, jumped over at least forty other generals who were ahead of him in rank and seniority.

Surely, some of the others were equal to or possibly were better strategists and tacticians than Eisenhower, but his ability to get people to work together smoothly caused him to be chosen. This was a most important ability when the job was to get full cooperation from generals of armies of other countries who were used to being first in command to follow the orders of a supreme commander from another country.

Nor are managers wholly free to choose the person they want in matters of hiring and promotion. Because of discriminatory practices in past years, there are few blacks or women in the ranks of management. This has caused programs of "affirmative action" to grow up, meaning that discrimination *in favor* of such groups is to be practiced now in order to remedy the disparity in higher-level jobs in the future.

Thus, the need to be fair to minorities and to give them equal opportunities has added a new dimension to both hiring and promotion. A minority candidate may need to be chosen unless he or she is obviously unqualified and is unlikely to become qualified with reasonable training. The failure to promote such a person may have to be defended in court if the unpromoted employee claims that it was because he was a member of a minority group. Consequently, today's promotion process is different and more complicated than it used to be. It must be more formally done and backed up by records and cannot be left up to department heads to carry out as they see fit.

Management by objectives is reported to be used extensively as a basis of appraisal because it results in reasonably objective appraisals.[3] Promotions based on MBO appraisals are, therefore, reasonably objective.

Legal restrictions are not the only factors which complicate the problem of trying to build up the quality of the organization's people. The statement, "We try to promote the employee who will do the best job," implies that superiors think that they can tell which one will do the best job. Yet, in almost all cases, none of the candidates has done the job which is open. When a person is promoted, his superior is forecasting that he will do well on a job he has never done before. Even promotions to jobs up only one level are usually promotions to jobs whose content is substantially different from the subordinate's old job.

The Cloning Tendency. It is unfortunate that probably most of us have a tendency to think well of people who are like us. We think that they are more capable. Managers, too, like subordinates who fit in well and who are usually like them in personality and capabilities. Over a period of time this has a cloning effect which works against the promotion of people who are different. This is unfortunate since the people who are different might contribute more to the organization's future well-being than the look-alikes who get promoted.

Training

Over the years, successful managers become effective because of what they learn — and most of this knowledge comes from what they have learned on the job through experience or from being coached or from organization training programs. Their early formal training, even college training, shrinks in importance as the years go by. It is important to recognize that their managerial capability can be improved considerably through further training. (See figure 13-4)

Most companies put a great deal of emphasis on the need to train managers, but, in fact, except in a small number of very large companies, very little formal training goes on. And where it does go on, it is usu-

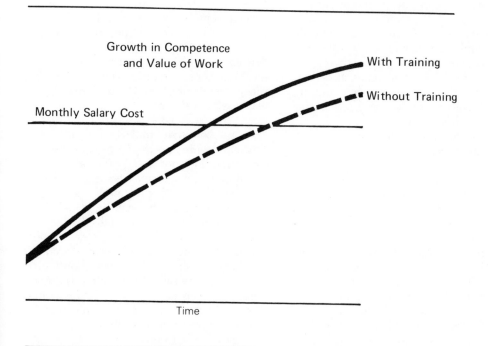

Growth in Competence
and Value of Work

With Training

Without Training

Monthly Salary Cost

Time

Figure 13-4
Relationship between the growth in a newly appointed manager's cost and his competence and value to the organization, with and without training.

Maintaining the Human Organization

ally in the order of magnitude of participation in a one- or two-week training seminar at the company's central education center. Very few managers participate in as many as two such programs during their entire careers as managers.[4]

The situation is worse in government work. Derek Bok, president of Harvard University, says that very few administrators in government work receive any serious training at all in administering their organizations.[5]

Training programs. Today it is popular to send young men and women with managerial promise to executive training programs conducted by universities and other groups for additional training. In these seminars the young manager rubs shoulders with managers from other companies and hears different viewpoints about various problems. Just what people get out of such courses is hard to determine but top officials seem to think that they have real value because companies continue to send their managers to them. A few companies, however, do not send their people to such training programs. They are afraid that "if you train them, you will lose them."

Companies located in metropolitan areas where colleges and universities offer evening courses usually support such training opportunities by paying tuition costs for all of their employees who enroll for courses which will help their development. This is a valuable aid in the training of people with access to such courses.

On-The-Job-Training. Most training, at all levels, is on-the-job training and coaching. In order for prospective higher-level managers to get varied experience, they can be put on varied jobs on the way up and can be coached so they will learn as much as possible. Ideally, this varied work should include experience in different functional work, in line and staff work, with different products, and with different geographical areas. Varied experience becomes a substitute for training as such.

On-the-job training sounds better than it often is. Often, all that a person learns on the job is how the work is being done. The method introduces no new element. A trainee does not learn anything about other ways that work could be done, or if it could be done better.

A difficulty is that no one in the organization, not even the president, is himself capable of training people for jobs which require specialized knowledge such as is needed by a purchasing agent, a personnel director, or a controller. Nor can a city mayor train his police chief or the head of the city's water works. On-the-job training is limited to the capabilities of the hierarchical superior who, in many cases, does not have any superior expertise relevant to the subordinate's job.

Self-Development. Some high-level managers make a big point of "self-development" as a way of developing future managers. They like to think that an energetic young employee will see to it that he develops himself. But since neither middle-level nor lower-level managers can transfer themselves around from job to job in order to learn, self-development has limitations.

Actually, when a superior says that it is up to subordinates to develop themselves, this may be only an excuse because the organization does not do any training. Possibly, however, a superior who says this has a more productive idea in mind. As we will say in Chapter 17, he may be thinking of subordinates developing the jobs they are on in maximum ways. What people do on jobs depends upon what they preceive as needing doing. A superior who talks about self-development by subordinates often is thinking about their seeing the need for doing things and then doing them. This kind of self-development makes them into better managers in the future.

Breadth Versus Specialties. The head of every organization has to be concerned with many different kinds of activities. The head of a manufacturing company has to administer production, sales, finance, and a variety of other specialized activities.

In order for him to be able to direct all of these diverse kinds of work, the chief executive officer needs to have breadth. He needs to become a "generalist," and to give up being a "specialist." He needs to know something about all of the different areas under his direction, although obviously, he cannot know as much about each specialized area as the heads of the individual specialized areas. But, if he has a reasonable acquaintance with the work of these subject areas, then, when he makes decisions, he will be able to appreciate the probable consequences in the various parts of the organization.

The process of becoming a generalist usually means, in the case of technically trained people, their learning to think more about people than about things. And they have to learn to think about the financial consequences of their actions.

Appraisal

High-level managers always need to appraise the *work* of their subordinates to see if the organization's goals are being accomplished. But *work* is done by the organization's people so appraisal becomes also the appraisal of the accomplishments of *people*, principally subordinate managers.

Appraisal is an evaluation process which has dual purposes:

First, it evaluates performance so that corrective actions can be taken if need be. Appraisal calls attention to areas where subordinates are not doing well and where the superior may be able to help them to do better and at the same time to develop into better managers.

Second, appraisal becomes the judgment of the quality of the performance of subordinates for reward-penalty purposes. Some subordinates will, on the basis of the appraisals of their work, receive pay raises and some will be promoted when the opportunity arises.

Appraisal is a management function which should always be consciously done because superiors have to act on the basis of appraisals. Both remedial actions and the reward-penalty system rest on appraisals.

Appraisals, if they are favorable, should give satisfaction to subordinates who then find out that their superior thinks well of their work. Curiously, many managers find it hard to tell a subordinate that he is doing a good job. They feel that the subordinate is being paid for doing his work and should not need praise besides.

Unfortunately, except in the case of excellent accomplishment, appraisal always contains a negative element. Any time a supervisor judges the work of a subordinate as being anything less than entirely satisfactory, this is negative and puts the superior into mental conflict with the subordinate. A subordinate whose accomplishment has been judged to be even slightly unsatisfactory is put on the defensive and this tends to tear down his ego and to discourage his future performance.

Perhaps this is one reason why so many managers shrink from appraising. It is so hard to accentuate the positive while actually calling attention to shortcomings. Showing a subordinate how to do better, even though this is intended to be a positive action and to be helpful, tends to downgrade the subordinate's past accomplishments. Appraisal needs to be done most carefully lest the harm it does to the organization's people outweighs the benefits.

In our discussions of appraisal we have assumed that all superiors want to have good subordinates and to promote their best performers. But this is not always so. Some managers do not want too much independence in their subordinates, preferring instead, more pedestrian don't-upset-the-apple-cart people. And they certainly do not want to promote capable subordinates into jobs where they will become rivals for their jobs. (Northcote Parkinson, many years ago, put this idea even more strongly. He said that managers select subordinates who are less smart than themselves in order not to develop rivals for their own jobs. As a consequence, as the years go by, organizations grow more stupid.)[6]

If very many managers are like this, then the matter of appraisal becomes, in fact, something quite different from choosing and promoting the most capable person. Managers who want to carry on without any disturbance to their usual ways of managing may very well rate plodding-along subordinates above those who accomplish more.

"Team players" who will be unquestionably loyal to the superior may also be chosen over more capable mavericks. John De Lorean reported that during his time as a vice president of General Motors, the emphasis on "team players" at the top was so strong that there were several instances where an "unobvious" candidate was picked for a top job. (The "unobvious" candidate was unobvious to his peers on the basis of their judgment of his capabilities.)[7]

The Appraisal Process

Appraisal is wholly a human activity. When one person judges the work of another person it is true that, just as beauty is in the eye of the beholder, so appraisal is in the eye of the appraiser. It is therefore incumbent on a subordinate who wants to get a good appraisal to try to do his work well *as the appraiser (almost always his superior) sees well done work.*

A difficulty with appraisal is that the measures of performance almost always fall short of reporting on a subordinate's whole performance. It is just not possible to design a report which will capture the full essence of a subordinate manager's accomplishment. Higher-level managers should, when appraising a subordinate's performance, not judge it wholly on the basis of the incomplete information provided by the reports.

Another appraisal problem concerns how to evaluate uneven performance. There are many facets, some of which are more important than others, to the jobs of subordinates and a subordinate may do well on some parts of his job and less well on other parts. A factory supervisor may do a fine job of producing quality products but he overspends his budget and does not get orders out on time. Should he be judged to have done well? Superiors have to weigh these uneven accomplishments together in order to arrive at an overall appraisal of a subordinate's performance.

There is also a danger of the "halo" effect operating. Because a higher-level manager is impressed with the subordinate's performance in certain directions, he concludes that he is good in all directions. It is also difficult to avoid overemphasis on recent happenings. Good or poor recent performance is likely to weigh more heavily than it should.

Job activities also vary from day to day. Some days a subordinate manager spends his time taking care of things which go wrong and putting out fires. During such days, although he works hard at getting things done, he doesn't get far. Other days go better. Also, in-process accomplishment doesn't show. What is counted is end-accomplishment. Work may be moving along in process for days but it only shows as accomplishment at its completion. Assuming that a manager always puts in the same effort, some days it shows up in accomplishment but not on other days.

Although these several difficulties stand in the way of perfect or even intelligent appraisals, superiors cannot escape having to make appraisals as best they can and acting on them.

Reluctant Appraisers. Partly because appraising is difficult to do, many managers do not like to do it. They don't like to be put in the position of having to judge, in a formal way, the work of their subordinates. They don't like to "play God." Not only is it distasteful to have to judge a subordinate's performance as being mediocre, but such a judgment reflects on themselves because it is part of every superior's job to develop his subordinates. Besides this, a judgment that a subordinate falls short of what he should have accomplished implies that the superior should now try to show him how to improve. And again, this is something which many superiors do not like to work at. Often they don't know enough about their subordinate's job to help him do better.

These tendencies to shirk the job of appraising are most unfortunate because the measurement-reward system is of great importance to the organization. It is also unfortunate when superiors do not see the appraisal process as an opportunity to work more closely with their subordinates and to try to upgrade their capabilities. How well superiors appraise has much to do with the determination of the organizational climate and with the development (or the lack of development) of motivation in the minds of subordinates.

Appraisal Interviews. In some organizations, managers are expected to have an appraisal interview with each of their subordinates once a year. During this interview, the manager is supposed to discuss with the subordinate his performance and his strengths and weaknesses. Such interviews,

common in the Federal government, are less common in business.

Appraisal interviews can be harrowing experiences. A person on the receiving end of such an interview hears all about his faults and shortcomings. It is true that a competent superior will also praise his strong points and discuss with him how the two of them can work together to improve his weaknesses. But unless the superior is very skillful, this doesn't nearly repair the hurt to a subordinate's ego that calling attention to his weaknesses inflicts. Going through the furnace refines metals and makes them purer, but going through an appraisal interview often flattens a person's ego and leaves him limp. It is unfortunate that managers who have to conduct such interviews are often poorly qualified to do the job. Many of them are quite unappreciative of how the interview sounds to the person on the receiving end.

Yet it is true that some subordinates need to be brought up short once in a while. Sometimes they don't even know that they are doing poorly, in which case they probably won't do better unless the superior tells them that their performance is unsatisfactory. Once they appreciate this they may well be receptive to suggestions from the superior about how to improve.

Summary

One of management's most important jobs, not always recognized as such, is to provide for its own replacement, and to be constantly bringing on capable junior managers as replacements.

The perpetuation of the organization's effectiveness is heavily dependent on its most capable men and women being selected and promoted to managerial positions. The choosing of these people is too important a responsibility to be left to chance. If an organization does not plan its future manpower requirements, then its future high-level managers will be those who were, years ago, given a promotion because lower-level managers liked their work. Given this start, they received further promotions. Such a method is too haphazard a way to insure that the organization's managers in the future will be capable and well-trained.

Consequently, most large companies have a high-level staff department make up plans showing future executive needs. They also make up inventories of the young people coming up and of their capabilities and their interests. Then, as openings arise, the best prospects for future high-level jobs are moved around and put into spots where they will gain the best experience to equip them for later promotion to high level positions.

But, in order to plan future managerial needs, the personnel staff needs to have reference to written position descriptions so they will know what kinds of training and experience prospective future managers will need. These position descriptions are at the same time the basis for job evaluation which sets wage and salary scales for jobs.

Appraisal, formal or informal, goes on all the time in every organization. Superiors are, consciously or unconsciously, always judging their subordinates. As a consequence of these appraisals, certain members of the organization are given pay raises and some are given promotions to higher jobs. There is need, therefore, for appraising to be done consciously and not haphazardly. Managers should consider it to be part of their jobs, and a very important part of their jobs, to appraise their subordinates as accurately as they can.

Review Questions

1. The text reports that one of management's biggest jobs is to prepare subordinates so that the organization will, in the future, be staffed with well-qualified managers. But the text also reports that many, perhaps most, managers do very little to train their subordinates in managerial matters. Why is this and what should be done about it? Discuss.

2. What three steps are essential to a good program of planning an organization's future managerial staffing needs? Are there problems here? Discuss.

3. Are position descriptions worth their cost? Discuss the pros and cons.

4. The company's policy is to promote the people who will do the best jobs. How can this policy be carried out?

5. Discuss the place that psychological tests can fill in the work of staffing the organization. Consider both the strengths and weaknesses of such tests.

6. Most people agree that high-level managers need to be "generalists" rather than "specialists." How can an organization go about training managers so that they will be good generalists?

7. The American Telephone & Telegraph Company tells its young trainees, "It is your personal responsibility to make sure that you develop yourselves." How can an employee train himself for higher-up positions?

8. Discuss the problems involved in appraising managers. What should a high-level manager do in order to be sure that appraisal is being well done in lower echelons?

Questions for Analysis and Discussion

1. Do you, as a student, have any good professors? How did you arrive at your appraisals of your professors? Do your ratings agree with those of the student sitting next to you? How can a college dean tell who his good professors are?

2. A General Electric policy says that, "Raises and promotions are to be based on merit, in proportion to the individual's contribution." How does a top manager determine merit and the value of an individual's contribution?

3. "We can't make John president because he's too effective as our sales vice president. While we're breaking in his replacement, our marketing position might slip. We'll have to go outside for our new president. Each of our vice presidents is a top person, but a specialist." How can an organization avoid such difficulties?

4. In order for operations to proceed, subordinates have to become followers, a role in which they stay for years. Yet, once in a while, one of them suddenly becomes the new head of a department and so needs to become a leader and an innovator. Isn't it asking too much for people to be followers and prospective leaders at the same time?

5. It is pretty well agreed that narrow specialization in top managers will keep them from being able to do the best job. Yet people have to advance upward to the top in areas of specialty. How can a company ever produce good top managers who are generalists rather than specialists?

6. The idea of training by coaching by the superior does not always work out very well. Often the superior does not want to do it and he doesn't really see any need for it. Furthermore, he really doesn't know enough about most of the jobs under his jurisdiction to be able to do a very good job. And, in any case, he is a busy person and just doesn't have much time to devote to this work. Discuss.

7. Most large companies have their principal offices in a large metropolitan center but some do not (Maytag in Newton, Iowa; Dow Chemical in Midland, Michigan; Caterpillar Tractor in Peoria, Illinois; etc.). Is there any merit in being located "where the action is"? Can a company's managers stay sharp in the hinterlands?

8. "We move our people around a lot. This breaks up their provincial interests in local activities and strengthens their ties to the organization." Should an organization try to destroy people's roots, leaving them with only the organization?

9. Discussing his company's appraisal method, an engineer said, "If your supervisor comes to believe that you are worth four points less than someone else and he begins to treat you that way, it's very hard to fight. You can tell yourself that you are still a good engineer, but you've got to have a very strong ego if your supervisor tells you that you are 20 percent less effective this year than last. If he continues to lower your rating, sooner or later it gets to you." The president hears about this comment. What should he do?

10. After returning from a conference at an Eastern university, the professor met a colleague who had attended the university as a graduate student. The first professor said, "While there I met Professor Porter, whom I believe you know." "Yes," answered the colleague, "and a very capable man he is. He is a great asset to the school." Later in the day, the professor met another colleague who had at one time taught at the Eastern University. Again he said, "While there I met Professor Porter, whom I believe you know." "Yes," answered the colleague, "and I never did understand how he ever got promoted. He impressed me as one of the weakest men there." Discuss this from the viewpoint of appraisal.

11. "When managers try to identify areas where subordinates can improve, this causes those being appraised to become defensive. They may even try *less* hard to improve in the criticized areas. Defensiveness should be expected since the manager, in discussing his appraisal of a subordinate's performance with him, is automatically cast in the role of judge and the subordinate becomes the defendant. The subordinate's defensiveness is, in effect, a denial of responsibility for the shortcoming cited. If, in the future he improved, this would be negating the validity of the defense." How can a manager appraise yet not have this happen?

12. Engineers and scientists are often said to think that managerial work is trivial and requires less expertise than their own work. Is this so? If so, should a higher-level manager do anything about this? What?

Case 13-1   Training at Genessee Tire

After graduation from a well known business school, Harry Davis went to work for the Genessee Tire Company. This company, with 2,000 employees, was small compared to the giants of the tire industry but nevertheless had managed to survive by emphasizing quality. Automobile tires made up most of its business but the company also made rubber heels and soles for shoes, rubber belting, and numerous other items such as bathing caps and rubber cushioning parts for automobile companies.

After a short time on a piece-work job in the factory, Davis was transferred into the office. There, his first assignment was in production control and scheduling. After one year on this work he was transferred to the time-study department by his superior, Harold Stevenson, who had charge of both of these departments.

After two years of time-study experience, Davis thought that he might learn more if he could get some cost accounting experience. Accordingly, he asked Stevenson if he could get transferred to the cost accounting department. Stevenson's reply was a surprise to Davis, "Why, Harry, what's the matter with the work here? Don't you like it here? Haven't I treated you right? If you have had any complaints why haven't you told me?"

• Discuss.

Case 13-2   The Promotion Choice

Unexpectedly, the head of a major department has had to resign because of a heart attack. You have to choose his replacement from among three candidates, all of whom work in this major department.

First, is Smith, a forty-four year old white man who is the head of one of the subsidiary departments. He has had fourteen years of experience with the company and has been head of his department for six years. For the last two years he has filled in for his boss (the man who had the heart attack) anytime during his absence, such as when he went on vacation. Smith is well thought of and has done a good job in his department.

Second, is Jones, a black man thirty-five years old. Jones is the head of a smaller subsidiary department. He started with the company eight years ago on an office job. Two years later he was made an "expediter," or trouble shooter assigned to help clear up difficulties anywhere in the major department. After three years in that capacity, he was made head of the subsidiary department that he now heads up. As a department head he has had more grievances than other department heads but these have diminished in the last year. Otherwise his performance has been good.

Third, is Winters, a white woman, thirty years old. She has been with the company for four years, the first two in a staff clerical job and the last two as an "assistant to" the man who has resigned. She is well liked, has an unusual amount of drive and seems to be competent in her work. She has a college degree in business administration, something which neither of the other two has.

• The question is, who should be promoted and why? But, before discussing this case, the students in a class should make a choice on a ballot. These ballots should be collected by the teacher. The count of the ballots can be used as a basis for the class discussion or it can be announced after the class discussion.

Endnotes

1. For a discussion on this subject, see, "Manager's Journal: The Public Sector," by Mitchell C. Lynch, *Wall Street Journal,* September 10, 1979, page 24.
2. These ideas are presented in *The Peter Principle,* by Laurence J. Peter and Raymond Hull, (William Morrow & Co., 1969). An interesting later article on this idea is, "Postscript to the Peter Principle," by Lane Tracy, *Harvard Business Review,* July-August 1972, pp. 65–72.
3. As reported in *Appraising Managerial Performance, Current Practice and Future Direction,* by R.I. Lazer, (The Conference Board, 1978).
4. As reported in a study of more than 2,000 managers' experiences and views on training, in *Manager to Manager,* by Robert F. Pearse (AMACOM, 1974).
5. As reported in the *Wall Street Journal,* 10 September 1979, page 24.
6. *Parkinson's Law,* by C. Northcote Parkinson (Houghton-Mifflin, 1957).
7. *On a Clear Day You Can See General Motors, John Z. DeLorean's Look Inside the Automotive Giant,* by J. Patrick Wright, Wright Enterprises, 1979, Chapter 3.

Suggested Supplementary Readings

Digman, Lester A. "How Well-Managed Companies Develop Their Executives." *Organizational Dynamics,* Autumn, 1978, pp. 63–80.

Schein, Edgar H. "Increasing Organizational Effectiveness Through Better Human Resource Planning and Development." *Sloan Management Review,* Fall 1977, pp. 1–20.

Walker, James W., and Michael N. Wolfe. "Patterns in Human Resource Planning Practices." *Human Resources Planning* 1, No. 4 (1978): 189–202.

Wooldridge, William D. "Fast Track Programs for MBAs: Do They Really Work?" *Management Review,* April 1979, pp. 8–14.

Objectives of Chapter Fourteen

1. To consider the nature of leadership as it applies in the ordinary day-to-day operations of organizations.
2. To analyze the relationship of the traits of leaders and the traits of non-leaders.
3. To look into the research on the subject of leadership which has been done by behavioral scientists.
4. To gain an understanding of the "contingency" theory of leadership which is widely accepted today.

Leadership

14

If you choose honest, Godly men
to be captains of horse,
honest men will follow them.
Oliver Cromwell, 1645

A leader is someone whom people follow because he has some kind of power which causes them to do what he wants them to do or to believe what he wants them to believe. He has effective influence over them.

In our study of management and organization, we are concerned with how leadership operates in organizations. And we are concerned with the nature of the leader's power and what it is that sets a leader apart from non-leaders. We will be dealing with two concepts of leadership:

· The formal power a leader has because of his position as the head of an organization.
· The power of a leader to draw out special or extraordinary effort and commitment.

The first of these concepts of leadership has to do with the formal authority of the person in charge. He is the leader by virtue of his position. This is "instrumental" leadership. He has the power to hire and fire people. He has the power to assign work, to dispense rewards or apply sanctions such as reprimands, and to commit the organization's resources. When he does these things, he is exercising instrumental leadership.

Such managerial or directional power (sometimes called "bureaucratic" power) has to exist in all organizations. Someone has to have authority or else the work simply will not get done. This type of leadership seems to dominate in the real world of organizations.

The second kind of leadership has to do with the powers of the leader to draw from his followers special or extraordinary effort, contributions, and commitment. This is "influential" leadership. Influential leadership is the kind of leadership which people

who talk about leadership usually have in mind.

This kind of leadership has to do with the extra increment of work and accomplishment which might be brought out above mechanical compliance with routine directives. It is the kind of leadership which gets most of the emphasis in the research and in the literature on organization and management, just as it does in this chapter.

The Role of Leadership

The role of leadership in organizations includes using both instrumental and influential leadership. Much of managing is exercising instrumental leadership but it is more effective if influential leadership is paired with it so that they are both used together. Our discussion of the role of leadership deals with certain of the problems that leaders face.

Leadership and Managing

Managers are almost always leaders in the sense that, as they manage, they exercise formal power. They exercise instrumental leadership. A manager exercises instrumental leadership when he gives directions to subordinates covering their work assignments. He leads when he discusses the objectives of their work with his subordinates and offers his assistance to help them get their work done. He leads when he coaches and trains his subordinates and decides whom to promote. He can do these things in ways which will generate greater acceptance and enthusiasm (usually by talking things over with his subordinates rather than being dictatorial) or he can use other methods which will generate less acceptance.

Similarly, a manager is exercising instrumental leadership when he weighs the strong and weak points of his organization and makes plans to strengthen the weak points. He leads when he marshalls the organization's resources and focuses them on accomplishing objectives. He leads when he sets up his organization to match the environment and the opportunities it presents and he leads when he compares accomplishments to plans.

Instrumental leadership of the managerial or directional kind is not itself strongly interpersonal and it can be reasonably effective by itself. But, its effectiveness is enhanced if the managers are also endowed with the charisma needed for generating enthusiastic support — if, in a word, they are also able to use influential leadership.

Leaders and Causes

Often the nobility of the cause of the leader is a very important factor to building enthusiasm in followers. A glamorous objective, such as conquering cancer or saving our forests, can stir the souls of followers. So can religion. Our epigram at the start of this chapter mentions Oliver Cromwell. In 1645, Cromwell was the leader of the Protestant insurgents in a religious war against England's Roman Catholic King Charles I. Cromwell's followers were probably as much or more dedicated to the Protestant cause as they were to Cromwell as an individual.

When a leader is a leader with a noble cause, it is relatively easy to enlist the support of followers. George Washington and Abraham Lincoln were surely much more effective leaders than they might otherwise have been because of the dedication of their followers to a popular cause.

It is less easy, however, to stir the souls of followers when the objective is to sell a new antiperspirant or to reduce the average duration of accounts receivable from sixty days to fifty days. The effectiveness of the leadership of the person in charge is often a function of the popular appeal of the objective.

The research evidence on leadership indicates that most followers are ready, or even eager, to become members of groups and to be numbered among the followers of strong leaders of popular causes. They also like to find meaning in the work they do. They respond and become interested and motivated when the person in charge tells them how important their work is and how it contributes to what the organization is trying to do.

Business history is replete with cases in which the leaders of rapidly growing companies were able to win high effort commitment from organizational members. In many cases there was, in such companies, an air of excitement and an impatience and a desire to accomplish. And even in large companies, such as IBM, similar attitudes have sometimes been developed. Unfortunately, managers in most organizations are not able to generate such enthusiasm and dedication to organizational purposes because organizational purposes are usually too prosaic and unglamorous.

The "Average Person" Dilemma

Although a ten-year old boy and a thirty-year old man have a combined average age of 20 years, it would obviously be wrong for a leader to treat either one of them as if he were "average," that is, as if he were a twenty-year old youth. Neither one is "average" in the sense that "average" implies a certain amount of commonality between them. Each one has, in fact, a different personality and different capabilities, and each one will respond to a given stimulus in different ways and not necessarily in any "average" way.

Similarly, in every group of people, the "average" of any human characteristic of the members of the group covers up many variations. Everyone has his own characteristics which may be close to the norm for the group or which may be quite different. The differences in people pose a serious dilemma for leaders.

So far as a leader is concerned, there are situations where he almost has to treat all of his subordinates alike (essentially as if they were all average). This is especially true at bottom levels in business organizations where union policies of equal treatment for everyone are the rule. If a lower-level supervisor tries to treat some of his people differently and in accord with his view of their individual personalities, he is likely to run into a great deal of resistance and lack of acceptance on the part of his *other* subordinates who see his acts as playing favorites or as acts which do not treat *them* as equals.

Treating people differently would, in many cases, violate the labor contract and aggrieved employees would sometimes file grievances claiming unequal treatment. On the other hand, if the supervisor treats everyone alike, he will be using methods which do not consider the individual differences among his followers.

Researchers on the subject of leadership have this same problem that leaders themselves have. The researchers want to generalize and to report how followers react to different styles of leadership, but they, too, are confronted with the fact that followers differ from each other. This has forced them to develop several generalizations (rather than one single generalization), each one applicable only to some people and to certain combinations of situational variables.

The Nature of Leadership

Leadership has to do with the relationships between leaders and followers. It is effective if the personalities of the leader and the followers are compatible and if the actions of the leader win the followers' support. We will consider, here, how leaders influence their followers.

Characteristics or "Traits" of Leaders

Studies of the characteristics of leaders have shown that there is no one pattern or mold into which effective managers all fit. Perhaps this finding should not be regarded as surprising since there are many kinds of jobs that leaders fill. Organizations are different from each other. The president of a university, the president of the United States Steel company, and the head of a research organization such as the Rand Corporation in Los Angeles have quite unlike jobs.

Some leaders direct entire organizations, whereas some other leaders head up only major departments. Their areas of operations vary a great deal. The job of a sales manager and a chief engineer are different.

It takes different kinds of people to lead in such diverse situations. The ideal person for each of these jobs would need to have a different set of characteristics. Any study of the characteristics of effective leaders in such diverse jobs, when they are all lumped together into one group, would find a great deal of variety. Effective leadership *is* related to the situation in which it is exercised.

Nonetheless, research studies have found that there are some personality characteristics which are stronger in leaders than in the general population. Ralph Stogdill analyzed more than 150 studies (and 3,000 articles and books) of leaders and found that the researchers concluded that leaders are emotionally well-balanced. They are strongly task and achievement oriented, aggressive and courageous, and willing to assume responsibility. They are ethical in conduct, and are articulate, persuasive, dominant, and energetic.[1]

In general, it appears that leaders are a little more intelligent than the general population, have greater feelings of responsibility, and are more dependable. They also show more initiative, are more self-assured, and are more socially participative. David McClelland and Donald Burnham say that they are also more "power motivated" than people in general. They want to have impact and to be strong and influential.[2]

Curiously, social scientist researchers seem not to have uncovered certain other characteristics which lay people believe are important in leaders. Thomas Murphy, a *Forbes* magazine writer reports that his interviews with successful managers show them to have unusually large egos. Murphy says that they need to have a great deal of self confidence to sustain themselves through the inevitable rough spots. He says that modesty here is no virtue.[3]

Research by social scientists aimed at finding out the characteristics of effective leaders has produced disappointing results. The purposes of these studies has been to determine the characteristics of leaders so that the selection of men or women to promote to higher jobs could be improved. The hope was that, if those being promoted had the same characteristics that established effective leaders have, then these newly promoted people would more surely also become effective leaders.

Unfortunately, as we have seen, the few traits which seem to be common among leaders are not really uncommon in the population in general. There is really not enough difference to be very helpful in predicting performance.

The Nature of the Leader's Power

A leader's ability to influence the attitude and behavior of others is supported by his power. A leader's power is, however, not actually one single kind of power. Stogdill reported that behavioral scientists consider a leader's power to be essentially of three kinds.[4]

1. "Legitimate" power, the power of position (including the power to reward and to censure).
2. "Expert" power, the competence and knowledge of the leader in the technical area involved.
3. "Referent" power, the degree to which followers like the leader and are willing to do what he says.

We will consider these kinds of power more fully in Chapter 19 when we take up the authority of managers.

Some people are motivated by a strong desire for power. Leaders almost always have this desire. This can, however, become a source of difficulty since, in many cases, there are also other people with similar desires for power. They also aspire to leadership positions, whereas only one person can emerge as the single leader. This can lead to friction and trouble in high echelons.

Once a leader emerges as the single leader, he may feel (and possibly correctly) that he has to eliminate the other strong personalities who covet his spot and who might usurp his position. The leader may exercise raw authoritarian power as he consolidates his position.

So we really should add the power of fear to our list given above. Adolph Hitler used fear very effectively to maintain his position as leader. And the use of fear by business leaders is not unknown. It may not be the best kind of leadership but it has its points.

Supportive Behavior by Leaders

Most leaders of businesses as well as of government organizations are not able to generate any great dedication of their subordinates to lofty organizational purposes, so they have to rely more on *winning* the support of their subordinates. Their respect has to be earned and this is where supportive practices on their part can be of great help.

Researchers have found that leaders who are the most effective are usually interested in their subordinates and they show genuine concern for their well-being. (If they are not actually interested, then, when necessary, they cover up their own feelings and act as if they have their subordinates' interest at heart.)

People tend to follow superiors in whom they see hope for satisfying their hopes and goals. Thus, the better a leader understands the needs of his followers, the more he may be able to create an atmosphere of support for his followers, and the better he can lead them. A good leader-manager notices and appreciates the good work that his subordinates do. He shows that he has confidence in them and builds up their self-esteem. ("I expect a lot from you because you are good," in contrast to "because I will fire you if you don't.")

Most behavioral scientists believe that a manager is likely to be more effective if he is employee-oriented and approachable, and behaves democratically and not arbitrarily. They believe that it helps for him to use only general supervisory methods and to try to help subordinates get their work done. And they say that it helps if he is considerate of his subordinates, thinks of their needs and preferences, treats them with dignity and kindness, and is not punitive. He is concerned about his subordinates as human beings and as individuals rather than as means for getting work done.

It would seem that if supportive leadership methods always produced good effects, then autocratic methods ought to produce reverse effects. And, indeed, quite a few studies have produced evidence that close non-participative and non-supportive supervision often does produce lower quality output. But the evidence from research studies is not altogether in agreement on this point. Research has shown that no one management style, not even a supportive and participative style, is the best in every situation.

"Path-Goal" Theory

"Path-goal" theory holds that a leader who makes it clear what he wants done has thereby shown the subordinate the path to follow to accomplish his own personal needs. The theory also holds that when a subordinate does what is wanted, he will be rewarded by accomplishing his personal goals at the same time.

There is more to path-goal theory, however. It implies also that the leader pays attention to his subordinates as individuals and that he tries to learn what motivates each one. Then he tries to help subordinates by supplying motivations which will suit each one. And he tries to help subordinates reach their goals by removing barriers which are keeping them from reaching the goals. Path-goal supportive leadership is reported to be very helpful on stressful and frustrating jobs.[5]

Path-goal theory needs to be used with discretion, however. As we said in Chapter 4, superiors can't know very much about the personal goals of very many of their subordinates. Nor can superiors really do very much to help beyond giving praise for well done work. If very many subordinates have high goals, most of them will be disappointed.

The "Great Man" Leader

Historically, many people have believed that leaders are born and not made.

Behavioral research has found that this is not so and that "great" leaders have usually been great because of fortuitous match-ups of the leader's characteristics with the needs of situations.

Our earlier discussions have suggested that "great" leaders are sometimes great because they are leaders of causes which generate intense emotional support. Sometimes they have even been "great" leaders and truly very effective in spite of their *not* having certain characteristics usually associated with effective leadership. Stogdill's research showed, for example, that effective leaders usually maintain close, friendly relationships with their followers. But this does not have to be so when followers are fundamentally dedicated to a cause and transfer their loyalty to the cause to the leader of the cause in spite of his not being warm and friendly.

Under these circumstances, leaders can be effective even when they are not loved by their followers. Both Hitler and Napoleon were effective leaders (they nearly conquered the world), but Peter Drucker remarks, "Napoleon has been called many things, but 'likable' is not one of them. The 'great man' leader is not always warm, a good many have been icy. He may not be outgoing or affable and he tends to be austere and aloof. He has little empathy; he makes demands. A good many leaders have not a trace of charisma. But a leader always inspires confidence, always commands respect."[6]

Both Hitler and Napoleon were effective leaders of the demanding type. They could lead effectively because of the strong commitment of their followers to the common cause.

Many people enjoy the second-hand glory, the prestige and the implied security which comes from being a part of a successful common cause led by a strong leader. They take pride in being a part of an organization which has the respect of outsiders and which is led by a strong leader.

Leadership Insights and Research

Although people have long been interested in leadership, its worth to an organization and how to develop it, actual research into the subject did not start until after World War II. Early research was largely centered in the work done at The Ohio State University and at the University of Michigan. After these pioneer efforts, many other scholars undertook further research aimed at refining the understanding of leadership.

The Leadership Increment

Favorable organizational empathy resulting from effective leadership surely improves organizational accomplishment, yet one can only guess at how much difference in effectiveness will come about from subordinates having a favorable attitude as against their being neutral or negative. Surely the difference in effectiveness can be as much as 25 to 50 percent. (See Figure 14-1).

Researchers have tried to isolate and to measure the contribution or increment added by effective leadership to total organizational accomplishment. This has proved impossible to do because organizational accomplishment is influenced by so many factors that the effects of leadership cannot be separated out for study and measurement. Often a leader's impact on organizational accomplishment is limited and muffled by environmental factors.

This is particularly true in government organizations. There the bureaucracy and the organizational inertia seem to be especially resistant to change. Arthur Schlesinger reported that President Kennedy found it almost impossible to change the State Department in spite of his power position as President of the United States.[7]

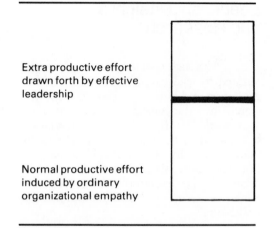

Extra productive effort drawn forth by effective leadership

Normal productive effort induced by ordinary organizational empathy

Figure 14-1
The order of magnitude of extra effort which effective leadership may induce.

Nonetheless, *business* history offers many examples where new top leaders were very influential and were able to cause their organizations to accomplish more. In Chapter 1, we noted the cases of Ernest Breech at Ford Motor in the 1940s and 1950s, Harry Cunningham at K mart in the 1960s, and Edward Carlson at United Airlines in the 1970s. In all these cases the new leader turned the business around and put it on a sound operating basis.

The ability of top managers can be of the utmost importance in business organizations where managers have more freedom and more power to produce consequential effects on organizational behavior than do heads of governmental organizations.

The Ohio State University Studies[8]

Shortly after World War II, a group of researchers at The Ohio State University began extensive research into leadership. Of these men, Ralph Stogdill is the best known. Edwin Fleischman and Alvin Coons were other well-known names.

The research that these men carried on soon led them to conclude that there were two different kinds of leadership, which they referred to as "initiating structure" and "consideration." Managers who followed the "initiating structure" pattern tended to be authoritarian, to define the jobs of subordinates rather carefully, and to establish well-defined patterns of organization, channels of communication, and ways for getting jobs done. In contrast, superiors who followed the "consideration" pattern were less authoritarian and were more associated with friendship, mutual trust, respect, and warmth in their superior-subordinate relationships.

Next, these researchers turned to the question of how well these styles of leadership worked. They concluded that the managers whose style was "considerate" achieved better results. Although these early Ohio State researchers did not develop good measures of effective managership, their conclusion was that the consideration style was the more effective kind.

The University of Michigan Studies

Studies of a similar nature were carried on at the University of Michigan at the same time but the approach was a little different from that followed at Ohio State. Under the general leadership of Rensis Likert, investigations were undertaken to see what differences there were between the leadership styles of managers of high production and low production organizational units.

The findings were similar to those of the Ohio State group. (See Figure 14-2) Daniel Katz and Robert Kahn of the Michigan group reported, "There is evidence that broad sharing of leadership functions contributes to organizational effectiveness under almost all circumstances."[9] Managers who were considerate of the feelings of subordi-

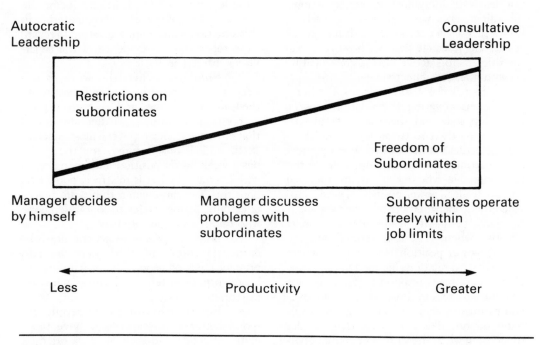

Autocratic
Leadership

Consultative
Leadership

Restrictions on
subordinates

Freedom of
Subordinates

Manager decides
by himself

Manager discusses
problems with
subordinates

Subordinates operate
freely within
job limits

Less

Productivity

Greater

Figure 14-2
The "leadership continuum" as suggested by the University of Michigan studies.

nates were found to be more effective leaders and the result was that the groups were more productive.

Likert and his group emphasized the need for participation by subordinates in decision making and thought that this style of leadership was better than more authoritarian methods.[10] According to Likert, supervisors of departments with good production records appeared to emphasize the interpersonal side of their leadership positions. They were "employee-centered" and used more reward power. They used general rather than close supervision. In contrast, superiors of low-producing sections tended to spend more time on their actual tasks and on paper work. They were more "production-oriented" and used more coercive power.

Fiedler's Research

In addition to the research already mentioned, the work of Fred Fiedler merits separate consideration. Fiedler started out over twenty years ago to find out whether lenient or demanding supervision would be more likely to lead to high-producing groups. From extensive research during the intervening years, Fiedler concluded that the type of leadership style which results in high group performance is contingent on:

· The leader's formal power position.
· The task structure of the subordinate's work.
· The relations between the leader and his followers.[11]

Leadership

Obviously, Fiedler's research could not deal with individual differences among subordinates nor with other factors such as how a new leader compares with his predecessor. His research showed, however, that the three factors above have a great deal to do with a leader's effectiveness.

Figure 14-3 summarizes Fiedler's conclusions covering the relationships of leadership style and these basic factors in determining the effectiveness of a leader.

Fiedler's work showed that a permissive, participative leadership style is the most effective where work is unstructured and the leader's power position is weak, provided the leader-follower relations are good. Similarly, permissive leadership is the most effective when work is structured and the leader's power position is strong but where the leader-led relations are moderately poor. Here subordinates respond better to leaders who use a more non-directive, participative, and permissive style of leadership. Subordinates do not like close over-the-shoulder supervision when the work poses minor challenges which they would rather work out for themselves.

A more conservative, directive style of leadership is more effective when the work is highly structured and specifically laid out if the leader is well liked. In such a case the power position of the leader is immaterial. In this situation many employees seem to regard close supervision as evidence of the supervisor's interest in their work.

Similarly, when the work is unstructured, directive leadership is best when the leader is well liked and has a strong power position. Curiously, Fiedler also found that directive leadership is the most effective when work is unstructured, and the leader has a weak power position and his relations with his subordinates is relatively poor. Perhaps this is because when things are highly uncertain, people prefer to follow someone who brings order out of chaos.

So far as people in general are concerned, Fiedler says that there are two primary types of people, those who are relationship oriented, and those who are task oriented.

Relationship-oriented people respond better when supervisors have moderate influence and control. Task-oriented people respond better either when the leader can exert a great deal of power, or in the reverse situation, when the leader has little power or influence.[12]

Task Structure	Leader's Power Position	Leader-Follower Relations	Most Effective Leadership Style
Unstructured	Weak	Good	Permissive
Structured	Strong	Moderately poor	Permissive
Structured	Strong	Good	Directive
Structured	Weak	Good	Directive
Unstructured	Strong	Good	Directive
Unstructured	Weak	Moderately poor	Directive
Structured	Weak	Moderately poor	Inconclusive evidence
Unstructured	Strong	Moderately poor	Inconclusive evidence

Figure 14-3

Leadership Styles and Situational Variables

Our examination of research into leadership brings out the point that few positive statements can be made about it. Researchers have sometimes used the terms "autocratic," "democratic," and even "laissez faire," to describe leadership styles. But they shy away from expressing their conclusions in such terms because leadership styles are so often not all of one and none of the other.

In fact, continuing research in recent years suggests that the conclusions of the early social science researchers, some of whom talked about autocratic and democratic styles, may have been somewhat overdrawn. Stogdill reported, for example, that by the mid-1970s researchers had come to believe that person-oriented leadership (democratic), taken by itself, did not seem to improve either motivation or productivity.[13]

Many people now believe that effective leadership is a function of the interplay of many factors and that no one specific leadership style, not even democratic, is the best in every case. It is now thought that the "best" leadership style is contingent on how the leader's style relates to the situation and to the kinds of people his followers are. Fred Fiedler says that because of this, it is not really meaningful to speak of effective and ineffective leaders.[14]

It is now believed that when work is routine and does not change much, then bureaucratic, directive supervisory methods (autocratic) are best. But if the work and how to do it are uncertain, then it is better to use participative (democratic) methods. Subordinates should be told about what is going on and consulted about how to do their work and asked for suggestions.[15] Temporary groups and multiple lines of authority and communications may be helpful in such situations.

The effectiveness of a leader depends also on his position and status in the organization. It is influenced by his age and previous experience and, when he is new, it is related to how he compares to his predecessor. The success of his style of leadership is also related to the specific work requirements of the group, such as the degree to which cooperation between individuals and groups is required. And it is also related to the size of the group, the personalities of the members of the group, and the expectations of group members.

The time allowed for decision making is also sometimes important. If a decision must be made quickly, there is not enough time for participation (which is a slow process) so a more authoritarian leadership style works better.

"Contingency" Theory

The preceding discussions show that researchers are largely in agreement that the most effective leadership style is contingent on the interaction of several factors, hence the term "contingency" theory. Contingency theory holds that "a leader's effectiveness depends on his personality and the degree to which the situation gives the leader power, control and influence over the situation."[16] Contingency management does not mean unsystematic or happenstance management. On the contrary, it means recognizing the style of management and the needs of the situation.

Indeed, Victor Vroom concludes that the *dominant factor* in leadership situations may well *not* be the autocratic or democratic inclinations of the leader. Instead, he concludes that, "It makes more sense to talk about participative and autocratic *situations* that it does to talk about participative and authoritarian *managers*.[17]

Some of today's organizational development proponents would disagree somewhat with Vroom on this point. They would hold to the position that the key to the most effective performance lies in the development of a healthy, cooperative *atmosphere*. The difference here from Vroom's point is the *emphasis placed on managers being able to develop a healthy climate*. A participative-type manager may be able to develop the needed atmosphere but autocratic managers probably would not be able to do this and would, therefore, not be as effective as more open, democratic-type managers.

A person could wish that contingency leadership theory were easier to use. To use it, a manager must:

1. Know about it and know about the conditions under which each different style of leadership will be the most effective.
2. Be perceptive enough to recognize the conditions he faces. Then he can decide which leadership style will be the most effective.
3. Be versatile enough to change to the style which will be the most effective or else change the conditions so that the style he wants to use will be the most effective.

The task structure, for example, can be made more structured by spelling out jobs in more detail. Or it can be made less structured by providing only general directives instead of detailed instructions. Similarly, it may be possible to change a manager's power position. Maybe his superior can give him more authority or give him a higher title.

Unfortunately, there are probably only a few managers who are knowledgeable and perceptive enough to appreciate the interplay of the several factors which bear on their effectiveness as leaders. And still fewer of them will be versatile and adaptable enough to be able to change their leadership styles or the job conditions or their subordinates or their own power positions to suit the situation.[18]

The Moderating Effect of Time. Actually, the passage of time probably improves the fit of the leader-follower relationship and reduces the need for a good inherent leader-follower-situation fit. As time passes, leaders and followers probably get used to each other and there is some adaptation on each side. Just as married couples learn how to get along with each other, so do leaders and followers.

Furthermore, there is a process of self-selection continually going on. Followers who do not like a leader's style sometimes leave. Over a period of time the replacements who stay on are those who are satisfied with his style. The effect is that the organization adapts to him.

Summary

Leadership and management have a considerable area of overlap yet they are not wholly the same. Both deal with influencing the behavior of subordinates and causing them to become more effective.

Leadership relates largely to motivating people, whereas management includes marshalling resources (including human resources) and directing them toward effective accomplishment.

Leadership is largely a matter of causing subordinates to develop organizational empathy to a cause or to a leader. And it has to do with the extra increment of output which can result from subordinates having high morale and enthusiasm which causes them to commit extra degrees of their energies to accomplishing organizational goals.

Studies of leadership styles have been disappointing in the sense that they have not found any panacea formula. They have shown that there is not any one style of leadership which is always the best. Instead, it has been found that the best style to use is related to how well liked the leader is, what his formal power is, and the degree of structure in the job situation, which includes the kinds of people his followers are. Neither authoritarian nor participative management is clearly the better in all cases. Each has its place where it is superior, but above all, a healthy, open, cooperative organizational atmosphere is important to effective organizational accomplishment.

Studies of the characteristics of leaders also have found that there is no one pattern of personal characteristics of effective leaders. Leaders have almost as varied sets of characteristics as does everyone else.

Review Questions

1. "An effective leader is what he *does,* not what he *is.*" Discuss.
2. When a manager manages, is he also leading? Discuss the relationship between managing and leading.
3. How is the "average individual" dilemma related to the study of leadership? How can a person escape this dilemma?
4. What have researchers found out about the traits of effective leaders? How can a high-level manager use this information as he manages?
5. The text reports that there is an increasing need for effective leadership. What reasons are there for this?
6. Review the reports of the findings of the Ohio State and the Michigan groups' studies of leadership. What similarities did these two groups find? What differences? What conclusions should a person draw from this?
7. Summarize Fiedler's findings so far as leadership styles are concerned. How could a superior use these findings to improve the leadership effectiveness of his subordinates?
8. What is "contingency" theory? What effect would knowing about this theory have on a leader as against how he would probably operate without knowing about it?

Questions for Analysis and Discussion

1. Is it possible to do good research on how people behave by doing studies and presenting *aggregate* or *average* findings which can be valid as predictors of how *individuals* will respond? Discuss.

2. "Normally, people who are *elected* to group leadership are the natural leaders of their groups." *Do* groups select the "natural leaders?" Doesn't this statement overlook the operation of politics and the misuse of the democratic process which sometimes occurs? (Several years ago an opposition candidate for the head of the United Mine Workers union was shot to death.)

3. The student in a graduate course in organization said, "I went to West Point and was in the Army. During my years, I took lots of courses in leadership and have seen others take them. But, from my observation, I believe that leadership can't be taught. Some men just have it and others don't." Comment.

4. Leading is said to be a dynamic activity in which a manager continually communicates with his subordinates in a way which he hopes will induce them to support organizational plans and objectives. But when there are several subordinates, should the leader try to lead in different ways according to each subordinate's individual personality?

5. A good many mature people have been employees of more than one organization. In each case, they probably felt a certain degree of loyalty to their current employer and to their immediate supervisor. Yet this statement suggests that loyalty is a relatively minor matter and is easily transferable. Is it realistic for an employer to expect loyalty from employees? How would a person's behavior differ if he were loyal versus his not being loyal?

6. Charles Perrow says that apparent leadership problems are often problems of organizational structure instead. The real problem may lie in the structure of the organization rather than in the characteristics of the people who head it. Yet, aren't organizational structural problems really the responsibility of the organization's head? So, aren't they leadership problems after all? Discuss.

7. Douglas McGregor once said, "Business leadership consists of a relationship between the leader, his followers, the organization, and the social milieu, and since these situational factors change with time, we cannot predict the personal characteristics of the managers that an organization will need a decade or so hence." How, considering this statement, can a company ever have a training program which will be effective? For example, what should the training director of International Business Machines do, so far as training is concerned?

8. Aren't participative and supportive leadership only more acceptable ways to manipulate employees? And, as such, aren't they poor practices? Can leaders lead without being manipulative?

9. Fiedler's three factors which he feels are important to effective leadership do not mention the acceptance theory of authority (see Chapter 19) nor do they say anything about subordinates developing their own jobs. Yet it seems illogical to conclude that these concepts play no part in determining the effectiveness of leaders. Discuss the relationships between these factors.

10. Are the *attitudes* of employees more important than *what they do?* Actually, isn't the important thing what a person does, not why he does it?

11. Behavioral researchers never seem to say, "If he can't do the job, get him out of there." Does this statement represent a healthy or an unhealthy viewpoint?

12. Quotation from a textbook: "Leadership is a function in the organization rather than a trait of an individual. It is distributed among the members of a group or organization, and is not automatically vested in the person with the formal authority. Good leadership and good membership therefore blend into each other in an effective organization. It is just as much the task of a member to help the group reach its goals as it is the task of the formal leader."

Comment by a part-time university student working on a full-time job: "Not for the money they pay me." Discuss.

Case 14-1   Effective Managerial Practices: A Self Evaluation

Chris Argyris asked several successful company chief executive officers what effect they thought that their managerial methods had on their subordinates. Here are several answers:[19]

"I believe that a real business leader is incapable of generating a climate where people can grow."

"Hell, none of us would work for people like ourselves."

"A real executive under any one of us would leave because he couldn't stand it."

"We couldn't work for dominant characters such as ourselves. We are leaders."

"Those who choose to work for us may need a security blanket. Maybe they need the feeling that 'I don't care if he tramples me or kicks me; I am drawn toward the success pattern.'"

"I wonder if a successful leader has the ability to breed another in his image. I think it would be almost self-defeating."

282

When Argyris next asked them if they had ever discussed the effects of their leadership styles on their subordinates with their subordinates, they said that they had not. (These chief executive officers all set difficult goals, were strongly committed to achieving these goals, set tight managerial controls (especially financial) and required subordinates to make highly detailed plans (especially in marketing, sales, manufacturing, and engineering).

- Why would the top managers think that their subordinates would not like their methods? Why would they use such methods if they caused such negative reactions?
- What effects would such managerial practices probably have on subordinates? What kinds of subordinates would be likely to develop?
- What future should a person project for these organizations? Why?

Endnotes

1. Stogdill, Op. Cit., Chapters 6 and 7. *Handbook of Leadership* by Ralph M. Stogdill, The Free Press, 1974.
2. "Power Is the Great Motivator," by David C. McClelland and Donald H. Burnham, *Harvard Business Review*, March-April 1976, pp. 99–110.
3. "Goodbye to All This," by Thomas P. Murphy, *Forbes*, September 1980, p. 144.
4. The research of social scientists on this subject is summarized in Stogdill, *Op. Cit.*, Chapter 22.
5. *Managerial Process and Organizational Behavior*, by Alan C. Filley, Robert J. House, and Steven Kerr (Scott, Foresman, 1976), pp. 256–260.
6. *Management: Tasks, Responsibilities and Practices*, by Peter F. Drucker (Harper & Row, 1974), p. 303.
7. *A Thousand Days: John F. Kennedy in the White House*, by Arthur M. Schlesinger, Jr., (Houghton Mifflin, 1965), Chapter 16.
8. A good summary of this extensive research is given in Stogdill, Op. Cit., Chapter 11. See also, "Leadership," by Victor H. Vroom, in *Handbook of Organizational Psychology*, by Marvin D. Dunnette, (ed.) (Rand McNally, 1976), pp. 1527–1551.
9. *The Social Psychology of Organizations*, by Daniel Katz and Robert L. Kahn (Wiley, 1966), p. 335. See also Stogdill, *Op. Cit.*, Chapter 34, and Vroom, *Ibid.*, pp. 1531–1533.
10. Likert, Op. Cit. *The Human Organization: Its Management and Value* by Rensis Likert, Prentice-Hall, 1967.
11. *Leadership and Effective Management*, by Fred E. Fiedler and Martin M. Chemers (Scott, Foresman), 1974.
12. "Hawthorne Revisited: The Legend and the Legacy," *Organizational Dynamics*, Winter 1975, p. 75.
13. Stogdill, *Op. Cit.*, Chapter 32.
14. This position is held today by most social scientists. See, *Leadership*, by James M. Burns (Harper & Row, 1978).

15. Perrow, Op. Cit., page 12 "The Short and Glorious History of Organizational Theory," by Charles Perrow, *Organizational Dynamics*, Summer, 1973, page 12.
16. "The Contingency Model — New Directors for Leadership Utilization," by Fred E. Fiedler, *Journal of Contemporary Business*, Autumn 1974, p. 65.
17. Vroom, *Op. Cit.*, pp. 1527–1552.
18. "Can Leaders Learn to Lead," by Victor H. Vroom, *Organizational Dynamics*, Winter 1976, pp. 17–28.
19. Reported in "The CEO's Behavior: Key to Organizational Development," by Chris Argyris, *Harvard Business Review*, March-April 1973, p. 57.

Suggested Supplementary Readings

Farrow, Dona L., Enzo R. Valenti, and Bernard M. Bass. "A Comparison of Leadership and Situational Characteristics Within Profit and Non-Profit Organizations," *Academy of Management Proceedings*, 1980, pp. 334–339.

Hunt, James G., and Lars L. Larson. eds. *Leadership, The Cutting Edge.* Southern Illinois University, 1978.

Likert, Rensis. *Past and Future Prospectives on System 4.* Rensis Likert and Associates, 1977.

Sayles Leonard R. *Leadership: What Effective Leaders Do — And How They Do It.* McGraw-Hill, 1979.

Objectives of Chapter Fifteen

1. To gain an acquaintance with the nature of the fundamental motivations common to most people.
2. To consider how managers can bring into play more of the motivations which are latent within us.
3. To study the effects of money as a motivator and how it should be used in the motivation process.
4. To consider the part that job enlargement and job enrichment can play in motivating people.

Motivation

15

"Your soul was not in your work?"
"Neither my soul nor my heart,
nor half my energies."
Lost Horizons, *by James Hilton*

What motivates a person to put his heart and soul and all of his energies into his work?

Questions such as this have intrigued philosophers over the ages just as they intrigue social science researchers and leaders of organizations today.

Unfortunately, motivation rarely goes so far in any organization as to cause heart and soul commitment. But managers of most organizations would surely hope to have their subordinates, especially their lower-level managers, be motivated enough to be willing to commit more than half of their energies.

Most people, in the Western world at least, are affluent enough not to have to work very hard to satisfy their most basic needs. Yet most people actually do work harder than they really need to so one could still ask, why? What motivates them? Could it be that the work itself is sometimes that interesting? Is it the personal satisfaction which comes from accomplishing something? Is it wanting to outdo other people? Is it the Protestant work ethic?

Managers of organizations who understand what motivates people may be able to manage in such a way as to appeal to the motivations of their subordinates and to cause them to direct their efforts more toward organizational accomplishment. Then they will manage better than will managers who do not concern themselves with what motivates people, because motivated employees work harder and get more done.

The Extra Increment From Motivation. As we said in the last chapter when discussing leadership, there is quite a difference between an employee's prosaic work-a-day performance and what he will do if he is enthusiastic and dedicated to making the best contribution he can to the organization's success. The difference is there even though, often, it can't be measured.

Motivation: Is It Latent or Can It Be Developed? In one sense, superiors cannot motivate subordinates. All they can do is to draw out or appeal to motivations, latent or active, which already exist in subordinates. The contribution which a competent superior can make, through communications, actions, or policies, is to appeal to a person's motivations and bring his motivations into play so that his behavior and his actions are turned to directions which will increase the amount and the effectiveness of his effort inputs, and consequently, his accomplishments. (See Figure 15-1).

Psychologist David McClelland would probably not agree with the statement just made (that motivations come from something deep inside people). McClelland has always held that the desire to achieve can be taught and can be developed in people and that the motivations of individuals are largely conditioned by cultures and by peoples' experiences. McClelland feels that motivation can be developed in people even in non-achieving societies.[1] Even if this is so, however, it is usually a long and slow process to change culture-inculcated ideas, and attempts to change them are not always successful.

Motivational Environment

Motivations operate within the limitations of certain constraints. There are individual differences as well as capability limitations on the part of subordinates. In order to focus the motivations of people on organizational goal accomplishment, it is necessary to make the reaching of personal goals conditional on organizational members reaching organizational goals.

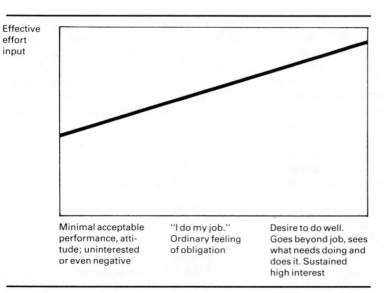

Effective
effort
input

| Minimal acceptable performance, attitude; uninterested or even negative | "I do my job." Ordinary feeling of obligation | Desire to do well. Goes beyond job, sees what needs doing and does it. Sustained high interest |

Figure 15-1
Good leadership helps develop motivations in subordinates so that they produce at levels toward the right of the diagram.

Motivation and Individual Differences

In a discussion of motivation, one needs to devote most of the attention to people in general and to the responses which motivations cause in most people. This approach emphasizes how alike people are.

But one should not overlook individual differences. People have different interests, different capabilities, and different backgrounds. Consequently, they respond differently to stimuli. David McClelland divides people into three groups according to their motivations:

1. "N-aff" people. People who have a strong need to affiliate. They like to be members of social groups and enjoy friendly participation in group activities.
2. "N-ach" people. People who have a strong desire to achieve. They want to succeed and like to work toward goals. They assume responsibility readily, are hard workers, and like to be their own bosses.
3. "N-pwr" people. People who want power over other people. They want to influence other people and are more verbal and persuasive. They are likely to be more autocratic and demanding. Entrepreneurs are usually high in n-pwr.

Probably most men and women respond at least to some extent to almost all of these motivating forces, but people differ in their evaluations of different goals and respond to stimuli in different ways. N-aff people are good followers whereas n-ach and n-pwr people are more likely to strive for leadership.

This creates the same kind of a dilemma that we had with leadership in the last chapter. Any discussion of motivation needs to keep in mind that people are alike, yet they are different. Unfortunately, in a limited space, it is not possible to consider individual differences at length. Our discussion must be largely devoted to the motivations of people in general, even though we recognize that such generalizations overlook individual differences and consequently cannot be descriptive of how every individual person is motivated.

Capability Limitations. Valuable as motivations are in drawing out the best from subordinates, they cannot directly cause a person to accomplish beyond his capabilities. A person's capabilities constitute upper limits which restrict how much he can achieve. Almost every job of consequential importance requires certain knowledge, skills and capabilities. An engineer needs to know how to design products and a computer programmer needs to know computer language. These are essential and no amount of motivation will suffice in lieu of such capability.

Motivation may help spur an unqualified person along the road to acquiring competence if the opportunity is provided, but until competence is acquired, motivation alone cannot do the job.

The "Will to Manage." Managers differ greatly in their "will to manage," their "drive to accomplish," and in their desire to have impact and to influence their organizations. Some managers have a strong urge to manage and they try hard to lead their organizations to greater accomplishments but other managers have less drive.

The motivation to manage, in its extreme degree, commands a price which some managers are not willing to pay. Sometimes it means long hours and dedication to the job at the expense of leisure time and time with one's family. (Long hours and work overloads sometimes also occur at low levels as well as at high levels but they are more common at high levels.) Sometimes, too, the stresses of the job give managers ulcers, high blood pressure, and heart attacks. Although only a minority of managers ever suffer these ills from job tension and worry, they are common enough to justify a person's thinking about them before he plunges in. (Actually, a mild amount of tension seems to help rather than hurt most people because tension and excitement tend to drive out boredom and complacency.)

Motivational Development

Newly hired employees usually come to their jobs in a frame of mind which is more favorable to the organization than mere complaisant acceptance. They have wanted the jobs they get and they come to work in a favorable frame of mind. Their organizational empathy at this point may, however, be more a matter of their having open minds than it is true organizational empathy.

From here on, their continuing empathy and motivation are more *results* which develop out of the way the job goes and from the work environment. It is here that managers can play a part in shaping and modifying their behavior and in developing and reinforcing employee attitudes toward their work and toward the organization. The motivations of subordinates are partly what their superiors cause them to be.

Job "Valence." Behavioral scientists sometimes refer to the interest and willingness of employees to apply themselves diligently as being a matter of what Victor Vroom has called "valence." Valence is the strength of a person's desire for a certain job after he considers the price he will have to pay in work.[2] The valence will be low if he thinks that he would have to work too hard or that the good results would not amount to much anyway.

Valence considers possible negative effects as well as positive effects. A person may find it highly preferable, particularly if other jobs are scarce, to do a job because if he doesn't do it he may be fired.

The strength of the motivation is the net attractiveness of the results (its valence) stemming from the activity, modified by the probability of this result coming about. If both the valence and the probability are high, the employee will be strongly motivated. But, even if the valence is high, the worker's motivation will probably be low if he thinks that good results are highly unlikely.

Fusing Personal and Organizational Goals. Effective motivation by managers lies in the tying together of organizational goal accomplishment and personal goal or personal satisfaction accomplishment. (See Figure 15-2) This is essentially the same as the "path-goal" leadership idea which was discussed in the last chapter. Motivation, in this case, comes not from the leader's style of leading, but from tying together rewards in the nature of personal goal achievement with organizational goal achievement.

The importance of tying personal goals and organizational goals together is illustrated by the case of a company which paid its salespeople a 10 percent commission on the sales of three items whose profitability rates differed.

The company's managers wanted to motivate the salespeople to sell more of the high profit items so they changed the commission plan so that the commissions were paid based on the *profitability* of the items sold rather than on the *sales dollars*. The sales of the more profitable items went up immediately because the salespeople were motivated by the plan.

Aside from commissions, piecework, and bonuses, it would seem that managers have several ways to fuse people's personal goals to organizational goals. Other kinds of rewards could be pay raises, promotions, more interesting work, and praise and participation in decision making.

Motivation Theory

Today's behavioral scientists are in general agreement with the theories of early investigators of motivation theory. Most of the research of recent years which we will consider in this section has been aimed at refining and improving upon the groundwork laid by the early theorists.

Early Motivational Theory

One of the early findings of motivational researchers has been called "expectancy" theory. This theory holds that needs alone do not explain behavior. A person's motivation is determined more by his *expectations* of job satisfactions and rewards than it is by the actual benefits or penalties. Another finding of the early social scientists was that the "habit strengths" of people and their "impetus to respond" and their "drive to accomplish" played important parts in their motivations.

Early Views of Money as a Motivator. As we reported in Chapter 3, Abraham Maslow was one of the early social scientists who was interested in motivation. Recall that he grouped people's motivations into five groups: physiological, security, belongingness, self-esteem, and self-actualization. These, he thought, operated in a sequential way with physiological needs being the most fundamental. Higher-level motivations came into play only after the lower-level motivations were fulfilled on a continuing basis.

We also reported that many of today's social scientists believe that Maslow's list is valid, except that, because of individual differences, *there is no hierarchy of needs*, no special order, in which higher-level motivators came into play, so far as people in general are concerned.

In Chapter 3, we did *not* emphasize the implications inherent in Maslow's idea

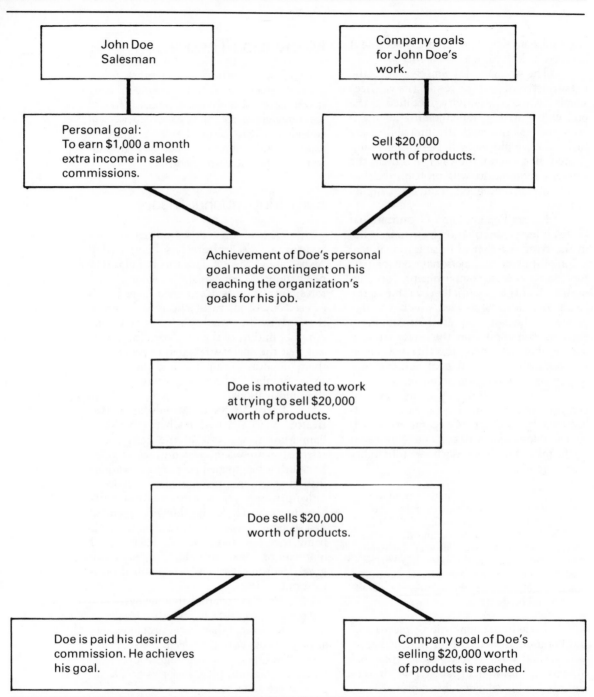

Figure 15-2
Effective motivation ties organizational goals and personal goals together and makes the reaching of personal goals contingent on a person's achieving organizational goals.

of a hierachy. He thought that low-level motivators had power only until they were fulfilled, then they lost their strength as further motivators and were replaced by the motivators which he considered to be higher-level motivators. Maslow, therefore, did not consider money to be a very important motivator. He accepted the idea that the money needed to meet people's needs for food and shelter would motivate them, but that beyond this point, money had a low motivational value.

Frederick Herzberg also had a low regard for money as a motivator. He held that more money can only reduce dissatisfaction but cannot generate satisfaction. It is surely true that many people are dissatisfied with the amount of their pay. They are dissatisfied because someone else makes more money than they do when they feel that this is not justified. And they are dissatisfied when their pay won't buy all of the things they want. So, sometimes they are dissatisfied with job pay differentials and sometimes they are dissatisfied with the absolute level of their pay. Reducing the causes of either of these dissatisfactions by adjusting a person's pay upward probably would, as Herzberg says, reduce his negative feelings more than it would improve his positive feelings.

At the same time, it is hard to believe that people getting pay raises are only less dissatisfied and never more satisfied. And, it will be recalled from Chapter 3, that there is some research evidence which shows that more money does increase satisfaction. We will consider more recent views of money as a motivator later in this chapter.

The Natural Inclination to Work. It will also be recalled from Chapter 3 that McGregor's Theory Y held that people putting effort into work was as natural as their putting effort into play.

We can admit McGregor's right to exaggerate to make a point. (His point was that managers did not need to try to drive people to work. Their inherent desire to work would cause them to work anyway if proper supervisory methods were used.) There is food for thought, however, in the fact that 80 percent of Americans retire at age 65 or earlier even when such retirement is not compulsory. Apparently, people's desire for work may not be so very great after all and it wears thin with the passage of time.

Sociologist Robert Schrank (who had thirty years of varied work experience before getting a Ph.D. degree in sociology) thinks that McGregor is wrong anyway and that people, at least employees, do not like to work. (Schrank's work experience included, among other things, being a plumber, a furniture factory employee, an automobile factory worker, a labor union official, and the Commissioner of the City of New York in charge of administering certain government-supported work programs.)

Schrank concluded that, "There seems to be a powerful inclination to do as little work as possible." He suggests that if people have job security and their basic needs are being met, there is no longer any motivation to work. He says, "My experience has given rise to serious doubts regarding humans' desires to work at all."[3]

Robert Vecchio tends to agree with Schrank. Vecchio went back over a 1955 study which concluded that most people want to work and will continue to work even when they can afford not to.[4] In 1955, 20 percent of the people interviewed said that they would not work if they didn't have to. In 1980, Vecchio found that 40 percent said that they would not work if they didn't have to. Vecchio concluded that the work ethic has slipped and is being replaced by the leisure ethic.

Responsibility and Challenge as Motivators. In spite of Schrank's and Vecchio's observations, it is surely true that most *managers* respond to Maslow's higher level motivators. In today's affluent society, no doubt a great many people are looking for much more than the physiological and security needs which can be satisfied by an ample pay check. Probably a great many of us want responsibility, challenge, and to use our own problem-solving abilities. Our real motivation may come from a sense of task accomplishment.

Yet, just as surely as some individuals *do* want responsibility and challenge, there are others who do *not* want such things. The work ethic is not universal nor is the desire to accomplish. One could wonder if motivation theorists do not overstate the desires of people when they say that most of us want challenge. There are surely more than a few people who do not want challenge and change. They want comfort, peace, quiet, a continuation of the familiar and the security of their present places in the organization.

And, as was noted in earlier chapters, managers just can't, in any case, give an employee who nails heels onto shoes in a shoe factory much self-actualization opportunity. It is unfortunate that many of the jobs to be done in this world can provide only very limited opportunities for self-actualization. At the same time, it is hard to believe that all people who do such work are dissatisfied.

Actually, worker dissatisfaction with their jobs is usually exaggerated in the literature. Several studies have found that 80 to 85 percent of working people say that they are satisfied with their work. They find their self-fulfillment outside their work and don't need to find it on the job.[5]

Power and Status as Motivators. On middle- and upper-level jobs, power and status are almost always very effective motivators. The responsibility for the work of a large department provides an exhilarating sense of power to most ambitious managers. High-level managers can heighten this sense of power in their subordinates by making more extensive delegations to them.

Status, too, seems to play an important part to a great many people. Arch Patton, executive compensation expert with McKinsey & Company, consultants, says that a great many executives would rather be made vice president than receive a $10,000 tax-exempt pay raise.

Actually, middle- and upper-level managers usually receive several kinds of added psychic income in the nature of status-showing extras. They may get a title, a private office, a private secretary, and other perks. But, and most important of all, they are members of the exclusive club of company bonus receivers where both status and money go together.

Scientists, on the other hand, are reported to respond to different motivation-type stimuli. Rarely do scientists want to become vice presidents, nor is a substantial pay raise of overriding importance to many of them. Probably a great many scientists would prefer an office off by themselves and freedom to work at what they like best to do and to come and go as they please. An article accepted by a learned society journal represents recognition to them and may mean more to them than either a title or a pay raise.

Organizational Success as a Monetary-Type Motivator. Top-level managers of businesses have to have an orientation toward the financial success of their organizations. The organization must take in more money than it pays out or go bankrupt. This forces such high level managers to think more in monetary terms and to put a monetary coloration on all of their decisions even if they, as individuals, are not very money conscious. They are motivated by the company's monetary future, no matter what their personal inclinations may be.

Intrinsic and Extrinsic Rewards

An *in*trinsic reward is an individual's feeling of satisfaction from something he has done or from the way something has worked out as a consequence of something he has done. In a sense, intrinsic rewards are rewards which the recipient grants to himself.

Intrinsic rewards are akin to Herzberg's "satisfier" motivators.

In contrast, an *ex*trinsic reward is something not included in job content. Extrinsic rewards include such things as praise, recognition, opportunity, pay, and so on. They are akin to Herzberg's "dissatisfier" motivators.

Researchers generally conclude that practitioners err in placing most of their emphasis on offering extrinsic rewards to motivate people. Practitioners assume that extrinsic rewards automatically produce a feeling of intrinsic reward inside people. This is usually the case but is not always so. Managers who are able to bring intrinsic rewards into play will generate greater motivation in their subordinates.

Monetary Rewards as Motivators

One can agree with those social scientists who say that more money by itself may not always be a very strong motivator, yet this does not deny that money can continue to be important to the recipient when he considers the things that money will buy.

A great many Americans own their own homes, on which they are paying on a twenty-five or thirty year mortgage. Most young couples have children who are expensive to rear and send to school. Even successful people are often not out of debt until they are sixty years old, and many people never get beyond living from pay day to pay day.

Money, as a motivator, continues to be important for many people until late middle age.

Curiously, most of the early social scientists gave little weight to the idea that a person's desires for the better things in life (travel, vacations, more opulent living) would motivate him to work for the money

which would make such a life possible. These theorists accepted money as a motivator for people as a requirement for subsistence but undervalued it as a motivator for people who want to live better.

Nor did most early social scientists consider the individual differences in people, nor did they put much stress on people's habits, which will, in some people, cause low-level motivators, including the desire for more money, to become a habit. It would be interesting to hear Maslow try to reconcile his theory with Pavlov's salivating dog's learned habits. And, to some people, more money is a measure of their achievement in society; it proves to them that they are better than other people.

In any case, it appears that in business organizations, the design of the compensation system is an important factor in the motivation of managers. In most American businesses the total remuneration of higher-level managers is made up of two or more parts: a base salary, plus one or more monetary extras whose size depends upon the individual's performance or on the organization's achievements, or both.

Thus, top administrators in business organizations, most of whom responded positively to monetary incentives on their way up, continue to believe that extra pay, contingent on good achievement, will motivate their subordinate managers. Stogdill's review of the research on monetary rewards showed that pay is a very strong motivator for managers at all levels.[6]

Top-level managers, too, need to try to avoid letting money become a Herzberg-type dissatisfier. They should use money to keep the organization staffed and to keep employees feeling that they are well treated. They can do this by paying wages equal to the wages of other organizations in the area. Similarly, job evaluation should be used to establish equitable pay differentials between jobs in their own organizations. Again, if this is done, it generates a feeling of being fairly treated. Workers are less likely to be dissatisfied over money matters.

Piecework Incentives. Factory production workers are sometimes paid on an "incentive" plan. Usually this is by the piecework method. Their pay is related to their output; the more they produce, the more their pay. Such plans used to be more common than they are today but they have by no means disappeared and are still the usual method of paying for work in the clothing, shoe, steel, and electrical appliance manufacturing industries.

The decline in use of wage incentive plans is related to the growth of service-type work where it is often impossible to set satisfactory production standards as well as from the use of more assembly line paced jobs in factories and to the frequently found dissatisfaction with the reasonableness of the production standards set.

"Cafeteria" Pay Methods. Edward Lawler is one behavioral scientist who thinks that money is more important than yesterday's behavioral scientists thought it was. Lawler says, "The writings of behavioral scientists such as Maslow and Herzberg seem to have convinced many executives that pay is not all that important to employees." Because executives believe this, says Lawler, they have tried to improve operating effectiveness through job enrichment, team building, and management training, but none of these things work very well unless pay is tied to performance. "Pay *is* an important part of the total system," says Lawler.[7]

Lawler suggests a "cafeteria" approach to all pay extras. Some people want extra pay for extra production, some want longer vacations, some want bigger pensions, etc. Why not let them take their choice? This is just what American Can, TRW, and a few other companies are doing.[8] These items are all wage costs to the employer who really does not care which benefits are chosen so long as their equivalent hourly cost is equal.

TRW reports that the extra bookkeeping work resulting from letting workers choose which extras they want, is minor compared to the extra job satisfaction generated. This is particularly helpful when both husband and wife work. If the husband's extras include hospitalization insurances for him and his wife, she can omit this coverage on her job and elect some other benefit.

Loyalty

There was a time — years ago — when loyalty played a strong part in motivation. Employees were expected to be, and usually were, "loyal" to the organization. They expected to work reasonably hard for organizational benefit in exchange for reasonable pay and reasonable treatment on the job.

Today, in the Western world, superiors can count very little on loyalty to cause subordinates to do their best. Fair wages and fair treatment on the job are the rule in most organizations. Consequently, they do not generate much feeling of loyalty. Only in Japan is there any carryover of the old feudal feeling of a loyalty obligation to a superior.

Such loyalty as can be developed is brought about through fair treatment and Likert system 4 managing. It has to be earned through a history of fair treatment and cannot be bought by high wages alone. But even a system 4 manager can expect only nominal loyalty. At best, loyalty plays only a minor part in motivation in most organizations in the United States today.

Nor is it different at high levels. High-level managers change employers almost as frequently as do low-level employees. One could wonder who or what a person should be loyal to.

Motivation in Practice

A great many practicing managers are aware of behavioral science theories on motivation and many of them try to apply them. This section discusses a number of practical areas where motivation is important. It closes with a consideration of job enlargement and job enrichment, concepts which have many supporters who place considerable faith in them as motivators at operating levels.

Supervision, Motivation and Reinforcement

Much of the theory of motivation deals with those influences or impelling forces which are inside the individual: personality factors, attitudes, perceptions, and the like. This is one side of the picture. The other side has to do with what managers can do or what appeals they can make to cause subordinates to do what needs doing and do it in a maximum rather than a minimum way.

As a usual thing, supervisors have, in their minds, a picture of what they want their subordinates to do. If the subordinates do what their supervisors want them to do, they will probably be rewarded in some way. Sometimes this is called the "carrot and stick" philosophy. Harry Levinson once called this the "jackass" theory (the employee is said to be treated like a jackass, with a stick threatening him from behind and a carrot dangling in front of him to produce forward motion).[9] Levinson is one of many people who believe that this is a poor way to motivate people.

Psychologist B.F. Skinner takes a different approach. Skinner believes that rewards *should* occur when people accomplish organizational goals and *should not* occur when people do not accomplish organizational goals. Only when rewards are withheld until after accomplishment occurs will there be a relationship between rewards and performance.

Skinner and the members of his school of thought emphasize that "reinforcement" is the most important cause of "behavior modification" (changes in behavior patterns) over a period of time.[10]

Reinforcement is something good (Levinson's carrot) *always happening, and soon,* to a person as a *result* of his performance of the desired behavior. The reinforcement is the repetition of the reward every time the preferred behavior occurs and the repetition of the penalty when the undesired behavior occurs.

When the favorable consequences for the desired behavior are strong, then such behavior will increase. Conversely, if the reinforcers motivate the wrong behavior, then that behavior will increase.

Sometimes supervisors unwittingly encourage wrong behavior. The supervisor who overlooks tardiness by employees is actually reinforcing tardiness. Or, if he assigns the most difficult jobs to those who arrive at work on time, again, he is reinforcing lateness. If he gives the early arrivals the right to choose the easy jobs, he is reinforcing arriving on time.

Skinner-type behavior modification programs are reported to have been very successful and have contributed to effective operations at 3M, B.F. Goodrich, Western Air Lines and in other organizations.[11] In practice, Skinner programs rely not only on reinforcement but also on the removal of impediments to productivity.

Controls as Motivators

Controls, the subject of Chapters 23 to 25, serve as motivators in that they influence lower-level managers to do things which will keep the organization moving in the direction of its goals. Control reports also motivate low-level managers by being evidence that higher-level managers care about what they do.

Properly designed controls motivate managers to undertake certain actions rather than other actions. They adjust their behavior and what they do according to the way budgets and reports are set up. They do things to make their records look good and to impress their superiors and their appraisers.

Even college students are motivated to do things to make their records look good. Many times professors are asked, "What kind of an examination are we going to have? What will it cover? How can I study for it?" The student wants to do whatever will make his record look good. He wants to be sure to study the things on which he will be examined. He does not want to "waste his time" studying things on which he will not be examined. The important thing, how much he learns, becomes secondary to his wanting to have a good record. His behavior (the things he does) is influenced by the way the controls operate.

Subordinate managers, as they respond to control, sometimes do things which are not in the best interests of the organization, but this only emphasizes that controls *do* motivate. Illustrations are given in Chapter 24 of both beneficial and harmful actions being taken in response to controls. And it was noted earlier in this chapter that salesmen paid a commission based on dollar sales sold certain products, but when their pay was based on the profitability of the items sold, they changed their emphasis and sold more of the highly profitable products and fewer of the low profit items. They were motivated by and responded to the design of the reward system which caused them to do things which helped accomplish organizational goals.

Job Limitations and Motivation

The opportunity for subordinates to develop the details of their own jobs is generally regarded as being a positive motivating factor. Yet this source of motivation will be limited if the job itself has limitations so far as development is concerned.

An apprentice bricklayer learns, during his apprenticeship, to do more and more difficult work. When he finishes his training, he is qualified as a journeyman in his craft. But from this point on, there is little more which is possible in the way of job expansion open to him. With further experience he will no doubt acquire even a little greater skill but the added skill needs of the work and the calls for skills beyond the capabilities of a newly qualified journeyman are almost nonexistent.

It is the same with most low-level managerial jobs. The job requirements can soon be mastered and the new manager can soon perform the work in a fully capable way — but there are limits to the job. It does not grow and is not expandable beyond rather confining limits. Once lower-level managers have reached these limits, there is little more that the job can offer in the way of challenge whose mastery can be a motivator. Therefore, it may be a mistake to train subordinates so that they can handle more responsible jobs when few such jobs will ever be open to them.

Middle-level managerial jobs are not wholly different. Such jobs have wider horizons, yet they, too, have limits. Eugene Jennings, specialist on executive mobility, says that a person promoted to a higher job can usually master the additional know-how required on the new job in from one and one-half to two years. The limits of the job's mission place restrictions on how much a person can grow on that job even though the specific man or woman on the job may have the potential for considerable more growth.

The difficulty of job limitations usually becomes even more pronounced for upper middle-level jobs because of the pinching pyramid. There are just not enough still higher jobs for very many lower-level managers to move up into so they may get to feeling "boxed in." After a while their motivation lags and they lose their enthusiasm.

The "Half-Life" of Motivation

The laws of physics tell us that radio-activity in matter decays as time passes, albeit often very slowly. The persistence of radiation is often described in terms of its "half-life," the length of time it takes for it to shrink to half of its original strength.

Motivation, too, has a strong tendency to decay. New jobs and new surroundings are usually stimulating and offer challenge. Newly promoted people are often highly motivated at the start. But, once they master their jobs, the challenge, the stimulation, and the motivation tend to die away. Half of the extra motivation (its "half-life") may die away before very long.

The failure to recognize the decaying and weakening strength of many kinds of motivation often causes disappointments over results from meritorious programs. In factories, a newly installed "zero defects" program almost always causes quality to improve. ("Zero defects" means that inspectors reject whole lots of parts already produced if they find even one defect in the small sample they inspect.) So, also, a newly installed "management-by-objectives" program usually produces improved initial effects. But, in both cases, all too soon many of the beneficial effects decay away; the programs get to be "old hat" and lose their power to motivate.

Superiors need to recognize the tendency for motivation to decay and, where possible, to insert new motivations from time to time. Perhaps they can change a subordinate's job in some way or the superior can ask a subordinate to investigate some problem even if it is more to furnish him something new to do than it is because the problem needs investigating.

Social scientists put self-fulfillment at the top of their pyramid of motivators.

They feel that after lesser objectives are reached they diminish in importance as motivators. Yet, actually, any goal reached, even self-fulfillment, probably diminishes as a continuing motivator.

The teaching profession illustrates this point. This profession is stimulating and carries with it rich rewards in self-fulfillment. Yet in universities (where professors do not have to retire until they are seventy years old) only 10 percent choose to stay so long. Eighty percent retire at sixty-five or earlier.[12] Even strong and deep-seated motivation reaching toward self-fulfillment tends to lose its appeal and even professors, doctors, and musicians sometimes get tired of their work.

Motivation Growing Out of Sanctions and Penalties

Superiors almost always have the power to administer sanctions and to withhold rewards or to impose penalties. They can discipline a subordinate, denying him privileges, or at low levels, they can lay him off without pay for several days. In extreme cases, the superior can even discharge a subordinate.

It is hard to avoid having to take punitive actions in some cases because some of the things that people do just cannot be tolerated. Consider, for example, these matters:

· Insubordination, refusal to do the work assigned, refusal to work overtime.
· Fights or altercations with superiors.
· Dishonesty, theft, falsification of records.
· Incompetence, negligence, poor workmanship, and violation of safety rules.
· Horse-play and trouble making.
· Illegal strikes, strike violence, and deliberate restriction of production.
· Absenteeism, tardiness, and leaving early.

· Intoxication, use of drugs on the job, bringing intoxicants or drugs into the plant.

This is an incomplete list of causes of some 300 cases of disciplinary actions at the plant level which went to arbitration in the late 1970s.[13] Actions such as these on the part of subordinates, call for some kind of action. Punishment appropriate to the misdemeanor is generally imposed.

Organization scholars usually oppose punitive actions. They point out that penalties may generate antagonism and lowered motivation. Richard Arvey and John Ivancevitch report, however, that, on the contrary, such penalties, fairly administered, usually generate better feelings, greater respect, and greater compliance with the rules.[14] (See Figure 15-3). Employees *do* come to work on time if they are taken to task for coming late. And drinking alcohol on the job *does* diminish when people are penalized for it. Fear of punishment motivates subordinates to modify their behavior.

Sociologist Robert Schrank, too, feels that penalties are worthwhile. He said, after his experience with New York City's civil service bureaucracy, that, "Managers in manufacturing have available tools of retribution (the measurability of work and penalties for poor performance), which are nonexistent in the public service sector. Civil service workers have little to fear since, if New York is any example, a civil servant is never fired. Experience makes me wonder if people will, in fact, work at all if we remove the punitive consequences of not working."[15]

Motivation From Nobility of Cause

In the last chapter we said that leaders of noble causes found it easy to enlist

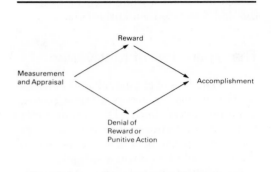

Figure 15-3
Depending on the appraisal which results from measurement managers can dispense rewards or apply sanctions as means for strengthening a person's desire to accomplish.

followers. Nobility of cause can generate strong motivation to goals. Unfortunately, organizational matters are rarely noble causes so it is not possible for managers to generate enthusiasm of this kind in the minds of their subordinates. Making the world safe for people to be free can motivate people to fight and possibly be killed. Religious fervor can stir people to put their souls into their work.

Few organization managers can, however, develop in their subordinates the motivation that nobility of cause can develop. Even government employees are likely to develop only bureaucratic job preservation type motivations even though some of their causes have elements of nobility about them. But very few business managers have missions which can generate much noble-cause motivation in subordinates.

These limitations should not, however, keep managers from motivating their subordinates as best they can. They can still manage in ways which draw out more than minimum effort from their subordinates.

Motivation From Comparisons With Peers

Whenever it is possible to compare the performances of people, a great many of them respond and compete strongly with each other to make the best showing. Part of the motivation lies in the competition itself apart from the rewards which go to the better performers. Reasonable competition, if not carried on so strongly as to be disruptive, often pushes people to higher accomplishment than they would otherwise reach.

Actually, it may be unnecessary for superiors to try to emphasize competition as a motivator. Every ambitious lower-level manager knows that he is constantly being evaluated by his superior and that his performance is being compared to the performances of other managers. There is a competitive urge in the minds of a great many people even though their jobs are not always capable of being compared directly to other jobs.

Job Enlargement and Job Enrichment

Physical Job Enlargement. At bottom levels, especially in factory work, many jobs are highly repetitive. An employee's complete task takes perhaps one minute and is done repetitively all day long. Most jobs of assembling stoves, refrigerators, television sets and automobiles are of this kind. Such specialization is usually highly productive, but many people find such jobs monotonous and boring (although not everyone feels this way). Admittedly, there seem to be many more repetitive, uninteresting jobs needing doing than there are people who are attracted to such work. Yet, since the work pays well (over $20,000 a year), there are usually many applicants for these jobs.

Sometimes these jobs can be expanded horizontally, or "enlarged" and made more interesting by allowing operators to do a few other things occasionally just to add a little variety and reduce the repetition a little.

International Business Machines tries to make its assembly line jobs in the factory more interesting by letting assemblers go after more parts when they need them and to do other things occasionally. Avon Products (facial creams, etc.) has production workers change jobs every hour.

The hope is, of course, that the more interesting (and less boring) the work can be made, the more productive the employee will be.

Psychological Job Enrichment. Much more promising is the idea of enriching jobs psychologically, or *vertical* job enrichment. The core philosophy here is to put more challenge and more achievement interest into jobs and to provide the employee with an opportunity to grow psychologically and mature in his job. Workers are allowed to make more decisions about their jobs. There is more participation and interaction between supervisors and employees. Superiors talk with subordinates, telling them the significance of their work and telling them what is going on. Superiors consult with subordinates and ask them for their ideas. Suggestions are welcomed and are either acted upon or reasons for inaction are given.

One kind of job enlargement has employees working in small groups rather than as individuals along an assembly line. This type of enrichment seems to contain one element of motivation which is lacking when employees work as individuals or when they work as members of very large groups. In small groups, when one member has difficulty, the others help him out because the group's performance will be impaired. This cooperative attitude seems not to develop under other work arrangements.

Sweden's Volvo and Saab companies, both makers of automobiles, have tried using small groups in assembling car components and report better satisfied workers, better quality from greater interest in work, and lower absenteeism, with total costs being reported to be about the same as with regular assembly lines. (Manufacturing costs are higher but total costs, considering the improved quality, are a little less.)

Merits of Job Enlargement and Job Enrichment. In spite of the considerable evidence supporting the desirability of job enlargement and job enrichment, there is other conflicting evidence.

In 1974, six Detroit autoworkers went to Sweden and worked in small groups in the Saab-Scandia company making component assemblies for automobiles for one month. Five of the six did not like the experience because it took too much concentration and the pace was too fast. One said, "If I've got to bust my ass to be meaningful, forget it; I'd rather be monotonous."[16]

General Motors tried using groups in its GMC division where it makes buses, but gave it up after it proved to be too costly.[17]

Other research studies have found that as many as half the workers themselves do not believe that enlarged jobs are better jobs. The employees interviewed often preferred jobs with less responsibility and less troublesome variety. Younger workers are just as uninterested in job enlargement and job enrichment as are older employees. Unions do not demand job enlargement. Job enlargement is usually imposed by management. In fact, Leonard Woodcock, when he was president of the United Automobile Workers, said that job enlargement is nonsense.[18]

Logic would suggest that the gains from job enlargement, particularly of the kind that merely adds a few more minor physical movements, might be limited largely to initial gains associated with newness which will wear off. A factory operative allowed to do his job his own way and to do a few more things than he used to do might well find this more interesting for a while. But most such jobs are just not inherently interesting enough to keep a person's interest high over a long period. The possibility of "humanizing" such jobs is quite limited.

Flextime. A different approach to making work more acceptable is the use of "flextime" (sometimes called "flexitime"). In flextime, as used at Metropolitan Life Insurance and at some places in General Motors, workers can come to work early and leave early or come late and leave late, or take time out during the day for shopping or appointments. Where workers perform work which does not have to be intermeshed closely with the work of others, this can work satisfactorily, and the workers like it since it gives them more freedom.

Although workers like flextime, it makes extra work-scheduling problems. There is some evidence that worker productivity improves but this is not clear.[19]

"Schmoozing"

Robert Schrank feels that the most effective way to improve life on the job, and, it is hoped, productivity, is to increase what he calls the "schmoozing" opportunities.

"Schmoozing" is camaraderie among workers. It is telling jokes, lining up at the water cooler, telephoning a friend on company time, wandering around the plant, and taking a long lunch break. It is talking about sports, sex, family, or politics. (It is, in fact, doing almost anything except work.)[20]

As Schrank sees it, neither job enlargement nor job enrichment of the kinds we have been talking about will improve the schmoozing opportunities on the job. People need to be able to see and talk to each other; they need a sense of community. When managers don't supply these opportunities, they overlook what, to Schrank, is the most important way to humanize work.

Schrank also does not see boring work as any great difficulty. He says, "My observation has been that there are more people who seem to accept boring repetitive work than there are those who are dissatisfied and complain about it. They accept it because it is the best they can do under the circumstances."[21]

At the American Telephone & Telegraph company, women who used to work for the company and are now homemakers frequently call in to see if there is any part-time work. Their usual comment is, "What we miss isn't the work, it's our colleagues and friends." When camaraderie can operate, it offsets many job shortcomings.

It is a little difficult to appraise the value of Schrank's viewpoint. His blueprint of what to do to humanize work calls for a lengthy list of time consuming non-work activities. One can wonder if the cost of all these non-work activities would be offset by greater productivity during the periods when workers do some work. He gives us no evidence that it would.

Summary

When organizational members are motivated, they try harder. In part, motivation is inside a person, yet his motivation can be heightened or reduced by the way superiors act and by the policies and practices of the organization.

Social scientists have found that motivation is a complex concept. People are individuals and so do not all respond to motivators in the same way. Some people want power, some want to achieve, whereas some others are not very highly motivated. Most managers, at least in the American culture, seem to want to achieve and to accomplish something they can call their own. This desire is not very apparent at lower levels where employees may be working primarily in order to meet life's necessities. But as soon as basic needs are met, then the more basic motivators (which include the desire for money) become less effective. Superiors need to recognize this and to provide motivators appropriate to the circumstances.

Positive motivation is not all generated as an outgrowth of good leadership or positive rewards. The reverse side of the coin, negative sanctions and the denial of rewards, also motivates people. So does the organization's structure of goals and its reporting system. Organizational members are motivated to do the things which will result in a favorable report.

The use of monetary rewards is regarded by social scientists as not having very strong motivating power. Yet, bonus plans based on accomplishments are, in fact, widely used in American companies. Business leaders seem not to be wholly convinced that money does not motivate. At least, they continue to offer monetary inducements.

Motivated people are so much more productive than unmotivated people that managers would like very much to make jobs more interesting to employees. But a great many of the jobs of this world are highly repetitious and boring. Job enlargement and job enrichment are both methods for making such jobs a little more interesting; it is hoped this will cause workers to be more productive.

Review Questions

1. What is a person's "interest reserve"? How big is it? How can it be tapped and drawn out so that it is applied instead of only being latent?

2. Is it true that superiors cannot generate motivation in subordinates and that, instead, motivations are something deep within us which can only be appealed to and drawn out? Discuss.

3. How do organizational scholars handle the matter of individual differences in their theories? Discuss.

4. It is pretty well agreed that it is a good idea to tie in the organization's reward-penalty system to a person's innate motivations. Then he will accomplish his personal goals if he accomplishes the organization's goals. What problems are there in trying to fuse these two sets of goals?

5. The text suggests that the horizon of challenge on many jobs is not very distant and that this limits the motivation which comes out of a person's desire to master the job. What can managers do to generate motivation under such circumstances?

6. Is there any way to counter the half-life or the decaying effect of motivation? Discuss.

7. Motivation theorists usually devote very little attention to the positive motivation that might come out of using negative sanctions. Do negative sanctions have a place in creating positive motivation? Discuss.

8. Discuss the possibility of using job enlargement or job enrichment to increase motivation.

Questions for Analysis and Discussion

1. "If I didn't have to eat every day, I'd give up my job." Do many people feel this way? How does this tie in with McGregor's Theory Y (work is as natural to people as play and people don't need to be driven to it)?

2. It is often said that directions to subordinates should include reasons why. Yet, isn't this irrelevant? Does a carpenter building a house really need to know why? What part do reasons why play in motivation?

3. The college football coach, after a losing season, extended his area of recruiting and his talks to alumni groups and covered more high schools. Should this be considered to be a change in "behavior"? What is the difference between a person changing his behavior and his mental attitudes? Does it matter which it is called?

4. As an experiment, a large electric company told a group of employees that they were very capable and that they were being paid more than the regular rate for their work. (This was office work where the employees themselves had no way of knowing whether this statement was true or not, and it was actually not true. They were not being overpaid.) The company kept drumming this idea in. The employees responded by being more productive. Wouldn't it be a good idea for a company to use praise in lieu of money? Discuss.

5. After several years in the top job, the company president said, "Perhaps the most important thing I learned is the need to help bring out the largely untapped potential of people in lower levels of management." Isn't there an implication here that the *job* potential is something more than lower people see? Is this so? Actually, it would seem that the potential which could be used on lower jobs is quite limited. Suppose that the *employee's* potential exceeds even the maximum that the job might call for—then what?

6. How can the managers of a utility company or a railroad be motivated? If the managers of either one try hard and earn a profit, the rates customers pay (which are regulated) will be set so as to limit the profit. But, if management does not do well, the regulating commission may allow a rate increase (since the company's managers claim that they can't make any profit on the present rates). How can there be much motivation to manage well under these circumstances?

7. How can motivation be held at high levels? Doesn't everything get to be less interesting as time goes along? Discuss.

8. Isn't it wrong to base a manager's pay on results instead of effort? What problems are there in this matter? Suppose that a superior believes that effort should be rewarded, how might he go about bringing effort into the reward picture?

9. How is it possible to keep middle-level managers enthusiastic and productive on jobs which they may hold for twenty years with little prospect for advancement? How can it be made clear to them that reaching and performing well on middle-level jobs is itself success of high order?

10. *Fortune* quoted a twenty-four year old assembly line worker in an automobile factory (who earned $16,000 in 1978) as saying, "I don't like nothin' best about that job. It really ain't much of a job. The bossman is always on our backs to keep busy." Is his a proper attitude for an employee

Motivation

who fastens wheels on automobiles? Does his attitude matter? Would job enlargement help? Discuss.

11. A senior partner of a large accounting firm says that most middle-level managers are underpaid. But, he says, this is helpful because it keeps them pushing hard to move up. Isn't this just a rationalization and just a convenient justification for underpaying middle-level employees? Discuss.

12. "Typically, people who are controlled by penalties for rule violations do not get rewarded for rule compliance." What should a manager do to produce a situation so that the net impact of the reward-penalty system will encourage the taking advantage of opportunities when there are good chances of success rather than encouraging the avoidance of even the slightest possibility of error?

13. If money is so unimportant, why is it that the big issue in almost all strikes by labor is their demand for more money?

Case 15-1   Teaching Summer School at State University

At the State University, professors are paid extra if they teach in summer school or in extension evening courses. Most professors do not take advantage of these opportunities (the pay is usually at a lower rate than that for regular classes) to earn extra pay because they prefer to do research, or to devote their time to writing or to other activities.

Last year Professor Collins did not teach in any extra programs. This year, however, he and his wife plan to take a trip to Africa so he is going to teach in the early summer term in order to help defray the cost of the trip in the latter part of the summer.

· Is it proper to say that money does not motivate except as a means for meeting people's basic needs for survival?
· Discuss this situation from the point of view of money being a motivator.

Case 15-2   Southern Company Hires College Graduates

Jack Helmers, owner of the Southern Company, a small company of 150 employees making plywood doors and other pre-fabricated items for houses, always put in long hours and usually worked on Saturdays as well.

His company was located near a large state university where he had several friends on the faculty. One of these professors remarked to him that

"Students nowadays are much more interested in going to work for small businesses than large companies." Consequently, Helmers hired two students but it wasn't long before each one quit and went to work for a large company. A second attempt to hire college graduates failed in the same say.

In describing his experience, Helmers explained, "They just don't want to work. They expect to be a success right away and by working only 40 hours a week. If a person is going to get ahead here, he has to work just as hard as I do. He has to have the interest of the business at heart just as I do."

· What are the advantages and disadvantages of the opportunities in small versus large companies?
· Would the people who quit the small company be likely to succeed in a large company?
· Discuss Helmer's problem and how he might solve it.

Case 15-3 Qualifying for ATTABOY Awards

The following communication appeared one morning on the company bulletin board. It was on a printed certificate form decorated with an orange scroll as a frame:

This CERTIFICATE for
Very Outstanding Performance
is awarded in lieu of a raise.

ATTABOY

Twelve ATTABOYS qualify you to be a leader of men, work overtime with a smile, explain assorted problems to management and be looked upon as a local hero.
Note: One AwHell, wipes the board clean and you start all over again.

· Discuss the thought implicit here. Should anyone in the organization do anything about it? Who? What should he do?

Endnotes

1. *Motivating Economic Achievement,* by David C. McClelland (Free Press, 1969).
2. For a discussion on this subject, see, "Motivation: A Diagnostic Approach," by David A. Nadler and Edward E. Lawler, in *Perspectives on Behavior in Organizations,* by S. Richard Hackman, Edward E. Lawler, and Lyman W. Porter, eds. (McGraw-Hill, 1977), pp. 26–38.
3. *Ten Thousand Working Days,* by Robert Schrank (MIT Press, 1978), pp. 111, 207.
4. "The Function and Meaning of the Job: Morse and Weiss Revisited," by Robert P. Vecchio, *Academy of Management Journal,* June, 1980, pp. 361–367. The Morse and Weiss study was reported in "The Function and Meaning of Work and the Job," by N.C. Morse and R.S. Weiss, *American Sociological Review* 20 (1955): 191–198.
5. *Most Americans Like Their Work,* a report of a survey of 3,000 people by The Conference Board, July 1978. See also, *The Quality of American Life,* by Angus Campball, Philip E. Converse, and Willard L. Rodgers (Russell Sage Foundation, 1976).
6. *Handbook of Leadership,* by Ralph M. Stogdill, The Free Press, 1974, p. 117.
7. "New Approaches to Pay: Innovations That Work," by Edward E. Lawler, *Personnel,* September-October 1976, pp. 11–23.
8. "Companies Offer Benefits Cafeteria-Style," *Business Week,* 13 November 1978, pp. 116ff.
9. *The Great Jackass Fallacy,* by Harry Levinson (Harvard University, 1973).
10. *About Behaviorism,* by B.F. Skinner (Knopf, 1974).
11. "Productivity Gains From a Pat on the Back," *Business Week,* 23 January 1978, pp. 56ff.
12. As reported in the 1979 annual report of The Teachers Insurance and Annuity Association, p. 6.
13. "Punishment in Organizations: A Review, Propositions, and Research Suggestions," by Richard D. Arvey and John M. Ivancevitch, *Academy of Management Review,* January 1980, pp. 120–132.
14. *Ibid.,* p. 125.
15. Schrank, Op. Cit., p. 208.
16. Reported in, *A Work Experiment: Six Americans in a Swedish Plant,* (Ford Foundation, 1976), p. 31.
17. "Job Enrichment: A Reevaluation," by Mitchell Fein, *The Sloan Management Review,* Winter, 1974, page 78.
18. "Union Response to Job Design and Work Innovation: An Explanatory Proposition," by Bernard J. White, *Proceedings of the Eighteenth Annual Conference of the Midwest Division,* Academy of Management, 1975, pp. 141–152.
19. "A Survey of the Empirical Literature of Flexible Workhours: Character and Consequences of a Major Innovation," by Robert T. Golembiewski, and Carl W. Proehl, Jr., *Academy of Management Review,* October 1978, pp. 837–852.
20. Op. Cit. p. 232.
21. "Worker Morale: Are There Solutions Abroad?" by Robert Schrank, *Management Review,* July 1979, p. 59.

Suggested Supplementary Readings

Arvey, Richard D., and John M. Ivancevitch. "Punishment in Organizations: A Review, Propositions, and Research Suggestions," *Academy of Management Review,* January 1980, pp. 123–132.

A Work Experiment: Six Americans in a Swedish Plant, Ford Foundation, 1976.

Dowling, William. "Are Workers Pigeons?" *Across the Board.* The Conference Board, November 1978, pp. 26–33.

Kearney, William J. "Pay for Performance? Not Always." *MSU Business Topics.* Spring 1979, pp. 5–16.

Objectives of Chapter Sixteen

1. To explain the concept of organizational development as a philosophy and as a method for improving inter- and intra-organizational relationships.
2. To familiarize the reader with certain techniques such as sensitivity training and transcendental meditation.
3. To offer examples of successful organizational development in operation.
4. To evaluate organizational development, reviewing its advantages and disadvantages.

Organization Development

The most effective kind of management is System 4, which reduces internal friction and develops harmonious cooperation.
Rensis Likert

Organization Development is an attempt to apply the research findings of behavioral scientists to improving the effectiveness of the operations of organizations by improving the quality of the working relationships of organizational members. OD tries to do this by developing a climate of helpful cooperation in communication, mutual trust, and more consideration for other people's feelings.

OD's thrust is toward improving total *group* performance rather than improving managers as individuals. The emphasis is not on how A can get B to do better, but on how A and B can work together and become more effective. OD relies heavily on group processes for unearthing and solving problems. OD is often very effective at lower managerial and at operating levels. At these levels, managers in OD applications almost become non-managers and joint participants rather than supervisors.

In Chapter 3, we reported that many business managers feel that managing in a heavily group-participative atmosphere, especially at bottom levels, is too loose and soft and is not results-oriented enough. Such a feeling overlooks the fact that this type of management has, in some cases, been very effective. General Motors, Procter & Gamble, and General Foods have each had outstanding success with OD-type management in one or another of their units. These companies are only three of many which have used OD successfully.

This points up an important facet of this concept. The open and relatively free participation and strongly communications-oriented atmosphere need not be loose and soft management. No doubt it could become so, as apparently it did (to the great misfortune of the company) in the early 1970s at Mattel (toys) and Boise Cascade (lumber and land development) and some others, but

it does not have to become so as is attested to by OD's successes.[1]

Properly used, OD is a goal oriented, practical form of management. For OD to work successfully, it must deal with a number of activities designed to improve the abilities of managers to get along with each other. Often, managers have to change their behavioral patterns and almost change their personalities.

Implementing Organization Development

Successful OD is almost a new way of life and of managing, so it is a matter of *educating* organizational members. This education is carried out by involving them in solving problems which exist in their areas of operation. The process starts with introductory-type "intervention" meetings, after which the group members are led into considering problems relating to their work and they, themselves have to solve these problems and have to carry on their work in the future so that such problems do not recur.

Interventions

OD practitioners refer to much of what they do as "interventions." A person could almost substitute the word "activities" for interventions as they use the word.

Interventions are attempts to influence. They are the means by which OD is brought to bear upon the operations of ongoing organizations. Interventions may deal with cultures, processes, and events at many levels in organizations. They deal with individuals, pairs, and small groups.

Interventions include any and all kinds of activities designed to improve the interaction capabilities of the organization's people. They, therefore, include, wholly or partially, many well known practices whose worth have been established in the past.

OD interventions, at times, use group meetings, job enlargement, job enrichment, management by objectives, work simplification, planning, goal setting, sensitivity training, Grid OD, team building, transactional analysis, relaxation responses, education and training, coaching, investigating and reporting, feedback, and problem solving.

Interventions include "confrontation" meetings, "diagnostic" meetings, and other actions and processes designed to improve the organization's interactive functioning, and its ability to deal with change and conflict resolution.

Interventions should not, however, stop with meetings and discussions but should include planned programmatic activities aimed at improving organizational effectiveness. They deal with real problems and are limited to explicit goals and objectives.

Confrontation Meetings

One of the best ways to start an OD program is to start with a "confrontation" meeting. This meeting is called by a high-level official who himself attends the meeting along with an OD consultant. The word "confrontation" here does not mean a meeting where antagonists confront each other. "Confrontation" here means that organizational members are confronted with or are brought to realize that there are certain problems which are holding down the organization's accomplishments.

In a confrontation meeting, the members of the group are asked to think about places where their units of the organization are not doing as well as they might because of difficulties between or-

ganizational units. The confrontation meeting is intended to bring to the surface problems and differences in beliefs, feelings, attitudes, values, and norms, and to start along the road to removing these obstacles to effective interaction.

The confrontation meeting thus shows the need for and sets the climate for improvement. It tries to loosen up the rigidities which tend to develop in bureaucracies. The first meeting may even go so far as to set priorities to the problems and to point out which problems are either the most pressing or are the most formidable.

OD Consultants

To be successful, OD programs seem to need the catalyzing effects of outside OD consultants. An external consultant is free from the cultural constraints of the organization and is more free to function as a change agent. Members of inside groups are often part of the problem and so cannot assume the proper detached and impersonal posture needed at times. Also the insiders are often not expert enough in OD to make it into the effective process that it can be. Even if they are expert enough, often the inside expert's peers do not accept him as an expert, and consequently he cannot be very effective.

The consultant can be of the greatest value to the group if he avoids taking the position of group leader and maintains a stance of being a coach, suggesting alternative courses of action for consideration rather than recommending or deciding. His purpose is to help the group members themselves learn to function more effectively. He should not lapse into the expert role just to please the client (he should resist answering questions such as, "What should we do?") but rather should help the group explore its problems and learn how to solve their problems themselves.

Consultant
provides:

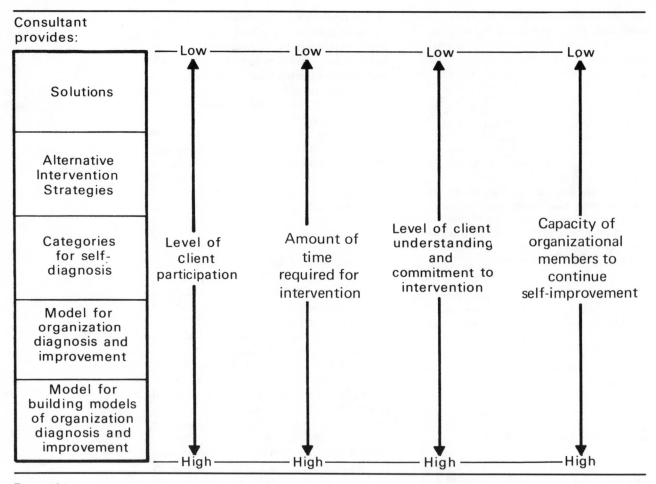

Figure 16-1
Levels of consultant interventions.

Diagnostic Meetings

Once an OD program has been start-ed it continues in the form of occasional "diagnostic" meetings. Diagnostic meetings can be focused on problem solving, decision making, role clarification, or task accomplishment. In these meetings information and data found during investigations carried on as a result of group discussions made in the last meeting are reported (and such things as group attitudes are regarded as data). The group then considers the data and plans programs of actions to remedy problems.

Diagnostic meetings are meetings in which *group members* jointly consider problems and alternative solutions. This is a very important part of OD. The *group* decides what the problems are; the *group* decides what information it needs; the *group* analyzes the data; and the *group* decides the planned remedial actions. The people involved in the problem are the same people who work out its solution.

Even though OD starts as a top-down program, it operates largely as groups carrying on from there. Only group members, not superiors, know about most of the problems, large and small, which are keeping them from being more effective. Not even the consultants can know about the problems. And, until a confrontation meeting calls their attention to the problems, even group members may hardly be aware of them.

It is just the same with problem solutions. Almost always these can be arrived at most satisfactorily by the group. Group members know most about which alternatives are feasible and what they can accomplish.

Feedback of Data

After data have been collected, the group studies and analyzes them. OD does not view facts as good or bad but looks at consequences. Facts are more *described* than *evaluated* (if they were evaluated, people would probably become defensive). Data are aids in solutions, not clubs to enforce. Data should be presented in a non-judgmental way, should be intended to be helpful, and should be offered in an atmosphere of mutual give and take. If there is anything that might embarrass an individual it might be better to tell him in private.

OD and Change

Since OD tries to improve organizational competence and effectiveness, it must deal with change. Sometimes this results in changes in job assignments which, in turn, cause changes in the status of people and of groups. Consequently, individuals and groups have to cope with all of the problems that changes can produce. OD assumes

that the best way to make changes become more acceptable is for them to be changes which have been recommended by the group itself. Many OD changes are made in this way and so usually do not meet with much objection. This approach is neither new nor is it peculiar to OD but without OD, it is often neglected.

Applied Learning from Using OD

In OD programs, the learning process differs from the usual situation in which management development activities deal with the individual manager by himself and away from the work situation. Learning and action are separated. In order to be effective, the learning must be transferred to actual operating situations.

The learning that comes out of OD differs in that, first, it deals with real problems and, second, the learning occurs as managers interact with each other and with groups as they work toward problem solutions. Problems deal with real people, those the manager works with as they work together at solving problems. In OD the skills are applied as they are learned. There is no need for a transfer of learning.

Conflict Resolution

"The marketing and engineering department heads are at swords' points right up to their hilts. They speak to each other only by memos or with eyes-averted antagonism at meetings. And, as disciples will, junior members of these departments work together only when they have to and with undisguised friction."

A common situation? No, not common, but not uncommon either. Top managers do sometimes have to contend with conflict among their subordinates. In the interests of harmonious relationships, they have to try to reduce conflict to a reasonable level. Common actions on the part of higher-level managers are persuasion, cajolery, head knocking, or even firing someone.

Actually, a minor amount of conflict can be helpful. Each group *should* stand up for its legitimate interests. Foremen acknowledged to be good foremen are usually known for the firmness of their positions tempered by a willingness to listen to the other side. Weak foremen allow themselves to be pushed around and then grouse about it.

Conflict may even be turned into something helpful. Standing up for one's position may bring things out into the open today which may result in changes which will reduce conflict in the future. Conflict, such as often arises in matrix management, can cause a better understanding of the other fellow's problems and more helpful cooperation in the future. In a similar way, the conflicts which sometimes arise between staffs and lines can often be ironed out so that cooperation in the future is enhanced.

A professional OD consultant can often help reduce conflict by serving as a "third party peacemaker." Above all, he needs to try to keep situations from becoming "win-lose" situations for conflicting parties. He needs to try to develop a "let's work it out ourselves" atmosphere instead of having conflicts turn into appeals to higher authority.

In one case, the foreman of the assembly department was not keeping the packing station clear and products were backing up and stopping the assembly line. The packing foreman complained that the assembly people changed labels and models without notifying him in advance, thus delaying the packing operations and causing the backing up. The assembly foreman reported that ample notification was always given.

When the trouble did not clear up, the general manager reversed the assignments of the two foremen, putting each one in charge of the other's department. The two foremen learned quickly to appreciate the other's problems. After two weeks they were returned to their old jobs more appreciative of the other's problems and the conflict disappeared.

When there is tension, competition, or outright conflict between groups, each group sees the others as enemies rather than as being neutral. Interactions and communications are frequently distorted and even inaccurate. Each group acts as if it were always right and the other always wrong.

Sometimes the difficulties can be improved upon simply by a greater interchange of information between the groups. Just talking things over face-to-face clears up many difficulties and helps develop cooperation. Usually, too, rotating one or two people between two areas, as was done in the example above, and having them work in the other department for a while, will improve their mutual understanding.

Sometimes, too, a problem need not be faced at all. If no one pays any attention to it, it withers away with the passing of time. Most of the time we get used to minor irritations. When traffic administrators put in a new fifty-five mile an hour speed limit or erect a new stop sign, it irritates most of us at first, but we soon learn to live with it. And, even if a minor problem doesn't go away, perhaps its consideration can be postponed. Problems are often more easily solved later after emotional feelings have died down.

Unfortunately, even minor irritations sometimes grow, like the irritation from a pebble in a shoe, rather than diminish in importance in people's minds. When this happens in organizations, irritations often lead to conflicts and managers need to try to resolve them.

An OD approach to conflict resolution might help here. When there seems to be a really consequential problem of internal conflict, the OD consultant might suggest that each group retire and have its own group meeting. In these meetings each group lists, in writing (see Figure 16-2), what it thinks the relationship ought to be and what the other group is doing or not doing which causes difficulties. Then the groups come back together and compare lists and find out what each dislikes about the other's list.

Donald Livingston suggests that two "rules of the road" are essential if making lists is to be productive. The first rule is that *one group does not tell the other group how to run its department.* The second rule is that *the lists should include only things which are going on now* and not what the other group did in the past. He suggests, too, that each group list only five items, put them in order of priority and then appoint a spokesman so that every-one is not talking.[2] Then the groups come together and consider their lists and how situations causing difficulties might be improved.

If the problems are not yet wholly cleared up, the groups can meet separately again and consider what they have now learned about each other and what else they might do to alleviate the problems the other group thinks they are causing for them. Then the groups come together again and agree on one list covering the action pro-grams they should undertake so that they will get along better in the future. Probably there should also be occasional review ses-sions later on where feedback information on results will be considered.

Possibly, too, internal conflict may

Engineering's Complaints

What marketing does that causes us problems:
1. Changes product manager assignments without telling us who is in charge of what.
2. Cost data format is inconsistent. We do not understand why some costs are budgeted against us rather than warranty.
3. Changes its mind on customer specs after we're told design is frozen; specs are sometimes incomplete and only added later.
4. Makes commitments to customers for delivery or performance specs we cannot meet.
5. Phasing of new orders makes work balancing very difficult.

Marketing's Complaints

What engineering does that causes us problems:
1. Changes its organization so often that we don't know who's in charge of some projects.
2. Doesn't always tell us when it makes a design change that affects customer acceptance; for example, the cover on a new widget.
3. Takes engineers off projects without telling us that there may be a delay in completion so that we can get back to customer.
4. Contacts customers without anyone in marketing or sales knowing about it.
5. R & D budget overruns catch us by surprise.

Figure 16-2
Lists of causes of conflict between two departments.
Source: Reprinted by permission of the publisher from PERSONNEL January-February, 1977 © 1977 by AMACOM, a division of American Management Associations.

Organization Development

316

be made worse just because the people are hurried and harried and overly irritable. If so, possibly their mental tensions could be relaxed by having them take up relaxation practices of the kinds described in this chapter.

OD at Bottom Levels

The primary thrust of OD is to improve the competence of managers to interrelate with each other both up and down vertically and also horizontally with peers. This same openness and cooperative atmosphere can also be developed at bottom levels between supervisors and operatives. The goal of OD is to develop a more effective operating organization at all levels and *it is at bottom levels where most end-accomplishment occurs.*

In the several outstanding successes of OD in operation, large increases have been achieved in bottom level productivity. These increases have been produced by developing a climate of trust and joint interest through open discussion of matters relating to the work of employees and by allowing employees a large amount of freedom to participate in all decisions relating to their work. Direct supervision is minimized and such supervision as remains casts the supervisor in a helping rather than in a directing role. Employees are given frequent progress feedback information so that they are informed at all times about how things are going so far as their work is concerned.

This improvement does not come from bottom level operatives being in on confrontation meetings but rather from their being supervised differently. An OD-type supervisor will, at bottom levels, try to treat people as full fledged members of the organization and try to get rid of any "closed club" atmosphere. The atmosphere of free and honest interchange of information that should be developed in middle-level managerial levels can carry down into superior-subordinate relationships at operational levels.

An OD-type supervisor tries to *maximize communications* between shop workers and management and tries to *eliminate "walls,"* social, hierarchical, or otherwise, between "us and them." OD-type supervisors try to avoid "adversary" feelings between themselves and their workers. OD-type supervisors answer questions and let workers in on news and tell them what is happening. Employees like to be brought in on the big picture.

Managers should give workers opportunities to become involved in solving problems relating to their jobs. It is frustrating to try to produce quality products on a machine which continually breaks down or which is hardly capable of producing high quality products. But the operator of such a machine might find his frustration turning into high interest if he were allowed to help try to develop a remedy for the problem and if his help and ideas were welcomed and not rebuffed.

Allowing workers to become involved in problem solving and even in goal setting and decision making, on matters relating to their work, offers interest and challenge to those workers who want this. Yet, at the same time, this places no obligation on those who don't want it.

Informal Groups

Cliques and groups inside organizations are sometimes of considerable importance. Such "informal groups" exist in almost all organizations and sometimes they have more to do with what gets done than do instructions from hierarchical superiors. Informal groups are discussed in Chapter 19, but groups also need to be mentioned here in our discussion of OD.

OD recognizes that two cultural systems are always operating in all organizations. There are, *first,* the formal elements such as policies, rules, procedures, and the hierarchy of formal authority positions. Besides this there is, *second,* the informal, almost wholly underground culture of feelings, attitudes and behavior which are hardly visible. Informal groups have no formally recognized being nor hierarchical status and they don't show on organization charts. Nonetheless, this informal hidden or suppressed domain of organizational life plays a part in what goes on.

OD tries to increase the congruency of these two domains. It emphasizes the collaborative aspects of the organization's subcultures by putting emphasis on work teams. OD assumes that the formal group leader needs the support and help of all members and groups of the organization, including the informal organization. In fact, OD strategy is often to work *more* through the informal system than the formal system. It assumes that the group culture is "owned" as much by subordinates as by the formal leader. It hopes to solve problems by bringing informal groups into the picture.

"QC" (Quality Control) Circles

A "QC" circle is a small group of employees who meet with or without their supervisor to discuss how the quality of the company's products can be improved, or how its production operations can be carried on more economically. Improvement suggestions are then made to management.

QC circles are common in Japan but are rare in the United States. (In Japan, workers used to meet in QC circles on their own time. Now it is on company time.) QC circles are not part of OD but we mention them here because they are an OD-like activity.

In Chapter 26, we will report that in Japan, there is an expectation of lifetime employment with the same organization.

This part of the employer-employee relationship generates an intense feeling of loyalty and of joint interest in Japanese workers. They are interested in the employer's success and they try to do all they can to help.

This whole idea of workers viewing themselves as partners in the organization is, of course, so praiseworthy, as a manager would see it, that attempts have been made to introduce it into the United States. But employee loyalty here seems not to be up to it. OD in the United States, as described in this chapter, has in it many elements which are similar to the Japanese QC circle idea but that is as far as it seems to be able to go.

Sensitivity Techniques

The changes needed to cause managers to operate in an OD fashion require them to change their mental "sets" and the way they manage. They need to become more perceptive and sensitive to the feelings of other people. This section deals with the ways managers can be trained to become more perceptive.

Sensitivity Training and "T-Groups"

Sensitivity training is a process where a group of people get together in "T-Groups" (for "training groups," also sometimes called "encounter groups") and tell each other the impressions they make on each other. Participants learn how they impress other people.

Most organizations using OD include sensitivity training as part of the program and some organizations which do not have OD programs carry on sensitivity training. Sensitivity training tries to train individuals rather than groups and is done away from the job and often among strangers. Hence it cannot be as effective standing alone as it can be as part of an OD program.

Over the years a great deal of evidence grew up pointing to the lack of awareness on the part of managers of the feelings of other people and how other people reacted to them. These were stumbling blocks to good communications and to good inter- and intra-group relationships.

Sensitivity training was developed to meet this problem. T-Groups are supposed to develop a greater sensitivity in people to the feelings of other people and to how people react to them. T-Groups help people become aware of their type III and type IV characteristics as depicted in Figure 16-3.

In T-Groups, people (usually 10 to 12 people make up such a group) come to-gether for, say, two weeks, and meet for two two-hour sessions daily in non-directed discussions where they talk about and explore their viewpoints, biases, and reactions to each other and delve into the reasons for their reactions. The discussions are not wholly non-directed. They are unstructured and agenda-less but there is a trainer present who acts as a catalyst and facilitator for the group. He probably tells the group that the purpose is "to explore their personal values and the impacts of their values on others." Frankness in discussions and criticism of each other is encouraged.

Participants are often baffled and even frustrated in the early days of T-Group programs from the lack of organization and the almost wholly non-directed sensitivity

	Known to self	Not known to self
Known to Others	Recognized by all **I**	Recognized by all but self **III**
Not known to others	Unrecognized by anyone but self **II**	Unrecognized by anyone **IV**

Figure 16-3
An "awareness" model. Sensitivity training would help people become aware of type III and type IV characteristics.

training sessions. (There are also lectures, general discussions, and sometimes competitive presentations of ideas by separate groups. These are in addition to the daily non-structured two-hour T-Group sessions.)

Reactions to such experiences are varied. Many participants are shocked to find their views and their reasons for their views rudely challenged and laid to biases. They often feel pilloried before the others, and they feel that their integrity has been attacked. Feelings sometimes run high. Probably most participants end up being considerably more perceptive of how other people react to them. They return to their jobs more aware of other people's feelings and will probably supervise their subordinates in a more understanding way.

For some, however, their T-Group experience is traumatic. People are not always benefited by the exposure of their inner feelings to raw criticism.[3] Even worse is to be criticized by strangers for biases imputed to them which they may not even have. In one case, two General Motors department heads needed psychiatric aid for six months after returning from a T-Group meeting. It took a long time to rebuild their shattered egos.

Some people believe that T-Groups, where the group members are strangers, are not very helpful. Chris Argyris, referred to in Chapter 3 in connection with his ideas on T-Groups, says that in these groups where people do not know each other, strangers make discourteous and unwarranted assumptions about their abilities to have insights into the personalities of other participants who are strangers to them. On the other hand, in groups where people know each other, it is hard to develop the proper candor. T-Groups are also negative. Participants find out how their views and actions upset other people but they don't find out how to generate acceptance for their ideas.

Nor do T-Groups improve the organizational climate which would allow an individual returning from a T-Group program to function differently now that he is himself a somewhat changed person. Instead, he experiences a "cold shower effect," a "reality shock," when he returns to his job in the real world. He returns to the same organizational situation he left and in it he has little opportunity to perform as a changed person.

Developing Cooperative Attitudes. Most OD programs include the T-Group approach but they modify it and try to make it less negative. They also try to broaden it so that it is not quite so much aimed at single individuals and so that the whole organizational atmosphere is improved. General Motors and Exxon have in-house programs of this type.

Improvement in cooperative attitudes is fostered by group discussions of problems and by face-to-face consideration of problem solutions. Conflict resolution efforts also improve cooperative attitudes.

These back-and-forth face-to-face contacts between members of different departments can be very helpful because, normally, most managers view almost everything only from the point of view of their own jobs. Even managers promoted or transferred to other jobs seem quickly to lose their appreciation of the problems in the departments they just left. Their views quickly take on the orientation of their present jobs. This seems to be even more pronounced with staff people than with line people. Because of this tendency to become insular, a certain amount of continual interaction and exposure to other people's problems is needed in order to develop and perpetuate understanding and cooperation.

Stress and Tension

Organizational conflict and lack of cooperation often result from managers being irritable or frustrated because of stress and tension. Stress and tension over prolonged periods sometimes finally cause high blood pressure and even heart trouble.

Stress and tension on the job come from conflict, role ambiguity and overloads. It comes from people having too much to do in too little time, from bosses demanding too much accomplishment and being too critical. And it comes from too little feedback, people not knowing how they stand.[4]

Besides these there are often off-the-job causes for anxiety and worry that most of us have to face from time to time. These include domestic problems such as divorce or alcoholism, health problems of family members or money problems from having too little money and too many bills to pay. People may feel "caught" in a chain of circumstances with no way out. Tension can also come from over-excitement and from poor sleep at night.[5]

Because of the trouble that excessive stress and tension cause, it is only to be expected that OD programs are usually concerned with them. Such OD attention is directed at reducing the troubles and thus improving organizational performance.

Avoiding Tension. There are a number of things which people might be able to do to help reduce tension. Job-caused tension is, unfortunately, usually hard to reduce. Some people report getting relief by deciding priorities for the things they have to do. Then they concentrate on doing the high-priority things first. Possibly, too, a discussion with the person's boss will result in his helping out by reducing his demands. Sometimes a manager in a stressful situation can delegate more and not carry the whole load himself.

Stress caused by excitement can be reduced just by staying away from excitement. An easily excited person can stop going to football and basketball games. And, if a person is a worrisome type, he doesn't have to look at the 11 o'clock news (which is usually depressing). Nor does he have to carry the weight of the world's problems on his shoulders.

Sometimes, just doing something different, breaking the routine, helps relieve tension. Often physical exercise helps by helping to induce restful sleep. Sometimes eating habits make for discomfort and interfere with normal sleep. Eating late at night, eating highly spiced foods, and drinking coffee or alcohol, all make such problems worse. These can be avoided.

Worry-prone people should also not plan too far ahead and should not set tight schedules. Nor should they compare what they get done with what other people get done. And, if at all possible, such people should arrange their money spending habits so that they do not get into financial binds and not be able to pay their bills. They should also have hobbies to which they can turn for relaxation and a change of interest.

Some of the most difficult problems arise in the health and domestic areas. Sometimes about all that a person can do is to try to accept life as it is and to try to remain tranquil. Possibly a "worry-hour" such as is described in Case 16-1 might help.

Meditation and Relaxation

A different approach to relieving stress and tension (different from trying to remove the *causes* of tension) and the irritability and conflicts which they so often cause is to try to reduce the mental tensions directly. Certain mental relaxation practices have been found to help relieve tensions and the harmful effects which they sometimes cause.

Interest in mental relaxation has grown since "Transcendental Meditation" (TM) became popular in the 1970s. TM is a method of relaxing the body and mind and of helping relieve mental and nervous tensions that build up in people. By relieving the body of tensions, TM brings about improvement in both a person's mental and physical well-being and in his performance on the job.

It is, therefore, not surprising that many OD programs include training in relaxation. It is reported to be used at Westinghouse, American Telephone and Telegraph, and many other organizations. And, as in the case of most of the practices used in OD programs, many organizations not having formal OD programs carry on relaxation programs.

"Transcendental Meditation" is the best known relaxation method. It comes from India where it has been associated with the practice of Yoga and where it has semi-religious overtones.[6] Neither of these facets of TM is of interest to managers trying to improve their organizations. But the relaxation part of TM *is* of interest to them because it has proven to be helpful in reducing tension and irritability.

The Meditation-Relaxation Process. There are five essential steps or requirements in a meditation-relaxation process.

1. A *definite relaxation period.* Effective relaxation cannot take place as a casual diversion at odd times on the job. It is much more effective if it is done at regular times when it will not be interrupted. Practitioners recommend two 20-minute periods a day, one in the morning before starting any activities and one in the evening before dinner.
2. A *quiet environment.* The relaxation session should be free from distractions. It helps to choose a quiet place where distractions, particularly noise distractions, will not inhibit the process.
3. A *word or phrase to be repeated.* The "meditation" part of the relaxation process is not really meditation at all. The person should *not* meditate on problems or troubles. Instead, he uses a mental device such as a word or phrase (TM practitioners call it a "mantra"). During the relaxing period this word or phrase is repeated mentally over and over again. This helps to keep other

things out of the mind and aids the relaxation process.

4. A *passive attitude.* During the relaxation session the person tries not to let things distract him. If thoughts come to mind and intrude, he tries not to dwell on them nor pay any attention to them but just to continue to think of his mantra. He should not worry if outside distracting thoughts occur. These will diminish with practice and the meditative state will predominate.
5. A *comfortable position.* A comfortable position allows for muscular relaxation which helps produce mental relaxation. The meditator should sit up, however, and not lie down, lest he go to sleep. The relaxing effects of sleep are different from those produced by conscious relaxing periods and are *not* as beneficial to tension reduction as is the relaxing period.[7]

Meditation-Relaxation Results. The results from these self-induced almost hypnotic trance-like relaxation periods are reported to be very beneficial. There seems to be a restorative process which counteracts and reduces the effects of stress. The blood pressure is reduced and the body uses less oxygen.[8]

Meditators are reported to become more tranquil, less tense, less anxious, more relaxed, more energetic, and more tolerant of life as it is and of conditions as they are. Mental patients and drug patients are often benefited by TM-like therapy.

Organization Development Evaluation

OD is no longer a new technique so it is widely known and widely practiced at least in limited ways. But OD users seem yet to be in the minority because it has not always been successful. It is like a delicate plant. It needs nurture and care and must be worked at continuously. On the good side, there are some cases in which it has been outstandingly successful. But OD has also had its failures. And there have been other cases in which OD has resulted in only minor adjustments in the organization's culture.

Advantages of Organization Development

The advantages of OD can be summed up as that it produces more effective management which results in better internal cooperation, higher morale, and greater productivity at lower levels.

A brief recounting of the experiences of two companies with OD will bring out its advantages. (General Foods' Gaines Dog Food plant experience at Topeka, Kansas, a third example, is written up as Case 16-3.)

OD at General Motors

General Motors has a successful OD application at its Lakewood plant in Atlanta, Georgia. Historically, this plant was a high cost and inefficient operation. OD was started in the early 1970s. It resulted in the usual OD pattern; initial great enthusiasm and lowered efficiency. Before long, however, direct labor costs improved and absenteeism and turnover declined. Scrap costs went from 4 percent to less than 1 percent and grievances went down from fifty to three per month. It took two years, though, for indirect costs to shrink, but improve they did after two years. By the mid 1970s, operations at the Lakewood plant had greatly improved.

General Motors also has a successful OD application at its Tarrytown, New York, automobile assembly plant. Before OD, this plant, too, had had a poor record of operations.[9]

OD at Procter & Gamble

Ted Mills reports that OD, which he calls, "Human Relations Development," (HRD) is, in some cases, so successful that companies don't want to talk about it. Mills reports that Procter & Gamble, in its Lima, Ohio, plant has found that, as a result of its HRD-type management, its production costs were only fifty percent of what they are in other comparable plants. But P & G denies access to its plants to researchers such as those from the National Science Foundation.[10]

Limitations of Organization Development

In spite of its many advantages, OD in its fullest form, which includes a great deal of worker participation at bottom levels, has not always worked out well. Mattel's and Boise Cascade's troubles have been mentioned. Another failure, that of Non-Linear Systems, is written up as Case 16-2.

The reasons for difficulties with OD are not altogether clear. Possibly OD is something which can be most successful only with small groups or with small organizations. Except for the two General Motors examples mentioned, nearly all reports of successful OD applications are with relatively small groups, and even the GM Tarrytown operation (2,000 employees) is relatively small.

Requirement of Changed Mental Attitudes. Another problem which seems to be a difficult one is that, in order for OD to succeed, most of the managers in an organization have to make substantial changes in their mental attitudes and in their behavior patterns. It appears that it is not always possible to bring these changes about.

Resistance of Middle-Level Managers. The most successful OD applications seem always to report a decrease in supervisory costs. This means fewer supervisory jobs. There is some evidence that middle- and lower-level supervisors are not enthusiastic because they feel threatened. Robert Schrank reported that he observed a successful OD application at the Philips Electrical company in Holland, but it was not being extended because middle-level people feared that they would lose control over the workplace.[11]

Requirement of Numerous Meetings. Meetings can also slow things down. With OD a good many meetings of groups are called for. These operate much like committee meetings and can easily take up too much time. They can also lead to indecisiveness. Both of these difficulties were reported to have occurred at Boise Cascade. At one time Boise Cascade was a heavily OD-oriented company, but today there is less OD there.

The Receding Horizon of Accomplishment. One seeming advantage of OD may well, in the long run, become a disadvantage. OD is on-going. It seems always to be "becoming" and "going toward" but it never arrives. This advantage (of always trying to perform better) contains the seeds of weakness. It tends to wear thin and to lose its drive. It also takes from three to five years for OD to become effective. During this time the normal promotions and retirements and personnel turnover in an organization cause numerous changes in managerial personnel which hamper the effectiveness of OD work.

Inadequate Rewards. Still another possible problem is the common lack of concern over the question, "What's in it for me?" OD literature seems to assume that most people have a drive toward personal growth and that they have a desire to and are capable of making a higher level of contribution to the attainment of organizational goals than most organizational environments bring out.

One can agree with this yet feel disturbed that the only kind of reward suggested for the individual is greater satisfaction on the job. He is allowed to share in everything except the extra profits. It would be only human nature for people who are doing a fine job and who are praised for doing well and who know that the company is profiting greatly from their good performance to expect more than a pat on the back or a kind word as a reward. It is hard to believe that greater satisfaction, by itself, will generate enduring motivation to do well for dear old General Motors, Procter & Gamble, or General Foods. Instead, the employee may feel exploited.

Summary

Organizational development is an attempt to create a healthy atmosphere of cooperation and improved interpersonal relationships in organizations. It uses both old and new techniques and focuses on developing better group relationships.

The thrust is on improving the effectiveness of interpersonal relations of managers working in groups rather than as individuals and it emphasizes group knowledge of problems and of attempts by groups to solve problems. During these activities, managers learn but they learn in context, they learn by doing and they learn while they are working with the people with whom they will work. Thus no transfer of learning from classroom to practice is needed.

Successful OD produces change in people and in organizational practices so it may cause some objections. These objections are, however, generally not great because the changes are changes generated by the groups themselves. Nonetheless, OD is not always successful and the programs are sometimes discontinued, in some cases because of opposition to change and sometimes from lack of internal high-level managerial support. Against this record, there are a number of successful OD applications where its effectiveness has produced extremely good results.

Review Questions

1. What is a confrontation meeting? How does it differ from a diagnostic meeting?
2. The text suggests that an outside OD consultant is highly desirable in an OD program. Yet one of the objectives of OD is for the organization to develop its own capabilities. Why the need for the outside consultant?
3. How does OD try to cope with resistance to change? Discuss.
4. Why should conflict resolution be discussed as part of OD? Is OD better than other methods of reducing conflict? Discuss.
5. What part do informal groups play in the functioning of organizations? Can a manager manage in such a way as to use informal groups to advantage? How?
6. What is "sensitivity training?" Discuss its strong and weak points.
7. How do meditation programs work? What good are they? How are they related to OD?
8. The emphasis in OD is almost always put on managers learning how to work together more effectively. Bottom-level employees are not brought into the picture. Yet the instances discussed in the text (and they are typical) describe situations where great gains in operating effectiveness were realized in bottom-level operations. Why is this? Discuss.

Questions for Analysis and Discussion

1. Behavioral Scientist Robert Blake says that, "It was learning to reject T-groups, stranger-type labs that permitted OD to come into focus." What does this mean? Discuss.

2. In the Academy of Management *OD Newsletter* of July, 1976, a behavioral scientist is quoted as saying that, "OD is a process which involves a conscious manipulation of the human side of the organization by specific and general interventions, the purpose of which is to identify its problems and improve its effectiveness." Yet, on the whole, it is thought to be poor practice to try to manipulate people. Discuss.

3. A manager told the OD consultant, "I am not very enthusiastic about your proposed OD program. The last consultant we had told us what a fine thing management by objectives was, but I have not seen much good come out of management by objectives in my plant. My subordinates just don't respond. I have spent hours going over my objectives with them, making sure that they understand and agree to them. But they just don't seem to apply themselves toward achieving them." Discuss.

4. Jack Tracy was a foreman who had been having more grievances than other foremen. Bud Hatcher, the personnel director, thought that this came partly from Tracy's never listening to what anyone else said. Grievants had told Hatcher that Tracy never really listened to them because he was always talking himself.
    Hatcher suggested to Tracy that when grievants started to tell him their story, not to talk back, but just to say, "Hmmm" and let them keep on talking. Hatcher told Tracy, "If you say anything at all, ask the subordinate a question, such as, 'What did you do then?'" Is there therapeutic value in letting people air their grievances? How well satisfied would most people be if they went in to see their boss with a complaint and he said, "Hmmm"?

5. "Not every supervisory position in the company carries with it responsibility for bringing about change and improvement. A warehouse foreman, for example, is not expected to develop better materials handling methods nor to improve the coordination of inbound and outbound shipments. So he is really an administrator and not a manager." Discuss. Should such a manager participate in an MBO program? In an OD program? Why?

6. "I can't get my major department heads to work together. My sales and engineering heads refuse to see each other's point of view. Right now my company is thirty days overdue with an important delivery, just because these men did not synchronize their schedules. This seems to be a problem which could have been avoided by a little cooperation." Couldn't the president solve this problem just by edict (tell them to cooperate)? If not, why not? What should be done?

7. One authority says that minor irritations and conflicts should be dealt with as soon as possible lest they grow in importance until they become destructive. Is this the right way to handle minor irritations? Or would it be better to pay as little attention as possible to them because if such irritations are not magnified, they might go away?

Case 16-1   "Worry-Hours"

At the end of the moving picture, "Gone With the Wind," Scarlet O'Hara's husband, Rhett Butler, leaves her just as she discovers, for the first time, that she really loves him and wants him. Alone, with her future in doubt, and at her wit's end, Scarlet says to herself, "I'll worry about that tomorrow. If I worry about that today, I'll go crazy." Some people are able to put off worrying about things until tomorrow. If they are able to do this, they don't have to worry today.

This is akin to the "worry hour" idea. A person selects, let us say, Tuesday at 4 o'clock as an hour to be set aside for worrying. Then he selects a drawer in his desk for worry notes to himself. If something worries him, he writes it down on paper and puts it into the drawer. This allows him to cease worrying about it until Tuesday at 4 p.m. In the meantime, he is free from worrying and can concentrate on doing what needs doing now.

At 4 o'clock on Tuesday, he sits down and goes through the accumulated notes. For some, the cause for worry is past, so these notes are discarded. Certain others, he can do nothing about now so they go back into the drawer until the next Tuesday. This leaves a few others for him to worry about now. So he worries about them until 5 o'clock. At 5 p.m. he stops worrying and puts whatever is left back into the drawer for another week. This frees him from the need to worry for another week.

All of this sounds like foolishness, but people *can* sometimes block out worry and the tensions it causes for the time being. And if they can do this even for short periods of time, they free themselves from some stresses and tensions. (It would be interesting to see what a research project on the worth of worry hours would produce. The idea is, apparently, not used much and there seems to have been no research on the subject.)

• Discuss the merits of worry-hours.

Case 16-2   Non-Linear Systems[12]

Utopia, 1965

In 1965, *Business Week* reported that, "A well worn path to the door of Non-Linear Systems is getting more deeply worn every week. It's not because the San Diego-based company has built a better mouse trap, but because it is trying to build a better kind of management along highly unconventional lines which seems nevertheless to be speeding up output." (Non-Linear had $6 million of sales and 300 employees in 1964. Its products were electronic instrumentation and test systems, largely for aerospace use and sold almost wholly to the government.)

To sociologists and professors of management, Non-Linear had become a laboratory for behavioral sciences. To corporate executives, Non-Linear was a test of some of the newest concepts in permissive, Likert System 4 and McGregor Theory Y management.

Andrew Kay, president and owner of Non-Linear, instituted this unusual type of management in 1960. He threw out all time cards and put all production workers on salaries at sixty cents an hour higher than the prevailing wage in San Diego. Then he tore down the assembly line which had carried electronic equipment through wiring, soldering, testing, inspection, and packaging, and replaced it with sixteen independent production groups of six or seven workers each.

Teams were free to organize their work as they wished. They could decide to break the work down and specialize different assembly operations, or they could decide to have single employees take an entire product unit through every phase of the operation, including test and final checkout, himself.

The first results were to boost morale sky high but also to disrupt production. It took three months to get output back to its old level. Thereafter production increased to thirty percent above earlier levels. Rejects almost disappeared and inspectors were eliminated. Customer complaints fell seventy percent. New model changeover time was reduced from ten weeks to two weeks.

(Similar methods tried in engineering, sales, and managerial ranks did not work out, however. There was confusion over responsibilities and the employees preferred to know what their jobs were.)

Utopia, 1973

In the 1960s and early 1970s when the government cut back on orders for space and defense products, Non-Linear's business fell off by more than 50 percent and the company lost money. Employment dropped to less than 150.

Even before 1973, Kay, who was still president and sole owner of Non-Linear Systems, had gone back to more orthodox managerial methods. He put in tightened financial controls and budgets, and developed an information flow system for control purposes. (He said that the company had lost a great deal of money in 1970 from his not knowing that inventories needed pruning long before they were reduced.)

Kay said that his earlier permissive method did not take into consideration that people were different and that some of them liked repetitive tasks. Also, since there had been no production standards, no one knew how well anyone was doing. Nor did the company know how costs had been affected by the introduction of participative methods. The costs of some items did go down, but the costs of other products went up. Kay said that, on balance, there was no productivity gain at all.

Kay was also disillusioned over his former pay arrangement which had everyone being paid a salary and at a rate of $1,200 a year above the area's rate in order to do away with the alleged "punishment-reward" psychology of hourly wages. Non-Linear employees now receive the same wages as do other workers in the San Diego area. Assembly lines have been reestablished and the decision-making powers of assembly line workers have been reduced to a minimum.

- How would perceiving that inventories should be reduced be related to the managerial methods used?
- How would it happen that Non-Linear experienced both substantial productivity as well as quality gains if the managerial methods used during the company's better days did not recognize the differing likes and dislikes of employees?
- Why would a company discard methods which had produced 30 percent extra production and almost eliminated rejects?
- Can a person draw any conclusions about the efficacy of OD from Non-Linear's experience? Discuss.

Case 16-3 Gaines Dog Food

General Foods has had considerable success with OD-type management at its Gaines Dog Food factory in Topeka, Kansas. This plant, which opened in the early 1970s, was designed to be run with a minimum of supervision. Many functions normally the prerogatives of management were to be performed by the workers themselves. Workers were to make job assignments, schedule coffee breaks, interview prospective employees, and even to decide pay raises.[13]

The plant was soon so successful that it was widely heralded as a model for the future. GF was so well pleased with it that, in 1976, it installed a similar system in a second dog-food plant in Topeka and in a coffee plant in New Jersey.

The system used in Topeka has fewer levels of management than are found in most factories. The work is divided into three areas of responsibility: (1) processing, (2) packaging and shipping, and, (3) office work. The responsibility for managing each of these three areas is assigned to self-managing teams of from seven to fourteen workers. Each such team is responsible for all of the work in its area including equipment maintenance.

There are no "foremen" in the usual sense; instead, one worker is the team leader. Workers rotate periodically from job to job to reduce job monotony. Pay is determined by workers voting on each other's pay raises with the amounts depending on the number of jobs a person masters. Managerial-type decisions affecting the group are decided by the teams.

After the plan had been in effect for some time, unit costs had come down to 50 percent less than in traditionally managed plants of similar nature and they have stayed there. Labor turnover is only 8 percent a year (one fifth of that found in typical factories) and the plant went nearly four years before its first lost-time accident. From the viewpoints of both humanistic working life and economic operations, this plant has been a success.

What more could one ask? The operation has been successful in every way.

Yet all is apparently not well at the Gaines Dog Food factory. General Foods, which used to encourage publicity about the Topeka plant, now refuses to let visitors inside. There has apparently been some let-down after the initial euphoria over the new system passed. Indifference is reported to have become common and hostility and conflict sometimes occur. Annoying jealousies and power conflicts have hampered the smooth operation of the system.

Part of the trouble is said to be that regular managers have felt that their power has been diminished. It didn't help that their workers performed almost too well without much supervision.

Staff people, too, apparently do not like to see worker groups doing things that they think is their work. The personnel staff has been concerned about work team groups making hiring decisions. It would be easy for worker groups to make decisions which would violate hiring laws.

Nor have all the problems been in the managerial levels. The matter of worker teams determining the pay of employees has been a thorny problem. As one worker put it, "You work with somebody for five years and get to be pretty good friends. It's a little tough to decide on a pay raise."

It has been reported that there has also been a groundswell in favor of some kind of profit sharing but none has been instituted. The company's other plants do not have profit sharing plans so that one at Topeka would probably cause complications.

Reports suggest that the Topeka system may be gravitating away from OD and toward more generally used practices.

- Is this a story of a failure of OD?
- Is it proper (or even legal) for employees to interview and hire new employees? Is it proper (or even wise) for them to discuss pay raises?
- How might management go about trying to get the organization to reach the goals that some people in the company feel it has not reached?

Endnotes

1. The results of OD-type management at Procter & Gamble and General Foods and in several other companies are described in, "The New Organization Man," *Forbes*, 15 June 1975, pp. 53–58.

Organization Development

2. "Rules of the Road: Doing Something Simple About Conflict in the Organization," by Donald G. Livingston, *Personnel,* January-February 1977, pp. 23–29.
3. For a discussion on this point see, "How Psychologically Dangerous are T-Groups and Encounter Groups?" by Gary L. Cooper, *Human Relations,* April 1975, pp. 249–260.
4. "An Examination of the Organizational Antecedents of Stresses at Work," by Saroj Parasuraman and Joseph A. Alutto, *Academy of Management Journal,* March 1981, pp. 48–67.
5. "How Much Stress is Too Much Stress?" by Herbert Benson and Robert L. Allen, *Harvard Business Review,* September-October 1980, pp. 86–92.
6. There are many books on relaxation and Transcendental Meditation. One good one is *The Relaxation Response,* by Herbert Benson, M.D. and Miriam Z. Klipper (Avon, 1976).
7. *Ibid.,* pp. 87–95.
8. Some of the medical evidence in support of this conclusion is given in, "Time Out From Tension," by Ruanne K. Peters and Herbert Benson, *Harvard Business Review,* January-February 1978, pp. 120–123.
9. See, "At General Motors: System 4 Builds Performance and Profits," [Likert's System 4], *Organizational Dynamics,* Winter 1975, pp. 23–38. See also, "Quality of Work Life — Learning From Tarrytown," by Robert H. Guest, *Harvard Business Review,* July-August 1979, pp. 76–87.
10. "Human Resources — Why the New Concern?" by Ted Mills, *Harvard Business Review,* March-April 1975, pp. 120–134.
11. Schrank, *Ten Thousand Working Days,* by Robert Schrank (MIT Press) page 220.
12. This case, which occurred in the early days of OD, is based on personal interviews with professionals close to the situation at Non-Linear Systems and on several magazine articles.
13. As reported in, "Stonewalling Plant Democracy," *Business Week,* 28 March 1977, p. 78ff.

Suggested Supplementary Readings

Albrecht, Karl. *Stress and The Manager: Making it Work For You.* Prentice-Hall, 1979.

Kilman, Ralph H., and Ian I. Mitroff. "Problem Defining and the Consulting Intervention Process." *California Management Review,* Spring, 1979, pages 26–33.

Thomas, Kenneth W. ed. Special section on "Conflict and the Collaborative Ethic" (six papers). *California Management Review,* Winter 1978, pp. 56–95.

Umstot, Dean D. "Organizational Development Technology and the Military: A Surprising Merger." *Academy of Management Review,* April 1980, pp. 189–201.

Veninga, Robert. "The Management of Disruptive Conflicts." *Hospital and Health Administration,* Spring 1979, pp. 8–29.

Case for Section Four   The Reluctant Miners[1]

"With a capital investment of about $50,000 per employee, we would prefer to work our company's coal mines around the clock, but we cannot persuade employees to come in on Saturdays. So we work the mines just five days a week, and even then almost one fifth of the men show up only four days.

"Uncertain how to change this uneconomic situation, I asked a bright energetic young fellow down in the mines, 'Tom, you've got a poor attendance record. You show up only four days a week and your absences are pretty regular. Why is that?' Tom's answer makes perfect sense if you work not because you feel you should, but because you want what the paycheck will buy. Tom said, 'I can't have what I want on three days' pay.'

"So we have, in effect, a four-day week in our mines, and we can't attain full economic use of our heavy capital investment until our employees once again want to work."

This new work ethic is by no means confined to blue collars. Many younger executives are willing to work hard forty hours a week, but they refuse to work before 9:00 or after 5:00, or let company duties override their own interests. They also refuse to move their families around the country. Like the young miner, more money may not motivate them. Perhaps the promise of good-sized chunks of time off, in return for a resumption of the Protestant work ethic, will do it.

Curiously, unions are always pushing for shorter work weeks and many are getting them. Ironically, the men often use their increased spare time to moonlight on a second job.

The automobile tire factories in Akron, Ohio, were among the first to go on the short work week (six hour days for many years but not so today). A manager of one of Akron's tire plants says that if a man spends most of his work time throwing pieces of rubber into tire molds, and then is given an extra eight hours a week off, he isn't likely to sit around reading Shakespeare and pondering Plato or Aristotle. He is either going to spend it in a saloon and have the old lady mad at him or he is going to spend the time at home and have her even madder at him. So he gets a job in a gas station, which keeps him busy and lets him bring home more money and have a more pleasant weekend.

- How might the mine manager get his mine working more hours?
- Discuss people, money, motivation, and work.

Endnote

1. This case was written up and described at length in "Executive Sabbaticals: About to Take Off?" by Eli Goldston, *Harvard Business Review*, September- October 1973, pp. 57–68.

Delegation means assigning work to lower-level people to carry out. Since there are several levels of hierarchy in all organizations of any size, the delegations to intermediate-level managers are delegations of managerial responsibilities to manage limited areas. The delegation of responsibilities, the subject of chapters 17 and 18 is the means by which members of organizations find out about what they are to do and at the same time it is the means by which subordinates receive authority to do things.

Some superiors are very careful, when they delegate, to spell out what they want done and what authority goes along with the delegation. Others delegate more generally, specifying only missions or general charges of areas of responsibility. When superiors delegate only generally, then subordinates have considerable freedom to develop the details of their jobs.

Sometimes subordinates don't really want to do what their superior wants them to do and so they drag their feet and don't get much done. This brings up the acceptance principle which holds that superiors have only such authority as subordinates are willing to grant them. This interesting idea is discussed in Chapter 19.

The degree of centralization of authority and decision making is also important. Things can't all be done centrally so the authority to decide needs to be delegated lower down in the organization. Often there is a question of just where certain decisions should be made. Chapter 20 considers the factors which bear upon where decisions are made.

Section Five

Organizations in Action: Delegation

Chapter 17
Delegation

Chapter 18
Responsibilities

Chapter 19
Power, Authority,
and Influence in
Organizations

Chapter 20
Decentralization
and Centralization

Objectives of Chapter Seventeen

1. To explore the nature of delegation as a means for assigning work and for freeing superiors from details so they can devote more time to larger matters.
2. To look into the process of delegation and the development of their roles by individuals.
3. To call the attention of the reader to the practical difficulties which creep up in the area of delegation as it takes place in organizational operations.
4. To look behind apparent delegation to see how it operates and to understand how to delegate successfully.

Delegation

17

*Choose able men
and place them over the people
as rulers of hundreds and of tens. Let them
judge the people in small matters
and bring great matters to you.*
Jethro to Moses, Circa 1500 B.C.

The Nature of Delegation

As we see from Jethro's advice to Moses, the recognition of the need for delegation goes back to the early days of history.

Delegation is assigning work to subordinates and is the process whereby a superior commissions his subordinates to become his agents and to act in his behalf. It is the process by which superiors pass on charges of responsibility and authority to subordinates.

At the same time, delegation is a means for relieving superiors of detail so that they will not need to be immersed in the details of their subordinates' work. When superiors delegate, they free themselves to do higher-level work.

This definition of delegation is, however, one sided. It is all in terms of what the superior does. But, in order for delegation to be effective, it must get through to the subordinate who must understand it and act upon it. Furthermore, there are some things a superior should delegate to his subordinates and other things which he should not delegate. Our discussion will cover these matters.

Major Mission Interpretations

Delegations of major responsibilities are stated in terms of desired end-accomplishments to be brought about or of subject areas to be administered. The recipients of such delegations have to interpret them into lesser goals and to develop action programs aimed at their accomplishment.

Our discussions deal with delegations downward within organizations. They presume the existence of top-level administrators who determine the general direction of the organization's activities. In businesses, the head of the organization, the chief executive officer (CEO) heads up everything. He decides the general directions the organization is to go. He does not have to interpret missions. He sets them. His delegations to the organization's major officers are, however, usually delegations of missions which *they* have to interpret.

In governments, the heads of major departments, such as the United States Department of Agriculture, or the Treasury, have broad-based sweeping delegations. A very important part of their delegation is to interpret their missions into action programs. The head of the Department of Agriculture has to decide what, if anything, the department should do to increase the yield per acre of farm products such as soy beans, for example. The head of the Treasury has to decide what, if anything, his department should do about inflation and the money supply.

Duties Which Superiors Should Delegate

When superiors delegate work to subordinates there are certain duties which they *should* delegate whereas they *should not* delegate certain other duties. The superior should retain certain responsibilities for himself. (See Figure 17-1)

The **general principle of delegation** is: Superiors should delegate all work for which there is someone lower in the organization who is capable of making an informed, responsible, and intelligent decision and who has available to him the resources needed in order to carry out the delegated work (provided, however, that the superior does not delegate away major portions of his own job).

Organizations in Action: Delegation

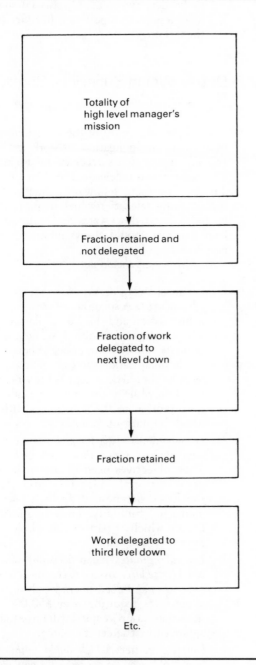

Figure 17-1
Mission delegation and retained and redelegated duties.

Delegation

Superiors should delegate to subordinates all of the work encompassed by their mission delegation except what they retain for themselves. There should be no gaps or work for which no one is responsible.

Work which *should* be delegated can be classified by the degree of supervision needed.

1. *Duties related to the making of higher-level decisions.* These are participative kinds of duties (fact collection, expert advising, idea-interchange, etc.) which help the superior make better decisions and which build up subordinate empathy and morale.
2. *Duties of the group responsibility kind.* In a manufacturing company, these could include activities such as product-design decisions, where representatives from several departments get together and make decisions concerning matters in which their several departments have a common interest.
3. *Matters which a manager would like to have his subordinate consider and to decide what he thinks should be done, but to check with him before doing it.* In a retail store, a special discount sale to move certain slow-moving items would be in this category. In a factory a decision by the superintendent to have the plant work ten-hour days during the next month would be in this category.
4. *Matters of lesser importance in which the superior would want his subordinate to decide what to do and then go ahead and do it but to tell him what he has done.* Disciplinary actions when employees violate the organization's rules would be in this category.
5. *Still lesser matters which the subordinate is to perform himself or redelegate to his subordinates to do.* Such duties would include establishing priorities among work orders, deciding whether to give a customer credit for goods returned claimed

to be defective, etc. Occasional summary reports to superiors will suffice for these duties.

Duties Which Superiors Should Not Delegate

Normally, most of the delegated authority and the obligation to work toward end accomplishments received by middle-level managers is redelegated to their subordinates. But there is always a fraction of the incoming delegation which ought not to be redelegated downward. Every middle-level manager should always retain certain responsibilities.

Managers *should not*:

1. *Let subordinates decide what their overall jobs are to be.* A subordinate's overall job is his mission and this he should accept as it is delegated to him. Usually a subordinate cannot know enough about the whole organization's work to know just what he should do except as his superior tells him while at the same time calling his attention to the constraints within which he must operate.
2. *Let subordinates have full power to set their own objectives nor their own budgets.* Their objectives need to contribute to organizational objectives and thus should be determined by higher-level managers. Similarly, budgets allocate money which is part of the whole organization's resource base.
3. *Let subordinates make decisions which could cause large losses.* A common limit even for major department heads is that all projects requiring over $50,000 of the organization's capital will have to be approved by the central office.
4. *Delegate matters which imply authority over people who do not work for him* (see Figure 17-2). Subordinates in one chain of authority should not be put in the

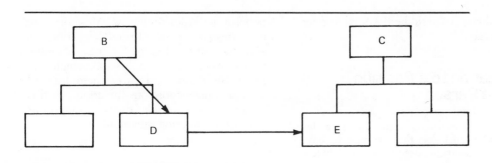

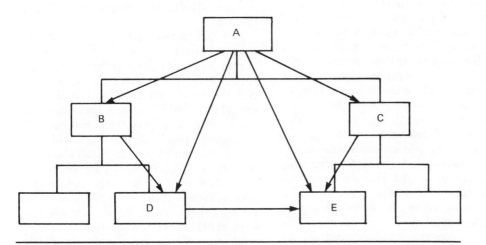

Figure 17-2
If *B* delegates to *D* the authority to tell *E* what to do, friction is almost certain to occur because *C* will not want his subordinate, *E*, to be receiving directions from anyone other than himself. But, if *A*, the common superior of *B* and *C* gives directions to *C* (or to *E* directly) to have *E* accept directions from *D*, this is not likely to cause friction.

position of giving directions to people in chains of authority which do not belong to their superior.

5. *Delegate responsibilities and authority without holding the subordinate accountable.* He should not delegate and then fail to check up; he should not abdicate. Furthermore, every subordinate should have a superior who holds him accountable.

6. *Let subordinates be the* final *judges of their own work, nor should they decide their own pay rates.* Probably everyone should judge his own accomplishments from time to time, but no one person's self-

Delegation

evaluation should be the final and total appraisal.

Delegation to a Position or to a Person

A purchasing agent directs a department which does the organization's buying. An advertising department head directs a department which develops advertisements and places them in magazines and newspapers, or on radio or television.

The delegation to the heads of such departments are missions and their delegations are primarily delegations to *departments* and only incidentally to the managers of these departments as individuals.

But departments are groups of people, each group being headed by a single individual. So delegations have, in fact, to be made to department heads, even though fundamentally, the delegation is to departments. *Such delegations are not the dispensing of personal prerogatives.* Furthermore, each department head is, in fact, only a temporary recipient of the delegation. ("Temporary" in the sense that, over the years, new managers are always coming on and replacing the old.)

The consequence of the need to delegate to a person, and a temporary incumbent at that, is to bring into play a whole host of possible "people problems." Sometimes, and unfortunately, the department head views his delegation as being a delegation to him personally and does not recognize that the delegation is really to the job he holds.

Delegation in Operation

Delegation, as a process, is not always visibly taking place since organizations are ongoing entities which are made up of people who performed activities yesterday, who perform activities today, and who will perform activities tomorrow. Most of these activities go on with little "delegation" as such happening. Except for the occasional person who is new on his job, employees know their jobs and carry them forward without much conscious direction. In this section we will consider the way delegations operate in on-going organizations.

How to Delegate

Delegating would seem to be simply a matter of managers telling their subordinates what they are supposed to do or to accomplish and then telling them to go ahead with the work.

But, in fact, telling a person that he is to do certain work is actually only a first step in delegation. As a further step, his superior needs also to give him the authority and the means for carrying out that responsibility. He has to give him tools, machines, materials, personnel, and probably the right to spend a certain amount of money. As still another step, he needs also to tell the other people with whom the subordinate will work that he has the assignment so that they will know that he has the right to ask for their help. And, besides these earlier steps in delegation, the superior needs to set target dates for the completion of the delegated assignments.

Delegation Interpretations

Earlier in this chapter we considered the need for heads of major departments to interpret their broad mission-type delegations. As we move down through the organization, delegations become more specific and there is less need for interpreting them. But the need for interpretation of delegations does not disappear altogether until we reach bottom levels. Middle-level managerial delegations still require a certain amount of interpretation.

In a factory, the engineering department is to design products and processes and to keep the physical plant operating. In a city government, the police department is to maintain law and order. Neither of these broad delegations spells out details. The heads of such departments have to decide what to do in order to carry out their delegated responsibilities. And they have to decide which work to delegate on downward to subordinate departments.

Managers at all levels thus receive delegations in more general terms than they pass on. By the time delegations have reached lower levels, they are largely in the form of directions to carry out specific duties and to reach specific minor goals.

Delegation in Context

As we have just said, although delegation operates all of the time, it is not often obviously in evidence. The roles of most managers are relatively stable over short periods of time. These roles are made up of the jobs originally delegated modified by minor additions and subtractions which have evolved with the passage of time. A manager's job also includes certain activities which he does because he feels that he ought to do them. They come out of his interpretation of his mission delegation.

In the list of Borden company accomplishments in Chapter 1, most of the specific things listed were probably almost wholly the result of middle level managers carrying out mission-type delegations, without specific directions from higher up administrators to undertake these actions. The manager in charge of Max Factor cosmetics probably himself saw the need to develop non-allergic cosmetic products and then followed through and developed them.

Delegation is a continuing relationship and job assignments are evolving totalities. Specific new assignments will be acted on by subordinates in different ways, according to the context.

An outsider cannot look at a single delegation and tell what it means because it is only part of the superior-subordinate relationship. The rest is embodied in context, unsaid at the moment. Both the giver and the receiver of any new order interpret its meaning in the light of the subordinate's usual work, the usual context of his authority and his ability.

"Trigger" Delegations

Usually some parts of a delegation cover conditional activities. Certain work is to be carried on *if and when* certain conditions exist but not otherwise. The subordinate is supposed to be ready to take action if the trigger event occurs or if the trigger situation develops. An army is authorized and expected to be ready but not to proceed with action without specific action authorizations.

In a sense, the original delegation is incomplete. For action to occur, the additional trigger delegation or directive is needed. On important matters, the trigger delegation would usually be a specific order from a superior. On less important matters it may be an event which the subordinate is expected to detect and react to. A supermarket manager would be expected to take action against a check-out cashier if he or she steals money. The trigger event would be the detection of the thievery.

Or the trigger may be a time trigger. Income tax reports have to be filed by certain dates and television advertisements have to be prepared in time for the TV programs. Time releases the trigger.

Delegation in General Terms

Delegations to managers at all levels almost always contain a certain amount of mission delegation. The manager is supposed to produce certain end conditions or results. His delegation is rarely phrased in terms of the specific activities he should take. This needs to be so in nearly all cases because his superior usually does not know just exactly what the subordinate will have to do in order to produce the results. The subordinate has to decide these things.

This is different for most bottom-level delegations which often can and ought to be quite specific. A factory supervisor tells an employee to drill two holes in each of fifty steel castings according to the drawing. This is a specific, clear directive or delegation. But, except where the job is quite clear and simple, managers don't normally delegate in such a sharply defined way. The outlines of the job the subordinate is to do are usually vague around the edges. The manager tells him what he wants him to do but lets the subordinate work out the details.

To illustrate, we might consider the job of maintaining the elevators in a large downtown building. This responsibility is a mission kind of delegation to the maintenance department which does not list duties as such.

> The building manager would expect the maintenance department employees to respond to emergency calls when elevators get stuck between floors and won't run. But, besides this, he would expect them also to decide when the elevators needed inspection and to inspect them. He would also expect them to grease and oil the elevators' moving parts whenever this is needed. And he would expect them to decide when repairs and replacement parts are needed and to carry forward all necessary repair work except major overhauls, without asking for specific approval.

The building manager would visualize the delegation as encompassing the maintenance supervisor or his employees seeing the need for doing these things and then actually doing them.

Ambiguous Delegations

Some managers think that a good way to develop middle-level or higher-level managers is to make only general delegations, even ambiguous delegations to them. This differs from the point just made that all delegations to middle-level managers are somewhat rough around the edges. In this case, the purpose of higher-level managers in being vague in their instructions is to give subordinates room to flex their muscles and to carve out their own niches as they develop their jobs.

Managers who subscribe to this theory believe that "cream comes to the top." Some people have called this the "jungle theory." Most of today's managers do not give their subordinates this much freedom. They would be afraid that they would recast their missions in ways which would let them omit doing certain essential work or they might impinge on the missions of other subordinates.

Unfortunately, too, ambiguous delegations do not always bring the best people to the top. (In nature, cream does come to the top, but so does scum.) The winner of internal company battles may be the best politician or the best at undercutting opponents to get them out of the way. Even if capable people emerge victors, other capable men or women may have been lost to the organization, and the scars of battle on those who remain may last a long time.

Another kind of ambiguous delegation sometimes occurs with newcomers to the organization. Sometimes such a new employee is given a general mission and is told, "Your future is up to you. It depends on what you do." (We mentioned this in Chapter 13 but did not follow it up there.) This would surely sound like an interesting challenge to an ambitious young man or woman. Presumably a senior manager making such a statement means it but only in a broad sense. Such a newcomer, mistakenly trying to change things, is very likely to run up against barriers and constraints which he was not told about. His colleagues may not like some of the things he wants to do. He finds out that his delegation was ambiguous.

We should not, however, denigrate too much the idea of subordinates developing their own jobs. Mission delegations to middle- and high-level managers anticipate that the recipients will interpret them into goals and action programs.

A chief engineer or a sales manager *should* make his job into his idea of what it should be to help the organization the most. He *should* develop his own job and his department into a unit which will help the organization. This is *his* responsibility, since his superior does not know enough about the mission area himself to be able to make a detailed delegation of exactly what should be done.

Saying that a manager should develop his job does not imply throwing one's weight around nor does it imply his overlooking carrying out his mission. It recognizes the need for the manager to get along with his peers. And it implies his recognizing his responsibility for interpreting his mission into goals and action programs which will implement his mission.

The Formalization of Structures and Delegation

Paul Lawrence and Jay Lorsch, in their studies of highly scientifically-oriented companies (which were not highly structured), found that broad, inexactly defined delegations were more appropriate in such organizations than in mature, highly structured organizations.[1] Specialists working with inexactly defined delegations found it easier to get their work done in situations where results from work are uncertain and almost always take a long time to come to fruition. Work in these organizations went better where organic structures (organizations with very little formal structure) were used. Vague and only generally outlined mission delegations worked well.

In contrast, Joan Woodward found a different situation in her classic study, done a number of years ago, of the operation of English companies. She found that, under stable conditions, such as exist in the factory production areas in mature industries, specialists had no trouble working effectively. This was true even though delegations were much more definite and were supported by formal procedures and frequent performance reviews.[2]

Failure to Delegate

"The trouble with old Joe is that he just won't delegate." This is a common failing of managers — they don't delegate enough. There are several reasons why.

Lack of Realization that the Delegation is Inadequate. Some managers give lip service to delegations but then insist on making every decision. They tell a subordinate that he is responsible but to "see me before you go ahead." Or they tell their subordinates that they are to do certain work, but then they don't give them enough authority or other support to allow them to get it done. They just don't realize that they have not really delegated enough.

Managers sometimes undermine the authority of their subordinate managers by going around them and giving orders which they don't know about to still lower subordinates. Or the manager listens directly to the complaints of these lower subordinates and takes actions or makes promises about matters which he should let his subordinate managers decide. Or he doesn't back up his subordinate and reverses his decisions. Sometimes he tells him to do something which requires his getting help from people in other departments but he doesn't tell the others.

344

Lack of Confidence in Subordinates. When a superior says, "See me before you go ahead," it is probably because he does not have full confidence in the subordinate's decision-making ability. He is afraid that something will go wrong and he knows that a failure of his subordinate is his failure too. His fear is quite understandable and a person can feel considerable sympathy for a manager who says, "I am personally responsible so I need to check very closely on what my subordinates do."

A manager who lacks confidence in his subordinate may also take away his supposed authority just by over-supervising him and watching over him too closely. This action is not often intended by the superior to be a recapture of authority but it amounts to the same thing.

Many superiors believe that, "If you want a job well done, do it yourself." It isn't so much that they don't have confidence in their subordinates, but just that they would still rather do it themselves. And, in any case, they want to keep in touch with everything that goes on. Making all of the decisions themselves raises their status (in their own eyes). Besides, as one superior put it, "Making decisions is fun, why give it up?"

Getting Things Done More Quickly. Henry Mintzberg found that managers rely heavily on verbally received information which they have in their minds and which is not written down. On this basis they decide that something should be done. But, explaining all of this to a subordinate would sometimes take more time than doing it themselves so they do it themselves and so delegate less than they might.[3]

Fear of Developing a Rival. Ultimately, every manager retires and is replaced. Usually his replacement comes from among his subordinates. But, as a manager sees it, there is no need to hurry the process along by developing a subordinate so that he becomes a rival for his job today and so might replace him before his normal retirement date! Holding down on delegation to

subordinates holds back their development into rivals.

Insufficient Delegation by Superiors. Managers sometimes cannot delegate enough to subordinates because they, themselves, have not been delegated enough. They might like to delegate more but they, themselves, have only limited delegations.

Cultural Differences in Delegation Practices. Still another reason for not delegating may be related to the culture. Robert Bass and his research colleagues found, in a study of managers in various countries, that American managers were more trustful than were most managers in other countries. They were willing to delegate more than managers in Europe and in other parts of the world.[4]

Limited Delegations and Aggressive Subordinates. The failure to delegate responsibility and the failure to delegate enough authority do not hold back every subordinate. Some subordinates, the aggressive ones, will go ahead and assume power anyway, and in many cases, will do good jobs. When this happens, the effect is the same as if the superior had delegated responsibility and authority to them.

Aggressive subordinates may need holding down. In the book about the United States Supreme Court, *The Brethren*, several instances were cited in which bright young law clerks for Supreme Court justices put their own views instead of the views of their Justice into the briefs they wrote for them. Justice William Douglas had to tell one of his clerks that if and when he got appointed to the Supreme Court, he could put in his own ideas. Meanwhile, he was to stick to Douglas' ideas.[5]

Error Tolerance

One of the prices which managers have to pay for developing subordinates by delegating to them the authority to go ahead on their own is the cost of their occasional mistakes. Subordinates cannot develop and learn to exercise authority without a certain amount of freedom to make decisions. They will probably make a mistake once in a while. And usually there is nothing that gets more attention than a good, big mistake!

Unfortunately, when things go wrong, nearly everyone, superior managers included, reacts by blaming someone — someone else. And the next reaction is often to punish someone. High-level managers should try to avoid this and not put too much stress on mistakes lest their subordinate managers avoid taking on authority and develop into timid decision makers.

Actually, superiors should go beyond error toleration. They should encourage subordinates to innovate and to try to make improvements. Risk is included. Not only should risks taken which work out poorly not be criticized unduly, but accomplishment of new and worthwhile things should be rewarded.

Delegation Concerns

There are several matters relating to delegation which managers need to keep in mind in the day-to-day operations of organizations. They have to do with how delegation is carried out. They deal with the relationship between delegation and supervision, with the giving of orders, with getting subordinates to delegate, and other similar matters.

Delegation's Relationships with Supervision

In one sense, delegating is almost the opposite of supervising and directing. The more a manager delegates the *less* close his supervision needs to be. If he has delegated wide decision making authority, he does not need to watch over the details of what the subordinates do very closely.

But the right to delegate includes the responsibility for seeing that the work gets done, and this in turn, includes an implied obligation to delegate only to subordinates who are capable of doing the work. So, whenever a subordinate does not have the necessary capabilities, then the manager needs to assume the role of a trainer. As he supervises and directs subordinates in their duties he works closely with them, coaching them, showing them how to do their work and sometimes giving them detailed instructions.

As such subordinates acquire competence, the close supervision can be relaxed and the apparent original delegation becomes more truly the actual delegation.

Written Position Descriptions and Delegation

Written position descriptions (which we discussed in Chapter 13) contain a listing of the regular duties of each job. They are not themselves delegations but are after-the-fact descriptions of what jobs are at the present time.

As we said in Chapter 13, written position descriptions are sometimes regarded as fixed and unchanging. Bottom-level workers sometimes refuse to do any work not listed. This is unfortunate because it tends to freeze job content and reduce flexibility. This is less of a problem with managerial jobs. Their position descriptions are written in more general terms so that normal variations in jobs are still covered by the generalized statements. The position description does not then stand in the way of job duty evolution.

Delegation and Order Giving

Part of delegation is giving orders. But the discussion so far has not mentioned giving orders. Actually, *when a manager gives*

Figure 17-3
Orders can be given just as orders or they can be offered together with explanations and with an interest in subordinates which helps win cooperation.

directions to a subordinate, he is making a delegation and *he is giving an order.* A supervisor might, for example, tell an employee to haul a load of materials to the next department, and he does. Or a manager might ask his engineers to develop an electric skillet, and they do.

These are delegations but they are also orders. Such orders are usually not resented as being dictatorial because that is what the subordinate's job is. If there were not such work to do there would be no job for the subordinate, but, even so, orders don't have to be given in an offensive way.

A manager should be particularly careful when giving a distasteful order and should try to think how it will sound to his subordinate and how his subordinate will receive it. He should try to tell him what he wants done in a way which will win his cooperation.

Communications and Actions as Delegations

Superiors sometimes make delegations which they don't intend to make. Subordinates interpret meaning into the actions and the interests of superiors. When a college dean promotes assistant professors who publish articles in learned society journals and does not promote those who only teach, he is defining the assistant professors' delegation as putting publishing first.

Even an expression of interest, or an idle comment, is sometimes converted into a delegation or is expanded from a small inquiry into a substantial delegation.

Case 25-1 describes a situation in which the head of the organization wanted to get a summer job for his friend's college student son. His inquiry about the company's hiring process resulted in him getting, later on, a complete report on all of the company's hiring procedures and practices.

In this case a casual question became a full-scale request for work to be done.

Getting Subordinates to Delegate

Just as higher level managers need to delegate, so do *their* subordinates need to delegate to their next-level subordinates. So, everything said so far also applies to middle-level managers. They, too, cannot do everything themselves so they must delegate work to their subordinates. The most obvious things that a manager can do to get his subordinates to delegate properly are to coach and advise them. Almost as important is setting a good example by delegating properly themselves. The behavior of subordinates is strongly influenced by the practices of their superiors.

Some companies try to force middle-level managers to delegate more by refusing to promote them until they have subordinates trained to take their places. Men or women who want to move up have to delegate things to their expected replacements.

Summary

Since higher level managers can't do all of the organization's work by themselves, they have to delegate work to subordinates and let each one of them do his part of the whole work. Logical though it is to delegate, some managers hate to let go and so they delegate poorly, with too many strings attached.

Most delegations to subordinate managers are general delegations to people to perform missions or to handle broad areas of activities. This means that subordinate managers have to redefine their general delegations and to decide just what they need to do in order to carry out their missions.

Some managers actually go too far and delegate almost to the point of abdication. This may not be harmful if the subordinates are capable people who will take such vague delegations and interpret them properly and so end up doing what needs to be done. Many times, however, vague delegations work less well. Subordinates don't know exactly what to do and consequently may feel frustrated. In other cases, aggressive individuals exercise power and undertake to do the things they believe are important. Often these actions impinge on the authority areas of others and result in frictions which hurt cooperation. It is usually better not to delegate so freely as to allow this to happen. Probably less delegation and more supervision would be better.

Review Questions

1. People receiving mission-type delegations have to interpret them into lesser goals and into action steps. Would it then be possible for two people receiving identical mission delegations to interpret them into quite unlike jobs? Discuss.

2. In the text, it was said that certain work *should* be delegated by superiors to subordinates. What were these kinds of work and why should they be delegated?

3. In the text, it was said that certain work *should not* be delegated to subordinates, but should be retained by superiors. What were these kinds of work and why should they not be delegated?

4. Why do superiors sometimes not delegate certain work and decision-making authority which really should be delegated? Discuss.

5. What is the point being made in the text in the discussion of "delegation in context"? Is this bad? Or good? Should anyone do anything about this? Explain.

6. What are the characteristics of an effective delegation? Explain and give examples.

7. Is it a good idea to use vague delegations? Do such delegations help to develop good managers? Discuss.

8. Is a written position description a delegation? What are and what should be the relationships between written job descriptions and delegations?

Questions for Analysis and Discussion

1. The foreman complained that his general foreman would never let him run

his department the way he wanted. Later he was promoted and made general foreman himself. His first remark was, "Well, by cripes, that department will be run right now." Would things probably improve?

2. The first Henry Ford, when asked what he expected of his workers, said, "We expect our workers to do the work that is set before them." Isn't this the best way to delegate?

3. In the text, it was said that newcomers to organizations are sometimes told, "Your future is your own. You can develop it into whatever you want to." Is this good delegation? If not, what are its faults? If the statement needs rephrasing, rephrase it so that it is appropriate.

4. When Maxey Jarman was head of Genesco several years ago, he told about a women's shoe company that Genesco had recently bought. The purchased company, now a division of Genesco, needed a new factory. Jarman said that its head couldn't believe it when he was told to select the site, hire the architect and engineers, place the contract, and get the plant built within the limit of his budget. Is this good delegation?

5. Professional employees (scientists and engineers) are not managers, nor are they bottom-level workers. Such professional employees often regard managers as mere record keepers and housekeepers. Yet, when professional people themselves become managers, often they become autocratic. What is the proper relationship between professional employees and managers? How can a higher manager make better managers out of scientists who get promoted.

6. "Formal organization is too restrictive. We want every employee to feel that he can go ahead and do things on his own." Discuss.

7. Jones says, "The way to develop an employee so that he can handle a load is to put that load on him." Smith says, "An employee does not work best when he is forced to deal with something he is not qualified to handle. I am not sure that he appreciates being held responsible for matters which he is not equipped to handle." Did you ever have to make a speech on a subject beyond your depth? Does it produce a good speech? Does this kind of experience make you into a better person?

8. "Joe," said the president to his "assistant to," "get out to Sacramento and straighten out that mess in Plant 3." "It's as good as done, Chief," said Joe. Discuss. How should Joe go about carrying out this assignment?

9. William O'Neil, who built General Tire Company into a billion dollar company, favored informal management techniques. He believed that the way to delegate was to tell a subordinate, "Here's a job to be done — do it." Reportedly, one of his favorite remarks was, "Who said you don't have the authority to decide that?" Discuss.

10. What should be done with a sales manager who makes a forbidden price concession in order to get business? Should the answer be any different if he gets the business than if he does not?

11. Expanding delegations to match a manager's development raises problems if written position descriptions are used. Should there be, say, three descriptions for a position — one for the limited job that a new manager

Delegation

will do, another for his expanded job after he has acquired reasonable competence, and still a third for the last stage of job expansion which covers everything that the most experienced and capable person might be called upon to do?

Case 17-1 The New Personnel Director's Delegation

The vice president in charge of staff services had recently hired a new personnel director. He told him, "Bill, will you write up a statement of the major requirements of your job as you see them? Perhaps you expect me to define your job for you and to tell you what I want you to do. But, if I did, it wouldn't be your job. Probably I won't see eye to eye with you on everything, but we both have a common purpose: We want yours to be a good personnel department."

Later the vice president asked the personnel director to think over how he might improve the personnel department's work and to set some targets. He said, "I don't want to tell you how to do your job, but if you will think over how you are going to proceed, maybe I can be helpful."

- Is this good delegation? How does Bill know how well his proposals will fit into the organization? What if Bill's ideas differ from those of the president or vice president?
- Suppose Bill wants to discontinue the company newspaper? Or suppose that he wants to hire three psychologists and to have them interview all of the employees?
- If this delegation should be restated, restate it so that it is more acceptable.

Endnotes

1. *Developing Organizations: Diagnosis and Action,* by Paul L. Lawrence and Jay W. Lorsch, Addison Wesley, 1969. Pages 43–49.
2. *Industrial Organization: Theory and Practice,* by Joan Woodward (Oxford University Press, 1965).
3. "The Manager's Job; Folklore and Fact," by Henry Mintzberg, *Harvard Business Review,* July-August, 1975, page 52.
4. *Assessment of Managers: An International Comparison,* by Bernard M. Bass, Philip C. Burger, Robert Doktor, and Gerald J. Barrett (The Free Press, 1979).
5. "The Brethren," by Bob Woodward and Scott Armstrong (Simon and Schuster, 1979), pp. 73, 98, 357.

Suggested Supplementary Readings

McConkey, Dale D. *No-Nonsense Delegation.* AMACOM, 1974.

Schleh, Edward G. "Handing Off to Subordinates — Delegating for Gain." *Management Review,* May 1978, pp. 43–47.

Steinmetz, Lawrence L. *The Art and Skill of Delegation.* Addison-Wesley, 1976.

Objectives of Chapter Eighteen

1. To consider the concept of responsibility as an obligation of subordinates to their hierarchical superiors.
2. To consider the reasons why subordinates sometimes do not accept responsibility and to consider what to do about this.
3. To study the way subordinates interpret their delegations and develop their work roles.
4. To get an understanding of the responsibilities of helping (staff) departments and how these responsibilities relate to the responsibilities of line managers.

Responsibilities

*Everyone wants to claim responsibility for successes; no one wants to claim responsibility for failures.
So, who is responsible?*

Locus of Responsibility

The Ultimate Responsibility of the Head of the Organization

In 1974, before he resigned, Republican President Richard Nixon came close to being impeached. This came about as a consequence of disclosures about wire tapping and breaking into the Watergate Hotel headquarters in Washington, D.C., of the opposition Democratic party in the 1972 presidential election campaign by certain Republican party workers. These were both illegal activities.

It was never established beyond question that Nixon himself knew about and approved these activities before they occurred (but he *did* resign). A great many people thought that he knew and many more people thought that, even if he had not known, it was still his responsibility. They thought that, as head of the Republican organization, the responsibility for its activities was his to bear. Many people believe that the heads of all organizations should make a point of knowing about everything of consequence that goes on in their organizations.

In a business organization, the company's president is the organization's top officer and so is "responsible" for its successful operation. He has more power than anyone else to cause the organization to carry on certain activities and not to carry on other activities.

Ostensibly and legally, the Board of Directors of a business organization is responsible to the stockholders and the president is responsible to the board. Practically speaking, the burden of directing the company successfully falls on its chief executive officer (the "CEO") who, in almost all cases,

is the president. Yet, even board members' responsibilities include certain things which are inescapably their own responsibilities when they accept their mantles as board members. Directors cannot evade responsibility for violations of their trustee position as representatives of the stockholders and they must not be in a conflict of interest position. They are obliged also to try to see that the president and other high officers operate ethically in such matters as honest operations and they have the obligation to see that the company obeys the nation's laws.

Unfortunately, neither directors nor presidents nor vice presidents can control such things as the activities of competitors, the responses of customers, conspiracies or acts of a criminal nature by subordinates; nor can they foresee events which are unpredictable.

So it is that, in a very real sense, no organization head, neither boards of directors nor presidents, ever has enough authority or power to carry out his apparent responsibility. If a Kroger grocery store manager embezzles money, it is really too much to blame the company president.

This is not to relieve a company's president of all accountability, but rather to refine his charge of responsibility. His responsibility would really be to see that he has chosen as capable and as dependable subordinates as he can and to instill in them the same feeling of responsibility for staffing the lower levels of the organization with capable and dependable people. They need, too, to develop control procedures which are normally adequate to protect the organization from serious mistakes.

The Insulation of Organization Heads

Although the head of every organization has the responsibility for seeing that the organization operates successfully, he has to try to accomplish this in spite of his not really knowing about some of the things that go on. People do not speak freely and openly to him because there is always the superior-subordinate barrier which inhibits open discussion.

Not only is he excluded from casual talk and therefore not kept informed on many things, but he finds that frequently he has no one else in the organization with whom he can discuss *his* problems. Often these problems concern the performance of some of his subordinates, but as chief executive, he can hardly talk over the performance of one of his subordinates with another of them. Neither he nor they can speak freely. The president of a company may have to join a president's luncheon club so that he can meet occasionally with the presidents of other companies so he can discuss his problems with someone.

That the organization's head is shielded from grass roots information is unfortunate because he is the only one in the organization with responsibility for the well-being of the whole organization. He is very likely to receive censored and distorted information about important problems. This difficulty does not, however, relieve him of his obligation to try to keep well informed about what is going on.

In giant companies, it isn't just the one single head who is shielded from bad news, it is the whole group of top officials.

In Company A, a billion dollar corporation, the development and marketing of product X was continued for over ten years. It was always a money loser. After the losses passed the $100 million mark, product X was discontinued.

It was reported that at least three plant managers and two marketing officials were convinced that product X was a failure *for more than six years before it was dropped.*

This story is told by Chris Argyris.[1] Why did the managers who were convinced that product X was a failure not tell the top administrators? Argyris reports that they almost did tell them. At first they didn't tell them because they had some hope hard work on their part might turn it into a success.

Later, when they had decided that they should tell the top administrators that it was a failure, they found that these top people were extolling product X to everybody and they would not have liked to hear that it was a failure. So, they condensed their reports so that they would not reveal very much. They tried, without saying it directly, to word their reports so that the administrators would be alerted to the bad news a little at a time. But the administrators did not discern the warning signs.

Not until the end did the top administrators learn the truth. The combination of distortion in the upward reports and the rosy colored views of the top administrators kept them from learning the truth for more than five years after the lower-level people had decided that it was a hopeless failure. Probably the presidents of many other companies could tell similar stories of their being surprised by sudden bad news of which they had not been warned. They cannot carry out their overall responsibilities when they don't get reliable information.

Who is Responsible?

Who made the shoes? In a shoe factory, one employee styles the shoes, another buys the leather, another cuts out the leather, another sews together the uppers, another puts them on the forming lasts, another puts on the soles, etc. If the shoes are good shoes, who deserves credit? If they are poor shoes, who did poorly?

These are not easy questions to answer. These questions will come up again in Chapter 24, on the subject of control, but they also need to be considered here.

High-Level Group Responsibility. Every organization of any size is really a collection of teams or groups working together. Usually top administrators talk important things over with their immediate subordinates before they make decisions. These subordinates participate in these decisions in that they offer their ideas.

Who, then, is responsible? Whose good work produces good results and whose failures cause poor results? The obvious answer, in the shoe example, is the top production manager. But this obvious answer is too simplistic. The top executive decides, but his subordinates with whom he consulted surely ought to share in the responsibility. In a very real sense, the whole group is responsible.

Surely, a high-level executive should not dismiss one of his subordinate managers because of a calamitous decision, while at the same time, keeping all of the other people, including this manager's subordinates who shared in making the decision by recommending that he do what he did. Just as these people should all share in the praise for well done work, all of them are somewhat at fault if things work out poorly. The responsibility should be a shared responsibility rather than just one superior manager's responsibility. It should be like that depicted in Figure 18-1, part III.

But, as soon as the shift in thinking is made away from individual responsibility to group responsibility, it is no longer possible to trace results to one person so it is much harder to improve performance. In the case of poor performance, high level managers need to know who did poorly so that they can try to help the manager who caused the trouble to do better.

But, with group accomplishments, it is more difficult to find out who did what that caused the poor results so that the people involved can be shown how to avoid future mistakes. It may be impossible, in practice, to improve a group, because the members of the group don't know how to do better (nor actually does the superior) nor how to train themselves so that they will be

able to perform better in the future. Possibly they just do not have the capability. A last place football team may just not be capable of doing any better.

Another unfortunate feature about group responsibility is that motivation is watered down since no one gets the satisfaction of being able to claim a result as his own.

Lower-Level Group Responsibility. One kind of middle-level group responsibility was called "splintered authority," in Chapter 12 on Committees. Splintered authority occurs when there is a middle-level interface problem which affects two or more departments. The middle level managers concerned could and should get together and decide rather than carrying the matter up to their common superior.

To illustrate, perhaps the engineering department's initial design of a product calls for costly operations and someone in a manufacturing department sees that the item can be made at a lower cost if the design is changed a little. In such a case, the design engineer and the production people really ought to get together and settle the matter themselves. Each has a splinter of the total authority; together they have full authority to decide. They have a shared responsibility to decide the item's design so that it can be manufactured economically, a responsibility which neither of them alone has.

Can Responsibility be Delegated?

A manager who delegates work to a subordinate is still, himself, responsible or accountable to *his* superior for seeing that the work gets done. Some writers (who are in the minority) conclude that, since the manager is still responsible, then he cannot have delegated responsibility. In fact, they say that responsibility cannot be delegated.[2]

They say that when a superior tells a subordinate to do certain work, he passes on

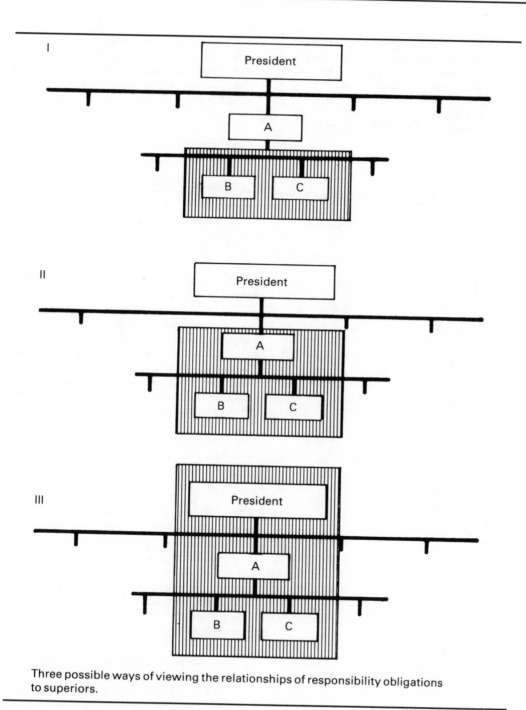

Three possible ways of viewing the relationships of responsibility obligations to superiors.

Figure 18-1
Three possible ways of viewing the relationships of responsibility obligations to superiors.

Responsibilities

to him only authority, not responsibility. They hold that since no superior can ever get rid of responsibility, he can't pass it on. They are willing to accept the idea that a superior passes on authority because having passed it on, normally he does not himself exercise authority, though he is still responsible.

But, if this is so, one might ask how anyone below the head of the organization can ever be responsible for anything? This is no problem to these people. They would say that a superior *assigns a duty* and *passes on authority* and that this *generates responsibility* in the subordinate. Responsibility is an *obligation*. The receiver of the work assignment *owes responsibility* to his superior. Thus, according to this view, responsibility can exist throughout the organization even though no one can delegate it.

Actually, a delegation of work accompanied by the necessary authority may not generate any reciprocal equivalent feeling of responsibility at all. A subordinate is just a person and he feels what he feels. When he receives an assignment, this may generate in his mind much, little, or no feeling of responsibility. If the feeling of responsibility generated in his mind proves to be a one-to-one inverse relationship to the assignment, this is pure happenstance.

This idea that responsibility cannot be delegated runs counter to common usage of the English language. When a person is newly appointed to a job, his new superior says, "Your duties will be . . ." "You are to . . ." "You are responsible for . . ." The assignment is phrased in terms of the work to be done or things to be accomplished, and either not at all in terms of the grant of authority or else with authority being mentioned only secondarily.

Most delegations are thought of by both superior and subordinate as delegations of *work* to be done or *responsibilities* to be carried out. And most writers are in agreement that responsibilities *can be delegated* even though the superior is still also responsible for the work he has delegated to his subordinate. It is like knowledge. After a person who has knowledge has passed it on to another, they both have it. It is not like money where A no longer has it after he has passed it on to B.

Getting Subordinates to Accept Responsibility

It's easy to delegate. What's hard is making sure, once something is delegated, that it gets done. One of the most common complaints of higher-level managers is that their subordinates won't accept responsibility. They don't go ahead and act in an entrepreneurial way. There are probably many reasons for this.

Unclear Job Assignments. Subordinates sometimes do not know exactly what is expected of them. Studies have found that the average manager and subordinate, upon being interviewed separately, don't agree on many of the details of the subordinate's responsibility. Sometimes, too, subordinates don't know what resources and help they can call upon to help them get their work done, or they get concerned over the lack of measurability of their work. All of these things make them hesitant and slow to accept responsibility.

The Reward-Penalty System. Subordinates may also have found that they get into a lot of trouble if they accept responsibility and do something which works out badly. They may have learned that, in the past, they rarely received any reward, praise, or even credit because of their taking on more responsibility. Instead, they have been criticized when they extended their responsibilities and took actions which worked out poorly.

Lack of Interest. Superiors would like for their subordinates to show initiative and to see things needing to be done and then to go ahead and do them and not to wait for them to tell them to go ahead. Normally, though, most subordinates are just not interested enough to see very many things that need doing.

Limited Trust. Subordinates are more likely to accept responsibility when they are trusted to proceed on their jobs without fear of reversal or second guessing. They grow in willingness to accept responsibility as the limits of the trust placed in them are extended. This tends to become a cycle. Trust a person and he accepts more responsibility, thus meriting more trust, and so on. Turn this cycle around and the reverse occurs. A trusted subordinate fails in one matter so he is given less responsibility and is trusted less the next time. He then seeks out and accepts less responsibility, which means less trust will be extended and thus the cycle goes downward.

Lack of Support by Subordinates. Another very different problem concerning subordinates' acceptance of responsibility is their lack of support.

High-level subordinate managers are themselves powers in the organization, perhaps not so strong individually as their superiors, but people with power nonetheless. Some of these people may have aspired to the top job itself, and when they did not get it, they felt jealous of the person who did become Chief Executive Officer. They may drag their feet, so far as cooperation with the CEO is concerned and possibly even try to sabotage his plans.

They may also be reluctant to do what the CEO wants them to do because of a very different reason, their belief that they know better than he what is good for the organization. So they put their effort into doing what they feel is best for the organization instead of what the CEO wants them to do.

Joint Responsibility and the "Upward Thrust"

An important area in which higher-level managers hope that subordinate man-

agers will use initiative concerns joint interface problems which affect two or more departments. Subordinate managers seem to feel responsible only for things which are theirs, and wholly theirs alone. Problems which concern two or more departments, they regard as their superior's problems, even when one of the departments is their own. They just don't step upward mentally and share the superior's responsibilities.

Duties

Responsibilities are assignments to do work or to accomplish goals. It is never possible, however, to describe fully and exactly what the recipient is to do. Thus, every subordinate always has a certain amount of latitude to interpret his instructions and to develop his job. This section will consider the factors which play a part in how jobs are developed.

Work "Roles"

Every job exists because some higher-level manager, at some time in the past, saw a need for certain work to be done so he set up the job and put someone on it.

Yet, in on-going organizations, it is not very likely that jobs, as they exist today, are what they are as a result of their having been consciously created as they now stand. Jobs are rarely created full blown. The specific duties, the subordinates' work "roles," are collections of duties which have evolved or developed over a period of time rather than having been created specifically and individually delegated.

Changes in jobs come partly from the need for the job content to change. Such needed changes can come from the superior seeing the need or from the subordinate recognizing a need for change. Changes also come from changes in personnel. A new higher-level manager will want his subordinates to do slightly different things from the things his predecessor wanted done. Changes in the subordinates also cause changes in job content according to *their* interests and capabilities.

Jobs also acquire traditional roles. People get preconceived ideas of how a manager should behave. An established role prescribes the behavior which is expected. A new incumbent is expected to act the part. An Army sergeant is supposed to be tough. A salesman is supposed to be dynamic, yet affable and easy going. These stereotypes help set the patterns of the roles that people develop on their jobs.

Individual Tasks in Work Roles; People Developing Their Own Jobs

A delegation to do certain work or to accomplish a mission is, by its nature, also a delegation for the recipient to figure out what specific work needs doing. Superiors should not try to specify every detail of subordinates' jobs or "work packages" but should phrase delegations in general terms. (Indeed, they couldn't specify all of the details even if they wanted to because, before a mission is accomplished, neither they, the superiors, nor their subordinates, know exactly what specific bits and pieces of work will have to be done.)

Some of these details of a subordinate's role concern important matters. Subordinates who have received general mission delegations often have to exercise considerable discretion as they interpret their mandates. A subordinate may believe that he sees the need to do important things not originally specified. For these he ought to get direct approval and should not consider them to have been covered by his mission delegation.

If a personnel manager decides that making a survey of the morale of the employees or that putting out a weekly company newspaper would help, he ought to get approval. He should not consider that his delegated mission allows him to go ahead with projects of such magnitude just because he deems them to be worthwhile. Only if he gets approval will this work become part of his role.

Nor should general delegations be so general as to leave subordinates wondering what they should do. Subordinates who are uncertain or confused as to what to do may become poor performers and may become dissatisfied. Most people seem to want to know what is expected of them. On the other hand, a certain amount of role ambiguity is welcomed by some subordinates, particularly the ambitious ones. General and slightly vague directions give them opportunities to develop their jobs with a good bit of freedom.

Perceived Duties

If a researcher were to follow a manager around for a day watching what he does, he would find him engaged in quite a few activities just because they need doing. Within his general delegation and his acceptance of the role, the manager does whatever he sees as being his duty to do. At the same time there are certain things he does not do. He develops his job while respecting the limits of his mission and the job roles of other people. (See Figure 18-2).

Yet he should not be left entirely on his own as he develops his role. Left to their own devices, some subordinates spend most of their time on what they like best to do and shirk the rest.

Foremen don't want their employees to get hurt but usually they do not work very hard at safety. One company appointed a

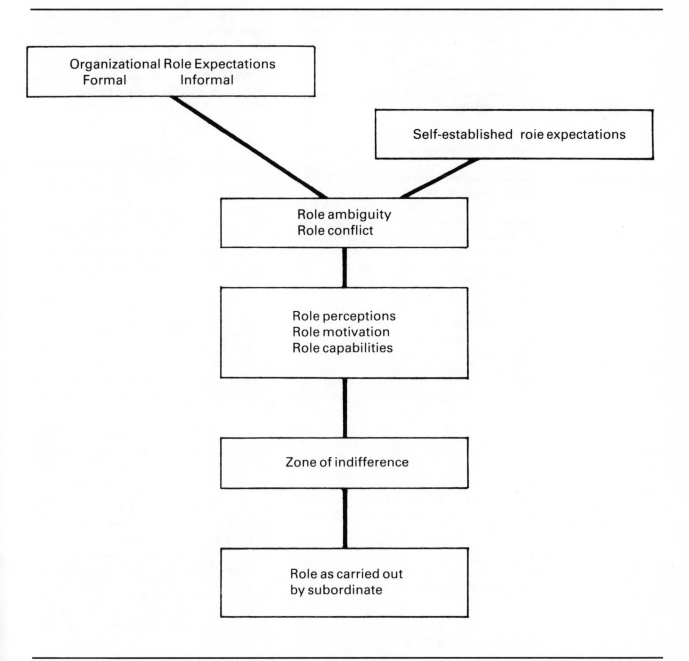

Figure 18-2
Role development from organizational expectations to role as carried out by subordinate.

safety engineer to help improve safety. Soon the company's accident rate went up because the foremen no longer perceived safety as being part of their jobs. The superintendent then put them straight on safety and told them that safety was still their job as well as the safety engineer's job. The accident rate went back down.

In his own mind, a subordinate has duties or not depending upon whether he recognizes them as such. But perceived duties are sometimes perceived because the superior makes sure that they are perceived.

The Need for Capabilities and Resources. A person's perception that certain work needs doing as part of his job is one of the first steps in its truly becoming a part of his job. Yet this is only part of the story since perception in a person's mind is unimportant if he can do nothing about it.

Several constraints act to limit the part perceptions play in determining a person's or a department's work assignment. There may be a lack of skill or capability (maybe neither the manager nor his subordinates know how to do operations research even if he thinks that doing an operations research project would be a good idea).

Or there may not be enough money. Or, maybe the organization does not have the right kind of personnel or equipment to do certain work even if it does have the money. Most companies cannot do atomic research work because they have neither the scientists nor the equipment needed for such work.

Thus, perceived duties become part of a manager's role only if the several constraints allow it. His mental perception of what his job ought to be is not allowed free play.

Conditional Duties

We said in Chapter 17 that delegations often include the obligation to be ready to respond to "trigger" directions or events. Some duties are conditional and are latent most of the time. *If* some specific thing happens, *then* these duties should be performed. *If* five employees are absent this morning, *then* the supervisor must reassign the work among the workers present so that the most necessary work is carried on.

Or, one might consider the instance of the United States enacting a new safety law such as occurred in 1970. This law affected most large employers in the country. No doubt, when this law was passed, nearly all of these companies immediately assigned certain staff people to analyze the effects of the new regulations on their operations. The trigger event (the passage of the law) resulted in the perceptions by certain managers that analytical work would need doing. Consequently, people were assigned to this work.

In this instance, there was no specific obligation to be prepared to analyze new laws since such new laws are infrequent. Rather, the standby obligation was to recognize that an important external factor was coming into play and to try to see how it would affect the company and what, if anything, should be done about it.

Triggered duties usually generate irregular work loads, yet, when their need arises, often they are high priority matters. Sometimes there is trouble because triggered duties are supposed to come into play as a result of an event or action which takes place in one department whereas the response and the work load fall on another department. For the duty to come into play, the trigger event has to be detected, its occurrence has to be communicated across departmental lines, and the communication has to be received and acted upon. If anything slips, the supposed-to-be triggered work does not get done and operations will probably suffer.

Ebbs and Flows of Work Loads

Work packages and responsibility roles are almost never static because the load of work continually changes. Seasonal changes in business volume and other changes increase a manager's load sometimes and leave him more free at other times. When he is swamped with work, as a department store manager is at Christmastime, he will probably lighten his load by delegating more than usual and by postponing everything that can wait. His most experienced subordinates will temporarily carry more responsibility. When things return to normal, he will return to delegating less and will catch up on the postponed jobs.

Responsibility roles change, too, when a manager gets tied up on big problems, or when he is out of the office for a few days, or when he takes a vacation. During his absence, his second-in-command has to keep things moving. Probably this subordinate does not take on quite the full job of the missing superior, but he does make the minor decisions. Bigger matters which his superior would normally handle are temporarily pushed up to the boss's superior for decision. Then when the manager returns, the regular responsibilities again hold.

Staff Department Responsibility Roles

Because Chapter 10 was devoted to staff departments, their responsibility assignments will be mentioned only briefly here.

Staff departments are delegated missions to help the rest of the organization. In business organizations, most staff work reaches into and impinges upon the domains of other department heads, which sometimes creates problems.

In this chapter, the interest is only in noting that staff departments have the right and the obligation to develop their own work roles but only within the limitation of helping other departments. And this help should largely be help as the recipient sees it and not just as the staff people see it. But delegations to other departments should not go so far as to allow them to turn down the help and advice of staffs without good reason. This is one of the constraints which limit the extent to which people in departments other than staff departments can develop their own roles.

Summary

Scholars sometimes differ about whether a top administrator can delegate responsibility since he is still responsible even though he tells someone else to do something. Such differences (about whether he delegates responsibility or authority or both) are largely matters of semantics because no one claims that superiors are relieved of their own responsibility just because they delegate work to subordinates.

In large organizations many activities are joint efforts of several departments. This makes it hard — almost impossible — to say who is responsible for total results. So, if something goes badly, it is hard to find out who should do something differently and what he should do, in order to improve things. Yet, in spite of these difficulties, top managers have to try to do things to improve results.

Delegations of work to individuals and to departments are often overall mission or responsibility-area delegations. Recipients of such overall delegations have to decide just what to do and then do these things. In a very real sense, managers and department heads develop their own jobs, the details of their "work packages" or their "roles."

They have considerable freedom in doing this yet their freedom is hedged; they have to operate within several constraints. Of these, the mission definition itself is perhaps the most important. But they also are bound by such other constraints as resource limitations, limitations of the capabilities of their employees, and obligations to other departments.

Review Questions

1. What is the actual responsibility of the head of an organization for its success? Discuss his responsibilities.
2. If it is true that the organization's head usually is not well informed about what goes on in the organization, isn't it his job to remedy the situation and to set up internal communication systems so that he will be properly informed? Discuss.
3. Does responsibility exist in the sense that it can be traced to one manager? And, if so, what good does it do to trace it to him?
4. Just what does a superior delegate? Responsibility? Duties? Work? Authority? Discuss the relationships between these concepts.
5. Why is there a problem in getting subordinates to accept responsibility? Or is this not really a problem? Discuss.
6. Discuss the development of the work "roles" of subordinates, how it occurs, and what is good and bad about this development process.
7. Discuss the part a manager's perceptions can play in the development of his role.
8. What part do such things as conditional duties and ebbs and flows of work loads have to do with the work role a manager develops for himself?

Questions for Analysis and Discussion

1. "Forward March!" said the captain, and the private marched forward. "Charge!" shouted the captain, and the private charged toward the enemy. Is this a delegation of responsibility? or authority? or what?

2. When Ford Motor bought a new subsidiary, a Ford manager said, "We found that some managers were reporting to more than one boss so that when something was wrong, the managers at the top found it impossible to place the responsibility and bring about a quick correction." How important is it to trace responsibility?

3. The text says that subordinates just don't "step upward mentally" and share their superiors' responsibility. Actually, why should they? Discuss.

4. The text recommends letting managers develop their own jobs and their own job duty sets. In Chapters 23 and 24, the text will say that people tend to concentrate their efforts on the things which get appraised as being either good or bad. These positions seem to be opposed to each other. Discuss.

5. The text devotes a good bit of space to people developing their own jobs. But, isn't it true that the main essential of nearly all subordinates' jobs is to accomplish some specific, rather narrowly defined mission? If this is true, then how much latitude do subordinates have in developing their jobs?

6. The Jones department store has just hired a new manager in the department which sells bed sheets and pillowcases. He does not want to have a January "white sale" (which is always an annual event in all such stores) of bed sheets and pillowcases because, he says, all that this does is to allow homemakers to load up at low prices. What should his superior do?

7. A & P's grocery store manager wants to buy all of his meats from a small local packing house. He also wants to put meats near the check-out counter so that they will stay cold longer for customers. And, since there is a fine baked goods shop next door, he doesn't want to carry bread. Should A&P let him do these things? Why or why not?

8. What should the head of one department do if he sees things going on in another department which ought to be improved upon? Is it true that, if he has the proper feeling of organizational empathy and concern for its well-being, he should do something? What if this person is a staff specialist and the work needing improving is in his area of specialty? Discuss.

9. One of the FMC company's machinery-making divisions had a rule of no trade-ins. But the manager of its San Francisco plant thought that he could sell more new machines if he accepted trade-ins. So he did, without telling his superior in Chicago. This put him in the used machinery business and, of course, violated his instructions. It proved profitable. The vice president in Chicago heard about it from the manager of the company's Philadelphia plant who wanted to do the same. What should he do about this?

10. A professor at a university in a remote part of the country says that supervising most workers in his area is different. They don't understand delegated authority. Tell them to use their own judgment and they don't think that they're paid to do that. Also, owner-managers in this professor's area don't really want subordinates to use much discretion. Isn't this a good way to operate, regardless of the section of the country? Discuss.

Case 18-1   The CEO's Duties and His Subordinates' Perceptions

Situation A

The company president came out of the board of directors' meeting where he had been roundly criticized for not getting the most out of his organization. He immediately called a meeting of his subordinates and told them, " I don't intend to subject myself to such humiliation again. You men are paid to do your jobs; it's not up to me to do them for you. I don't know how you spend your time and I don't intend to try to find out. You know your responsibilities, and these figures bear out that you haven't discharged them properly. If the next report doesn't show a marked improvement, there will be some new faces around here."

Situation B

Hillcrest College had been trying to get accredited by the National Association of Colleges. Accreditation depends on a favorable recommendation by an examining committee appointed to check into the college's resources, both material resources, such as library facilities, as well as the training (particularly the number of Ph.D.'s) of its faculty and its strength in various departments.

The president of Hillcrest was happy to hear that the accrediting committee had recommended the accreditation of the school. Yet he was chagrined by some of the negative criticism — the lack of scholarly publications by his faculty members, their lack of participation in scholarly organizations, and even their lack of membership in such organizations.

Accordingly, he called a meeting of his faculty and announced the good news. Then he moved on to the shortcomings the investigating committee had found. In fact, he laid down the law and told them that future promotions would depend on improvement in these matters. He told his faculty members that, in the future, they would have to measure up.

- Aren't both of these men excusing themselves too readily? Why should they have had to learn about the shortcomings of their organizations from someone else? Shouldn't they feel that such shortcomings are their shortcomings too?
- Can managers of businesses do very much to improve their organizations? Can college presidents do more or less to improve the quality of their organizations?
- How much is "laying down the law" likely to accomplish? What merit is there in such an approach?

Endnotes

1. "Double Loop Learning in Organizations," by Chris Argyris, *Harvard Business Review*, September-October 1977, pp. 115–125. Although Argyris does not identify the company or the product, product X could easily be the DuPont company's artificial leather, "Corfam."
2. This view is held, for example, by Koontz, O'Donnell and Weirich. See, *Management*, 7th ed., by Harold Koontz, Cyril O'Donnell, and Heinz Weirich (McGraw-Hill, 1980), p. 428.

Suggested Supplementary Readings

Graen, G. "Role Making Processes Within Complex Organizations." In *Handbook of Industrial and Organizational Psychology*, by M. Dunnette, ed. Rand McNally, 1976, pp. 1201–1245.

Henschell, Harry B. "The President Stands Alone." *Harvard Business Review*, September-October 1971, pp. 37–45.

Posner, Barry Z., and D. Anthony Butterfield. "Role Clarity and Organizational Level." *Journal of Management*, Fall 1978, pp. 81–90.

Schuler, R.S. "Role Perceptions, Satisfaction and Performance Moderated by Organization Level and Participation in Decision Making." *Academy of Management Journal* 20 (1977): 159–165.

Objectives of Chapter Nineteen

1. To investigate the base of power of managers and how this power can be transferred down through organizations.
2. To relate power and authority to each other and to see how managers use them in managing their work.
3. To examine the role of informal power groups in organizations and how their existence affects the organization's accomplishments.
4. To consider the "acceptance principle," its nature, how it operates, and how managers can avoid being too much constrained by it.

Power, Authority, and Influence in Organizations

19

*The exercise of power,
the management of people,
is the ultimate challenge.*

Relations between Power, Authority, and Influence

Power is the ability to change the thinking or behavior of others. *Authority* is the right to exercise power. *Influence* is low-grade power.

The dictionary defines power, authority, and influence as being to some extent coextensive with each other and as sometimes being synonyms. And although the word "influence" does not connote the strength that the words "power" and "authority" carry, the difference is largely a matter of degree. In a political campaign, a leader has a great deal of influence, but no strong power over a large number of volunteer workers.

If one person can influence another and cause him to think or to behave differently or to perform different activities, he does, in fact, have a degree of both power and authority over him even though it may not rest on any formal grant of authority. In most organizations, the leader's power is, of course, much greater than that of a political campaign leader because the organization's members have already accepted their normal work assignments on the basis of their making contributions to the organization in exchange for proper and fair wage payments.

The Power Base. Managerial actions in all organizations always rest on a base of power which is embodied in authority. In business organizations the stockholders delegate the authority to oversee the organization's activities to the board of directors, whom they elect. The board then chooses officers to whom they delegate the power and authority to operate the organization on a continuing basis.

In government units, the heads of major departments get their power and au-thority from constitutions, from state or municipal charters, or from laws passed by elected representatives of the people.

Limitations on Power. The power of managers at all levels is subject to many restrictions. A manager, having received delegated authority, is presumed to have the power to do the things necessary to accomplish his mission. He has the power to give directions, to pass judgment on the work done by his subordinates, and to dispense rewards or censure, even to removing individuals from the organization.

Power and authority are, however, rarely what they seem. They are restricted and hedged about and intertwined with personal as well as hierarchical relationships. Modern management theory and practice recognize, for example, that certain actions are simply not acceptable. An angry manager does not just fire a subordinate for little reason even if he has the power to do so. Nor do managers actually have enough power always to get subordinates to do what they want them to do. Subordinates may not be able to do what the superior wants done or they may not want to do what he wants them to do, so they drag their feet. Formal power is greatly overrated and is much weaker than it would seem.

In today's organizations even the power to give directions and to dispense rewards or to mete out censure has been watered down, diminished, and, in some situations, taken away. We mentioned earlier that managers of government organizations, for example, find that civil service regulations severely curtail their power to dispense rewards and to mete out censure. Labor contracts covering unionized workers also restrict the power of managers.

The Kind of Power and Authority Delegated

Presumably, when a manager makes a delegation to a subordinate, he gives him all of the power and authority he will need in order to carry out the task. There is a real question, however, of whether the subordinate manager has received enough power and authority. He actually needs to have four kinds of authority and not all four can be delegated in the usual sense. We mentioned these kinds of power in Chapter 14 when discussing leadership, but we need to consider them more fully here as they relate to managers' authority.

1. *A manager needs to have the authority of position.* This is the formal right to direct the work of subordinates, to allocate resources, and to take other kinds of actions in support of his directives. Normally, this is the most important part of a manager's authority. A manager has positional authority when he is appointed to the job and given the insignia and rank associated with the job. Positional authority implies also that the recipient is entrusted with sufficient resources, including capable personnel, so that he can accomplish his mission.

   Organization scholars sometimes call this "legitimate" or "institutionalized" power. Superiors *can confer this kind of power* on their subordinate managers. An authoritarian manager relies considerably on this kind of power. Usually, however, authority based on the power of the position is not enough, by itself, to allow a subordinate manager to be very effective. David Bowers says that "legitimacy of position is a rubber crutch."[1]

2. *A manager should have the authority of expertise.* He needs to have a certain amount of know-how relating to the work of his subordinates. To some extent, expertise knowledge is power. If the manager knows the work of his subordinates fairly well, they will respect him because of his knowledge and will follow his directions more readily.

3. *A manager should have reasonable skill in*

administration. This kind of authority is like that in point two. It is a matter of expertise in how to delegate and supervise and not expertise in the work of the subordinates. If the manager is a skilled administrator, he has more power to cause his organization to accomplish goals.

4. *A manager needs to have personal skill or charisma in dealing with people.* He needs to be able to influence people by virtue of his human relations skills. Presidents Eisenhower and Kennedy were both known for having this kind of skill. In Chapter 14, we called this "referent power," meaning that subordinates identify with the manager, possibly to the point of desiring to emulate him.

   A manager who has these last three kinds of authority has "inner authority" to buttress his positional authority. Managers with inner authority don't need to rely on rank when giving orders. Subordinates of a manager with inner authority look to him for directions and orders because they believe both that he *is* the boss and furthermore, that he knows his business.

Limitations to Superiors' Power to Delegate Full Authority. A superior cannot confer inner authority directly and quickly. A considerable amount of inner authority can, however, be conferred or "delegated" over a period of time through training. New managers or prospective managers can be trained in administrative and personal relations skills.

Inequality of Responsibility and Authority

Ideally, the authority of every manager should go hand-in-hand with and be co-extensive with his responsibility. This tenet of scholars of organization, the *prin-*

ciple of parity of responsibility and authority, goes clear back to Henri Fayol.

But such an ideal state of affairs rarely exists. Responsibility is almost always greater than authority. A sales manager is responsible for selling products and he has the authority to do it, that is, all the authority that the president can give him. But the president cannot give him any real authority over external factors nor can he give the sales manager the authority to make customers buy the company's products. The authority the president can give to his sales manager is limited to allowing him to use the resources, including salespeople, assigned to him to best advantage and to try to sell all that he can.

Probably everyone recognizes that responsibility and authority cannot be wholly commensurate. When someone says that responsibility and authority ought to be equal, surely he means "within reason." He knows that the sales manager has to operate within constraints and that his control over the sales of products is limited. When a person says that the president is responsible for the company's well-being he recognizes that the president cannot control everything.

In Chapter 10 we mentioned product managers and project managers and discussed their having responsibility but without very much authority. As we said there, this lack of enough authority sometimes causes minor conflicts and, at times, a certain amount of frustration. But there seems to be no better way to get this kind of job done, and the difficulties rarely become major problems.

None of these things, however, should be any excuse for managers of every organization not trying to back up the responsibilities of their subordinates with commensurate formal authority insofar as possible. Many managers fail on this point and grant subordinates too little formal authority when they could grant them more. This point was discussed in the last chapter.

Authority and Latent Power

Most managers actually have more power and authority than they use. Their true power is greater than their formally granted power. Their actual power is embodied in a complex hierarchy of position and status. Their failure to use all of the power they have may stem from their not realizing that they have this much power.

A manager who wants to find out how much power he really has should ask himself, "Can I do anything about it?" When he answers this question he will often find that he has a good bit of informal latent power. Perhaps it even extends beyond his own departmental confines. He may find that he is able to persuade another department head to do something for him.[2] If he can do this, he has power and authority, perhaps not of the formally delegated kind, but real power nonetheless.

Organizational Change and Resistance to Change

An organization should be a dynamic entity. This means that managers should change their organizations, at least in minor ways, as a continuing activity so that they will fit in with the ever-changing environment.

When managers try to make changes, they often encounter resistance. When a manager tries to change the job of one or more of his subordinates by delegating different work to them, they sometimes object, particularly people who have been on their jobs for a long time. To many managers this is illogical. Subordinates are members of the organization and they willingly accept their pay checks so why shouldn't they be willing to earn these checks by doing what they are told?

Parenthetically, we should say that John Miner[3] reports that it is easy to be over-

Organizations in Action: Delegation

ly impressed with resistance to change. He says that resistance to change is far from being a universal reaction. Without considerable group support, it rarely becomes much of a problem.

Barriers to Change. Even though Miner may be right, it is still true that subordinates *do* sometimes drag their feet on changing. No doubt there are many barriers which impede the making of changes in organizations. Most of these have to do with what will happen to employees.

1. Change often upsets comfortable established jobs. Sometimes, when an employee resists changing, his objection is, in fact, more a feeling against change as such than it is an objection to the proposed change. A good many people, particularly older people, just don't like change at all. They have become comfortable on their present jobs and would rather stay with them as they are even though a change might be for their own betterment. Their opposition is not based on any opposition to organizational well-being but on their personal feelings of not wanting to change.

2. A great many changes result in changes in status and in skills requirements. Unfortunately, changes are often changes which improve the status of only some of the organization's people. Other employees may also have their jobs and status changed, but not for the better. Some may even lose their jobs.

    Employees may properly feel that their security is threatened. They are already on jobs where they have acquired specialized competencies, and where they have proven their capabilities and they are secure. A change will take some of them off their present jobs and put them on new jobs. Such employees might well lose some of their competence because not all of their expertise relevant to their old jobs is relevant to the new jobs. The change might easily strip them of their present skills (as when their present skills are not needed on the new job), downgrade them, and cast them in roles of beginners on strange jobs.

    Nor is it only bottom-level operatives who feel threatened by changes. The jobs of heads of departments are rarely in jeopardy but a change might reduce the size or status of a department. So department heads, too, are often fearful over the results of changes.

3. People have to learn to live with new internal social structures. Changes usually change the internal social structure and the communications networks already built up. The circle of people a person deals with will change and so will the way they will have to interact and communicate.

4. An organization is, among other things, a social order. In this social order, individuals and groups develop possessive "ownership" feelings about their activities and areas of responsibility. They resist change, particularly encroachment types of changes, which disturb their established areas of responsibility.

Reducing Resistance to Change. Although change is disruptive and there are barriers standing in the way of making changes easily, managers can do several things to make change more acceptable.

It helps to start early and give an early warning about changes and it usually helps to make changes slowly rather than all at once. This avoids the shock of sudden change and helps keep the change from being in the nature of a confrontation. It also helps to explain the need for change and to ask people who will be affected for suggestions about how to go about it. Resistance to change often melts away when the way it is done has been suggested by those who will be affected. They may even become supporters for the change.

Beneficiaries from Change. Change does not, of course, upset everybody because almost every change will benefit someone. Those people are usually enthusiastic. Change is usually exciting to the people who will be better off. Change, when it is not threatening, often boosts productivity.

Informal Power Groups

In most organizations there are informal internal power groups which exercise much of the real power in the organization. This informal power system, in general, follows the formal hierarchical structure power delegations—but not always. Sometimes it operates in opposition to the apparent power structure. In other cases, its operation distorts the operation of the formal system.

We will consider the operation of informal power groups at three levels in organizations; at high levels, in the middle levels; and at lower levels.

High-Level Power Groups

Power in organizations can be considered from the viewpoint of the interests and power positions of departments. It is unusual for all of an organization's departments to be equally important to its successful operation.

In a new manufacturing organization, the real power may be the creative area, such as engineering or research. Managers in these areas have the most to say in the most important decisions being made. Later, after a company's products are developed, power is likely to shift to the marketing people. Important decisions are heavily influenced by marketing considerations. Still later, after markets have been established, power often moves to the financial people. Other factors also sometimes come

into play. Today, because of anti-discrimination laws, the director of industrial relations has become more powerful and is often a vice president.

Such dominance by power groups, which is entirely natural and reasonable, nonetheless poses a danger to the organization. Presumably the current power group came to the fore because of the greater importance of its part of the business at the present time. The danger is that other facets of the operations will not receive the attention they should get. John De Lorean, at one time a vice president of General Motors, for example, decries the strong centralized financial control in General Motors. The financial group has been the power group in GM since the late 1960s. De Lorean feels that this emphasis has resulted in too little attention being given to marketing and to engineering and design. He blames the financial people for blocking GM's development of small cars in the 1970s to meet Toyota and other small imported cars on a directly competitive basis.[4]

Infra-Structure Politics.[5] At high levels, infra-structure groups and subcultures sometimes play important parts. Competition for determining courses of action is sometimes close to outright conflict as one group tries to gain an advantage over other groups. This sometimes happens when a manager is promoted to a high office. The decision to promote one person to be a major department head instead of someone else may be like choosing the President of the United States. Not that organization employees get to vote, but that the promotion of the individual who is chosen produces a winner and one or more losers.

Furthermore, in large organizations, a manager who wins does not win all by himself. Both he and the losers are probably leaders of informal power groups which include other people. When one person wins, the whole group benefits. He will probably move his supporters into positions having more power. And when the leader loses, so do his followers.

When Semon Knudsen, a highly regarded vice president of General Motors, was passed over several years ago for the presidency of GM, he resigned. Probably other managers in General Motors who hitched their wagons to his star found that their further advancement was slowed down or stopped.

Infra-structure power politics also play a part in decisions other than filling high-level jobs. Power groups build their power by their members being in on making important decisions which work out well. Organizations, being social and political entities, operate by distributing authority and this sets the stage for the exercise of power. Highly motivated individuals find in this an opportunity to secure and use more power. Even job changes are seen to be acceptable or not depending upon the power positions involved and upon whom one will work with and what decisions he will be in on making.

Back in Chapter 15 we reported that psychologist David McClelland felt that some people were "n-pwr" people. They wanted power. Top level people seem, nearly all of them, to want power, just plain unadulterated power for its own sake. This desire frequently is so strong that it breaks out in open conflict between power-hungry executives. Friction, lack of cooperation, and undermining the position of rivals occur in the struggle for power.

It has long been axiomatic in the study of political science that "uneasy rests the head that wears the crown." Rivals constantly try to usurp the crown and take it over themselves. It is not surprising that the same thing sometimes happens in organizations. The desire to contribute to organizational effectiveness gets lost sight of in the internecine conflicts.

Power conflicts are likely to arise when a top-level job opens up as contenders vie for the job or when a major success or failure occurs. Everyone wants to claim credit for the success and no one wants to be blamed for the failure.

Informal Groups at Middle Levels

Informal groups also exist at middle levels in organizations. Here, the people concerned are middle-level managers and their supporting office groups. People who speak of "bureaucracies" usually are referring not only to the middle-level part of the organization but also to its common intractability. Both middle-level managers and their supporting office staffs are regarded as being resistant to change.

The bureaucracy could be regarded as being an informal group since it usually has its own subculture, its own norms, and its own goals. Bureaucracies as informal groups differ from high-level power groups in that they are not always sharply evident or recognized. They are really informal and to the extent that they exist, the strengths of the ties and bonds are only slight for some people, especially those on the outer fringes of the group. Many people hardly recognize that such groups exist or that they themselves are in any way associated with (or excluded from) a power group. Besides, both the people concerned and the strength of their interest and support may well vary according to the issue at hand. A person may find himself aligned on one side on one issue but with another group on another matter.

We reported, in earlier discussions, that behavioral scientists usually believe that the bureaucracy has a great deal of power, even as much as that of their hierarchical superiors. This thinking lies behind much of the popularity of the idea that participative, consultative, democratic-type management is usually the best kind and that if they are not consulted, the informal organization members will not support their hierarchical superiors.

Psychologist David McClelland is one of a few social scientists who believe that this idea goes too far, particularly so far as office people and bureaucracies are concerned (McClelland's ideas are presented more fully in Case 19-1, at the end of this chapter.) McClelland feels that McGregor, Maslow, Likert, Herzberg, Argyris and others who subscribe to these ideas overemphasize the existence of and the power of informal groups and bureaucracies in organizations. He thinks also that these social scientists overemphasize the extent and strength of the opposition of informal groups to their organizational superiors making decisions and giving directions.[6]

Informal Groups at Lower Levels

Informal groups seem to grow up in the lower levels of almost all organizations. The effect of such groups on organizational behavior is much as if they were incipient power or anti-power groups.

As is true at higher levels, informal groups at lower levels are made up of people who from friendship, community of interest, fear, enmity, or other common bond, feel alike about something and act in a way to protect their common interests even if this distorts or works against managers' attempts to reach organizational goals.

In a retail store paying salespeople on a commission basis, the group may decide that they don't like the plan. They may then ignore it so far as motivation is concerned. They may take turns waiting on customers and also report sales in each other's names in order to equalize earnings.

Informal group subcultures often determine how much work employees do. The workplace subculture is a social environment which prescribes certain behavior patterns as

"appropriate" and penalizes other behavior as "inappropriate."

Groups have probably always imposed restrictions on their members.

Three hundred years ago in England a man who violated group codes was "sent to Coventry." (No one would speak to him for several days.) Nearly one hundred years ago in the United States, Frederick Taylor tried to get men to quit "soldiering on the job" (holding production down).[7] Twenty-five years ago, Herbert Simon reported that groups could and did withhold group membership from men who produced more than the group's norm.[8]

At bottom levels, if an employee violates the group's code, usually by doing too much work or by otherwise failing to behave in the prescribed manner, he may, even today, be "sent to Coventry." Or, if he leaves his machine to go to the washroom, his machine is likely to be out of adjustment when he gets back. Or some of his tools or his lunch disappear. In rare cases, he may find flat tires or even broken windows in his car.

Sometimes groups take collective action against the organization, instead of against individuals, as when they engage in wildcat (spur-of-the-moment and unauthorized by the union) strikes.

Subcultures usually are, to some extent, affected by individual differences. The feelings of some people are strong but others care less. Some people never develop much in the way of intra-group feelings. Usually, no strong action is taken by an informal group unless it has a leader who crystallizes latent feelings and who stimulates group action. Usually, too, the strength of informal groups ebbs and flows over time depending upon the issue at hand and the strength of the opposition to it or support for it.

We should not, however, be wholly negative toward informal work groups. Sometimes they are supportive of organizational goals and work to further organizational benefit. They help keep recalcitrant people in line and they sometimes help circumvent organizational rules when these rules are actually hindrances to accomplishment.

The Acceptance Principle

Back in 1938, Chester Barnard wrote that the only real authority and power that a manager has is that which his subordinates are willing to let him exercise. This was mentioned briefly in Chapter 2. Barnard said, "The necessity of the assent of the individual to established authority for the superior is inescapable."

He continued, saying that a person can accept only if four conditions are met:

· The subordinate understands the communication.
· He believes that it is in accord with the purposes of the organization.
· It is compatible with his own interests.
· He is mentally and physically able to comply.[9]

Power and the Acceptance Principle of Authority

Barnard's idea, which is now called the *Acceptance Principle,* holds that the real authority and power in an organization resides in the *subordinates* and that a superior has no real authority or power other than what the subordinates confer upon him. This principle also holds that subordinates will grant authority to their superior only if doing so is in their best interests as they see them.

Fundamental Validity of the Acceptance Principle

Acceptance by subordinates *is* fundamental to getting work done through other people. Subordinates *do* do the end-product or end-service work of the organization. They *make products,* or *sell products,* or *perform services.* And, if they don't do these things, they don't get done. So, fundamentally, the acceptance principle must be valid.

Furthermore, subordinates *can* deprive or deny power to superiors. On July 4, 1776, the American colonies deprived England's King George III of his authority and power over what became the United States. And, on July 14, 1789, when the Bastille fell, King Louis XVI lost his authority in France.

People in all organizations do sometimes deprive their superiors of power over them by quitting. Furthermore, when subordinates are unwilling, they don't always go so far as to refuse an assignment or to say that they are unwilling to do it. Instead, they just go along half-heartedly. Managers will endure a good bit of such lack of support before they discipline an employee because his reluctance is usually not overt and often it is not sharply evident.

Acceptance and Willingness. Perhaps the most important strength of the acceptance principle is the *willingness,* even *enthusiastic willingness,* which whole-hearted acceptance can generate. As we said in Chapter 15, there is a big difference, possibly half or more, in how much work and how effective work a person will do when he is willing and enthusiastic as compared to his prosaic work-a-day sense-of-obligation performance.

Some companies have benefited greatly from the sometimes even exciting atmosphere generated by enthusiastic employees engaged in the purposeful pursuit of demanding goals. People who were close to IBM, Xerox, Polaroid, Texas Instruments, and other growth companies in their periods of rapid growth often commented about the unified sense of mission that members of these organizations had. There was great enthusiasm to get things done. The people worked hard and they worked long hours; but there was apparently little or no negative feeling of being pushed, and results were outstanding.

Zones of Acceptance. The acceptance principle is not always a seriously constraining factor because everybody has an area or zone of acceptance of indifference. Within this zone, the subordinate expects to do what his superior wants him to do.

People usually do not accept jobs on which they expect to refuse to do the work assigned. They expect to meet the job's requirements. An employee refuses to do the work assigned (at the risk of losing his job) only if it is against his principles, such as falsifying the records, or if it is clearly beyond his ability (not everyone can do nuclear physics work just because he is willing), or is beyond his physical abilities (a five-foot basketball player just can't do what a seven-foot player can do). But, within his zone of acceptance, he accepts the supervisor's authority over him.

Inability of Subordinates to Confer Full Power and Authority. Earlier in this chapter, it was brought out that subordinate managers really need four kinds of power and authority, only one of which (formal or positional authority) could be clearly delegated by a superior. This raises an interesting philosophical point; that is, can subordinates, by accepting their superior manager, confer on him the other three kinds of authority which a manager ought to have (the authority of job knowledge, the authority of administrative ability, and the authority of human relations skills)?

Probably subordinates cannot, through acceptance (see Figure 19-1), do this wholly. But, by cooperating with their superior, they can improve his effectiveness, whatever his qualifications may be.

Reluctant Acceptance. Acceptance is not always accompanied by enthusiasm among subordinates. Sometimes the accept-

ance principle works like a person going to the dentist. He doesn't "want" to go to the dentist, but he goes.

In 1980 and 1981, Chrysler's employees agreed to postpone their expected pay raises and agreed also to move their future expected pay raises back for several years as their part to help the company avoid bankruptcy.

Several years earlier Schwayder Brothers' (card table makers) employees in Detroit, took a fifty-cents an hour wage cut rather than see their jobs go to Tennessee.

In each of these two cases, the employees "accepted" the wage limitation, albeit reluctantly.

The "Psychological Contract." Some scholars feel that employees and employers enter into what Edgar Schein calls a "psychological contract" (see Figure 19-2) which holds that each one expects certain behavior on the part of the other and that there is an implicit agreement which is the product of mutual expectations. Ordinarily, this includes the acceptance of all normal job requirements by the employee and it implies fair treatment and normal job security from the employer.

But, since this "contract" is implicit and not expressed, not all parts of the expectations of either party are known to the other. Consequently, one or the other of them sometimes inadvertently does something which the other regards as being in violation of the contract — at least it violates *his* expectations. When an employee feels that the psychological contract has been violated, he is likely to be dissatisfied and may even quit — and for no apparent reason, as the employer sees it.

The Ultimate Strength of the Power of Managers

Although managers cannot always

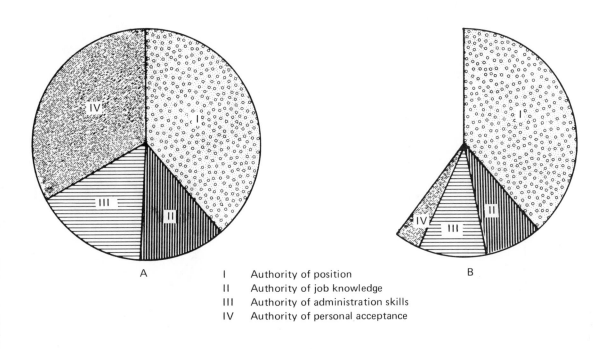

Figure 19-1
A manager needs to have the four kinds of authority which were discussed in chapter 18. Diagram A depicts the authority of a superior with full authority. But, as depicted in diagram B, subordinates have it in their power to delegate *only part*, not all, of the authority a superior needs.

I   Authority of position
II   Authority of job knowledge
III Authority of administration skills
IV   Authority of personal acceptance

cause subordinates to accept, this is not quite so hard and fast a limitation on managerial actions as it at first sounds. Managers have the power to allocate resources and they control the reward-penalty system. They can promote workers who accept and who produce and can give them pay raises. And, except at bottom levels where union membership protects employees, managers can dismiss men or women who do not accept and hire others who do accept. They can, in the long run, often work around the acceptance principle. Voluntary attrition probably helps too. Non-accepters are probably dissat-

isfied and some of them quit, thereby making room for others who accept.

Accountability

Accountability means being answerable to a superior for one's actions and accomplishments.

Accountability is an accounting which one person renders to another person. It is not possible to hold a building, machine, or product accountable. Any of these

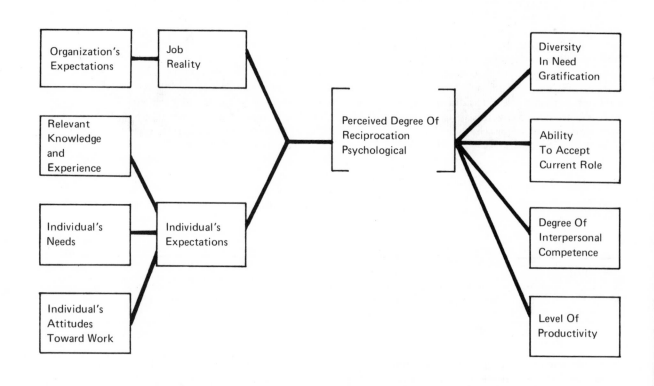

Figure 19-2
Psychological contract model.

may have caused trouble, but only a person can do anything about it.

Probably the greatest value of accountability lies neither in reports nor in the checking up by higher-level managers. Instead, just as we found in the case of motivation, the greatest value in accountability lies in the *expectations* by both manager and subordinate that the manager will be watching the progress and accomplishments of his subordinates.

Subordinates who know that the superior maintains an interest in what they are doing will almost always try harder than they will if they think that no one is paying any attention to their work. Subordinates expect and want their superiors to pay attention to their work and to know whether things are going well or not. They hope that their good work will be noticed and rewarded.

The Principal of "Unity of Command."
Ideally, every employee should have one superior only. This is the principle of *"Unity of Command."*

Serving two masters is usually difficult although it may not be so bad as it is pictured in the Bible where it says, "No man can serve two masters." Earlier discussions considered how group decision making blurs the pin-pointing of responsibilities because no one person is responsible. Having two or more superiors, in a similar way, blurs accountability.

One danger in a subordinate having two or more superiors is that, without their knowing it, the total of their assignments of work may overload him. Or his several superiors may give him conflicting instructions, and friction and bad feelings may result. (See Figure 19-3).

Another danger when a person is accountable to several superiors, is that he may not, in fact, end up being accountable to anyone at all. He may even become inefficient without it being noticed when no one person watches over his work. When several people are supposed to watch over a person's work, often no one does. The employee may even get to establish his own work priority list and do only the work he likes best, or to do work for the people he likes best because he has, or claims to have, in total, too much work to do. He does any one superior a favor if he does his work. This is unfortunately the way it works sometimes when office secre-

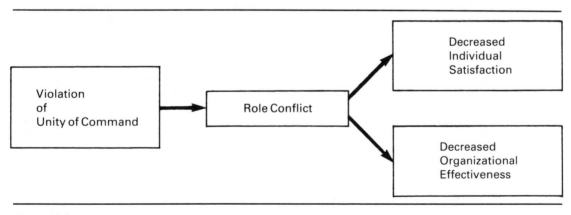

Figure 19-3
Possible results from violations of the unity of command.

taries serve several people. Single accountability helps resolve such situations.

Actually, the evils of double accountability are probably exaggerated. There are businesses situations in which employees have two or more superiors, but no friction develops because they are cooperative. Differences are resolved quickly and without animosity. Small companies, especially, often have unclear lines of accountability yet things go along well because everyone is so cooperative. Lower-line supervisors often think that they have several superiors, but they get along.

Double accountability may not even be all loss. Having two or more pairs of eyes looking over proposals adds insurance against anyone taking unrecognized critical risks and exposing the organization to substantial losses.

Summary

It seems wholly logical and reasonable that responsibility and authority and power should be equal but in fact this cannot be. Managers at nearly every level in all organizations are supposed to accomplish results in spite of their having authority and power over only some of the factors which bear upon results.

Besides constraints from the outside, middle- and lower-level managers have to contend with superiors sometimes not delegating enough power and authority to them. Although when this happens it hampers operations somewhat, it is usually not a serious problem because it is not common.

One theory of granting power and authority, the "acceptance principle," holds that managers have only such power and authority as subordinates grant to them. This principle is not always apparent on the surface because people who join an organization almost always accept its goals and constraints when they accept their jobs. Yet managers should know of its existence because lack of acceptance may come to the surface if they issue directives which are unpopular.

Subordinates who are responsible for work should expect to be held accountable for it and should expect surveillance from their superiors. It is usually best for them to be accountable to one superior only, because things are likely to go better when there is but one superior.

Review Questions

1. At the start of this chapter, it was said that a department manager's power is watered down and less than it seems. Yet a little later it says that managers usually have more power than is apparent. How is this? Explain.

Organizations in Action: Delegation

2. What kinds of authority does a subordinate manager really need? Can a superior delegate them all? And, if not, how does a subordinate acquire authority?

3. Is it true that authority and responsibility are necessarily equal? Discuss the relationships between these two concepts.

4. What common barriers exist which make it hard to make changes in organizations? What can be done about them?

5. What is the "acceptance principle"? How does it differ from other theories? What are its strong and weak points? How should it affect a manager's methods of managing?

6. Compare the short- and long-term constraints which the acceptance principle imposes on managers. Which constraints are stronger in the short-run and less strong in the long-run? Are there other effects which become stronger with the passage of time instead of becoming weaker? Discuss.

7. It is said that members of organizations often resist change. Why is this and what can be done about it?

8. Why is "single accountability" or "unity of command" important? What are the dangers from not recognizing this principle? How likely are they to be serious?

Questions for Analysis and Discussion

1. If responsibility is often greater than authority, how does it happen that managers are able to carry out their responsibilities?

2. Suppose that Smith is a dissatisfied foreman (his present acceptance of his job is very reluctant acceptance) in a shoe factory in a small town in mid-state New York. He is the foreman of the department which cuts "uppers" for shoes out of leather. If Smith decides that the job does not offer enough challenge (he does not accept it) what should he do?

3. When a subordinate says, "I do only what I am supposed to do," is this a result of his trying to equate authority and responsibility? Is this good? What should be done about it?

4. When Dwight Eisenhower was elected President, his predecessor, President Harry Truman, said, "Poor Ike, when he was a general he gave an order and it was carried out. Now he is going to sit in that big office and he'll give an order and not a damn thing is going to happen." Since Truman spoke from experience, it is highly probable that it is true that people respond differently to the orders given by the President and by a general. Why the differences and why is the President less powerful than a general? After becoming President what should Eisenhower have done about this?

5. A manager was quoted as saying, "I agree that something should be done, but I'm not going to do anything about it myself." Discuss this from the point of view of the acceptance principle. If his superior hears of his having said this, what should the superior do?

6. According to the acceptance theory of authority, a superior has not really delegated when he tells someone to do something. Delegation occurs when the subordinate accepts the delegation. Does this mean that there can be a time lag when delegation is sort of held in abeyance and no authority can be exercised and nothing happens?

7. "I have seen men come and go in our place just because they believed that their positions entitled them to argue with the boss. In some cases they even refused to do the job as requested. If my boss askes me to do something, I do it. If I disagree, I voice my opinion, for my boss is a reasonable man. But I do the job as he wants it done, just the same. He is paying me — and it makes no difference to me if I have to do it over and over again. I figure that a man is boss because he knows what he is doing." Is this a common attitude? Is it a good attitude? Discuss.

8. The marketing director has price-setting authority. He set the price of item A at $15. Then one of his salesmen told him that a competitor was charging only $13 for a similar item so the marketing director changed the price to $13. Who, in this case, has price-setting authority? Discuss.

9. "Oldtimers have been around for a long time and know the ropes in a way that no newcomer can. They will resolutely prevent any newcomer from moving fast unless he first pays them the attention and obeisance which they feel they have earned." Can they really be such roadblocks? What can a higher-level manager do about this?

10. How can an organization use the "team" idea and yet preserve a unity of command? Aren't these two ideas at odds with each other?

11. "This man has been with the company for thirty years and his experience is really valuable. But it's impossible to get him to budge an inch from his own way of doing things. I've been trying to get him to introduce a new work simplification program in his department for months. If only he would try it for one week, he'd be sold on it completely." Why not just tell him to do it? What should the superior do in this case?

12. B can only accept a responsibility from A to *try* to see that certain work is done or that certain accomplishments are reached. Yet, if so, is it possible for him to have carried out his responsibility and yet not have gotten the work done or not have reached the desired accomplishment? Discuss.

Case 19-1   Managers and the Need for Power[9]

Psychologist David McClelland is the maverick of the behavioral scientists. He favors less participation and more autocratic managerial methods.

McClelland believes that there are three main motivational characteristics — the needs for power, for achievement, and for affiliation. He reports that his research shows that the best managers are high in their need for power but low in their need for affiliation. They are not interested in people. They are interested in discipline. And, contrary to McGregor, McClelland reports that his research clearly shows that the subordinates of such managers have high morale.

McClelland suspects that part of the emphasis on participation and the relaxing of authority comes from society having become disillusioned with power. "I see two faces of power, says McClelland. "The face that social science has presented has been the NAZI face, which depicts power as bad, and so we must do away with it. But there is another face of power — the one to be found in successful managers."

McClelland says, too, that too much participation can be harmful to an organization. He reports the experience of his own firm. "We founded this firm twelve years ago under very democratic management. Even the secretaries sat in on the board meetings. We had endless staff meetings which drove me up the wall. The first thing we did was to lose money and run ourselves into a debt of $800,000." After that they changed to less participative methods and became successful.

By no means does McClelland see eye to eye with his teaching colleagues. Of his Harvard colleague Argyris, he says, "Chris Argyris has this big thing about how awful it is that he studied 200 American companies and found them all to be very authority conscious. He is dead set against that. I said, 'Chris, did it ever occur to you that the reason you didn't get a chance to study democratic organizations is because they didn't stay in business long enough?'"

McClelland also differs from most other psychologists about changing people's motivational patterns. He says, "When I started out in this field years ago, Americans were prejudiced against the idea of changing people's motivations. They had bought the Freudian model, which says that things like motives are laid down in early childhood and that you can't really change people. But, through training, we *can* change people."

"When I first started, one of the main methods for determining what motivated people was to ask people what their motives were and then count answers. I felt then as I still feel that that wasn't a very good method because people obviously didn't know.

"Maslow never got out of this bind. All the leading behavioral scientists of that generation — Rensis Likert and all of them — ended up asking people questions in more or less subtle ways about what their interests were. This is not a very accurate way of finding out what's on people's minds. People aren't used to observing themselves systematically and there is a lot of retrospective falsification. If you interview a successful industrialist, he will probably say that he was motivated by a strong desire to achieve. This may be largely untrue. The most common thing is that people in the Western world say that they were motivated by the profit motive because it is part of their ideology, but they may have not been motivated by that at all in any true psychological sense."

· If it is true that you can't get at people's motivations by asking them questions, then how can you do research on the subject of motivation? Assume that you are a doctoral graduate student and having just read this case, have been told to write a critique of it; what would you say?

Case 19-2   Aftermath of Watergate

At the start of Chapter 18, the text reported that in the summer of 1972, prior to the voting for the president of the United States, certain Republican party supporters violated the law by tapping telephone wires and breaking into the headquarters of the Democratic party at the Watergate Hotel in Washington, D.C. Since the Congress was dominated by Democrats, they instituted an extensive investigation which proved to be embarrassing to Republican President Nixon and which finally culminated in his resignation in 1974.

One sequence of events in this whole affair saw Attorney General Elliot L. Richardson resign. This brought Deputy Attorney General William P. Ruckleshaus to the top at the Attorney General's office. Nixon fired him. This brought Solicitor General Robert N. Bork to the top as Acting Attorney General.

All of this activity came about because President Nixon wanted Special Watergate Prosecutor Archibald Cox, who worked for Richardson, fired. Neither Richardson nor Ruckleshaus would do it but Bork did. Cox was fired on October 20, 1973.

Cox was fired because of his announced intention to defy an order from President Nixon that he cease a court battle to obtain certain electronic tapes of telephone calls and other conversations related to the Watergate case.

In Richardson's letter of resignation, he said, "At the time you appointed me, you gave me the authority to name a special prosecutor if I should consider it appropriate. I said that I would appoint a special prosecutor and give him all the independence, authority and staff support needed to carry out the tasks entrusted to him. While I fully respect the reasons that have led you to conclude that the special prosecutor must be discharged, I trust that you will understand that in the light of your commitment to me, I have no choice but to resign."

Nixon said of Cox, "In his press conference today, Cox made it apparent that he will not comply with the instructions I issued to him through Attorney General Richardson. Clearly, the government of the United States cannot function if employees of the executive branch are free to ignore in this fashion, the instructions of the President."

· Discuss this situation from the point of view of the authority relationships.
· Are such relationships different in government than they are in business?

Endnotes

1. *Systems of Organization,* by David G. Bowers (University of Michigan Press, 1976), p. 61.
2. "Informal Influences in the Formal Organization: Perceived Sources of Power Among Work Unit Peers," by Anthony T. Cobb, *Academy of Management Journal,* March 1980, pp. 155–161.
3. *Management Theory,* by John B. Miner (Macmillan, 1971), p. 58.
4. De Lorean, Op. Cit., Chapters 10, 15. *On a Clear Day You Can See General Motors John Z. De Lorean's Look Inside the Automotive Giant,* by J. Patrick Wright, Wright Enterprises, 1979.
5. A good discussion on this subject is given in *Power and Politics in Organizations,* by Samuel B. Bacharach and Edward J. Lawler, (Jossey-Bass, 1980).
6. "McClelland: An Advocate of Power," *International Management,* July 1975, pp. 27–29.
7. Copley, Op. Cit., Chapter 2 *Frederick W. Taylor,* by Frank P. Copley. Harper & Brothers, 1923.
8. *Administrative Behavior,* 2d ed., by Herbert A. Simon (Macmillan, 1957), Chapter 7.
9. *The Function of the Executive,* by Chester I. Barnard (Harvard University Press, 1938), pp. 165, 166.
10. Abridged by special permission from the July, 1975, issue of *International Management.* Copyright © McGraw-Hill International Publications Company Limited. All rights reserved.

Suggested Supplementary Readings

Gandz, Jeffrey, and Victor V. Murray. "The Experience of Workplace Politics," *Academy of Management Journal,* June 1980, pp. 237–251.

Kotter, John P. "Power, Success, and Organizational Effectiveness." *Organizational Dynamics,* Winter 1978, pp. 26–40.

McClelland, David C. *Power: The Inner Experience.* Wiley, 1975.

Mowday, R. "The Exercise of Influence in Organizations." *Administrative Science Quarterly* 23 (1978): 137–156.

Pfeffer, J. "Power and Resource Allocation in Organizations." In *New Directions in Organizational Behavior,* by B. Staw and G. Salancik, eds. St. Clair, 1977, pp. 235–265.

Objectives of Chapter Twenty

1. To become acquainted with the centralization-decentralization dilemma: what it is, and how it affects the operations of organizations.
2. To survey the factors which bear upon the amount of centralization or decentralization which is most suitable in given cases.
3. To note the underlying tendency toward centralization, its causes, its effects, and what to do about it.
4. To note the underlying counter tendency toward *de*centralization, its causes, its effects, and what to do about it.

Centralization and Decentralization

*It is the policy of General Motors
to have decentralized operations
and centralized controls.*
Alfred Sloan

Centralization and decentralization have to do with where decisions are made and where things are done.

In the United States, the Federal government handles all matters relating to national defense. Individual states have no armies. All matters of coinage and currency are also centralized in the Federal government.

In contrast, each of the individual fifty states handles matters of interest at the state level. Almost everything relating to highways, outside cities, is decentralized to the states but is centralized within the state.

At the next step down, we find that police and fire protection as well as all educational matters below the college level are decentralized to cities.

Business organizations, too, have to deal with centralization and decentralization matters.

In the K mart company, all purchasing for the K mart stores is done centrally. The central office also sets maximum selling prices for all items. Managers of individual stores may, however, set lower prices whenever they think that local conditions merit them.

Product lines are also determined centrally, with individual K mart store managers having no authority to decide whether to sell Polaroid cameras, garden equipment, or other items.

Centralization and decentralization, as concepts, deal with both the making of decisions and with work done. We have, however, already dealt with the decentralization or dispersion of operations, such as road-building or operating grocery supermarkets or branches of banks, in Chapter 9, where we discussed the setting up of departments.

Our interest in this chapter, therefore, is directed to the centralization and decentralization of decision making and of the places where service work for the whole organization is performed. (See Figure 20-1) We are also concerned with the level in the organization where these kinds of work are done. And, although these matters are also important in governmental departments, our discussion will be largely in terms of how this is done in business organizations, because managers of business organizations have considerable freedom to decide matters of centralization and decentralization in their organizations. Managers in governmental organizations have much less freedom to make centralization-decentralization choices.

The Centralization-Decentralization Dilemma

Whether to centralize or decentralize a great deal or very little is not an easy question to answer. Most companies grow from small to large under strong centralized management. But, the larger they become, the less suitable strong central control becomes because central managers cannot keep close to everything. Managers of growing companies need to decentralize a little more all the time to match their growing physical decentralization and product diversification.

The Dilemma

Centralization and decentralization each has advantages and disadvantages; hence, managers face a dilemma. No matter what degree of centralization an administrator chooses, there will be some beneficial and some harmful effects.

If an administrator centralizes, he may get overburdened managers and consequently slow decisions. Centralization may also result in inappropriate decisions being

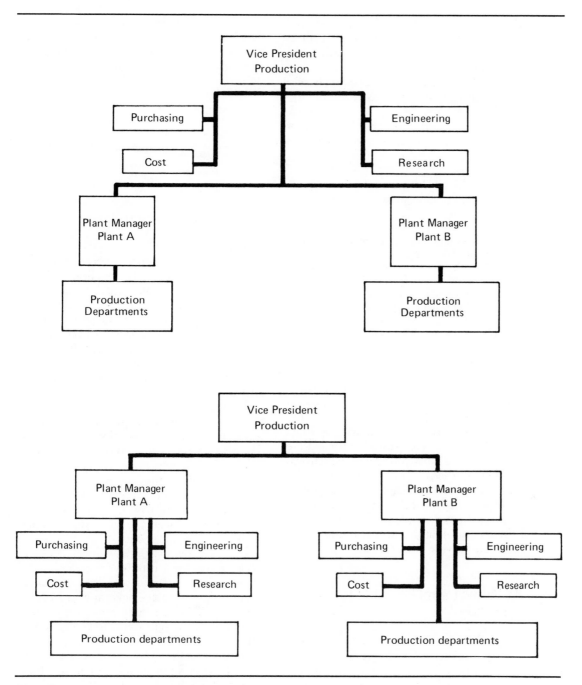

Figure 20-1
Centralized and decentralized staff departments.

Centralization and Decentralization

made by managers who are far removed from the point of action. Furthermore, central decision making stultifies subordinates' ambitions.

If, however, an administrator chooses decentralization, these weaknesses are reduced but other weaknesses are introduced. Higher-level managers lose a degree of control and the organization sometimes suffers from unwise decisions made by poor subordinates.

In the 1970s, quite a few large companies moved to more centralization because of this weakness.

> Westinghouse, for example, centralized its financial controls in the 1970s after it suffered severe losses from too much decentralization. It lost $60 million on low income housing construction, water pollution control, and making elevators in France. In each of these activities, the individual divisional managers overcommitted the company on fixed price contracts during times of rising prices.

It is, of course, possible that Westinghouse might have suffered similar losses if these decisions had been made centrally. But, at least, central decision making would have allowed the company's total exposure to loss to have been considered; which was not done in the actual case where each decentralized divisional manager made his own decision independently. In a great many cases, either extreme, high centralization or high decentralization, seems not to work very well for very long.

At What Level Should Decisions Be Made?

Major decisions, such as one concerning whether to distribute a company's products through wholesalers or through company owned warehouses, clearly need to be made at high levels. But decisions of lesser import, such as deciding whether to spread out employee vacations over the summer or to close down operations for two weeks and let everybody take his vacation at the same time, can be made lower down.

Low-Level Decision Making. In Chapter 17 on Delegation, we said that decisions ought to be made low down in the organization, provided that the lower manager has the requisite knowledge and capability.

This is particularly true when operations are widely dispersed and where managers have wide-scope jobs.

Local managers know local situations better than anyone in a distant home office can know them. Allowing local managers leeway pays dividends in local goodwill. They can buy materials, supplies, and services from nearby sources and can use local contractors for construction. Hiring local managers and salespeople helps too. They know local conditions and the kinds of people they deal with and sell to. In foreign operations, decentralization lets decisions be made by local managers (often local nationals) who know the language and customs of the country.

Despite what has just been said, however, the case for decentralization is not quite so strong as it sounds. Locally made decisions are not guaranteed to be good decisions just because they are made locally. Local managers are not all highly qualified and their judgment, even on local matters where they are on the scene, is not always superior to home office judgment.

A great deal of low-level decision making goes on within every company. In doing their ordinary day-to-day work, low-level people have to make any number of decisions. When a new customer with a poor record of paying bills wants to charge something, the credit manager decides, on his own, whether or not to extend credit. When the supply of a raw material item runs low, the stock clerk orders more without asking anyone. Higher level managers may never know about such decisions.

Apparent and Actual Decentralization. The amount of centralization or decentralization that an administrator wants and what he gets are probably not the same. Most organizations are probably more decentralized than their top executives think they are, in spite of most organizations having their share of authority hoarders.

People in lower echelons just don't obey every rule laid down nor do they come in and ask the superior all the time either. Most instances of subordinates going ahead and doing things their own way and ignoring rules concern minor matters where direct action speeds things up and does little harm. This is unfortunate, however, if it goes so far as to cover up poor practices and poor performance.

Decentralization and Control

When managers decentralize and allow and encourage subordinates to make decisions, they will not know what goes on unless they develop good control reports. So, decentralization should be accompanied by good control reports, especially for subordinates who have not yet proven themselves.

But whether managers try to use close controls or looser controls, they should, with decentralization, outline missions more carefully than if they were more centralized. Carefully outlined delegations of missions operate as controls in advance of performance.

Factors Bearing on Centralization-Decentralization Decisions

The most effective degree of decentralization in decision making in any given case depends upon the mix of several factors, all of which are operating at the same time. Of these, the possibility of large losses is always important and even the most important, but other factors are also important in individual cases.

Economic Factors

Several of the factors which bear upon centralization-decentralization decisions are economic in nature. They have to do with the probable financial consequences of the alternatives.

Possible Loss. Frequently the most important factor to consider in determining whether or not to decentralize decision-making authority is the question of the possible loss or harm to the organization. Admittedly, it is not always possible to estimate the loss possibilities ahead of time, but the difficulty of estimation should not cause managers to overlook them. If large losses could result, then low-level subordinates should not decide.

In a bank, the president could safely allow his subordinate loan officers to make loans to customers to buy automobiles without their asking him. But he should not let one of them, on his own, lend a million dollars to someone to build a large apartment house or a new race track.

Large companies need to watch the possible loss angle just as carefully as small companies. A small company can lose all that it has or can borrow, but no more. But a division of a giant company could conceivably lose all the money the whole company has or can get. If the parent company does not stop it, a money-losing division can go on losing, even losing heavily, for years.

The possible loss from decentralizing is not always related to market place losses but instead it may be a matter of operating economies.

In 1977, International Harvester changed from decentralized to centralized designing for its world-wide operations of its Pay Line (construction equipment) division.

When the designing was decentralized on a geographical basis, the German and Japanese engineering staffs not only designed different models for their own markets, but they also made them from completely unlike parts. This practice kept the company from realizing the gains from large scale production of interchangeable parts which the use of common parts allows. Since the centralization move, common parts have been used wherever possible and costs have been reduced.

We see this same problem (as reported in Chapter 26) in the case of Ford Motor. Ford's English and German subsidiaries also made their automobiles from completely different parts. Ford had them centralize their design work and they now make cars using many common parts, thus reducing costs materially. Now the wheels on English and German made Ford cars are alike and can all be made in the same plant.

Back in Chapter 9 we noted a case of gains from *de*centralizing rather than from centralizing. In the case of Joy (mining equipment maker), the central engineering department was eliminated and the design work was decentralized to the product-line divisions. In this case, the products were too different to use common parts very much and it had been found that the central engineering department was not responsive enough to the differing needs of the different product-line divisions.

Possible Gain. It would seem that it is just as important for all decisions where possible gains could be large to be made centrally. This is not so, however, because large losses suffered can bankrupt companies but large profits missed are not as harmful as that. Companies can survive missing out on large profits. Sears, Roebuck has suffered because of K mart's success, much of which could have been greater sales for Sears if Sears had followed different policies, but Sears is still a profitable company and is certainly far from bankrupt. A company's top executives should want to know about and to

be active in all decisions where large sales gains appear possible, however.

Capital Expenditures. Final decisions over large expenditures, even where small risk is involved, should remain centralized. Only the people in the central office can know how much money is available and how much more is coming in. And only they can know the company's total needs and its investment opportunities so only they can allocate large amounts of money to major projects intelligently.

Organizational Factors

Some of the factors which bear on centralization-decentralization decisions have to do with the organization itself — either with the organization's capabilities or with the effects of the choice on the organization's operations.

Abilities and Work Loads of Superiors. Every organization's best managers ought to be at the top. If the home office people are the organization's best people, their knowledge should not be wasted by letting lower, less capable managers make most of the decisions. This comment should not be taken too literally, however, because centralization holds down bright upcoming managerial prospects. There is also the matter of how busy the home office managers are. If they are overloaded, decentralization helps ease their burdens.

Capabilities of Subordinates. Another factor bearing on the proper amount of decentralization is the capabilities of subordinates. If they are experienced and capable, they can be given a great deal of freedom in decision making. Decentralizing decision-making authority also helps develop young subordinates coming up.

Personalities of Superiors and Subordinates. The ideal amount of decentralization also depends in part on the manager's willingness to let go and to trust subordinates even to allowing them to make an occasional mistake. And, as we have mentioned before, cultural differences may play a part. European managers decentralize less than do their American counterparts.

The amount of decentralization will also depend on the personalities of subordinates. Ambitious and motivated subordinates will act more independently than will less ambitious subordinates. No matter what the top managers' desires are, strong subordinates will act in a more decentralized manner than more submissive subordinates. So, the degree of decentralization which actually operates is a function of the personalities of both superiors and subordinates.

Scope of Decision. Another question is, will the decision affect the whole organization? And, if it will, does it need to be consistent throughout the organization? If the answer is yes to either of these two questions, then decisions should be made centrally. If lower managers are allowed to decide policy matters, the result will be a variety of policies. This may be all right for minor policies, but major policies ought to be consistent throughout the organization and should be decided centrally. In a divisional company, one division cannot be allowed to give large pensions when other divisions can afford only more reasonable pensions.

This is not to say that decisions about everything which is common throughout the whole organization should be centralized. Many things are done in many places in the organization, yet decisions concerning these matters should be decentralized because each one affects only one department. Many personnel decisions are of this kind. Who, for example, in Department A, Smith or Jones, gets promoted? Should a branch store put a half- or a full-page advertisement in the newspaper? Such decisions have to be made in many places in the organization, but since they need individual treatment, they need to remain decentralized.

Information and Knowledge of Effects of Decisions. Decision makers ought to know about the effects of their decisions, both in their own departments and in the rest of the organization. So, when considering whether to allow a subordinate to decide, one question is, does the subordinate have enough information about the consequences of a decision to allow him to make an intelligent decision? If not, and if he himself cannot get such information, the superior should not allow him to decide.

In organic-type structures, decisions are often made by the several individuals concerned who are technical experts. Hierarchical superiors do not have the technical expertise to decide intelligently so they leave it to their experts in the several chains of command to get together and decide.

Coordination. Whenever activities in several chains of responsibility have to be coordinated, they need overall directives. The work itself can be decentralized, but each department's directives need to be coordinated with the directives of other departments and this can better be accomplished if they all get their directives from a central office.

"My Department" Thinking. Decentralization makes subordinate managers become more "my department" conscious and less "organization" conscious. A department head might say, "Look, Joe, I've got my own department to run and I have troubles enough of my own. You'll have to work out your own problems."

It is well for managers to want to run their departments effectively, but cooperation with other departments is also necessary for the good of the whole organization.

Decision Process Factors

Certain other factors relate to the process of making centralization-decentralization decisions. These often have a direct bearing on the proper choice.

Susceptibility to Decentralization. Most sales matters need to be handled close to the customer and to stay decentralized. Customers will not inconvenience themselves to suit a company's desires.

In the mid-1970s, the United California Bank took away from individual branch bank managers the right to approve or disapprove installment sales loan applications. It set up special loan offices in each geographical area to handle these loans.

But this move worked poorly because customers balked at having to go to separate loan offices in inconvenient locations to get loans. And, of course, local branch bank officers didn't like it because they no longer handled the loans.

The number of loans went down. Then the bank went back to the old method of letting individual branch managers approve or disapprove installment loan applications and the loans went back up.[1]

Some functions are more susceptible to decentralization than others. As we have mentioned, selling usually needs to remain decentralized. But the setting of general price policies and the handling of most legal and income tax matters relate to the whole organization and consequently are less susceptible to decentralization.

Accounting controls, too, are not well suited to being decentralized. Major departments should use consistent policies on such matters as depreciation, the way payrolls are handled, and similar things. This allows reports to be made up in such a way that different departments' results can be summed up and compared.

Laws and Outside Factors. Decentralization and centralization practices are sometimes affected by laws. We have noted in earlier chapters that laws such as those covering non-discrimination and affirmative action in employment have to be obeyed. In order to comply with these laws, their provisions have to be translated into policy guidelines for the organizations to follow. Such guidelines need to be set centrally lest some organizational subunits develop inappropriate policies and cause the company to be in violation of the law.

The Occupational Safety and Health Act (OSHA) is so written that it induces more centralization. This runs directly counter to the more decentralized practices which progressive companies have found to be so helpful. OSHA provides, among other things, that managers of organizations found guilty of non-compliance with safety regulations could go to jail. Obviously, a manager faced with such a threat is not going to delegate very much to subordinates whose actions could land him in jail.[2]

On the other hand, some laws and regulations require decentralization, at least of certain record keeping. Many state laws require that companies keep certain records, such as those for sales of products and employee records, divided up, state by state, so that the company can make the reports and pay sales taxes, workmen's compensation taxes, state income taxes, etc., which each state requires.

Distance from the Point of Action. We have already mentioned that physical distance in decentralization can harm the quality of decisions. But distance does not have to be physical distance to become an impediment. It can be hierarchical. As we saw in Chapter 8, John De Lorean reported that when he was head of Chevrolet in General Motors, he found that information from plant managers of a plant only two miles away from his office had to go through five layers of intervening managers to get to him. If a proposal got through all of these levels and De Lorean made a decision, it had to go back down the same hierarchical chain. The process was very time consuming and introduced numerous chances for higher levels not understanding local conditions.

Which Work Should be Decentralized?

Although the discussion in the last few pages does not say exactly which activities to decentralize, it furnishes guidelines. This is all that it can do because the best action depends on the circumstances. It would be reasonable for a top manager to ask, "Should I allow geographical division heads to choose their own product lines?" The proper answer to this question would have to relate to the factors which have been discussed. What might be the possible loss? How necessary is it to have consistent practices on this matter everywhere in the company, and so on.

The answer to the question posed, "Should division heads be allowed to choose their own product lines?" should probably be "yes" for at least some items if a company operates retail stores which sell a wide variety of products in many locations. It would surely be unwise for Macy's department store's home office in New York to tell Macy's San Francisco store what items to carry in stock and what items not to carry.

But the answer might have to be "no" if a company's own nationally advertised products are available. A & P grocery store managers can't cut out A & P's Ann Page line of canned foods and put in Kroger's Avondale line instead. And Sears managers would never be allowed to put in Montgomery Ward's Airline home work tools instead of Sears' Craftsman tools.

This is both a matter of company policy and of economics. Each company has advertised and tried to build up customer demand for its brands of products. And, just as important is that adding another brand line would split the sales volume and lose part of the gain from mass production of the company's own brand of products.

Decisions about the extent of decentralization would need to be made individually in the cases of many other decision making areas such as price setting, purchasing, labor matters, and so on.

Difficulties Caused by Geographical Dispersion

When a company has stores or factories all over the country or, indeed, all over the world, its managers run into a good many problems about where to do things, in the home office or out in the individual units. And they run into communications problems just because some things are a thousand miles apart.

There seems to be no extensive recent research on this subject, almost none, in fact, since the classical study done thirty years ago by George Smith. Smith investigated the operations of a number of geographically dispersed companies. He found that smooth working relationships were sometimes disrupted by problems which were caused by or made worse by geographical dispersion. Smith divided these problems into two groups.

His first group included problems which he said he found often, but which could probably be overcome:

1. Arousing needless fear or false expectations through poor communication.
2. Confused organizational thinking.
3. Talking and acting in contradictory ways.
4. Blaming people when administrative arrangements are at fault.
5. Expecting people to adjust quickly to new status relationships.
6. Expecting people to play conflicting roles.
7. Refusing to alter arrangements to fit people, or to fit new circumstances.
8. Judging people by standards that are unrealistic.

Worse, however, are the following problems, which he said are stubborn, always present, and hard or impossible to solve.

1. Friction between central and local offices.
2. Jockeying for power between headquarters and local offices.
3. Disagreeing over basic organizational arrangements.

4. Belief that the "other level" is not doing its part.
5. Resistance to changed status relationships.
6. Tendency of people at each level to overstep prescribed bounds.
7. Fear of being judged unfairly in the absence of clear standards.
8. Impossibility of finding a common mold into which all local units fit.
9. Resentments that occur when managers are transferred between regions and between regions and headquarters.[3]

Most of Smith's group one problems are problems that all companies (whether they are widely dispersed or not) still seem to have, at least at times. They are probably worse when operations are widely spread out. His group two problems are caused more directly by widespread operations and they too seem to come to the surface at times.

Of all the problems Smith listed, perhaps the most common were (and still are):

1. The feeling on the part of both central office people and people out in the decentralized operations that *they* are doing most of the work and that the other group is not doing its share.
2. Along with this, there is almost always a feeling that the people in the other group are not as capable as they ought to be.

A plant manager in Los Angeles, whose home office was in Pittsburgh, Pennsylvania, said:

"We make the money for the company. The big boss can see that we earn our way because we make the profits. How much, if anything, those men at headquarters produce, is hard to say. A good many of those mahogany-desk boys at headquarters are just parasites."

But his superior in Pittsburgh saw things differently. According to him,

"This company would be a lot better off if our men out in the field would wise up and follow our advice instead of getting their backs up every time anyone suggests anything."

Some friction between headquarters and field personnel should be expected. Capable people both in the home office and in the field want more power and they want bigger jobs. Probably nearly all of them want to expand their areas of responsibility. A company president should not want them to be any other way. Fortunately, these differences rarely become large enough to hurt cooperation seriously.

Decentralization in Operation

R.H. Macy is one of the nation's largest department store chains. One of its subsidiaries is the LaSalle & Koch company with headquarters in Toledo, Ohio. LaSalle has seven satellite stores in northwestern Ohio.

Ann Arbor, Michigan (population 100,000), is only fifty miles away and until recently had no branch stores of any large national department store chain. Clearly there was an opportunity for LaSalle to open up a satellite store there.

We will use this as an example to see how decentralization would work. If Macy were extremely decentralized, the managers of LaSalle would have it wholly in their power to decide that there might be an opportunity in Ann Arbor. They would have the power to make a study, decide to go ahead, buy the land, have the store built and open it up, all without special permission from Macy's central office in New York.

But, if Macy's were extremely centralized, the home office would be responsible for seeing the opportunity and for doing everything clear down to opening up the store and overseeing its getting started and then turning it over to LaSalle to operate as another satellite store.

Actually, LaSalle and Macy did not take advantage of the Ann Arbor opportunity. (But both Minneapolis-based Dayton-Hudson and New York-based Lord & Taylor, did move into Ann Arbor.) A person could suspect that Macy's inaction came from a high degree of centralization (too high a degree?) in the New York office. Such centralization does not, however, extend down into LaSalle's day-to-day operations. LaSalle satellites decide on their newspaper advertisements and merchandise displays.

Tendencies Toward Centralization and Decentralization

There are factors constantly at work which push an organization toward centralization in decision making. At the same time, other factors are operating in the direction of decentralization. Unless these tendencies just happen to offset each other, or unless managers consciously counteract them, organizations will drift one way or the other.

Danny Miller and Peter Friesen concluded, from a study they made on this point, that momentum tends to perpetuate trends toward centralization or decentralization. Obviously, these trends cannot go on forever, lest all become centralized or decentralized. But, because of momentum, they often go too far before their harmful effects are recognized. Then major changes, often of revolutionary proportions, become necessary.[4]

The Drift toward Centralization

Although the factors tending toward decentralization are numerous and ever present, there are other factors tending to push organizations in the other way, toward centralization. These include the following:

Growth From Internal Expansion. Growth from internal expansion tends toward centralization because everything is centralized at the beginning and tends to stay that way even after decentralization might be preferable. Ford Motor and NCR (formerly National Cash Register) are both companies which grew from internal expansion rather than by merger. They had centralization without ever deciding to have it. Growth companies don't have decentralization unless they deliberately decide to decentralize. Ford Motor and NCR are both still more centralized than many large manufacturing companies.

Autocratic Managers. Some people are autocratic by nature and whenever they move up in an organization, they tend to retain decision-making power so the organization ends up more centralized than it was before. People who like to hold onto power can be found almost everywhere up and down in all organizations.

Weak Subordinates and New Subordinates. Sometimes managers claim that they have to make most of the decisions centrally because of the perennial scarcity of good subordinate managers. In the long run, however, this is not a valid reason because, if there is a shortage of good subordinates, it occurs because the superiors themselves have failed to develop their subordinates.

Frequently, newly appointed subordinates are not quite up to handling their new job. Superiors always expect, temporarily, to watch closely over them. They re-centralize some decision-making power until the new subordinate acquires competence. Supposedly, as the subordinates master their jobs, superiors then relax their close watch and let the subordinates handle matters in the usual decentralized manner. There is a temptation, however, not to relax enough and to remain too centralized.

Superiors are not alone in causing operational-type decision making to gravitate upward. A great many subordinate managers are all too ready to ask their boss what they should do. They try to push the job of making difficult decisions upward. If the superior lets them do this, the result will be more centralization.

Trouble and Emergencies. When trouble or emergencies occur, most superiors tend to move in and try to straighten things out. For the moment, they decide more things themselves. This seems reasonable; they *should* devote extra attention to trouble spots. The effect, however, is that they take back, temporarily, some of the decision-making power which they had previously delegated. This is particularly likely to occur in the making of decisions relating to cost control and sales efforts. And, again, temporary re-centralization tends to become permanent.

Centralizing Effects of Outside Factors. Earlier in this chapter, the operation of outside factors and outside organizations such as labor unions and governmental regulating agencies on centralization practices was mentioned. Usually these pressures are toward more centralization. In dealing with such outside agencies, the organization usually has to adopt a specific posture and to have a spokesman who speaks for the whole organization.

The Drift toward Decentralization

A number of factors are always pushing organizations in the decentralization direction.

Growth by Merger. Companies which grow by merger tend to stay decentralized. Years ago, both United States Steel and International Harvester were put together this way. They were combinations of companies. R. H. Macy, too, is made up of merged department stores, as is Federated Department Stores.

Before a merger, officers in each company make all their own decisions, and even though they give up power when their company merges with a larger one, they still keep a great deal of power. None of the changes which shift decision making to central offices is automatic in any short period of time. Top administrators in the main organization have to decide to centralize work and then they have to centralize it. Such moves probably come late and slowly rather than early and quickly, thus perpetuating decentralization.

There are sometimes good reasons for remaining decentralized. If a newly bought or merged company is doing well, there is merit to not upsetting a smooth operation. If its managers are doing a fine job on their own, it is usually a good idea to let them keep on operating as they did before, with few home office restrictions, so the company ends up being decentralized.

Still another reason why decentralization persists is the attitude of the officials of the merged company. Rarely are more than one or two of them promoted to higher offices in the new parent company's home office. (Usually they do not want to sell their homes and move a thousand miles to the new central office.) Most of them stay on as executives in their former company, now a division of the large company. These managers, accustomed to deciding everything on their own, resist the new top home office cutting down their power. They don't want to give up power, so again, so long as things go well, the buying company ends up being decentralized.

Geographical Dispersion. Geographical dispersion has already been mentioned as still another factor which forces at least some decentralization of decision making, even if top managers want centralization and even if they think they have it. Local managers of distant plants or offices are more independent than they would be if they were in the building next door.

Diverse Activities. Another factor tending toward decentralization is the diversity of activities.

> Armour is well known as a meat-packing company. But Armour also makes Dial soap. Since running a meat packing-house and making soap are different, it is natural for Armour to decentralize and to set up, apart from the meat business, a soap division and to give its manager a good bit of autonomy.

Centralization is logical when the product and how to make it and sell it are much the same in different parts of the company. But when the products, technologies, and consumer groups differ, decentralization is usually better.

Weak Top Managers. Still another factor which sometimes contributes to decentralization is weak managers at the top. Probably such situations are rare because weak top managers usually don't last long, but when they exist, they make for decentralization. Lower managers probably make more decisions.

This kind of decentralization should not be condemned unrestrainedly, however. It is a misfortune to have poor top managers, yet if this happens, centralization is probably worse than decentralization. Decentralization may be preferable if middle managers are not held down by the decisions of poor top managers. If the top managers stay out of their way, some of these subordinates will do good jobs for them.

Capable Subordinates. Still another factor in the drift toward decentralization is the ability of the organization's decentralized major department heads. It is reasonable to decentralize more to capable subordinates.

Poor Control. Poor control methods also result in decentralization. There may be no intent, in the home office, to decentralize, but if home office people don't know what is going on, then the lower managers are either managing by drift or they are making their own decisions. The organization is, in fact, decentralized whether its top level managers know it or not and whether they want it to be or not.

Ebbs and Flows of Decentralization

Since there are some factors which tend toward centralization and other factors tending toward decentralization, it is difficult to say which tendency will win. Yet, with the passage of time and with growth in size, the factors working toward centralization seem to outweigh the factors which work toward decentralization. If a company's top managers do nothing consciously toward either centralizing or decentralizing, time and growth seem to pull toward more formal structuring and more centralization of operational-type decision making.

Decentralization needs to be consciously worked at. It may even need an occasional specific decentralization program to offset the tendency for things to centralize. There is a need to back up consciously, perhaps in jerks. General Electric has done this in the past about once in every ten years.[5]

Considering the tugs and pulls of centralizing and decentralizing tendencies, it is not surprising that there is some evidence of an ebb and flow effect. It would be surprising if these tendencies always balanced each other out. Yet underlying it all, the continual growth of the nation's economy makes established companies grow in size. Consequently, most companies probably should finally decentralize and adopt a divisional structure.

Summary

Decentralization has to do with where, in the organization, decisions are made. Since there are so many decisions to be made in large organizations, they can't all be made centrally (although important decisions should be made centrally or else controlled centrally). Consequently, every organization is decentralized to some extent. In general, it is well to have lower unit heads make decisions in their areas of responsibility because this will mean that decisions are being made by the managers who are best informed on the subjects at hand.

Both extreme decentralization and extreme centralization usually work poorly in the long run but in between these extremes, there is a fairly wide zone of indifference. This exists because neither decentralization nor centralization has all of the advantages and none of the disadvantages.

Several underlying conditions are always operating to shift decision making to more or to less decentralization. Probably, in the long run, the tugs and pulls of the various elements in operation here do not wholly offset each other. The conditions tending toward centralization seem ultimately to be stronger so organizations slowly become more centralized. Since this is not the best for large companies, top managers need continuously to try to remain reasonably decentralized.

Review Questions

1. What are the arguments for and against decentralizing decision making? What conditions favor decentralization as against centralization?
2. Usually, an organization's higher-level people are its best people. Why should the organization decentralize and put decision making in the hands of less capable people?
3. If a manager decentralizes and pushes decision making down, what happens to control? Isn't he more or less abdicating and letting his subordinates run the organization? Discuss.
4. Which is more important for managers to consider, the possible gain or the possible loss when allowing decentralized decision making? Why?
5. What organizational factors should be considered in the matter of centralized or decentralized decision making? Discuss.
6. Give examples in which the susceptibility of a factor to decentralization should play a part in whether or not decisions in its area should be decentralized. Give reasons.

7. Is it true that geographical dispersion makes certain problems and heightens certain other problems? What problems? Does it minimize other problems? What problems?

8. If managers do nothing to bring about centralization or decentralization, which way will the pendulum swing? Why? What factors bear upon the direction that decision making may swing?

Questions for Analysis and Discussion

1. How should a person answer a company president who asks, "How can I decentralize yet still know what is going on? How can I decentralize yet control?"

2. An official of Standard Oil of California said, "We know that a head of operations in New Orleans can operate more effectively if he doesn't have to wait for telegrams from San Francisco." Can he? Will he?

3. "It is unwise to attempt to decentralize authority unless and until you have good, strong, centralized control." Is this so? Discuss.

4. "Decentralization means that managers set up units to operate autonomously in such a manner that they operate against standards, objectives, and goals, rather than against supervision." What does this mean? Is it true? How about situations where standards can't be set?

5. At Bethlehem Steel Company, every customer's order clears through the home office. Presumably Bethlehem's managers know all about the advantages of decentralization. What circumstances might indicate that it would be better for orders to clear through the central office?

6. The sales manager described it thus: "In our company, marketing is decentralized. Headquarters does not sell products, but headquarters determines the product lines, approves the hiring of salesmen, conducts sales training programs, sets salary limits, moves salesmen from one region to another, and handles the company's advertising. Headquarters also keeps sales records by products and by salesmen and advises regional sales managers." Curiously, men in regional offices say that marketing is highly centralized. Which is it? Should it be changed? How?

7. During economic recessions, most companies show a tendency to re-centralize authority. It may be expected then, that decentralization will be seen most frequently in periods of prosperity. Does this actually happen? Discuss.

8. The sales manager wants to hire his own salesmen but the personnel department argues that recruitment and hiring are specialized activities and that it should hire the salesmen. Similarly, the sales department does

Centralization and Decentralization

not like the automobiles that the traffic department has been buying for its salesmen, so it wants to buy its own automobiles. Nor is the sales department satisfied with the quality of repair work done out in the field by the service repairmen who are hired and trained by the manufacturing department and then assigned to the sales department. Which, if any, of these activities should be decentralized to the sales department? Why?

9. The text reported that K mart store department managers have price-setting authority — yet a K mart policy is to stock fairly good quality products but to discount everything. Also, certain product specials are advertised in an insert put into area newspapers which commit all K marts in the area to meeting the advertised price. How can K mart's department managers have price-setting authority when price policies and many individual prices are set for them?

10. In a university, where should admissions be administered? Should each college decide for itself which students to admit? Or should there be one central admissions office where admission decisions are made?

11. Should a manufacturing company's purchasing department buy the food used in the company's cafeteria? Why?

Case 20-1   The Hess Company Labor Negotiation Problem

The president of the Hess Company asks a consultant to advise him on how best to handle labor contract negotiations. He has been using an outside law firm which specializes in this work. Members of this law firm actually represent the company in all contract negotiations. They do the talking and settle with the union on contract details. Several Hess men are, of course, present at all negotiating sessions and the lawyers agree to proposals only after frequent recesses and conferences with company officials.

The question the president puts to the consultant is whether it would not be better for the company to give the personnel director of the company the job of conducting negotiations with the union and to relegate the law firm to the background.

· Sometimes an outside agency can do a better job in a specific area than an inside department because they are not themselves part of the problem. Also, outsiders report very high in the organization and automatically have the ear of the organization's top men. Does this apply in this case?
· What are the advantages and disadvantages of delegating to the outside law firm in this case?
· What recommendations should be made?

Organizations in Action: Delegation

Case 20-2 The Leather Products Company's Decentralization Problem

The Leather Products Company had factories in San Francisco, Atlanta, Detroit, and Fort Worth. Its home office was in St. Louis, although it had no factory there. In a decentralization move, the president issued a directive to the effect that each manager was to operate his factory independently, just as he would do if he owned the business. But he would be relieved of accounting and finance responsibilities which would be handled at the home office.

All went well until the manager in San Francisco, contrary to company policy, made a commitment for an entire year's supply of natural leather. Soon afterward he permitted the rewriting of the specifications for the principal products, changing the material from natural leather to synthetic leather, and he canceled the contract for the balance of the year's supply of leather. A contract for the synthetic material was signed with a different supplier. The leather company sued the Leather Products Company for breach of contract.

The company's lawyer, who was a member of its board of directors, brought the matter before the board. The president was reminded that, years before, the board had ruled that the company must not speculate in raw materials. The price of leather was so unstable that a positive rule had been made limiting purchases of leather to not more than two months' supply. Moreover, the directors intended that a standard product would be made at all factories. A change from leather to a synthetic material was a change in the type of product. The president admitted that the San Francisco manager had used poor judgment, but disclaimed any responsibility. He said that the board of directors had concurred in the decentralization policy and that they understood that each manager was to have unrestricted authority to make decisions. If the policy was faulty, as apparently it was, the board had better change it, declared the president.

· Has the San Francisco manager violated his mission delegation?
· How ought the board react to the president's disclaimer of responsibility?
· What should be done now?

Case 20-3 Wyandotte Company Centralizes Purchasing

The Wyandotte Company has twenty plants, each of which has been doing its own purchasing. The president has been convinced that this is a costly arrangement since it precludes the company placing large orders and getting lower prices from buying in quantity.

Accordingly he appointed a new vice president of purchasing. The new man, with the approval of the president, sent out a general directive to the company's twenty purchasing agents at the twenty plants telling them to submit all contracts for over $10,000 to the home office for review at least a week before they were to be signed. Several of the purchasing agents wrote back letters saying okay. But in the next six months, no one sent in any proposed contracts.

- Discuss the action of the president, the vice president in charge of purchasing, and the decentralized purchasing agents.
- As for the present situation, who should do anything and what should he do?

Endnotes

1. As reported in, "Joe, the Giant Waker," by Paul Sturm, *Forbes,* 10 July 1978, p. 31.
2. James L. Hayes has a good discussion on this point in, "Memo for Management," *Management Forum,* January 1977, p. 2.
3. *Managing Geographically Decentralized Companies,* by George A. Smith, Jr. (Harvard University Press, 1958), pp. 106–108.
4. *"Momentum and Revolution in Organizational Adaptation,"* by Danny Miller and Peter Friesen, *Academy of Management Journal,* December 1980, page 592.
5. Reported in,"New Templates for Today's Organizations," by Peter F. Drucker, *Harvard Business Review,* January-February 1974, p. 46.

Suggested Supplementary Readings

Chandler, Alfred D., and Herman Daems, eds., *Managerial Hierarchies,* Harvard University Press, 1980.

Porter, D.O., and E.A. Olsen. "Some Critical Issues in Government Centralization and Decentralization." *Public Administration Review* 36 (1976): 72–84.

Perrow, Charles. "The Bureaucratic Paradox: The Efficient Organization Centralizes in Order to Decentralize." *Organizational Dynamics,* Spring 1977, pp. 2–14.

Moves in the 1970s to more centralization as recounted in several periodicals include:
Sears, Roebuck: *Wall Street Journal,* 9 August 1977, pp. 1ff.
Union Carbide: *Business Week,* 14 July 1973, pp. 88ff.
Bendix: *Forbes,* 15 March 1974, pp. 48ff.

Case for Section V   Hanson Stores

Hanson Stores was an expanding chain of supermarkets operating largely in Ohio and Indiana. In recent years it had been adding some 10 stores a year and currently operated 150 stores. The president felt that the company's highly centralized direction of the stores was probably not the best arrangement and that it would become even less satisfactory as the company grew larger.

Each store had three managers, one in charge of groceries, one in charge of meats, and one in charge of produce items. Each store was under the direct supervision of the district manager who had charge of a dozen or more stores. He had three assistant managers, one each in charge of the three product lines. The assistant managers supervised each store manager of their product lines.

The new proposal was to put each store under one single store manager who would then make many of the decisions formerly made in the district manager's office. It was also proposed that the former assistant managers in the district manager's office be made into staff merchandising advisors (with the title of "merchandise managers") over their lines instead of having direct line supervisory power over lower product specialists.

When the changes were put into effect it was found, in several cases, that the product-line managers in the individual stores did not go ahead and do things, even such things as arranging the display of their products, until the central staff men gave the word. This was not surprising since, in a few cases when they had gone ahead, the staff men (the "merchandise managers") had "raised hell" about how they did things. The merchandise managers would even insist on certain arrangements of items on the shelves and they also specified their lower department's inventory levels.

· What would have been the matter with the old arrangement which would not have been suitable to the company as it grew?
· If the merchandise managers were not doing what they should have been doing — what should they have been doing? Were they doing anything which they should not have been doing?
· If these changes result in some conflict where there was none before, is this something which will pass as the men get used to the new system? If this happened, would it result in more effective operations?
· If the store manager thinks the system is causing difficulties, to whom should he talk?

Actions occur in organizations only after someone has decided that they should occur. Thus the making of decisions is central to managing organizations.

Decisions are made by human beings and consequently reflect the personalities of the decision makers almost as much as they reflect the merits of the matters being decided. Human judgment is required at all stages, in seeing the need for making decisions, in analyzing the merits of alternative actions, and in making the decisions and carrying them out.

The power to make decisions is usually assigned to individual managers according to their positions of responsibility. Decisions are often improved if such managers consult with their subordinates when they make important decisions. The quality of the decisions themselves may be improved as is their acceptability to subordinates. This makes it easier to carry out decisions. These matters are discussed in Chapter 21.

Management science, too, with its operation research techniques, is being used more and more by managers as they make decisions. Whenever quantitative relationships are involved, formulas and mathematical models can often be developed which will tell managers what the results of certain actions will most likely be. Such models are discussed in Chapter 22.

Objectives of Chapter Twenty-One

1. To emphasize and illustrate the importance of managerial decision making to an organization's success.
2. To bring out that decisions need to consider all limiting factors and also be reviewed from time to time to see if they are still appropriate to current conditions.
3. To discuss the decision-making process and see how decisions are arrived at and how they are sometimes not based altogether on the merits of the situation.
4. To study the value of participation by subordinates in decision making from the point of view of the quality and the acceptability of the decisions to the organization's members.

Decision Making

21

Decisions come from power in operation — with a heavy overlay of human vicissitudes.

When Ralph Cordiner was president of General Electric he had a caller, a vice president of one of General Electric's smaller divisions. This man had a problem which he thought needed higher-level thinking. He outlined the problem and the several alternatives to choose from.

"Now, Mr. Cordiner," said the caller, "What should I do?" "Do?" answered Cordiner, "You'd damn well better get on an airplane and go back to your office and decide." The vice president got on an airplane and went home and decided.[1]

An important part of all managerial jobs, high-level, middle-level, and low-level, is to make decisions. Managing, at all levels, means causing actions to take place and one of the first steps in causing actions to take place is making decisions at appropriate levels in the organization.

Nor should high-level managers allow minor decisions to float up to them. It is only natural for a timid subordinate manager to want the boss to decide but, as Cordiner did, high-level managers should require subordinate managers to make their own decisions in their areas of responsibility. If the delegation is not clear on a point, it should be clarified.

Not only does making managers decide for themselves help them to develop their decision-making ability, but it probably also produces better decisions. Superiors do not know as much about local situations as their subordinates know.

At first glance, the decision-making part of the work of managers would seem to be simple. Everybody makes any number of decisions every day, so everyone is used to making decisions. Often we "just decide" without much study and weighing of alternatives. Yet, decision making in organizations usually is not really simple. (See Figure 21-1) It can be simple when a manager makes deci-

sions in his area of expertise, where the problem is familiar and the manager has been through similar problems before. He probably knows intuitively what to decide.

Decision making is also simple in "programmed" situations. If the payroll is due out on the fifteenth of the month, there is no problem in making decisions about when to start calculating employee earnings and deductions nor about how to do it. These programmed decisions carry over from the past.

But in non-repetitive or first-time situations there is much more to good decision making. Managerial decision making for unstructured and uncertain matters ought to be a blend of investigating, consulting, discussing, thinking and deciding. This should happen when the problem is new in some way so the manager's normal decision making methods don't cover the situation. Here, decision making is a creative, innovative activity. It involves a good bit of what Herbert Simon once called, "mental stirring about, deliberation, discussion, and often vacillation" as is suggested in Figure 21-2.

An important decision is only the last event in a process which requires a succession of thoughtful consideration of activities and numerous lesser decisions along the way as well as consideration at every point of how the decision will be carried out.

The Decision-Making Environment

Decision making is carried out in an organizational environment in which managers have to consider both the nature of the organization and the effects of the decision on the organization. Usually the possible organizational responses to decisions will be constraints to the higher level managers' freedom to make decisions. We will consider these matters in this section.

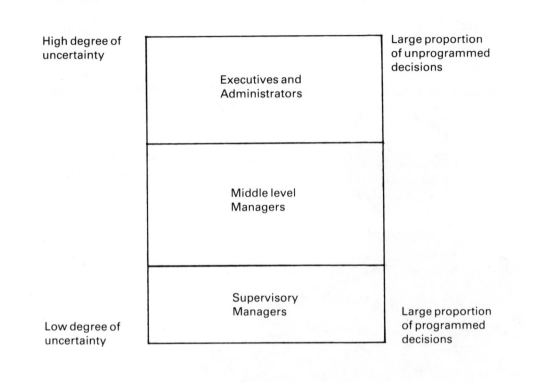

Figure 21-1
Uncertainty, programmed decisions, and organizational levels.

Limiting Factors

Although deciding implies freedom to choose from among alternatives, managers are almost always limited by certain constraints. Every company's established place in the economy places limits on the decisions its managers can make.

American Motors Corporation does not make and sell road grading equipment. If its managers decided to go into this business, they would find the way hard indeed because AMC is totally unequipped to make and sell such products and it would have very little consumer acceptance of its new products.

Nor can managers send employees out to get jobs in competitors' plants in order to steal their secrets or to sabotage their machines or products. The culture, ethics, and laws prohibit this.

Probably many decisions are as much to satisfy a collection of limiting factors as they are to reach goals.

A complete list of things that limit a manager's realm of choices in decision making would be too lengthy to consider here. Many of them have to do with the organization's being capable of doing only certain things. Other limitations are caused by union rules, government regulations, and

Figure 21-2
Despite uncertainty even after studies and analyses, decisions finally have to be made based on expectations about future conditions and the results which the actions taken produce. The best choice is by no means always clear.

other environmental factors. Still other limitations stem from the abilities of the managers themselves, and we will consider those here.

New Jobs and New Horizons

Middle-level managers can usually make good decisions in the areas of their competences. But when they move up the ladder, they come up against questions which are larger and more complex and where their past knowledge does not give them enough background on which to base decisions. Higher jobs are usually not just "more of the same," but are different *kinds* of jobs, requiring different competences and different decision-making skills.

When a salesman becomes a sales manager or an engineer becomes a chief engineer, he does not become just a bigger salesman responsible for more sales or a bigger engineer responsible for more complicated designs. The work itself is different.

And when these same people move up still another step and a sales manager or a chief engineer becomes the executive vice president of a business, again there is a change in the *nature of the job*; neither one becomes just a bigger *functional* manager.

On the contrary, such a manager finds that he has moved up into a profit-and-loss, risk-taking, decision-making area. He no longer makes decisions based on his own thorough technical and functional competence. More and more, he accomplishes whatever he accomplishes through other people. He doesn't do end-result work himself. He also finds that results are influenced by factors, such as economic conditions and the actions of competitors, which he neither makes or controls. And, he finds that he is supposed to produce results in spite of these limitations. When he makes decisions, he has to remember more things than he used to.

Value Judgments and Perceptions in Decision Making

Managerial decisions are by no means wholly dependent on the relative merits of the alternatives. Everyone has his own set of personal values and objectives and his own scale of what he thinks is important. Probably subconsciously, every manager regards certain goals as being more desirable than certain other goals.

Furthermore, most people, managers included, cannot really identify all of the factors which actually play a part in their decisions. We all make many decisions without consciously thinking much about the factors which influence them. Many decisions made by almost everyone are as much intuitive or emotional as they are rational and it is the same with managers. Their decisions incorporate their value systems, without their having given much thought to the matter.

Ann Brown tells this story:

The recent MBA graduate spent many long hours proving that television advertising was not producing the desired results for the company's products and that the money would be better spent by increasing the sales force.

The research was flawless, the logic was impeccable and the conclusion was textbook perfect. *But* the Chairman of the Board of Directors enjoyed seeing television commercials about his products and reveled in the plaudits he received because of the creativity displayed in the 60-second TV commercials. So the television advertising continued and the sales force was not enlarged.[2]

The company's decision to continue the TV advertising was based on the board chairman's value system which put receiving favorable comments from his friends above economic benefit to the organization. The MBA graduate learned that decisions are not always based on logical reasoning.

There is a good bit of truth to Leon Festinger's "cognitive dissonance" idea (deciding to do what you want to do instead of what, logically, you really ought to do), which we will discuss later in this chapter. Cognitive dissonance operates in the making of business decisions as well as in the area of personal decisions.

Decision makers are also probably always biased by their interest in their own survival. Whenever a decision will affect a decision maker's personal well-being in any way, his view of how he will be affected becomes a biasing consideration bearing upon his decision. It may even become the main consideration and push all other factors into secondary roles. There seems to be no way to prevent this sort of thing from happening. It plays a part in a great many decisions and reduces the part that the fundamental merits of alternative decisions get to play.

Cause and Effect Premises in Decision Making

Aside from cognitive dissonance biases and self protection biases, a manager, when he makes a decision, probably tries to make the choice which he thinks will work out the best in the future. But, in order to make the best choice, he has to decide, first, what conditions he thinks will exist in the future. These (his anticipations) are his premises or assumptions about the future.

Premises, as they relate to long-range planning, were discussed in Chapter 7. But premises, particularly cause and effect premises, are also important in decision making. These are also "controllable premises" in that the manager has it in his power to take actions intended to bring about the desired situation in the future. Macy could have put a store in Ann Arbor, in which case, a premise made earlier that there would be such a store would have become a valid premise.

The higher one goes in an organization, the more he needs to consider implicit cause and effect premises as against fact premises because higher level managers need to be concerned with results which will come about in the future from causes which operate today. Managerial decisions are usually concerned with the need to take certain actions today which the managers hope will produce certain results tomorrow.

The important point here is that causes do not always produce the hoped-for effect. Many "controllable" premises prove to be not entirely controllable. More advertising and hiring more salespeople may *not* produce more sales or profits. Spending money for research may *not* produce any new products. High-level managers have to make many decisions in which cause and effect expectations often do not work out. These are "predictive" judgments.

Decisions and Risk-Taking Propensities

One important aspect of individual differences in decision making is risk-taking propensities.[3] Some people prefer a small sure thing rather than even a high probability, though not certainty, that there will be a large payoff. Most young people probably make different decisions from older people. Engineers and accountants probably differ as do other groups.

Cultural differences also play a part in risk taking in decision making. Research has shown that European managers are less likely to take risks than American managers. And managers in India are reported to be even more averse to taking risks.[4]

Since risk-taking propensities differ, when different managers are faced with exactly the same situation and the same probable payoffs, some of them will choose one alternative and some will choose a different alternative. Consequently, business decisions reflect the risk-taking propensities of managers as individuals as much as they reflect the relative merits of alternative actions.

Organizational Climate and Risk-Taking Propensities. Another quite different aspect of risk-taking propensities is the organizational climate.

No matter what a person's personal risk-taking propensity might be, he will be influenced by the organizational climate as he or she makes decisions. If the atmosphere is one of openness and confidence by superiors in their subordinates, the subordinates will feel more free to make decisions involving some risk. If, on the other hand, the organizational climate is more restrictive, or perhaps punitive, even venturesome subordinates will be more conservative in their decision making. The risk taking propensities of individuals will be modified by the organizational climate.

Rigidity and Flexibility of Decisions

Decisions are made at the expense of flexibility. Before an advertising manager places an advertisement, he can choose from among several alternatives. But, after he has placed his advertisement in *Fortune*, he cannot spend the same money on a television program.

Costs of Changing. If decisions will result in actions which, once started, will be costly to change, then a manager ought to be careful and not decide too quickly. It helps, too, if he can try out the decision on a small scale before making a big commitment.

Creeping Commitments. Surely no manager ever "decides" to lose a great deal of money on any program. Yet large sums are sometimes lost, witness General Electric's half billion dollar loss on computers (see the next section). When they first went into computers, GE's officials knew that many

millions of dollars would have to be spent before there would be any payoff. They were prepared to face several years of loss, but they did not expect such large losses nor such continued losses as actually occurred.

General Electric's big loss is an illustration of the possible unfortunate effects of creeping commitments. Often a manager's first decision is to commit and risk a certain amount of money to develop a product and to develop a paying market for it. In due time, this money is spent but either the product still does not work very well or sales are disappointingly low. Yet, success appears nearer and more probable if only a little more time and money are spent. So, the managers spend more money, after which success appears to be nearer, but it is still not yet achieved. This calls for another reappraisal. Success now seems so close that once again good money is sent after bad but this money disappears too.

Americans are all too familiar with how creeping commitments sometimes work out. A great many Americans, possibly most of them, seemed to favor the original military commitment in Viet Nam in the early 1960s. Later, as further commitments grew, there was more feeling against this activity. And surely there would have been very strong opposition originally if the magnitude of the ultimate costs in men and money had been appreciated in the beginning.

Unfortunately, pride often makes this problem of being locked into creeping commitments worse than it needs to be. It hurts a manager's pride to have to admit failure and to admit that substantial losses have occurred. The failure's becoming a public admission of failure only makes it worse. The French and English supersonic Concorde airplane was an obvious financial failure when it was still in the design stage. It could have been cut off in the early 1970s with a loss of $4 billion. But national pride caused its production and operation to be carried on. By 1980, its losses had amounted to $6 billion.

Risks From Decisions Made

The axiom says that *effective managers act;* that *they decide to act and then they do act.* They do not behave like caretakers who relax and let things go so long as all seems to go well without their doing anything. Nor do effective managers just adapt themselves to conditions. On the contrary, they recognize when decisions should be made. Then they make the needed decisions and take actions intended to create, innovate, or to change conditions, or to change their organizations.

Taking action is not, however, without its risks; losses sometimes occur. In fact, the last decade saw an unusual number of huge loss write-offs by companies which had taken actions which worked out poorly. A few of the big losses are listed below. [5]

Unfortunately, in order to continue to be successful, a company must take some risks. Its managers need to try to see what customers want or might want even though they are not actually demanding them. Years ago, General Foods had to *create* markets for frozen vegetables and instant coffee. First, it had to spend money developing the products and then it had to spend more money advertising and setting up an appropriate sales organization. Until it did these things, there was no "demand" for these products. The market place often rewards companies which produce innovations and punishes companies which do not innovate even when there is no evident demand for the innovations.

Undecided Decisions

The Wilson Company, a meat packer, also made tennis balls until the 1970s when it sold its athletic equipment business. Armour, another meat packer, never made tennis balls. Yet Armour's not making tennis balls was probably not a consciously made decision.

Possibly almost the whole universe of the things which a company does not do is made up of things which its managers never thought about doing. They are not in their "field of vision," and are not related to the organization's operating objectives. These, together with the much smaller universe of activities which they considered doing and turned down, make up the whole universe of what the company does not do.

The great limitless outside area beyond an organization's characteristic and established activities is rich in possibilities. It is the domain of most other companies and is by no means barren. Managers should, at times, consider possibilities in these other areas. Decisions not to engage in activities should, where reasonably possible, be consciously made decisions and not undecided or *de facto* negative decisions made by default.

Undecided decisions are also tremendously important in another way which is

Company	Loss	Activity
General Electric	$500 million	Computers, competing with IBM
RCA	$500 million	Computers, competing with IBM
Anaconda	$350 million	Chile copper mines seized
U.S. Steel	$300 million	Competing with imported steel
W. T. Grant (went bankrupt)	$175 million	Emulating K mart
United Technology	$140 million	Making jet airplane engines
Uniroyal	$120 million	Tires, competing with Goodyear
Occidental Petroleum	$110 million	Chartering oil tankers

not often thought about. Whenever a new company grows quickly to large size, its growth is evidence of a failure on the part of the companies which were there first. The established companies did not take advantage of an opportunity, so the newcomer did.

Xerox's phenomenal growth (to six billion dollars in sales in ten years) should have been growth for A.B. Dick (mimeograph) or Addressograph-Multigraph (multilith) or 3M (Thermofax). All of these companies were well established in the office paper-copying field before Xerox came along.

Still another aspect of undecided decisions has to do with timid or lethargic managers. Some decisions are not really urgent yet they should be made and they become more urgent as time passes. This sometimes happens when higher-level managers don't face up to getting rid of poor performing subordinate managers.

One president tells this story:

"Our sales had been declining relative to the rest of the industry. I knew for a long time that the core of the problem was the lack of leadership in our sales department. It was the hardest decision of my whole life, but I finally fired my sales manager, who was also my close personal friend. This act revitalized the whole organization."

A second story was without an end at the time of telling:

"Our maintenance methods are completely outdated. My production head has not been able to effect operating savings to offset increasing wage and salary benefits, and our profit margins have dropped steadily. I can't convert his thinking and have failed to fire him because of his age."

In both of these cases, the failure to decide and the failure to act, or to act soon rather than late, resulted in harm to the organization. To keep from hurting the

feelings of one individual, these two presidents held back their whole organizations' accomplishments.

The Decision-Making Process

Major decisions should be the last steps in a process which starts with problem recognition. Problem recognition may come from unusual events or from managers asking questions. After problems are recognized, they need to be defined and the alternative courses of action to be investigated can be decided.

Decision Making and Problem Solving

Decision making and problem solving are closely related but not all decisions relate to problems, at least not to situations which already have been regarded as problems. The word "problem" carries a connotation of trouble. Something is not working right and needs attention.

Not all decisions concern problems of this nature. Managers sometimes have to make decisions when all is well and there is really no problem. They might have to choose between buying a Ford or a Chevrolet delivery truck, or K mart might have to decide whether to put a new store in Chattanooga or in Indianapolis. Probably deciding neither of these matters would actually be aimed at correcting a troublesome problem. Figure 21-3 shows several choices faced by one company.

Sometimes, too, managers have to choose between two or more alternatives when they can hardly tell which is best, yet, where one alternative may prove to be better than the others.

The oil companies which decided to drill for oil in Northern Alaska in 1968 made

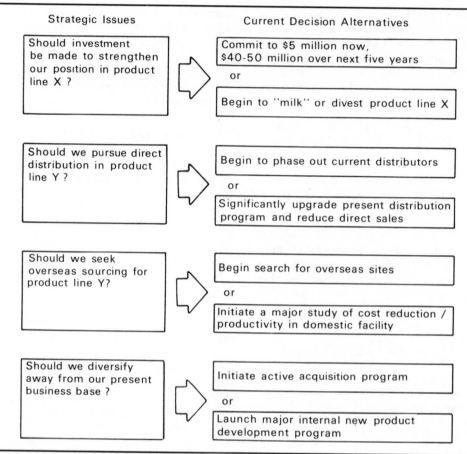

Strategic Issues | Current Decision Alternatives

Strategic Issues	Current Decision Alternatives
Should investment be made to strengthen our position in product line X ?	Commit to $5 million now, $40-50 million over next five years or Begin to "milk" or divest product line X
Should we pursue direct distribution in product line Y ?	Begin to phase out current distributors or Significantly upgrade present distribution program and reduce direct sales
Should we seek overseas sourcing for product line Y?	Begin search for overseas sites or Initiate a major study of cost reduction / productivity in domestic facility
Should we diversify away from our present business base ?	Initiate active acquisition program or Launch major internal new product development program

Figure 21-3
Relationships between strategic issues and decisions. This is from: "Can Strategic Planning Pay Off?" by Louis V. Gerstner, Jr., *Business Horizons*, December, 1972, page 10.

wise decisions because they discovered large supplies of oil. These companies have benefited substantially from these decisions. But when the managers made their decisions to drill, with the evidence then available, it appeared to be so risky and so costly that, at that time, only two oil companies (Atlantic Richfield and Humble Oil) decided to go ahead.

Problem Prevention. Sometimes there is no problem for the present but one could arise. Most companies carry on product-development research because their managers know that most of their present products will eventually phase out. There is no problem today but they are trying to avoid problems in the future by having new products coming along.

Decisions concerning problem prevention need to be made just as do decisions aimed at solving problems. Unfortunately these are sometimes neglected because all is well today. The possibility of problems arising will be better appreciated if managers make a habit of asking questions, probing questions, which give clues to tomorrow's problems.

Organizations in Action: Decision Making

Opportunities and Decisions. Questions may also reveal opportunities instead of problems. Decisions then have to be made about objectives and strategies.

People all over the world have become more affluent year by year and now take more vacations and more expensive vacations. But until recent years, hotels in many parts of the world were poor or non-existent so not very many vacationers went there. Consequently, and to encourage travel to remote places, both Pan American and TWA airlines made decisions to build or buy good hotels in such out-of-the-way places as Samoa and Tahiti.

Opportunities are often not "problems" since no one has to do anything about them. In fact, they may not even be recognized; most opportunities do not force themselves on anyone. Pan Am and TWA did not have to do anything about the growing affluence of people.

All managers at all levels face opportunities, many of which can be seen only by middle-level people. Possibly, for example, a soap company could sell more of a special detergent to hotels in, say, Southern Europe, if the attempt were made. The opportunity to do this might be visible to the manager of Southern European sales but not to the company president in New York. In a factory only lower-middle managers can know that a machine is needing costly repairs too often and should be replaced. To operate economically, managers at all levels and not just those at the top need to see and act on opportunities.

Problem Recognition

The president of the Home Service Company sees, in his reports, that sales are down in the kitchen appliance department but not in other departments. He also notes that one department has an absentee rate of 8 percent whereas other departments have 6 percent rates. And he sees that the com-

pany sells 5 percent of its total sales in one territory and 15 percent in another territory.

These are all reports of *facts* and there may be *problems* associated with any or all of them. Any or all of these situations may be unsatisfactory, so much so as to need remedial actions, although this is not certain.

A situation becomes a "problem" only when someone decides that it ought to be changed or that something should be done about it.

In the case of the Home Service Company, the president should certainly ask some questions about why these differences exist. After getting answers, he would be very likely to think that he has one, two, or even three problems here.

It is the same with a great many matters which need to be decided. There is, first, a fact or situation. The fact or situation may come to the attention of a manager through the organization's information flow system. Or it may come to him solely because he asks probing questions trying to get deeper insights into how things are now going and how they will soon be going. The manager then has to decide that something should be done about it.

People, in this case managers, therefore, make "problems" in the sense that they decide that something should be done about a situation; they "recognize that there is a problem." This is the start of decision making so far as problem solving is concerned.

Defining Problems and Unearthing Reasons Why

Once a problem has been recognized, managers need next to try to define and clarify it. They need to ask, "What are the main issues, or the one main single issue? What are the root causes? They need to search for the key obstacles. The small foreign car "problem" will illustrate this point.

Small imported cars have been a problem for American car manufacturers since the late 1960s. By the late 1970s, more than 2 million small imports were coming in every year (out of a total American passenger car sales of some 10 million cars a year).

Why do Americans buy these cars? The answer has never been clear. Some people apparently believe that the imports are better cars and/or they are lower priced. Or it might be their economy of operation or the extra miles per gallon of gasoline. Or it might be that they are easier to park.

It is not always easy to see what fundamental things are causing trouble and which need correcting, just as it is not always easy to see opportunities. Yet managers have to try to find out what the core problems are and to see opportunities.

Interrelationships Between Problems. Rarely does a problem stand alone, rather it is intermixed with many other problems. There have been times in recent years when the electric power companies in the eastern part of the United States could hardly produce enough electricity to meet their peak demands. Yet, expansion of their electricity-generating capacity through building more power plants has been seriously hampered by the reactions of environmentalists to the air and water pollution caused by electricity-generating plants, to despoiling the scenery by building new power plants, and to the question of the safety of nuclear power-generating plants, to say nothing of the high interest rates on borrowed money. In many cases a problem is not one but many.

Selecting Alternatives to Investigate

Decision making implies freedom to choose from among two or more alternative courses of action. This implies that the managers making the decisions are aware of the alternatives and of the important factors which they need to consider. Alternatives are, however, often not self evident. Managers have to think them up. If they do not do this, they may overlook some of the better alternatives.

Gathering Information

After identifying and formulating a problem and deciding the alternatives to be investigated, the next step is to gather information relating to these alternative courses of action. Gathering information requires a new set of decisions.

Thus, part of any problem is deciding what information to try to get since this is not always evident. It is like a person who has to decide between renting and buying a house. It is not clear just what information will enable him to make a better decision.

Availability of Data. Another part of the problem is to decide how to get the information and the data wanted. Unearthing information may be expensive or even impossible. When managers investigate problems, they need to include, early in their analysis, how much time and money they are willing to spend to get the information and data which they think they need.

Incomplete Information. Almost always, managers end up having to decide without complete information. Unfortunately, too, a manager getting more information may find that this only makes it harder to decide because some of the evidence will be conflicting. The data needed for high-level decisions are often conflicting and are *less* conclusive than are the data needed for low-level decisions. Tradeoffs are more difficult to assess.

Nor are "facts" always what they seem. When researchers ask people questions and tabulate answers, they seem to have collected facts. They ask people such questions as, "Would you buy a second color television set if the price were only $150?" And they get answers, but such answers are not wholly reliable. Often, given an actual choice, people don't do what they said they would do.

"Facts" are also sometimes biased. A government agency set up to help the poor has one job to do if poor people are defined as those who have less than $4,000 a year but it has a different job to do if poverty is said to exist up to $8,500 (which was the government's figure for the poverty level for a family of four in 1981). Hospital care needs "facts" have also been biased so frequently that government planners have been misled and have provided too many or too few hospital facilities.[6]

Time may also be important. Managers have to decide some matters with whatever information they have or can get quickly. They may have to decide with only incomplete information because it takes too long or costs too much to get complete information.

Congealing Decisions and Getting Ready to Carry Them Out

Major decisions are seldom made all at one time. Instead, most such problems evolve toward a final decision. Often the investigations, as they progress, build up a stronger and stronger case for a specific action. Managers have subordinates look into problems and study possible solutions and make recommendations. They talk over the alternatives and the recommendations with their subordinates and finally they decide. The decision incubates as they digest pertinent information.

Cyert and March, in their classic research done years ago on how managers actually go about making decisions, found that managers try to reduce complex problems

into a number of small problems, each of which is more manageable. Some of these smaller problems then turn out to be similar to other problems faced before, so the decision-maker is able to use the same analytical process since it is familiar to him.[7]

Cyert and March also suggested that reducing complex problems to simpler elements often allows managers to make sequential decisions, thus freeing them from deciding everything all at once. Deciding one thing at a time turns a big problem into a number of little problems and reduces uncertainty. It also allows managers to try to solve the most pressing problems first. When this technique can be applied, the quality of the overall decisions is usually improved.

Reliance on Experts. Many decisions can be made intelligently only if they are based on the expert knowledge of staff specialists. A matter may require analysis and study from the point of view of scientists, engineers, economists, lawyers, accountants and others. When this is so, the decisions may, in fact, be virtually made by these subordinate specialists through recommendations which are well supported by investigation and analysis.

Because managers have to rely so heavily on the advice of specialists there is a danger that they may fall into the habit of just following, uncritically, their specialists' recommendations. When this happens, it amounts to splitting off technical decision making from the manager's job. Managers should try not to let this go too far because the specialists do not know the overall picture. Their recommendations are sometimes not the best when all things are considered and unfortunately, too, specialists are sometimes mistaken. This happened at International Harvester in one instance:

When Brooks McCormick became president of International Harvester several years ago he was told by his engineers that Harvester's tractors were better than those of competitor John Deere. But farmers didn't think so. Deere's sales went up and Harvester's sales went down.

Because McCormick relied on the assurances of his engineers he did not order the tractors to be redesigned, yet later events showed that his experts had been wrong. Redesigns were then ordered but Harvester has not yet made up the lost ground.

There seems to be no good way for a manager to escape the dilemma of having to make final decisions in areas beyond his own expertise. Probably he should try to unearth weak points in specialists' recommendations by going over their reports with them and asking questions about the possibilities of unexpected contingencies.

Authority to Decide versus the Ability to Decide. We have just said that managers need to hear and consider the views of experts, yet not quite let the experts decide. At the same time, managers should try to avoid the other extreme of just deciding because they have the authority to decide.

In World War II, Adolph Hitler made numerous military decisions against the advice of his generals which proved to be catastrophic blunders. Wrong decisions both in the invasion of Russia and in the defense of Northern France against the Allied invasion contributed to Germany's loss of the war. Hitler had the authority to decide but not the capability for making good military decisions. Nonetheless he decided.

Cognitive Dissonance and Perceptual Distortion. "Cognitive dissonance" is a term originally popularized by Leon Festinger.[8] Festinger regarded dissonance as the uncomfortable feeling which people have when most of the logic favors one course of action which they don't want to follow. So they are inconsistent. They act logically *except* where this conflicts with what they want to do. Where the illogical things conflict with the logical actions, they choose the illogical action anyway. Ciga-

rette smokers keep on smoking in spite of well-founded health danger warnings.

People who do this are, nonetheless, somewhat uncomfortable because they know that there are arguments against what they have chosen to do. They rationalize their choice by denying the facts or reweighting the evidence in their minds ("Smoking helps keep my weight down and that is important") so that it seems to support what they want to do. They create a distorted picture of the facts so that the picture supports their position. We are all facile at thinking up reasons for doing what we want to do.

Computers in Decision Making

Computers are important in managerial decision making in their role of supplying information and data on which managers base their decisions. And, because of their incredible speed in making calculations they have made it practicable to use the whole array of operations research techniques now available to help managers make decisions.

The use of computers goes even farther. Computers are beginning to assume the role of being decision-makers themselves. They have taken over the making of many low-level decisions of kinds formerly made by clerks, thus reducing the human aspects of decision making.

A computer can be given a list of materials which are carried in stock and the quantities of each which are on hand. Then it can be given a list of instructions to change the quantities in its memory when material is issued or when more material is received. The material identification, the quantities on hand, and the instructions are all retained in the computer's memory. When material is issued the computer subtracts the quantity and puts the new remaining balance into its memory as the quantity now on hand. Materials received are reported in a similar way.

The computer can also be told, for every kind of material, that when the supply gets down to a certain minimum quantity, a new replacement order for more should be originated. Following out this instruction, the computer will, after each issue of materials, ask itself if the minimum quantity has been reached or passed and if so the computer will make a note of it. Then, at the end of every day, it will print out a list of all materials needing reordering. The computer, following its programmed instructions, has "decided," for every kind of material, whether it needs reordering or not.

Computers are used today to make many other similar kinds of low-level decisions. In payroll work, they "decide" the amount of an employee's pay and the amount of his deductions for Federal, state, and social security taxes, hospitalization insurance deductions, etc.

Many factory operations done on semi-automatic processing equipment are also controlled by mini-computers used just for this purpose. In a steel rolling mill, electronic sensors monitor the thickness of the steel strips being rolled. These monitor reports are fed continuously into a mini-computer which makes comparisons to what the measurements should be. If the actual measurements get out of line, the computer "decides" that corrections are needed. Then it "decides" what corrections to make and tells the machine to make them. The machines are programmed electronically to carry out the instructions.

Improving Decision Making

Scholars studying decision making have concluded that while one-person decision making is often not bad, as such, it is usually not the best way. Letting subordinates in on what is going on and letting them make suggestions is thought to improve both the quality and the acceptability of decisions which in turn contributes to organizational effectiveness. This section will consider the part that participation can play in decision making.

Participative Decision Making and Organizational Climate

There is perhaps no other single subject area in organizational theory which has come in for as much attention in the last twenty years as participative decision making and how its use can add to organizational effectiveness.

We have touched on this subject before so only a short summary will be given here. Briefly, the idea is that if subordinates are allowed to participate in organizational decisions, especially as they relate to their own jobs and their own responsibility areas, they will respond by becoming more enthusiastic and more productive.

It is wrong, however, to put all of the emphasis on subordinates participating in *decision making.* As we saw in earlier chapters, the important thing is *participation.* All managers and supervisors at all levels should *show interest and concern in subordinates,* both as people and as fellow organizational members, and in their work as well.

The essential element is not so much that subordinates participate in the making of decisions as it is that they be treated as full participating members of the organization.

Participation and Sincerity. Managers who embrace participation and open communication may find that it backfires unless they are wholly sincere about it. They have to be honestly willing to discuss matters with subordinates and to receive suggestions and to follow them wherever it is reasonably possible. Subordinates quickly become disillusioned when superiors ask for suggestions but rarely follow them. If a suggestion has to be turned down, the person who made it should be told why.

Better Decisions and Greater Acceptance. Major decisions which affect the whole organization should rarely be made until there has been considerable participation and discussion among high-level managers. Such decisions, when made, almost become joint decisions and are better accepted. As we will see in Chapter 26, decision making by consensus, as is done in Japan, appears to help develop a harmonious, cooperative atmosphere which contributes to effective operations.

Participation in Decision Making to be Limited. Participative decision making is a slow and even a costly process since it entails groups meeting together. So, even though it is usually beneficial, participation in decision making should be restricted to people who will be affected by the decision or who might be able to help solve the problem to which the decision relates. Victor Vroom says that, "It is wrong to think that group decision making is always more effective than autocratic decision making."[9] There is really little reason for subordinates to participate in decisions where there is little possibility that their participation will be meaningful to the organization or to themselves.

Effects of Participation on Productivity. One of the conclusions of early social scientists was that satisfied workers were productive workers and that participation in decision making increased their satisfaction and consequently their production.

Later research has shown that by no means always are satisfied workers productive workers, and although participation does increase the satisfaction and morale of many people, this is not universally so. Dudley Bennett even goes so far as to say, "We know now that it is naive to assume that if a worker is satisfied, he must be a productive performer."[10]

Nor does participation appeal to everyone.[11] Some people are comfortable in a highly authoritarian situation which demands little of them. At lower levels in particular, many people don't want to get mixed up in their boss's problems. Some of them would say that the boss is paid to do this work, so let him do it.

Business managers' experience with participation has produced mixed results. Usually the results reported are good but American Airlines once found that its version of participative management worked out poorly.

George Spater, who became president of American Airlines in 1968, was a great believer in management by participation. The result was, "They were committeeing the company nearly to death and no one was making any decisions."[12] After several years of losing money (which resulted in Spater's resignation in 1973), his successors changed to more authoritarian methods and the situation improved immediately. Within one year a loss of $28 million was replaced by a $35 million profit.

Participation should not be allowed to degenerate into indecision and excessive use of committees.

Winners and Losers. Participation in decision making encourages subordinates to make suggestions. But when several people are involved, different suggestions will be made, yet as a rule, only one of these suggestions can be accepted. Because of this it is necessary to reject and not to carry out the other suggestions. This has the unfortunate effect of producing winners and losers. Worse even, there are more losers than winners.

Managers need to be especially tactful about rejected suggestions and to explain why they are not followed. Unless this is done, people whose suggestions have been rejected are unlikely to care much for participation from this point on.

Decision-Making in Government Units

Philip Carroll, a vice president of Shell Oil, worked for the government in Washington for a year on an executive exchange program. After his year he reported that, "There is really no good, established mechanism by which you can make a decision in government.[13]

Charles Percy, one-time president of the Bell & Howell company, makers of moving picture cameras, and later Senator to the United States Congress from Illinois, agrees that the decision-making process operates quite differently in governmental units than it does in business units.[14]

Percy emphasizes the greater need, in governmental decision making, for horizontal participation between the heads of different departments. He noted also that decision making and its implementation is a slower process than in business.

Percy feels that the essential difference is the *absolute need*, in government units, to *win* cooperation from other units and other levels in the same organization. In contrast, the manager of a *business* has much more *power* to cause a program to be carried through or to cause actions to be taken.

So it is that decisions made by the head of a government unit are not his decisions alone. Others have to concur even on such a matter as the selection of assistant secretaries and undersecretaries.[15]

Furthermore, top administrators come and go frequently so the supporting bureaucracy is more powerful than it is in business. If the bureaucracy supports a decision, it has a good chance of being carried out but if the bureaucracy does not support a decision, it can often frustrate higher level decisions. The bureaucracy's power to do this restricts the power of the formal department heads and forces them to use more permissive methods, including participation, rather than dictatorial methods.

Summary

In the process of making decisions, the first and very important step is the initial decision that a problem and the need for a decision exists. Once this recognition occurs a whole set of activities is normally started. Managers try to see what the important factors are and what alternative actions seem to be available.

Often, as the evidence comes in, the most promising alternative more or less sorts itself out and stands out above other possible actions. But in other cases the possible actions are more equal in their advantages and disadvantages. Nonetheless it is usually necessary to make a decision. The difficulty of making decisions does not relieve managers from making them.

There are always a great many possibilities that could be considered but because there are just too many, most possible actions have to be ruled out and not even considered. Managers then devote their study to the alternatives which they have chosen as possibilities.

Decisions are heavily influenced by the value scales of the managers who decide. Some managers aim for one set of goals, whereas other managers would choose differently. Some managers accept risks whereas others avoid them. Some managers make decisions more or less after problems arise. Others try more to prevent problems from arising. Some managers look into opportunities more than do others. And some allow subordinates to participate extensively in the decision-making process whereas others do not.

Review Questions

1. The text says that higher-level managers should not let decisions "float up" to them. But, if the higher-level managers are the most capable people the organization has and if they have better overall views of the total situation, why shouldn't they decide? Discuss.
2. What difference does it make whether a decision is a "programmed" decision or not? What other kinds of decisions are there? When should each kind be used?
3. Isn't it a good general idea to promote the person who has the best record of performing in the lower job? When the sales manager's job opens up, this would mean promoting the best salesperson. Discuss.
4. What is the relevance of the discussion of value judgments to the subject of decision making? Discuss.
5. The text reports that people have different "risk-taking propensities." Of what importance is this observation? What is its relevance to a study of decision-making?
6. What are "creeping commitments"? Is it good (or not good) for managers to make decisions which involve creeping commitments? Why?
7. What is "cognitive dissonance"? What might it have to do with decision making? What, if anything, should a manager do about cognitive dissonance?
8. To what extent should subordinates participate in the making of decisions? Discuss participative decision making.

Questions for Analysis and Discussion

1. At the start of this chapter, an example was given in which a General Electric manager came to the president for help but instead got a curt brush-off. Was this a good way to handle this situation? Discuss.
2. A president said, "I know that my top men's decisions are choices made

only after they have considered several alternatives. For me to impose my will would be presumptuous because I can't know, with little study, better than they which course is best. I'd be foolish to do that. So I only ask pointed questions to see that all alternatives have been investigated. Then I accept their decisions." Isn't this president almost abdicating his job? Revise this statement so that it is more acceptable.

3. How much conflict between organizational members is good in the decision-making process? Does conflict improve or harm the searching for better alternatives, the quality of the analysis, and the likelihood of reaching an acceptable group decision?

4. At what level in Macy's department store should the decision be made on the retail price of a Zenith television set? At what level in General Motors should the price of a Chevrolet be set? Compare these situations from the point of view of decision making.

5. In every problem-solving process there is effort put into searching out information, and then more effort is put into screening. It would seem that a good bit of randomness would get into the process. Is this the way it works? How did you, for example, choose the school you are now attending? How did you choose the subject in which you are majoring?

6. To decide, a person needs adequate information. What information does a person need to have before he decides whether to buy a house or to rent one? Discuss the relevance of information in decision making.

7. It seems so incisive to say that there is no one best answer, yet there is always a tallest, heaviest, etc. Isn't there one best answer after all?

8. If a manager calls a meeting and asks subordinates for their views on problems which he has to decide, what does this do to his prestige? Suppose that he gets conflicting suggestions? Doesn't his calling a meeting heighten the expectations on the part of subordinates of potential influence? Suppose that the subordinates make poor suggestions?

9. When lower managers participate in the decision making of their superiors should they not be held jointly accountable with him for the consequences, something they clearly would not be accountable for had they not participated in their superior's decision making? Discuss.

10. Today is the new plant superintendent's first day. Yesterday he was a general foreman reporting to his predecessor superintendent. Yesterday there were certain decisions which he could not make. Today he can make them. But he is no more capable today than he was yesterday. Discuss.

Case 21-1 Sandage Medical Center's Research

The Sandage Medical Research Center is a nonprofit organization whose funds come from the government, from contributing hospitals and from private donations. It has, for years, devoted its main efforts toward working on diseases and disabilities of the nervous system. Because of a medical break through, almost complete success has been achieved in halting the advancing harmful effects of disease X. In the past, research aimed at alleviating or curing disease X has been Sandage's principal single activity and, in fact, had consumed 60 percent of Sandage's available research funds.

Harold Wilson, Sandage's Administrative Director is now considering the organization's future activities. There are questions of whether not to continue research against disease X since a complete cure has not been developed. If the research on disease X is to be reduced, then there is a question of what direction to take in new areas of research.

Besides these, there are several operating problems to consider. New research areas would require different expertise capabilities on the part of Sandage's staff and would require different and expensive supporting research apparatus and facilities. Furthermore, qualified personnel are becoming very hard to find and there is a good bit of pirating of personnel by companies and schools. Their salaries have also been skyrocketing.

Wilson recognizes that while it is healthy for two or more research organizations to be studying the same diseases, there is at the same time an element of waste, when this is done, from the duplication of efforts by different organizations. Because of this concern over what might be wasteful duplication, Wilson believes that if Sandage does change its course, it should try to pick a subject area in which few other organizations are working.

· What information should Wilson want before he tries to make a decision in this matter about where to allocate Sandage's research efforts?
· Who among Sandage's present staff should participate in this decision? Why?

Case 21-2   Ibex Company's New Marketing Methods

Last year the Ibex Company had sales of $5 million, on which it earned $250,000 of profit. The president, James Brown, decided that the company ought to do better. So he called in the company's fifty salesmen for a two-day strategy-developing session where he outlined his hopes and the actions which he proposed to take.

First, he noted that the company needed more sales and that this would require more aggressive efforts by the salesmen. He recognized, however, that the company needed to do market research (which it had not carried on before). To remedy this lack he reported that he had just hired an experienced market research man from the outside.

Brown also reported to his salesmen that he had devised a new schedule for determining the costs of products sold. Most of these were upward adjustments made to cover certain selling costs not formerly charged to products directly.

Other than this, he did not propose any changes in the salesmen's compensation plan. Under the existing plan, salesmen were regarded as independent salesmen and not as employees. Essentially these men bought the company's products at its prices and sold them to customers at whatever price they could get. Suggested selling prices were 25 percent over the salesmen's purchase prices. Most of the time, the salesmen realized a little less than 25 percent yet this provided them with good income.

Brown also announced a new product line which would be phased in beginning some nine months later. The same commission plan was to apply to this new product line except that the company planned to redivide the sales territories and to hire 5 more salesmen. Because of the broader total product line, each salesman would, according to Brown, have the same sales potential that he had before. (A smaller geographic area, but a wider product line.)

Six months later, Brown found that both sales and profits had gone down. Since part of the profits decline came from the costs of the new market research work, Brown considered prorating this cost to the salesmen since it was being done to help them. The salesmen objected vociferously to this.

The salesmen had also not proven to be very cooperative with the new market research man. He had suggested that he should work up a sales manual to help them. And he asked each salesman to send in to him a write-up of how a new customer was gained, how a sales objection was overcome, and how an old customer was won back. None of the salesmen supplied any such write-ups.

- Discuss the way Brown has handled his problem. How should matters such as this be handled?
- What should be done now?

Endnotes

1. This incident was reported to the author by another GE vice president.
2. "Things You Never Learn in Graduate School," by Ann C. Brown, *Dividend*, Spring 1979, p. 6.
3. *Systems Analysis for Engineers and Managers*, by Richard de Neufville and Joseph H. Stafford (McGraw-Hill, 1974), Chapter 6.
4. *Assessment of Managers: An International Comparison*, by Bernard M. Bass, Philip C. Burger, Robert Doktor, and Gerald J. Barrett, The Free Press, 1979.
5. We are not including losses in the 1979-1981 depression because they were not caused primarily by managerial decisions. In this depression quite a few companies lost over $100 million. General Motors, Ford Motor and Chrysler, together lost over $4 billion.
6. "The Influence of Biased Information in Regulatory Decision Making," by Paul C. Nutt and David Miller, *Proceedings* of the meetings of the Midwest Section of the Academy of Management, 1981, pp. 272–283.

7. Reported in, *A Behavioral Theory of the Firm*, by Richard M. Cyert and James G. March (Prentice-Hall, 1963).
8. *A Theory of Cognitive Dissonance*, by Leon Festinger (Row, Peterson, 1957).
9. "Industrial Social Psychology," in *Handbook of Social Psychology*, by G. Lindsey and E. Aronson, eds. (Addison-Wesley, 1970), p. 239.
10. *Transactional Analysis and the Manager*, by Dudley Bennett (AMACOM, 1976), p. 69.
11. Jay Lorsch says that early behavioral scientists erred in thinking that nearly all employees had strong needs for participation and group membership. "Making Behavioral Science More Useful," by Jay W. Lorsch, *Harvard Business Review*, March-April 1979, p. 172.
12. Reported in *Forbes*, 15 November 1974, p. 39. The actions taken by Spater's successors are reported in Chapter 23.
13. "When Bureaucrats and Executives Swap Jobs," *Business Week*, 12 February 1980, p. 99.
14. Percy's views on decision making in businesses and in governmental units are presented in, "You Simply Cannot Impose Your Will," *Business Week*, 15 May 1973, p. 270.
15. In the United States federal government, a secretary is an important administrator and not a stenographer. Assistant secretaries and undersecretaries are also important managers.

Suggested Supplementary Readings

Hy, Ronald J., and Walter M. Mathews. "Decision Making Practices of Public Service Administrators." *Public Personnel Management*, May/June 1978, pp. 148–154.

Locke, E.A., and S.M. Schweiger. "Participation in Decision Making: One More Look." in *Research in Organizational Behavior*, Vol. 1, by B.M. Staw, ed. JAI Press, 1978, pp. 265–339.

Simon, Herbert A. "Rational Decision Making in Business Organizations." *American Economic Review*, September 1979, pp. 493–513.

Stumpf, Stephen A., Richard D. Freedman, and Dale E. Zand. "Judgmental Decisions: A Study of Interactions among Group Membership, Group Functioning, and the Decision Situation," *Academy of Management Journal*, December 1979, pp. 765–782.

Objectives of Chapter Twenty-Two

1. To acquaint the reader with the several classes of quantitative techniques available to managers to aid them in their decision making.
2. To give examples illustrating the use of trade-off mathematical models in decision making.
3. To introduce the concept of probability and to show how it can be used to help improve decisions.
4. To demonstrate how simulation and linear programming work and how they provide answers for decision makers.

Quantitative Methods in Decision-Making

Numbers standing alone are meaningless but if they can be related to each other in mathematical models, they can serve as guides to managerial decisions.

Managers have always relied a great deal on quantitative data such as sales forecasts, budgets, and planning in their decision-making. But, today's quantitative techniques go beyond just supplying basic data. Operations researchers have learned to construct mathematical "models" (formulas) which can be used to provide answers to many problems. If a problem with its required data is given to them, these models will supply answers (usually the calculations are done on a computer). And, if a manager wants to consider the probable results for several possible future states of the economy ("What if this?" "What if that?"), these models will provide him with whole arrays of answers, one for each scenario. With the help of such operations research techniques (also called "management science") managers can make better decisions.

These techniques, several of which are described in this chapter, are all methods for determining the best choice from among several alternative courses of action. These methods all share two weaknesses, however.

· They help managers to find answers to questions but they do not tell managers what questions to ask.
· They are all based on numbers. When accurate numerical input data are not available, these methods cannot produce valid answers.

Because they need numbers, quantitative methods are poorly suited for dealing with organizational matters where people are concerned since matters of interpersonal relationships and group cultures cannot be validly quantified.

Although this weakness rules out certain areas of decision making, there are other places where such procedures are apropos and where they can help managers make better decisions.

Models to Aid Decision Makers

There are several types or "families" of quantitative techniques which managers can use to help them make the best choices when they have several alternatives to choose from. Of these, we will consider, in this section, trade-off models and cost-benefit analyses, break-even models, inventory control systems, and PERT.

Trade-Off Models and Cost-Benefit Analyses

Many managerial decisions have to do with the economic concept of "trade-offs" or with "cost-benefit analyses." Trade-offs (see Figure 22-1) come into play when two or more elements, which work in opposite directions, need to be balanced off at the point of least cost. Cost-benefit analyses set the value of benefits off against costs and so help managers make decisions.

There are many trade-off situations in managerial decision making. Large inventories mean low losses of sales from running out of stock but high inventory carrying costs. Conversely, low inventories reduce inventory carrying costs but run up the losses from being out of stock. In a retail store, the more sales clerks there are, the better the customers are served, but at a cost of considerable idle clerk time. Fewer clerks mean poorer service and more lost sales but low costs for the clerks. The most economical operating point is somewhere between these extremes. Figure 22-1 shows this graphically.

Break-Even Models

Break-even models constitute another quantitative tool for businessmen to use in

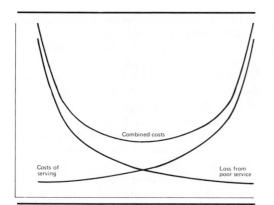
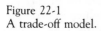

Figure 22-1
A trade-off model.

decision making. As Figure 22-2 shows, break-even models show how much sales volume a company will need to have for it to break even financially. They also show how much profit a company would earn at sales volumes above the break-even point and the losses it would suffer at sales volumes below the break-even point.

Break-even models rest on the assumption that most costs are one of two kinds. Either they are relatively fixed in amount regardless of sales or production volume or else they are costs whose total is closely related to volume. These latter costs are "incremental" in that their total goes up and down with changes in volume. These two kinds of costs are called "fixed" costs and "variable" costs.

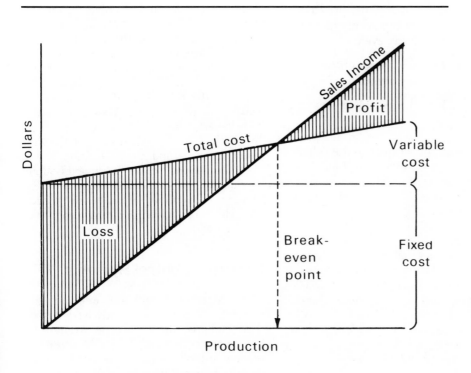

Figure 22-2
Break-even model.

438

In a motel, the costs of heating, depreciation, and real estate taxes are fixed costs. They are independent of the number of rooms rented. But the costs of laundering bed linens and washing towels are variable. More customers increase these costs. In a factory, machinery depreciation is a fixed cost but the costs of material and of labor performed on the product are variable costs.

In order to calculate the break-even point for any given period of time, it is necessary to know the total fixed costs and the variable costs and the selling price per unit. In formula form, the relationships among these are:

$$P \times Q = F + (V \times Q)$$

where P = the price per unit

Q = the quantity needed to be sold in order to break even

F = the fixed costs for the period

V = the variable costs per unit

Since Q, the quantity, is the volume we want, it helps to restate this formula as follows:

$$Q = \frac{F}{P - V}$$

If an item's variable costs are $30 per unit and the fixed costs associated with making this item during one month are $2,000 and its selling price is $50 per unit, then:

$$Q = \frac{\$2,000}{\$50 - \$30} = \frac{\$2,000}{\$20}$$
$$= 100 \text{ units}$$

It will take a volume of 100 units a month for the company to break even on this item.

Contribution Ratios. If an item costs $30 per unit in variable costs and sells for $50, as in our example, the $20 difference contributes toward paying for the fixed costs. Or, if volume is high and all fixed costs have been recovered, the $20 will be left over as profits. Such a product is said to have a "contribution ratio" of 40% ($20 ÷ $50).

Uses of Break-Even Models. Break-even models provide managers with answers to "what if?" questions such as, what would the profit (or loss) be if sales were higher (or lower)? Moreover, contribution ratio comparisons between products call the managers' attention to the products which contribute the most and so justify greater sales attention. Doubling the sales of an item which sells for $50 but which contributes only $10 (a 20% contribution ratio) is not as worthwhile to the company as doubling the sales of items with 40% ratios. Dollar volume sales increases or decreases in the sales of different products have different effects on profits.

There are many possible applications of break-even models. They can be used to compare the relative merits of buying or making component parts. They can be used to help in deciding which of several processing methods to use when each of the different methods under consideration has a volume range (or "domain") where it is more economical than other methods. In the sales area, break-even models can be used to decide whether an advertising campaign would pay for itself.

Inventory Control Systems

Merchandising and even manufacturing companies frequently have half of their total investment tied up in inventories. Governments, schools, hospitals, and most other non-business organizations also have to maintain inventories of thousands of kinds of materials for use in rendering services and for maintenance repair. Controlling such inventories requires the continual making of many decisions in most organizations.

Economic Order Quantities (EOQ). One of the most widely used methods for trading off the costs of carrying inventories against the costs of buying or making new supplies is the "economic order quantity" (EOQ). In a store, every time that a new order for products or materials is made out, there is a cost of doing the paper work. Or, in a factory, there is the cost of the paper work for bought items. For items made inside the company, the machines to make the products have to be made ready ("set up") by having the appropriate tooling attached and properly adjusted. The costs of the paper work and the set-up costs for each order are called "costs of acquisition" and are not related to the quantity ordered. So long as the item will be needed on farther into the future, its ordering quantity should be high enough to hold down the acquisition costs per unit.

At the same time, orders for large quantities will result in larger inventories when the new orders come in. These large inventories will last longer before they are used up so the average inventory size will be increased. The costs of carrying these inventories are called "costs of possession."

The larger the reorder quantities, the less the cost of acquisition *per unit* but the larger the cost of possession *per unit*. The proper size of the lot to order becomes a tradeoff problem.

The quantity to order which produces the lowest combined cost per unit is the low point on the top line in Figure 22-3. This is the point where the acquisition cost per unit and the average carrying cost per unit are equal and is also the point of lowest total cost.

The decision maker can find this point by using the following formula (which is sometimes called the EOQ model):

EOQ, in units =

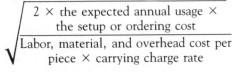

$$\sqrt{\frac{2 \times \text{the expected annual usage} \times \text{the setup or ordering cost}}{\text{Labor, material, and overhead cost per piece} \times \text{carrying charge rate}}}$$

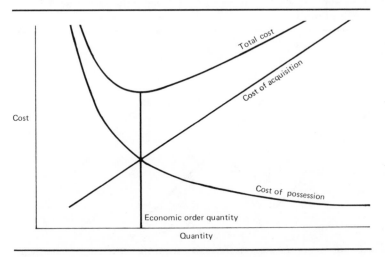

Figure 22-3
The EOQ model. This is a special case of trade-off situation where one factor decreases in a diminishing fashion whereas the other factor increases in arithmetic increments.

440

Working this out for an expected annual usage of 3,000 units used more or less steadily throughout the year and with an ordering cost of $25 per order, a $5 per unit value, and an inventory carrying cost of 25 percent, we get:

$$EOQ = \sqrt{\frac{2 \times 3,000 \times \$25}{\$5 \times 25\%}}$$

$$= \sqrt{\frac{150,000}{1.25}} = 346 \text{ units}$$

The EOQ formula rests on the assumption that when new supplies come in, the inventory will be large but that it will be used up more or less steadily until the next replacement supply comes in, after which the process repeats. The average inventory is assumed to be halfway between the maximum and the minimum levels.

Figure 22-4 is a model of the way inventories of individual items often fluctuate. This model also shows a "safety stock" or "buffer stock," a small amount of reserve stock which is supposed to be still on hand when a new order arrives. This safety stock provides a cushion to protect against running out of the item if more than usual are used during the replenishment time or if the replenishment time turns out to be unusually long.

The "reordering point" indicated in Figure 22-4 is a quantity representing the number of units normally used up during the procurement time plus the safety stock. When the stock level gets down to this point, it triggers a reorder which, in companies using EOQ's, would be for the EOQ quantity.

PERT

Managers have, in the past, frequently found that it helped their planning of complex interrelated activities if they could depict these relationships graphically. Then they could see when certain work should start and when it ought to finish. PERT-type network charts do this. PERT (for *P*erformance *E*valuation *R*eview *T*echnique) also show which work has to follow other work in sequence and which will therefore be delayed if the earlier work is not completed on time.

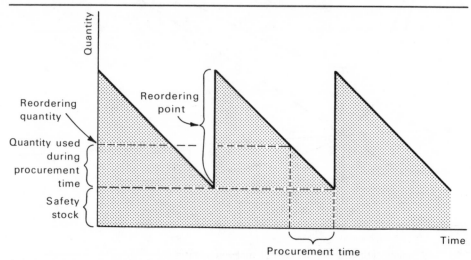

Figure 22-4

Figure 22-5 shows a simple PERT chart. This chart has no horizontal time scale. Instead, the times that it will take to do work are indicated by numbers (of days or weeks) put in along the lines. In Figure 22-5, the connecting lines represent "activities" or parts of the total work. The circles indicate "events," the end of one activity and the start of the next following activity. This makes it easy to see the sequences of events and to see which activities cannot start until earlier work has been completed.

A person can add up the times shown on a PERT chart and find out how long the project will take. When this is done for different pathways (the PERT method is sometimes called the "Critical Path Method" CPM.), it will be found that some chains of activities take longer than others. The one which takes the longest time is called the "critical path" and its time determines the total project completion time. This being so, all shorter paths contain some "slack" time (not every activity will have to start as soon as it possibly could start). And, should the critical path show that the whole project will take too long to meet overall schedules, it can sometimes be shortened by "crash" work and the assignment of more resources to the activities in the critical path (you can paint a house in a day if you put enough painters to work).

PERT is particularly helpful in the planning of large complex non-repetitive projects. It was used, for example, in the 1970s, to plan and control the thousands of activities needed in the construction of the Alaskan pipeline for oil. It has also been used for other kinds of construction such as building stadiums, hydro-electric storage dams across rivers, refitting ships, and installing new computer systems.

Large projects are far too complex to depict graphically in chart form so PERT, as it is used on such projects, is all done on computers. The end-products of the computer work are lists of activities and their start and finish dates which will need to be met in order for the final project completion date to be met. As time passes and as work is done, whether on time or not, reports to the computer allow it to update its records and to print out new lists of the current status of the work.

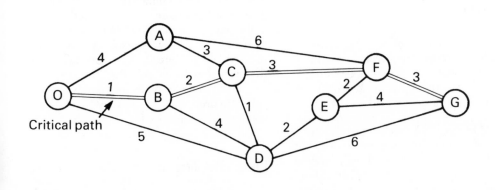

Figure 22-5
A simplified PERT model.

Computers are also usually used to monitor costs. (This is called PERT/Cost.) As activities are completed, the *cost* of getting that far are reported and compared to the planned or budgeted costs. If costs are rising too high, this becomes known right away so that remedial action, if this is possible, can be undertaken right away.

The United States government, for years, required contractors on large contracts to use PERT in their planning and control. They no longer require this very often and PERT is used rarely rather than commonly. Like so many things, PERT was oversold by its advocates, at first, and it was used where it was not worth its cost. Today, PERT is used only in limited applications.[1]

Mathematical and Statistical Tools

A second group of quantitative methods which can be used to help decision makers uses probability theory. Our discussion will concern probability and its uses in decision trees and payoff matrices. We will also discuss the use of probability in statistical quality control and in queuing models.

Probability

Since almost all managerial decisions deal with the future, they deal, at the same time, with uncertainty. There are almost always several results which are possible, but some of which are more likely to occur than others.

Mathematical procedures can help here. They do not eliminate uncertainty but probability theory provides a rough method for evaluating results. Probability allows managers to weigh the likelihood of different results more realistically than if they have to rely only on their intuition and thus improves their decision making.

In our discussion on break-even analysis, we found that the break-even point for an item selling for $50 and having variable costs of $30 per unit and fixed costs of $2,000, was 100 units. Starting from this, suppose that our present sales come to 150 units, thus producing $1,000 profit ($20 profit on each of the 50 items above the break-even point).

It is suggested that we spend $700 for advertising hoping that the sales will increase by enough to cover the $700 and more. This would change the break-even point to $2,700 ÷ $20 = 135 units. If we spend this $700, the sales department thinks that sales will go up as follows:

Units sold	Probability	$S \times P$
150	.00	0
170	.20	34
190	.60	114
210	.15	32
230	.05	11
	Total	191

Although the probability of each sales level is just an estimate, it nonetheless allows managers to make more intelligent decisions. In our example, if the estimates are reasonable, the managers can proceed as if the expected volume would be 191 units. They now have more to go on than they had at the start of our problem when the proposal to spend the $700 was made. In this case, they should go ahead. The best evidence they now have indicates that the sales increase will more than pay for the advertising (41 extra units × $20 = $820 − $700 advertising = $120, net extra).

Decision Trees

When a person comes to a cross road in the highway, he has to choose which one to take. Having chosen one, this opens up a whole set of possibilities while cutting off other sets. And, having chosen one road and pursuing it for a distance, he comes to another cross road. Again he has to choose, and again he opens up certain possibilities while closing off others.

Managers of organizations have to make similar decisions. As they look ahead for a given time, they try to make the choice which will advance them toward their goals. When they make their first decision, they need to consider the probable end results of the several courses of action open to them at that time. The initial choice should be one which will lead, through later decisions, to the most promising result.

A decision tree is a model, a graphic portrayal, of the choices together with probable payoff figures for each possible end situation. Figure 22-6 shows the possibilities for the following example:

The Tasty Pizza restaurant chain is considering going into a new area where the managers believe that ten Tasty Pizza shops could be profitable. They can approach this problem either by putting in one restaurant first to test the market or they could put in ten restaurants right at the start. It costs $50,000 to open a store and should business be so poor that it has to close down later, the loss would be $100,000 per restaurant closed. A successful restaurant would produce a $30,000 profit per year. If Tasty Pizza tried out one store first and found it to be successful, the company would plan to add nine more after one year.

The company's managers feel that there is a 75 percent chance of the restaurants being successful and producing $30,000 each in profits each year, except that if they open only one restaurant at first, the prospective profits for the nine others which might be added after one year would be only $20,000 per restaurant because competi-

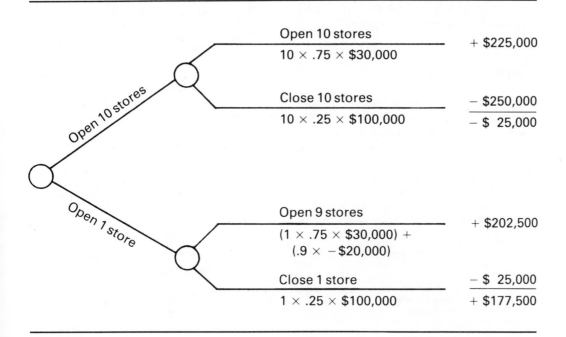

Figure 22-6
A decision tree.

tion might become better established. The analysis is to cover a ten-year period of operations.

Figure 22-6 shows that Tasty Pizza's managers should start with only one restaurant and if it is successful, should add the other nine stores. Otherwise the possible loss from having to close ten restaurants after one year are too great. Considering the probabilities which reflect the average results if such a problem were faced many times, the company would average a loss of $25,000 over a ten-year period each time it put in ten restaurants at the start. But it would average a gain of $177,500 during a ten-year period if it made a practice of starting with only one restaurant and then adding nine more if the first one was successful.

In practice, decision-tree type problems would be far more complex than our simple example. They could hardly be depicted graphically at all, but, would be handled on computers. But the decision-tree process could still be used to shed light on the merits of different alternatives.

Payoff Matrices

Since all decisions have to do with the future, the appropriateness of the choices made from among alternatives depends upon what the future proves to be like. A decision to spend money to expand in anticipation of prosperity could be calamitous if, instead of prosperity, a depression ensued. *Payoff matrices (sometimes called Bayesian analyses) provide managers with a means for comparing the*

expected results of the several possible choices under differing "states of nature."

Consider, for example, the Apex Airlines example:

Apex flies airplanes to a number of remote, yet exotic places. There is some demand by tourists to go to these places but not many tourists go because local hotels are very poor. Apex has been considering building modern hotels in several of these locations in order to generate more tourist traffic. The profitability of such undertakings is, of course, somewhat problematical and depends in large part on how many tourists would visit these interesting locations if they had good hotels.

Apex's managers are considering building hotels in ten locations. Four would be in one general area and all would be built or none would be built. Another four would be in another general area while the last two would be in another more remote area. Apex is, therefore, considering building four, eight, or ten hotels. Figure 22-7 shows the expected monetary returns from each of these choices under different conditions of tourist demand:

With these estimates of the expected results before them, Apex's managers must next estimate the probability of each level of demand. These estimates of the probability of each situation are purely subjective and are decided by the managers. We will suppose that they believe that, once the hoteis are available, there is a 30 percent probability that demand will be low, that there is a 55 percent chance that demand will be moderate, and a 15 percent chance that it will be high.

	Low	Moderate	High
Four hotels	−$3,000,000	$2,000,000	$5,000,000
Eight hotels	− 5,000,000	3,000,000	8,000,000
Ten hotels	− 8,000,000	4,000,000	10,000,000

Figure 22-7
Tourist Demand

These estimates allow Apex's managers to set up a "payoff" matrix in a form which will yield a "total expected value" for each of the contemplated actions while giving consideration to the probabilities of the various levels of tourist demand. This is done by multiplying each expected value figure in Figure 22-7 by the probability shown at the top of each column respectively in Figure 22-8. This is how the figures in the body of Figure 22-8 were calculated.

sured to very exact measurements and the frequency of each measurement is plotted on a chart, the plot will be "bell-shaped," as is shown in Figure 22-9A. The items measuring very close to the average size will be the most frequent, with measurements farther away being less common.

It is possible to calculate the proportion of items which will be close to the center and the proportion which will be less

	Low	Moderate	High	Total
Probability	.30	.55	.15	
Four hotels	−$ 900,000	$1,100,000	$ 750,000	$ 950,000
Eight hotels	− 1,500,000	1,650,000	1,200,000	1,350,000
Ten hotels	− 2,400,000	2,200,000	1,500,000	1,300,000

Figure 22-8
Tourist Demand

The total expected value for each of these three choice alternatives is the horizontal summation of the expected values for the different demand levels. In our example, it comes out that the highest prospective profit ($1,350,000) would be to build eight hotels and not to build the last two hotels at this time.

Statistical Quality Control

One very common use of probability in decision making is in statistical quality control. SQC is widely used in manufacturing to control the quality of products and its use in office work and in service industries is growing.

Statistical quality control is based on the idea that perfection is almost impossible to achieve. It assumes that any time anyone tries to make many items to an exact size, most of them will be almost exactly the size wanted but there will be variations in size and a few items will be too small or too large to be acceptable.

If a large number of items are mea-

close. To do this, the "standard error" of the distribution of all the measurements is calculated. How to calculate this is explained in statistics books. The arithmetic mean (the average) plus and minus one standard error will set measurements between which 68.3 percent of the actual item measurements fall. The mean plus and minus two standard errors shows measurements between which 95.5 percent of the items fall, and plus and minus three standard errors, sets measurements between which 99.7 percent of them fall.

If a factory operation is producing nearly all acceptable parts, then these measures (plus and minus three standard errors) can be used as "control limits." Samples (perhaps as few as four or five items) of ongoing production of parts are measured periodically (say, every half hour) and the average measurements of such samples are plotted on a chart such as Figure 22-9B where the control limits have been set at plus and minus three standard errors. So long as the averages of the measurements of these

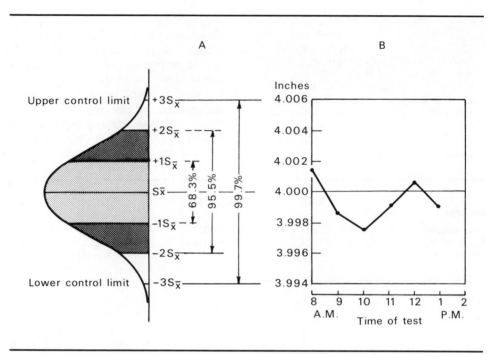

Figure 22-9
A. The "normal curve" showing the probability of substantial variations in measurements from the mean measurement of a population and showing their uses in setting control limits for quality control purposes.
B. Control chart for use in monitoring the quality of parts being made.

limits, the operation is "in control" and is not producing very many items which will have to be rejected.

Quality control charts can also be used to monitor errors which occur in office work. The Chase Manhattan Bank, for example, processes over two million checks a day. Obviously, an error will occur occasionally. Ratios of the number of errors to the number of checks handled are set up and compared, clerk by clerk, and day by day. A limit is then set to the number of errors to be tolerated. The charts will show whenever these limits are exceeded. If the limits are exceeded, the managers need to investigate why this is happening and to take action to reduce the number of errors to within the acceptable level.

Although we will not describe it here, another widespread use of statistical quality control is "acceptance sampling." A sample of items from a lot already produced or bought from a vendor is inspected and the whole lot is accepted or rejected according to the characteristics found in the sample.

Statistical quality control has been, for years, widely used in decision making in quality matters. It reduces quality decisions to a level where low level employees can make the necessary decisions just by following simple rules based on mathematical probability.

Queuing Models

Earlier in this chapter we discussed trade-off models. One of the examples used there was that of a retail store manager trying to give good service to customers while having to contend with the cost of rendering good service increasing with its quality. The point where the worth of good service and the cost of good service equal each other is the trade-off point.

Queuing models provide a way for managers to make more intelligent decisions in many trade-off situations. These models deal with situations in which customers arrive and need to be served. If service times exceed the time intervals between arrivals, an ever growing queue of customers will build up. Temporary queues can also build up, as frequently occurs in banks, if either the service times or the arrival intervals are irregular even though the service capacity is, in total, more than adequate to take care of the total need for services. Such a situation is quite common in real life. Most of us have experienced waiting in lines at super-market check out stations even though in the end the lines are all taken care of.

At the same time, something similar occurs on the serving end. The servers can be regarded as constituting a queue waiting to serve. If fewer than usual customers arrive or if their service times prove to be short, there will be excess service capacity and the servers will essentially constitute a queue of waiting servers.

There are many kinds of queuing situations, each of which needs its own formula for calculating answers. A single-channel, single-phase situation would have only one server who performs the complete service. Two or more servers, each performing the same complete service for the next customer in a single line of customers (as in a bank customer service line) would be a multiple-channel, single-phase situation.

To illustrate queuing models, we will use a single-channel, single-server type example. It concerns a gasoline filling station in a remote area staffed by only one attendant. Customers arrive at an average rate of five cars per hour but the time intervals between these arrivals are irregular. Service times average six minutes (ten per hour) but this, too, varies.

With these figures it is possible to use queuing formulas to get answers to questions about how often a newly arrived car will have to wait because its predecessor is being served, how long such a wait might be, how much idle time the attendant will have, and so on.

Queuing models are formulas using Greek letters to represent certain data. Arrival rates are indicated by λ (the Greek letter lambda) and service rates by μ (the Greek letter mu). So, in our case $\lambda = 5$ and $\mu = 10$. The formula for the average number of cars waiting in line (called L_q) is:

$$L_q = \frac{\lambda^2}{\mu(\mu - \lambda)} = \frac{5^2}{10\,(10 - 5)} = 0.5 \text{ cars}$$

The average number of cars waiting in line and being served (called L) is:

$$L = \frac{\lambda}{\mu - \lambda} = \frac{5}{10 - 5} = 1 \text{ car}$$

The average time a car spends waiting in line (called W_q) is:

$$W_q = \frac{\lambda}{\mu(\mu - \lambda)} = \frac{5}{10(10 - 5)}$$

$$= 0.1 \text{ hours or 6 minutes}$$

The average time a car spends waiting in line and being serviced (called W) is:

$$W = \frac{1}{\mu - \lambda} = \frac{1}{10 - 5}$$

$$= 0.2 \text{ hours or 12 minutes}$$

The average proportion of time that the attendant spends servicing cars (called ρ, the Greek letter rho) is:

$$\rho = \frac{\lambda}{\mu} = \frac{5}{10} = 0.5 \text{ hours or 30 minutes}$$

The average proportion of the time of the attendant not spent serving customers then becomes $1 - \rho = 0.5$ hours or 30 minutes per hour.

It will be noticed that the last two answers did not really need to be calculated by a formula. An attendant serving five customers per hour for six minutes each will be busy for thirty minutes and not serving customers the other thirty minutes. The formulas given here only illustrate that these ratios could be calculated for other combinations of more cars and more attendants where the answers would not be so obvious.

Queuing models can be developed for a great many of the different combinations of numbers of serving channels and phases. Unfortunately, such models become very complex when they deal with several service channels and several phases of work all in the same problem. Consequently, queuing model use is uncommon. The simpler simulation method often proves to be a better method to use.

Computerized Operations Research

A third set of operations research techniques which are helpful in decision

making includes several techniques which are so complicated that computers have to be used for nearly all of their applications. In the case of one of these techniques, simulation, the process is simple but the volume of data needing to be handled usually necessitates using a computer. We will present a simulation example which is simple enough to be solved without a computer.

The other two operations research techniques which we will discuss, linear programming and input-output analyses, require complex calculations which almost always require computers. We will discuss these two techniques without working through any sample problems.

Simulation

Simulation (sometimes called "Monte Carlo" simulation) is a conscious attempt to imitate a sequence of happenings so that managers can test and evaluate various possible actions. It is a technique whereby a system and its associated possible sequences of events are produced on paper on a make-believe basis.

In order to use simulation it is necessary to have, (1) a listing of the number of instances of each measurement of a variable and, (2) a table of random numbers, such as is found in every statistics book. With these basic data, managers can investigate the merits of different courses of action. The data about the variable can even be hypothetical rather than actual. A manager might, for example, want to see what the probable results would be in the event of some unlikely situation which has not as yet actually occurred.

Suppose that a small city airport is finding that more and more airplanes are using its facilities. At the present time there is no problem of airplanes arriving at the same time and having to wait. But if the present rate of increase in use continues, in four years, there will be twice as many airplanes coming in as now arrive. The airport managers want to find out if their present landing strip will be adequate.

Figure 22-10 shows how the arrival pattern shapes up. The numbers in Figure 22-10 are the actual arrival rates during a recent typical nine-hour day when 100 airplanes arrived. Figure 22-10 also shows the accumulated percent of arrivals by time intervals. These last figures, the accumulated percent figures, are necessary so that blocks of random numbers can be assigned to the various arrival times in accord with the pattern shown in the basic data. The random numbers assigned in our example are shown in Figure 22-10:

Minutes between arrivals	Number of Cases*	Accumulated % of cases	Random Number assignment
1	0	0	—
2	3	3	1-30
3	8	11	31-110
4	14	25	111-250
5	30	55	251-550
6	25	80	551-800
7	10	90	801-900
8	7	97	901-970
9	2	99	971-990
10	1	100	991-000

*Since there are 100 cases in our sample, these numbers individiaully, also represent the percent distribution of the arrivals by time intervals.

Figure 22-10

Once the assignment of random number blocks has been made, the simulation of arrivals can proceed. If one were to simulate a whole day's arrivals he would consult a random number table and draw off, perhaps the first one hundred numbers in the table. Then he would convert these numbers into minutes between arrivals and would have a simulated list of arrival intervals for the day. (In practice, all of this would almost surely be done on a computer.)

Because of space limitations, we will carry through a simulation for the first twenty airplane arrivals only. The first twenty numbers we found in our random number table were:

965	845	098	115	133
366	018	407	681	297
370	730	195	354	756
918	033	543	491	685

These translate into arrival intervals (in minutes) of:

9	7	3	4	4
5	2	5	6	5
5	6	4	5	6
8	3	5	5	6

By accumulating these intervals, we develop a simulated history of arrival times. The times shown here are consecutive minutes.

9	34	48	66	86
14	36	53	72	91
19	42	57	77	97
27	45	62	82	103

Supposing that at the present time it is felt to be unsafe to allow airplanes to land more often than one every two minutes. We can now investigate how often new arrivals will have to wait. Actually, in our sample, no airplane had to wait at all since none arrived in less than two minutes after its predecessor. It is highly probable that it is rare today for an arriving airplane to wait.

But we have not yet investigated the question of what the situation would be if twice as many airplanes were trying to use the single landing strip at this airport. If twice as many airplanes arrived, then the time intervals between arrivals would be only half of what they are in our sample. In that case, our simulated arrival experience would become:

4.5	30.5	46.5	64	84
9	34	48	66	86
11.5	35	50.5	69	88.5
14	36	53	72	91
16.5	39	55	74.5	94
19	42	57	77	97
23	43.5	59.5	79.5	100
27	45	62	82	103

The simulated use of the landing strip for the 103 minutes of our simulation is worked out in Figure 22-11.

These new figures indicate that, in our, now forty-item, simulation, there would be twelve cases of airplanes waiting to land if the number of arrivals doubled over today's level. In no case, however, in our simulation, would the delay in the air exceed two minutes, so the single airstrip would still be adequate and a second landing strip would

Arrival	Runway clear	Airplane in air waits	Arrival	Runway clear	Airplane in air waits
4.5	6.5	—	57=58	60	1 minute
9	11	—	59.5=60	62	.5 minute
11.5	13.5	—	62	64	—
16.5	18.5	—	64	66	—
19	21	—	66	68	—
23	25	—	69	71	—
27	29	—	72	74	—
30.5	31.5	—	74.5	76.5	—
34	36	—	77	79	—
35=36	38	1 minute	79.5	81.5	—
36=38	40	2 minutes	82	84	—
39=40	42	1 minute	84	86	—
42	44	—	86	88	—
43.5=44	46	.5 minute	88.5	90.5	—
45=46	48	1 minute	91	93	—
46.5=48	50	1.5 minutes	94	96	—
48=50	52	2 minutes	97	99	—
50.5=52	54	1.5 minutes	100	102	—
53=54	56	1 minute	103	105	—
55=56	58	1 minute			

Figure 22-11

not be needed until traffic became still heavier. Obviously, of course, such a conclusion, if it were actually made in our case, should rest on a much more extensive simulation than we have provided here.

Our example did not consider airplanes taking off and the problems they might cause. Since the number of airplanes coming in and going out are equal, perhaps our second simulation above would come close to describing how the landing strip would be used for in and out traffic at today's traffic density. The pattern of departures might very well, however, differ from the arrival pattern we used. If so, a more extensive simulation, covering arrivals and departures, should be carried through.

Simulation is such a simple process that one could easily under-estimate the capability of this technique for solving complex waiting line problems. As we said earlier, queuing-type mathematical formulas quickly become too complex to use when several variables interact. In such cases, simulation can often fill the bill.

Linear Programming

When a company makes several products in considerable volume using the same production machines, it sometimes happens that their combined machine time requirements exceed the capacity of some of the machines. Then the least profitable items are usually cut back to allow the production of the more profitable items to continue without being reduced.

It is easy to say "cut back on the least profitable items" but it is hard to work this out when there are several products which:

· yield different amounts of profit
· require different amounts of machine operating time on different machines in some cases and on the same machines in other cases

· and which have differing amounts of operating hours available

Linear programming is a mathematical process which determines how many of each kind of product to make which will use the available machine capacity to best advantage considering the profits to be earned on each product. Linear programming determines the most profitable product mix.

Linear programming is not, however, confined to problems having to do with the allocation of limited production resources to their most profitable use. It can also be used in other kinds of production problems, such as exist in a canned foods company with customers in many locations and with several of its own warehouses in different locations. (Although linear programming methods can solve such problems, a simpler variant, the "transportation method," can be used for this type of allocation problem.) There are many times when such a company's managers need to decide which warehouses should serve which customers and which items to ship from which warehouse. In this case, the object is to minimize costs rather than to maximize profits directly. Linear programming can be used either to maximize one thing, such as income, or to minimize something else, such as costs.

Most linear programming problems are solved by the "simplex" method. This method allows the problem solver to start with the assumption that nothing at all will be made and then to consider making products in various combinations until the best solution is found. It utilizes successive steps ("iterations" or "tableaus") as it moves toward final solutions.

Linear programming is an algebraic procedure but it differs from regular algebra in that it can solve for unknowns where there are more unknowns than there are equations. (In regular algebra, answers can be found only when there are the same number of equations as there are unknowns.) In real life applications of linear programming, problems might have hundreds of equations and possibly hundreds of unknowns. Solving such problems requires computers.

To show what linear programming can do, we will pose a problem of a lawn mower manufacturer who makes two kinds of mowers, one, the old shear-type mower and the other a rotary mower. Shear-type mowers produce a gross profit margin of $35 each and rotaries, $60 each.

These mowers are made in four departments: parts fabrication, engine assembly, shear mower assembly, and rotary mower assembly. The parts fabrication department can, in a week's time, make parts for 3,000 shear type mowers or 6,000 rotary mowers or any combination of the two on a proportional basis. Engines are assembled at either a maximum rate of 5,000 a week for shear mower engines or 4,000 a week for rotary mower engines or any in between combination on a proportional basis. The two kinds of mowers each has its own specialized assembly line. Capacities are shear mowers, 2,500 a week, and rotary mowers, 3,500 a week. Both departments can operate at the same time and the operations of neither is affected by the operation of the other.

A manager can use linear programming to find the balance point between these two products which will produce the greatest profit, considering the limitations of his manufacturing facilities. Although the calculation is too lengthy to present here, the answer proves to be to make 625 shear mowers and 3,500 rotary mowers. At that point (point *F* on Figure 22-12), the total gross profit contribution from making the two kinds of mowers is $232,000 a month.

In most actual situations, the managers who are making decisions would also like to get answers to other related questions, such as, should we operate the rotary mower assembly department extra hours at overtime even though this costs extra? How much can we afford to spend to expand the capacity of this department? If we expand the rotary assembly capacity how far can we go before we

will come to some other department's capacity limit? etc.

All of these questions can be answered by using the output figures that appear in the final tableau of a simplex linear programming solution. The obvious main answers to linear programming problems (what is the best program for the problem as posed?) are only part of the information also provided as by-product answers in simplex method solutions.

Input-Output Models

As management science comes of age, companies are turning more to mathematical models of the "input-output" type. These are the same kind of sophisticated models that economists use to forecast the nation's economy. Figures for a large number of the elements of the economy's operation (such as employment, interest rates, retail sales, inflationary trends, bank deposits, etc.) are put into a model in a computer. The computer will then calculate the effects of changes in any one or any set of these elements on all others.

Union Carbide, Monsanto, General Electric, and many other companies have such models. Their models include all of the general information relating to the whole economy and they also include information pertinent to their industry. Their managers can ask the computer, "What will happen to us if there is a strike in the steel industry which lasts two months?" "What will happen to the economy and to us if the long term interest rates go up?" "How will it affect us if personal incomes go up three percent?" Answers give these managers clues about what the future may be like and what the future conditions will do to their operations.

Planning models are still, however, a long way from perfect. Because of their imperfections, some companies, among them Boeing and Sun Oil, have abandoned their

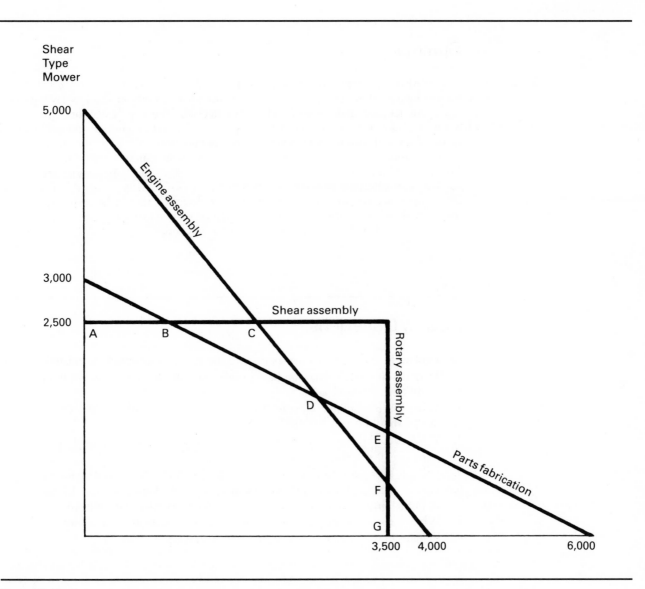

Figure 22-12
Production capabilities of four departments concerned in making lawn mowers.

overall models. Such models also failed the Federal government badly in the 1970s by not forecasting high inflation rates, high interest rates, and high unemployment rates.

To be helpful, models need to be very carefully designed. It usually takes five years or more to develop models which are capable of producing reasonably reliable projections. And, even then, of course, they need accurate numerical input data.

Quantitative Methods in Decision-Making

454

Summary

Although important decision making will always have to be done by human beings, there are actually a good many areas, mostly of the low-level repetitive decision-making kind, where the decisions are largely economic in nature and depend on the interaction of only a few factors. When this is so many of these decisions can be handled mathematically.

Standardized procedures for solving problems such as how much inventory should we carry and how many should we order when more are needed, can often be worked out. When this is so, managers can rely on quantitative methods to tell them what their decisions should be. Already, many low-level decisions are made in accordance with mathematical programs and the areas of such applications continue to expand.

Review Questions:

1. Explain how the break-even point and the contribution ratio are related.
2. In trade-off models what are being traded off? What does one learn from using trade-off models?
3. What is the economic lot size? When can it be used in inventory control? When should it not be used?
4. What is a PERT system? How does it work? Where can it be used best? Why is it not commonly used?
5. What is a decision tree? How can it be used to improve decision making?
6. How does a payoff matrix (Bayesian analysis) work? How does it make use of probability to give managers better estimates of what will happen?
7. What is the "normal curve"? How is it used in statistical quality control?
8. Explain how random numbers are used in simulation.

Questions for Analysis and Discussion:

1. Suppose that some variable costs prove not to be wholly variable, particularly as volume decreases and some fixed costs prove not to stay wholly fixed when volume goes up. What would this do to break-even

analyses? How often are either of these possibilities actual factors in real situations?

2. If statistical quality control neither makes nor gets rid of risks, what does it do? Discuss.

3. Would it ever be true that the economic order quality curve is not relatively flat for volumes of, say, 25 percent above and below the EOQ? If yes, explain how it could be.

4. If PERT activities are, in fact, *work load* assignments, why are they so universally spoken of in terms of the calendar time they will take? Isn't the time a direct function of the resource inputs? Discuss.

5. When using probability figures in a calculation, how is the answer in any way improved since there is only one case at hand? What good does it do to know how things would work out "on the average"?

6. Aren't decision trees rather worthless in that the organization finally ends up going down one and only one path? What good does it do to know all about what might have been?

7. "Although Monte Carlo methods are useful for helping managers see what average conditions will be like, they are of little help to a manager who is interested in extremes." Discuss.

Problems:

1. What is the break-even point for a product with $25,000 of fixed costs and which will sell for $10.00, with variable costs of $6.20 per unit? If $1,000 were spent for advertising costs what would be the new break-even point before there would be any gain from the advertising?

2. An item is used at the rate of 7,000 per year. Because of minor irregularities in usage and in replenishment lead times, it is felt that reordering should allow for the need of a safety stock of 200 units. Normally, it takes one month to get a new supply. What should the reorder point be? If the company uses EOQs, what should the reorder quantity be if the cost of the item is $3, the carrying charge is 20% and the ordering cost is $50?

3. The following data are for part of a large PERT diagram:

Event	Immediately preceding event	Immediately following event
O	—	A, B, D
A	O	C, F
B	O	C, D
C	A, B	D, F
D	O, B, C	E, G
E	D	F, G
F	A, C, E	G
G	D, E, F	—

The expected time required to perform the necessary activities (in weeks) are

O–A	4		C–D	1
O–B	1		C–F	3
O–D	3		D–E	2
A–C	3		D–G	6
A–F	6		E–F	2
B–C	2		E–G	4
B–D	4		F–G	3

Draw up a PERT diagram for this set of activities. What is the critical path and how long will it take to complete this project?

4. A $100,000 advertising campaign is expected to produce the following results: If it is highly successful, $500,000 more profits; if moderately successful, $200,000 profit; if unsuccessful, 0 profits. A less extensive program would cost $50,000 and would produce $200,000, $75,000, or 0. The chances of excellent results are .30, mediocre results .55, and poor results .15. What action should be taken?

5. The office issuing drivers' licenses has the following experience with people coming in to have their automobile drivers' licenses renewed:

Time between arrivals minutes	Per cent of cases
4	10
5	30
6	30
7	20
8	10

The service time experience has, in the past, been

Service time minutes	Per cent of cases
3	10
4	20
5	40
6	20
7	10

Using simulation, find out what proportion of the people will have to wait and, for those who have to wait, how long their waits will average to be. Use the random numbers given in the text for this. For constructing a simulated table of arrivals use the random numbers as they are. For service times, use the random numbers in reverse order, starting at the end and working back.

Endnote

1. "Management Practices and Research—Poles Apart," by William G. Ryan, *Business Horizons*, June 1977, pp. 23–29.

Suggested Supplementary Readings

Beard, Larry R. "Economic Profit Maximation and Break-Even Analysis." *Michigan Business Review*, September 1977, pp. 18–22.

Heenan, David A., and Robert Addleman. "Quantitative Techniques for Today's Decision Makers." *Harvard Business Review*, May-June 1976, pp. 32–70.

Rosen, Gerald R. "New Vogue in Forecasting." *Dun's Review,* October 1979, pp. 94–100.

Weist, Jerome D. "Project Network Models: Past, Present and Future." *Project Management Quarterly* 4 (1977): 27–36.

Case for Section VI: The Retail Gamble Case[1]

The Signature Shop at Higbee Company, one of Cleveland's three major department stores, carries this store's trendiest men's wear. Its racks are filled with slacks, shirts and suits by fashion-plate designers. As of June, 1977, everything was classy, in fact, but its sales.

"Last fall was disastrous and sales this spring are not very hot either," said Robert Clay, a nattily dressed twenty-seven-year-old who buys the trendy clothing. "We had more European goods than ever before, but with the high prices we chased a lot of business away."

For department store buyers, uncertainty has always been a way of life but today's customers seem to be more unpredictable than they used to be and this makes buyers' tasks tougher. Here's how these problems are being tackled by the buyers in the men's clothing division at Higbee.

Higbee has 10 menswear buyers—nine men and one woman. Among them they spend some $15 million a year buying men's clothes. These buyers have to know the customer's quirks. For instance, blue collar workers dislike imports. Only clergymen buy black raincoats. Green clothing generally does not sell well. Large-sized goods sell big for Father's Day (wives and daughters think their men are bigger than they actually are).

But these are the easy things. The hard part of the job is buying the right merchandise in the right quantities at the right price and setting up deals so that orders can be canceled if the items don't sell. What makes it really hard is that purchase contracts with manufacturers are usually placed six months ahead of delivery. Consequently, sudden changes in what customers buy upset plans that are hard to change.

"This job of buying is the hardest job I've ever had," says Bob Erwin, buyer of sportswear for the youth market. To Peter Mohn, who oversees five buyers, buying menswear is "kind of like gambling—intelligent gambling—but risky."

Purchasing the wrong merchandise can cause big headaches for a buyer, especially since buying wrong is frighteningly easy to do, as Hank Kloots, a buyer of moderately priced sportswear, knows. Recently, he bought a big batch of Donegal brand "canned packages"—a $60 blazer with a variety of matching pants and sports shirts. Stocking these items in all ten Higbee stores cost between $30,000 and $60,000 and, to Kloots's dismay, it turned out to be a real bomb. "We expected to sell 50 percent of them in the first month; instead we sold only 15 percent."

A buyer can sometimes hedge his bets by buying his goods at a discount. That's what buyer Mike Daniels did in April on an order of sport coats. "I bought 385 sport coats at 20 percent off," or at $36 each instead of the regular $45, he says, because a supplier was overstocked.

Buyers can sometimes hedge by buying from suppliers who will accept cancellations. For example, a few months ago, Kloots bought some white slacks under a Higbee private label. "On the basis of 125 sold in January, I figured that I could sell 4,600 during the spring season. I knew that this was a high estimate but I could cancel orders for coming months so long as I gave them thirty days notice." Recently he cut his estimate to 3,600 without penalty. It isn't always that easy, though, because suppliers sometimes drive harder bargains.

Economic downturns also play havoc with plans. The pause in the economy recovery in mid-1976 caused the Higbee men's department to become overstocked. This happened at the same time that the United Rubber Workers strike against the "Big Four" tire companies deflated sales at the company's Belden Village store near Akron. The Midway Mall, in the Lorain-Elyria area west of Cleveland, had similar problems in early 1977 because of a major strike and weather-related local plant closings.

Economic policies in Washington also have a heavy impact on sales. When the 1975 tax rebates came out, things went wild, said one buyer. On the other hand, President Carter's decision to kill the proposed $50 rebate in early 1977 went down hard at Higbee. "I think that a great number of those checks would have gone for suits," says Ray Bushnell, the suit buyer, who noted that the average family of four would have received $200 in rebates.

Inflation fears and price resistance seem to produce a sort of battle between the store and its customers. To the store's buyers, it sometimes appears that there must be hordes of bargain hunters who wait for sales. They buy only when goods are marked down.

How is Higbee dealing with this hot-and-cold customer behavior? For one thing, "We are looking for customers who are more resistant to the economy," says Peter Inglin, merchandising manager of the men's division. The company hopes to get a piece of the affluent action by stocking such merchandise as $27.50 neckties by Polo and by courting customers who give cocktail parties, by means of timely direct mailings and an elegant atmosphere in the store. By stocking more higher quality, higher priced items, the company hopes to get more business from affluent customers who are less affected by strikes and layoffs and less hurt by soaring energy bills.

Some of the moves already made: low-priced Hickok belts have been moved to the bargain basement. Hathaway and Gant dress shirts are being promoted more strongly than cheaper Arrow and Van Heusen shirts. Higher-priced suits are being given more display racks and the company has considered changing the salesmen's commission structure on suits to give them a bigger percentage on higher priced lines.

Meanwhile, Higbee plans to introduce lower-priced high-fashion goods for the younger, less affluent customers. It will beef up its supply of $25 cotton twill slacks, for example. "The look has to be right and the price has to be very right," says Clay.

Assume that you have been appointed to survey the literature and to make recommendations about how to improve the quality of the decisions being made in the men's clothing department at Higbee. Assume also that the chapters in this book on decision making are about what you would find in the literature. What recommendations do you make?

Endnote

1. This case was written up at length in, "The Retail Gamble: Store Chain's Buyers Take Big Risks Trying to Guess Sales Trends," by Bernard Wysocki, Jr., *Wall Street Journal,* 6 June 1977, pp. 1ff. Abridged and reprinted by permission of Dow Jones & Co., Inc., Copyrighted, 1981. All rights reserved.

In order to be effective, organizations need to operate as total entities. Individual subunits need to function as if they are parts of one entire integrated organization; they need to coordinate their separate activities. A certain amount of control from the top must be exercised over the activities of the separate units.

The first two chapters in this section, Chapters 23 and 24, have to do with control, as such. They consider how high-level managers find out what is going on, and how they judge whether what is going on is satisfactory or whether something else needs to be done.

Control does not operate perfectly. Attempts to get work done do not always get it done. And down within organizations, the jobs of subordinates are often hard to define as are the measurement and appraisal of degrees of accomplishment.

Control is usually exercised in one of three ways. First is for the superior to supervise subordinates closely; second is to put a capable subordinate manager in charge and hope that he will do well; third, a superior can rely on communications, principally in the form of reports. The merits of these methods are considered in Chapter 24.

A continual flow of information is essential. Communications flow from person to person, group to group, top to bottom, and bottom to top. And information, requests for information, and barriers to the flow of information, exist throughout the organization. These matters are the subject of Chapter 25, the last chapter in this section.

Organizations in Action: Controlling

Objectives of Chapter Twenty-Three

1. To explore the concept of control and its pervasive need throughout organizations.
2. To emphasize the need for the control of *costs* in both business and in nonbusiness organizations.
3. To consider the difficulties encountered by managers as they try to operationalize control over their organization's activities and accomplishments.
4. To put the need for using comparisons into perspective as it relates to control.

Nature of Control

23

I   If anything can go wrong, it will.
II   Of the things that can't go wrong,
some will.
Murphy's Laws.

Control is the process by which managers direct and monitor the organization's actions trying to cause the organization's people to accomplish its goals. Control is not an activity wholly apart from regular supervision and direction. Rather, it is more a matter of surveillance plus action when action is needed.

Control helps managers to counteract Murphy's Laws. It is the means for defending the organization against the internal decay and the aggressive factors mentioned in Chapter 1.

Our discussion of control is going to be a little unrealistic. It will have to do with how managers *can try* to cause their organizations to operate effectively. Unfortunately, many managers, particularly middle-level managers, do not care a great deal whether their departments operate effectively or not, just so they continue to operate in a prosaic fashion and get their daily work done in a reasonable way. Such managers do not really try to bring about controlled and effective operations.

As we use it, the word "control" comes close to being just another word to describe effective management. In trying to control, managers set goals, make plans, start to carry them out, get reports of what is being accomplished, appraise performance, make new plans if they are needed to correct deviations from plans, and try to carry out these new plans. (See Figure 23-1) In order to do all of these things, managers have to set up objectives and policies, provide for up and down communications, delegate work, and motivate people — all of which are parts of effective management.

It may sound as if there is almost no new element in control unless it is the extra emphasis on the need for good communications so that surveillance can operate.

Yet communications and getting information, of themselves, do not constitute control. A manager might get unimportant information or get too much information to digest or he might not do anything even when he gets the proper information. The communication systems can be operating well and a manager can be well informed and still not really be trying to exercise control.

Managerial control seeks to insure that performance conforms to plans. It starts with plans and then tries to follow through to achievement. Managerial control is more oriented to the carrying out of plans by correcting deviations from plans than it is to the making of the plans themselves.

In this process, appraisals are perhaps the most highly essential element. Taking corrective actions rests on appraisals that accomplishments are unsatisfactory. Managers try to bridge the gap between planning and achievement, first by appraising, and then, if performance is falling short, by causing subordinates to do still different things in order to achieve goals. In Chapter 21 we mentioned the American Airlines experience in 1973. It is also relevant here.

In 1973, American Airlines was losing money so it brought its former president, C.H. Smith, out of retirement to see if he could reverse the trend.[1] When Smith returned in the Fall of 1973, the company's forecast was for a loss of $68 million in 1974. Smith told American's top echelon managers that, "American is not going to lose $68 million in 1974, nor anything like it." Nor did it. In the first nine months of 1974, there was a profit of $28 million whereas there had been a loss of $35 million in the same period a year earlier.

Smith, together with his successor, Albert V. Casey, accomplished this turnaround by, among other things, eliminating several money-losing flights, including routes across the South Pacific. These moves allowed for the reducing of uneconomical employment. Smith and Casey also sold off several giant Boeing 747 airplanes which had been flying with too many empty seats.

Organizations in Action: Controlling

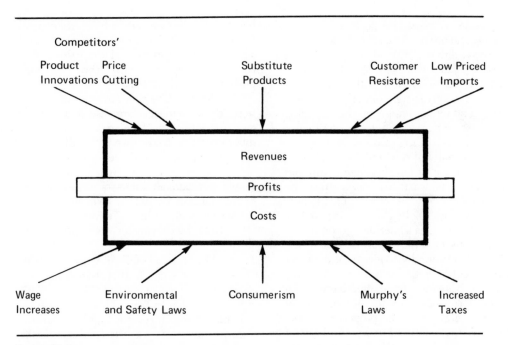

Figure 23-1
Control tries to reduce the vise-like pressures that are always working against effective operations.

They also reduced the extremely participative decision making which was popular at American at the time. They centralized decision making more and the greater decisiveness was reported to have improved employee morale.

Their actions put the company back into healthy financial shape again. Without these attempts to control costs, American might well have lost the $68 million which the forecasts had anticipated.

Control is relative and is not an all-or-nothing matter. A department head can "control" labor costs in his department in that he can do something about them. Controlling labor costs does not mean that he can eliminate them, but only that he can do something about them. If he controls them, they will be less than if he does not control them. Similarly, a retail store manager can control the store's sales, in the sense that he can do something about them.

Is Performance the Test of Effective Control? The answer to this question is a qualified no. Control *tries* to produce results according to plan. But sometimes a department head does all of the things normally needed for producing results yet, because of unfavorable outside conditions, does not get far in the direction of reaching his department's objectives.

Should such a manager be appraised as not having exercised control? It seems reasonable to say that a manager *has* exercised control even if he fails to reach his goals, if he has influenced accomplishment in the direction of more effective accomplishment.

Our discussion more or less assumes that control results in progress toward goals.

Nature of Control

The discussion takes the position that, in one sense, *no one in a managerial position produces results directly.* Instead, a manager does things, *he takes action steps,* which normally lead to results. The view is that control is planning, exercising surveillance, appraising, and replanning, even though doing all of these things does not, in every case, result in the achieving of objectives.

Internal Politics and Control. Our discussion on control in this chapter assumes that managers want to have their organizations operate effectively. This is not, however, always so. In Chapter 19, we saw that power struggles sometimes go on in upper echelons of large organizations. Such conflicts between departments and power groups are likely to undermine effective operations. Organizational effectiveness as a goal takes second place to the winning of power struggles. Ideas and proposals are not judged on their merits but on the basis of whose idea it is and who will get the credit. Nor are people judged on their accomplishments but on their loyalty to the power group. It is unfortunate when control is subverted and is not aimed at the better accomplishment of organizational goals.

Control as Evidence of Managerial Interest. Our discussion of control has been in terms of trying to insure that work gets done, with the emphasis on the work itself. Actually, many subordinate managers feel that control is also evidence and is an expression of their superior's interest in what they are doing. Subordinate managers are motivated to do better because they know that the higher-ups care about their work and about them. This keeps subordinates from developing a feeling that management doesn't care so why should they care.

The Pervasiveness of the Need for Control

Except at the very top, attempts to control are always two-sided. On the one hand, all managers are subject to control from above. They are subordinates to and agents for their superiors. Their superiors try to cause them to bring about accomplishment in their areas.

At the same time, in their dual position, these managers are also superiors to *their* subordinates. They try to cause *their* subordinates to do things which will result in accomplishment in their subordinate areas.

Attempts to control, therefore, should pervade all kinds of organizations. Every manager should be trying to control the activities under his direction while at the same time he is subject to control from above.

The Importance of Cost Control. Our discussion so far in this chapter has emphasized the need to control the *activities* of organizational members. This is, however, only half of the story. It is highly important to control *the* cost *of activities and of achieving results.*

Money is only one of several motivators which cause people to act. But, *money is the lifeblood of all business organizations.* In a person, *blood flows* keep the individual alive. In a business, *money flows* keep it alive. It cannot be emphasized too strongly that if the money being spent for the costs of activities and for achieving goals exceeds the amount of money coming in from sales, *the company goes bankrupt.*

It should never be forgotten that, at least in business organizations, everything aimed at the development of people, everything concerned with motivating people, and everything having to do with their interfacing with each other effectively — everything — must result in the organization's work being done economically, or else it doesn't matter. If the organization does not operate effectively, it goes bankrupt.

Most managers in business organizations have nothing to do directly with bringing in more money. But every manager has discretion over things which *cost* money. And, in almost every case, he has some control over the actions and accomplishments of his group. He has some control over costs. *Cost control* should, therefore, be recognized as a very important part of the mission assignment of every manager.

An important corollary to the need for controlling costs is the need to have a good cost accounting system. Without a good cost accounting system, the data needed for controlling costs will not be available and it will be impossible to do a good job of controlling costs. It will be impossible to make cost/benefit analyses, or to compare the costs of alternative ways of doing things, or to compare costs of doing things to their planned costs.

Control in NonBusiness Organizations

One of the most striking differences between business and nonbusiness organizations lies in the area of control. Control, as we have been discussing it, hardly exists in most nonbusiness organizations. Goal setting is rare and measurement of accomplishments against planned goals is even more rare. And still more rare is the taking of remedial actions when performance is poor. The kinds of actions taken by Smith and Casey in the 1970s at American Airlines just don't occur in nonbusiness organizations.

Control is lacking because it is almost impossible to judge the accomplishments of nonbusiness organizations such as hospitals, schools, and government agencies. Such organizations do not have identifiable, quantifiable, and countable goals so plans and reports of accomplishment compared to goals are rare. Appraisals are usually lacking. It is, therefore, almost impossible to have effective controls. Unfortunately, too, this lack of control in government and other nonbusiness organizations usually includes a lack of control of costs as they relate to accomplishment.

Such controls as non-government organizations have are usually over the money spent and not over the resulting accomplishments. Usually they can't overspend their budgets so there is a control over the costs. But there is no parallel control to see that the concomitant achievements are reasonable considering the money spent. Sometimes, nonbusiness organizations can overspend their budgets as well. If a highway bridge costs more than was planned, it just costs more (and it may take longer to build as well) and some other project gets less money.

Operationalizing Control

Control can be effective only if it is operationalized. In this process there are several elements to be considered. Because control can be more effective in business organizations than in nonbusiness organizations, the matters we will discuss will relate to operationalizing control in business organizations.

Importance of Surveillance

Surveillance is a primary essential of control. Surveillance is a showing of interest, a watching over, a monitoring, and an appraisal of the work done by the organization. It is not, however, a furtive, under cover, watching over. Nor is there anything sinister or dictatorial about surveillance and control. Nor should control imply over-control of every detail.

Surveillance does not imply any lack of confidence except that newly promoted subordinates need closer watching over. At the same time, even with experienced subordinates, the superior should not abdicate control altogether. He should still think of himself as a principal whose subordinates are his agents even though they are also team members and junior partners at the same time.

If all goes well, a manager's control is little more than a watching over and light-handed kind of monitoring. But, if his appraisal is that the desired results are not being accomplished, then the second phase of control should come into play. It should change from surveillance and appraisal to remedial action initiation. (Nor should the action which is initiated be a "ready to pounce" punitive action, but a helpful joining of hands of superiors and subordinates.)

Lest this imply that this monitoring and appraising is rather casual and incidental, it should be noted that this is a very important part of the manager's job. It envisions the superior's getting reports of what goes on and his going through the reports and acquainting himself with the details. He needs, all the while, to be alert to detect evidences of places where goals are not being reached. If his appraisals reveal any such places, he needs to institute remedial actions or to see that his subordinates institute remedial actions as is indicated in Figure 23-2.

All of this means that the superior ought to do a good bit of somewhat onerous detailed and even uninteresting work, or at least it is often onerous and uninteresting to him. He *should* be willing to dig into these details, because they cover the work of *his* organization. The performance of these people is *his* performance. Nonetheless, it is probably only human nature for higher-level managers to prefer to work on bigger things, particularly when they really do have competent subordinates and therefore feel that they do not need to spend their time following what they do very closely.

Looking *down* into the details of what subordinates do may seem demeaning to some superiors. It is not big-picture work. The down below activities are so routine and so minor compared to some of the other work that superiors have to do. Some managers

don't take their surveillance and appraisal responsibilities seriously enough. They almost abdicate their responsibility and so do not really try to control as much as they should.

The tendency for superiors not to give enough attention to monitoring the work of their subordinates is usually abetted by the subordinates themselves. The subordinates feel competent and they like to be left alone to carry out their delegated work. And they like to think that the superior should and does have confidence in them and should not keep checking up on them and appraising their work. They may even resent his watching over their work and take it as an affront to their abilities.

Nonetheless, subordinates do not have fiefdoms. They are still agents for their superiors and are not full partners. Managers do not, however, need to watch so closely as to deprive their subordinates of their jobs. There needs to be some trust and confidence.

Policy Surveillance in Large Companies. The many new governmental regulations over businesses which came into being in recent years have increased the need for surveillance. Lower-level managers' practices in such matters as non-discrimination, safety, anti-pollution, quality assurance, and energy conservation, must be watched over. Besides these, lower units must not offer bribes to customer purchasing agents nor contribute to political campaign funds, nor sell munitions abroad. Surveillance by the central office has become necessary in all of these matters to be sure that lower units know about and obey all of the laws and regulations.

Olin Corporation's failure to check up closely enough on the actions of two subordinate units cost it $750,000 in fines in 1978 as well as damage to the company's corporate image.

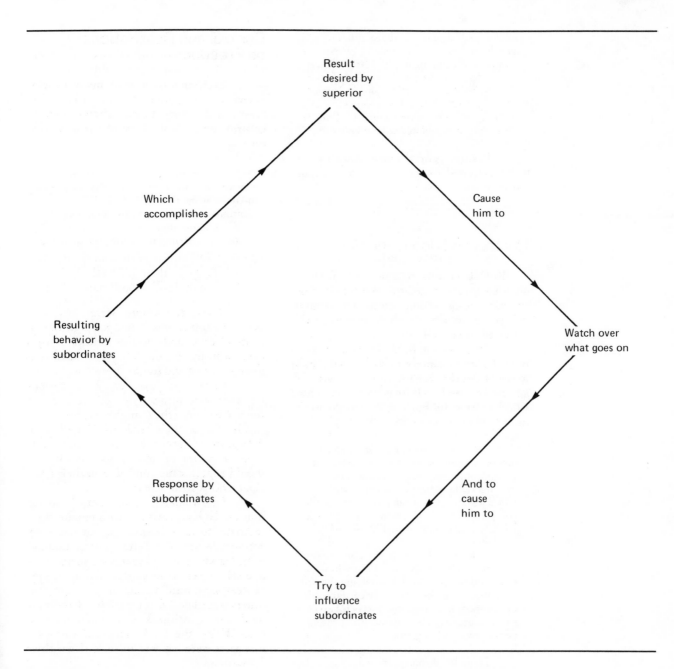

Figure 23-2
The control cycle.

Its Niagara Falls division falsely and grossly understated the amount of mercury waste it was dumping into the Niagara river.

Its Winchester division sold more than $1 million of sporting guns and ammunition to South Africa, but reported the sales as being made to other countries.[2] Both of these activities violated federal laws.

Positive central office control needs to be exercised to try to keep such occurrences at a minimum.

Control and Job Definition

Delegations to sales managers or chief engineers and many other kinds of department heads are delegations of missions or delegations to achieve whatever needs to be achieved in general areas.

The interest here, in control, is to note that the recipient of such a delegation may not develop his job in accord with organization needs. He may not even know whether what he has decided to do is the most helpful thing to do.

A chief engineer may do an excellent job of improving the factory's processing equipment and making it more efficient. He may rightly feel that this is important. But, if he does not also make improvements in the company's end-products which will help sales, he is not carrying out his assignment to the fullest.

Or, at a lower level, a stockroom clerk may keep big supplies of everything on hand and believe that he is helping the organization by giving good service. Probably he does not realize that the costs of his excessive inventories exceed the worth of the superior service he is giving.

High-level managers may not realize that their subordinates are defining their missions in these ways. The normal reporting procedures will not call it to their attention.

Control and Restrictions on Freedom

Even though a great many people, perhaps most people, do not like to be "controlled," they do not always react to control, even strong control, as if it were onerous.

A college professor has to meet his classes and this restricts his freedom, but men or women who regard this as burdensome usually do not take such a job.

College students are also controlled. A student studying engineering is required to take certain engineering courses. If he doesn't want to take these courses, he should not enroll in engineering.

These restrictions seem, however, not to be unreasonable and millions of students elect to undergo this kind of control every year. In fact, they clamor for admission to engineering and some other subject areas.

Control is, however, often unpopular with subordinates because it restricts their freedom (they might express it as "infringing" on their freedom). Nonetheless, delegation of authority is not license but is more a matter of agency so subordinates should expect some control from their principal who is their superior.

Unfortunately, too, control has, at times to be hard control which requires subordinates to take disagreeable but necessary actions. When the Penn-Central railroad went bankrupt several years ago, many of its operations were consolidated and many employees were retired early on pensions and others were laid off (operations of the railroad were continued on a much reduced basis during the bankruptcy). Lower-level managers were *required* to scale down their operations.

Sometimes directives from above are not so hard as to require absolute compliance by subordinates. When this is so and when the subordinate doesn't want to carry them out, he may move slowly or even disobey (at the risk of losing his job). Normally, of course, most people would carry out the directives even if they didn't like to because of the superior's coercive power.

People do not, however, always yield to mild coercive power. Not all directives are of such import that a subordinate manager must comply or leave. Possibly the matter itself is relatively minor, or possibly the subordinate is a valuable employee or maybe there would be other undesirable side-effects if the superior took strong coercive action.

The superior might endure even major insubordination rather than require a subordinate to leave. Attempts to control and to restrict the subordinate's freedom somewhat do not always rest on strong power to enforce compliance and even when they do, the strong formal power is not always used.

Control Before the Fact

It was said earlier that control tries to detect variations from planned courses and, when variations are found, to set corrective measures into action. But, in order for control to operate effectively as a future-shaping mechanism, planning, and particularly plans for cost control, should begin before there are any costs to control. If a company plans to make a stove to sell for $100, it can't have everything. So control over the cost of doing things starts long before there are any costs to control by ruling out many alternatives.

Most kinds of control should, in fact, be as much or more preventive as they are corrective. Before actions take place, managers should work with subordinates, helping them to develop their plans and working out with them what it will probably cost to do things. Prospective actions which will not reach toward objectives or which will cost too much are ruled out. They just don't take place. Such joint development of plans and

expected implementation actions operate as controls in advance of action.

Control before any action takes place and control during early action stages is much more effective than people sometimes appreciate because failures which do not occur and losses which have been prevented don't show on reports at all. Yet such losses would have been real and, in some cases, substantial. The study, analysis, questioning of assumptions and premises, and development of alternative plans are all part of control before the fact. Taken collectively, these parts of control are very worthwhile.

Control and Behavior Modification

In organizational literature, attempts by managers to direct the work of their subordinates are often said to be attempts to influence or modify their "behavior." And this, in turn, seems to imply that control deals largely with changing mental attitudes, which is often hard to do. The literature also sometimes uses the word "manipulative" as if it were a wrong thing to do. But, of course, a manager is not controlling unless he influences what his people do. He does "manipulate" them.

The literature also often plays down the matter of control having largely to do with the directing of the *activities* their subordinates engage in to their most effective applications. This is something which normally is not nearly so resistant to change by superiors as would be changing their mental attitudes.

Most attempts to control are not of the kind which require subordinates to change mental attitudes. Frequently, they are merely clarifications or amplifications of a delegation. Often they are nothing more than minor work directives.

A sales manager telling a salesman to call on customers next week in Indianapolis instead of customers in Cincinnati is trying to influence the salesman's behavior. So is a factory supervisor who tells an employee to work on the Jones company's order next instead of the Smith company's order.

In both of these cases, this is control in operation. It could be said to be manipulative. It gets people to do what the manager wants them to do. Yet, in neither of our two example cases is it the upsetting kind of control which a manager might get involved in if he tried to change an employee's mental attitudes. When control is confined to controlling activities, it is usually easier to be effective than when mental attitudes are involved.

Comparisons and Appraisals in Control

We have said that control depends on comparisons and appraisals. Managers have, first, to know what performance is expected, then, second, to get reports telling them what is being accomplished. Then follow comparisons and appraisals on which to base corrective actions. This section discusses the problems associated with developing valid comparisons and appraisals.

Degrees of Accomplishment and Limiting Conditions

Possible performance is a continuum with in-between degrees all the way from very little accomplishment to a great deal of accomplishment. A goal is a specific degree of accomplishment along this continuum which a manager is expected to achieve. If he accomplishes this much, he would be regarded as having done a good job and remedial action would not be taken by his superior. But, if a subordinate manager falls a little short of a difficult goal, he may

still be appraised as having done a good job and again, no remedial action would need to be taken. This would be particularly true if he inherited a difficult situation or if outside factors were against him.

Throughout the 1970s, over-capacity in the fertilizer industry held down the profits of all fertilizer making companies. There was little opportunity, under these conditions, for fertilizer company managers to achieve reaching goals. Managers of companies which broke even or lost only a small amount of money were actually doing good jobs.

The point is that managers who avoided losses were actually doing well and no remedial action from the top really needed to be taken.

Changing outside conditions, however, themselves need study. If they are permanent and the organization's present strategies and action programs are not suitable, then the strategies need to be changed — not because the subordinate managers did poorly — but because the organization's fundamental strategies are not appropriate to the new environment.

Discount stores grew up because big city department stores did not realize that people would go out of their way to poorly located discount stores just to save a little money. Later it turned out that the discount stores, which were usually located in outlying areas and had plenty of parking space, actually had better locations than downtown stores.

Here an outside environmental factor did hold down accomplishment and a reaction to it was called for. But most department store higher-level managers did not realize how important its effects would be and that hard work on their part would not be enough to overcome it.

Measurability of Performance

In other places in this text, we have said that quite a few parts of many jobs are not measurable in an absolute way. For example, many people go to church on Sunday and listen to the preacher give a sermon. If these people were asked to appraise the sermon, there would surely be differences of opinion about it.

It is easy to say that, to control, managers should set up standards and goals and compare accomplishments to them. But this cannot be done very well in the case of the preacher's sermon. His product, the sermon, cannot be evaluated satisfactorily in measurable countable terms, and it is thus not possible to judge his sermon objectively. And when accomplishment can't be judged, there are limited possibilities of devising methods for improvement.

Unfortunately, appraisals must be made whether or not the accomplishment is measurable. In the many situations in which accomplishment is not measurable, the appraisal must be based on subjective judgments.

Results in the Future

Time lags between effort and action steps and results also complicate appraisals for control purposes. The effectiveness of an advertising campaign cannot be judged for some time. Nor can the increases in sales which improvements in products cause be evaluated in the short run. The full worth of the improvements will show up only over a longer period of time. It is, therefore, not clear for a long time whether the original action was effective or not. The longer it takes before performance can be appraised, the more difficult it is to control by means of taking corrective actions.

One should not, however, give up on appraising difficult to appraise work just because it can't be done perfectly. Actions leading to goal achievement in the future have to be taken even though little accomplishment will show in the short run.

Comparisons

No matter how managers control, whether by supervision, by telephoning, or by reports, the essence of appraisal in control is through *comparisons*. First, it is necessary to try to find out what is going on. Then comparisons can be made with what was supposed to happen, or to what happened yesterday, or to what is happening elsewhere. These comparisons unearth unusual situations and allow managers to focus their attention on them.

Individual Numbers. Almost always, reports of what is going on are reports of facts, expressed as individual numbers. But reports of individual figures standing alone do not reveal much about how well things are going. Their magnitude is known but their meaning and their effects cannot be appreciated until they are related to other relevant data. Each piece of data needs another piece of data to compare it to.

Statements of hours worked, payrolls, pieces produced, or sales, do not, by themselves, provide any basis for action. They do not tell a manager whether productivity is high or low, and whether products are selling well, etc.

Let us consider the following information about last month's business:

Accounts receivable billings for the month	$62,000
Sales of new products	33,000
Customers paid us	71,000
Number of new orders received	30
Number of calls made by salesmen	147
Standard hours of work produced in Department A	9,000

No one can get any real meaning out of this list. A manager looking at these figures cannot tell from them whether the company had a good month nor whether it reached its goals. Nor can he tell whether he should do something about any of the items.

First-Degree Comparisons. To evaluate an event or fact, it must be related to other facts or events. Figures begin to take on meaning and to tell a manager something when he makes comparisons. It is necessary to express data as totals, averages, ratios, proportions, and per cent differences.

But even totals, averages, ratios, etc., are only steps toward meaningful comparisons. Most of these are only "first-degree" comparisons which do not help much.

Let us make first-degree ratio comparisons out of the list and look at it again:

The average collection period for receivables was 64 days.

New product sales came to 12 per cent of total sales.

The average cost per salesman's call was $27.32.

We received 30 new orders from 114 sales department bids on contracts.

During the last period, department A produced at 112 per cent of standard efficiency.

Every item in this list is a ratio, a first-degree comparison between two things. But the list is still not very helpful. A manager still cannot tell which figures reveal satisfactory performance and which reveal unsatisfactory conditions and which call for remedial actions.

Second- and Third-Degree Comparisons. In order to unearth the significance of these numbers it is necessary to go on to second- and third-degree comparisons. Second- and third-degree comparisons are comparisons of ratios to ratios, etc. With such comparisons, a manager begins to get

clues which tell him whether his organization is doing well or not and where it is headed. Expenditures should be compared to sales. Department A's should be compared to that of department B. And yesterday's ratio should be compared to today's, etc.

Trends should be shown — there should be figures showing where the organization is headed. The movement of ratios, week by week, should be watched. Products, departments, geographical areas, and actual performance against goals should be compared.

Returning to our illustrative list of ratios: it shows that the average collection period last month was 64 days (on the average, customers paid their bills 64 days after their purchases). This was up for the fourth consecutive month. The trade association reports that, for the industry, this figure is standing still at 56 days. The figure 64 is now revealed as being unusual and the manager now knows that something is probably wrong here and the situation needs looking into.

The manager might also look at new orders. The company got 30 new orders from making 114 quotations, a ratio of 26 percent. This ratio has been slowly creeping up from 20 percent a year ago. This is probably healthy, yet it is not healthy if the sales department has not been quoting on as many jobs as it should. If the company used to get 20 percent orders from 200 quotations, that, 40 orders, was better than 30 orders, even though 30 is 26 percent from 114 quotations. Maybe the sales manager is not bidding on enough jobs.

There is no need to go on. But the figures can come alive and tell managers a good bit if they are used correctly.

Lack of Comparability

In order to compare and appraise, it is necessary to have numbers which are comparable. Numbers can be misleading and can imply a comparability which does not exist.

Changes in the "product mix," for example, upset comparability. If a factory department is making more eight cubic-foot refrigerators today and fewer of the six-foot size, the average labor cost per refrigerator almost has to go up. Yet the supervisor may be controlling his costs as well as he did before.

When a department makes several kinds and sizes of any product, product mix changes, all of which affect operating costs, are going all the time. Superiors have to be careful when they try to interpret overall cost per unit figures. They need to try to find out if the changes in the numbers are from better (or worse) performance or whether they come from product-mix changes.

Summary

Control deals with directing the organizational sub-units and with implementing plans. It is a two-sided activity. In its surveillance function, control watches over and gets reports of what goes on. Then it compares what goes on with what should go on and starts remedial action whenever it is needed in order to try to get the organization back on the track.

Control falls short, however, of guaranteeing desired results. All it can do is to try to keep the organization moving in the direction of goal accomplishment. The performance of subordinates should always, therefore, be judged on a relative basis. The measure of a job well done is not always in terms of end-goal accomplishment. Rather the measure is in progress toward goals, or reasonable achievement in spite of difficulties. Although appraisal is an imprecise process, it is a necessary activity in order for control to operate because unsatisfactory performance needs to be detected so that remedial actions will be undertaken.

Review Questions

1. Would it be proper to say that a man has controlled his department's work if he does not reach his objectives? Discuss.
2. The text takes the position that cost control is almost the essence of true control. How is this justified? Is it true? Discuss.
3. How does control operate in non-business operations? How can it be improved? Discuss.
4. What part does surveillance play in control? How can surveillance accomplish anything?

5. Are delegation and control opposites? Isn't control just getting matters back into the superior's hands after a delegation?

6. If it is truly possible to control before the fact, why not always do so and avoid no end of trouble? Discuss.

7. The text reports that it is actually quite difficult for a superior to judge the accomplishments of subordinates. Discuss these difficulties and how to overcome them.

8. What effect does affluence have on the effectiveness of control in operation? Discuss.

Questions for Analysis and Discussion

1. A company president said, "I don't know whether my organization is good, bad or indifferent because I don't know with what to compare it." Should not a company get rid of a president who does not know whether his organization is good or not?

2. The general manager, speaking of his foremen, said, "I have no idea what they are doing today and I care less." Is this a proper attitude on his part? Why?

3. "In the Army, the Captain thinks that he is running his Company, but it is really the top sergeant who runs the show." Is this really so? Should it be so? Discuss.

4. How can a manager tell a good engineer from a poor one? Or a good supervisor? How can he identify a good subordinate? And if he cannot tell who is doing a good job, how can he control?

5. In a bank, what is output? Is it lending money? Or refusing loans to doubtful credit risks? What is output in a department store? Is it selling merchandise? Or buying merchandise? Or advertising? How can a superior control if he doesn't know what output is?

6. Can performance effectiveness be evaluated without defining the amount of resources required to produce a given level of output? Discuss.

7. A number of years ago, several officials of companies making electrical products went to jail for violating the law by conspiring and fixing prices. Some were from General Electric where the president had, every year for three years, issued instructions forbidding this practice. Why wouldn't the control procedures of these companies have prevented this?

8. How can what managers do not do be measured? Earlier in the text, it was reported that Macy's Toledo LaSalle & Koch store had not put a satellite store in nearby Ann Arbor, Michigan. How remiss were L & K's managers? What information should Macy's managers want to have if they asked and tried to answer this question?

9. How might an administrator evaluate the sins of omission of subordinates? Money not spent for research or for new machines does not show up as opportunities neglected. Neither does the sales campaign that a manager did not put on. How can performance against potentials be appraised?

10. The company's president has decided that the company's salesmen are not very productive. What information would have caused him to think this? What might he try to do about it? (Do not answer, "try to improve it." That is an insufficient answer.)

11. The Bono Company had seen its sales slide off bit by bit for four years. Profits disappeared. The executive vice president put on a cost-reduction drive and fired three hundred office people. At the stockholders' meeting held a month later, a stockholder demanded that the vice president resign. "If firing three hundred employees is now suddenly necessary," asked the stockholder, "what has the vice president been doing for the last several years?" Isn't this evidence that he has been doing a poor job?

12. After Paul McCracken, who was Chairman of the Council of Economic Advisors under President Nixon during his first term, resigned, he said in a speech that, "The Federal budget is out of control." What does this mean? Could it happen in a business organization? If yes, who should do what to remedy the situation?

Case 23-1   The Specious Performance Record at Rocktown Manufacturing Co.

When Stanley Horne was promoted to the home office of the Rocktown Manufacturing Company after having been in charge of Rocktown's Kelwood, Ohio, plant, it was partly because of his consistent record, over four years, of holding down costs at the Kelwood plant.

Horne's successor, Frank Taylor, naturally felt a need to continue Horne's record. Within a month, however, a large milling machine had broken down, requiring two weeks to repair. The following month, the plant's forge had to be taken out of service when its hydraulic system failed, almost injuring the operator. At this point, Taylor asked the maintenance foreman to produce the maintenance records for all of the major machines in the plant.

After inspecting the records, Taylor realized how Horne had kept his overhead costs down (apparently he had undermaintained the equipment and had done almost no preventive repairs). Taylor did not know exactly how to proceed from this point. He felt, judging from Horne's promotion, that keeping repair costs down was critical, yet it looked as if several thousands of dollars would have to be spent to overhaul practically all of the plant's machines or else there would be still more machines going down like the miller and the forge.

Nature of Control

- This case suggests that it is unwise to undermaintain. On the other hand, is it wise to let the auto mechanic fix everything he says the car needs?
- This case also suggests that Horne was very fortunate in not having costly breakdowns, yet the month he left, things started to go badly. Assuming that events actually occurred as the case relates them, should Horne's superiors not have recognized what was happening and judged Horne accordingly?

Case 23-2   Rubinoff's Controls at Holiday Inns

David Rubinoff, as Holiday Inns' largest franchisee, operates some fifty Holiday Inns, largely in Canada but with others in the Caribbean, England, and Portugal. Rubinoff's Holiday Inns are a little more sumptuous than others of this chain and represent a greater investment per room.

Therefore, in order to be successful, Rubinoff believes that he needs to control costs closely. He has built a planning, marketing, and advertising organization which parallels that of the parent company. But, in cost controls, he has gone farther and has developed his own system of cost controls. He uses a "report system" which keeps a tight control over the financial operations of every inn in his chain.

Under his system, the manager of every inn in the chain is required to submit reports — sometimes daily — to the main office's accounting department, covering all aspects of their operational costs. The reports are analyzed to detect any variances from budget and are compared for performance. Thus if the costs of one inn for, say, food and maintenance, rise sharply or appear to be out of proportion with the rest of the system, the home office will work with the innkeeper to try to rectify the problem.

In addition, the management performances of all of the system's innkeepers are compared, as are the results of the various district directors and other executives up the line to the main office, in order to spotlight achievers and to pinpoint individuals whose operations have fallen behind.

- How can an innkeeper who is trying to operate under such close controls get to exercise any ingenuity of his own or respond to local conditions?
- In the evaluation process, how can such close control make allowances for local conditions? Is innkeeping the same in Lisbon, London, and Toronto?

Endnotes

1. Reported in *Forbes,* 15 March 1974, pp. 38ff.
2. As reported in, "The One-Two Punch That Shook Olin," *Fortune,* 5 June 1978, pp. 120ff.

Suggested Supplementary Readings

Hinrichs, John R. *Practical Management for Productivity.* Van Nostrand Reinhold/Work in America Institute, 1978.

Jarrett, Jeffrey E. "Hospital Capital Expenditure Controls: Their Desired and Expected Results." *Michigan Business Review,* September 1979, pp. 20–26.

Lane, Robert E. *Administering and Controlling Plant Operations.* Prentice-Hall, 1979.

Lynn, Laurence E., Jr., and John M. Seidl. "Bottom-Line Management for Public Agencies." *Harvard Business Review,* January-February 1977, pp. 144–159.

Objectives of Chapter
Twenty-Four

1. To consider the several ways available to managers for controlling organizational activities and to consider the merits of each.

2. To examine the inherent fundamental internal factors which are always operating to hamper managerial efforts to control their organizations.

3. To analyze the controllability of different kinds of work, such as staff work as compared to line work.

4. To consider the matter of using strong versus soft controls and the strengths and weaknesses of each of these philosophies of control.

Control in Operation

The number of office workers grows at the rate of 5.5 percent a year even when the work to be done remains unchanged.
Parkinson's Law

If Parkinson's Law is true, and there is some evidence that it is, then obviously, organizational controls, so far as the number of office employees is concerned, are not as effective as they should be. Control tries to keep Parkinson's Law from operating.

Methods of Controlling

Managers have several methods available to them for trying to control the work of their subordinates.

1. Among these methods is direct supervision, which can be used when people are nearby. Where it can be used, this method is, perhaps, the most effective method.
2. When subordinates are farther away, superiors have to rely on their subordinates more and to use indirect methods of control. Here there are two alternatives. The first of these is to try to make the subordinates into more capable managers by training and coaching them. The other alternative is here called the "competent man" theory. Using this method, a manager tries to control by choosing capable people to become subordinate managers but without emphasizing their training.
3. Superiors also, as they try to control, rely on reports. This is the most common method of all. Reports are discussed in Chapter 25.
4. Business meetings help the control process. They are particularly useful as means for passing out information to members of geographically separated units of the organization. When they

come together at a central location they all hear the same information and learn about the operations of the whole organization. When managers meet their peers from other units on a face-to-face basis it helps build cooperation between units.

Control through Direct Supervision

Much the most common method for trying to control the work of organizational members, so far as direct subordinates are concerned, is direct supervision. The manager works closely enough with his subordinates so that he knows rather well what is happening and he knows when things are going well and when they are not going well. He directs his subordinates and helps them produce the desired accomplishments. Managers influence the activities and behavior of their subordinates through their directions and coaching. This is the most common method of controlling at bottom levels.

Control Through Training

Middle-level subordinate managers often cannot be supervised very well by their superiors by means of face-to-face daily contacts because they are physically separated and work in different buildings or even in different parts of the country. Often, too, they are in charge of specialized activities in subject areas in which the superior is not himself an expert.

Consequently, these managers are more on their own. In such cases, their superior managers have to try to control their work indirectly. One way to do this is to try to make them into capable managers through training, including formal training in courses and seminars. The reasoning is that if they learn management fundamentals and how to apply them, they will be better managers. Control is therefore accomplished because the training has made the subordinates into more capable people.

The "Competent Man" Theory

Another approach to controlling the activities of organizational sub-units is here called the "competent man" theory. This theory uses extreme delegation to competent men or women with a minimum of controls.

This philosophy is followed by many managers in America and is reported to be even more commonly used in England. Derek Pugh reports that, "The average American manager is subjected to considerably more control than his British opposite number."[1]

The competent man theory relies heavily, almost wholly, on the idea that the subordinate is a capable person. The superior more or less stands back. He does only a minimum of supervising and he does not get detailed nor frequent reports of what is going on in the subordinate's area of responsibility.

The competent man theory is a little different from developing capable subordinates by means of training, coaching, and exposing subordinates to varied job experiences. The difference lies in the lack of emphasis on *developing* subordinates and causing them to acquire competence. The superior feels little or no obligation to train subordinates; rather the theory largely overlooks how people acquire competence.

The theory more or less implicitly assumes that a competent person will be good at anything he does. There is a tendency for managers who are impressed with a person's capabilities in one area to inpute equal capabilities to him in other areas. ("He's a good man.") Unfortunately, such capabilities in other areas do not always exist. The important thing is whether or not the subordinate has capability relevant to the job to be done.

Because a manager using the competent man theory operates with loose controls, he does not meet with his subordinates very often, nor does he get frequent and detailed reports, nor does he do much appraising of accomplishments. Consequently, he will not really know whether his subordinates' performances are satisfactory or not. A subordinate can perform ineffectively for a good while before his superior finds out that this is so.

Indirect and loose controls are not, however, so inadequate as the preceding discussion suggests. This is because

1. The subordinate will sometimes prove to be competent, so all is well. Left to his own devices he will do a good job.

2. The competent man philosophy allows for quick decisions. The subordinate is at the point of action and can go ahead with little or no time-consuming checking with the home office.

3. It is not always true that the higher-level manager, even with specialized staff at his disposal, can do any better than the subordinate. The higher-level manager is not himself superior in competence in every area which he supervises, so his closer attention to a troubled area, which he would give if he had less confidence in his subordinate, might not be of much help.

In such a case, whether he uses close controls and detailed reports or whether he uses looser indirect controls relying more on the competence of his subordinates is somewhat immaterial. The manager actually has to rely on the subordinate regardless of how he would like to control performance.

Control Through Reports

In almost all organizations, written reports are the main control technique.

They report on the performance of every minor department. Reports for major departments are then made up by combining the reports of their subsidiary departments. And finally, the reports for major departments are combined into performance reports for the whole organization.

Reports also show the performance of product lines, geographical areas, or of any other important aspect of the organization's operations. Reports are so important that a considerable portion of Chapter 25 is devoted to them.

Ramifications of Control

Control has to operate in organizations as they carry out their work. Operations are dynamic and control needs to be flexible enough to continue to be effective under changing conditions. Control, although it has the objective of controlling performance, has to operate through people so reports have to deal with the responsibility areas of specific people. Control has also to recognize that work loads vary and performance needs to be judged with these variations in mind.

Control and Single Responsibility

Control works best when *one* manager is supposed to get certain work done. Superiors need to try to design reports which cover the work under *each* subordinate manager's jurisdiction so that they can see how well each one is functioning. If higher managers can trace responsibility, then they will know who should get credit when things go well and who needs help when things go poorly.

Unfortunately, responsibility can rarely be traced to one manager and one manager only, because so many things are

the results of the efforts of several people. Important decisions are usually group decisions and important accomplishments are usually group accomplishments. Sometimes hundreds of people contribute to a plan's success or its failure. A large organization tends to be a galaxy of specialists. So much joint effort is involved that responsibility cannot be nailed down.

This weakens control because higher managers can't fix responsibilities. They can't even, with certainty, tell who their best qualified subordinate managers are. And, if things go poorly, the top administrators can't quite say who should do what to improve the situation.

At bottom levels, the effects of one person's work are usually not very far reaching and often it is possible to trace responsibility to one single individual. If two holes in a piece of metal are too far apart, either the drawing was wrong or the holes were drilled in the wrong places. In either case, it would probably be possible to find out who was responsible and to straighten things out.

The Organizational Work-Multiplier

Control tries to produce the desired accomplishments at the lowest possible cost. Here the manager has to contend with what might be called the "organizational work-multiplier."

The organizational work multiplier concept holds that, for every extra level in the organization's hierarchy, a certain amount of extra work is added. This is the extra work caused by employees needing to talk to each other about their work and the passing out of directions and getting back reports. It is the extra work which grows out of interactions between people and between groups.

To see how the organizational work-multiplier works, let us assume that one individual can do a certain amount of work. And suppose that this work grows to five times the first amount (see Figure 24-1). It would seem that five people could do it. But, actually, because of the extra work which creeps in, it will take six employees to do the work. (A multiplier of 20 percent is just assumed here. The actual multiplier could be larger or smaller.)

Some of the extra work generated by the organizational work-multiplier is caused by up and down communications. Besides this, lateral communications, integrative relationships, and slippages also grow.

This example can be carried one step farther by thinking of the total amount of work growing again by five times. The fundamental work load is now twenty-five times what it first was. What the six employees did in the first stage now takes thirty employees, *plus 20 percent more!* All told, it takes thirty-six people to do twenty-five times the original individual's work.

It is obviously impossible to avoid all of this extra work, but there is a good bit of truth to the statement that people make work for each other. When two or more people meet to talk about something, the multiplier is operating, because the talk is extra work. Managers should try to hold their organization's multiplier to as low a ratio as possible.

Work Ebbs and Flows and the "Ratcheting Effect."

As time passes, the ebbs and flows of work loads in middle levels tend to work like a ratchet so far as the number of employees is concerned. When loads go up, so does the work force. But when the load goes down, the work force tends to stay the same, with the employees' spare time being taken up by less urgent work which was not done during the rush period. Then the work load goes up again, and so does the work force. And again there is no work force reduction when the work load declines. Before long, the middle-level organization is considerably larger than it really needs to be.

To counteract this ratcheting effect, managers should try to hold to some kind of ratio between bottom- and middle-level employment. Probably middle-level employment should move up or down with bottom-level employment but not proportionally.

Organizational Slack

James Miller, a college student, was pleased to get a summer job in the nearby automobile factory. His work was somewhat varied since he had no regular assignment. Most days he filled in along the assembly line for someone who was absent that day. One day, he fastened left front headlights into place, another day he attached rear bumpers. Some days he worked out of the stockroom delivering materials to production workers.

One day when he arrived and checked in, his boss told him to "get lost," meaning, keep out of sight (but not meaning go home). There were only a few absentees that day and no stockroom work to do so the boss had no work for Miller to do.

To his surprise, Miller found out that he wasn't alone in his "get-lost" assignment and he found out from the others that this was not an unusual occurrence.

Absenteeism had been running so high (10 percent or more on Mondays and Fridays, and 8 percent or more on other days) that the company had been following a practice of being over-staffed. It had been found that it took 108 employees on the payroll in order to keep at least 100 employees on the job. Then, on days when absenteeism was low, there wasn't enough work for all of them to do.

Absenteeism is not the only factor which creates a need for organizational slack. Departmental workloads vary, yet it is

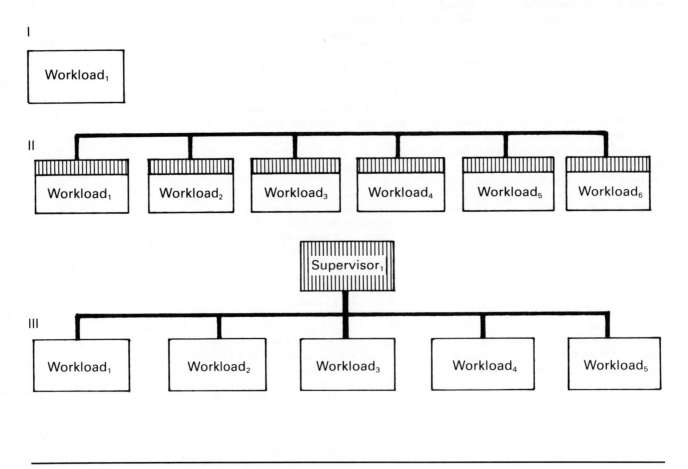

Figure 24-1
The operation of the organizational work-multiplier. Section II depicts the need for six men to do the equivalent of five times the work done by the one man depicted in section I. The shaded areas of the blocks in section II depicts the part of the time of each man being covered by interactive extra work. Section III shows the same loss in effectiveness. Here again, it takes six men to do five times the work of one man. In section III, the extra work is all shown as making up the workload of a superior of the five subordinates, each doing as much work as the one man in section I.

not feasible to increase and decrease the number of employees with every fluctuation in workloads. It is necessary to have a certain amount of organizational slack and to maintain a workforce large enough to handle average workloads and workloads during vacation periods when over 10 percent of the workforce is on vacation, recognizing that this will be somewhat uneconomical during valleys in workloads. Usually workers won't have to "get lost" during valleys but will be able to do less essential work which gets pushed aside during busy periods. They may also be transferred temporarily to other departments where the current workloads are larger.

The problem of organizational slack is especially pernicious in the case of staff work and in all types of service organizations. One problem is that it is not possible to stockpile services. The calls for service in a city fire department, a taxicab company, or a hospital, are quite irregular, yet it is not possible to give the employees fill-in work in all slack periods. Nor is it practicable to reduce the size of individual departments to the size where they will always be busy on essential work. The control process needs to allow them a certain amount of slack.

This complicates the job of controlling because it is hard to know just what amount of slack to allow for, while still judging a department head to be doing an effective job.[2]

The "Backlog Syndrome"

A century ago when Frederick Taylor was an apprentice at the Cramp Shipyard in Philadelphia, the incoming orders sometimes slowed down. With layoffs in sight, the men slowed down in order to keep their jobs from finishing.

The owner would go through the plant to see if everyone was busy, but he had no good way of telling except by the amount of noise. At such times, it was young Taylor's job (an assignment made by his fellow workers, not by management) to go around behind the boiler and hammer on it, thus making a lot of noise and impressing the boss with how busy everybody was.[3]

This stretching out of work is the "backlog syndrome" or the "contractor's dilemma." When companies work on large contract jobs, such as putting an oil pipe line across Alaska, this is just as much a dilemma

today as it was in Taylor's day. As backlogs of future work shrink, or as the one large contract approaches its end, and there is no other work in sight, work slows down and almost stops.

It was reported that the United States Department of Commerce had a little trouble of this sort during the taking of the 1980 census. Some of the temporary workers hired just for the census intentionally left loose ends which needed later checking over and which kept their jobs going longer.

Fortunately, most organizations do not have many backlog syndrome problems because only in serious depressions does the backlog of work ahead almost disappear. But in construction, shipbuilding, and airplane manufacturing, it is sometimes a real problem. Managers need to have good controls to counteract this tendency and keep the work moving.

Group Restrictions on Output

The power of informal groups was discussed in Chapter 19. It will be recalled that, particularly at bottom levels, groups of workers sometimes decide how much work they will do, and no matter what management tries to get them to do, they won't do any more.

Such restrictions by informal groups are facts of life and they limit the effectiveness of the attempts by managers to control operations. Managers can accomplish results only within the limits permitted by group restrictions.[4]

Controlling the Work and Costs of Staff Departments

It is just about as hard to judge the work of staff departments in business organizations as it is to judge the work of the preacher who was mentioned in Chapter 23.

The work of most staff departments is similar in that it is most difficult to appraise accurately and hence to control.

Since very little of the work of staff departments can be measured or counted, it might seem that high-level managers ought to give up and not to try to control the costs of such staffs. But service is not always good service and whether it is good service or not, it often costs too much. Since uncontrolled work seems always to cost more than controlled work, managers should try to control staff costs even though they recognize that there is a strong element of subjective judgment in their appraisals.

One reason why staff service sometimes costs too much is that it is sometimes too good, and is done too thoroughly. When business is slow, staff personnel often use the extra time to do their work very thoroughly (too thoroughly, in fact). They investigate every alternative to every problem, however trivial, fully.

A "civil service mentality" seems to operate here, meaning that there is a dedication to serve but without raising the question of the cost of serving versus its value. Staff people usually take pride in their work and want to do it well; sometimes they do it too well. Often they seem unable to distinguish between necessary things and things which are "nice to have" but which are costly and not very necessary.

Value and Cost of Staff and Service Work. As we said in Chapter 10, people nearly always seem to expect service staff departments to give good and fast service all the time. They are quick to complain about poor service. So, and not unnaturally, in response to such demands, and also in response to their innate desire to serve well, staff departments try to expand and to give everybody good service.

Service organizations live in a similar world. Everyone wants better hospital care, better schools, better police protection, etc. Then, after they get it they complain about the costs.

A manager should try to get his staff department heads to think about both whether they are doing satisfactory jobs *and* whether what they are doing is costing too much. When the personnel manager asks for $50,000 to remodel the cafeteria, perhaps he should be reminded that it will take half a million dollars of sales to generate the profits needed to pay for the remodeling. Probably he does not normally think this way, but getting him to think about value and cost relationships should help.

Staff Responses to Pressure Budgeting. It has been mentioned in other places that higher-level managers need to be careful and not put too much pressure on staff departments to make individual control ratios look good because there are so many ways for a staff manager to produce a good ratio by cutting down on the quality of the service provided. Some of these reductions may not be economical. It would be unwise for the personnel department just to hire the first person who comes along or for the purchasing department to stop shopping around for the best buys just because their budgets are tight.

Although it is a crude method, managers sometimes try to keep staff costs in check by just not allowing a staff department to hire a replacement when anyone leaves unless his job is proved to be essential. The department head has to make a strong case of need or he gets no replacement. This method is not a perfect solution to the problem, however, because staff department heads soon learn to make strong cases regardless of true need. In fact, they usually sincerely feel that their need is great.

Managers actually set the service level of staff departments when they set their budgets. They usually try to set budgets at levels which do not allow the staffs to "overserve." But, in fact, higher-level managers usually do not have very good evidence about where this point is. They don't always get staff budgets set at the right cut-off points. Unfortunately, the difficulty of not being able to set budgets at the ideal cut-off point does not relieve them from the need to set such cut-off points. They have to do the best they can.

Pros and Cons of Strong Controls

Nearly all social scientists differ from a great many business managers about control. Most business managers try to control the costs of the making of products or the rendering of services directly. They try to use "hard" controls. In contrast, nearly all social scientists feel that managers should pay more attention to weak or "soft" goals, to creating a healthy atmosphere of mutual cooperation among the organization's people. They feel that if soft goals come first, then effective operations (reaching hard goals) will follow.

Possible Harmful Effects of Strong Controls

Strong pressure on subordinates to produce results usually causes some kind of reaction on their part. Pressure to accomplish "hard goals" (meeting production goals, low cost objectives, budgets, etc.) assumes that the resulting actions on the part of subordinates will be the kinds of actions which are likely to lead to improved results. Sometimes, though, the reverse happens and subordinates do things to meet goals which actually harm the organization's accomplishments.

Sacrifice of Forward-Looking Work. Subordinate managers under pressure to make a good showing sometimes respond by reducing the money spent today for tomorrow's good. In merchandising, this could mean their reducing market research. In manufacturing, it could mean cutting down on product development. Normally, control reports will not reveal whether today's reduc-

tions are being made at the expense of tomorrow's good.

Although pressure for short-run accomplishment does tend to result in the over-emphasis of short-run goals, this tendency does not get to operate altogether freely because higher-level managers are fully aware of this danger and try to prevent it from happening. They went through all of this themselves on their way up. They appreciate the need for evaluating the performance of their subordinates on their total performance and not just on good facade performance. Moreover, lower managers usually have enough feeling of responsibility not to do things which hurt the organization's future.

Harm to "Intervening Variables." Certain behavioral scientists, Rensis Likert in particular, feel that pressure controls aimed at hard goal achievement will cause harm to what he called "intervening variables" (attitudes, motivations, perceptions, willingness to cooperate and to help the other fellow, organizational empathy, etc.). Likert feels that this harm will hurt the organization's performance in the future. Unfortunately, the hurt that comes from deteriorating intervening variables takes time, sometimes up to two years, to become apparent. Meanwhile, a higher-level manager might not know that harm has been done.

Strong pressure to meet hard goals probably does do harm to the willingness of department heads to cooperate with and to help the other fellow if this in any way harms a manager's own showing. In the case of staff departments, a busy staff department may become arbitrary about whose work requests it will respond to. It may not listen to the plea of another department that its work is important and consequently do harm to the organization's accomplishments.

Wrong Appraisals of Accomplishments and of Managers. Furthermore, says Likert, short-run producers (who may actually be undermining the organization's long-run good) are wrongly judged to be doing a good job. This misjudgment would be a Type II error as depicted in Figure 24-2. Consequently, the organization would be promoting the wrong people, those who are actually hurting the organization (either by not doing things for the organization's future benefit or by tearing down the value of its human resources) and the organization suffers. The promoted individuals then go on somewhere else in the organization to repeat their good facade work and leave other people to correct the unsatisfactory conditions they generate but leave behind.

Likert argues for better measures of performance. He would like to see better reports developed, reports which would

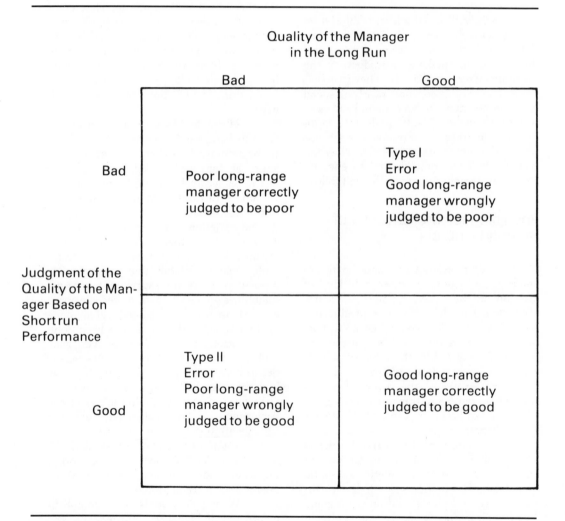

Quality of the Manager
in the Long Run

	Bad	Good
Bad	Poor long-range manager correctly judged to be poor	Type I Error Good long-range manager wrongly judged to be poor
Good	Type II Error Poor long-range manager wrongly judged to be good	Good long-range manager correctly judged to be good

Judgment of the Quality of the Manager Based on Short run Performance

Figure 24-2
Likert's concern is that top managers will make both type I and type II errors (but particularly type II errors) and thus promote the wrong men, to the detriment of the organization in the future.

more truly show the quality of a manager's performance, by including coverage of *all* the variables. The improvement of or the harm to intervening variables would be included along with the accomplishment of hard goals. Unfortunately, such reports appear to be impossible to develop since the effects of actions on intervening variables cannot be isolated and evaluated.

Actually, it is probable that not very many good facade performers escape having to clean up any poor conditions they might create. According to Likert, it takes up to two years for some of the injurious effects to show up. There are just not enough higher jobs to allow very many managers to be promoted within each two-year period. So most good facade managers will still be there when the harmful effects show up. And even the individuals who do get promoted usually get promoted to the next job up the line. If they leave unsatisfactory conditions behind, these conditions are still theirs to clean up.

Admittedly, executive trainee prospects sometimes do move from job to job across departmental lines fast enough to escape having to live with the consequences of possibly unwise decisions. It is also true that higher-level managers' knowing about the possibility of subordinates following unwise short-range goals or of their doing injury to intervening variables is often not enough. Their mental concern over such unwise actions does not keep these things from happening.

Possible Beneficial Effects of Strong Controls

Managers reacting to strong controls by no means always respond by taking actions which are harmful to the organization. Many action responses to strong controls neither tear down Likert's intervening variables nor do they sacrifice long-range good. On the contrary, they build up the intervening variables.

Putting Forward-Looking Work into Proper Perspective. The argument concerning the sacrificing of forward-looking work can easily be overdrawn. It assumes that all jobs have substantial forward-looking content and that all forward-looking work is inherently good. Both assumptions are true only sometimes. There is little need for distant future thinking in mature industries such as making bread.

Nor are forward-looking activities always helpful to the organization. Elsewhere in this book, stories have been told of large losses suffered by some companies. Many of the greatest losses were suffered by companies which looked ahead, took actions, and suffered losses because they misguessed markets, costs, or because of their inability to compete in the new areas. By no means is it always harmful for managers *not* to spend the organization's money on what they believe are forward-looking activities.

Emphasis On Improving the Capabilities of Subordinates. When a subordinate performs unsatisfactorily, a higher-level manager who uses strong controls might very well himself respond by working more closely with the subordinate, coaching him and training him and giving him help so that he can perform better. Such a reaction would build up rather than tear down intervening variables and would contribute to both short- and long-range organizational good.

Still another response to pressure may be that the subordinate does his job as it should be done. A supervisor may want so much to be a "good guy" to his employees that he does not make them measure up. He may let them arrive late, double the length of the coffee break, quit early, and turn out too little work and too poor work. A little pressure often makes him do a better job and make his employees do the same.

Reexamination of Relationships with Environment. Strong pressure to improve may also result in the reconsideration of economic matters as they relate to the environment and in the making of new choices of actions to follow. We reported earlier about how, in the mid 1970s, American Airlines, as a result of pressure caused by several years of losing money, cut out several money-losing flight routes.

In another company, an ice cream making company, declining profits caused the Board of Directors to insist that the managers do something and to take strong action.

As a result of this pressure, the managers called in a consulting firm. The consultants analyzed the different markets for ice cream (summer road-side ice cream stores, supermarkets, hotels, restaurants, etc.) and found which were the most profitable, which were growing, etc., and drew up plans to push harder in the areas of greatest promise. More salesmen were added in those areas, and sales and profits soared. At the same time low profit items were dropped.

Another reaction to the pressure in this same company was to train middle-level managers to recognize the profit impact of their decisions. Before this, they had not known.

As a result of all of these actions, profits doubled. This reaction to pressure produced improved organizational performance.

Summary of Effects of Strong Controls

Short-range improvements can, as our discussion indicates, often be effectuated without interfering with long-range goals or harming intervening variables. And, although the results from pressure control can be either harmful or helpful, there are so many kinds of possible beneficial actions that it would seem that there is a high probability that the beneficial results will outweigh the harmful results. Managers should not forget, however, that there can be harmful effects and that these could outweigh the beneficial effects.

Summary

Intriguing though the idea is to control the activities of organizations by means of using standards and goals, these methods are just not suitable for many of the activities of organizations. It is therefore often necessary to use controls which depend largely on subordinates being competent people. Higher-level managers rely on the abilities of subordinates as well as on their sense of organizational empathy and responsibility to see what needs doing and then to go ahead and do whatever needs doing.

Control should be heavily oriented toward cost control because this economizes on the organization's resources. This is necessary because costs always tend to creep up, thus eroding away the organization's resources. This is particularly important in staff departments where the work is so hard to measure. Perhaps the best that can be done here is to hope that the heads of such departments will keep in mind the cost-value relationships of their work. They should try to serve the rest of the organization but to do it while remembering the need to do it in an economical fashion.

Some managers have faith in strong controls. It is dangerous, however, to push too hard for current performance lest subordinate managers become short-range decision makers and lest they do things which will hurt the morale and empathy of the organization's employees. This danger is real but is not always serious. Managers under pressure to accomplish often respond by doing things which help rather than harm the organization. As they exercise control, higher-level managers should try to watch how their controls are working and try to have the beneficial effects outweigh the harmful effects.

Review Questions

1. What alternative methods do managers have for trying to control their organizations? Compare and contrast them.
2. How is the "competent man" theory supposed to work? What are its strengths and weaknesses?
3. What position does the text take about single and double or multiple responsibility? Which is better? If there is a problem here, what can be done about it?
4. How can a manager control the work of his organization if he can't tell for sure who his best managers are?
5. What is the "organizational work-multiplier?" What has it to do with control?
6. What is organizational slack? What should a manager do about it?
7. The text offers certain suggestions with respect to controlling staff costs. Discuss them.
8. Managers sometimes use pressure controls to accomplish "hard" goals. What are these and what effects may they be expected to produce?

Questions for Analysis and Discussion

1. A book on organization says, " The superior must be willing to create and to maintain a realistic environment of freedom from interference around the subordinate. This means that he must adopt an attitude of 'hands off' once the grant of freedom is made. Also he must create such an administrative structure that the freedoms of different individuals do not clash, and that orderly relationships will evolve. This means that he must provide an adequate system of information for the making of decisions. He becomes, literally, a resource to those below." Isn't this carrying delegation too far? How can a superior control operations if he delegates this way?

2. The Eastern Railroad set up an economic research department and, since this was a new activity for it, its managers retained a professor of economics and statistics from the nearby university to help them train the research department's people by working with them one day a week.

   The department's work went along very well and its personnel soon became proficient in all of the kinds of work on which the professor could offer help. After some six months he had little more to offer so he asked the research department's head when he should stop coming. "Oh," he said, "You don't stop coming, you are on the payroll." Discuss.

3. Suppose that a manager decides that costs are somewhat out of control. What evidence would have made him think so? And how does he know that it is so?

4. It is almost impossible to trace the parenthood of a failure because no one wants to be blamed. It is perhaps even harder to trace the parenthood of a success because everyone wants to claim credit for it. If these statements are true, how can superiors control anything? How can they even tell who their most capable subordinates are?

5. Can a company cost control itself into a profit? Can it build a healthy company on the basis of cost control?

6. "We go through this every four or five years. They tell us that profits are down so we can't hire replacements when people leave." Does prosperity undermine control? And, isn't it easier to reduce costs when sales are down? Then the message gets through more easily and more effectively. In other words, isn't having cost control drives when sales are down the way things ought to operate?

7. A manager says that refusing to allow staff departments to hire replacements as a method for controlling costs is a stupid way to try to control costs. Industrial engineers don't *cost* money, they *save* money. What better suggestions might be offered?

8. A retiring university financial vice president said, "If we had all the money we thought we needed, it would mean that someone had run out of imagination." Is this the way service workers feel? How can the costs of service work ever be controlled if this is the way they feel?

9. In the discussion of organizational slack, it was indicated that under some conditions, managers should keep their organizations overstaffed. What are the implications of this on managerial controls?

10. When objectives conflict, how does a subordinate know which to put first? Should budgets be taken more seriously than schedules? What should a foreman do whose superintendent tells him, "It is your job to keep costs down, but don't forget the Simmons job, keep it moving." What if he would have to have his employees work overtime at extra costs to get this order out on time? How do such conflicts affect control?

11. Wouldn't it be a good idea just to cut 5 to 10 percent off the office payroll every three or four years? Discuss.

12. "Some people like to be pushed and feel better being given a stiff goal to work toward. Then they feel elated when they accomplish it." Is this so? If it is so, then what about all of the objection to the use of hard goals?

Organizations in Action: Controlling

13. "In my experience in government work, and in my present capacity as an administrator of a large hospital, I have concluded that there is no incentive whatever in either case for anyone to save money. Everyone just wants more of everything." How can a manager who would like to control costs go about doing it?

Case 24-1　The Organization's Hatchet Man

"Every organization needs to have a good strong action man as the second or third in command. He needs to be someone who will knock heads together when they need it and who will not hesitate to fire someone when that is needed. He can do the organization's hatchet work.

"Furthermore, that is just what our organization needs right now only we need him at the top and we have just such a man in Joe Bannerman. I vote for making him president."

So spoke one of the outside board of directors at the meeting of directors called to decide what to do in the company's present crisis.

· Is such a person an asset to an organization? Is he likely to do the organization more harm than good?
· Should he be the number one man? If not, how can his natural progression to the number one spot be prevented?
· If he is the second or third in command in a company, how can he really serve the whole organization since he has no power other than in his own chain of command?

Case 24-2　Belloc and the New Manager

Douglas McGregor told this story as being told to him by a union agent: "A new manager appeared in the textile mill. He came into the weave room the day he arrived. He walked directly over to the agent and said, 'Are you Belloc?' The agent acknowledged that he was. The manager said, "I am the new manager here. When I manage a mill, I run it. Do you understand? The agent nodded, and then waved his hand. The workers, intently watching this encounter, shut down every loom in the room immediately. The agent turned to the manager and said, "All right, go ahead and run it."
· Although this case sounds most unlikely, it could have happened. In many labor contracts, there is a provision which binds the union not to foster wildcat strikes, and if a wildcat strike occurs (a "wildcat" strike is one in violation of the contract), this provision calls for the union's officials to help

stop it and get the employees back to work. Belloc's action would be a clear violation of such a contract provision and the company could sue the union for the loss caused by the shutdown. And, if Belloc were an employee of the company, he could be fired.

· Supposing that the labor contract in this case contained such a provision, then what?

· Discuss this situation, aside from any labor contract considerations.

Case 24-3 The Anti-Productivity Attitude at Mills Appliance

In the last seven years, the profits of the Mills Appliance Company had fallen from 11.4 to 0.3 percent on the investment. Employment had fallen from 2,000 to 1,400 at its Philadelphia plant (the company's total employment was 5,300 at last count).

The president of the company sent out a four-page letter to the Philadelphia employees aimed at altering an "antiproductivity" attitude there. The president said that costs would have to come down or the plant would probably have to be closed.

· Suppose that, in this situation, a new manager is put in charge of this factory. What should he do?

· Which ideas in this chapter might be of help to him?

Endnotes

1. "The Measurement of Organization Structures," by Derek S. Pugh, *Organizational Dynamics*, Spring 1973, pp. 19–34.
2. See Bourgeois, L. J., "On the Measurement of Organizational Slack," *Academy of Management Review*, January 1981, pages 29-39.
3. Taylor's experiences as an apprentice are recounted in, *Frederick W. Taylor* by Frank B. Copley (Macmillan, 1923), vol. 1, page 493.
4. At bottom levels, unions sometimes set output ceilings on jobs and impose fines on employees who "overproduce." In the United States, their right to do this has been upheld by the Supreme Court, so these are very real restrictions. On the other hand, it will be recalled that in Chapter 3, Robert Dubin was quoted as having found that worker groups were by no means united on such matters as holding back on work.

Suggested Supplementary Readings

Successful and unsuccessful control in five companies.

American Airlines:
"Competitive, Streamlined Management Mark Style of American Airlines" (An interview with Albert V. Casey, Chairman of the Board at American Airlines), *MBA Executive,* April/May 1978, pp. 1ff.

ELTRA (Formerly Electric Autolite):
"In the Grip of 'Hands-On' Management," by Arthur M. Louis, *Fortune,* March 1977, pp. 170ff.

W.T. Grant (Chain of Retail Variety Stores):
"W.T. Grant's Last Days — As seen from Store 1192," by Rush Loving, Jr., *Fortune,* April 1976, pp. 108ff.

Singer (Sewing Machines):
"How the Directors Kept Singer Stitched Together," by Patricia Hough, *Fortune,* December 1975, pp. 100ff.

United Airlines:
"An Interview With Edward Carlson" (Chairman of the Board of United Airlines), *Organizational Dynamics,* Spring 1979, pp. 49–62.

Objectives of Chapter Twenty-Five

1. To emphasize the importance of communications and to consider the reasons why poor communications so often occur.
2. To look at the communications systems and see how information gets into the system and how information flows operate.
3. To note how the reports used in the information system become, themselves, motivators to action and to consider how to keep them from motivating wrong actions.
4. To consider budgets and their use in control as well as considering the typical difficulties which often impair their use.

Communication Systems and Control
Reports

If it can be misunderstood,
it will be misunderstood.
Murphy's Law of Communications

Pearl Harbor was the United States' worst military defeat. In one half hour on the morning of December 7, 1941, Japanese airplanes, in a surprise aerial attack on the Pearl Harbor base in Hawaii, sank or damaged severely, more than half of the American Pacific fleet of warships and two hundred airplanes as well. Thirty-three hundred American sailors and soldiers lost their lives and thirteen hundred more were wounded.

And all because of a communication failure. *Ten days earlier* the high command in Washington had sent word to the commanders in the Pacific that, *"This dispatch is considered to be a war warning, an aggressive move by Japan is to be expected in the next few days. Assume an effective deployment and expect hostile action at any moment."*

Yet through an incredible mix-up and delay in encoding this message, transmitting to Hawaii, decoding it and transmitting it up through several military echelons, the Pacific commanders did not receive this message until several hours *after* the Pearl Harbor attack.[1]

Had the message gotten through and been acted upon, the Japanese attack on Pearl Harbor would probably have failed and the subsequent four years of war in the Pacific might have been averted.

Fortunately, such critical misunderstandings do not occur very often but the fact that they occur even on rare occasions emphasizes the need for all managers in all kinds of organizations to appreciate the need for good communications. It also emphasizes the point that successful communication depends upon whether communications are received and acted on and not on whether they are sent.

Communications: The Human Element

Communication is a process of translating information from one human being to another. There is some truth in Murphy's Law that if it can be misunderstood, it will be misunderstood. In this section we will consider how misunderstandings in communications can arise and how communications can be improved.

Impediments and Hazards to Communications

Successful communicating depends upon the skills and perceptions of both the senders and the receivers, and, in some cases, on the means of transmission as well. There are also possible impediments and hazards at every stage. The Pearl Harbor failure was a failure in transmission.

How well people communicate depends on (see Figure 25-1):

1. *The clarity of the idea in the sender's mind.* Senders of messages cannot send clear messages unless they are clear in their own minds about the ideas they want to transmit.

    Superiors are, however, sometimes not clear in their delegations to subordinates because they are not clear in their own minds. This may not be their fault. As we said in Chapter 17, there are times when the superior does not know just what the subordinate will have to do. Often the desired *result* can be communicated rather clearly but the actions and means will have to be developed by the subordinate.

2. *All messages must be encoded and put into words,* either spoken or written. This stage of communication is often not well done and so becomes a source of misunderstanding. The ability of people to express themselves, whether orally or in writing, varies greatly. Many times, the message is not expressed clearly and so the import of the communication is not clear.

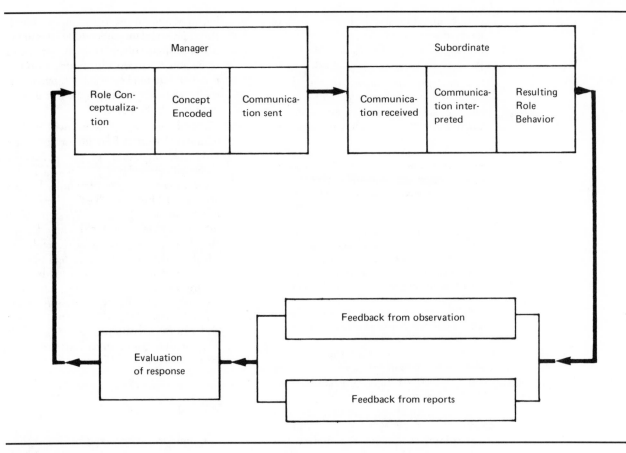

Figure 25-1
A model of the communication system as it relates to superior-subordinate relationships.

3. *Transmission is the next stage in communication.* When the people in the back row at a speech can't hear the speaker, it is a transmission failure. Maybe it is because the speaker doesn't speak loudly enough or it may be that there is too much interfering noise. Communicators need to try to avoid faulty transmission.

In the case of written communications there is an added possibility of errors being made in the transmission of the message itself. Sometimes, too, too much time is consumed in the transmission process, as happened at Pearl Harbor. Today, there are said to be cases in which it takes a letter a week to travel from one part of New York City to another part of the city. Worse yet, messages sometimes get lost altogether in the transmission process.

4. Following transmission, comes the *reception and decoding* of the communication. Receivers sometimes miss getting the essence of the communication because they aren't listening or else they don't interpret the words in the same way the sender intended. The im-

port of the message is lost because of faulty translation.

5. *Perception difficulties* frequently arise. Personal biases sometimes play a part in the perceptions of people receiving communications. In the case of statistical reports, superiors often interpret them as showing what they want to see.

There was the case of the bridge playing partner of an economist who specialized in keeping up with consumer attitudes and whose views were regularly quoted in many newspapers who one day met his partner's personal secretary. Knowing the economist very well and knowing him to be a very opinionated man, and not very open-minded, he asked the secretary how it happened that the economist could be so objective and free from bias in his professional work when he was not fundamentally that kind of man. "Oh," said the secretary, "I think that Henry sees in the figures what he wants to see."

People hear what they want to hear and in reports they see what they want to see. And, unfortunately, too, they sometimes forget.

The situation is sometimes even worse. It is not just a matter of the organization head seeing it as there when it isn't there. The head thinks that if he wills something to happen, it will happen, and he will not even listen to unfavorable news.

Some of Adolf Hitler's wrong decisions in World War II came about because he did not want to hear unfavorable news. People bearing bad tidings were berated by an infuriated Fuhrer. So they had to distort what they reported to him. Toward the end of the war no one reported any bad news to him so even if he had been a superior strategist he could not have made appropriate decisions.

6. *Sometimes managers are swamped with a plethora of information* and get lost in it. This happens more now than it used to because computers turn out so much data. This applies particularly to numerical information where managers need to be able to interpret meaning into the flood of data made available to them. In such cases, less information, if it is relevant, would be better.

7. *Cultural differences,* as we will see in Chapter 26, are often important. The Japanese, for example, put politeness above all else. They give you a polite answer even if it is not a wholly honest answer. (They say "yes" when they mean "maybe.") So do Westerners in many cases, but not to the same degree. We don't say exactly how we feel if it will hurt the other person's feelings.

We also avoid conflict by distorting meaning or choosing our words carefully. And, on the receiving end, we draw conclusions, evaluate, judge, and jump to conclusions. It is small wonder that communications are often misunderstood!

Listening

Communications experts suggest that too many managers are not good listeners. Instead, they interrupt and talk too much themselves. Consequently, they don't even hear the views of their subordinates. Subordinates sometimes need to have courage and tenacity in order to make them hear.

The experts suggest, too, that communication is often like an iceberg in that nine-tenths of it is under water and not visible. (The point is that in communications, so much is unsaid that what *is* said is not very revealing.) They suggest that managers give thought to what is not said as well as to what is said, and try to come to a fuller understanding of the feelings of the subordinate.

For most of us, this suggestion has merit yet, if followed, should be used with caution. We are on dangerous ground when we presume to have competence to read meaning into what is not said. We could easily mislead ourselves. We mislead ourselves all too often even when we try to get meaning from what *is* said.

Actions as Communications

We have been emphasizing communications as overt actions, verbal or written communications. But we are all acquainted with the use of facial expressions and "body English" such as a shrug of the shoulders to convey meanings.

Besides these, however, the *actions* of superiors become communications. When a superior *says* one thing and *does* another, subordinates quickly learn to regard the *actions* as the real communications.

College deans usually insist on good teaching as being necessary for Assistant Professors being promoted to Associate Professors. But then they promote those who publish articles in learned society journals. Assistant professors soon learn that it is better for them to publish even if this means neglecting their teaching and their students. The true message is the one which is supported by actions which, in this case, differs from the message given verbally or in writing.

Managers need to recognize that their enunciated communications will soon lose their power to affect the behavior of subordinates if they are not adhered to. In any enduring relationship, the follow-up actions become the enduring communications.

The "Grapevine"

All organizations seem to develop a "grapevine," an informal system of downward flow of information. By means of this grapevine, information, passed by word-of-mouth, sometimes reaches lower levels even faster than it does through regular channels.

Unfortunately, too, the grapevine does not always get the facts straight and transmits misinformation as it often does in "whispering-gallery" (where things get distorted more and more in successive retelling) type situations.

Keith Davis says, however, that the information is right 75 percent of the time or more.[2] Davis sees the grapevine as not always harmful even though it sometimes does misinform people. In contrast, James Hayes, president of the American Management Associations, warns that, if you don't tell people what is happening, the grapevine will probably magnify problems out of proportion and generate more insecurity, which in turn may breed criticism, short tempers, and internal competitiveness.

Communications: Information Flows

The purpose of communications in organizations is to inform people. They are either instructions to subordinates to do work or upward reports to superiors of actions and results. Downward flows of information — delegation — were covered in Chapter 17. Here we are concerned almost altogether with the upward flows of information, with reports of actions and results.

Management Information Systems

Although every means by which a higher-level manager learns about organizational activities and organizational accomplishments is truly part of his management information system, the term "management information system" (MIS) has come to refer to the flow of recorded information. Normally, this term does not refer to the information learned by a superior from direct observation nor from face-to-face contacts with his subordinates.

Written Reports. Since face-to-face communications are necessarily limited, the main burden of upward communications falls on written reports. To higher managers, reports are tangible evidence of what goes on (see Figure 25-2). Collectively, they should communicate knowledge of events, acts, information, and circumstances for every cost causing, cost saving, growth determining, and every result achieving area in the organization. And although they are less than perfect for reporting everything that goes on,

usually most of the main parts of a subordinate's job and his accomplishments can be covered in regular formal reports. When this is so, the superior can be well informed from reading the reports.

Often, however, some parts of the job cannot be covered very well by the usual record-type report. If several people look out the window and write down what they see, they will write down different things because they notice different things and because a whole picture can never be captured in words. Neither can an event be captured in words or numbers in a report. It is thus im-

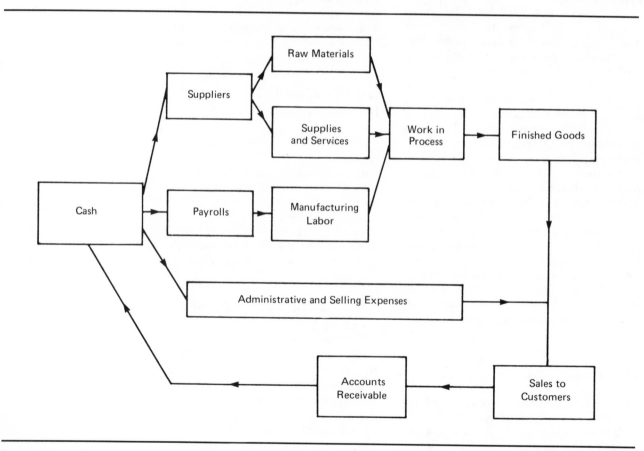

Figure 25-2
The manufacturing-sales-finance information flow system.

possible to communicate in a report the totality of what goes on. If the unreported parts of the job are consequential, then the regular reports will not tell the superior the whole story.

One source of difficulty with reports is in the multiplicity of minor events. When a piece of primary data is born, it causes reactive data, some in the same department and some in other departments. Events are never single, but double, triple, or more in their effects.

A sales clerk sells a pair of shoes. This decreases the company's inventory of shoes and increases its cash or its accounts receivable. The sales clerk has made a sale, the department has made a sale, and perhaps there is now a package to deliver. This one transaction generates half a dozen or so side effects.

Events having multifaceted effects are always going on in every part of the organization. It is as impossible as it would be undesirable to report every facet of every event.

A more serious shortcoming of reports is that they usually omit information on *how results were obtained*. Normally, reports are expressed in numbers and do not give reasons why. Yet, remedial actions, if they are to be applied, deal with trying to change the reasons why.

Most things which are not normally reported upon fade quickly from people's memories. If, on Monday, a manager tries to go back and find out why last Friday's sales were down, he will probably find that the reasons why are hazy in everyone's memory. The clerks may not have noticed that the sales were down and weren't really conscious of any reason at all.

To illustrate how hard it is to unearth the past, the reader might ask himself, "What was I doing at 10:30 last Saturday morning?" Most of us can't even answer this question on Sunday, to say nothing of a week

later. And, if people cannot remember *what* they were doing, they can hardly, days later, decide whether what they were doing was contributing effectively to organizational goal accomplishment and what changes might be desirable to make their work more effective.

One-Sided Reports. Since reports can never show the whole picture, they are always more or less "one-sided" or "single-fact" reports. They show salespeople's salaries, credit losses, and such things. But a manager should not act on the basis of any of these figures by themselves lest he do the wrong thing.

If a manager cuts off salespeople in order to save their salaries, then sales will go down. If a superior tells a subordinate to keep overtime down, he may do it by having too many people on the payroll. If the subordinate is told to keep costs down, he may skimp on quality. Conversely, if the pressure is to improve quality, he will have his employees do things too carefully and at too high a cost.

Even an unfavorable-looking single figure on a report may be fully justified when looked at as part of a whole picture. If machine repair costs go up, this looks unfavorable. But, before doing anything, the manager should look at the hours of work. If the machines have been working sixteen hours a day instead of eight, machine repair bills should go up. A taxicab needs more repairs than a family car.

The results enumerated on reports are also often results from the combined efforts of several rather than just one manager. Yesterday's managers' actions may also have contributed to today's results. Often it is just not possible to separate out the results of one single manager's work.

To summarize, there are a number of practical difficulties with reports and these can cause a superior to get a wrong picture of what is going on. Fortunately, however, reports do typically show how the main parts of the work are going. They need not mislead the higher manager if he uses them with discernment and discretion.

Government Accounting. We spoke earlier about the typical lack of effective controls in government work. One of the worst of common government practices lies in the way they keep accounts.

Accounts are nearly always kept on a cash basis. The budget is balanced if today's income equals today's expenses. Commitments for future costs don't show. No provisions are made, for example, for replacing buildings or other capital equipment when it wears out. Also, today all governments have large commitments to pay pensions to their employees when they retire. Businesses lay away money every year during a person's employment for paying him a pension after retirement. Government agencies, except for schools, don't do this. So, in the late 1970s, when pension costs began to mount, many governmental organizations couldn't keep up with the financial drain. First, New York City, then Cleveland, then Philadelphia and Chicago, began to fall behind in paying their bills.

Cities also almost always count back taxes (overdue taxes) as an asset which they would be able some day to collect. But, in fact, a considerable portion of back taxes always proves to be uncollectable.

Thus most cities and some states always understate their true cost of operation and overstate their prospective incomes. This allows them to think that they are better off than they are. So, they don't try to control their costs as they might if they kept better accounts.[3]

Distorted Upward Communications

In Chapter 19, we discussed the insulation of top administrators from full knowledge of what goes on in the organization.

The same difficulty exists, although to a lesser degree, on down through the organization. Managers at all levels probably never do learn the whole truth about what goes on in still lower echelons. Subordinates tell superiors only what they think the superior wants to hear, modified by what they are willing to have him hear, and which will not be threatening to them.

When the news is bad, subordinates try to sugar-coat the bitter pill and to sweeten the things which might otherwise sound unfavorable. "We didn't get this done because _____." A great many lower managers fill in the blank space with any reasonable excuse, valid or invalid. In such a person's mind, this frees him from blame.

We should not, however, blame only lower-level managers for passing up distorted information. Sometimes the superior is at fault. We saw earlier in this chapter that Hitler did not want to hear bad news. Shakespeare said, "Though it be honest, it is never good to bring bad news." Obviously a superior who won't listen to bad news will be misinformed.

Reasonableness of Reasons for Nonaccomplishment. When accomplishments are falling short of goals, managers should sit down with their subordinates and try to unearth the reasons why so that remedial actions can be taken.

"Reasons why" are often hardly more than excuses. Sometimes these concern the message itself,

- "The message got to me too late."
- "I did not understand the message."
- "It seemed better to do it that way."

One manager reported that when he discusses budget variances with his subordinates, he believes that he hears a mixture of truth, half-truth, and even fantasy — that these are all one to some of his subordinates.

Three seemingly basic laws, which we will call the "laws of reasons" seem to operate. They are:

· Excuses become reasons.
· When necessary, small reasons become large reasons.
· If there is no reason, one will be invented.

If a manager asks a factory department head why results in his department were unsatisfactory, he will explain that his employees had trouble with materials, or with the machines, or that the new employees just aren't much good and don't learn fast enough, and so on. In any case, the unsatisfactory results were not his fault which, in his mind, frees him from blame.

In addition to excuses, subordinates sometimes try to give their superior managers the "snow job" by offering optimistic reports. They give optimistic reports of corrective actions already being carried on and how things are already much better and will soon be fine. Or a researcher who has missed his deadline will report that at least he has learned something and has advanced the state of the art.

Managers need to be wary of taking such reports at face value. They should try to find out just what is really going on and then decide whether the remedial action already under way will accomplish better performance.

Information Origination

In every organization, information is generated at certain places and enters the communication system at various input stations. These are "reporting points" or "gates" where information relating to performance is reported. Someone at these gates has first, to realize that an event is newsworthy enough to report and, second, to report it.

If either requirement is not met, this information bit does not get into the communication system and is not recorded. The event or fact or condition exists but superiors will not know about it.

The regular reporting system should, of course, always provide a flow of current information about what is going on even when plans are, for the most part, still being carried out. With reports of this sort, managers may be able to find out when things are headed downhill even though conditions are not yet serious. Maybe at this point there will still be enough time for them to do something different and so improve performance.

Unrecorded Information. Many events are recorded but some are not. Sales slips record sales, time cards record time and labor costs, and invoices show what materials cost. But, in many companies, the cost of repairing machinery is not reported separately for each machine. Such repair costs are just part of the cost of keeping all of the machines operating. If only one machine is causing high repair costs, no one will ever know about it because the reporting system does not show it. In this case, *the lack of separate records keeps the information from getting into the reporting system.*

Sometimes the gatekeeper who has to report information can't report it because he doesn't know about it. A customer who gets his order late or who thinks that the products are too high priced or are not of good enough quality may just go somewhere else the next time. No one inside the company knows about his dissatisfaction if he doesn't complain. In this case, *the lack of knowledge by the gatekeepers keeps the information from getting into the reporting system.*

Similarly, direct perceptions of customer attitudes toward retail stores is restricted largely to salespeople. If the way a store or its sales clerks do things irritates customers, it is the salespeople who are in a position to notice it. These people probably do not want to report this, in which case, the managers will not know that they exist. In this instance, *the lack of a desire on the part of the gatekeepers to have the situation reported keeps the information from getting into the reporting system.*

Boundary Spanners

Almost all daily newspapers have "Action Please" columns listing customer complaints about unsatisfactory products or services where the customer's attempts to get satisfaction have been unsuccessful. Often they are unable to get past the clerk at the desk or on the telephone to someone who might help them. All of us can remember instances where we, too, have been irritated and frustrated by bureaucrats or just uninterested clerks.

These people are "boundary spanners."[4] They are gatekeepers at the boundary of the organization. A sales clerk is, in effect, a boundary spanner in that he sees and can report on customer reactions to certain organizational practices.

Boundary spanners have contacts with people outside the organization and receive information from them which they can incorporate into the flow of information

passing through the organization. They represent their organizations to customers, suppliers and the public. They are the organization's agents of influence over the environment. They have a great deal to do with the flow of information going out from the organization and with the information which enters the organization's inside information flow system (see Figure 25-3).

Boundary spanners, being at the organization's perimeter, also serve as buffers to the internal organization, shielding the people there from environmental uncertainties. They absorb all sorts of external pressures. This may be helpful or harmful, but, in any case, it has the effect of screening off the internal organization from environmental uncertainties. Most of the time, this would probably be harmful since organizations usually need to be responsive to changing outside conditions.

Organizations in many service industries, those where the service has to be rendered by a person, need to be especially aware of boundary spanning roles. In a retail store, a bank, a restaurant, a motel, or a bus company, the organization's end product,

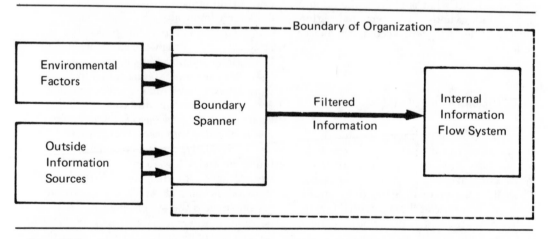

Figure 25-3
The position of the boundary spanner in the linking up of outside sources of information with the organization's internal information flow system.

in this case a service, is rendered at the organization's boundary.

This service is usually rendered by a relatively low-level employee, a sales clerk, a bank teller, a waiter, a room clerk, or a bus driver. These people are the customer's contact with the organization. Often these representatives of the company have little empathy with the organization and its purposes. Their jobs, which have them dealing with customers who, all too often, complain, are sometimes wearing and exasperating.

These people need to be chosen with their ability to endure these annoyances being kept in mind. And they need to be trained so that they will be courteous in spite of their jobs' disagreeable features. If they become surly and discourteous, the organization will suffer.

Certain organization members perform a similar boundary spanning function *within* organizations. They are the people who are at the boundary limits of departments and who receive or pass out information or products or services which flow between departments. Often they have a liaison responsibility. The way these people carry out their work can contribute greatly to or can seriously hamper the working relations between departments which ought to be cooperating and coordinating their work. They can also color or bias the information which superiors receive.

Lateral Communications

The discussion about communicating has, so far, been confined largely to communicating up and down lines of responsibility and authority and not, except for boundary spanners, laterally or horizontally across department lines. Lateral communications between departments go on all the time too. Since this kind of communication was discussed in earlier chapters, we will not go into it further here.

Reports as Motivators

All communications downward, except where they are purely informational, should motivate subordinates to do something. Less obvious is the fact that reports upward are also motivators. Subordinates are motivated to do things which they think will make their reports look good. In this section we will consider how these motivations operate.

Induced Harmful By-Product Actions

The reason we mention reports as motivators here is to call attention to the by-product actions which are sometimes caused. Superiors sometimes emphasize certain goals while at the same time failing to appreciate the harmful by-product actions which are induced at the same time.

In a manufacturing company, the high-level managers may emphasize good customer service and regard meeting factory delivery schedules and giving good customer service as being very important.

When this occurs, factory supervisors do not feel fully accountable for costs, such as for overtime, hurry-up maintenance, and large inventories. They have been told that good service is of utmost importance so they provide good service while feeling no concern over the extra costs which this entails.

Often the superior does not realize that his policy of good customer service is being accomplished at considerable cost in the factory. If he realized the cost of his good service policy, he might relax it and let the factory operate more economically.

The matter of induced harmful effects of high-level goals on the actions of subordinate managers is much worse, however, than this example illustrates. Earlier in this chapter, when discussing one-sided reports, we cited a number of by-product harmful actions which sometimes occur as subordinate managers try to make their records look good. Our point here is that reports *do* motivate managers to do things. High-level managers should try to see that reports are designed so that they will motivate helpful actions and not harmful actions.

Organization Structure and "Responsibility Accounting"

Reports should be patterned to parallel the organization's structure so that they will reflect work done in areas controlled by one person.

"Responsibility accounting" charges costs to the causing department and so to the person in charge of it. *He* is the one who might do something about controlling such costs. Only when costs are charged directly to one person does this individual think that he has responsibility for them and so will try to control them.

Responsibility accounting reports leave out cost figures for elements beyond a manager's power to correct. They *ex*clude, for example, in a subordinate's report, any share of the company's real estate taxes or any share of the president's salary since subordinate managers can't do anything about these expenses.

One company, troubled with too many "rush" sales orders, solved its problem by using responsibility accounting. Half of the orders were rush orders and this boosted factory costs. There seemed to be no way out because so many customers just had to have their orders right away. Then the company started to keep a record of the extra costs caused by rush orders and charged them to the sales department, and not the factory, as before. Suddenly customers were much less anxious. The number of rush orders dropped way down.

By charging the costs of rush orders to the department responsible for them, the company reduced the problem.

Unfortunately and as we have noted in past chapters, it is not always possible to use responsibility accounting in an effective way because responsibilities do not always clearly belong to one person. We also said earlier that this is one of the weaknesses of matrix organizations, which are so popular in high-science companies.

The "Exception Principle"

Reports should be designed to facilitate the use of the "exception principle."

The "exception principle" (or "management by exceptions") holds that subordinates should take care of routine matters but should call the superior's attention to anything unusual.

Such reports would not only keep managers informed about what is going on but they would call the superior's attention to exceptions. Events or conditions which are not following the usual pattern or are not conforming to expectations, should be flagged so that the superior will be alerted. Higher-level managers, once alerted, can insert themselves more actively into the situation and try to initiate remedial actions.

It might happen, for example, that, for the second time in one week, a report shows that inspectors have rejected a lot of purchased parts from one supplier. This causes the manager to have the buyer in the purchasing department call up the supplier and do some checking up.

In another case, three customers in one week called the company complaining that their orders for component parts were arriving late. Investigation showed that all three orders had been delayed because of an overload of work in the electroplating department. The manager then authorized this department to work overtime until all delayed orders got back on schedule.

In both of these cases, no higher-level action would have been taken if all had gone along normally. But things did not go normally. The reports communicated to the superior that something unusual or exceptional was occurring. He was alerted and inserted himself into the picture. The result was corrective actions resulting from the use of management by exceptions.

Ideally, management by exceptions operates by subordinates calling the superior's attention to exceptions. It should operate as if the superior had said to his subordinates, "Here are the results for which you are responsible. I expect that when an exception occurs you will notify me early enough so that I can help, or at least I won't be surprised." Such a delegation would free the subordinate to proceed on an autonomous basis unless an exception occurs.

Budgets

"Expenses rise to meet the amount of money available." — Parkinson's Law of Expenses.

At the beginning of the last chapter we quoted Parkinson's Law to the effect that the number of office workers tends to grow. So do expenses. Control tries to keep these things from happening.

Budgets and accounting reports for budgetary control are the most common methods for trying to control expenses. They are plans for money coming in or going out or both and with how the money flows are related to accomplishments. They show the basic reflections of the economic consequences of managers' actions.

This section will deal with the kinds and uses of budgets and with their strengths and weaknesses.

Budgets as Cost Limitations

Budgets are, to almost all managers, *cost* plans and *cost* limits and do not deal with generating income since, except in selling, most managers have nothing to do with bringing in money. They are allowed to spend up to the budget limit of money in order to get their work done.

Actually, budgets are often not truly hard and fast upper limits to spending money. Department heads sometimes overspend their budgets because things can't always be done for the expected cost. A taxicab trip budgeted for $4 may cost $5 if the cab gets caught in a traffic jam. Similarly, in a manufacturing company, department heads have to get the work out cost what it may, and budget or no. Then, after the work has been done the higher manager looks at the costs and, if they ran over the budget, he talks it over with the department heads. They try to figure out how to avoid having this happen in the future. Because he will have to explain and because cost overruns are held against him, the department head tries not to go over the budget.

Budgets for staff departments are usually easier to meet than those for manufacturing departments because, as has been pointed out elsewhere, a staff department head can simply cut out some of his department's less essential work.

Budget Flexibility

Most budgets show the expected costs for certain expenses during a week, month, or longer period of time during which certain production or sales are expected to occur. But production and sales never follow plans exactly (they turn out to be higher than expected, or lower than expected, or the sales of some products go up and the sales of other products go down) so actual expenses *should* differ somewhat from the original budget. They *should* be affected

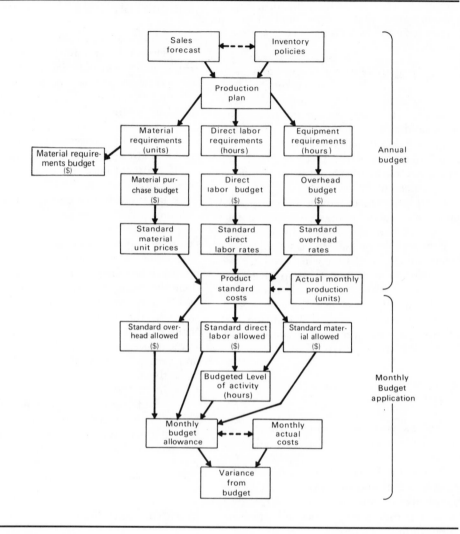

Figure 25-4
Budgetary information flow system.

by what does happen as against what was supposed to happen.

When this occurs, the budget should be changed because the results actually wanted and the results obtained are both different from the original plans. "Flexible" budgets take care of this by providing new budget figures appropriate to the level of accomplishment. ("Flexible" budgets merely means setting up several budgets, one for each of several levels of accomplishment. The one used is the one which is appropriate to the accomplishment.)

Expense Class	Prior Year Total Actual	Budget Year Total Budget	Fixed Budget	Variable Budget	January
Molding (machine hours)	642,000	792,000			57,000
Indirect labor	$ 386,400	$ 454,600	$ 72,000	$ 382,600	$ 37,800
Employee benefits	882,000	1,010,400	23,800	987,600	70,000
Repairs:					
Machinery	972,000	1,227,600	—	1,227,600	82,000
Molds	842,000	1,029,600	—	1,029,600	70,800
Other	130,000	174,200	—	174,200	11,600
Supplies	1,296,000	1,523,200	324,000	1,199,200	129,400
Utilities	484,000	577,400	86,400	491,000	41,000
Miscellaneous	162,000	198,000	—	198,000	13,400
Depreciation	426,000	440,000	440,000	—	36,300
Total	$5,575,400	$6,636,000	$946,200	$5,689,800	$497,600

Figure 25-5

A budget for a factory foundry department. The expected expenditures for the whole year are shown as are the expected figures for January which are set apart by themselves. The complete budget would show figures for the other months as well. As each month passes, comparisons are made of the actual costs with the budgeted amounts and variances are investigated.

Budgeting Gamesmanship

When higher managers make up budgets, they usually ask their subordinate department heads how much money they will need for each expense considering the level of operations expected. Each subordinate makes an estimate for every expense item.

Higher managers almost never have enough money available to cover all of the budgetary requests submitted, so they have to cut some of the requests down. Subordinates, knowing that this is likely to happen, often add their anticipation of the expected cuts into the figures they provide. They overestimate their probable costs. This is their padding. They suggest high numbers and the superior tries to cut off their overestimates. Maybe he will cut off the right amount and maybe he won't.

It is unfortunate that budgeting gamesmanship goes on because it keeps a useful management tool, budgets, from being as worthwhile as it could be. It seems to

be a game that is played everywhere. In fact, administrators who have worked in government and other nonbusiness organizations as well as in business organizations, report that it is even more prevalent in government and non-government organizations than it is in businesses.[5]

The word "overestimates" is used above, but this may not be the way a subordinate looks at it. Rather, he asks for enough money to allow him to do everything he would like to do plus a little extra to cover troubles that always come up and which always increase costs. Should he not get as much money as he asks for, he will omit doing some of the perimeter work.

High-level managers want to allow, in budgets, only enough money for expenses when they are "controlled" (held down). A subordinate will have to perform effectively to keep within these figures and he will not get to do quite all of the things he would like to do.

We need not, however, be too hard on lower department heads as gamesmanship players. They don't play the game alone. The higher-level boss is not at all opposed to having large subordinate departments himself. He doesn't really want to hold down their budgets because the sum of the budgets of his subordinate departments is *his* budget and he wants to be the head of a *big* department. Nor is the situation improved much if we move up another layer in the hierarchy. Tight budgets, the kind that foster effective control of costs, have to start at the top.

Too Large a Budget

Probably no department head has ever been known to admit that his budget was too large and probably such a budget is rare, but some budgets are more liberal than others.

If a budget is too liberal and allows too much money, Parkinson's law of expenses seems to operate. Expenditures rise to meet the amount available. Everything conspires to make the department head spend it all. He feels disloyal to his function and to his staff if he does not spend all of the money available. After all, he did ask for the money and claimed that he would need it. If his padding went through and was not cut off, he feels required to use the money. It allows him to do some of the extra things he usually can't do for lack of money.

As a department head sees it, it is best for him just barely to beat the budget (spend a little less) but not to beat it very much. This "proves" that he did an effective job of running his department. And he will not be saddled with too stiff a budget for the next period. (If he beats the budget very much, he receives praise for a job well done and a cut in his budget for the next period.)

Too Small a Budget

Sometimes a department gets too small a budget. Then one of two things happens. Either the department meets the budget figure or it does not.

As has been said, staff departments can usually meet low figures just by cutting down on some of their services. A maintenance department can cut down on all except critical repairs. The budget "controls" expenses in that it holds down expenses, possibly wisely, possibly unwisely.

Line department heads, such as a factory department supervisor, however, cannot always live within budgets which are too low because they have to get the work out. A line head may not be able to manufacture an electric toaster for two dollars even if this is the budget figure. Nor can the sales manager meet his sales quota if his salary budget is so low that he can't pay his salespeople enough money to keep them. If he does pay them enough, and so meets the sales quota, he may have to overspend his salary budget.

Budget Strengths

Budgets are really not so bad as they are being painted here, however. Everybody, budget-makers, managers, and subordinate managers, lives with budgeting all the time and they learn to use budgets intelligently.

In most cases, budgets probably really do save most of the money that they seem to save. Holding down budgets does cause departments to cut out relatively unimportant work. And holding down expenses often really does save money rather than just postpone costs. If a person eats hamburger today instead of steak in order to save money, he does save money. Saving money this way is not just postponing an expense as occurs when a person puts off having the dentist fill a tooth or buying a new tire for his car. And when people need to conserve their own cash, they can get along forever without a large remote controlled color television set. They can cut down on necessary expenses and cut out less necessary expenses.

In a factory, a supervisor can often save money if he has to meet a close budget.

He can keep his employees from stretching a ten-minute coffee break into a half-hour of wasted time. He can cut down his people's lost time between jobs by having next jobs ready. And he can keep his employees from starting to wash up a half-hour before quitting time. Probably, too, he can get them to be more careful and not to produce so many rejects.

Budgets in Government Organizations

In government departments, budgets are more strictly both income and outgo than they are in business. The budget is the amount allocated for operating a department or for conducting a program and, once approved and allocated, is very likely to remain fixed for the year. Extra calls for service, or fewer calls do not, most of the time, change the amount allocated or spent. Neither income nor outgo are very responsive to variations in the calls for service.

In contrast, in business, a budget is a department's allocation of money to spend, but if sales levels go up or go down very much, a department is allowed to spend more or is expected to cut its expenditures accordingly. Governmental units are much more likely to scale their service level to the money available, whereas in business, the budget is more likely to be adjusted to meet the service level needed.

There is a pernicious problem in the budgets of government departments (almost all of which are wholly supported by budgetary allocations since almost none of them get any of the money which supports them by selling services to customers). Peter Drucker says that the "importance " of government departments is measured by the size of their appropriations and the size of their staffs. "Performance" becomes a matter of maintaining their size or growing. To achieve results with a small budget is not regarded as "performance."[6]

This is a chilling thought since it suggests that it is almost impossible ever to reduce the size of such departments and to get them to operate at levels appropriate to their usefulness. A good many people agree with Drucker on this point and believe that there is no incentive in government work for anyone to hold costs down.[7]

Zero-Base Budgeting

In 1977, newly elected President Jimmy Carter brought with him to Washington the idea of "zero-base" budgeting. Carter had tried this out as Governor of Georgia and felt that it would be effective in improving the operation of Federal government departments.

The idea of zero-base budgeting is to have every department rejustify its existence every year by showing what it will accomplish or how it will contribute to organizational purposes. The idea is, when making up budgets for the next year, to consider only a department's future justifiable needs while paying little attention to past expenditures and activities. All requests for monies need to be justified almost as if the department were being newly created. In regular budgeting, usually a department head has to try to justify only the added increment of money he is asking for.

Successful zero-base budgeting includes attention to priorities. Requests for money are itemized by cost centers or work programs and each item is given a priority rating. Managers have to say how they will use the money before they get it. Later on, if the money made available is less than that requested, the low priority items drop out up to the point where the amount available will support the remaining items.

Reports from Washington indicate that zero-base budgeting is not having much impact on the budgets of government departments. Established departments are too well entrenched.

Summary

An organization's communication system is its nervous system. It is the means by which information flows throughout the organization and is the immediate cause of many of the actions of organizational sub-units. For the most part it is like a human being's nervous system in that it operates almost autonomously and with little thought being given to it so long as it works well.

A great deal of the day-to-day surveillance and control work done in organizations depends upon the organization's written reporting system. Such reports are necessary since managers cannot be everywhere all of the time and cannot observe everything which goes on at first hand.

In order for reports to function well as control devices they need to be designed to parallel the organization's structure. They should be designed to show accomplishment or its lack in each department head's domain. Then each head will make a favorable impression or not depending upon how his area performed. It is not possible, however, to design reports which accomplish this purpose perfectly because some activities are joint activities which affect two or more departments. Nonetheless, reports still are the principal control device. And, among reports, budgets and comparisons of performance against budgets are the most common. They do the job reasonably well, albeit a little crudely at times.

A serious weakness of all management information systems is that not everything can be reported. The unfortunate part of this is that subordinate managers respond to the way reports are made up by trying to make the reports look favorable by doing things which will look well on the reports. This is laudable except when it is accomplished at the expense of something else, something important, but which does not show on the reports. Too much pressure to have a good report should therefore be avoided. Higher managers need to use reports with discretion.

Review Questions

1. It sounds perceptive to say that a person should listen to what is not said as well as to what is said. Discuss the merits of this idea.
2. Why do upward communications tend to become distorted? What can a superior do to prevent this happening?
3. What is an organizational "grapevine"? Should it be developed? Or pruned away? Why?
4. What is "responsibility accounting"? How can it be used by managers to help them control their organization's activities?

5. What is "management by exceptions"? In what way would a manager using MBE operate differently from a manager who is not using this idea? Discuss.

6. Budgets fall short of being ideal devices for controlling an organization's activities. What are their weaknesses and how can they be minimized?

7. What are the "laws of invalid reasons"? Discuss their effects on organizational performance and control.

8. Discuss the differences in accounting procedures between government and businesses. What has this to do with the control of operations? Explain.

Questions for Analysis and Discussion

1. In the Pearl Harbor disaster mentioned at the start of this chapter, what could General Marshall and Admiral Stark, Joint Chiefs of Staff in Washington, have done to have averted this disaster? Who should have done what in order to make sure that the communication reached its destination and was acted upon?

    After the Pearl Harbor attack who should have done what? Should the Generals and Admirals in Hawaii have been dismissed? Again, who should have taken what action?

2. Supposing that a superior appreciates the fact that what people do not say is often significant and may be pregnant with meaning, what kind of preparation should he engage in before he embarks on interpreting meaning into what subordinates do not say?

3. If the bridge playing economist who "saw in the figures what he wanted to see" recognized this weakness, what might he do in order to be more sure that he sees in the figures only what is there?

4. Some managers like to keep in touch by "getting out on the mill floor." One manager who did this every now and then said, "We have a splendid work force here. Every time I go through the plant — and I go unannounced, mind you — the employees are hard at work. There's no fooling around here." How reliable are his observations? How can their reliability be improved upon?

5. The world of top executives is more shadow than substance. The reports that they get can never capture the whole of events or of performance. They are more shadowy than X-ray pictures. Top managers are likely to be screened off from lower managers and not to know what is going on. Is the president "wrapped in cellophane?" Does this matter? How can it be remedied?

6. Go into a supermarket and look around. Is the manager doing a good job? What makes you think so? If you want to get more information than you have, what further information do you want?

7. "How do you like our country?" This is a familiar question put to travelers. But the traveler does not give the person asking a wholly honest answer because he does not want to hurt his feelings by saying anything negative. So, he picks out something he can praise and tells him how much he likes that. The person asking does not really find out how the stranger feels about his country. How can an organization keep reports from being equally misleading?

8. The young manager trainee in charge of inventory control wants to do a good job. What information will he need in order to judge his performance, and how can he get the information he needs?

9. In one recent year, the University of Michigan asked the State legislature of Michigan for $136 million to carry on its operations but got 21 percent less ($108 million) (which was nevertheless an increase from the year before). Is this unusual? How can an administrator operate a facility without the money he needs? Of how much value is participation on budget setting?

10. In the text it was said that reasons why escape fast. Actually, what were you doing last Saturday morning at 10:30? And why were you doing it?

11. A consultant working for a large textile company found that the company had a twelve-years' inventory of peacock-picture printed bedsheets on hand. Why would this be? Discuss this from the point of view of control.

12. When should sales be listed as having occurred? In the period when the order was booked? Or when the project or product is delivered? Or in between? And, if in between, how should the total dollar value be split up? Westinghouse at one time, reported the sales of big projects all in the period of delivery. Is this good? How about Brunswick selling bowling alleys on the installment plan? When should it report sales as having occurred?

Case 25-1   The Summer Job Applicant

A corporation president sent this note to the personnel office: "I would like to know what procedure we follow in hiring people at our X plant."

Three weeks and fifty consultation hours later, the president got a fifty-page report. It gave full details of all of the aptitude and intelligence tests used, all of the sources of manpower that were tapped, what percentage of applicants were able to make the grade, and the cost of the hiring program.

He looked at the report and almost strangled. "All I wanted to know," he said, "was where I should send a neighbor's young son who was interested in a summer job. It doesn't matter now, he'll soon be going back to college."

• Discuss.

Case 25-2   The Monday Foremen's Meetings

Joe Schlender was the newly-appointed foreman of the electroplating department at the Lock-Nut Nut and Bolt Company. Formerly he had been the assistant foreman with the main duty of filling in for the foreman in his absence.

In his new capacity he found himself invited (and expected) to attend the weekly foremen's meeting in the office of the superintendent on Mondays at 3 P.M. At these meetings, subjects of general informative nature were discussed and explained. Problems of joint interest to several or all of the foremen were discussed and actions were often decided upon.

The superintendent wanted these meetings to be as helpful as possible to the organization's operations so he always made a point, before they broke up, of asking the foremen if any of them had any problems.

Sometimes this produced reports of problems but Schlender noticed that Sam Hardy, foreman of the Heat Treating department never reported any problems although he knew that Hardy had several problems which were making trouble.

Schlender asked him about this since the superintendent probably could have helped on some of them. Hardy answered, "When they ask if we have any problems, hardly anyone speaks up. I never do. If I bring up a problem, the superintendent might think that I can't handle my job and I might get fired."

· What ideas in this chapter ought to improve things here?

Case 25-3   Sales Quotas and Motivations

"I spend a great deal of time battling the octopus — all the emanations of this big organization. The district manager, the regional manager, the staff men — I'm always on the phone squawking to them about something. I'm always pounding the desk in conversations with my bosses. If I think the competition may beat us out because we can't get delivery for the customer on time, I'll fight to get the equipment out of the normal priority sequence.

"Of course, I say we'll lose the order for sure if we don't get the equipment — that's what my salesmen say to me. But headquarters is getting pretty hardened to that argument by now. They hear it from everybody and it becomes more or less routine. So I say that if we lose the order we may lose some related opportunities; the customer may give us a black eye in the whole area. If I think something serious may go down the pipe, I'll really howl to New York, Chicago, everywhere.

"My salesmen are all on base salary plus commission. I am myself — we have an annual quota and if we make it, it could mean a $10,000 bonus to me personally. If we make double the quota, my bonus is doubled. The company fixes the quotas in some weird way. Nobody understands it, but it isn't very scientific. I really scream when I get the quota, telling them how impossible it is and how unfair. Then I work like hell to make it.

"That quota means all kinds of pressure on me. But if we lower our prices after we hear about a competitor's bid, we're in trouble. I've got to move carefully. Yet I want the business and, within limits, I know they want me to get it. I go pretty far sometimes, I even make some commitments in writing about what we're going to be able to do. I'm taking a hell of a risk — if a customer ever passed on a letter like that to New York, I'd be out in the street, no question about it. I go around all day with my neck out a mile. But I wouldn't change it."

- Is this man typical in his reactions to his pay arrangement? How would most employees react?
- Is this manager reacting in a typical way to controls from headquarters?
- Is he carrying on his job in the way his superiors would want? If they knew all about what he does, should they judge him to be doing a good job?
- How does all of this square up with the popular idea that strong pressure management hurts organizational performance?

Endnotes

1. Details of this unfortunate mix-up were later unearthed in Congressional investigations which are recounted in the *Encyclopedia Brittanica's* article on Pearl Harbor.
2. "The Care and Cultivation of the Corporate Grapevine," by Keith Davis, *Dun's*, July 1973, pp. 44ff.
3. A good article on this difficulty is, "You Can't Fight City Hall — If You Can't Understand it," *Business Week*, 3 March 1980, pp. 92–97. This article reports that a Coopers and Lybrand (public accounting firm) report found that three-quarters of the fifty largest cities in the United States do not show, in their reports, what their future obligations are.
4. "Characteristics and External Orientations of Boundary Spanning Individuals," by Michael L. Tushman and Thomas J. Scanlon, *Academy of Management Journal*, March 1981, pp. 83–98.
5. As reported at the meetings on planning at the annual meeting of the American Institute for Decision Sciences, held in Cincinnati, Ohio, November 5–7, 1975.
6. *Management: Tasks, Responsibilities and Practices*, by Peter F. Drucker, Harper & Row, 1974, page 142.
7. "Why Bureaucracy Keeps Growing," by Tom Alexander, *Fortune*, 7 May 1979, pp. 164ff.

Suggested Supplementary Readings

Leifer, R., and A. Delbecq. "Organizational Environmental Interchange: A Model of Boundary Spanning Activity," *Academy of Management Review* 3 (1978): 40–50.

McCaskey, Michael B. "The Hidden Messages Managers Send," *Harvard Business Review,* November-December 1979, pp. 135–148.

Mitroff, I.I., R.H. Kilmann, and V.P. Barabba. "Avoiding the Design of Management Misinformation Systems: A Strategic Approach." In *The Handbook for Managers in Non-Profit Organizations,* by G. Zaltman, ed. American Management Associations, 1979.

Robey, Daniel. "User Attitudes and Management Information Use." *Academy of Management Journal,* September 1979, pp. 527–538.

Case for Section VII   Eclipse Tire Company

The Eclipse Tire Company was an energetic small automobile tire producer whose president was particularly anxious to get a foothold in the original equipment business of the automobile companies. He believed, as did tire industry officials generally, that people buying replacement tires often bought the same kind of tire that the car had on it when it came from the automobile factory.

Accordingly, Eclipse's president concluded a deal with the head of the Standard Car Company, number four in the car industry, to furnish a special tire for Standard's low cost line of cars. These would be put on all of those cars except when customers specified some other make of tire.

The final negotiations were concluded at the same time that there was a meeting of Standard's dealers and Standard's president thought it would help to show the dealers what the new tire would look like. Accordingly, he asked Eclipse's president if he could get two sample tires made up the next day and delivered (150 miles away) to Standard's home office by the day after. Eclipse's president was only too happy to comply.

Accordingly, the next morning, he sent through a special order on a rush basis for the factory to prepare the two tires specially that very day. This order was conveyed in a written memorandum to Bill Payne, the head of production control for the factory. He made the necessary schedule changes to get the two tires produced. It was late in the day, however, before they were actually finished, and was, in fact, 5:30 in the afternoon. It happened that Payne was working late that afternoon and he was pleased to see the night shift foreman, at 5:30, carrying the two tires to the shipping room.

Payne was quite surprised, therefore, to be called in to the president's office at 9:30 the next morning. The president was nearly apoplectic. Why weren't the tires at the Standard Office as had been promised? Where were they?

Payne felt relieved to be able to tell him that the tires had been produced and delivered to the shipping room late the previous afternoon (the shipping room was not under Payne's direction so it was not his responsibility to oversee their actual shipping.)

Unfortunately, this proved not to have been enough. When the second shift foreman, who had come on duty at 3:30, had arrived at the shipping room, he found it locked up. He didn't know what to do with the tires so he left them at the shipping room door where they still were. Payne was glad that he had not fallen down on his part of the work since the president was greatly upset about the tires not having been delivered to Standard.

- Obviously there was a failure here; whose failure was it?
- Did anyone fail to carry out his delegation? Who?
- What might be the best thing to do to prevent similar things occurring again?

Case for Section VII   Whose Fault Was It?[1]

In Shakespeare's play, *Hamlet,* Hamlet is greatly preoccupied with the question, "Whose fault was it?" This is a question which seems to preoccupy us all, at least in the Western world. The impulse to assign blame seems to be obsessive. It comes from a man feeling personal guilt which disturbs his reasoning as he struggles to escape this guilt feeling to trying to place the blame elsewhere.

"Whose fault was it?" postulates a prejudgment by the questioner. Something bad has come to pass and someone is to blame. It seems that for every unfortunate event we must parcel out blame.

"Whose fault was it?" is always a complicated and often an unanswerable question. It is also a disturbing question which all too often produces waste and much fruitless discussion.

It is even a futile question because the questioner is no further along. He is looking back and is focusing on punitive rather than on remedial actions. It is a harmful question because the man who stands accused finds his point of view becoming distorted. He becomes defensive and less capable of making rational diagnoses which will provide the proper bases for future actions.

"Whose fault was it?" is a very different question from "What happened?" or "Who did it?" These two questions are straightforward questions to which answers can usually be found. They are more objective and less subjective and less emotional. Yet there seems to be something about an objective approach to problems which repels people and something in an emotional which appeals to them.

"Whose fault was it?" looks backwards. How much better it would be to ask: "How can we do better in the future?" or "Can I do anything to help?"

All persons in positions of authority over others can choose between holding those under them responsible for their actions, good or bad, or holding them responsible only for what goes wrong. The superior who holds his subordinates responsible for both good and bad actions will surely find himself better served than if he holds those under him responsible only for what goes wrong.

Further, if he applies this kind of thinking to himself as well as to others, he will have his own full resources and abilities free for constructive thought and action.

- How pervasive is the tendency to blame others? Is it as harmful as Gragg puts it?
- If we ignore fault and fail to fix blame, what becomes of responsibility and control?

Endnote

1. Adapted and condensed from "Whose Fault Was It?" by Charles I Gragg, *Harvard Business Review*, January-February 1964, pages 107–110.

Most people appreciate the fact that there are many cultural differences between societies and ethnic groups in the various parts of the world. It is curious that this appreciation of differences in attitudes, motivations, and behavior seems to be less general in the study of organization and management.

Both scholars and practitioners like to think that there are certain fundamentals of organization and management which apply everywhere. And, although this may be true, it is also true that cultural differences in values and behavior constitute an overlay which produces different colorations to organizational relationships. Effective managerial practices need to be different in different societies and to be appropriate to the local cultural environment.

The problem of managing in diverse cultures is the subject of our chapter on Local Customs and Managerial Styles, Chapter 26.

Management Throughout the World

Objectives of Chapter Twenty-Six

1. To highlight the fact that cultural differences exist in different parts of the world and to relate these to the need to adjust managerial practices accordingly.
2. To look into the cultural differences between countries and note the need for foreigners to be aware of local customs and to observe them.
3. To consider the differences in the business climate in different parts of the world and how these affect business operations.
4. To inquire into the managerial problems faced by multi-national organizations and how they handle the differences they find.

Local Customs and Management Styles

528

All the world's a stage.
  Shakespeare

The world is not one world and, contrary to Shakespeare, it is not one stage. It is many worlds, many stages, and many cultures. Organizations, public and private, and large and small, exist in all of these worlds and managers manage them using many variations of managerial practices.

Historically, before World War II, the subject of management was hardly recognized anywhere in the world, even including the Western world, as a subject with principles and knowledge content which could be generally applied and which could contribute to organizational effectiveness. It is true that, in the United States and England, there was earlier recognition of the contributions that management could make but much of the understanding of how to manage *people* lay in the future.

Prior to mid-century, managers in different parts of the world developed their own managerial philosophies and procedures based on what their predecessors had done, on their own individualities, and on the cultures of their different countries. Usually their methods were autocratic and dictatorial, with power and decision-making being highly centralized. There were exceptions, however, notably in Japan. In most countries, the managers of private companies were owner-managers and high-level positions were filled by members of the family.

There was considerable change after World War II as the interest in how to manage *more effectively* became widespread. Since the United States was the leading industrial nation in the world and was one which had not been devastated by World War II, American methods were introduced into many other parts of the world.

These were often effective but often, too, they were not very effective. In many cases they were not appropriate to local customs and cultures. In subsequent years, continuing research into effective management methods as they apply in different countries has been carried forward.

Over the years there will probably be a slow gravitation toward similar managerial practices everywhere. Multi-national companies operating in many countries try to operate in each one as effectively as they can. Most of them have a good understanding of how to operate effectively but they have to adapt their more or less universal methods to local conditions. Their methods take on a different coloration in every country. But at the same time, the methods used in different countries are themselves drawn toward the multi-nationals' ideas of effective universal methods.

Management in Three Countries

There are so many differences in managerial practices in different countries that it is not possible for us to describe them all. At the same time, they are so different that it is equally not possible to make very many generalized statements about them all of which would have complete validity.

In spite of this, however, and in spite of there being differences among individual managers in every country, there are many similarities so that it is possible to say that Japanese managers, or German managers, etc., operate in certain ways.

For our discussion of management practices in the world, we will consider those of three countries as examples of differing cultures. We will use Japan, West Germany and England.

Managing in Japan[1]

Perhaps no other country's management practices are so unique as those of Japan. Japan's culture is very different from

Western cultures and its management practices are just as different. Not only that, but Japan's economic success has, in recent years, outstripped every country in the world including the United States.

Lifetime Employment. At the heart of the Japanese system is the expectation that the employee-employer relationship will last for life. The employer more or less takes on a parental role. The company helps the employee in matters of housing, transportation, and medical expenses. Managers often find spouses for employees. Vacations can be taken at company owned cabins in the mountains or at seaside resorts at very reduced rates. Workers all wear company supplied uniform-like work clothes while on the job. Operations are closed down twice a day for short periods of calisthenics at the workplace. Noon meals are available at very low prices. Promotions and pay raises are largely dependent on a person's age, his length of service, and the size of his family and not on his productivity.

The company tries never to lay off any worker and will take losses, anything short of bankruptcy, rather than lay people off. If certain jobs are eliminated, the employees are retrained and put on other work.

Workers respond to being treated with dignity and respect and to this concern for their welfare by being very loyal and cooperative. They think of themselves almost as partners in the company so they try to help it. They try to see places where they can improve quality or increase productivity and make suggestions to management. This extends to the use of labor-saving machinery. They welcome it instead of objecting to it. In crisis situations, they may work long hours at no extra pay in their interest in the continuing well-being of the company and absenteeism is almost unknown.

The bond between employer and employee stemming from the lifelong employment expectation has several side-effect consequences.

New employees are not taken on lightly, not unless it is highly likely that they can be kept on into the future (also new employees are not considered to be permanent employees until after two years). Business up-swings are met, at first, by working longer hours, and then by more subcontracting out of work to other companies. Reductions in business cause reductions in the subcontracting and shorter hours. Employees of the subcontracting companies, which may go out of business, do not, therefore, benefit from the lifetime employment expectation.

Promotion. Both in initial employment and in promotion, so far as managers are concerned, a person's status, the university he went to (it is very important that he should have gone to one of Japan's six prestigious universities), and his family count more than do his skill capabilities.

Appraisal of work, in the Western sense, is not carried on. Promotions at low levels are almost always on a seniority basis and go to the longest service employees. And both at low levels and farther up, getting out the work is rated as less important than status and developing harmonious relationships with and among subordinates. Among managers, old school connections also count; graduates of the same university cooperate with each other. But different university groups do not cooperate with each other.

Decision Making. Decision making, as it concerns subordinates' jobs, is very participative, so much so that it is a slow process and often produces bland noncommital decisions. Decision making relating to matters of minor consequence often come up from the bottom in the form of suggestions. Such suggestions are then discussed with everyone who might be concerned so that everyone's views will receive consideration. Superiors are very careful not to hurt the feelings of subordinates and to see that they do not lose face. If a suggestion has to be turned down, the superior will probably not turn it down directly but will suggest to the subordinate that he consider the matter further.

In spite of what we have just said about the Japanese participative style of making decisions, this is not the procedure at all levels. Peter Drucker reports that management in Japanese companies is notoriously autocratic. Drucker reports that the typical Japanese company is tightly structured and that formal lines of command are clearly drawn and meticulously observed. There is an appearance of participation but no one should ever mistake a polite request by the company president as being anything other than an order.[2]

Organization Structures and Delegations. Japanese organizations are vertical structures. The vertical lines of responsibilities and authority are more clear and unequivocal than are responsibilities laterally for cooperation with other chains of command. Delegations of responsibility are more delegations to departmental groups than they are to the individual department heads. Within groups there is often considerable group unity. But departmental groups are largely indifferent to problems of other departments.

Responsibility delegations to individuals are often not clear because there is so much group participation in middle and low level decisions. Often this results in people not knowing what they are to do. This sometimes results in duplicate effort, overlapping authority, confused reporting, and inefficient operations.

Objectives and Policies. In the past, most Japanese companies did not have any stated organizational objectives, nor did they do much planning for the future. This often resulted in the poor application of organizational resources. And, since there was no internal appraisal of performance, there was little coordinated control over activities, except as it came out of all of the joint discussions.

Japanese methods have been changing for several years. They still manage largely in the way we have described but, with larger companies, and being subject to the vagaries of foreign trade (with its irregular sales patterns), the old closely knit, family style of management is changing. Lifetime employment is still the rule but this does not apply everywhere. There is more changing jobs and labor strikes are not unknown.

There is more use of planning, appraisal, and promotions on the basis of merit. Policies and objectives are more clear. Even delegations, decision making, and control procedures show Western influence.

Managing in West Germany

German managers (our discussion is wholly about West German managers) are autocratic rather than democratic. John Tarrant says that the German top manager considers himself, and is considered by others, to be the possesser of a "divine right" to complete power to direct the organization. He feels strongly that *he* should run the enterprise.[3]

There is a sharp line of demarcation and a gap between top echelon managers and their next-level subordinate executives. And, these next level executives, too, believe that *they* belong to an executive elite and that they have a moral right to authority and obedience. German managers at all levels seem to believe that most subordinates do not have it in them to contribute ideas and that they want to be and should always be told what to do.

The "Mystique of the Engineer." In Germany there is a "mystique of the engineer." They put great emphasis on technical training. Engineers who have never done anything but engineering are accepted without question as being able to manage any kind of business.

This mystique is not wholly confined to engineering training. There are actually two courses to the top, engineering and law. Both of these kinds of training (particularly if they have been supplemented with stints of working for the government) are presumed to prepare a person for any high level managerial job, be it in government or industry.[4]

"Rank" Consciousness. Higher-level managers do not mix with their subordinates, who are at a lower level and are their juniors in the hierarchy and in status. Top executives treat their subordinates more as menials than as near co-equals. Meetings of groups do not include people from different levels. High-level managers also respect the hierarchy in the echelons below them. They do not go around their subordinates and talk to *their* subordinates. If they did, the subordinates would get quite upset.

Emphasis on Vertical Chains of Authority. Below the top level, German organizations are strictly functional and vertical. There is little across chain of authority communication or cooperation. This makes it difficult for engineering improvements to become incorporated into product designs. Customer reaction to product performance and design tend not to be communicated across functional lines of authority and thus are not likely to be incorporated into product improvements. Promotional progressions are also vertical. Young managers coming up are not given experience in varied lines in order to prepare them for top jobs in the future.

The extreme emphasis on vertical chains of authority also makes it difficult for a German company to form a task force made up of representatives of several departments to study a problem. Juniors from different departments, even in a committee, would not be allowed to agree to something and to commit their superiors to agreements which they make.

German managers work hard (Tarrant says that they overwork) and they do not go in for participation in decision making by their subordinates, nor do they share information with their subordinates. This practice of non-participation is, however, modified somewhat through "co-determination" and works councils which are described below.

German managers don't even give praise to their subordinates for their good achievements. And since higher managers delegate so little, it is necessary for them to make most of the decisions themselves. This results in an overconcentration of decision making at the top.[5]

Because higher level managers delegate so little, their subordinates do not get much experience in decision making. And since subordinates cross departmental lines so rarely, they do not develop any feel for the total organization or its problems. Furthermore, most of them never receive any formal training at all in management, so they are not really well equipped to move up the managerial ladder.

Dedication to the Job. Even though they often work long hours, European managers, including German managers, do *not* dedicate themselves to the job as completely as do Americans. Americans consider that their jobs have first call on their time. If the job requires their working weekends, they work weekends. But not so with a German, a Frenchman, or a Dutchman. Family and social life come first. A Dutch executive spends Saturday with his family. This comes first. In France, this private-life-first priority extends also to vacations. If it is time for a French manager's vacation, he takes it, company crisis or no. Many Germans, other than the top executives, feel the same way.

Objectives and Policies. Like most managers in other European countries, German managers consider more sales volume to be more important than more profits. They are satisfied with normal profits and don't push hard for more.[6] They do, however, have bonus systems for executives.

German managers are usually more production than sales oriented. (Historically, they often sold their products through cartels or syndicates and thus did not engage in marketing at all.) Usually, too, German managers were, and still are, not as customer conscious as are American companies.

German managers are also, as are most European managers, conservative and less willing to take risks than are Americans.[7] This shows up in German managers' reluctance to delegate much to subordinates. German managers also have less interest in time than Americans. They are not in a hurry. They are, however, more time conscious than are Southern European managers, such as those in Spain.

Use of Staffs. Within their organizations, German managers do not build up large staffs to study problems and to advise and help them. Consequently, their staff costs, except for engineers of whom there are plenty, are small. Presumably they pay a price for this economy, at times, in the inadequate study of problems. Usually, too, German companies have proportionally fewer salesmen and do less advertising than do their counterpart American companies.

There is one area, however, where German managers do very thorough staff work. They try to organize and plan everything ahead of time down to the last detail. Because of their thorough planning, they are often not very flexible.

Labor Matters. In Germany, as in Scandinavian countries, the law requires "co-determination." This means that company boards of directors must include representatives of workers. Even though labor is represented on their boards, German managers have more freedom to hire and fire employees than do most European managers. In some countries, managers must justify, to a government agency, the need to dismiss a worker before he can be fired or laid off. In Germany, most such matters are settled by the company's works council, which is made up of representatives of workers and management. These councils must approve layoffs, extreme disciplinary measures, hiring, promotions, safety matters, vacation schedules, and other matters related to employees' work. This arrangement seems to settle most matters because there are few strikes.

Labor unions in Germany do not always see eye to eye with management but their leaders have been cooperative with the government and with industry's need to keep wage levels within reason and thus to hold inflation down. This seems not to be so much because of their greater social consciousness, but rather a second and third generation memory of Germany's 1921 inflation which reduced the value of the country's money to zero. They know the effects of inflation. They also know that 30 percent of Germany's Gross National Product goes into exports. They realize the need to be price-competitive in world markets.

German workers also work hard and are productive. This, too, helps managers keep inflation under control and holds down the costs of products for export.

As we move into the 1980s, however, the labor atmosphere in Germany is changing. Germany's labor costs per hour were, in 1981, the highest in the world, higher even than labor costs in the United States and double the Japanese labor costs. This has caused the prices of German made products to rise and exports to fall. This has, in turn, caused layoffs and labor unrest. No longer are labor relations in Germany harmonious.

Customer Awareness. In the domestic market, German managers are not very customer conscious. The attitude is more one of making a well made product and letting the customer buy it than it is of trying to find out what the customer wants and then making it. They put technical excellence above style. In the export market, however, the Germans are quite customer conscious. They try to give customers what they want and are always willing to do something more if that will help.

Managing in England

"The productivity of British workers in various branches of industry is only a quarter of that of the German or Japanese and is rising much more slowly. Real incomes for workers have stagnated. For managers, real incomes have declined over the last decade. Industrial friction is chronic. There is an atmosphere of skepticism about the value of work and achievement. Workers are class-conscious and alienated; workers are hostile and managers are lofty."[8]

This quotation from an article by Robert Wesson in *Business Week* is typical in its appraisal of the British economy. It is a story of management and management-worker relations failures on a national scale. Worker productivity in England is very low. It takes twice as many labor-hours to put an automobile together in England as it does in Germany or France. Old equipment explains this in part but even where the same machines are used, it takes British workers 50 percent more time to turn out work. In the steel industry, it takes three workers to do what one employee does in the United States. If West Germany productivity per worker, in the overall, is rated at 100, the United States is 124, and England is 52.[9]

The Class Struggle. One of the principal causes of England's poor showing in productivity is the class struggle. The English system of industrial relations, so far as labor unions are concerned, is based on adversary roles and is not one of cooperation and participation. The outlook is "them and us," and not "we." If cooperation is ever considered, the question is "whether" to cooperate, not "how."[10]

Labor unions in England do not have strong central national organizations; rather their strength is on the shop floor. This means that there is no discipline within the union itself. Consequently, local and minor matters often flare up and cause little local strikes. With a strong central union organization (as there is in the United States), such little things are not permitted by the national union to erupt into small strikes.

Robert Wesson says that English unions put jurisdiction over jobs first in their priority lists, then job security, and a distant third, efficiency. They suspect that any new machine is intended by the uncaring upper class to cut out some of their jobs. They prefer more jobs, even at lower pay, to fewer jobs at higher pay. Their work restriction rules result in companies having too many employees considering the number of products they turn out.

The "Competent Man." In Chapter 24, we discussed the "competent man" theory. Superiors holding to this theory rely on having chosen capable people as subordinates and they rely heavily on such people doing their work well.

This idea is commonly used in England. Historically, it has usually been the basis on which managers were chosen. Becoming a competent man was not, however, a matter of his having proven appropriate capabilities. Instead, a man was judged to be competent if he had the right background (if he had gone to Oxford or Cambridge university and had studied liberal arts). Family, status, and friends also helped.

In recent years this has been modified somewhat. Peter Drucker reports that, for those not born and educated to the purple, the road to the top is through accounting. Marketing people also sometimes make it.[11] Management itself, as a skill, and particularly in manufacturing, has, historically, been held in low esteem in England. Good young people do not go into manufacturing. Government civil service work and banking are held in higher esteem. Training in management itself is, however, common today in English universities.

Attitudes and Practices of Managers. The attitudes and practices of English managers have also contributed to England's troubles. In the labor relations area, managers, as well as workers, seem to get a dour satisfaction from having problems. Managers seem to get satisfaction out of having problems and then "muddling through" them. They seem to feel that trouble breeds character.

So far as the managerial job itself is concerned, English managers are not very customer conscious. They do not innovate and introduce new products very often. And they are careless about delivery schedules. Customers often get their products long after the delivery promise date.

Managers in England have been slow to put in new machinery and have continued to emphasize old mature industries such as coal, iron and steel and textiles. They have not moved aggressively into new technologies such as computers even though they actually invented electronic computers.

English managers have numerous costly perquisites such as company owned cars with chauffeurs. Nor are class distinctions only between top and bottom. There may be several strata of classes. In one company with only 100 employees, there are five lunch rooms; a workers' canteen, a foremen's room, a junior staff room, a senior staff room, and an executive dining room.[12] All of these things add to operating costs and they stratify rather than unify the organizaion.

Internal Managing. Down within organizations, British management methods vary considerably. Typically, there is reasonably clear delegation of work assignments to subordinates. But the amount of control exercised varies a great deal, particularly in overseas operations. Local managers in far off countries have a great deal of autonomy and little surveillance. But subordinates not considered to be in the competent man class are supervised much more closely and are not given much decision making authority.

Large organizations tend to be quite formal. They have organization charts, detailed corporate policies, job descriptions,

authority limitation statements, and systematic job titling. They do less training of managers than do American companies. Bonus pay plans for middle level-managers are not unknown but they are not common.

Behavioral scientists have had some success with introducing participatory methods but they are still uncommon rather than common.

English companies usually have smaller staffs than similar American companies. Normally they do less planning, both long-range planning and internal short range planning. This, in part, is where muddle through practices take the place of planning. Normally, too, they do less setting of short term internal objectives and they do not use so many internal control reports, preferring instead to rely on the capabilities of their subordinate managers.

Government and Business. In England, companies are not required to go the co-determination route such as applies in Germany where there must be worker representatives on company boards of directors. English managers are free, so far as the law is concerned, to lay off excess workers. But job protection in England is nonetheless regarded as very important. Often, companies in financial trouble and needing to lay off employees, are given government subsidies so that they can continue to operate and maintain employment. (Perhaps we will see more of this in the United States, too, since the government bailed out Chrysler in 1980.)

This produces results which are a mixture of good and bad. Jobs are preserved, but so are inefficient operations. Cartels, which apportion different segments of the market to certain companies are also permitted (as is true also in Germany) and this, too, gives protection to inefficient producers. The most unfortunate part of subsidies is that, without them, a company's managers would try very hard to operate more efficiently, but with them, they probably don't try so hard.

Summary of Management Styles in Three Countries

Our capsule descriptions of how business managers operate in Japan, Germany and England, would probably draw objections from some people in each of these three countries because, in each of these countries managers differ. And there are differences between the management methods used in multi-national, large domestic, and small domestic companies. They don't all manage in the same way.

But, it is true, nonetheless, that cultures *do* have characteristics and that managers in each of these cultures do, for the most part, manage in similar ways. The pictures we presented of these three countries are those expressed by people who have been there or who still are there, including managers native to each of the countries. Furthermore, all large American companies carry on operations in all of these countries and they have experienced the local cultural customs. They have first hand experience with managerial methods in other countries.

A person can hardly read the discussions above about management in Japan, West Germany, and England, without being impressed with how different these cultures are. It becomes evident that no one management style would be highly effective in all three countries.

Weaknesses of Management Styles in Japan, Germany and England. As Americans would see it, there are several weaknesses in the practices in all three of these countries:

1. There seems to be little feeling that management is itself a subject area with skills and knowledge content.

2. Because of this, there is rarely any attempt to fill high level jobs with people who have this kind of capability. Formal attempts to train people so that they will acquire this capability are rare.

3. And related to this, is the almost universal lack of appraisal of either the capability of people or appraisal of the work they do.

4. Except for Japan, there is little participation in decision making. Managers are secretive and do not share decision making, problem solving, nor even information with subordinates.

5. Consequently, the managing which is done tends more to be status quo, hold-the-line managing rather than reaching, greater accomplishment managing. There is little setting of reaching objectives and of developing plans for reaching them.

Strengths of Japanese Management Style. In spite of what Americans would consider weaknesses in the managerial styles of managers in our three countries, the Japanese in particular and the Germans to a lesser degree, have competed very successfully against the Americans. Because the Japanese have been so successful, we will examine the Japanese strengths.

The Japanese accomplishments seem to rest on several advantages. Perhaps the greatest advantage is that they work hard and are very loyal and supportive of organizational objectives. Employees try to help develop effective operations. American workers are much less supportive. Similarly, the Japanese government helps whereas the United States government often holds down industry.

The Japanese industrialization and the reindustrialization of Germany after World War II have been more recent than the industrialization of the United States. Their factories are newer and more efficient. Their workers are younger. Japan also has a wage advantage, wages there are only half of what they are in the United States and in Germany.

The Japanese have been very protective of their home market. They are past masters at protectionism by red tape. An imported American or European car has, for example, to pass numerous inspections and get certification and be repainted before it can be operated in Japan. All of this makes such a car cost a great deal more. Foreign automobile companies are not allowed to make cars in Japan. In the computer area, until 1981, IBM was not allowed to bid for any Japanese government business nor is it allowed to bid for business in certain industries, such as the telephone industry. (In 1981, this prohibition was relaxed but only if IBM disclosed its technical and trade secrets.)

The Japanese also cut prices to suit the market. Their television sets sell for less in New York City than in Tokyo. This pays so long as they get more than their out-of-pocket costs back. Economists call this "dumping." Most nations, including the United States, have laws prohibiting this because it kills their own industries. But the United States has not taken any action. Meanwhile our own television businesses have all but disappeared.[13]

In summary, the Japanese success seems to be built on hard work, wide supervisory spans, few hierarchical managerial levels, relatively low wages, an emphasis on high quality, harmonious labor relations and government support as well as on several questionable trade practices. (Japan also has no anti-bribery law.)

Their performance has been impressive but there may be clouds on the horizon. France, Italy, and some other countries are beginning to put retaliatory restrictions on Japanese products.

The Japanese emphasis on harmonious employee relations has a familiar ring. It sounds very much like the era of benevolent paternalism in the United States. It sounds very much like life at National Cash Register, Endicott Shoe, or Hershey Chocolate in 1910. In the United States, that melted away with the coming of

unions and more belligerent demands by workers.

This could happen in Japan. The lifetime employment expectation is already showing some cracks at the seams. (In 1981, Mitsubishi eliminated automatic annual pay increases for workers over 45 years of age and reduced the level of pensions for future retirees.)[14] The effectiveness of Japanese industry in the future will be further slowed down as their factories and their workers both grow older. Their concensus decision-making method tends to stifle risk taking and creativity.

The vagaries of foreign trade will also, at times, cause slow-downs in industries, which if prolonged, will force layoffs and interruptions to the lifetime employment policy. If this happens it will put a serious strain on the reasons for harmonious labor relations. Serious interruptions in foreign trade will also cause bankruptcies since many Japanese companies are heavily financed (75 percent) with borrowed money.

The early reports from Japanese owned factories in the United States and England are generally favorable but not altogether so. They have also been quite successful in remaining non-union.

The World Environment

We have said that the world is a world of many cultures. Any company, American, European, Japanese, or other, which wishes to do business in other countries, needs to know about the cultures of these countries so that they can adapt their managerial practices to suit the needs of local customs.

Social Cultural Customs

Managers need to know both the social customs and the business customs of the countries in which they expect to operate. Otherwise they may inadvertently do unacceptable things and they will be regarded as being discourteous or rude. They will be disliked and their effectiveness will be hampered.

Personal Acceptability. Customs relating to personal acceptability are perhaps the most important of social customs. And in this area there are almost no universals. Customs differ everywhere.

In Europe, people shake hands when they meet someone they know and again when they part company. In Russia, they may get kissed on both cheeks, as Carter did in Figure 26-1. But not in India. An Indian does not want to touch other people. An Arab likes to carry on a conversation more or less eyeball to eyeball from less than two feet away, as Sadat did with Carter in Figure 26-2. Latin Americans also like to be close to the other person. Americans want more distance, but if they draw away, an Arab or a Latin American will not like it. And, in Arab countries, a person is uncouth indeed if he eats with his left hand.

In Thailand, if a man sits with his legs crossed, he is rude. If a man places his hands on his hips, a Chinese will think that he is angry. A friendly slap on the back by an American will insult an Indonesian. In England a person who is aggressive is a boor. In Italy, if a person waves to someone else with the palm of his hand toward them, he is saying "go away." A friendly wave is palm towards the waver,

In Norway and Sweden, anyone invited to dinner at someone's home should take flowers for the hostess. And in all of Scandinavia, after the meal, the guest shakes hands with the hostess and thanks her for the meal. In the Far East, the guest brings some small thoughtful gift. Foreigners need to be aware of such local customs lest they unknowingly offend someone and thus preclude doing business with him.

Americans are often regarded as having bad manners. At the table, they hold the fork in the wrong hand. They even talk business during meals where they are guests. Americans do not shake hands with all of the ladies at a party. Many people in other lands think that Americans talk too loudly.

Time in Social Events. The part that time plays in social events also differs among cultures. If a person is invited to someone's house in Sweden for a meal, he should come on time. The meal will soon be served. But, in Latin America, he should come at least an hour late. In Spain, two hours late is better yet. (This is the case for business appointments as well as for social events.) In all of these cases, it is discourteous not to observe local customs.

Cultural Customs in Business

Cultural customs are not confined to social life in foreign countries. They bear upon business relationships and affect how business is carried on. There are several aspects to these relationships.

Friendship. In most parts of the world, people do business only with people they know and like. If a new company offers them a product at a lower price, local customers will say no if this company's managers are new to the community or are otherwise unacceptable. They may also think that the price is low because the quality of the product is low. In order to carry on business, a company's managers have to become a part of the local social structure. They have to be around for a while and to develop friends.

Politeness. In Far Eastern cultures it is customary to value politeness over truth. The Japanese, for example, conceal their sentiments. They are not likely to say "no" directly lest it offend someone. With Japanese, too, a "yes" at first is not to be taken as a firm "yes." It may be just a politeness "yes" which keeps the door open for further negotiations which later on may become a "no."

Figure 26-1
President Jimmy Carter and President Leonid Brezhnev of Russia meet in Vienna.

Fate and the "Will of Allah." Most people in the Western world and Americans in particular, believe that their future is partly within their own control and that it will depend partly on what they do. But, people in many parts of the world are more fatalistic. What happens is the "Will of Allah," or "Que sera, sera," (Whatever will be, will be). Buddhist, Hindu, and Moslem societies (as well as conservative Christians) regard what happens as being the will of God. Obviously, local managers in such cultures will

ularly in such countries as Spain where the mañana complex is so pervasive.

Foreigners like to spend more time on preliminary discussions. Talk, negotiating, and bargaining are all parts of the game. In South America and in the Near East and the Far East, haggling over price is expected. Nor should the discussion be hurried. Pressing to get down to business right away will offend an Argentine just as pressing for a deadline will offend an Arab.

The relative unimportance of time often shows up in sellers failing to meet delivery dates. Failures to meet delivery schedules on time are common in much of the world. This unreliability extends also, so far as emerging countries are concerned, to quality. The quality of the product delivered is often not as good as it should be.

Language Problems.

In December, 1977, United States President Jimmy Carter was a guest in Poland. On the occasion of his arrival speech in Warsaw, he said, "I am interested in the Polish people's desires for the future." But this is not what the Poles heard in Polish. His translator translated it as if he had said, "I am interested in your lusts for the future."[15] And when Carter said that he had left the United States to visit Poland, the audience heard it as his having abandoned the United States. Obviously, he needed a better translator.

Multi-national companies have to carry on their business in each country in its own language. This makes a problem within the company when people from different subsidiary units in different countries try to talk to each other. There has to be some common language for use within the company. English is the language most commonly used, so one of the qualifications for top level managers of foreign subsidiaries is to be fluent in English.

Translation difficulties of the Carter kind are ever a danger so it is always desirable to have a *good* translator present. The Italian

Figure 26-2
President Jimmy Carter and President Anwar Sadat of Egypt say goodbye at Cairo airport.

not do very much creative managing. They won't plan ahead or try to do anything to mold the future.

Attitudes toward Time. Americans are in a hurry. They want to get on with whatever it is. But time is of less consequence in other parts of the world, partic-

word for "ask" is "demand." If it is translated into English as "demand" it distorts the meaning. In Spain and Portugal, "America" often refers to South America. United States is "Los Estados Unidos." In England, a "billion" is a million million and not a thousand million as it is in the United States (in England, a thousand million is a milliard).

The nuances of language differences are often so subtle that even good translators do not catch all of them and so they sometimes translate incorrectly.

Social Position and Occupational Status. In both India and England, educated people would rather go into government work than into "trade." Business is lower on the social scale than government work, or teaching, or office work. In Arab countries, too, most capable people will not go into business because business is held in low esteem.

A difficulty in some parts of the world is that education elevates a person above doing anything manual. In India, an educated man is too superior to engage in any kind of manual work. In Venezuela, a sixth grade school drop-out is too good to do manual labor (that is fourth grade drop-out work). An American who handles his own suitcase degrades himself in local eyes.

In many parts of the world, educated people and those with high social position do not like to dirty their hands, so they won't take low-level managerial jobs. In contrast, they will accept high-level managerial jobs. High social position is almost always an important qualification for a man's becoming a successful executive. Having social position adds to a manager's power position and makes his decisions more effective.

In a Latin American country or in most of Europe, should a man with low social position reach a high managerial post, his lack of blue blood would reduce his effectiveness. And, in India, promoting a lower caste person over a high caste person would wreak havoc in the organization.

In a study on this point, Rodger Griffeth and his colleagues found that, in France, subordinates associated the authority of their superiors with their status much more than with their hierarchical position. They regarded authority more as personal than hierarchical. Superiors without status had little genuine authority. This same relationship was found to exist in several other countries.[16]

The Business Climate

In most countries the governments want business companies to locate there because businesses create jobs. But they are ambivalent toward foreign businesses out of fear that the country will lose its economic independence.

Many countries are so small (Holland and Pennsylvania are equals in population, as are Switzerland and Massachusetts) that their own economies are too small to support the production of mass produced products at economical levels without the extra volume supplied by foreign trade. A much larger part of their Gross National Products depends on exports than is true of the United States (United States' exports are 6 percent of the GNP. But Holland's exports come to 42 percent of its GNP while Switzerland's exports amount to 28 percent of its GNP.)

Because so many countries are small, business organizations which operate only in the domestic market are small. In Europe there is a "small is beautiful" fetish. And it is true that in small companies everyone knows everyone else and they usually get along well together and work cooperatively with each other.

Large-scale operations lose this group loyalty that grows out of small group cohesiveness. The point here is that, in many countries, because of their industrial organizations being small there is a spirit of mutual support between employer and employee which is usually lacking in the United States where so many of the companies are large.

This smallness of the country and the need to support exports bring business and government closer together. Governments are actively supportive of locally owned businesses and are not antagonistic as is so often the case in the United States. Locally owned businesses in small countries receive favored treatment over foreigners in many ways. Often there are tariffs and quota limitations on competing imports. Local companies are also allowed to form cartels and to follow restrictive market area practices. "Trading groups" also operate in many countries to fix the prices of coffee, cocoa, etc. The climate is one of joint cooperation.

In most emerging countries, the atmosphere is more hostile to business by foreign companies. The political leaders in these countries want business, foreign business included, but in spite of this, most of the people there are anti-foreign-business. They distrust foreign companies doing business within their borders and place restrictions on them. In many parts of Africa and Asia, "capitalism" connotes plutocracy, social irresponsibility, and materialistic greed.

Government and Business. In most Western countries, a "business" is a privately owned business. But this is frequently not so in developing countries and sometimes is not so in developed countries. The governments of most countries own their nation's airlines, railroads, power companies, and their telephone and mail systems.

They also own some of the heavy industry organizations, such as steel mills. In England, the government owns not only the steel mills but the coal mines as well. In Italy, the large oil company, "ENI," is government owned and the giant Fiat automobile company is partly government owned. In France, the government owns part of the Renault automobile company.

Governments also pass laws requiring foreigners to favor local employees and local companies. In Mexico, 90 percent of a foreign company's employees must be Mexicans. Nor can foreign managers be brought in if there is a qualified Mexican available for the job. In many emerging countries, foreign companies are required to train local nationals and later to promote them into managerial jobs.

Quite a few countries do not allow foreign investors to own any more than 49 percent of important local industries. Nor do they permit products to be made wholly from imported parts. In Mexico, 63 percent, and in Argentina, 83 percent of the value of light automotive trucks must be locally made. In Japan, foreign automobile companies are not allowed to produce either whole automobiles or parts in Japan.

Most less well developed countries have central governmental planning. Decisions are made to favor the development of certain industries and certain activities and to discourage others. Foreign investors may also have to undertake certain activities (such as to build a hospital, or schools, or roads) in order to get a permit to do business.

Investing in developing countries is a chancy undertaking because of the many restrictions and the very real possibility of expropriation. Every now and then a new government takes over the government of one of these countries and then it repudiates agreements made by the previous government and it takes over foreign investments. This occurred in the Arab oil producing countries in the 1970s. Sometimes the old owners are offered token payments or payments in the distant future. But sometimes, as when Castro took over Cuba, no payment at all is made.

Ethics. In Chapter 5, we reported that small under-the-table payments facilitate trade and business relationships in many parts of the world. Such payments are accepted practice and are regarded by most people in these parts of the world as not being reprehensible. Rather, they are regarded as evidence of appreciation. Facilitative payments are essential to the successful carrying on of business where this custom prevails.

Job Security. For many years, Europe has been moving toward giving workers more say in company decisions. They have, through "co-determination," had worker representatives on company boards of directors for several years. This is to give workers greater protection against arbitrary actions by managers, particularly against layoffs and reductions in the workforce.

Job security is important everywhere in the world, the United States included, but the job protection rules are more rigid and much more costly to employers almost everywhere in the world than they are in the United States.

There is a danger in trying to protect workers' jobs too completely when the products they make do not sell. The danger is that the company will go bankrupt if it has to maintain a large workforce when customers are not buying products. This happened to a Raytheon subsidiary in Sicily several years ago.

This subsidiary (majority owned, but not wholly owned by Raytheon) in Palermo, saw its sales go down so it tried to lay off forty workers. The Sicilian government refused permission and the subsidiary went bankrupt. Then 200 employees lost their jobs.

Naturally, employers react to costly job protective measures just as do the Japanese. They don't hire anyone unless they feel *very* sure that they will have enough work in the future to keep the employee busy. Job protectionism thus holds down employment. It also causes employers not to respond quickly to market changes. If business picks up, they let customers wait instead of expanding production by hiring more workers, lest they be unable to release them later.

Job security operates at top levels, too, in most non-American companies. Such companies rarely dismiss a top-level manager. In most social orders, top managers are regarded as competent and are not removed. One does not presume to blame *them* if things go poorly. Instead, company owners accept their explanations that outside conditions caused the trouble. The managers themselves, too, have no feeling that they did poorly if things go poorly. They just accept events and results as facts of life which call for no action on their part. Barring outright catastrophe, overseas companies rarely change top managers.

Managing Overseas Subsidiary Units

Foreign trade is essential to the world's economic prosperity. Most of it is carried on by large companies which produce products in one or more locations and which sell them in many other countries. Thus they have subsidiary producing and/or selling units operating in different countries. In this section, we will consider the problems they have having to do with operating in two or more countries and the solutions to these problems.

Centralization Versus Decentralization

For large companies with extensive overseas operations, there are always a number of questions to answer all along the way. Managers have to decide where, in what parts of the world, to sell in and what products to manufacture overseas. They have to decide where to make parts and where to assemble them into end-products. They have to decide whether to have wholly owned subsidiaries or to join hands with a foreign company, and many other questions of major importance.

There are also matters of organization structure to decide. Some companies organize on a functional basis and have all heads of overseas manufacturing plants report to the head of manufacturing in the home country. Other companies organize on a geographic basis.

Local laws also bear on centralization-decentralization matters. We mentioned, for example, several instances of countries where laws require a large proportion of the value of a product to be made with local labor. Companies may have to set up small scale production facilities in countries where they would not otherwise be put.

Local units may also have to be set up as domestic corporations in each of the countries requiring this. When this is so, there is usually an additional requirement that 51 percent or more of the shares be owned by local people. Local majority ownership usually also extends to requiring the employment of local managers in all low level managerial jobs and in most of the high level managerial jobs too. Obviously, under these conditions, there is a great deal of decentralization.

Coordination Problems

Multi-national companies have greater coordinative-type problems in their international operations than they have in their domestic operations

After a company has become large and has operations in several countries, problems of where to do things arise. In one company operating in Latin America, there has been almost outright conflict between its Mexican and its Brazilian subsidiaries over the question of which one should supply the Venezuelan market.

Home office managers often come up against conflicts between differing local groups. Such groups, even within one subsidiary, frequently will not work together cooperatively. In Belgium, the Flemish and French speaking people don't work well together. And, in India, Hindus, Moslems and Christians will almost never work together cooperatively. And the English, French and Germans don't really like to do business with each other. Historically, they have often been at war with each other.

Ford Motor had to reorganize its European operations a few years ago in order to achieve operating economies which the subsidiaries had not been able to work out for themselves. Ford of Germany and Ford of England each designed its own automobiles with no thought of using the same parts so that some of them might be interchangeable. Because the parts were not interchangeable, production quantities in each country were limited to the number of cars made in each country. The result was that each factory had too many short production runs which were uneconomical and this caused high costs.

Ford combined the two operations and redesigned the cars so that Ford Germany and Ford England cars now contain many identical parts, all of which are made in larger production lots and at lower costs.

Adapting to Foreign Conditions

Overseas managers of all multi-national companies have to adapt their home country practices to the new cultures in which they try to operate. The kinds of adjustments they have to make depend on the practices of their home countries since this determines the practices they start with. As an example to illustrate the kinds of changes they have to make we will discuss the adjustments which a newly appointed manager of an American owned subsidiary ought to try to make:

1. He should try to understand the people

Local Customs and Management Styles

in his new country. He should try to learn all he can about local customs of the kinds we mentioned earlier so that he will not unwittingly commit faux pas. He should be careful not to be a reformer nor to judge local customs to be inferior just because they are different from what he is used to at home.

2. He should try to learn the language of his new country. Even if he doesn't succeed very well, his trying wins local good will.

3. He should try to see himself as the local nationals see him. If he knows what the local people think of him and if he knows their stereotyped picture of people from his country, he can act in such a way as to avoid being tarred with the stereotyped view which the local people have of his countrymen and of him.

So far our suggestions would apply to all foreigners, not just Americans when they are foreigners. There are, however, many Americanisms which he should be aware of. People in many parts of the world, and particularly in Europe, consider Americans to be naive, lacking in culture, and they used to think that Americans were wealthy. In the business world, they consider American managers to be arrogant because they believe that American managerial methods are superior and because of that they try to put them into effect in place of locally accepted methods.

They look down on us for the first two of these things and resent us for the third and fourth. Europeans think that things on the surface are probably different underneath. Americans accept things more at face value so they are believed to be naive. Americans put deals largely on a take-it-or-leave-it basis, leaving no room for negotiations. People in many parts of the world regard this as a sign of being both naive and arrogant. Nor is the American "holier-than-thou" attitude toward "facilitative" payments (considering them, if made to high officials, to be bribes rather than tips) well received in many parts of the world. *Business Week* reports that Europeans and Japanese laugh at our naivete as they take over the business we have spurned.[17]

American managers also expect good performance from their subordinate managers and sometimes fire those who don't measure up. This shocks the local nationals who see it as an arbitrary, heartless and uncalled for action.

Probably no American manager can manage in such a way as to avoid some of these negatives. But he can know about them and try to do things which will be more acceptable. Only if he can do this, will he be able to manage effectively.

Summary

There are many nations in the world and many more cultural groups. Multi-national companies, therefore, carry on their operations in many different varieties of cultures.

In order to do this, they have to adapt their managerial practices so that they are suitable to local conditions yet not so much as to lose the essence of effective management. This can be done only if they are fully aware of local customs and that they respect them.

In this chapter we have made such a strong case for managers adapting their methods to local needs that it might sound as if we are saying, give up Western world and American practices and adopt local methods.

This position would go too far. Nearly all of what has been discussed in this text as effective managerial procedures can be used effectively in other cultures if it is adapted to these cultures. It is not necessary to give up the fundamentals which make effective managers effective.

Planning, setting goals, allocating organizational resources to the support of activities designed to reach organizational goals, keeping track of what is going on. taking corrective actions, motivating subordinates — all are useful to managers in every culture.

Review Questions

1. Discuss the ramifications of the Japanese practice of trying to give lifetime employment to employees. What side effects does this generate? What are the good effects? the bad?

2. What should an ambitious young man do to get promoted and to move up the managerial ladder in Japan?

3. How do decisions get made in Japanese organizations? What are the advantages of their method? What are the disadvantages?

4. What is the "mystique of the engineer"? Does it contribute to managerial effectiveness? Explain.

5. What is "co-determination"? What are its advantages and disadvantages? Would it probably help if American managers adopted this idea?

6. Discuss the matter of many companies having an "ambivalent" attitude toward business. Why would they feel the way they do?

7. How do governments of small countries around the world protect their home companies? What can a foreign multi-national company do about this?

8. If three American managers were to be assigned to manage their company's subsidiary in Japan, Germany, and England, respectively, which one would have the most difficult adjusting to do? What adjustments would he have to make?

Questions for Analysis and Discussion

1. In earlier chapters we noted that one of the difficulties with American civil service is that people essentially have their jobs for life. Yet this seems only

to induce laziness instead of a Japanese-type loyalty and dedication. Isn't this likely to happen in Japan? Discuss.

2. When American companies start foreign trade operations in a country, they usually staff the operating unit with American managers and local nationals at operating levels. As time passes and the operation grows, the nationals tend to move up and there are fewer Americans in managerial spots. How far should this be permitted to go? Why?

3. The economies of emerging nations are usually heavily dependent on their exporting agricultural and mineral products, or of other products of nature. Can a nation build a thriving and enduring economy on such exports? What else can such nations do? Should they go in for subsidized heavy industry?

4. In the text, it was said that in the rest of the world outside the United States, job security for employees is considered as one of the most important of the responsibilities which managers have. In the United States, job security also ranks high yet there is more of a feeling that customers (not employers) make jobs (and the lack of customers reduces jobs). Is the rest of the world ahead of the United States on this matter?

5. In Japan, executives are expected to retire at fifty-five years of age. In Holland, it is usually sixty. In the United States, it is customarily sixty-five. Would the United States economy be better off to lower the retirement age to sixty or fifty-five? Or, should Japan and Holland go up?

6. The British system (which is about the same as what the text calls the "competent man" theory) uses managers more fully than does the American system. Also British senior managers look over their juniors longer before they promote them. British executives are allowed to "grow up on the job" where Americans are more limited to their jobs and are not allowed to go beyond them." Discuss these statements.

7. Foreign companies usually have low turnover in managerial ranks. Although this gives junior people more opportunity to develop seasoned judgment over more years, it also keeps them down longer. Is this good? Discuss.

8. Several years ago, psychologist Mason Haire studied more than 3,000 managers from all over the world. He found that nearly all foreign managers thought that the average person has little capacity for initiative and leadership. Is this so? What are the implications? Discuss.

9. The American working for an Italian company noticed that his secretary was making two carbon copies of his letter to a man in another company. Upon asking why, she explained that the extra one was for the head of the company. A copy of all letters to people outside the company always went to his office. Otherwise he would not know what was going on. Comment.

10. In India, labor is plentiful. In Germany it is scarce. Yet in neither country is there much low-level decision making. Would it not seem that the scarcity or plentitude of labor ought to be a factor in the centralization of decision making? Discuss.

Management Throughout the World

11. An American manager working in Turkey reports that in Turkish companies there is no decentralization of decision making authority. And, he reports that the workers there have no ambition, no discipline, and time means nothing to them. The authoritarian way of life and of managing does not disturb them at all. Would it not be smart for a foreign company to go in there and improve things by using more participative methods?

12. What are the good and bad points of a multi-national company being organized on a product line basis worldwide, instead of being organized geographically, with an International division, or a European division?
    • Discuss[1]

Case 26-1   Mining Copper in Angola

The Magenta Mining Company mines copper in the United States and is considering opening up mines in foreign countries. Magenta's engineers have found substantial high grade copper ore deposits in Angola in Africa. The government there wants to develop its resources and so is favorable to allowing Magenta to develop mines there.

The Angloa government has offered to grant Magenta complete tax exemption for ten years. Thereafter it asks for 25 percent of the profits, half of which would be paid in cash and half would be spent for roads, schools, hospitals, water and sewage systems, and other activities for the public good. Besides this the government would require that another 25 percent of the profits be reinvested in developing local businesses. There seems to be no question that there will be an adequate supply of labor although the men available would be tribesmen who have no skill relevant to mining.

If Magenta should go into this project, it would probably require at least a $30 million investment before any copper would be produced at all and possibly the investment would go up to $50 million before break-even operations were reached.

• What information should Magenta's managers still want before making a decision on this matter?
• What premises should they make regarding the future of this operation?
• How should Magenta plan to organize the operation of the mining activity? As a jointly owned company (jointly owned with one or more nationals?) or as a wholly owned subsidiary? Why?
• How should it staff the new organization? With Americans or local nationals? Why?

Local Customs and Management Styles

Endnotes

1. There are many good sources of information about Japanese managerial methods. One good brief one is, "Sources of Management Problems in Japanese-American Joint Ventures," by Richard B. Peterson and Justin Y. Shumada, *Academy of Management Review,* October 1978, pp. 796–804. See also, *Assessment of Managers: An International Comparison,* by Bernard M. Bass, Philip C. Burger, Robert Doktor, and Gerald J. Barrett (The Free Press, 1979).
2. *Management: Tasks, Responsibilities and Practices,* by Peter F. Drucker, Harper & Row, 1974, page 21.
3. See, "Worldwide Variations in Management Styles," by John J. Tarrant, *Management Review,* April 1976, p. 38.
4. Drucker, op. cit., p. 21.
5. Tarrant, op. cit., p. 38.
6. See, *International Management Practices,* by Gunnar Beeth (AMACOM, 1973) p. 98.
7. *Assessment of Managers: An International Comparison,* by Bernard M. Bass, Philip C. Burger, Robert Doktor and Gerald J. Barrett, The Free Press, 1979.
8. See, "Why Britain is Floundering," by Robert Wesson, *Business Week,* 14 August 1978, p. 11.
9. *Wall Street Journal,* 21 August 1978, p. 1.
10. "Worker Participation: Contrasts in Three Countries," by Nancy Foy and Herman Gadon, *Harvard Business Review,* May-June 1972, pp. 73–83; this quote is from p. 76.
11. Drucker, op. cit., p. 21.
12. Foy and Gadon, op. cit., p. 76.
13. The Mitsui Company's practices in the United States were investigated very thoroughly in 1980 and 1981. Early reports were that the practices found would lead to prosecution of the company for violating our laws. See, *Business Week,* 13 April 1981, p. 44.
14. See *Business Week,* 20 April 1981, p. 72.
15. As related in the *New York Times,* 23 July 1978, Sec. 1, p. 27.
16. See, "A Multivariate Multinational Comparison of Managerial Attitudes," by Rodger W. Griffeth, Peter W. Hom, Angelo DeNisi, and Wayne Kirchner, *Proceedings of the Academy of Management Annual Meeting,* 1980, pp. 63–67.
17. *Business Week,* 3 September 1979, p. 151.

Suggested Supplementary Readings

Amano, Matt M. "Organizational Changes of a Japanese Firm in America," *California Management Review,* Spring 1979, pp. 51–59.

Bartolme, Fernando, and Paul A. Lee Evans. "Professional Lives Versus Private Lives — Shifting Patterns of Managerial Commitment" (A study of 500 European middle managers). *Organizational Dynamics,* Spring 1979, pp. 2–29.

Hofstede, Geert. "Motivation, Leadership and Organization: Do American Theories Apply Abroad?" *Organizational Dynamics*, Summer 1980, pp. 42–63.

Jacoby, Neil H., Peter Nehamkis, and Richard Eells. *Bribery and Extortion in World Business*. MacMillan, 1977.

Mazzolini, Remato. "The Influence of European Workers Over Corporate Strategy," *Sloan Management Review*, Spring, 1978, pp. 59–82.

Except for historical interest, the whole purpose of studying management practices is to learn how to manage better in the future.

It would be relatively simple if we could just study the best of past practices and assume that they will be just as suitable in the future as they are today. But this cannot be because every factor that bears on effective operations will be different, in small ways, if not in large ways.

It is necessary, therefore, to try to look ahead and to see what the future will be like and then to try to see what changes will be needed in management methods so that managing can still be done effectively in this future.

Chapter 27, The Changing Environment, discusses the future environment and how managerial methods might be adapted so that they will be effective under these changed conditions.

Management in the Future

Chapter 27
The Changing
Environment

Objectives of Chapter Twenty-Seven

1. To try to look into the future and see what it will be like with a view of trying to see what effects there will be on managerial practices.

2. To try to appraise the effects of the continuing growth of service-type activities in the nation, paying particular attention to the difficulty of managing this type of work effectively.

3. To give thought to the more restricted areas of managerial freedom and to the effects of these restrictions on managerial effectiveness.

4. To get some appreciation of what tomorrow's managers will have to be trying to do and how they will be trying to do it.

The Changing Environment

27

What's past is prologue.
Shakespeare

Fifty years ago, when Calvin Coolidge was President, he said, "The business of America is business."

His statement was a typical viewpoint of the time. We needed more goods and services and it was up to business to supply them. At that time there was little feeling that either government or business should assume social responsibilities.

Obviously, we have come a long way from that viewpoint. Today, everyone in private life, in business, and in government is aware of and accepts the idea that the social well-being of people should have a high place in every organization's list of objectives.

In this chapter, we will consider how tomorrow's managers will need to manage. We will look at tomorrow's economy and the probable social and cultural environment and give thought to how these factors will bear upon the way organizations need to be managed.

The Social/Cultural Environment

Since managers must always manage their organizations in the existing environment, what they do and how they do it are affected by the current environment. The environment sets limits to what managers can do and at the same time, sets up demands and requirements which they have to pay attention to.

In this section we will consider the expected changes which will come about because of the increasing importance of government and/or social responsibilities. We will consider also, the part played by ecology, ethics, and demographic changes.

The Increasing Importance of Governments

In 1980, one person out of every five who was working in the United States, worked for the government, either national, state or local. In total, this came to nearly 20 million people working for some government agency. At the same time, governments, through taxes, took 40 percent of the national income.

Both the number of people and the fraction of our national income used for government activities has always increased year by year although taxpayer revolts, such as those occurring in 1978 in California and in other parts of the country may halt the process.

A large part of the money spent by governments goes for activities where the government is better equipped to perform the service than are private businesses. Police and fire protection at the local level and national defense at the national level, can be better done by governments. Schools, streets and road, sewage disposal, and many other public services, can best be provided by governments. So also, welfare programs can be better administered by public agencies.

Some of the cost of government is, however, spent for regulatory activities. This is the area where the greatest expansion has taken place in recent years. And it is the area which has the strongest impact on how managers will have to carry out their work in the years ahead.

Since the mid-1960s, Congress has passed more than eighty new federal laws regulating the operations of business in one way or another. This legislation produced a number of new regulatory agencies, all serving as quasi-legislative and quasi-judicial bodies, producing complex sets of regulations which have the force of law. We are now being governed as much by regulations promulgated by government agencies as we are by laws passed by legislative bodies.

Management in the Future

Many of these new regulations put the regulating agencies in the position of making managerial decisions. These relate to prices, product designs, product performance and reliability. In the food industry they cover food ingredients.

Unfortunately, some government regulations seem to be made without consideration being given to their cost impacts or to their reasonableness.

In 1977, the Pure Food and Drug Administration banned the use of saccharin, a sugar substitute, because it might cause cancer. The evidence for this was a Canadian study that showed that large amounts of saccharin caused cancer in mice. Public outcry against this regulation was so great (saccharin had long been used in the diets of diabetics) that Congress delayed its enforcement.

In fact, the Canadians had fed the mice the equivalent of *100 gallons of diet soda per day* for an adult person for a lifetime, so the evidence of the cancer danger to human beings from normal usage of saccharin was slight indeed!

Three years later, in 1980, after several studies covering 4,000 people in the United States, it was found that there was no evidence that saccharin caused cancer in people. The proposed ban on its use was lifted.[1]

In another case, in 1979, the Occupational Safety and Health Administration moved to restrict the use of benzine in industry because of its hazard to human life. The companies objected, pointing out that it would cost $300 million per life saved. OSHA answered that their mission was to save lives and not to consider costs. The case went to court where the court upheld the objections. It was suggested that $300 million spent in other ways could save many more lives.[2]

This type of irresponsible use of regulatory power by government agencies occurred in other cases and in the operation of other government agencies as well. By the beginning of the 1980's, there was a groundswell of anti-regulation feeling because of unnecessary and costly regulations. (Automobiles, for example, cost at least $700 extra each because of regulations.)

Managers in the 1980s may get some relief from extremely burdensome regulations since the Congress is turning toward requiring its agencies to make risk-benefit-cost analyses before they issue new regulations. The American Congress seems finally to be conscious of the need to be supportive of business after a long history of negativism. The success of Japanese companies, which enjoy the complete support of the Japanese government, in competition with American companies, has driven home the message that cooperation rather than harassment is needed.

Social Responsibilities

Starting in the late 1960s and continuing on into the 1970s, the social climate in most Western civilization countries went through great changes. In the United States, these changes concerned equal rights for all groups in our social order, safety and health protection for consumers and workers, protection of consumers in matters of the quality of products and services, and concerns about the quality of life.

Some scholars say that the Western world is now entering a "post-industrial" era where the production and distribution of goods and services will be secondary in importance to quality of life considerations. By 1980, it was generally accepted that business managers needed to have more direct concern for social problems. These changes have greatly modified the work of managers since *they* have to try to bring about most of the improvements being demanded by society.

Equal Rights in Employment. Civil rights in employment movements, starting with equal rights for blacks and women during the late sixties and progressing to other minority groups, became even more important in the 1970s. Obviously, fairness in employment relations is wholly reasonable from a humanitarian viewpoint and few people would argue today against this requirement. Tomorrow's managers must manage under more restrictive restraints than used to apply. This is an area where high level managers must see that lower level managers operate this way too.

The result of equal rights for women and minorities will be an increase in their numbers in managerial jobs in the 1980s. During the 1970s, the progress of such people into managerial ranks was slow. This was probably caused in part by the scarcity of qualified candidates since it takes time to develop managerial competence. In the 1980s, and with the passage of time this hurdle will be removed as minority people move up the managerial ladder. Within a few more years we should find more women and blacks in managerial ranks.

Safety and Health Protection for Consumers and Workers. In the United States we have a long history of protection of consumers from products which might endanger our health. The Pure Food and Drug Administration has, for example, monitored matters within its scope since before World War I. In a similar way we have had safety laws to protect workers against hazardous working conditions for over 100 years. And we have had, for over 60 years, workmen's compensation laws to provide monetary help for workers injured on the job.

In 1965, Ralph Nader's book, "Unsafe at Any Speed," which charged that General Motors' Chevrolet new small Corvair car was unsafe, came out.[3] (There had been several serious accidents with Corvairs not being able to take sharp turns at high speeds.) This book sparked a wave of consumer protection sentiment which resulted in Congress passing many new safety laws covering both consumers of products and workers on jobs. Job hazards which might cause injury or health impairment and even

noise levels on jobs were covered and new standards were set up limiting these hazards.

Protection of Consumers: The Quality of Products and Services. Consumer protectionism spilled over from safety and health into product and service quality in use. Spokesmen, presuming to speak for consumers, attacked business, claiming that the quality of goods and services offered by business should be better. Such attacks drew considerable support. Consequently, both products and services must live up to their promise and their claims in a reasonable fashion or else the producer will have to make good.

Associated with this is a greater emphasis on truth in advertising and sales claims. And, in the case of charge account purchases, interest charges must also be spelled out and not be hidden or misrepresented. In a great many cases where foods, beverages, cosmetics, or medicines are concerned, the ingredients must be listed on the label.

Consumer protection laws have, in the areas where they apply, supplanted the traditional forms of consumer protections which used to be largely matters of producers cautioning consumers to use discretion in the use of their products. Consumers also had the freedom to vote their preferences in the marketplace with their dollars by buying what they wanted and going elsewhere if they couldn't get what they wanted or if they did not like what they got.

Today, consumerism seems sometimes to go too far (by ruling out low quality products, it has denied customers who want such products the opportunity to buy them). But whether it goes too far or not, managers have to live with it as part of the environment.

Quality of Life. As we move into the 1980s, there is an increasing interest in the "quality of life." One of our national purposes is to improve the quality of life and the well-being of people in our society.

In the United States (and much of Europe) the standards of living of people in terms of material well-being surpass anything the world has ever known. This affluence manifests itself in home ownership, possession of consumer durable goods, expenditures on travel, health, education, and savings of individuals.

Nor is the affluence confined to only a few. Angus Campbell and his colleagues found that fewer than 5 percent of the people living in the United States live at or below the poverty level.[4]

Our growing material improvements have, however, been accompanied by other disturbing changes. A decade ago, there was an increase in drug addictions and in civil disorders. There was also an increase in crime and in violence, and a deterioration of confidence in public authority. All of these things appear to be moving toward improvement as we head into the 1980s. But the fact remains that we do not have a Utopian level of social harmony and personal fulfillment.

Meaning of "Quality of Life." The "quality of life" or "well-being" of people is hard to define since it has to do with many things. It is psychological and sociological and economic as well. It includes material things — food, shelter, and consumer durable goods — and it includes health, happiness, and satisfactions. All of these things exist in context with other things and they differ from time to time and they differ among individuals. A given achievement level will give satisfaction to one individual but not to another. Quality of life is partly in our minds so it is partly an individual matter.

Campbell and his colleagues define the quality of life in terms of happiness and satisfactions. As we reported in Chapter 15, these researchers, as well as others, found that 80 to 85 percent of the people studied said that they were mildly happy or very happy with their work life.[5]

Young people reported themselves as being happier than did old people but old people were rather well satisfied even though they were often not exuberantly happy. Married people are happier than other groups and separated and divorced people are the least happy. Interestingly, uneducated people were found to be better satisfied (but not necessarily happier) than better educated people. Perhaps they are better satisfied because they don't expect so much.

Sources of Happiness and Satisfaction. Campbell and his colleagues reported that the new rhetoric about the quality of life and well-being takes for granted the basic essentials of life — adequate food, housing, and other material goods. The quality of life comes from the realization of less tangible values such as, achievement in one's work, a sense of fulfillment of one's potential, a feeling of identification with one's community and appreciation of beauty in nature and in the arts.

The achievement of these values comes from the individual's achievements in one or more of the several "domains" of his association with the social order in which he moves. These domains include marriage, family life, religion, friends, organizations to which he belongs, and his life on the job. Of these a successful marriage is, according to Campbell's study, the most important of all domains.

Also important are the individual's on-the-job relationships and accomplishments. Most adults who have jobs spend close to half of their waking hours on the job so, to them, quality of life is divided into two nearly equal parts, life on the job and life off the job.

Even having a job is part of the quality of life. Most women do not have to work outside the home (see page 560) but many of them want outside jobs so, to them, having a job improves their satisfactions with life. But for women who would rather not work outside the home but who have to take a job, having a job does not increase their satisfactions directly. A job does increase their satisfactions indirectly, however, in that it provides the money for paying the necessary bills. In fact, forty per cent of the women working said that they would quit if they didn't have to work (twenty-five per cent of the men said this too). For such people, non-work domains have more to do with generating a sense of well-being than do their jobs.

At the same time, people, men and women who want jobs and cannot find them, regard themselves as unemployed. This experience is, to almost every unemployed person, a deleterious experience. Unemployed people are almost always unhappy people.

The burden of trying to improve the quality of life of people will be an important concern to tomorrow's managers, both in government and in non-government organizations.

Ecology

Protectionism has also embraced protecting the environment. No longer does land ownership confer on its owner full authority to use it as the owner desires. For over fifty years, city zoning laws have put restrictions on the development of land in cities so that adjacent owners would not be harmed.

But now land use restrictions have been considerably broadened outside of cities and even in remote wild areas. The Sierra Club and similar groups lobby continually for the preservation of our natural areas. Other groups want "endangered species" of wildlife to be left alone in their natural habitats.

On the whole, this type of ecology activity affects only land developers. But sometimes, as in the case of the construction of the trans-Alaska oil pipeline, other parts of our economic life are affected.

The most far-reaching effects of ecological considerations are, however, felt in urban areas. The Environmental Protection Agency (EPA), has power to issue regulations covering air and water purity as well as to set maximum permissable noise levels.

These regulations affect all businesses and all cities. They all create trash and sewage. Electric power generating plants and manufacturing companies are also faced with the problem of cleaning up the air and water pollution which their processes create. Some companies also produce considerable amounts of other waste such as ashes and chemical waste.

Today's society is requiring that all of these situations be improved and brought under control. Much of the burden of improving these conditions falls on the managers of businesses.

An unfortunate by-product associated with ecology programs is that they are almost always negative and are not constructive in a positive way. Ecologists delayed the Alaskan oil pipeline for a year and caused it to cost several billion dollars more money. And they have opposed strip coal mining even when attractive replacement land contours have been assured. They have delayed our badly needed self-sufficiency energy program and have made us more dependent on imported Arabian oil. In the process of our changing more to coal, some ecological goals will have to be compromised.

Ethics

The 1970s saw extensive disclosures of bribery by many large Western civilization companies, among them many large American companies. Governmental investigations were made because bribery payments are illegal under American law and companies making such payments in order to gain a competitive advantage are not allowed to consider bribes as costs of operations so far as the calculations of profits for income tax purposes are concerned.

We discussed ethics briefly in Chapter 5 but we did not go into certain aspects of this very difficult problem. Since the dawn of history, bribes, favoritism, sex, and blackmail have played a part in the operations of every society. So also, all of these practices have long been part of worldwide political intrigue.

Probably there is less of this in Western civilizations than elsewhere but even today there are many parts of the world where these practices are the order of the day. You do business in this kind of an atmosphere or you don't do business. And it is unlikely that any laws passed by, or any pronouncements by, the United States Congress or the United States Department of Justice, will change it. This is the way business is done in many parts of the world.

What can and what should an ethically thinking American or Western European manager do when faced with such a choice? A great many of today's managers have made their choice. They try to do business only on a high ethical standard. No doubt this often puts them at a competitive disadvantage but most Americans seem to feel that this is better than engaging in questionable practices. Tomorrow's managers will sometimes have to make hard choices in matters of ethics.

Demographic Factors

Changes in the make-up of our population go on all of the time. These are part of the ever changing environment within which managers must operate. We will look at the following aspects of demographic changes in the environment: changes in age groups, changes in the educational level of employees, changes in the nation's workforce and women in the workforce, and the growth of the "Sun Belt."

Changes in Age Groups. The population of the United States passed the 200 million mark in the early 1970s and is on the way, even with a slowing down of the rate of increase, to 240 million in 1990.

Today, over 80 million or 40 percent of the population is made up of the very young, those who are under twenty-one years of age. But, because of declining birth rates, there will be no increase at all in this group in the future. Rather, it may go down. If it holds at 80 million, it will, in 1990, make up only 33 percent of the total.

At the other end of the age spectrum, today there are 20 million, or 10 percent, of the population who are sixty-five and over. By 1990, their numbers will increase to 28 million or 12 percent of the total. (See Figure 27-1).[6]

These two things, the lessening importance of youth and the growing importance of the elderly, will be the salient points of the population changes in the next decade.

Businesses supplying products and services for babies and infants will have a stagnant market. Teenagers, too, will become relatively less important. We may see less of "new, improved, advanced, bold, pacesetter, and innovative" emphasis. The emphasis may change to "price, quality, durability, performance, and serviceability."[7]

The relative scarcity of teenagers will help solve today's unemployed teenager problem. Since the whole population will grow while the number of teenagers stands still, job opportunities for teenagers will improve. By 1990, there will be a shortage of workers in this age group. This will hurt service industries such as hotels and fast foods companies because they depend on the young as low-wage employees.

One might suspect that the growth in the number of the elderly would block off jobs for younger people. This appears not to be a serious danger. In 1980, almost 70 percent of social security pensioners had retired before age sixty-five, even though there was no compulsion for them to retire early.

Today's elderly people usually live in their own homes and do not live with their

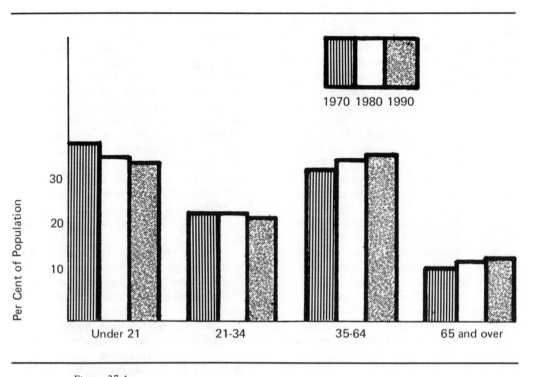

Figure 27-1
Age group changes in the United States in the 1980's.

children so they spend more money than old people used to spend. There being more older people and their spending more will boost the markets for things that older people like, such as eating out and travel.

Changes in the Educational Level of Employees. It is estimated that, before 1990, the proportion of young people who will have had at least some college training will go up to 35 percent.[8] Their motivations and responses to organizational life will differ from those of today's employees, fewer of whom have gone beyond high school. Furthermore, so far as job requirements are concerned, young people, as a group may be over-educated (see Figure 27-2). In the business education area, it is expected that the number of MBAs will double in the next decade. Doctors, lawyers, and teachers will probably be in oversupply. Some of these

educated people will have to take routine, uninteresting jobs. Problems may arise from their lack of interest in jobs which offer little challenge.

The Nation's Workforce and Women in the Workforce. The nation's workforce (people working and wanting to work) stood at 103 million at the start of 1980. Of these, 43 million were women. Ninety-seven million people were actually employed. Of these, 40 million were women.

The increase of the number of women in the workforce has been the outstanding change in workforce demography since World War II. Most of this increase has come from the ranks of married women. As late as 1970, only 40 percent of all married women were working outside of the home. By 1980 this had risen to just over 50 percent, and the trend toward more working

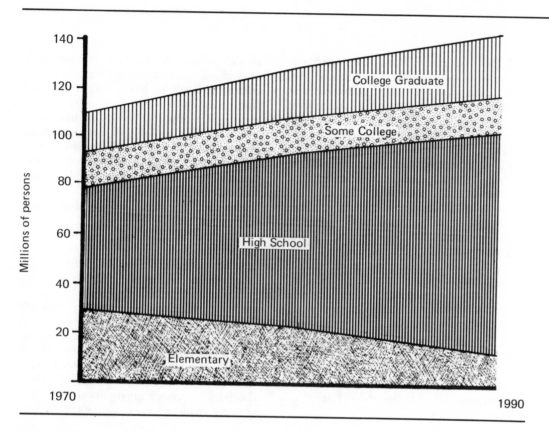

Figure 27-2
Educational attainment changes of the adult population (25 years and over) of the United States, 1970-1990.

women seems to be continuing.

The "Sun Belt." The population in the South and West has grown, for a number of years, at double the national rate. Employment in these areas, particularly manufacturing employment, has grown just as rapidly. As we noted in Chapter 4, this has come from heavy government spending for defense products in these areas and from lower wages. Other factors include the greater use of air conditioning and the migration of older people to warmer climates.

These factors all seem to be operating still so it is probable that the Sun Belt areas will continue to grow at faster rates than in the North although perhaps at a slower rate than today's growth.

The Economy

The economic environment is a second broad area where outside conditions will play a part in the way managers will operate in the future. We will address ourselves to the growth in the size of organizations, the growth in service-type work, inflation, and the future of labor unions.

Organization Size

Since populations almost everywhere in the world continue to grow, most of today's organizations, both public and private,

The Changing Environment

will also grow in size. Tomorrow's managerial methods will, therefore, need to be suitable, even more than heretofore, to large scale operations. In the late 1970s there were more than 1,000 companies in the world with over 10,000 employees each and there probably were 100 or more companies with over 100,000 employees. And, of course, in addition to these, many governmental units employ far more than 100,000 people.

In business, the further growth in prospect would seem to indicate that the divisional form of organizational structure will become even more common than it is today since it is usually the best form to use for large scale operations.

Other problems associated with large size will also be accentuated. Large organizations have greater problems trying to control what their many subordinate managers do. This is partly because of the new stringent laws. Higher level managers need to see that the requirements of these laws are known and obeyed by lower-level people.

Growth of Service Work

As we move through the last quarter of the century, we find, in the United States, that we are an urban and largely a white collar society. Today, very few people (only three percent of the workforce) work on farms. And even factory and other blue collar workers make up only an additional 25 percent of our working population.

The big swing in employment in the last twenty years in the United States has come in the service industries and in service work in all industries. Today, over sixty per cent of all of the people working in the United States are white collar workers and workers performing service activities, either in service-type organizations or service-type work in manufacturing organizations. Service-type organizations include governments, schools, hospitals, and such private business companies as those in marketing, advertising, accounting, law, entertaining, insurance, banking, hotels and motels, and transportation.

This growth in service organizations, and it is still going on, will mean that more of tomorrow's managers will be managing in difficult situations than was formerly so. Because there is no tangible, countable output, the work of service organizations is almost always hard to define, hard to direct, and hard to control.

The fact that managing service organizations is difficult will not be new or different in the future. The change will be that, because of the growth of service-type activities, more and more people, both managers and other employees, will be engaged in this difficult-to-manage service area. Unfortunately, too, because these organizations are difficult to manage, they usually do not operate very effectively. Trying to develop more effective operations and increasing productivity in service organizations will be a growing challenge to tomorrow's managers.

Inflation

Today, there are few people who do not believe that inflation is here to stay in the United States and in the rest of the world too. Prices everywhere keep going up and up. Very few things lag behind for very long.

During most of the 1970s, inflation averaged some 7 percent a year, but, in more recent years, it worsened and has stayed well above 10 percent a year.

It might seem that inflation should not be much of a problem for tomorrow's managers because although inflation makes everything cost more, every company can raise its own selling prices too. So it would not seem to cause any consequential problem to managers.

It doesn't seem to work out quite this way, however. Many companies (utilities, railroads, etc.) can't increase their rates without permission because their rates are regulated. And such increases as are permitted are often slow in coming. But even companies which can increase their prices frequently find it hard to do because of customer resistance.

It takes quite a bit of managerial effort to hold the increases in money outflows to the same rate as the increases of money inflows. One obvious reaction to the expectation of more inflation is for managers to spend money today for the things which will be necessary in the future because tomorrow they will cost even more.

Labor Unions

With the growth of service industries and the migration of industry to the sun-belt areas, there has come a slight decline in the strength of labor unions. Unions have been less successful in organizing workers in the service industries and in the South than in the industrial North and in manufacturing industries. Unions have even lost a little of their power to influence congressmen in Washington.

In 1981, the combination of a nation-wide depression and the continued invasion of Japanese cars hit the American automobile industry very hard. For the first time in many years, management and labor in the automobile industry began, truly, to cooperate and to join hands to try to operate more efficiently. The United Automobile Workers Union no longer pressed for various make-work rules as they had in the past. On the contrary, they were willing to give up many practices which had, in the past, made extra costs.

This reduction in union militancy has rubbed off on unions in other distressed industries. Managers will, in the early 1980's at least, be able to make more economies than they could in the past.

Managers in the Future

If our premises about the look of the future are right, then we can anticipate certain changes in managerial methods and in points of emphasis. The jobs of managers will be a little different from those of today's managers. Public relations will come in for more attention and the present greater emphasis on social responsibilities will continue.

Public Relations

In the United States, business has an impersonal image. It is faceless to the public and has no personality. Heads of large companies assume a low profile image. There are very few Henry Ford IIs who speak up to represent business sides on issues.

Perhaps, in part because of this, the American public is skeptical of business companies and distrusts them. More people are growing less willing to accept the operation of the market place and are turning to the government to control things. Unfortunately, this is often because they have the wrong idea about how businesses operate and about how much money they make. Studies have shown that many people think that profits are 30 to 40 percent of sales dollars, whereas, in fact, they are rarely more than 3 to 5 percent of sales. Companies need to do a better job of presenting their case to the public and of clearing up such misconceptions.

If business companies are to have a better public image in the future in this country, more high level managers will need to assume some of the public relations obligation themselves and become spokesmen for their companies' positions.[9] The need to say "yes" to invitations to make speeches before public groups where they will have an opportunity to acquaint the audience with the problems of their organizations and with the economic relationships which the public so often does not understand.

They may even, at times, have to appear and testify before Congressional committees. For such appearances they need to be well prepared and to make good presentations. They will need to be more aware of their organization's public image and to public reactions to what they say than used to be necessary.

In order for them to do this well, they will need to be articulate and to have good platform presence. They will need to make their positions clear. Furthermore, their positions need to be defensible positions both for their organizations and for their industries. Managers will need to show that they are giving consideration to social needs as well as to the long-term implications of their actions.

Maintaining a good public image does not, however, imply that managers should not stand up for their rights. In 1977 the Equal Employment Opportunity Commission (EEOC) filed charges against Sears, Roebuck claiming that the company had violated their regulations. Sears countered with a lawsuit against the government asking for it to clear up its conflicting regulations. The suit was dismissed by the court, but, in the light of Sears' defense, the EEOC decided that it didn't have a very good case and it dropped its charges. Sears' public image was probably enhanced because it no longer stood accused of wrongful discrimination.

The Quality of Life on the Job

Since workers spend half of their waking hours on the job, the quality of life on the job is an important part of the total quality of life so far as employees are concerned.

Quality of life on the job is a three sided affair. It has to do wtih "creature comforts," and with organizational relationships and with peer relationships.

"Creature Comforts." Working conditions are part of life on the job. Temperature extremes, noise, dust, and fumes are distasteful to most employees. Sometimes workers have to have their hands in oil all day. Sometimes they have to work in awkward positions and sometimes they have to exert considerable physical effort. Most of these working conditions are now covered by law requiring employers to improve jobs so that there is now little hazard to employees' health. Physical creature comfort on the job is today usually well taken care of.

Organizational Relationships. Organizational relationships are also part of the quality of life on the job. These include open communications between superiors and subordinates and include pay and job security. They also include designing jobs, where possible, so that they offer some challenge and satisfaction for work well done. Although it is not possible to make all jobs interesting, managers ought to do what they can in the direction of making them more interesting.

A different way to improve the quality of life on the job, is to transfer monotonous and highly repetitive or dangerous manipulative work to machines or robots. Most of the welding done on bodies of automobiles is done by robots. Robots and machines don't mind heat, cold, dust, noise, monotony, or repetition. The use of robots takes certain jobs out of the realm of worker jobs, leaving for employees the jobs which call for higher degrees of mental application. The least "humanized" jobs go to the machines and the robots.

Peer Relationships. A third factor in the quality of life on the job is peer relationships. Almost everyone wants to be accepted by his fellow workers and to feel that he is a member of the group. This is a part of the quality of life with which managers have little to do. It is part of the social culture of groups themselves.

Robert Schrank feels, however, that managers can help here. He feels that workers need to have opportunities to socialize and to "chew the fat" with each other. They need to have opportunities to visit with each other and not be tied to their jobs too tightly. These things, Schrank feels, will improve peer relationships and the quality of life on the job.[10]

The Objectives of Tomorrow's Managers

Tomorrow's social goals will be aimed at improving the national welfare just as much as they will be aimed at increasing the gross national product. This poses a question for managers of businesses. What should be their role? Should it be to produce goods and services as needed by the marketplace at reasonable prices? Or should it be something more? Do managers have a greater responsibility to contribute to the well-being of the nation?

The answer today seems clearly to be that producing goods and services economically is *not,* standing alone, enough. Business managers cannot, themselves, solve very many social problems, but they can contribute a great deal to alleviating some of them if they do what they can by hiring their share of handicapped people, of minority groups, and by doing other things, to help the social order. When managers make decisions they should consider their broad social effects as well as how they will contribute to effective operations.

Lest this seem to underplay the responsibility of managers to operate efficiently, it should be said that effective operations must still be *the fundamental* ojbective of business organizations. Without this, bankruptcy ensues and all objectives, social and otherwise, fail.

So we see that *managers* have to become the agents to make the many improvements now called for by law. But they are costly to make. At Dow Chemical, for example (and Dow is only twenty-fourth in size among the nation's largest companies),

the costs of specially mandated work and extra record keeping comes to $150 million a year.[11]

It seems anti-climactic to add that even though managers have to humanize jobs, lessen air and water pollution, reduce noise levels, and make products and jobs safe, in the final analysis, the consuming public has to pay for it all, including Dow's $150 million, through higher prices.

Managerial Processes

We have said that tomorrow's managers will have to manage in a more humanistic and more participative way. Hard authority will be used less. This will come about partly from there being a more general recognition that this kind of management is usually more effective than commanderism management.

Another reason for this will have to do with tomorrow's employees, many of whom will be overeducated, so far as job requirements are concerned. This will probably make them less willing to tolerate autocratic management.

They will also be relatively affluent. By 1980, average factory wages had passed the $15,000 a year mark and many families had two wage earners. Furthermore, wages go up still more every year. The ties that bind employees to jobs get looser with their greater affluence. Both absenteeism and turnover go up. Managers have to counteract these tendencies by managing in a more acceptable way.

The apparent diminishing of the work ethic will also increase the need for managers to use more motivation oriented methods. So will our laws concerning the fair treatment of employees. Employees may now question the decisions of managers so far as hiring and promotions are concerned.

Managers themselves, may however, not be inherently more participative in their methods than are today's managers. So tomorrow's managers will need training in a more tolerant managerial style. They will need to be able to make sophisticated applications of organizational knowledge.

Tomorrow's managers will also have to carry on with less full authority than their predecessors had. Their authority is continually being eroded by government agencies and the intervention of powerful interest groups such as unions and consumer groups.

Growing Importance of Staff Work. Earlier we reported the growing importance of staff work. This trend seems likely to continue because of the growth in organization size and the complexity of the problems organizations face. And the growth in staff departments in turn causes more internal problems associated with internal flows of information and confused chains of authority.

Mathematical Models. The use of mathematical models, described in Chapter 22, will probably continue to expand as operations research analysts develop additional procedures and develop new adaptations of present procedures to current problems. Tomorrow's managers will not themselves have to become operations research specialists but they will need to become knowledgeable about the contributions which such techniques can make.

Summary

Effective management tomorrow will no doubt have many similarities to effective management today. Tomorrow's managers will still have to choose able people, define their responsibilities, provide them with help and the resources they will need, monitor their work, hold them accountable, and reward performance.

Managerial fundamentals, the essential activities of management which are discussed in this book will largely continue to apply. But as we have seen, the many different combinations of people, activities, and environments are so different that they require different applications of these fundamentals — so much so that it becomes really true that different kinds of management are called for. It seems evident that the changes going on today will require tomorrow's managers to manage somewhat differently from the way today's managers operate.

The social atmosphere has changed in the last decade from one of allowing managers of businesses largely to manage as they saw fit. The change, which is still in progress, is in the direction of incorporating broad social goals into managerial objectives.

This new atmosphere poses a most difficult challenge to the managers of businesses in the future. (The change will be much less in nonbusiness organizations such as governments because they do not have to generate their own funds in order to support their organizations and they already operate in the social service area toward which the emphasis is moving.) The challenge to business managers is in their having to generate profits in order to stay alive, yet while at the same time having their organizations engage in many non-profit-making and costly activities which are for society's benefit. But, bridge this gap they must or see the government move into more business areas.

Review Questions

1. Service industries have, for many years, been growing faster than industries which produce physical products. If this tide continues, what impacts is this likely to have on managerial methods?
2. What changes in business goals is society imposing? How will the adoption of such goals affect managerial methods?
3. In what way has the growing importance of government work affected managerial work? What has it caused managers to do or not to do which differs from past practices? Discuss.
4. How can an employer discriminate in favor of minorities in employment without discriminating against members of the majority? (The law forbids discriminating against any and all groups.) Discuss.
5. How has the consumerism wave affected business? Which industries have felt the strongest impacts from consumerism and what adaptations have managers had to make to keep their organizations' practices in tune with the environment?
6. What does "quality of life" mean? How about the quality of life on-the-job? How do you measure it? What can managers do to improve it?
7. Do managers have to get involved in ecology matters? Discuss and give reasons for your answer.
8. How will demographic changes affect the work of managers? What changes in their practices seem to be indicated? Discuss.

Case 27-1   God Plans to Create the Earth

Apparently our legislators in Congress have their lighter moments. They recognize that some of their actions make problems for managers. In her syndicated column of October 20, 1976, Erma Bombeck quotes the following from the *Congressional Record* where it appeared with no author's name:

IN THE BEGINNING GOD CREATED HEAVEN AND EARTH. He was then faced with a class action suit for having failed to file an environmental impact statement with the Heavenly Environmental Protection Agency (HEPA, an angelically-staffed agency dedicated to keeping the universe pollution-free). God was granted a temporary permit for the Heavenly portion of the project but was hit with a cease and desist order for the Earthly part, pending further study by HEPA.

Then God Said, "LET THERE BE LIGHT," and he should never have brought up this point since one of the Council was active in the Sierrangel Club and immediately demanded to know how the light would be made. Would there be strip mining? How about thermal pollution? Air pollution? God explained that light would come from a huge ball of fire.

Nobody in Council really understood this, but it was provisionally accepted assuming (1) no smog or smoke would result from the ball of fire; (2) a separate burning permit would be required, and (3) since continuous light would be a waste of energy it should be dark at least half of the time. God agreed.

When asked how the Earth would be covered for darkness, God said, "LET THERE BE FIRMAMENT AMIDST THE WATERS" and one ecologically radical member accused him of double talk, but action was tabled since God would be required first to file for permit from Angelic Bureau of Land Management (ABLM) and further would be required to obtain water permits from appropriate agencies.

God said, "LET THE WATERS BRING FORTH THE CREEPING CREATURES HAVING LIFE AND THE FOWL THAT MAY FLY OVER THE EARTH." Here again, Council took no formal action, since it would require approval of the Game and Fish Commission, coordinated with Heavenly Wildlife Federation and Audubon-angelic Society.

Everything appeared in order until God said He wanted to complete the project in six days. At that point he was advised by Council that his timing was completely out of the question. HEPA would require a minimum of 180 days to review the application and impact statement. After that, there would be public hearings. It would be 10 or 12 months before a permit could be granted.

God said, "To hell with it."

· Tomorrow's managers will surely have some frustrating as well as interesting days. Theirs will not be monotonous jobs.

Endnotes

1. The results of these studies were reported in *Time,* 17 March 1980, p. 86.
2. Reported in *Dun's Review,* September 1979, p. 87.
3. *Unsafe at Any Speed,* by Ralph Nader, (Grossman, 1965).
4. See, *The Quality of American Life,* by Angus Campbell, Philip E. Converse, and Willard L. Rodgers (Russel Sage Foundation, 1976). (By 1981, the Federal government defined the poverty level for a family of four as $8,500.)

5. Ibid., Chapter 1. See also, *Most Americans Like Their Work* (The Conference Board, July, 1978).
6. "Demography's Good News for the Eighties," by Walter Guzzardi, Jr., *Fortune,* 5 November 1979, pp. 92ff. See, also, "America's New Demographic Profile," by George H. Brown, *Conference Board Record,* October 1975, pp. 53–56.
7. "America's Adults, In Search of What?" *U.S. News & World Report,* 21 August 1978, p. 37.
8. Brown, op. cit., p. 53.
9. See, "The Top Man Becomes Mr. Outside," *Business Week,* 4 May 1974, pp. 36ff.
10. *Ten Thousand Working Days,* by Robert Schrank, MIT Press, 1978.
11. As reported in *Management Review,* May 1978, p. 20.

Suggested Supplementary Readings

Bohlander, George W. "Implementing Quality-of-Work Programs: Recognizing The Barriers," *MSU Business Topics,* Spring 1979, pp. 33–40.

Carlson, Howard C. (Interview). "GM's Quality of Life Efforts." *Personnel,* July-August 1978, pp. 11–23.

Driscoll, James W., Gary L. Cowger, and Robert J. Egan. "Private Managers and Public Myths — Public Managers and Private Myths." *Sloan Management Review,* Fall 1979, pp. 53–58.

Meadows, Edward. "How Three Companies Improved Their Productivity." *Fortune,* 10 March 1980, pp. 92–101.

Terborg, J.R. "Women in Management: A Research Review," *Journal of Applied Psychology* 62 (1978): pp. 647–664.

INDEX

Glossary of Terms

Acceptance theory of authority   Superiors have only such authority as subordinates are willing to give them.

Accountability   To be answerable to a superior for doing one's work or for the use of organizational resources or for accomplishing certain ends.

Appraisal   Judging by the superior of the quality of work or accomplishment of a subordinate.

Authority   The right to exercise power over the actions of people or over the use of resources.

"Average person" dilemma   The difficulty that all people have who try to make general statements about how people behave caused by people not all being average thus precluding generalized statements from being descriptive of everyone's behavior.

Backlog syndrome   Tendency for workers to slow down in their work as the backlog of future work shrinks.

Behavior modification   Changes in the behavior of subordinates brought about by actions of the superior intended to influence them and to produce these changes.

Behavioral science   The use of scientific research methods to study the behavior and reactions of people to stimuli in the human relations area.

Boundary spanner   Person at the boundary or outer limit of a department or organization who has to transmit communications from the department to other departments or from the organization to the outside environment and vice versa, to transmit communications inward.

Break-even model   A mathematical model with which the amount of profits or losses from given levels of business can be calculated ahead of time.

Budget   A statement of money outgoes or income or both, related to expected activities or accomplishments.

Bureaucracy   The organization's people working at their jobs in the structural hierarchy of levels and departments.

Cafeteria pay methods   Allowing employees to select whichever fringe pay benefits they want, providing only that their total cost to the employer equals that allowed for everyone.

Centralization   The withholding of decision making power from lower echelons and retaining these powers largely at the top of the organization. Contrasts with decentralization.

Chain of command   The vertical hierarchy of several levels of departments from high to low with delegations of authority being passed downward from major departments to subordinate departments.

Classical theory   The views of early scholars of management (Taylor, Fayol, Weber) where managers made all of the decisions and made all job assignments which subordinates carried out in a wooden fashion. Workers were instruments for getting work done but were not personalities.

Co-determination   The requirement in northern European countries that there be one or more representatives of workers on company boards of directors.

Cognitive dissonance   A term originated by Leon Festinger referring to the feeling of discomfort which people have when they consciously make an irrational decision because of emotional reasons.

Comparisons   Relating two or more variables to each other to see if accomplishments are following plans. Comparisons can be of raw data but they have more meaning if they compare ratios to ratios and trends to trends. These are first and second degree comparisons.

"Competent man" theory   Choose good subordinate managers and give them free rein. Because they are competent they will do good jobs with a minimum of supervision and control.

Conditional duties   Latent job duties to be brought into play and carried forward if and when some specific event occurs.

Confrontation meeting   Part of an organizational development program. Internal group meetings of managers where they are confronted with the idea of the need to unearth internal problems which are holding back organizational accomplishment.

"Consideration" leadership   Term used in early studies of leadership at Ohio State University to refer to managers consulting with subordinates and asking them for suggestions.

Contingency theory   Theory of leadership which holds that the managerial style of the leader which will be the most effective in any given situation depends on the situation and upon the kinds of people the leader and his followers are.

Contribution ratio   The fraction of the sales dollar in excess of the variable costs (usually labor and materials) or products. This extra amount is available to cover overhead costs and after all such costs are recovered, any added extras are left over as profits.

Creeping commitments   The result of initial decisions to commit certain resources to an activity but which prove to be inadequate to produce the desired accomplishment so these first commitments are followed by successive greater resource commitments not originally contemplated.

Cultural customs   The differing customs found in different cultural environments which bear upon the appropriateness and effectiveness of different managerial practices.

Decentralization   The delegation of decision making power to lower levels leaving only the making of major decisions at the top. Contrasts with centralization.

Decision making   The process of choosing from among alternatives and settling on one choice as being the one to follow.

Decision tree   A quantitative method for comparing the merits of the several end result possibilities for each of several possible choices where the initial choices are followed by further choices, each of which, considering the probability of certain states of the environment, will produce its own unique end-result.

Delegation   The process of passing on of work assignments and authority to act to subordinates.

Demographic factors   Changes in the make-up of sub-groups, sex, age, etc., in the population part of the environment.

Departmentalization   The process of setting up departments so that work of common nature is assigned to groups specializing in certain work. This process, at the same time, sets each kind of work apart from other kinds of work. It also subdivides work vertically as lesser and more specialized assignments are made to smaller subsidiary departments.

Diagnostic meeting   Part of an organization development program. A meeting confined to diagnosing one or more problems.

Dissatisfiers   (see also hygiene factors)   A term used by Frederick Herzberg. Contrasts with satisfiers.

Divisionalization   The subdividing, in large companies, of major departments on the basis of product line or by geography instead of by function. Divisions can thus operate largely as complete entities, each one with its own profit making responsibility. Contrasts with functional structure.

Economic order quantity (EOQ)   An inventory control tool. A mathematical model for determining the least cost order quantity considering the reduction in the unit cost from ordering large quantities of an item at one time and the increasing cost per unit from carrying inventories if large quantities are ordered.

Employee-centered leadership   Leadership style which features open communication and participation in information and personal interest in subordinates as human beings. Regarded by behavioral scientists as more effective than production-centered supervision.

Exception principle   Set up rules and policy guidelines telling subordinates what to do in certain situations. Exceptions to situations covered by the rule are referred upward for decision.

Extrinsic rewards   Rewards which come from outside the person. They include praise, recognition, and pay. In contrast to intrinsic rewards.

Feedback   Information reported frequently and quickly back to managers so that they can tell how well they are doing.

Flat structure, Horizontal structure   An organization whose chart is flat and wide. Because managers have many rather than few direct subordinates, there are few vertical layers in the structure. Contrasts with tall structures.

Flextime   (also Fleximite) Giving workers considerable freedom to come and go so long as they put in their required work hours in a day or in a week. A growing practice which is practicable whenever an employee's work is not closely tied in with the work of others.

Functional authority   The authority that a superior has over a subordinate so far as the kind of work he does is concerned. Also the authority a staff specialist has over the way his specialty is performed throughout the organization including in departments which are not otherwise subordinate to him.

Functional department   A department which does one kind of **work**, be it operational, as in the case of a foundry making steel castings, or a staff department, such as the personnel department. Non-functional departments are those set up by product, geographic area, or other bases.

Functional structure   One whose top level line departments are set apart on a functional basis and not by product line, geography, customer group, or other basis. In a manufacturing organization, a functional structure would be set up with manufacturing and sales departments as major departments. Contrasts with divisional structures.

"Good Enough," policy of   Policy of setting upper limits to the quality of products or services depending on the value of the extra quality related to its cost to provide.

"Grapevine"   The informal information flow system which exists in organizations. The grapevine by-passes and is outside of the formal information flow and communication system.

Group dynamics   (see also informal groups) Organizations are made up of people and groups of people. Groups develop identities of their own and people in groups behave differently from the way they behave as individuals. Often the reactions of groups need to be considered in managerial decision making.

"Half-Life" of motivation   Motivation of the emotional kind tends to decay away much as does radioactivity in the elements of nature. The half life period is the length of time it takes for motivation to decline to half.

Hard goal   Goals such as production quantities and quality, meeting budgets and schedules, holding down scrap, etc. Regarded by behavioral scientists as often being injurious to long-run operational effectiveness. Contrasts with soft goals.

Hawthorne experiments   The experiments carried on at Western Electric's Hawthorne factory by Elton Mayo and his colleagues in the 1920's which showed that worker reactions on jobs were complex sociological matters.

Hawthorne effect   Any research project being carried on among workers to find out how they react is likely to cause increased production, not because of the superiority of any new methods, but just because the workers know they are the subjects of investigation. This may well fade away after the research is stopped or the newness wears away.

Hierarchy of needs   Maslow's hierarchy of five most fundamental needs listed in sequence from the most fundamental to the less basic (need for food and shelter, then security, then belongingness and love, then self-esteem and acceptance by others, and lastly self-actualization).

Human asset accounting   An attempt to appraise the performance of managers on the basis, not only of their achievement of hard goals, but also on the basis of the good things they do in building up the human organization or in tearing it down. Popular as an idea in the 1960's and early 1970's but apparently impossible to apply in practice because of the subjective nature of the elements involved.

Hygiene factors   Term used by Herzberg, also called dissatisfier factors. These are working conditions, interpersonal relations, policies and administration, money, status, and security. Herzberg says that managers cannot, by improving these factors, increase satisfaction, but only reduce dissatisfaction.

Informal groups (see also group dynamics) The groups which grow up within organizations held together by some kind of bond of common interest. Often such groups respond to organizational directives in ways which defend the group's interest against encroachment, whether this coincides with organizational interests or not.

Initiating structure A term used in early studies of leadership at Ohio State University to refer to managers who use more directive and authoritarian rather than consultative methods in their relations with subordinates. Contrasts with consideration leadership.

Instrumental leadership Leadership viewed as managers directing the organization's activities in an instrumental way, carrying on managerial activities but with little emphasis on human relations.

Intervening variables Term used by Rensis Likert to refer to attitudes, motivations, perceptions, and willingness to cooperate and help other organizational members, and organizational empathy. These would, Likert felt, be harmed by the use of hard controls and consequently organizational performance would be harmed.

Intervention groups Part of organization development (OD) programs. Groups set up to search out causes of organizational ineffectiveness and to work out solutions to such problems.

Intrinsic rewards Rewards that a person grants to himself; his feeling of personal satisfaction from what he does and what he accomplishes. Contrasts with extrinsic rewards.

Inventory models (see also economic ordering quantities) Mathematical formulas for calculating least cost inventory levels and reordering quantities.

Job descriptions Lists of job duties for each job title. Describes what employees on the job are to do.

Job enlargement Adding more duties to a job to make it a little less routine, and, hopefully, more interesting.

Job enrichment Adding more duties of a discretionary nature to a job, such as letting workers decide how they will do their jobs, with the purpose of making the jobs more interesting.

Job evaluation The process by which job pay rates are established. Based on their job descriptions, jobs are awarded points which in turn determine the pay rate for each one.

Jury of executive opinion The composite of what the organization's executives think about some matter. Often used in forecasting the future environment or forecasting the company's future sales.

Law of inefficient service departments The most effective level of performance of the whole organization will be achieved only when service departments operate at some point below their individual optimum efficiency levels.

Law of invalid reasons Where reasons for malperformance are weak or non-existent, subordinates often offer excuses as reasons. Inconsequential reasons are magnified and if no reason exists, one will be invented.

Leadership power Often regarded as being made up of four kinds of power: the power of position, the power of expert knowledge, the power of knowledge of administration, and the power of acceptability to subordinates.

Leadership traits The peculiar traits or characteristics of leaders. These are neither numerous nor very pronounced. Leaders are believed to be intelligent, emotionally well balanced, achievement oriented, dominant, and energetic.

Line organization The vertical chain of authority of departments doing the organization's main stream work.

Linking-pin concept The idea that all middle level managers are in a dual position. They are at the apex of the triangle of subordinates below them but they are themselves across the bottom line of the triangle of people reporting to the next layer above. Thus they are the linking pins between top and bottom in the organization.

Long range plans Plans for the organization's future for from three to five years or more into the future. Contrasts with short range plans.

Management by objectives (MBO) Procedure of having manager and subordinate sit down together and jointly describe and define the accomplishments expected in the coming period by the subordinate. These are his objectives.

Management information systems (MIS) The whole system or collection of procedures by which information flows through the organization with emphasis on managers receiving the appropriate information so that they will know what is going on.

Management principles   Statements of fundamental relationships of management which have widespread applicability both over geographical space and over time.

Managerial grid   Square schematic diagram developed by Robert Blake and Jane Mouton to show the orientation of managers. The horizontal scale is marked off in degrees of interest in production and the vertical scale is marked off in degrees of concern for people.

Matrix management   (see also organic management.) Project manager's authority to see that his project's work is done is quite strong authority and overrides the normal functional department heads' authority. Project manager's authority extends across several departments and into their internal operations so far as his project is concerned.

Missions   A delegation expressed more in terms of what is to be accomplished than in terms of what the recipient is to do and how to do it.

Motivation   The inner urge to do something. Managers have to try to develop motivation to accomplish organizational objectives in subordinates.

"Mystique of the engineer"   The feeling in some countries (Germany and Holland in particular) that engineering training automatically equips a person to be a good manager.

"N-ach," "N-aff," "N-pwr." people   Terms used by David McClelland to describe the urges and uppermost driving power in people. Some are n-ach people (they want to achieve), some are n-aff (they want to affiliate), others are n-pwr (they want power).

Objectives   Goals, what it is that the organization is trying to accomplish.

"Open" management   Consultative type management. Superiors share information, problems, solutions, and decision making with subordinates.

Operations research   Mathematical models which can be of many kinds for use in helping managers to solve business problems.

Organic structures   (see also matrix management) Ordinary pyramidal structure but with technical staff departments and specialists

such as project managers having strong power to cross regular departmental lines to confer and to decide matters and the use of resources in areas under the line department head's ostensible direction.

Organization structures   The arrangement of major and minor departments into vertical work mission groups and the arrangements of the necessary staff departments to each other and to the line departments.

Organization development   An attempt to improve organizational performance through getting middle and lower level managers to cooperate better with each other and with lower level operatives as well. Requires the development of a participative and cooperative frame of mind on everyone's part.

Organizational slack   Temporary excesses in the organization's personnel needed to carry on the necessary work in situations where the workload fluctuates up and down. The number of employees needed should take care of typical needs but will be in excess of the needs during short term downswings in workloads.

Organizational work multiplier   As workloads increase, more people are required and more levels have to be added to the organization. Both the horizontal and the vertical expansion call for more interacting contacts and communications, all of which increase the number of employees at a rate greater than the increase in the workload.

Parity of authority and responsibility   Ideally, all managers should have enough authority to carry out their responsibilities. Unfortunately this ideal can rarely be achieved, almost always responsibilities outweigh authority.

Parkinson's Law   C. Northcote Parkinson put forward several Parkinson's Laws. The best known is that office workers go up in number at the rate of 5.5 per cent per year even if the workload stands still. Another of his laws is that expenses rise to meet the amount of money available.

Parochial thinking   Thinking by managers in a narrow way. Functional managers usually think only of their function. Divisional managers think only of their divisions. Both, often do not give enough thought to total organizational good.

Participative management   Subordinates are consulted and their suggestions welcomed in matters, particularly decisions, relating to their jobs. They are told what is going on and let in on things.

Path Goal theory   Theory of leadership which holds that subordinates try to do the things which will lead to their promotion and their own good, if their superior tells them what he wants done (lays out a path for them to follow).

Payoff matrix   A matrix which shows the possible payoff results for several possible courses of action for each of several possible future states of the environment. When each of the possible payoff figures is multiplied by the probability of its occurrence, a total most probable payoff figure can be arrived at.

Perceived duties   (see also role development) A subordinate regards duties as being part of his assignment or not as he perceives his delegation. He may end up doing some things which his superior did not intend or to neglect doing other things the superior did intend for him to do.

PERT (Program Evaluation Review Technique) A graphic and mathematical method for planning complex projects and for controlling their progress while production or construction goes on.

Peter principle   Because they do well on their present jobs, Laurence J. Peter says that people are promoted and then promoted again and again until they advance to a level beyond their competence. Upper level managers are therefore often incompetent.

Policies   General rules or guides to action to help keep the organization on the track and to help increase the effective use of resources for reaching goals.

Premises   The assumptions which planners have to make about what the future environment will be like when they make plans. Some premises are assumptions about facts and some premises are assumptions relating causes to effects.

Principles of management   see management principles.

Product manager, Project manager   (see also matrix management) Product and project managers are staff people, without departments but whose authority to watch over the production of their product or project is strong authority and often extends to allowing them to tell regular line department heads to assign people to their products or projects.

Production-centered leadership   Behavioral scientists belief that superiors who are primarily concerned with getting out production and less interested in their employees as people, will be **less** effective than supervisors more interested in their employees as people. Contrasts with employee-centered leadership.

Profit center   Section of a company which incurs costs for products or services and which has its own income, thus generating its own profits. This allows the managers of these centers to be judged on the basis of the profits they earn.

Profit planning   One kind of long range plan. It starts first, with a forecast of expected sales, costs, and profits. Then, these are regarded as being unsatisfactory, so higher profit figures are inserted. Then managers work backwards and try to figure how to increase sales or to decrease costs in order to arrive at the new profit figure.

Protestant ethic   The idea that is it not only acceptable but also socially desirable that people be motivated by the profit motive which will cause them to work and produce goods or services. This idea, introduced by Max Weber, was in contrast to the ethic in most societies in the past.

Psychological contract   This idea, introduced by Edgar Schein, held that, when an employee accepts a job, both he and the employer, have certain expectations, unsaid at the moment, which constitute a psychological contract. Since neither one knows what the other expects, it is quite possible that one of them will violate the contract, as the other one sees it, thus leading to misunderstanding.

Pyramidal structure   The typical triangular inverted tree structure with one person at the apex and a spreading out of departments, layer by layer, as one moves down through the hierarchy. Sharp lines of demarcation between duties and authorities of separate lines are characteristic.

Quality of life   The satisfactions of life, both on the job and off the job. These are not all related to the quantity of physical possessions. Most of these satisfactions come from life off the job but some of them come from life on the job and to job related conditions. Managers need to try to make life on the job tolerable or pleasant.

Queuing models   An operations research technique which allows managers to decide how much, in the way of service facilities, to provide, considering their cost as against their irregular use when the calls for their services are irregular.

Reinforcement   Immediate rewards for desired behavior and immediate penalties for unwanted behavior will increase the frequency of the desired behavior occurring and diminish the frequency of the unwanted behavior.

Responsibility   The duty to perform actions or to produce end-results. Responsibility is usually assigned in somewhat general terms, leaving it up to the recipient to develop the details.

Responsibility accounting   Setting up the organization's records so that incomes or costs or both are shown separately for the separate responsibility areas of single individuals. Results can then be more readily ascribed to each person's efforts.

Risk taking propensities   The differences between people in their willingness to take risks in decision making.

Role conflict   Duties within one's job assignment which conflict with each other as could occur if a manager had to choose between promoting a long service employee with a good record or a black or a woman also with a good record but with considerably less service.

Role development   (see also perceived duties) Work assignments are usually in general terms or in terms of missions to be accomplished. The recipient figures out the details of his assignment.

Satisfiers   Herzberg's motivators: challenging work, increasing responsibilities, growth and development, achievement, and recognition for accomplishment. According to Herzberg, only improvement in these factors can improve satisfaction. Contrasts with dissatisfiers.

"Schmoozing"   Term used by Robert Schrank to refer to camaraderie on the job and relative freedom of workers to leave their workplaces for short periods of time for socializing.

Scientific management   Term used to describe the methods of Frederick Taylor. Included were; time study to set production standards, carefully analyzed production methods, careful selection of workers to fit jobs, and their training in the best methods, and piece work pay.

Self actualization, Self fulfillment   The deep seated need that people have for accomplishing something and for using their abilities to the fullest.

Sensitivity training   (see also T-Groups) A process where small groups of people meet together to explore their reactions to each other for the purpose of becoming more aware of how other people react to them.

Service departments   Staff departments, such as the maintenance department which do not advise other departments but rather do work directly for them.

Short range plans   Plans for up to one year or two. Contrasts with long range plans.

Simulation   An operations research technique which simulates a problem and its solution through a make believe history of events as they might actually occur, thus allowing a manager to make a more informed decision about a proposed action.

Social contract theory   Historical antecedent of the acceptance theory. Theory held, centuries ago, by Jean Rousseau, John Locke, and Thomas Hobbs, that people, in need of the protection of a strong protector, gave over some of their freedom to a protector in exchange for his protection.

Soft goals   Empathy, willingness to cooperate, constructive attitudes, etc. Contrasts with hard goals.

Soldiering in the job   Old term used in Frederick Taylor's time meaning that workers are not working very hard.

Span of control, Span of supervision   The number of direct subordinates which can be supervised best by one supervisor.

Staff departments   Those departments which do **not** do the organization's main stream work but rather serve in a helping capacity.

Statistical quality control   Mathematical procedures used to help keep up the quality of production.

Strategic planning   See long range planning

Strong controls   (see hard goals) Controls based on the accomplishment of hard goals in contrast to soft goals.

Surveillance   Part of control, a watching over of the work of subordinates by superiors.

Systems   The complete circuit idea. Plans, actions, reports of actions, evaluation of performance, decision concerning corrective actions. This system of control repeats itself continually. Systems can be "closed," so that outside information cannot enter in or they can be "open," in which case information from the outside can enter the system.

System 4 Rensis Likert's "system 4," type of management. This system, which is strongly participative, was believed by Likert to be the best way to manage of the four systems he discussed.

Tall structures, Vertical structures An organization which is narrow and tall. Managers have small numbers of direct subordinates and there are several layers of departments between top and bottom. Contrasts with flat structures.

Task force groups Special temporary committee-like groups made up of representatives of several departments set up to tackle some special problem.

T-Groups See sensitivity training.

Theory X, Theory Y Douglas McGregor's postulate about the nature of people and how their nature is misunderstood by most managers. Theory X holds that people are lazy and need authoritarian managing. Theory Y, which McGregor believed to be true, holds that people like to work and that supervisory methods should recognize this and offer their employees an opportunity for self actualization.

Time study Method of using a stop watch to set production standards for factory operations.

"Trigger" delegations Delegations which cover activities to be called into play only if some trigger event occurs.

Transactional analysis Considers discussions between people to be transactions but often not as between equals. In discussions, people act as if they are adults, parents, or children. Communications will not be clear unless the discussants are on the same wave length. So a manager should try to put all discussions on an adult to adult plane, but if he cannot do this, misunderstanding may occur.

Transcendental meditation Relaxation method which uses silent meditation periods each day to relax bodily and mental tensions. People become refreshed mentally and physically.

Transfer prices The prices charged by one division of a divisional company for products or services for another of the company's divisions.

Unity of command Subordinates should not report to two or more superiors.

Valence The importance of the satisfactions from doing what the organization wants done compared to the cost in work to be done to get these satisfactions. A positive valence would motivate a person to do the organization's work.

Vertical structure See tall structures

Wall between The conceptual barrier between departments which impedes lateral communication and cooperation.

Work roles (see also role perceptions) The collection of duties which make up a person's job. This set of duties partly results from the operation of evolutionary factors.

Zero base budgeting Requiring departments to rejustify their existence each year before they get a new budget. Hopefully, this will hold down budgets and save money.